OXFORD PAPERBACK REFERENCE

The Concise Oxford Companion to
Irish Literature

Professor Robert Welch is Professor of English
and Director of the Centre for Irish Literature
and Bibliography at the University of Ulster at
Coleraine. His novel, *The Kings Are Out*, will be
published in 2001.

Editorial Assistance: Anne McCartney and Wendy
Taulbutt

Oxford Paperback Reference

forthcoming

The Concise Oxford Companion to

Irish Literature

Edited by
Robert Welch

OXFORD
UNIVERSITY PRESS

OXFORD
UNIVERSITY PRESS

Great Clarendon Street, Oxford OX2 6DP

Oxford University Press is a department of the University of Oxford.
It furthers the University's objective of excellence in research, scholarship,
and education by publishing worldwide in

Oxford New York

Athens Auckland Bangkok Bogotá Buenos Aires Calcutta
Cape Town Chennai Dar es Salaam Delhi Florence Hong Kong Istanbul
Karachi Kuala Lumpur Madrid Melbourne Mexico City Mumbai
Nairobi Paris São Paulo Singapore Taipei Tokyo Toronto Warsaw

with associated companies in Berlin Ibadan

Oxford is a registered trade mark of Oxford University Press
in the UK and in certain other countries

Published in the United States
by Oxford University Press Inc., New York

British Library Cataloguing in Publication Data
Data available

Library of Congress Cataloging in Publication Data
Data available

ISBN 0-19-280080-9

1 3 5 7 9 10 8 6 4 2

Typeset in Swift with Frutiger
by RefineCatch Limited, Bungay, Suffolk
Printed in Great Britain by
Cox & Wyman Limited,
Reading, Berkshire

for Angela

Acknowledgements

My deepest debt of gratitude is to the Leverhulme Trust under its Chairman in 1989, Sir Rex Richards, which gave most generous financial assistance for three years towards the compilation of the full *Companion*, on which this volume is primarily based. This help was augmented by further and timely assistance from the Central Community Relations Unit at Stormont Castle, Northern Ireland. Without these generous grants the work could not have been completed in such a relatively short space of time, if ever. I am grateful to the Trustees of the McCrea Research Fund of the University of Ulster, under its Chairman Professor Robert Gavin, CBE, for an initial start-up grant and I thank the Faculty of Humanities of the University for its warm and enthusiastic support.

Special thanks are due to: Professor Norman Gibson CBE for his practical and moral support at a crucial moment; to Professor T. G. Fraser and the members of the Department of History at the University of Ulster who showed complete professionalism and solidarity at the eleventh hour; to Professor Terry O'Keeffe, Dean of Humanities at the University of Ulster and Felix Agnew, Faculty Administrator, who cleared away many difficulties; to the Gaelic advisers, Professor Séamus Mac Mathúna and Professor Seán Ó Coileáin; to Robert Hogan (now, alas, no longer with us) who generously brought his bibliographical skills to bear on the first reprint of the full *Companion*; and to Tony McCusker and John Carson at the Central Community Relations Unit, Stormont. Contributors with particularly demanding responsibilities in various areas were: Diarmaid Breathnach and Máire Ní Mhurchú; Professor Pádraig Breatnach, UCD; Professor Sean Connolly, QUB; Seán Hutton; Professor Proinsias Mac Cana, DIAS; Professor Máirín Ní Dhonnchadha, UCG; Professor Breandán Ó Buachalla, UCD; Tomás Ó Cathasaigh, Harvard; Professor Donnchadh Ó Corráin, UCC; Professor Brian Ó Cuív, DIAS (now deceased); Dr Diarmaid Ó Doibhlin, UUC; Professor Máirtin Ó Murchú, DIAS; and Professor Pádraig Ó Riain, UCC.

My thanks to Sarah Barrett for her meticulous and incisive copy-editing; and to John Palmer who turned proof-reading into a gracious art-form. I am grateful to Kim Scott Walwyn, Andrew Lockett, and Angus Phillips of Oxford University Press for guidance and decision; and especially to Frances Whistler at the Press whose practical and imaginative support and advice greatly enhanced the range and quality of the full *Companion* and of this abridgement. My thanks also to Mrs Lyn Doyle, Mrs Beth Holmes, Mrs Rosemary Savage, Mrs Mary McCaughan, Ms Chris Clements, Ms Cindy McAllister, Mrs Eleanor McCartney, Mrs Wendy Tarlbutt, Ms Sharon Lowry, Ms Maeve Patton, and Ms Louise Gagen; and to my colleagues and students in the University of Ulster. A special word of thanks is due to Dr Bruce Stewart, Assistant Editor of the full *Companion* for his assistance in the preparation of that volume; and for this version the unfailing assistance and encouragement of Dr Anne

McCartney, British Academy Fellow in the History of the Irish Book at Coleraine and QUB. My deepest gratitude also to those many friends and fellow scholars who took the trouble to alert me to the inaccuracies that crept into the full *Companion*, and to omissions, all of which I now hope are corrected here. I also thank the many writers who responded to the questionnaire distributed to them so I could update and verify the contemporary record.

Contributors to the Volume

Abbot, Vivienne
Addis, Jeremy
Ahlqvist, Anders
Andrews, Elmer
Arkins, Brian
Bareham, Margaret
Bareham, Tony
Bayliss, Gail
Berman, David
Boyle, Terence
Bowe, Nicola
  Gordon
Bradford, Richard
Breathnach,
  Diarmaid
Breatnach, Pádraig A.
Brown, Terence
Burnside, Sam
Cahalan, James
Campbell Ross, Ian
Coleman, Tony
Connolly, Sean
Corr, Christopher
Croghan, Martin
Cronin, John
Dalsimer, Adele
Dantanus, Ulf
Davies, Gordon
  Herries
de Bhaldraithe,
  Tomás
Denman, Peter
Denvir, Gearóid
Devi, Ganesh
Devine, Kathleen
Dillon, John
Elmore, Gráinne
Eska, Joseph F.
Farren, Seán
Fitzgibbon, Ger
Fleischmann, Ruth
Foley, Imelda
Fraser, Grace
Fraser, Thomas G.

Gamble, Jack
Gibbs, A. M.
Gillespie, John
Gillies, William
Gilligan, David
Hadfield, Andrew
Harmon, Maurice
Harrison, Alan
Hastings, Caitríona
Herbert, Máire
Hill, John
Hillan King, Sophia
Hofman, Rijklof
Hooley, Ruth
Huber, Werner
Hughes, Éamonn
Hunter, Robert
Hutton, Seán
Jeffares, A. N.
Jeffrey, Keith
Jones, Mary
Kelly, Fergus
Kiberd, Declan
Kosok, Heinz
Kreilkamp, Vera
Laurie, Hilary
Lavery, John
Lee, Joseph
Longley, Edna
Loughran, James
Lucy, Seán
Mac Cana, Proinsias
McCartney, Anne
Mac Craith, Micheál
Mac Eoin, Gearóid
Mac Lochlainn, Alf
McLoone, Martin
McMahon, Seán
Mac Mathúna,
  Séamus
McMinn, Joseph
McNamara, Leo
McVeagh, John
Mallory, James

Maxwell, Daphne
  K. P.
Mays, James C.
Mhac An tSaoi, Máire
Morash, Christopher
Morgan, Hiram
Moynihan, Julian
Murphy, James
Murphy, Maureen
Murray, Christopher
Ní Bhrolcháin,
  Muireann
Ní Chuilleanáin,
  Eiléan
Nic Eoin, Máirín
Ní Dhonnchadha,
  Máirín
Ní Mhurchú, Máire
Nicholson, Robert
Ó Briain, Máirtín
O'Brien, George
O'Brien, Gerard
Ó Buachalla,
  Breandán
Ó Canainn, Tomás
Ó Catháin, Séamus
Ó Cathasaigh, Tomás
Ó Ciardha, Éamonn
Ó Coigligh, Ciarán
Ó Coileáin, Seán
Ó Conchúir,
  Breandán
Ó Conncheanainn,
  Tomás
O'Connor, Emmet
Ó Corráin, Ailbhe
Ó Corráin,
  Donnchadh
Ó Crualaoich,
  Gearóid
Ó Cuív, Brain
Ó Doibhlin, Diarmaid
O'Donoghue, Jo
Ó Dushláine, Tadhg

Ó Fiannachta, Pádraig
Ó Háinle, Cathal
Ó hAnluain, Eoghan
Ó hÓgáin, Daithí
Ó hUrdail, Roibeárd
O'Keeffe, Terence
O'Leary, Philip
Ó Luing, Seán
Olinder, Britta
Ó Macháin, Padráig
Ó Madagáin,
  Breandán
Ó Murchú, Máirtín
Ó Murchú, Mícheál

Ó Snodaigh, Pádraig
Ó Trathaigh,
  Gearóid
Oram, Hugh
Reynolds, Lorna
Riordan, Maurice
Ronsley, Joseph
Russell, Paul
Scowcroft, Mark
Sharpe, Richard
Sheeran, Patrick
Siegmund-Schultze,
  Dorothea
Sloan, Barry

Smythe, Colin
Stewart, Anne Millar
Stewart, Bruce
Swift, Carolyn
Tilling, Philip
Titley, Alan
Tucker, Bernard
Walsh, Patrick
Watt, Stephen
Whelan, Kevin
Welch, Angela
Welch, Robert
York, Richard
York, Rosemary

Contents

Editor's Preface

This book aims to be a guide and companion to the student and reader of Irish literature in all its phases, from the earliest times to the present day. Irish literature in Irish, one of the oldest vernacular literatures in Europe, reflected a society with its own language, institutions, and traditions. The first written records of this literature, preserved in manuscript compilations, date from as early as the sixth or seventh centuries, but many of them were already very old when first inscribed. It is no exaggeration to say that Irish literature represents the continuing literary expression of Irish people over a period of nearly two thousand years.

The reader will find entries on authors and their works; on movements, genres, and branches of learning; on tales, cycles of tales, and types of tale; on annals, manuscripts, and institutions; on history and major historical figures and events; on Catholicism and Protestantism in Ireland; on translation; on mythology, folklore, and folksong; on archaeology and the Celts; on Irish, Celtic, Indo-European and Hiberno-English; on the Troubles; on Latin and Norman-French writing; and on writers such as Spenser and Arnold, who, though not Irish, greatly influenced the cultural context of Irish literature.

A carefully designed system of cross-referencing allows the reader to travel across the borders between one language and another, between different branches of learning, and between centuries, to explore the entire interconnected network of relationships that is Irish literature. There are brief outlines of many texts, as diverse as *Táin Bó Cuailnge* and *Finnegans Wake*; and they too are cross-referenced, thereby radiating out to other works, authors, and periods. The coverage of contemporary writing in both Irish and English is not exhaustive but it is as comprehensive as restrictions of space allowed.

It is my hope that this book will allow the reader to cross over many of the internal boundaries that run athwart the corpus of Irish literature. These crossings-over, translations if you like, may help the reader to recognize that all the different territories and voices that comprise and animate Irish literary tradition go to make up one coherent but manifold cultural expression, something to be experienced and delighted in, not asserted.

My thanks and love as ever to my wife Angela, agus ár gceathrar álainn: Rachel, Killian, Egan, and Tiernan.

Samhradh 1999
Cúl Rathain   ROBERT WELCH

Notes to the Reader

Entries are in alphabetical order and are not capitalized unless the entry heading is a name or a title of a work: hence ogam, but Otway, Caesar. Surnames precede given names. Titles of novels, plays, and other full-length works are in italics: *Irish Cousin, An*. Titles of shorter works are in roman with single quotation marks: 'After the Race'. Modern names beginning with Mac or Mc are ordered as if they were spelled Mac. For the period before the Norman Invasion names with the patronymic 'mac' are alphabetized according to the forename: hence *Cormac mac Airt with 'mac' in lower case. Thereafter 'Mac' began to function as a part of the early form of modern surnames, so it is listed under 'M' with the 'Mac' capitalized. Saints are listed under their given name: St Patrick is under P not S.

The orthography of Irish presents special difficulties in that there is no settled system of spelling for Old, Middle, and Early Modern Irish. In general the orthographical conventions adopted have been those of the period in which the author, scribe, or person lived, or in which the manuscript, poem, or tale was written down: hence *Lebor Gabála*, reflecting a medieval orthography, is used although in commentaries it is often spelled *Leabhar Gabhála*, a modern standardization. The titles of works are translated when the work is the subject of the entry, hence *Lebor Gabála* [*Book of Invasions*]. Titles of longer works are also translated if they occur in the course of an entry and there is no separate entry devoted to them. An asterisk before a name or a title or a subject indicates a separate entry for that person, or work, or area. Square brackets are used to contain other cross-references e.g. [see *folklore]. The term Gaelic is used interchangeably with Irish to avoid undue repetition of the latter word and for the satisfying reason that it derives from Gaeilge, meaning the Irish language, which often helps to make useful distinctions.

Abbreviations

A Chronology of Historical Events

The purpose of this Chronology is to provide a sequential listing of historical events mentioned in the *Companion*. Readers will also find entries on most of the events and people listed here.

BC

*c.*6000	Probable date of first human settlements in Ireland
*c.*3000	New Grange
*c.*450	Traditional date for founding of Emain Macha in Ulster
*c.*300	Possible date of arrival of Celts

AD

*c.*130	Ptolemy, the Alexandrian, writes a geography of Ireland based on much earlier sources (*c.*300 BC)
*c.*366	Traditional date of Cormac Mac Airt's death
432	Traditional date of the beginning of St Patrick's mission in Ireland
546	Traditional date of foundation of Clonmacnoise by St Ciaran
*c.*550	Beginning of Irish manuscript tradition as Irish monasticism develops; inscription of Irish law begins
563	Iona established by St Colum Cille
575	Convention of Druim Ceat called to resolve conflicting Irish and Scottish territorial claims
*c.*770–850	Céle Dé [Culdee] movement in Irish church
795	First raids of Viking Invasion
807	Monastery established at Kells
841	Viking fleet in Dublin
1006	Brian Boraime recognized as high king
1014	Battle of Clontarf
1134	Cormac's chapel consecrated at Cashel
1142	First Cistercian monastery established at Mellifont
1169	Norman Invasion begins
1315	Invasion of Ireland by Edward Bruce, brother of the Scottish chieftain Robert; Edward proclaimed 'king of Ireland'
1366	Statutes of Kilkenny proscribing Irish customs amongst the colonists
1494	Sir Edward Poynings appointed as Lord Deputy of Henry VII, after the Anglo-Irish support the Pretender Perkin Warbeck; 'Poynings' Law' binds Irish Parliament to English governance
1541	Declaration Act by which Henry VIII is declared king of Ireland, leading to his policy of 'surrender and regrant'
1558	Accession of Elizabeth I
1570	Elizabeth I excommunicated
1579	James Fitz Maurice Fitzgerald, Earl of Desmond, arrives in Kerry with a Continental Catholic force

1580	Arthur Lord Grey de Wilton crushes Munster Rebellion
1586	Plantation of Munster
1588	Defeat of Spanish Armada
1595	Hugh O'Neill, Earl of Tyrone, assumes his Gaelic title and heads rebellion with Red Hugh O'Donnell
1599	Essex in Ireland as Lord Deputy after Tyrone Rebellion spreads and Munster planters ousted
1601	Battle of Kinsale
1606	Foundation of St Anthony's College, Louvain
1607	Flight of the Earls
1609	Plantation of Ulster
1641	Rebellion
1642	Catholic Confederation at Kilkenny
1649	Cromwell begins his Irish campaign after Charles I executed
1654	Cromwellian Plantation
1660	Restoration of Charles II
1681	Execution of St Oliver Plunkett, Catholic archbishop of Armagh
1689	James II lands at Kinsale; Williamite War begins
1690	Battle of the Boyne
1695	Penal Laws restricting rights of Catholics
1782	Henry Grattan's Parliament
1785	Royal Irish Academy established
1791	United Irishmen founded in Belfast
1792	Relief Act allows Catholics to become lawyers
1795	Foundation of Orange Order
1798	United Irishmen's Rebellion
1800	Act of Union
1803	Rising of Robert Emmet
1829	Catholic Emancipation
1831	Tithe War begins; introduction of 'national' schools
1840	Daniel O'Connell founds Repeal Association
1842	*The Nation* founded
1845	First year of the Great Famine
1848	Young Ireland Rising
1858	Irish Republican Brotherhood founded
1859	Ulster evangelical revival
1866	Paul Cullen becomes first Irish Cardinal
1867	Fenian Rebellion; Manchester Martyrs
1873	Home Rule League founded
1879	Michael Davitt founds the Land League
1880	Parnell elected leader of the Irish Parliamentary Party
1882	Phoenix Park murders
1884	GAA founded
1886	First Home Rule Bill defeated in the House of Commons
1891	Death of Parnell
1893	Gaelic League founded
1899	Opening season of the Irish Literary Theatre

1903	Wyndham Land Act
1904	Abbey Theatre opens
1908	Arthur Griffith founds Sinn Féin
1912	Ulster Covenant declares loyalty to Crown
1913	Ulster Volunteers, Irish Volunteers, and Irish Citizen Army formed; Lockout Strike; Larne gun-running
1914	Third Home Rule Bill signed by George V, then suspended
1915	Irish Republican Brotherhood reorganized and a military council formed
1916	The Easter Rising and proclamation of the Irish Republic; Battle of the Somme
1918	First Dáil Éireann formed after general election
1919	Anglo-Irish War (the 'Troubles') begins
1920	'Better Government' of Ireland Act introduces partition between north and south of Ireland
1921	Treaty between Sinn Féin leaders and British government signed
1922	Irish Free State established with Northern Ireland remaining within the Union; Civil War begins
1925	Partition confirmed by agreement between Irish Free State, Northern Ireland, and Westminster
1928	Gate Theatre opens
1931	IRA banned in Irish Free State
1932	Stormont opened by Edward, Prince of Wales
1937	De Valera's Constitution
1939	IRA bombing campaign in Britain; Ireland's declaration of neutrality in Second World War
1940	IRA hunger-strike
1941	German air-raids on Belfast
1948	Irish Free State declares itself a Republic
1966	Nelson Pillar in Dublin blown up
1967	Northern Ireland Civil Rights Association founded
1968	'Troubles' begin again in Northern Ireland
1970	Provisional Sinn Féin and Provisional IRA formed
1971	Internment introduced in Northern Ireland
1972	'Bloody Sunday' in Derry; suspension of Stormont; Direct Rule imposed in Northern Ireland
1973	Ireland and UK join European Community; Sunningdale conference on power-sharing between Unionists and Nationalists held
1974	General strike in Northern Ireland; Guildford and Birmingham bombings
1976	Christopher Ewart-Biggs, British Ambassador to Ireland, killed in Dublin
1979	Earl Mountbatten killed in Sligo
1980	Field Day founded
1981	Republican hunger-strike
1983	All-Ireland Forum

1985	Anglo-Irish Agreement sets up inter-governmental agencies between British and Irish governments
1993	Downing Street Joint Declaration on Northern Ireland by British and Irish governments
1994	IRA and Loyalist ceasefires
1996	IRA ceasefire ends with Canary Wharf bomb
1997	Labour victory in UK General Election; Dr Mo Mowlam, Secretary of State for Northern Ireland; IRA ceasefire renewed
1998	Good Friday Agreement
1999	Devolution of government to Northern Ireland Assembly
2000	Assembly revoked

Select Bibliography

General guides, literary histories, bibliographies

ALSPACH, RUSSELL K., *Irish Poetry from the English Invasion to 1798* (1943)

BAUMGARTEN, ROLF, *A Bibliography of Irish Linguistics and Literature 1942–1971* (1980)

BELL, SAM HANNA, *The Theatre in Ulster* (1972)

BEST, RICHARD IRVINE, *A Bibliography of Irish Philology and of Printed Irish Literature* (1913)

——, *A Bibliography of Irish Philology and Manuscript Literature: Publications 1913–1941* (1942)

BRADY, ANNE M. and BRIAN CLEEVE, *A Biographical Dictionary of Irish Writers* (1985)

BREATHNACH, DIARMUID, and MÁIRE NÍ MHURCHÚ, *Beathaisnéis*, 5 vols. (1986–97)

BROWN, STEPHEN, *Ireland in Fiction: A Guide to Irish Novels*, vol. 1 (1919); see also Clarke, Desmond

CAHALAN, JAMES, *The Irish Novel: A Critical History* (1988)

CLARKE, DESMOND, ed., STEPHEN BROWN, *Ireland in Fiction*, vol. 2 (1985)

CLARKE, WILLIAM SMITH, *The Early Irish Stage, The Beginnings to 1720* (1955)

——, *The Irish Stage in Country Towns 1720–1860* (1965)

CORKERY, DANIEL, *The Hidden Ireland: A Study of Gaelic Munster in the Eighteenth Century* (1925)

CRONIN, JOHN, *The Anglo-Irish Novel*, vols. 1 and 2 (1980–1990)

DEANE, SEAMUS, ed., *The Field Day Anthology of Irish Writing*, 3 vols. (1991)

——, *A Short History of Irish Literature* (1986)

DE BLÁCAM, AODH, *Gaelic Literature Surveyed* (1929)

DE HAE, RISTEÁRD, and B. NÍ DHONNCHADHA, eds., *Clár Litríocht na Nua-Ghaeilge 1850–1936*, 3 vols. (1938–1940) [see also Hayes, Richard]

DILLON, MYLES, *Early Irish Literature* (1948)

EAGER, ALAN, *A Guide to Irish Bibliographical Material: A Bibliography of Irish Bibliographies and Sources of Information* (1960; rev. 1980)

FINNERAN, RICHARD J., ed., *Anglo-Irish Literature: A Review of Research* (1976)

——, ed., *Recent Research on Anglo-Irish Writers* (1983)

FLANAGAN, THOMAS, *The Irish Novelists 1800–1850* (1958)

GREENE, DAVID, *The Irish Language* (1966)

HARMON, MAURICE, *Select Bibliography for the Study of Anglo-Irish Literature and its Backgrounds* (1977)

HAYES, RICHARD, *Manuscript Sources for the History of Irish Civilization*, 11 vols. (1965); Supplement, 3 vols. (1979)

——, *Sources for the History of Irish Civilization: Articles in Irish Periodicals*, 9 vols. (1970)

HOGAN, J. J., *The English Language in Ireland* (1927)

HOGAN, ROBERT, ed., *The Macmillan Dictionary of Irish Literature* (1979, rev. 1996).

HOGAN, ROBERT, et al., *The Modern Irish Drama: A Documentary History*, 6 vols. (1975–1992)

HYDE, DOUGLAS, *A Literary History of Ireland* (1899)

JEFFARES, A. NORMAN, *Anglo-Irish Literature* (1982)

JOHNSTON, DILLON, *Irish Poetry After Joyce* (1984)

JOYCE, PATRICK WESTON, *English As We Speak It In Ireland* (1910)

KENNEY, J. F., *The Sources for the Early History of Ireland: An Introduction and Guide* (1929)

LEERSSEN, JOEP TH., *Mere Irish and Fíor-Ghael* (1986)

MACCANA, PROINSIAS, *Celtic Mythology* (1970)

McCORMACK, W. J., ed., *Blackwell's Companion to Irish Culture* (1999)

MAXWELL, D. E. S., *A Critical History of Modern Irish Drama 1891–1980* (1984)

MIKHAIL, E. H., *A Bibliography of Modern Irish Drama 1899–1970* (1972)

MURPHY, GERARD, *Early Irish Lyrics* (1956)

Ó'BRIEN, FRANK, *Filíocht Ghaeilge na Linne Seo* (1968)

Ó BUACHALLA, BREANDÁN, *Aisling Ghéar: Na Stíobhartaigh agus an tAos Léinn* (1996)

O'CONNOR, FRANK, *The Backward Look* (1967)

Ó CUÍV, BRIAN, ed., *A View of the Irish Language* (1969)

O'DONOGHUE, DAVID JAMES, *The Poets of Ireland* (1912)

Ó MUIRITHE, DIARMUID, ed., *The English Language in Ireland* (1977)

Ó TUAMA, SEÁN, *An Grá in Amhráin na nDaoine* (1978)

RAFROIDI, PATRICK, *Irish Literature in English: The Romantic Period, 1789–1850* 2 vols. (1980)

STANFORD, WILLIAM BEDELL, *Ireland and the Classical Tradition* (1976)

STOCKWELL, LA TOURETTE, *Dublin Theatres and Theatre Customs 1637–1820* (1968)

TITLEY, ALAN, *An tÚrscéal Gaeilge* (1991)

VANCE, NORMAN, *Irish Literature: A Social History* (1990)

WEEKES, ANN OWENS, *Unveiling Treasures: The Attic Guide to the Published Works of Irish Women Literary Writers: Drama, Fiction, Poetry* (1993)

WELCH, ROBERT, *The Abbey Theatre 1899–1999: Form and Pressure* (1999)

——, *A History of Verse Translation from the Irish 1789–1897* (1988)

WILLIAMS, J. E. CAERWYN, agus M. NÍ MHUÍRIOSA, *Traidisiún Literartha na nGael* (1979)

A

Abbey Theatre, the (Irish Literary Theatre; later Irish National Theatre), grew out of the *literary revival that took place after the death of *Parnell in 1891. Irish writers had nothing like the same access to a history of theatrical achievement as those in other European countries. Anglo-Irish dramatists as various as George *Farquhar, R. B. *Sheridan, Dion *Boucicault, and Oscar *Wilde had written successfully for the stage, but with London and even American audiences in mind.

The Abbey had its beginnings in the summer of 1897 at Duras House, Kinvara, when W. B. Yeats, Lady *Gregory, and Edward *Martyn discussed the founding of a theatre for new Irish drama, Martyn acting as guarantor of the Irish Literary Theatre, as Yeats called it. Martyn also persuaded his cousin George Moore to produce the first two plays, performed at the Antient Concert Rooms in Great Brunswick (now Pearse) Street on two successive nights: Yeats's The *Countess Cathleen (8 May 1899) and Martyn's The *Heather Field (9 May). Before the first night a pamphlet by Frank Hugh *O'Donnell, Souls for Gold, had been distributed attacking The Countess Cathleen on the grounds that it showed the Irish people selling their souls. Further allegations of anti-Catholicism from prominent figures including Cardinal Logue aroused sectarian feelings which led to jeering and hissing on 8 May.

In its second season, the Irish Literary Theatre staged Maeve, a two-act drama by Edward Martyn and The Last Feast of the Fianna, by Alice *Milligan on 19 February 1900. The *Bending of the Bough by Edward Martyn, a realistic full-length play rewritten by Moore, under whose name it appeared, followed on 20 February. The third season, in 1901, featured the three-act *Diarmuid and Gráinne, a collaborative effort from Yeats and Moore (with music by Edward Elgar); and *Casadh an tSúgáin, written by Douglas *Hyde, President of the *Gaelic League.

Now William and Frank *Fay, amateur actors and Gaelic enthusiasts, approached George *Russell, who promised to finish his play Deirdre for them. Yeats gave them *Cathleen Ni Houlihan, for staging with Russell's, and these plays were produced by Inghinidhe na hÉireann, Maud *Gonne's republican women's group. She played the title role in Cathleen, electrifying the audience in St Teresa's Temperance Hall in 1902. A National Theatre Society was now formed, with Yeats as president, and William Fay as stage-manager.

At the Antient Concert Rooms the Irish National Theatre Society produced The Sleep of the King by James *Cousins and The Laying of the Foundations by Ryan (29 October 1902), followed by The *Pot of Broth by Yeats, The Racing Lug by Cousins, and Eilís agus an Bhean Déirce by P. T. Mac Fhionnlaoich (30 October). At the invitation of Stephen *Gwynn the Society performed in South Kensington, impressing Annie *Horniman, Manchester tea heiress, astrologer, and Yeats's friend, who became the Society's patron. In October 1903 J. M. *Synge's first produced play, *In the Shadow of the Glen, was staged, but it caused disquiet amongst the actors in rehearsal, who thought it a slur on Irish womanhood. *Riders to the Sea was staged in January 1904. In 1904 Miss Horniman acquired the Mechanics' Institute Theatre, in Abbey Street, for the Society. The new theatre was called the Abbey, and opened on 27 December with two new plays: Yeats's *On Baile's Strand* and Lady Gregory's *Spreading the News*, as well as *Cathleen Ni Houlihan* and *In the Shadow of the Glen*. Synge's *The *Well of the Saints* was staged in 1905, followed by Lady Gregory's *Kincora*, William *Boyle's realistic *The *Building Fund*, and Padraic *Colum's *The *Land*.

Miss Horniman agreed to make an annual subvention to the Society in order that salaries be paid to William Fay and the actors. In 1905/6 the Company toured in Ireland and Britain, and staged *The Eloquent Dempsey* by Boyle, a political farce; *The Doctor in Spite of Himself*, the first of Lady Gregory's translations of Molière into Kiltartanese, her version of the *Hiberno-English dialect of Galway; and Yeats's *Deirdre*. On 27 February 1907 the Abbey produced Synge's *The *Playboy of the Western World*, with Fay playing the lead, the apparent amorality of which caused an uproar. *The *Country Dressmaker*, a first play by George *Fitzmaurice, was staged in October. The Fay brothers, angry that Yeats kept all power to himself, Lady Gregory, and Synge, resigned in 1908. In that year a first play by Lennox *Robinson (*The *Clancy Name*) was staged.

Synge died in 1909 and the Abbey revived *The Playboy* to acclaim. In 1910 Lennox Robinson became manager. In his first season he produced Padraic Colum's *Thomas Muskerry*, followed in the same year by Robinson's own *Harvest*, R. J. *Ray's *The Casting Out of Martin Whelan*, and T. C. *Murray's *Birthright*, thus inaugurating a new school of realistic drama. When Robinson did not close the theatre on 7 May, the day of Edward VII's death, Miss Horniman withdrew her subsidy. A new patent was granted to the Abbey, despite an attempt by the Theatre of Ireland (a rival group founded in 1906 and headed by Martyn and George *Russell) to secure concessionary rights.

An American tour in 1911 caused much protest, the Irish-Americans dis-

liking *The Playboy*. In 1914 A. Patrick Wilson replaced Robinson as manager, and was followed in 1915 by St John *Ervine who produced *John Ferguson*, a play about Northern Protestantism. In 1916 a number of players saw active service in the *Easter Rising, while the Proclamation was printed on the premises. Ervine resigned and J. Augustus Keogh took over. In 1916–17 six of Shaw's plays were staged, including *John Bull's Other Island*, *Arms and the Man*, and *Man and Superman*. In December Robinson's *The *Whiteheaded Boy* was produced.

In 1918 Yeats organized the Dublin Drama League, with himself as president and Robinson as secretary, to promote foreign and European theatre. In 1919 Robinson returned as manager.

Robinson was made a director with Yeats and Lady Gregory. George *Shiels, from Ulster, had a play, *Insurance Money*, performed in 1921, followed by *Paul Twyning* in 1922. Sean *O'Casey's *The *Shadow of a Gunman* was produced in 1923 at the height of the *Civil War. After complex negotiations with Ernest *Blythe, the Abbey became a subsidized National Theatre in 1924. This year also saw the première of O'Casey's *Juno and the Paycock*. In 1926, when O'Casey's *The *Plough and the Stars*, was produced, there were violent scenes, Yeats declaiming to the audience that they had disgraced themselves again. O'Casey's next play, *The *Silver Tassie*, was disliked by the directors, who rejected it.

Lady Gregory died in 1932, and in 1935 Yeats decided to expand the board, making F. R. *Higgins, Brinsley *MacNamara, and Ernest Blythe directors, along with himself, Robinson, and Walter *Starkie. When the new board staged *The Silver Tassie* MacNamara resigned on the grounds that it was blasphemous, and Yeats replaced him with Frank *O'Connor. The years after Lady Gregory's death began a bleak phase of the Abbey's history, extending to the 1960s, in which there was an emphasis on 'PQ' ('peasant quality', a degraded version of Synge's poetic intensity). Good plays, such as Carroll's *Shadow and Substance* (1937), or M. J. *Molloy's *The *King of Friday's Men* (1948), were often badly served by a stereotyped production style.

F. R. Higgins, managing director since 1938, died in 1941, and Blythe succeeded him. In the 1940s theatre in Irish improved, with Tomás *Mac Anna staging plays by Mícheál Mac *Liammóir and Piaras *Béaslaí. A School of Ballet, whose productions were choreographed by Ninette de Valois, ceased production in 1933.

On 18 July 1951 the Abbey burnt down. The company moved to the Queen's Theatre until 18 July 1966 when a new theatre opened on the old site. At the Queen's, the company relied upon the established classics of the Irish theatre and plays by well-known authors. In 1962, however, the Abbey presented Brian *Friel's *The Enemy Within*, and many of his plays have had their first staging there, including *The *Freedom of the City* (1973), *Aristocrats* (1979), and *Dancing at Lughnasa* (1990). A new, experimental, tone was set in 1967 with Tomás Mac Anna's production of Brendan *Behan's *Borstal Boy*. Tom *Murphy's first play for the Abbey was *Famine* (1968), and the theatre continued to produce his work with plays such as *The Sanctuary Lamp* (1975), *The *Gigli Concert* (1983), and *The Wake* (1998). Thomas Kilroy's *Talbot's Box* (1977) made exciting use of stage-space to convey states of mind.

The 1980s and 1990s brought fresh experimentation and work of high quality, in particular Frank *McGuinness's *Observe the Sons of Ulster Marching Towards the Somme* (1985); Tom *McIntyre in *The *Great Hunger* (1983) chose a non-naturalistic imagist-style;

while Stewart *Parker anatomized the competing nationalist rhetorics of Ireland in *Northern Star* (1985). Joe Dowling, Vincent Dowling, and Tomás Mac Anna were artistic directors in the 1970s and 1980s, and in 1990 Garry Hynes, who founded the *Druid Theatre in Galway, assumed the post, vacating it in 1993, to be followed by Patrick Mason, Ben Barnes succeeding in 1999.

See Robert Welch, *A History of the Abbey, 1899–1999: Form and Pressure* (1999).

Abernethy, John (1680–1740), leader of the non-subscribing Presbyterians in 1727. Born near Moneymore, Co. Tyrone, he was educated in Edinburgh and held ministries in Dublin and in Co. Antrim. Abernethy opposed the Anglican Test Act and challenged *Swift's view of dissenting religion as fanatical. He was cited by William *Drennan as a formative influence on the *United Irishmen. His published writings include *Scarce and Valuable Tracts &c.* (1751).

Abraham, J[ames] Johnston (1876–1963), naval surgeon and author, born in Coleraine, Co. Derry, and educated at TCD. *The Surgeon's Log* (1911) gives a frank account of maritime and colonial life in the Far East. *The Night Nurse* (1913) was a novel set in a Dublin hospital during a typhus epidemic. Johnston practised successfully in London.

Absentee, The (1812), a novel by Maria *Edgeworth first published in *Tales of Fashionable Life* (2nd series), deals with the ill-effects of landlord absenteeism in Ireland. An Irish landowner, Lord Clonbrony, and his ambitious wife are living in London amid growing debts. Their son, Lord Colambre, fails to persuade them to return to Ireland. He travels back, incognito, to find his father's estate being rackrented. Colambre falls in love with Grace Nugent, of a Gaelic family.

Acallam na Senórach (*Colloquy of the Ancients*), a monastic compilation of materials from the *Fionn cycle, made in the late 12th cent. The narrative tells how Oisín, son of Fionn, and Caoilte, son of Rónán, the last surviving warriors of the Fianna, emerge from the woods of the Fews Mountains, to encounter St *Patrick, engaged on his Christian mission. The priests with Patrick are frightened by these strange-looking men with their enormous wolfhounds; when the saint exorcises the warriors, legions of devils leave them. Patrick and Caoilte then travel Ireland together, the old pagan narrating the lore of places that they pass [see *dinnshenchas], interweaving myth and legend as he interprets the terrain. The travellers complete their circuit ending at *Tara and the court of the High King Diarmait mac Cerbaill, where they find Oisín has arrived before them. The Feast of Tara (Feis Temrach) is in progress, and both warriors tell of the brave deeds of their former comrades. With its glorification of a legendary past, and its perception of Ireland as a storied landscape, the *Acallam* is a characteristic and central group of texts in Irish literature. See Nessa Ní Shéaghdha *Agallamh na Seanórach* (3 vols., 1942–5).

accentual verse, see Irish *metrics.

Act of Union, see Act of *Union.

Acta Sanctorum Hiberniae, see John *Colgan.

Adamnán (?627–704), Abbot of Iona from 679 and biographer of *Colum Cille; born probably in Donegal. His *Vita Columbae* (*Life of Colum Cille*), composed some time between 690 and 700, includes an appeal for the peaceful celebration of the Easter season. He also wrote a description of the Holy Land (*De Locis Sanctis*). A vision attributed to him forms the subject-matter of *Fís Adamnáin, in the *Book of the Dun Cow.

Adams, Gerry (1948–), politician and writer. Born in West Belfast, he joined the Republican movement in 1964 and was later imprisoned for IRA activities. He was elected MP for his native constituency in 1983 but did not take up his seat. As President of *Sinn Féin he advanced a constitutional policy in the Republican movement, leading to the IRA ceasefire of 1994. His political thought is outlined in *The Politics of Irish Freedom* (1986), *A Pathway to Peace* (1988), and *Before the Dawn* (1996), an autobiography. *Falls Memories* (1982) deals with the spirit of resistance in Belfast. *Cage Eleven* (1990) and *The Street* (1993) are prison sketches and stories, displaying humour and humanity.

Adrigoole (1929), a novel by Peadar *O'Donnell set in West Donegal in the early 20th cent. Hughie and Brigid Dalach are invited to farm the land of an old bachelor who leaves them the property on his death, but they render themselves destitute by feeding and clothing the Republicans during the *Anglo-Irish war.

adventures, see *tale-types.

AE, see George *Russell.

Áed mac Crimthainn, see *Book of Leinster.

Aeneid, see *classical literature in Irish.

Aengus [Oengus] see *mythological cycle, Irish *mythology, and *Aislinge Oenguso.

áes dána ('men of art'), a collective term in Early Irish for the practitioners of the professions, trades, arts, and crafts. The social rank of the áes dána is reflected in Gaelic *law and literature. The most important literary treatment of the áes dána is in *Cath Maige Tuired*, in which the professionals practising at the court of the king of *Tara are listed as carpenter, smith, fighter, harper, warrior, poet and historian, sorcerer, physician, cupbearer, and brazier.

Uraicecht Becc (*Small Primer*), a tract of the 8th or 9th cent., makes a broad distinction between two classes of person enjoying certain immunities in Irish law. Of the áes dána, the poets (filid) belong in the upper rank with the landowners (lords and freemen) and the clerics. The lower rank comprises 'the people of every art besides', who include wrights, blacksmiths, braziers, craftsmen, physicians, judges, druids, and others. Irish law distinguishes between the principal professions (prímdánae) and the lesser professions (fodánae), which are practised by various types of entertainer and by all musicians with the sole exception of the harper, who enjoys a higher status.

The most highly developed of the professional hierarchies is that of the poets. In *Uraicecht Becc*, seven types of poet are ranked from the ollam downwards. In addition to the poet (fili), there is another type of versifier, the bard, who lacked the professional training of the fili. There is no mention of the bard in *Uraicecht Becc*, but other texts supply classifications of bards. Three grades of judge are distinguished in *Uraicecht Becc*, the lowest grade being competent to decide on matters relating to the áes dána. There are many indications of the close interaction between Church and laity, and it is clear that in early Ireland the áes dána served both ecclesiastical and secular patrons. The term Aos Dána was adopted by the Irish Arts Council (An Chomhairle Ealaíon) for an affiliation of artists receiving pensions from the *Irish State, set up in 1983 by Charles J. Haughey, advised by Anthony *Cronin.

African Witch, The (1936), a novel by Joyce *Cary, set in southern Nigeria and based on his experiences in the colonial service. An African witch uses juju to kill the enemies of Aladai, heir to the emirate of Rimi.

'After the Race' (1904), a story in James *Joyce's *Dubliners* (1914). Jimmy Doyle, a butcher's son, attends a motor-race with other young men more cosmopolitan than he, and struggles to keep up with them in hilarity and recklessness.

Agreeable Surprise, The (1781), a comic opera by John *O'Keeffe, first produced at the Haymarket Theatre, London. Eugene and Laura are in love but her father, Sir Felix, insists that she must marry someone else. The surprise is that he has been teasing them.

aided, see *tale-types.

Aided Cheltchair maic Uthechair (*Violent Death of Celtchar mac Uthechair*), a short saga of the *Ulster cycle preserved in the *Book of Leinster*. By way of atonement for killing a guest Celtchar is obliged to free the Ulstermen from their three greatest afflictions: Conganchess, an invulnerable warrior; a fierce dog called Luchdonn; and another dog that attacks livestock. Celtchar is killed by a drop of the second dog's blood.

Aided Chon Culainn (*Violent Death of *Cú Chulainn*), also known as *Brislech Mór Maige Murthemne* (*Great Rout at Mag Murthemne*), a saga of the *Ulster cycle in which Cú Chulainn meets his death on the plain of Mag Muirthemne in Co. Louth. Pierced by a spear, he fastens himself to a pillar-stone so that he may die standing up. When a raven dares to settle on his shoulder, it is taken as a sign that he is dead, and he is beheaded. There is a version in the *Book of Leinster*.

Aided Chon Roí (*Violent Death of Cú Roí*), a saga of the *Ulster cycle. Cú Roí, a West Munster king married to Bláithine, is slain by *Cú Chulainn with her connivance. The court poet Ferchertne avenges his patron by casting himself of a cliff with the treacherous wife. A version is preserved in the 14th-cent. *Yellow Book of Lecan*.

Aided Chonlaích, see *Oidheadh Chonlaoich*.

Aided Chonchoboir, see *Conchobor mac Nessa.

Aided Oenfhir Aífe (*Violent Death of Aífe's Only Son*), an Early Irish saga of the *Ulster cycle preserved in the 14th-cent. *Yellow Book of Lecan*. While learning the arts of war in Scotland, *Cú Chulainn has fathered a son, Conlae, with the woman-warrior Aífe who lays down an injunction (*geís) that the son should come to Ireland at manhood, but also that he should never reveal who he is. Cú Chulainn fails to recognize his boy, and kills him.

Aifreann na Marbh, a long poem by Eoghan *Ó Tuairisc included in *Lux Aeterna* (1964). Written in the form of a requiem mass, it commemorates the victims of the atomic bomb attack on Hiroshima, and depicts a journey through Dublin at the same time.

Ailill, see *Táin Bó Cuailnge.

Airbertach mac Cosse (?–1016), poet; lector and later superior of the monastery of Ros Ailithir (now Rosscarbery), on the coast of south-west Co. Cork. 'Rofessa i curp Domuin Dúir', a poem on the geography of the world, is ascribed to him in both the *Book of Glendalough* and the *Book of Leinster*.

airchinnech, see *coarb.

Airec Menman Uraird maic Coise (*Stratagem of Aurard mac Cosse*), an Irish saga which tells how the 10th-cent. poet Aurard mac Cosse received compensation for losses sustained by him from the King of *Tara, Domnall mac Muirchertaig (d. 980). Aurard lists the titles of the stories he can tell, thereby providing one of the two extant versions of the medieval Irish tale-list.

aisling (vision or dream), a Gaelic literary genre, primarily associated with the *political poetry of the 18th cent. though having roots in early Irish literary texts dealing both with love and sovereignty [see Irish *mythology]. Although the love-aisling was still in wide use in the 18th cent. (particularly in Ulster), the genre was by then being used more frequently to express the hope of political deliverance after the *Williamite War. The vehicle of this message is the female persona of Ireland, often called the spéirbhean ('sky-woman'), and specifically named Caitlín ní Uallacháin by Liam Dall *Ó hIfearnáin [see also *Cathleen Ni Houlihan].

The political aisling was especially favoured by the 18th-cent. Munster poets, and in the hands of Eoghan Rua *Ó Súilleabháin it became very formalized, encapsulating a set pattern of conventionalized themes. The poet wanders forth and meets a fairy woman [see *sídh] of outstanding beauty, who is described in terms of traditional and conventional formulas; he engages in dialogue with her and asks her name, and she identifies herself as Ireland, forsaken by her legitimate spouse. The aisling ends with the woman declaiming a prophecy of the return of the rightful Stuart king. See Breandán *Ó Buachalla, *Aisling Ghéar: Na Stíobhartaigh agus an tAos Léinn*, 1603–1788 (1997).

Aislinge meic Conglinne (*Vision of Mac Conglinne*), a parody of the medieval físi and immrama (vision and voyage tales [see *tale-types]) which also mocks the conventions of heroic literature and the institutions of Church and State. Influenced by goliardic satire, the tale was composed in the 12th cent. and is preserved in *Leabhar Breac*. Ainíer Mac Conglinne, a scholar and satirist from Roscommon, decides to become a poet and goes to Cork to seek patronage, where he is meanly entertained.

Aislinge Oenguso (*Vision of Oengus*), an Old Irish saga which survives in a manuscript of the early 16th-cent. Oengus, son of the god Dagda and the goddess Boann [see Irish *mythology], falls in love with a beautiful woman whom he has seen in a dream.

aithed, see *tale-types.

Albigenses, The (1824), Charles Robert *Maturin's last novel. Set in early 13th-cent. France, it is a loose historical account of the campaign of Simon de Montfort against the Albigenses led by Count Raymond, and the vicissitudes encountered by two brothers involved in it, the vengeful Paladour and the gallant Amirald, who respectively love Isabelle and Genevieve on the other side.

Alciphron, or The Minute Philosopher (1732), George *Berkeley's longest book and his most sustained defence of theism and of Christianity, consisting of seven dialogues in which Crito and Euphranor represent the author's position while Alciphron and

Lysicles are the 'minute philosophers', taking the part of contemporary free-thinkers such as Mandeville and Shaftesbury.

Alexander, Cecil Frances (née Humphreys) (1818–1895), poet and author of 'All Things Bright and Beautiful'. She was born in Dublin, daughter of a land agent, and married William *Alexander in 1850. Her religious poetry includes *Hymns for Little Children* (1848), *Verses for Holy Seasons* (1846), and *Narrative Hymns for Village Schools* (1853).

Alexander, Mrs, see Annie French *Hector.

Alexander, William (1824–1911), churchman and poet. The son of a clergyman in Derry, he became Archbishop of Armagh and Protestant Primate of Ireland in 1896. Although the author of theological works such as *Primary Convictions* (1893), he wrote poems as in *St. Augustine's Holiday* (1886) and *The Finding of the Book* (1900).

Allgood, Molly (pseudonym 'Máire O'Neill') (1887–1952), actress. Born in Dublin, she was brought up in an orphanage and joined the *Abbey Theatre in 1905. She played Pegeen Mike in the first productions of *The *Playboy of the Western World* and was engaged to the author, J. M. *Synge.

Allgood, Sara (1883–1950), actress; sister of Molly *Allgood and, like her, brought up in a Dublin orphanage. A member of Inghinidhe na hÉireann, she joined the *Abbey Theatre in 1904, playing in Lady *Gregory's *Spreading the News* and as Maurya in *Synge's *Riders to the Sea*. In 1916 she married Gerald Henson and left the Abbey, returning to play in a revival of Lennox *Robinson's *The *Whiteheaded Boy* in 1920.

Allingham, William (1824–1889), poet. Born in Ballyshannon, Co. Donegal, and educated there, he worked in a bank before entering the customs service in 1846. As a young man he wrote words to popular folk airs and had them printed as *broadsheets. *Poems* (1850) contained the popular lyric 'The Fairies'. He knew D. G. Rossetti, Thomas *Carlyle, and Tennyson, whom he met in 1851. *Day and Night Songs* (1854), illustrated by Rossetti, was followed by *The Music Master* (1855). *Laurence Bloomfield in Ireland* (1864) was issued by *Fraser's Magazine* in twelve instalments during 1863, dealing with the Land War [see *Land League]. In 1870 he settled in London, where he became sub-editor on *Fraser's Magazine*, taking over as editor in 1874. In that year he married Helen Paterson, the water-colourist. Among his major collections are *Songs, Ballads and Stories* (1877); *Evil May-Day* (1882); *Blackberries* (1884); *Irish Songs and Poems* (1887); and *Life and Phantasy* (1889).

All-Ireland Review, The (Jan. 1900–Jan. 1906), a weekly literary journal edited by Standish James *O'Grady in Kilkenny, offering a conservative perspective on Irish affairs.

All That Fall (1957), a radio play by Samuel *Beckett. Maddy Rooney goes to the railway station to meet her blind and domineering husband Dan, returning from work. The train is delayed, caused by the death of a child falling from it.

Altram Tighe Dá Mheadhar (*Fosterage of the Houses of the Two Milk-Vessels*), a tale probably dating from the 14th cent., set among the Tuatha Dé Danann [see *sídh] after they have been banished to the fairy-mounds, it relates how Eithne is fostered in Oengus's dwelling at Brug na Bóinne [see *New Grange].

Amergin, the name given to several legendary poets in medieval Irish literature, signifying wonderful birth. Amergin is included in pseudo-historical accounts of the settlement of the Gaels in Ireland as found in *Lebor Gabála*. Coming ashore, he sings a cosmic hymn in which he identifies himself with the whole of creation.

amhrán, see Irish *metrics.

Amongst Women (1990), a novel by John *McGahern. Michael Moran, a veteran of the *Anglo-Irish War, lives in the north-west midlands with his second wife, Rose, and family. His moods and sense of superiority over his neighbours impede his relations with his children.

Amory, Thomas (?1691–1788), novelist. Brought up in Ireland, he was educated at TCD and later lived at Hounslow and Westminster. Amory wrote two eccentric works of fiction, *Memoirs of Several Ladies of Great Britain* (1755) and *The Life of John Buncle, Esq.* (1756–66). The former deals with a community of learned women sequestered on a certain 'Green Isle' in the Hebrides. *John Buncle* deals with the repeated marriages and philosophy of an Anglo-Irishman in England.

Amra Choluim Cille (*Eulogy of *Colum Cille*), the earliest surviving verse composition in the Irish language, probably composed shortly after the saint's death in AD 597, in which Colum Cille is depicted as heroic in his asceticism.

Androcles and the Lion: *A Fable Play* (1913), a play by George Bernard *Shaw exploring the politics of religious persecution and the nature of religious commitment, and set in Imperial Rome.

Angel of Pity, The (1935), a novel by Francis *Stuart, set in the future during 'the next great war' and exploring the concept of spiritual renewal through suffering. The narrator, a writer, is led to an awareness of love through his relationship with Sonia, whose rape and death parallel the sacrifice of Christ.

Anglo-Irish chronicles see Anglo-Irish *chronicles.

Anglo-Irish dialects, see *Hiberno-English.

Anglo-Irish literature, a term used to describe Irish writing in English which helps to distinguish this tradition from English literature and literature in Gaelic. The term Anglo-Irish was applied increasingly by 19th-cent. historians of the Protestant *ascendancy to register growing awareness of the political and social circumstances of British settlers in Ireland. It came into general use as a term to describe Irish writing in English only after the Anglo-Irish had ceased to be the dominant class following the Land War [see *Land League]. Thomas *MacDonagh, in *Literature in Ireland: Studies Irish and Anglo-Irish* (1916), argued that Anglo-Irish literature could express Irish cultural identity, and that the use of *Hiberno-English would help further its distinctness. In *Anglo-Irish Essays* (1917), John *Eglinton applied the term generally to Irish writers after John *Bale. It had already gained currency as a term for modern Irish writing in English when the bibliographer Stephen *Brown employed it in 1919 to describe the body of writing investigated in Ernest Boyd's *Ireland's Literary Renaissance* (1916). In *Synge and Anglo-Irish Literature* (1931), Daniel *Corkery associated it with an attitude of mind, expressed in the work of *Somerville and Ross, *Yeats, and Lady *Gregory, which he saw as alien to Irish life.

Since then the term has been adopted for all periods in literary histories and bibliographies. In 1968 A. N. *Jeffares founded the International Association for the Study of Anglo-Irish Literature (IASAIL, later IASIL, where the term is dropped to refer to 'Irish Literatures') which has done much to promote world-wide academic study of all of Irish writing. The term cannot comfortably be applied to most Irish writing after 1922, for there is something less than satisfactory in describing Thomas *Kinsella, or Seamus *Heaney as Anglo-Irish writers, hence IASIL rather than IASAIL.

Anglo-Irish literature has taken as recurrent themes the country of Ireland itself, its land, government, and laws; its different and often mutually antagonistic political and religious cultures; and matters of history and society, language and tradition. As a literature of a country colonized by Britain, it has been especially preoccupied with questions of national identity.

Language was always a crucial issue, in that the history of Anglo-Irish literature was co-extensive with the substitution of English for Irish as the language of the majority. An enriching consequence of the displacement of Irish has been a questioning or comic attitude to language, leading to subtlety and nuance in the use of Hiberno-English, as well as to crude *stage-Irish misrepresentation. It has been profoundly influenced by the indigenous literature in Irish, from which it derived an atmosphere imbued with ancient Celtic *mythology, a love of nature's intricacy and detail, and an earthy realism. The *literary revival, a late flowering of Anglo-Irish literature, drew extensively upon the variety of its sources, with Lady Gregory and Synge building upon native elements.

See A. N. *Jeffares, *Anglo-Irish Literature* (1982) and Seamus *Deane, *A Short History of Irish Literature* (1986).

Anglo-Irish of the Nineteenth Century, The (1828), a nationalistic novel published anonymously by John *Banim, which offers an analysis of the political caste system of the period and a sardonic portrait of the *ascendancy. The plot is a variant on the reformed absentee theme pioneered by Maria *Edgeworth.

Anglo-Irish War, the (1919–1921), the War of Independence whereby a parliament of the Republic of Ireland asserted its sovereignty in arms and won dominion status from the British Government under the terms of the Anglo-Irish Treaty. Following *Sinn Féin's 1918 general election victory, that party constituted itself as Dáil Éireann in Dublin on 21 January 1919, declaring allegiance to the Republic proclaimed in the 1916 *Easter Rising. The same day, a party of *Irish Volunteers killed two members of the Royal Irish Constabulary (RIC) escorting gelignite at Soloheadbeg, Co. Tipperary. The ensuing guerrilla operations were conducted by the *IRA under the brilliant direction of Michael *Collins. The government raised the *Black and Tans and the Auxiliaries, two forces recruited from ex-servicemen in Britain. By the spring of 1921 the administrative processes of the State were in abeyance and neither side could see any prospect of military victory. On 10 July a truce was declared leading to the signing of an Anglo-Irish Treaty in London on 6 December 1921 and the foundation of an Irish Free State. The Treaty was repudiated by Eamon *de Valera, and those who left with him formed the Republican leadership in the ensuing *Civil War.

Annála Ríoghachta Éireann, see *Annals of the Four Masters.

annals, Irish. The Irish annals contain records of facts and dates concerning the inaugurations and deaths of kings, battles, the founding of abbeys and monasteries or their destruction, dynastic marriages, and other such material, all listed under the year of their occurrence. After the monastic reform of the 12th and 13th cents. the work of preserving and compiling historic records passed into the hands of secular learned families such as the *Ó Maoilchonaires, the *Ó Cléirighs, and the *Mac Fhir Bhisighs, who perpetuated the records independently of liturgical requirements. The resultant annals, based on earlier materials, vary greatly in their geographical as well as chronological spread, and are preserved in *manuscripts written between the 14th and 17th cents. The *Annals of the Four Masters, latest of them all, was compiled in Donegal by Mícheál *Ó Cléirigh and his associates during the 1630s. The *Annals of Ulster, one of the sources for this synthesis of Gaelic records, itself comprises copies of earlier material and is the most reliable source for the medieval period. Most of the annals deal with the pre-historical period from the Creation to the coming of Christianity, and share a body of quasi-historical and historical lore based upon the Bible, Latin sources, and the Irish synthetic history *Lebor Gabála. See Gearóid Mac Niocaill, *The Medieval Irish Annals* (1975).

Annals of Clonmacnoise, the, record events from the earliest times to the year 1408, and survive in an English translation made in 1627 by Conall *Mac Geoghegan of Lismoyny, Co. Westmeath. The original manuscript is lost, and nothing is known of its compilers or scribes. These *Annals* draw on materials probably assembled at the monastery of *Clonmacnoise.

Annals of Connacht, the, surviving in a manuscript written in the 15th and 16th cents. mainly by three members of the *Ó Duibhgeannáin family (most probably), record events from 1224 to 1544.

Annals of Inisfallen, the, record events from the earliest times to the year 1326, and are the main source for the history of early medieval Munster. The first part, chronicling events to 1092, was probably written at Emly, Co. Tipperary.

Annals of Loch Cé, the, record events from 1014 to 1590 and survive in two manuscripts; they provide, along with the *Annals of Connacht*, invaluable material for the history of Connacht in the later Middle Ages.

Annals of the Four Masters, the (properly *Annála Ríoghachta Eireann/ Annals of the Kingdom of Ireland*), a compilation of *annals recording events in Ireland from the earliest times to 1616. They were written by Mícheál *Ó Cléirigh at Bundrowse, Co. Donegal, between 1632 and 1636, with the help of Cúchoigríche Ó Cléirigh, Fearfeasa *Ó Maoilchonaire, and Cúchoigríche *Ó Duibhgeannáin, collectively called the Four Masters following the designation used by John *Colgan. The whole project, initially devised in the Franciscan community at *Louvain, was made practicable in Ireland by the patronage of Fearghal Ó Gadhra of Coolavin, Co. Sligo. See John *O'Donovan, *Annála Ríoghachta Éireann: Annals of the Kingdom of Ireland by the Four Masters* (6 vols., 1848–51).

Annals of Tigernach, the, a compilation of *annals made at *Clonmacnoise, and so called because of a mistaken notion that they were the work of Tigernach ua Braein (d. 1088). In addition to some prehistorical material, they record events AD 489–766 and 974–1178.

Annals of Ulster, the (*Annála Uladh*, or *Annála Senait*), begun by Cathal Mac Maghnusa (d. 1498), Dean of Lough Erne, and carried on after his death, record events from the earliest times to the year 1541, with some additional entries up to 1588. The manuscript was written on the island of Senait (now Bell Isle) in Lough Erne for Mac Maghnusa by Ruaidhrí Ó Luinín.

Anster, John [Martin] (1793–1867), poet and scholar. Born in Charleville, Co. Cork, he was educated at TCD, where he eventually became Regius Professor of Civil Law. His verse translation of the first part of Goethe's *Faust* as *Faustus: A Dramatic Mystery* (1835) was acclaimed immediately. The second part followed in 1864. *Xeniola* (1851) was a collection of poetry.

Aoife, see *Aided Oenfhir Aife* and *Cú Chulainn.

aonach, see *oenach.

Aonach Tailteann, see *oenach.

Aongus [Oengus], see *Aislinge Oenguso*, *mythological cycle, and Irish *mythology.

Aos Dána, see *áes dána.

Aphrodite in Aulis (1930), a historical novel by George *Moore, and his last published work, is a family saga of ancient Greece set in the Aulis of the 5th cent. BC.

Apple Cart, The: *A Political Extravaganza* (1929), a play by George Bernard *Shaw. Set in the latter part of the 20th cent. the play is a satirical sketch of democracy in disarray. King Magnus, an urbane ironist and skilful tactician, has precipitated a crisis by refusing to accept the role of a constitutional rubber-stamp.

'Araby', a story in James *Joyce's *Dubliners* (1914), written in 1905.

Aran Islands, The (1907), a travel work in four books by J. M. *Synge, written as a chapter of contemplative autobiography; it arose from W. B. *Yeats's advice that Synge should live on the islands in order to find an artistic purpose. Between May 1898 and summer 1902 he spent eighteen weeks in all on the islands. Besides translating stories and poems recited to him, the author describes a mixture of Catholic belief and pre-Christian custom and the physical colours and texture of island life.

Arbuckle, James ('Hibernicus') (1700–1742), schoolmaster and poet. Born in Dublin, and educated at Glasgow, he associated in Dublin with leading figures of the 'New Light' intelligentsia. His essays were published as *Hibernicus's Letters* (2 vols., 1725–7). *Snuff* (1719) is a mock-heroic poem on tobacco and *Glotta* (1721) a poetic description of Scottish scenery.

archaeology, Irish. The study of the human past in Ireland, through analysis of the material remains of different cultures, has established that when New Stone Age (neolithic) farmers arrived about 3000 BC they encountered very few inhabitants, though evidence exists for earlier settlements near beaches in Antrim, Down, and Louth, and along the River Bann extending back as far as 6000 BC. The presence of neolithic settlers from about 3000 BC is deduced from artefacts such as pottery and flint arrow- and axe-heads, as well as by the form of megalithic long-barrow and passage tombs—tombs constructed of large stones covered over by elongated earth barrows or circular mounds. The long-barrows are of two types: the court tomb and the portal tomb (the latter also frequently known as the portal dolmen). The court tomb is so called because the passage leading into the burial chamber at the recessed end of the barrow opens out to an open space or court immediately in front of the burial chamber itself. There are more than 300 court tombs sited mostly in the northern half of the country with concentrations in Mayo, Sligo, north Donegal, and around Carlingford Lough. Portal tombs are so called from the two large upright stones forming the entrance to the burial chamber; a capstone is set over these and slopes backwards to rest on backstones. Originally covered by a barrow, in their denuded state they are striking features of the Irish landscape. Ireland has some 150 examples of portal tombs, mostly in the court tomb area.

The passage tombs are a separate category to the long-barrow types, and include some of the most remarkable megalithic constructions in Europe, among them *New Grange, Knowth, Dowth in Co. Meath, and Carrowkeel in Co. Sligo. The passage tombs are most often set on a hilltop inside a large circular mound surrounded by kerbstones. The burial chamber is entered by a passage, often of considerable length. Many of the stones are engraved with ornamentations such as spirals, interconnecting loops, lozenges, and circles with lines emanating from them. The tombs are mainly concentrated along an axis from the mouth of the Boyne to Sligo, with other examples on the Antrim coastline and in Leinster. They date from roughly the same period as the long-barrow tombs but would appear to represent a more advanced culture.

In the Bronze Age remains were interred with food vessels or beakers, hence the term 'Beaker Folk'. During the Bronze Age Ireland had a significant metal industry, and exported artefacts in bronze, copper, and gold to Britain and the Continent. Bronze rapiers and gold torcs survive from *c*.1000 BC, while from *c*.700 BC there are trumpets and cauldrons in bronze, as well as many types of gold ornament. From this period the type of lake-dwelling known as the crannóg, wooden platforms built near the lake's edge, make their appearance. With the *Celts, who probably began to arrive *c*.300 BC, came the Iron Age culture known as La Tène, after a site in Switzerland, which had a characteristic style of ornamentation seen on such monuments as the Turoe Stone, and in metalwork. The Celts also introduced the ring fort, which remained the basis of the social structure of pre-Christian Ireland.

Amongst the hill forts are *Emain Macha, Ráth na Ríogh at *Tara, Grianán Ailigh in Donegal, and Dún Aonghusa on Aranmore. There are other field monuments. The standing stone (gallán) was used to mark burial sites and boundaries, and the many examples date from the early Iron Age down to the early Christian period. Some carry *ogam inscriptions. There are also stone circles which belong to the early Bronze Age. These are mostly concentrated in south-west Munster and mid-Ulster. See Michael Herity and George Eogan, *Ireland in Prehistory* (1977).

Archdall (or Archdale), Mervyn (1723–1791), antiquarian and author of *Monasticum Hibernicum* (1786), a survey of Irish ecclesiastical ruins. Born in Dublin and educated at TCD, Archdall served as chaplain to the Bishop of Ossory and held several livings before finally becoming rector of Slane, Co. Meath.

Archdeacon, Matthew (?1800–1853), novelist; born in Castlebar, Co. Mayo, where he became a schoolteacher. His *Legends of Connaught* (1829), *Connaught in '98* (1830), *Everard* (1835), and *The Priest Hunter* (1844), were based on local traditions.

ard-rí (high king), see *kingship.

Arden, John (1930–), English Marxist playwright who produced, while living in Ireland with his wife Margaretta D'Arcy (1934–), plays on Irish subjects. These include *The Non-Stop Connolly Show*, a twenty-six-hour cycle on James *Connolly's conflicts with capitalism (Dublin Theatre Festival, 1975), *The Ballygombeen Bequests* (1972), a farce on the British history in Ireland, and *The Little Grey Home in the West* (1982), dealing with the exploitation of a housing-estate family.

Arena (Spring 1963–Spring 1965), a literary magazine published in Wexford and edited by Michael *Hartnett, James *Liddy, and Liam O'Connor.

Aristocrats (1979), a play by Brian *Friel chronicling the disintegration of a Catholic *big house family at a reunion in Ballybeg Hall.

Arms and the Man (1894), a play by George Bernard *Shaw, set in Bulgaria at the time of the Serbo-Bulgarian war of 1885–6 and dealing with the glorification of war and idealized conceptions of human love.

Armstrong, G[eorge] F[rancis] (later Savage-Armstrong) (1845–1906), poet. Born in Co. Down, he was educated at TCD and became Professor of English and History at Queen's College, Cork, 1870–1905. His poetry includes effusive depictions of Renaissance Italy and Ireland in collections such as *Poems Lyrical and Dramatic* (1892), and dramatic poems such as *Ugone* (1870), *Victoria Regina* (1887), and *Mephistopheles in Broadcloth* (1888).

Arnold, Matthew (1822–1888), English poet-critic and Professor of Poetry at Oxford from 1857. His lectures *On the Study of Celtic Literature* (1867) were a formative influence on the Irish *literary revival, besides leading to the establishment of the Chair in Celtic at Jesus College, Oxford. Arnold conceived of *Indo-European culture as a unity in which the genius of the marginalized Celtic race was an underrated strand. He saw the Celtic psyche as 'essentially feminine', ambiguously praising the Celts for their indifference to the 'despotism of fact'.

Arrah-na-Pogue, or *The Wicklow Wedding* (1864), a political melodrama by Dion *Boucicault, set in the Wicklow Mountains during the Rebellion of 1798 [see *United Irishmen]. Beamish MacCoul has returned from exile in France to organize an insurrection, and also to marry Fanny Power. He hides in the cottage of the heroine, Arrah-na-Pogue, and is discovered there on the eve of her wedding to Shaun the Post.

Art Maguire, or *The Broken Pledge* (1845), a temperance novel by William *Carleton published as part of James *Duffy's 'Library of Ireland'. Having unsuccessfully sworn off drink three times, Art dies in the poorhouse, almost killing his own son when he breaks his pledge for the third time.

Arthurian literature, as redefined by Geoffrey of Monmouth (*fl.* 1140) and developed in the romances of Chrétien de Troyes (*fl.* 1180), found its way back to Britain and eventually to Ireland, where a group of adaptations into Irish form an identifiable subgroup within early modern prose literature. *Lorgaireacht an tSoidhigh Naomhtha,* a 15th cent. translation of the *Queste del Sant Graal,* is the best-known of these. An Arthurian element surfaces in later genres of literature such as stories or apologues in *bardic verse, *ballads and oral tales, and even *genealogies. Early texts of the *Fionn cycle make reference to an Artúr who led a British war-band, while the 11th-cent. Irish translation of Nennius' *Historia Brittonum* supplies glimpses of a supposedly historical Arthur. The early Irish saga *Scéla Cano meic Gartnáin* has been suggested as a source for the Tristan and Isolde theme.

As I Was Going Down Sackville Street (1937), the first of several volumes of reminiscence by Oliver St John *Gogarty, subtitled 'A Phantasy in Fact', and covering a period from the 1900s to the 1930s. The book shows a close familiarity with the poorer parts of Dublin and its people.

As Strangers Here (1960), a novel by Janet *McNeill which addresses the *Troubles through the eyes of Revd Edward Ballater, a Presbyterian clergyman who has an invalid wife and unhappy children as well as a bigoted and demoralized congregation.

ascendancy, a term generally used to refer to the Protestant upper classes of Ireland in the 18th cent. and later. The defeat of the Jacobites [see *Williamite War] in 1689–91 left local political power entirely in the hands of a Protestant landed class. Their dominance was based partly on a near-monopoly of landed wealth, partly on the exclusion from full citizenship of Catholics and Presbyterians. Landlord control was dented when Daniel *O'Connell and others began to mobilize the Catholic masses from the 1820s. The decades after the Act of *Union had seen a steady widening of Catholic access to the civil service, judiciary, and other former Protestant preserves. Land-ownership itself, for more than two centuries the key to political and social authority, was dismantled by a series of measures, notably the *Wyndham Land Act of 1903. The term 'Protestant ascendancy' first came into use in the 1780s to define the constitutional arrangements that conservatives felt were being jeopardized by recent moves to allow greater political and religious freedom to Catholics [see *Catholic Emancipation]. Its use was popularized during the bitter debates that accompanied the passage of the Relief Acts of 1792 and 1793.

Ashbury (also Astbury), Joseph (1638–1720), manager of the Theatre Royal at *Smock Alley. He came to Ireland as a soldier and took part in the capture of Dublin Castle for Charles II, for which he received a commission. In 1666 he took over the management of the theatre, becoming Master of the Revels the year after.

Ashe, Thomas (1770–1835), soldier and memoirist. Born to a down-at-heel *ascendancy family in Glasnevin, Co. Dublin, he ran away to join the army. His *Memoirs and Confessions* (1815) is an autobiographical account of 'criminal and delinquent' escapades beginning with the seduction of a girl in France. In America he edited the *National Intelligencer*, and was arrested when attempting to steal treasures from churches in Latin America. Other works were: *Travels in America* (1806) and *The Soldier of Fortune* (1816).

Ashton, Robert (?1706–?), author of *The Battle of Aughrim* (1727; earliest extant edition 1756), a four-act play in bombastic verse, much reprinted and frequently acted in Ulster country towns down to the early 20th cent. It celebrates the Protestant victory in a crucial engagement of the *Williamite War.

Assassin, The (1928), a novel by Liam *O'Flaherty loosely based on the assassination in 1927 of Kevin O'Higgins, Free State Minister for Justice.

Asses in Clover, see *Cuanduine trilogy.

Aston, W[illiam] G[eorge] (1841–1911), philologist, born in Derry and educated at QUB. He wrote grammars of Japanese, a translation of the chronicles of Japan (*Nohongi*, 1896) and studies of Japanese culture, *A History of Japanese Literature* (1899) and *Shinto, the Way of the Gods* (1905).

At Swim-Two-Birds (1939), a novel by Flann *O'Brien influenced by pulp fiction and Old and Middle Irish tales. A student is living uneasily at his uncle's house in Dublin while writing a book about an author called Trellis. The latter has borrowed his characters from literary stereotype, including cowboys who run riot in Ringsend. His own characters bring Trellis to trial on charges of maltreatment. Caught up in these events are characters from Gaelic legend and *folklore, such as *Fionn mac Cumail and the Pooka [see *sídh].

Atkinson, Joseph (1743–1818), playwright. Born in Dublin and educated at TCD, he wrote dramatic comedies and comic operas such as *Mutual Deception* (1785), *Match for a Widow* (1788), and *Love in a Blaze* (1800) which were produced successfully with music by Charles Dibdin and Sir John *Stevenson.

Audacht Morainn (*Testament of Morann*), a 7th-cent. *gnomic text in Old Irish consisting of advice by the legendary judge Morann to a young king, stressing the importance of justice in bringing about peace and stability.

Aughrim, Battle of, see *Williamite War.

Auraicept na nÉces (*Scholars' Primer*), an Old Irish text on language, possibly written by *Cenn Fáelad, covering topics such as the origin of the classification of letters in the Latin and Irish alphabets, *ogam, and grammatical gender.

Autobiographies (1955), a compilation of previously published autobiographical writings by W. B. *Yeats, comprising: 'Reveries Over Childhood and Youth' (1915, though actually appearing in 1916); 'The Trembling of the Veil' (1922); 'Dramatis Personae' (1935); 'Estrangement' (1926); 'The Death of Synge' (1928); and 'The Bounty of Sweden' (1925). Macmillan had earlier issued 'Reveries over Childhood and Youth' and 'The Trembling of the Veil' as *Autobiographies* (1926).

Autobiographies (1963) by Sean *O'Casey, comprising *I Knock at the Door* (1939), *Pictures in the Hallway* (1942), *Drums under the Windows* (1945), *Inishfallen, Fare Thee Well* (1949), *Rose and Crown* (1952), and *Sunset and Evening Star* (1954), and frequently reprinted in a two-volume edition by Macmillan after 1963. Though factually unreliable, these third-person narratives present a moving chronicle of a poverty-stricken childhood in Dublin and the author's struggle for literary recognition.

Autumn Fire (1924), a three-act play by T. C. *Murray, staged at the *Abbey Theatre, telling of the growing attraction between Owen Keegan, a widower, and the young Nance Desmond.

Autumn Journal and **Autumn Sequel,** see Louis *MacNeice.

Avatars, The, see George *Russell.

Back to Methuselah: *A Metabiological Pentateuch* (1922), a five-part play cycle by George Bernard *Shaw, written in 1918-20. It is partly an expression of his belief in Creative Evolution and partly a satire on human folly. The framing conception is that only the extreme longevity of Methuselah and other biblical patriarchs could provide humanity with the necessary wisdom for self-government. Part I is set in the Garden of Eden; in Parts II and III the population of the world divides into 'short-livers' and the more highly evolved 'long-livers' and England is run by Africans and Chinese; Part IV moves to Galway Bay in AD 3000; and Part V is set in AD 31,920. The cycle concludes with Lilith, who proclaims a final transition to a state of pure intelligence.

Baile Chuin Chétchathaig (*Ecstasy of *Conn Cétchathach*), a 7th-cent. text on the kingship of *Tara, preserved in two 16th-cent. manuscripts, cast in the form of a prophecy naming the kings of Tara from the prehistoric Art, son of Conn, down to 697.

Baile in Scáil (*Phantom's Vision*), a text on the kings of *Tara composed in the 9th cent. *Conn Cétchathach is brought to the otherworld [see *sídh], where he meets a woman identified as the sovereignty of Ireland [see *mythology].

Bailegangaire (1985), a play by Thomas *Murphy, set in a cottage in the west of Ireland, telling how the small town of the title (Town Without Laughter) came by its name. Mommo, who embodies a variety of female personifications, tells the story of a laughing competition and its aftermath.

Bairéad, Riocard (?1740–1819), poet. Born in Barrack, Erris, Co. Mayo, where he worked as a teacher and small farmer. Amongst his poems are a vigorous drinking song, 'Preab san Ól', and a vicious mock-lament on a bailiff, 'Eoghan Cóir', written in 1788.

Bairéad, Tomás (1893–1973), writer of short stories in Irish. Born near Moycullen, Co. Galway, the son of a small farmer, he was educated locally. He joined the *Irish Independent* in Dublin in 1922, and became Irish Editor in 1945. Among his collections are: *Cumhacht na Cinniúna* (1936), *Ór na hAitinne* (1949), and *Dán* (1973). *Gan Baisteadh* (1972) contains autobiographical recollections.

Balcony of Europe (1972), a novel by Aidan *Higgins, set in an artists' enclave on the southern coast of Spain. It concerns an affair between Dan Ruttle, an Irish painter, and Charlotte Bayliss, wife of an American academic.

Bale, John (1495–1563), Anglican Bishop of Ossory and playwright. Born in Norfolk, he became a Carmelite friar before entering Jesus College, Oxford, where he converted to Protestantism. Around 1534, he wrote a number of plays on Protestant themes. *King John* (1538) is regarded as a first step towards the Elizabethan English history play. After the accession of Edward VI, he wrote the flagrantly sectarian, *The Image of Both Churches* [in] *the Revelation of St. John* (1550), and gained preferment to the See of Ossory. *The Vocation of John Bale* (1553) is a justification of his refusal to be consecrated under the Roman rite, still in use in Ireland. His attempts to root out 'idolatry' in his diocese with performances of his plays at the

Kilkenny market cross resulted in civil disturbances.

Balfe, Michael [William] (1808–1870), singer-composer of operas. Born in Pitt St. (now Balfe St.), Dublin, he was chosen by Rossini to appear as Figaro in *The Barber of Seville* (Paris, 1827). His *The Bohemian Girl* (1843) became a favourite Irish opera. Other operas include *Falstaff* (1838) and *The Sicilian Bride* (1852) in English, and *Puits d'Amour* (1843) in French.

Balfour, Mary (1780–?), schoolteacher and poet, Born in Derry, she provided eight poems for Edward *Bunting's *General Collection of Ancient Irish Music* (1809). Her collection *Hope* (1810) contains some translations of Gaelic poetry and carries an epigraph from Charlotte *Brooke.

Ballad of Reading Gaol, The, a prison poem written by Oscar *Wilde in 1897–8, after his release and during his self-imposed exile in France and Italy; and published anonymously over his prison number, C33.

ballads in Ireland. The ballad came to Ireland from England and Scotland from around the beginning of the 17th cent., its popularity increasing as the English language spread. The ballad in Irish is almost unknown [but see *lays]. Ballads are most often first-person narratives told in rhyming quatrains of *Hiberno-English, and dealing with matters such as love and war. Non-literary in origin, they were circulated orally by itinerant singers and through the sale of *broadsheets. Ballads reflecting the physical and emotional traumas of emigration were composed throughout the latter part of the 19th cent. Many published Irish ballads arose from the 19th-cent. attempt of Thomas *Davis and Charles Gavan *Duffy to provide a 'ballad history of

Ireland' in *The *Spirit of the Nation* (1843) as a means of raising political awareness. A dolorous attitude towards the lost kingdoms of Gaelic Ireland, combined with a more practical aspiration towards modern nationhood, is characteristic of the verse that featured prolifically in *The *Nation, The Shamrock, The Irishman,* and various publications launched by James *Duffy & Co. The ballad proved adaptable for the drawing-room as in the comic entertainment of Percy *French. Writers of the *literary revival made extensive use of the form, e.g. Padraic *Colum in 'She Moved Through the Fair'. See Hugh Shields, *Narrative Songs in Ireland* (1990).

Ballroom of Romance, The (1972), the title-story of a collection by William *Trevor, in which Bridie resigns herself to marrying Bowser Egan, a whiskey-sodden bachelor.

Balor, see *mythological cycle.

Banim, John (1798–1842), novelist and poet. Born in Kilkenny, the second son of a farmer and small shopkeeper, he was educated at Kilkenny Grammar School, before studying art at the *RDS. In 1816 he returned to Kilkenny and set up as a drawing-master. He moved to Dublin in 1820 and began writing full-time.

His first significant production, *The Celt's Paradise* (1821), a poem, was admired by Sir Walter Scott. *Damon and Pythias*, a classical tragedy, was produced at Covent Garden in May 1821. Following the failure of other plays, John visited Kilkenny in 1822 and suggested to his elder brother Michael (*Banim) that they collaborate in writing a series of Irish tales in the style of Scott, begining with *Tales by the O'Hara Family* (1825). His best-remembered poems are 'Aileen' and 'Soggarth Aroon'. Banim issued a collection of satirical essays in novel form as *Revelations of the Dead Alive* in 1824.

John's contributions to the first series of the *Tales of the O'Hara Family* were *The *Fetches* and *John Doe*. The collection was followed by a second series of O'Hara tales in 1826. John's individual work here included *The *Nowlans*, a story of clerical life. *The Denounced* (1830) includes two studies of Catholics under the *Penal Laws (*The *Last Baron of Crana* and *The Conformists*).

Supplied with research material by Michael, John specialized in historical romance focused on the history of religious persecution. *The *Boyne Water* (1826) attempts to emulate Scott while appealing to an English readership to understand the wrong done in dishonouring the Treaty of Limerick [see *Williamite War]: *The *Anglo-Irish of the Nineteenth Century* (1828), is a satirical account of political divisions between the social classes in colonial Ireland. His last novel, *The *Smuggler* (1831), is an improbable melodrama.

Banim returned in a state of near-paralysis to Kilkenny in 1840. See John Cronin, *The Anglo-Irish Novel: The 19th Century* (1980).

Banim, Mary (?–1939), a daughter of Michael *Banim, was born in Kilkenny. *Here and There Through Ireland* (1891) is an account of a journey through post-*Famine Ireland.

Banim, Michael (1796–1874), novelist. Born in Kilkenny and educated there, he abandoned legal training to rescue his father's shopkeeping business in Kilkenny, unlike his younger brother John (*Banim), the better-known member of the 'O'Hara Family'. When his brother returned from London in 1822, Michael responded to his plans for a collection of national tales with *Crohoore of the Bill-Hook*, the first of the stories in the *Tales of the O'Hara Family* (1825). During 1826 Michael visited his brother in London, meeting Gerald *Griffin. *Peter at the Castle* in the second series of *Tales* (1826) appears to be mostly his work. Michael's subsequent novels *The Ghost Hunter and his Family* (1833) and *The *Mayor of Windgap* (1835) both appeared under the O'Hara name rather than his own. Actual collaboration resumed in the eighteen stories of *The *Bit o' Writing* (1848). *Father Connell* (1842) shows Michael's hand throughout. In about 1840, shortly after his marriage to Catherine O'Dwyer, the shopkeeping business failed. *The *Town of the Cascades* (1864), a temperance novel, was the only book-length work to bear his name. From 1852 to 1873 he was postmaster in Kilkenny.

He tried to dissuade his more radical brother from writing *The *Boyne Water* (1826), while his own novel about the Rebellion of 1798, *The *Croppy* (1828), is deferential to an English readership. His familiarity with the Irish landscape and the mentality of the peasantry are reflected in a keen insight into the rural life of pre-*Famine Ireland. Banim wrote the introductions and notes for the collected works of the O'Hara Family issued in Dublin in 1865.

banshee, a *folklore figure whose lamentation portends a family death. In the form of a solitary woman, *bean sí* in Irish meaning 'woman of the *sídh', she derives from the *mythological construct whereby a goddess presides over the fortunes of a *kinship group. She is generally heard at night rather than seen, though some late stories portray her as a small, wizened old woman who combs her hair as she makes her cry.

banshenchas (lore of women), a body

of writing about women, surviving in both metrical and prose form. The original metrical version was composed by Gilla Mo-Dotu ua Casaide on Devinish Island, Lower Lough Erne, in 1147. The poem catalogues the history of the famous women of Ireland. An expanded prose version also survives.

Banville, John (1945–), novelist; born in Wexford town and educated by the Christian Brothers, he worked as a sub-editor on *The Irish Press*, before becoming literary editor of *The Irish Times*, 1988–99. His first collection of short stories, *Long Lankin* (1970), was followed by a novel, *Nightspawn* (1971), a thriller set in Greece just before the military takeover of 1967. *Birchwood* (1973) revisits the *big house theme of Irish fiction in surprising and disturbing ways. Banville embarked on a series of novels exploring the imaginative life of scientists, producing *Doctor Copernicus* (1976), *Kepler* (1981), The *Newton Letter* (1982), and *Mefisto* (1986). The *Book of Evidence* (1989) is a confessional account of a murder. *Ghosts* (1993) is a sequel. *Athena* (1995) is a meditation on love, while The *Untouchable* (1997) is a dark tale of betrayal and sexuality, based on the spy Anthony Blunt. All of Banville's creations are fascinated by images of ordinary beauty, and the texture of the writing is poetic. The big house motif provides a recurrent structuring device.

Banville, Vincent (1940–), novelist; born in Wexford, and educated by the Christian Brothers and at UCD, he worked as a secondary teacher until 1988. *An End to Flight* (1973) was a novel, followed by a couple of thrillers: *Death by Design* (1993) and *Death the Pale Rider* (1995). Children's fiction includes *Hennessy* (1991) and sequels in the Hennessy series.

barántas (warrant), a literary genre in Irish that flourished mainly in Munster during the 18th and 19th cents., is a legalistic satire, occasioned by a petty crime or the breach of literary good manners. Couched in the form of a warrant of arrest, it cites the offender and his crime. Its witty realism gives valuable glimpses of contemporary Irish life.

Barber, Mary ('Sapphira') (1690–1757), poet. Born probably in Dublin, she published verse that attracted the attention of Jonathan *Swift, who raised subscriptions for her *Poems on Several Occasions* (1734). Swift presented the manuscript of *Polite Conversations* (1738) to her, and its income from publication improved her fortunes.

bardic poetry (also schools, learning, etc.), also known as classical poetry, is used to refer to the writings of poets trained in the bardic schools of Ireland and Gaelic Scotland down to the middle of the 17th cent. Poetic schools existed in Ireland before Christianity, and the training poets received in them had its origins in the druidic learning associated with the religion of Celtic Gaul, Britain, and Ireland. In early writings the terms 'bard' and 'fili' are both used for 'poet', a fili being someone with a special responsibility towards traditional knowledge, *laws, language, grammar, and senchus (lore, including *dinnshenchas, place-lore), whereas a bard was a poet or versifier. The term 'bard' is used, most often pejoratively, in the Anglo-Irish *chronicles to refer to members of the poetic caste in Gaelic Ireland, and it was, though with some misgivings [see Osborn *Bergin], adopted to refer to poetry composed in the variety of syllabic rhyming metres known as dán díreach [see Irish *metrics] practised by Irish and Scottish poets from the 6th to the 17th cents. With the advent of Christianity the fili's role and functions were gradually absorbed into the Church's pastoral and educational activities.

In the 12th cent. the poets established schools throughout Ireland comparable to the monastic centres of learning. Each bardic school was associated with a poetic family: the *Ó hUiginns had theirs in Sligo, the *Ó Dálaighs in Cork, and the *Ó hEódhasas in Fermanagh. Teaching was conducted orally, but there was also instruction from Irish and Latin *manuscripts; the course of study often lasted seven years; and tuition was given in language, *metrics, *genealogy, Latin, dinnshenchas, *mythology, and history. Students composed alone in the dark on allotted subjects and in given metres, reciting their verses in public performance. Each poetic family had a head, who would have the support of a Gaelic dynastic lord (the patrons of the Mac an Bhairds, for example, were the O'Donnells), in return for which the poet would compose eulogies, exhortations, and elegies.

From the 12th to the 17th cents. the bardic caste enjoyed high prestige, and became the secular chroniclers and interpreters of a society which was deeply conservative and based on privilege. They developed a formalized literary language which changed little, if at all, over this period. Poets could, and often did, move from one part of Ireland to another, or between Gaelic Scotland and Ireland, with little difficulty. Their approach to their official duties, whether of inauguration, advice, or lament, was to appeal to the past. Not all of this verse was official: many of the poems that figure in the *Fionn, *Ulster, *mythological, and *historical cycles were composed by poets trained to some degree or other in the schools of the learned bardic families. The craft, sophistication, and self-conscious linguistic wit of bardic poetry also inform the *dánta grádha.

The fortunes of the bardic order were closely involved with those of the Gaelic aristocracy, and when that began to collapse under the Elizabethan and Tudor reconquests the poetic institution also declined. See Michelle Ó Riordan, *The Gaelic Mind and the Collapse of the Gaelic Order* (1990).

Bards of the Gael and Gall, see George *Sigerson.

Bardwell, Leland (1928–), poet and novelist. Born in India to Irish parents, she returned at an early age to Ireland. Poetry collections include: *The Mad Cyclist* (1970), *The Fly and the Bed Bug* (1984), and *Dostoevsky's Grave* (1991). *Girl on a Bicycle* (1977), *That London Winter* (1981), *The House* (1984), *There We Have Been* (1989) are novels, while her short stories were collected in *Different Kinds of Love* (1987).

Barlow, Jane (1857–1917), poet and fiction writer, born in Clontarf, Co. Dublin. Her poetry in *Bogland Studies* (1892), *The End of Elfintown* (1894), and *The Mockers and Other Verses* (1908) is generally sentimental and fantastic. *Irish Idylls* (1892), contains stories set in the Connemara village of Lisconnel. *Strangers at Lisconnel* (1895) was a second series, while further collections were *Maureen's Fairing* (1895), *Mrs. Martin's Company* (1896), and *A Creel of Irish Stories* (1897). In novels such as *In Mio's Country* (1917) she comments stringently on landlordism. *Kerrigan's Quality* (1894) describes the effects of the *Famine. *A Bunch of Lavender* (1911) was staged at the *Abbey Theatre.

Barney Maglone, see R. A. *Wilson.

Barrett, Eaton Stannard ('Polypus', etc.) (1786–1820), poet, and novelist. Born in Cork and educated at TCD, he practised as a barrister in London. *All the Talents* (1807), contains sharp-tongued portraits of Charles Fox and

Richard Brinsley *Sheridan. A shorter poem, *All the Talents in Ireland*, appeared in the same year. *Women* (1810) eulogizes female virtue. Other works are a comedy, *My Wife, What Wife?* (1815), and *The Heroine* (1822), an Ossianic romance.

Barrington, George (1755–c.1830), convict and author. He was the son of a British officer stationed in Maynooth, Co. Kildare. He was a pickpocket in London until arrested, when his eloquence and bearing in court gave rise to several popular accounts of his life, at least one by himself (*Memoirs &c.*, 1790). He was transported to New South Wales in 1790, and later became High Constable of Parramatta. He published *A Voyage to Botany Bay* (1801), a *History of New South Wales* (1808), and a *History of New Holland* (1808).

Barrington, Sir Jonah (?1760–1834), lawyer and historian of Anglo-Irish society before the Act of *Union. Born at Knapton in Co. Laois, he was educated in Dublin and at TCD. He became an Admiralty Court judge in 1798. From 1815 he lived mostly in France to escape creditors. His *Personal Sketches of His Own Times* (vols. i and ii, 1827; vol. iii, 1832) contain vivid portraits of contemporary political and legal figures, besides a gallery of bibulous landlords and their *stage-Irish retainers.

His last work, *The Rise and Fall of the Irish Nation* (Paris, 1833; Dublin, 1853) purports to do for the Protestant *ascendancy what Gibbon did for the Roman Empire. A skilful recorder of witty repartee and extravagant hoaxes, Barrington is the unequalled chronicler of his period.

Barrington, Margaret (1896–1982), fiction writer; born in Malin, Co. Donegal, she was educated at TCD and married the historian Edmund *Curtis. She then married Liam *O'Flaherty the novelist and moved to England where she was a journalist and assisted German refugees during the war, after which she settled in West Cork. *My Cousin Justin* (1939), a novel dealing with life in the Donegal of her childhood, was followed by the posthumous publication of the short stories *David's Daughter, Tamar* (1982).

Barry, David (1580–1629), author of *Ram Alley, or Merry Tricks* (1611, 1636), a bawdy verse comedy performed in London in 1608, believed to be the first play in English by a writer of Irish extraction. Baptized in Putney, London, Barry incurred debts as a theatre-owner at Whitefriars and escaped to Ireland. As Lodowicke Barry he was tried and acquitted of piracy in Cork, and sailed to Guiana with Sir Walter Ralegh in 1617. *Ram Alley* contains no Irish material.

Barry, James (1741–1806), painter; born in Cork the son of a ship's master, he went to sea before turning to painting. He attracted the patronage of Edmund *Burke and exhibited at the Royal Academy, becoming a member in 1773. That year he published *An Inquiry into Obstructions to Arts in England*. His writings were issued in 1809.

Barry, Michael Joseph (1817–1889), Cork-born poet and journalist. He was imprisoned in 1843 as a *Young Irelander, contributed frequently to *The *Nation, and edited the *Southern Reporter*, as well as issuing *Songs of Ireland* (1845) and an anthology of Cork poets called *Echoes from Parnassus* (1849). His verse contributions to the *Dublin University Magazine* were collected as *The Kishogue Papers* (1872). Other works include *Lays of the War* (1855), *Heinrich and Lenora, an Alpine Story* (1886), *Irish Emigration Considered* (1863), and some legal treatises.

Barry, Sebastian (1955–), poet,

novelist, and dramatist. Born in Dublin and educated at TCD, his novels include *Macker's Garden* (1982), *Strappado Square* (1983), *The Engine of Owl-Light* (1987), *The Whereabouts of Eneas McNulty* (1998). *The Water-Colourist* (1983) and *The Rhetorical Town* (1985) are collections of poems. *Boss Grady's Boys* (1988), produced at the Peacock [see *Abbey Theatre], uses the convention of peasant realism only to subvert it. *Prayers of Sherkin* (1990) concerns a Protestant fundamentalist sect. Though set in the Wild West, *White Woman Street* (1992) embraces Irish and American traditions. In *The Steward of Christendom* (1995) the former head of the Dublin Metropolitan Police, incarcerated in a lunatic asylum, relives family tragedies. It was followed by our *Lady of Sligo* (1998).

Barry Lyndon, see *The *Luck of Barry Lyndon*.

Barton, Harry (1916–), playwright and fiction-writer; born in Belfast, educated at Bangor, Wrekin College, Shropshire, and Naval Staff College, Greenwich. He served in the Royal Navy on 'Ramillies' and the aircraft-carrier 'Formidable' during the Second World War, laying offshore during the atomic bombing of Japan. He became Deputy Director of the Staff College at Greenwich. *With a Flag and a Bucket and a Gun* (1959) was a novel, followed by many pieces for stage, TV, and radio, among which are: *A Borderline Case* (1975), *The Giant Lobelia* (1976), *Hoopoe Day* (1981), *Fire at Magilligan* (1982), and *Battleships* (1985). *Yours Till Ireland Explodes, Mr Mooney* (1973), and *Yours Again, Mr Mooney* (1974) were collections of radio pieces.

Battle of . . ., see under *Cath . . . and *tale-types.

Bax, Sir Arnold Edward Trevor (pseudonym 'Dermot O'Byrne') (1883–

1953), composer and writer. Born in London, he came to Ireland in 1905 out of enthusiasm for W. B. *Yeats's poetry, according to the autobiographical account in *Farewell My Youth* (1943). Besides publishing his own poetry as *Seafoam and Firelight* (1909) he set poems by Padraic *Colum to music. *The Sisters and the Green Magic* (1912), *Children of the Hills* (1913), and *Wrack* (1918) are story collections depicting life around Glencolmcille. His best-known Celtic work is the symphony *Tintagel*. In later life Bax was knighted for his services as Master of the King's Musick.

Beacon (or Becon), Richard (*fl.* 1594), colonial administrator. Born in Suffolk and educated at Cambridge, he served in Ireland as an administrator of the Munster *plantation. *Solon His Follie* (1594) is a long analysis of Elizabethan policy cast in the form of a dialogue.

Béal Bocht, An (1941) a novel by Myles na gCopaleen (Flann *O'Brien), translated by Patrick C. Power as *The Poor Mouth* (1964). It describes a series of episodes in the life of the narrator who inhabits the fictitious *Gaeltacht community of Corca Dorcha. The book satirizes classic Gaeltacht autobiographies such as *Ó Criomhthain's *An tOileánach*.

béarla na bhfileadh (earlier bérla na filed), literally 'the language of the poets', a term applied in early Irish literature to rhetorical passages in texts, containing obscure forms of speech employed by poets, druids, prophets, and mythical heroes.

Béaslaí, Piaras (1883–1965), revolutionary and writer. Born in Liverpool to Irish parents and educated there, he learnt Irish on holidays in Kerry. From 1904 he worked for the *Dublin Evening Telegraph*. A member of the IRB [see *IRA], he fought in the *Easter Rising, and was elected TD for West Limerick,

1921–3. During the *Civil War he acted as director of propaganda for the Government. In 1913 he founded a theatre company to tour Irish-speaking areas, writing many plays himself. *An Sgaothaire* (1929) is a collection of six comedies. Other writings include the poems in *Bealtaine 1916* (1920), the stories in *Earc agus Áine* (1946), and a novel, *Astronár* (1928).

Beatha Aodha Ruaidh Uí Dhomhnaill (Life of Red Hugh *O'Donnell)

(c.1616), a biography by Lughaidh *Ó Cléirigh. Written chronologically in the manner of the *annals, it covers events from Red Hugh's capture and imprisonment in 1587 to his death in 1602. It closes with a sorrowing account of the dispossessed Irish nobility living on the Continent after the *Flight of the Earls in 1607.

Beaux' Stratagem, The (1707), a

comedy by George *Farquhar, first produced at the Haymarket Theatre, London. Archer and Aimwell plan to entrap Dorinda, an heiress, into marrying Aimwell so that the two rakes may divide her dowry. Aimwell falls truly in love, whereupon Archer takes the money and separates from his friend. Foigard, actually an Irish priest called MacShane, is a sombre version of the *stage-Irish stereotype.

Beckett, Samuel [Barclay] (1906–

1989), novelist, dramatist, and poet. Born in Foxrock, Co. Dublin, the son of a quantity surveyor, he was educated at Portora Royal School, Enniskillen, 1920–3, and at TCD. In 1928 he taught French at Campbell College, Belfast, before moving to Paris, where he met James *Joyce. His first publication was 'Dante … Bruno. Vico . . Joyce' for *Our Examgination Round the Factification for Incamination of Work in Progress* (1929), a collection of essays on *Finnegans Wake. *Whoroscope* (1930) was written in a

night to win a competition sponsored by the Hours Press in Paris. His study of *Proust* (1931), in its discussion of the breakdown of traditional relations between the subject and the object, prefigured many concerns of his later work. *More Pricks than Kicks* (1934) was a volume of short stories, centering on college life in Dublin. *Dream of Fair to Middling Women* written around this time, remained unpublished until 1992. In 1937 he settled in Paris. *Murphy* (1938) reflected his disillusion with post- *Treaty Ireland. Beckett was stabbed in the street in Paris in 1938, and was helped by Suzanne Deschevaux-Dumesnil, who became his companion. He became a member of a Resistance cell in Paris, then escaped to Roussillon in the Vaucluse, where he worked as a farm-hand and wrote *Watt* (1953). Around this time he decided to write in French. After *Mercier et Camier* (written 1946, published 1970) came various novellas, such as *Premier Amour* (1970) (*First Love, 1973). At his mother's death in 1947 he began work on *Molloy* (1951), the first volume of a trilogy which includes *Malone Dies* (1951) and *The *Unnamable* (1953). These novels enact the break-down between the perceiving mind and so-called reality that Beckett saw as lying at the heart of the modern condition. Writing in French purified his style, and his translations into English of his work retain a penitential rigour and asperity.

Waiting for Godot (written c.1948–9) translated the despairing self-questioning of the prose fiction into stark dialogue between two tramps. The plays *Endgame* (1957), *All That Fall* (1957), *Krapp's Last Tape* (1958), and *Happy Days* (1961) project images of the exhausted (predominantly male) ego of twentieth-century Western man. In *How It Is* (1961) the tale is told in urgent bursts of speech set out in unpunctuated paragraphs. The later writings continue this mode: voices come out of silence and pick up threads of a story. From the 1960s onwards his work became ever more minimalist, as in *Play* (1964), *Come and Go* (1965), *Eh Joe* (1966), *Breath* (1969), *Not I* (1973), and *Rockabye* (1982)—all plays. The fiction, too, grows ever more concentrated, as in *Imagination Dead, Imagine* (1965), *The Lost Ones* (1972), *Company* (1980), *Worstword Ho* (1983), and his final work, *Stirrings Still* (1988). Beckett was awarded the Nobel Prize in 1969. See Anthony *Cronin, *Samuel Beckett: The Last Modernist* (1996).

Bedell, William (1571–1642), Church of Ireland bishop and translator. Born in Black Notley, Essex, he was educated at Emmanuel College, Cambridge. In 1627 Bedell was made Provost of TCD and introduced lectures and prayers in Irish, which he also studied. His *Aibigtir.i. Theaguisg Cheudtosugheadh an Chriostaidhe* (*ABC or the Institution of a Christian*) (1631), a short catechism, contains extracts translated from the Bible. In 1634 Bedell called for a translation of the entire Bible to complete the work of Uilliam Ó Domhnaill [see William *Daniel], who had co-ordinated the translation of the New Testament in 1602. The 'Bedell Bible' was completed in 1640, but did not appear until 1685 [see *Bible in Irish].

Behan, Brendan (Breandán Ó Beacháin) (1923–1964), playwright. Born in Dublin into a talented Republican family, he was taught by the Christian Brothers until 14. Behan joined Fianna Éireann, the junior branch of the *IRA, at an early age. He became a house-painter like his father. In 1939 he was arrested in Liverpool for taking part in an IRA bombing campaign. During his three-year sentence, spent mostly in Borstal in Suffolk, he began to write. Shortly after his release in 1941 Behan attempted to kill a detective and served five years in prison. The autobiograph-

ical *Borstal Boy*, not published until 1958 was begun around this time. He also wrote poetry in Irish. He wrote his first play, *The Landlady*, while in prison at the Curragh, and The *Quare Fellow*. The *Quare Fellow* was rejected by both the *Abbey and the *Gate before being staged at the experimental Pike Theatre by Alan Simpson and Carolyn Swift. A successful London production directed by Joan Littlewood followed in 1956. Behan's self-destructive career as showman began after a notorious BBC television interview in which he appeared drunk and belligerent. His next play The *Hostage* (1958), first produced in Irish as An *Giall* at the Damer Hall in Dublin (1958), has proved to be his most enduring work for the stage. Behan's marriage to Beatrice ffrench-Salkeld in 1955 failed to tame his damaging life-style, even after he was diagnosed as diabetic. A trip to New York in 1960 proved disastrous. He wrote very little subsequently, although he discovered the tape-recorder and, with *Brendan Behan's Island* (1962), found he could make books from anecdotes. See Ulick *O'Connor, *Brendan Behan* (1970).

Bell, Robert (1800–1867) playwright; born in Cork, educated at TCD. He founded the *Dublin Inquisitor* (1821) before becoming a journalist in London (after 1828). He wrote the comedies, *Marriage* (1842), *Mothers and Daughters* (1843), and *Temper* (1847); and two novels, *Hearts and Altars* (1852) and *The Ladders of Gold, an English Story* (1850).

Bell, Sam Hanna (1909–1990), fiction-writer and broadcaster. Born in Scotland to an Ulster family, he went to live in Belfast in 1921. For a time he attended the Belfast College of Art. He began writing documentary scripts for BBC Northern Ireland and became a producer, 1945–69. Short stories contributed to The *Bell* were collected as *Summer Loanen* in 1943, the year in which he founded *Lagan* with John *Boyd and Bob Davison. His first novel, *December Bride* (1951), was based on a story of his mother's family. *The Hollow Ball* (1961) depicts Belfast, poverty and unemployment. *A Man Flourishing* (1973), set in 18th-cent. Belfast, follows the progress of James Gault, a *United Irishman. His final novel, *Across the Narrow Sea* (1987), shows the effects of the 17th-cent. Ulster *plantation. *Erin's Orange Lily* (1956) concerns Ulster *folklore. He edited *Within Our Province* (1972), a miscellany of Ulster writing. *The Theatre in Ulster* (1972) is an authoritative history. Bell used his position with the BBC to encourage fellow writers.

Bell, The (1940–1954), a monthly literary and cultural journal founded by Sean *O'Faolain, who was editor until 1946, with Peadar *O'Donnell as business manager, and later editor when O'Faolain signed off. Many contemporary Irish writers contributed. Besides poetry and fiction, *The Bell* offered commentary on social, political, and cultural issues. In the first issue O'Faolain promised that the journal would stand 'for Life before any abstraction, in whatever magnificent words it may clothe itself'. It frequently challenged the notion of Irish nationhood and the simplistic views of Irishness it fostered, attacking also the literary *censorship sponsored by the new State.

Bellamy, George Anne (1727–1788), actress and author of a theatrical autobiography; born Co. Dublin, the illegitimate daughter of Lord Tyrawley. She joined her mother in London and prevailed on the Drury Lane manager to put her on the stage. From 1744 she often appeared opposite Garrick. Thomas *Sheridan the Younger recruited her for *Smock Alley, 1745–8. On retirement she issued an *Apology* (6 vols., 1785).

Beltaine (Bealtaine), the day marking the beginning of Celtic summer, celebrated on 1 May. On this day fairs were traditionally held, labourers began their term of hire, rent was paid, and summer welcomed in.

Beltaine (1899–1900), the earliest publication of the Irish Literary Theatre [see *Abbey Theatre], of which three issues, edited by W. B. *Yeats, appeared before its function was taken over by *Samhain.

Bending of the Bough, The (1900), a rewriting by George *Moore of Edward *Martyn's play *The Tale of a Town* in which W. B. *Yeats assisted, though the two fell out in the course of collaboration. The town of Northhaven feels it has been swindled in its dealings with richer, more powerful Southhaven. Jasper Dean looks like being the leader they need, but he is torn by divided loyalties.

Bennett, Louie (1870–1956), feminist and novelist; born and educated in Dublin. After studying singing in Bonn, she helped establish the Irishwoman's Suffrage Federation in 1911, becoming President of the Irish Trade Union Congress in 1932. *The Proving of Priscilla* (1902) is a modern tale of differences and reconciliation in a marriage, while *Prisoner of His Word* (1908) is set in the aftermath of the *United Irishmen's Rebellion of 1798.

Bennett, Ronan (1956–), novelist; born in Oxford he returned to Ireland aged 2 and was brought up in Belfast, attending St. Mary's Christian Brothers School. He was imprisoned in Long Kesh under suspicion of Republican activities 1974–6, then in England, 1977–9. On release he attended King's College, London, and published *The Second Prison* (1991), a novel, followed by *Overthrown by Strangers* (1992), and *The Catastrophist* (1998), a novel of sex and social conflict set in Africa.

Bergin, Osborn [Joseph] (1873–1950), scholar; born in Cork and educated at Queen's College there [see *universities], where he joined the *Gaelic League. In 1897 he was appointed university lecturer in Celtic, but later went on to study under Rudolf *Thurneysen at Freiburg in 1905-6, becoming professor at UCD in 1909. His scholarly work includes an edition of the *Book of the Dun Cow (1929), with R. I. *Best. An early song that evokes the West Cork *Gaeltacht was collected with others in a volume of that title (*Maidin i mBéarra*, 1918). A lasting interest in *bardic poetry led to a posthumous collection, *Irish Bardic Poetry* (1970).

Berkeley, George (1685–1753), philosopher and Bishop of Cloyne; born at Dysart Castle, Co. Kilkenny, and educated at Kilkenny College, and at TCD. In 1709 he issued An *Essay towards a New Theory of Vision, followed in the next year by The *Principles of Human Knowledge, the main exposition of his immaterialism. Berkeley went to London in 1713 and published *Three Dialogues between Hylas and Philonous*. He became friendly with Addison, Pope, and Richard *Steele, through Swift, who presented him at Court. *De Motu* (1721) criticized Newton's philosophy of nature and Leibniz's theory of force. He returned in 1721 to Ireland. In 1724 Berkeley was appointed Dean of Derry, but he wished to establish a missionary college in Bermuda. He sailed for Rhode Island in 1729, and established himself in Newport, awaiting funds, returning in 1731 when the money was not forthcoming. *Alciphron (1732), written during his stay in Rhode Island, is an apologetic work designed to combat atheism and free-thinking. His *Theory of Vision Vindicated* (1733) defends his first essay. A polemical work on mathematics, *The Analyst* (1734), shows that free-thinking mathematicians are themselves guilty of logical absurdity. In 1734 he was appointed Bishop of Cloyne, and he took up residence in Co. Cork in the following year. He was particularly exercised by the poor economic state of Ireland at the time. He gave an account of the facts and proposed remedies in The *Querist, published in three parts in 1735, 1736, and 1737. He wished to promote harmony between the established Church and the Catholic clergy, and in *Words to the Wise* (1749) he appealed for conciliation. One of Berkeley's last published works was *Siris: A Chain of Philosophical Reflexions and Inquiries concerning the Virtues of Tar-Water* (1744). He believed in tar-water as a universal medical panacea. His philosophy is a rejoinder to John Locke's on the nature of perception and the material world. Berkeley took the view in his *Principles* and *New Theory of Vision* that a sufficient explanation of knowledge can be found in the claim that our perceptions constitute what there is (hence *esse est percipi*, 'to be is to be perceived'). This denial of objects independent of minds and their contents is immaterialism. He had, also, recourse to a God who underpins human experience of a common rather than a private world. See David Berman, *George Berkeley: Idealism and the Man* (1993).

Berkeley, Sara (1967–), poet; born in Dublin and educated at TCD and California. She studied in London, and worked as a computer manual-writer. Her charged verse first appeared in 1983. She went on to produce the collections *Penn* (1986) and *Home Movie Nights* (1989). *The Swimmer in the Deep Blue Dream* (1991) is a story collection, while *Facts about Water* (1994) contains poems of loneliness, exile, and the end of intimacy.

Bertram, or The Castle of St Aldobrand

(1816), a tragedy in blank verse by Charles Robert *Maturin, first staged at Drury Lane with Edmund Kean in the title-role. Bertram is shipwrecked near the castle of Lord Aldobrand, a noble who had forced him into exile and who has married his beloved Imogine. Bertram seduces Imogine and kills Aldobrand; then, appalled by what he has done, he kills himself. To the disgust of Coleridge, *Bertram* was chosen over his own *Zapolya*.

Berwick, Edward (1750–?1820), translator. Born in Co. Down and educated at TCD, he became chaplain to the Earl of Moira, and then vicar of several parishes, among them Leixlip, Co. Dublin. He made the first complete translation of Philostratus' *Life of Apollonius of Tyana* (1809), and his *Lives of Marcus Valerius, Messala Corvinus, and Titus Pompinius Atticus* (1812). George *Moore maintained that Berwick wrote the best prose to come out of Ireland, and used the *Apollonius* typeface as the model for the Heinemann edition of his works.

Best R[ichard] I[rvine] (1872–1959), scholar. Born in Derry and educated at Foyle College, he lived in Paris, where he met Kuno *Meyer. He translated Henri d'Arbois de Jubainville's lectures at the Collège de France (*The Irish Mythological Cycle and Celtic Mythology*, 1903). In 1904 he became a librarian at the National Library of Ireland, and was appointed Director in 1924. His *Bibliography of Irish Philology and of Printed Irish Literature* (1913), was followed by *Bibliography of Irish Philology and Manuscript Literature: Publications 1913–1941* (1942).

Bible in Irish. The translation of the Bible into vernacular languages came about as a result of the Reformation, but in Ireland an added incentive was given by the need to convert the Gaelic-speaking Irish from *Catholicism to *Protestantism. Soon after the beginning of her reign (1558) *Elizabeth I paid for founts and a printing press in order that the New Testament be translated into Irish. Nevertheless it was not until 1602 that the translation appeared, the outcome of work conducted since the early 1560s, but delayed, according to Uilliam Ó Domhnaill [see William *Daniel], by 'Sathan' and 'Romish seducers'. In 1634 William *Bedell called for the translation of the Old Testament. He was helped by Muircheartach Ó Cionga (d. 1639) and others at his house in Kilmore. The translation was complete by 1640, but it remained unpublished until 1685, when it was revised under the patronage of Robert *Boyle (1627–91). In 1690 Boyle paid for the reprinting of the Old and New Testaments together for use in Scotland, and the entire Bible was issued for the first time as *An Bíobla Naomhtha*, published in London using Roman typeface. In 1810 the Bible Society reprinted the New Testament, under James McQuige's editorship, and in 1817 he edited the entire Bible for the Society. In 1945 the Irish Catholic hierarchy established a commission to undertake a translation of the New Testament. In 1966 a steering committee, including Tomás *Ó Fiaich and Pádraig *Ó Fiannachta, was set up to translate the entire Bible, based on the original texts, resulting *An Bíobla Naofa* (1981). See Nicholas Williams, *I bPrionta i Leabhar* (1986).

Bickerstaff[e], Isaac (?1733–?1810), playwright. Born in Ireland, presumably in Dublin, he became an ensign in the Northumberland Fusiliers in 1745. Bickerstaffe turned to musical comedy and became the acknowledged master of the form. *Thomas and Sally* (1760), appearing at Covent Garden, was followed by *Judith* (1761), an oratorio with music by Thomas Arne. Other works include: *Love in a Village* (1762),

The Maid of the Mill (1765), *Lionel and Clarissa* (1768), and *The Padlock* (1768), a farce with music by Charles Dibdin. In 1771 he fled to France to avoid prosecution for homosexuality, then a capital offence, where he lived under an alias at St Malo. *The Farce of the Spoil'd Child* appeared in London in 1790, and in Dublin in 1792.

Bickerstaff, Isaac [pseudonym], see Jonathan *Swift.

Big Chapel, The (1971), a novel by Thomas *Kilroy. Set in the 1870s in the village of Kyle, Co. Kilkenny, it deals with the conflict between the parish priest, Fr. Lannigan, and his Bishop. Lannigan manages the interdenominational school run by Martin Scully, where the numbers are being depleted by the new, strictly Catholic, Christian Brothers institution, supported by the Bishop and the curate, Lutterell.

big house, a theme in *Anglo-Irish literature referring to the big houses of the *ascendancy, reflecting the anxieties and uncertainties of the Protestant landowning class in their decline, from the late 18th cent., through *Catholic Emancipation, the *Tithe War, the *Famine, the *Land League, and the growth of modern militant Irish nationalism, to the founding of the *Irish State. Maria *Edgeworth's *Castle Rackrent* (1800) initiated enduring conventions in *Anglo-Irish literature: the decaying house and a declining gentry family; the improvident, often absentee, landlord; and the rise of a predatory middle class. Such conventions were developed in the novels of Charles *Lever, William *Carleton, Sheridan *Le Fanu, and Charles Robert *Maturin; and in W. B. *Yeats's poetry and drama. Other writers to explore this theme included: George *Moore, *Somerville and Ross, Elizabeth *Bowen, Lennox *Robinson, Sean *O'Casey, Brendan *Behan, Padraic *Colum, Sean *O'Faolain, Joyce *Cary, Mervyn *Wall, Julia *O'Faolain, Brian *Friel, John *McGahern, Jennifer *Johnston, William *Trevor, Molly *Keane, Aidan *Higgins, and John *Banville.

Big House at Inver, The (1925), a novel by *Somerville and Ross chronicling the decline and fall of the Prendevilles, an *ascendancy family in the west of Ireland who have abandoned their class, producing illegitimate successors with their tenants. Shibby Pindy strives to restore the family fortune by marrying off her half-brother Kit to a wealthy heiress, but fails.

Bigger, Francis Joseph (1863–1926), solicitor and nationalist. Born in Belfast, and educated at the Royal Academical Institution, he organized with Roger *Casement and others cultural events such as the Glens of Antrim feis (festival). He wrote extensively on local history, notably in *The Ulster Land War of 1770* (1910).

Binchy, D[aniel] A[nthony] (1899–1989), scholar of *law in Gaelic Ireland. Born in Charleville, Co. Cork, he was educated at Clongowes Wood College, at UCD, and later at Munich and Paris. He became Professor of Jurisprudence and Roman Law at UCD in 1929, then entered the Irish Diplomatic Service. He became Senior Professor at the School of Celtic Studies at the *DIAS. His life work was the study of early Irish law, resulting in the *Corpus Iuris Hibernici* (6 vols., 1978).

Binchy, Maeve (1940–), short-story writer and novelist; born in Dublin and educated at UCD. Beginning as a teacher, she became a journalist in the late 1960s and has published several selections from her long-running *Irish Times* weekly column. Her career in fiction began with collections of London stories linked by place, *Central Line* (1977) and *Victoria Line* (1980), followed by two with Irish settings, *Dublin 4* (1982) and *The Lilac Bus* (1984). Her first novel, *Light a Penny Candle* (1982), became a best-seller, while *Echoes* (1985), *Firefly Summer* (1987), *Silver Wedding* (1988), *Circle of Friends* (1990), and *Evening Class* (1996) have secured her international standing as an immensely popular author. Her warm-hearted novels are tinged with nostalgia for the Ireland of a few decades ago in which they are generally set, offering a tolerant view of ordinary, sympathetic characters involved in episodes of Irish family life. *The Copper Beech* (1992) and *The Glass Lake* (1994) concern small-town loves and jealousies, and the search for freedom.

Birchwood (1973), a novel by John *Banville, set in 19th-cent. Ireland in the form of a confessional memoir by Gabriel Godkin, survivor of violent and tragic events related to a struggle for possession of the Birchwood *big house.

Bird Alone (1936), a novel by Sean *O'Faolain set in Cork in the *Parnell period, describing the love affair between Corney Crone and Elsie Sherlock.

Birmingham, George A. (pseudonym of Canon James Owen Hannay) (1865–1950), novelist, playwright, and religious writer. Born in Belfast, and educated in England and at TCD, he was rector of Westport, Co. Mayo, 1892–1916. He joined the British army as a chaplain, serving in France and Budapest before settling in a London Parish. He shared the cultural nationalism of his friends Arthur *Griffith and Douglas *Hyde, presenting the case for the *Gaelic League in a pamphlet, *Is the Gaelic League Political?* (1906) and in a novel, *Benedict Kavanagh* (1907). He wrote between *The Seething Pot* (1905) and *Two Scamps* (1950) nearly sixty comic novels gently satirizing Ireland. *Spanish Gold* (1908) established his popularity, with its central figure, the Revd J. J. Meldon; while Dr Lucius O'Grady, Birmingham's ideal Irishman first appeared in *The *Search Party* (1909) and returned in the controversial *General John Regan* (1913). *Up The Rebels* (1919) gives a comic account of a bloodless Irish insurrection. His study of representative contemporary types in *Irishmen All* (1913) purveyed an inclusive notion of Irish nationhood. *The *Red Hand of Ulster* (1912) contains ominous forebodings of Partition, while *The *Northern Iron* (1907), his novel of the *United Irishmen's Rebellion, showed an appreciation of Presbyterian tradition. His non-fiction includes *The Spirit of Christian Monasticism* (1903), *Isaiah* (1937), and an autobiography, *Pleasant Places* (1934).

Birthright (1910), a two-act play by T. C. *Murray on the Cain and Abel theme and dealing with a fratricidal conflict over the inheritance of a farm in Co. Cork, first performed at the *Abbey Theatre.

Bishop's Bonfire, The (1955), a play by Sean *O'Casey in which the Codger—something of a self-portrait—stands firm against clerical oppression.

Bit o' Writing, The (1838), a volume of short stories by John and Michael *Banim (mainly the latter). The title-story by John deals with the attempts of an old sailor to obtain a naval pension by letter.

Black and Tans, the name given to non-Irish personnel enlisted into the Royal Irish Constabulary (RIC) who fought against the *IRA between March

1920 and July 1921; it was derived from a pack of hounds of the Skarteen Hunt in Co. Limerick. Together with the Auxiliary Division of the RIC (the 'Auxies'), they acquired a reputation for ferocity and indiscipline.

Black List, Section H (1971), an autobiographical fiction by Francis *Stuart, dealing with people and events of his own life including his activities in the *Civil War, and his troubled marriage to Iseult Gonne, while recounting journeys to Paris, London, and Berlin in 1939.

Blackburn, Helen (1842–1903), feminist author; born Kingston (Dún Laoghaire), Co. Dublin, she wrote *Women's Suffrage* (1903), a standard work.

Blackburne, E. Owens (pseudonym of Elizabeth Casey) (1848–1894), novelist. Born in Slane, Co. Meath, she became a London journalist in 1873. *A Woman Scorned* (1876) concerns the predicament of women in a male-dominated society. There followed *Molly Carew* (1879), *The Glen of the Silver Birches* (1880), and *The Hearts of Erin* (1883). *A Bunch of Shamrocks* (1879) contains tales of Irish rural life including 'Biddy Brady's Banshee'.

Black Prince, The (1973), a novel by Iris *Murdoch, narrated by Bradley Pearson, a middle-aged novelist who has been sentenced for murdering a more productive rival, Arnold Baffin.

Black Prophet, The: *A Tale of Irish Famine* (1847), a novel by William *Carleton, written in response to the *Famine and first published serially in the *Dublin University Magazine*. It concerns a murder committed by Donnel Dhu, the 'prophecy man', and the shadow of suspicion which hangs over the Daltons, a family of small farmers. Its searing depiction of the effects of starvation and disease in a peasant community are based on Carleton's personal experience of the famine of 1817. Donnel Dhu was modelled on the wandering prophets of pre-Famine Ireland, who based their predictions on *Pastorini.

Black Soul, The (1924), a novel by Liam *O'Flaherty set on the Aran island, Inishmore. It concerns a wild love affair between Fergus O'Connor and the wife of the man he lodges with.

Blacker, William (1777–1855), Orangeman and poet. Born in Carrickblacker, Co. Armagh, he was the author of *Orange ballads such as 'Cromwell's Advice'. The title-poem in *Ardmagh* (1848) is a verse chronicle of Armagh Cathedral from *druid times to the Act of *Union.

Blackwood, Caroline (1931–), novelist. Born in Co. Down, daughter of the 4th Marquis of Dufferin and Ava, she married Lucien Freud, and later Robert Lowell. Her first novel, *The Stepdaughter* (1976), is a wry tale of the emotional neglect of a girl by a deserted wife. *Great Granny Webster* (1977) is a black comedy dealing with cruelty and madness in an Ulster *big house. *The Fate of Mary Rose* (1981) describes a murder, and *Corrigan* (1984) recounts an Irishman's intrusion into the house of an elderly widow.

Blackwood, Frederick Temple (1st Marquis of Dufferin and Ava) (1826–1902), diplomat and author; born in Florence, son of Helen *Blackwood, and a descendant of Richard Brinsley *Sheridan. Governor-General of Canada and Viceroy of India, he wrote a moving *Narrative of a Journey from Oxford to Skibbereen in the Year of the Irish Famine* (1847). His *Letters from High Latitudes* (1859) is a journal of a yachting voyage to Iceland.

Blackwood, Helen Selina, Lady Dufferin (née Sheridan) (1807–1867), poet; granddaughter of Richard Brinsley *Sheridan. Brought up at Hampton Court, she was the author of well-known lyrics including 'The Lament of the Irish Emigrant'. *A Selection of the Songs of Lady Dufferin* (1895) was edited by her son Frederick *Blackwood.

Blake, Nicholas, see Cecil *Day-Lewis.

Blasket Islands, see Tomás *Ó Criomhthain, Muiris *Ó Suilleabháin, Peig *Sayers.

Blathmac, son of Cú Brettan (*fl.* 760), poet. Born in present-day Co. Monaghan, he was educated in a monastic school and became a monk, having been influenced by the *Céle Dé (Culdee) movement. The manuscript containing his two surviving compositions, meditations on the Virgin, is in the National Library, where it was rediscovered by James *Carney.

Blessington, Countess of, see Marguerite *Power.

Blindness of Dr. Gray, The, or *The Final Law* (1909), a novel of clerical life by Patrick *Sheehan describing an old priest's last years and how he learns that the final law is love.

Blunt, Wilfrid Scawen (1840–1922), English poet and traveller. He retired from the British diplomatic service in 1869. In 1878 he explored Saudi Arabia, going on to India, where he acquired the anti-imperialist convictions in *Ideas about India* (1885). He founded *The Egyptian Standard* in Cairo in support of the nationalist movement, and recruited W. P. *Ryan as its editor. During 1888 he involved himself in the Irish *Land League, leading to *The Land War in Ireland* (1912). In Galway gaol he

wrote the poems *In Vinculis* (1889). He celebrated his amours in English society more or less openly in *Sonnets and Songs by Proteus* (1875), and published Lady *Gregory's love-poems to him as 'A Woman's Sonnets'.

Blythe, Ernest (Earnán de Blaghd) (1889–1975), revolutionary, and Director of the *Abbey Theatre. Born near Lisburn, Co. Antrim, he joined the *Gaelic League and the IRB [see *IRA]. He was a TD from 1918 to 1936, held ministerial posts (Commerce, Finance, and Post and Telegraphs) until he lost his seat in 1933. Blythe made the first government grant to the *Abbey Theatre and served as managing director 1941–67, presiding over the rebuilding of the theatre after the fire of 1951. He advanced drama in Irish and kept the Abbey going during its sojourn at the Queen's. He published two volumes of autobiography, *Trasna na Bóinne* (1957) and *Slán le hUltaibh* (1969), and a volume of poems, *Fraoch agus Fothannáin* (1938).

Boann, see Irish *mythology.

'Boarding House, The', a story in James *Joyce's *Dubliners* (1915), written in 1905. Bob Doran, clerk in a vintner's business, is trapped into marriage to Polly Mooney, the daughter of a domineering lodging-house keeper.

Bodhrán-Makers, The (1986), a novel by John B. *Keane set in the fictional townland of Dirrabeg, Co. Kerry, and dealing with a conflict between the wren-boys and a puritanical parish priest.

Bodkin, M[athias] McDonnell (1850–1928), novelist. Born in Co. Galway, he wrote popular story collections and novels including *Poteen Punch* (1890), *Patsy the Omadhaun* (1904), and *Kitty the Madcap* (1927). His historical novels include *Lord Edward Fitzgerald*

(1896), *In the Days of Goldsmith* (1903), and *True Man and Traitor* (1910).

Boland, Eavan [Aisling] (1944–), poet. Born in Dublin, daughter of the diplomat F. H. Boland, she was educated in London, New York, Killiney, and TCD. *New Territory* (1967) contained poems written mostly while at university. *The War Horse* (1975) deals with the *Troubles in the north of Ireland. *In Her Own Image* (1980) confronts women's issues. *Night Feed* (1982) celebrates the value of domestic life. *The Journey and Other Poems* (1986) considers the repressed histories of women. The poems of *Outside History* (1990) uncover fresh nuances of freedom and delight. *In a Time of Violence* (1994) sets the routines of work against savagery.

Bolg an tSolair (1795), an Irish-language magazine, compiled by the Gaelic scholar Patrick *Lynch and containing poems with translations by Charlotte *Brooke.

Bolger, Dermot (1959–), poet, novelist, dramatist, and publisher. He was born in Dublin and educated at Beneavin College before working as a factory hand, 1978–9, library assistant, 1979–84, then writer and publisher. He founded the Raven Arts Press in 1979, issuing also in that year *The Habit of Flesh*, poems. Further collections include *No Waiting America* (1981), *Internal Exiles* (1986), and *Leinster Street Ghosts* (1989). His first novel *Night Shift* (1985) tells how Donal Flynn copes with the brutality of city life. *The Woman's Daughter* (1987) deals with the physical and sexual abuse of women. *The Journey Home* (1990) was followed by *Emily's Shoes* (1992), an exploration of the roots of a man's unhappiness. Other novels include: *A Second Life* (1994), *Father's Music* (1997), and *Finbar's Hotel* (1997, with others). *Blinded by the Light* (1990) was a play staged by the *Abbey Theatre; *In High Germany* (1990) was produced at the *Gate as was *The Holy Ground* (1990). He became executive editor of New Island Books in 1992.

Book of Armagh, the (*Liber Armachanus*), a Latin manuscript compiled at Armagh in AD 807–8, contains the complete text of the New Testament, a collection of early texts on the Life of St *Patrick, and a text of St Patrick's *Confessio*. It was presented to TCD in 1855.

Book of Ballymote, the (*Leabhar Bhaile an Mhóta*), a *manuscript compilation of the late 14th cent. Its contents include *genealogy, *Auraicept na nÉces, *Dinnshenchas Érenn, and *Lebor Gabála. The book was presented to the *RIA in 1785.

Book of Clan Sweeney, see *Leabhar Clainne Suibhne.

Book of Clandeboye, see *Leabhar Cloinne Aodha Buidhe.

Book of Duniry, see *Leabhar Breac.

Book of Durrow, the, one of the earlier Irish illuminated *manuscripts of the Gospels, compiled around 650. Known to have been in the possession of the Columban monastery at Durrow, Co. Offaly, it is now in TCD.

Book of Evidence, The (1989), a novel by John *Banville, set in contemporary Ireland, and taking the form of a prison notebook in which Freddie Montgomery presents his explanation of the murder which has landed him in gaol.

Book of Fermoy, the, a *manuscript dating from the 14th cent. and written for the Roches of Fermoy. It contains a collection of thirty poems composed by the 3rd Earl of Desmond, *Gearóid Iarla.

Book of Glendalough, the (*Lebor Glinne Dá Loch*), a *manuscript compiled c.1125–30 and known until recently as Rawlinson B 502, its pressmark in the Bodleian Library, Oxford. Besides *Salt-air na Rann*, it includes *Senchas na Laignech*, a collection of historical texts with a Leinster bias.

Book of Invasions, the, see *Lebor Gabála*.

Book of Judas, The (1991), an epic poem in twelve parts by Brendan *Kennelly which allows Judas as betrayer, informer, and man of letters to speak out of the corner to which he has been consigned by society.

Book of Kells, the, compiled some time in the 8th or 9th cent., and written on calf vellum. In the 11th and 12th cents. it was kept in Kells, Co. Meath. Scholars differ on its provenance: whether Iona, Kells, or even Northumbria. The manuscript is a Latin copy of the four Gospels. It is written in a majestic large-lettered script. Richly decorated initials mark the text, but sumptuous paintings and so-called carpet pages— for example the famous Chi-Rho, and the Evangelists—make the *Book of Kells* one of the great achievements of the early Church of the insular *Celts. The book may have been intended as the centrepiece at the commemoration of the bicentennial of the death of Colum Cille on Iona, 797.

Book of Lecan, the (*Leabhar Leacáin*), compiled between 1397 and 1418 by Giolla Íosa *Mac Fhir Bhisigh and assistants. It includes *Dinnshenchas Érenn, *Banshenchas*, and two recensions of *Lebor Gabála*. It is now the property of the *RIA.

Book of Leinster, the, one of the great 12th-cent. *manuscript collections, compiled under the patronage of Diarmuid mac Murchada (Mac Murrough; see *Norman invasion) and formerly known as *Lebor na Nuachongbála* after Nuachongbáil, now Oughaval, Co. Laois. R. I. *Best believed that the manuscript was the work of a single scribe, whom he identified as Aed ua [mac] Crimthainn of Terryglas, Co. Tipperary. A treasury of medieval Irish learning, it contains *Lebor Gabála, *Táin Bó Cuailnge*, parts of *Dinnshenchas Érenn*, an account of the banqueting hall (Tech Midchuarta) at *Tara, and a list of the 350 tales [see *tale-types] a poet should know. The book is mostly preserved at TCD.

Book of Lismore, the (also known as the *Book of Mac Carthaigh Riabhach*), an Irish *manuscript compilation made by Aonghus Ó Callanáin and other scribes for Finghin Mac Carthaigh Riabhach (d. 1505), but named after Lismore Castle, Co. Waterford, where it was found by workmen in 1814. It includes religious texts, saints' lives, poems, sagas, and tales including *Acallam na Senórach, and a translation of the voyage of Marco Polo.

Book of Mac Carthaigh Riabhach, see *Book of Lismore.

Book of Rights, the (*Lebor na Cert*), a *manuscript compilation dating from the 12th cent. and preserved in the *Book of Lecan. It contains a collection of poems on the stipends and tributes of each of the kingdoms of Ireland; St *Patrick's Blessing of the Irish; and a poem on *Tara.

Book of the Dean of Lismore, the, a *manuscript collection of varied material mostly in Irish, but also containing items in Latin and Scots. It was compiled in the early 16th cent. by

Duncan and James MacGregor at Fortingall in Perthshire, the latter holding the Deanery of Lismore in Argyll. It includes examples of *bardic poetry, lays from the *Fionn cycle, *dánta grádha, and satire.

Book of the Dun Cow, the (*Lebor na hUidre*), an Irish *manuscript collection, probably dating from the late 11th cent. and so called because it was believed to have been written on vellum from the hide of a cow that followed St *Ciarán to *Clonmacnoise. The main scribe, Eugene *O'Curry believed, was Mael Muire of Clonmacnoise. The collection contains an early version of *Táin Bó Cuailnge, *Tochmarc Emire, and *Fled Bricrenn, along with other tales of the *Ulster cycle, and a poem attributed to *Dallán Forgaill in praise of *Colum Cille. The manuscript was acquired by the *RIA in 1844.

Book of the O'Conor Don, the, a 17th-cent. paper *manuscript containing a large collection of *bardic poetry. The manuscript was written by Aodh Ó Dochartaigh for Somhairle Mac Domhnaill, a captain in Tyrone's Irish Regiment in Flanders (see also *Duanaire Finn). In the 18th cent. it came into the possession of Charles *O'Conor the Elder of Belanagare, Co. Roscommon, and today it is in the O'Conor-Nash family home, Clonalis, Co. Roscommon. With the exception of a few earlier items, the poems span practically the entire bardic period from the late 12th to the early 17th cent. Among the many poets represented are Eochaidh *Ó hEódhasa and Tadhg Dall *Ó hUiginn.

Book of Ui Mhaine, the, a *manuscript compiled in the late 14th cent., formerly known as *Leabhar Uí Dhubhagáin*, from a connection with that learned family. It includes *Lebor na Cert* [see *Book of Rights], *Dinnshenchas Érenn,

*Auraicept na nÉces, and apocryphal matter. It is now in the *RIA.

Books Ireland (1976–), edited by Jeremy Addis, a monthly periodical reviewing and listing books of Irish interest or Irish authorship in English or in Irish.

Boran, Pat (1963–), poet. Born in Portlaoise, Co. Laois, and educated by the Christian Brothers, he was an administrator for *Poetry Ireland*, 1989–91. His collections include *The Unwound Clock* (1990), *History and Promise* (1990), *Strange Bedfellows* (1991), *Familiar Things* (1993), and *The Shape of Water* (1996). Under pseudonyms he has written *Sex: An Encyclopedia for the Bewildered* (1996) and *A short History of Dublin* (1996).

Borlase, Edmund (?1620–1682), colonial historian. Born in Dublin and educated at TCD and Leiden. His *Reduction of Ireland* (1675) is an account of the *Rebellion of 1641. It was reissued as *History of the Execrable Irish Rebellion* (1680).

Borstal Boy (1958), an autobiographical account of Brendan *Behan's experiences in an English reformatory following his arrest in November 1939 for possession of explosives during an *IRA campaign in Britain.

Boucicault (or Boursiquot), Dion[ysius] Lardner (1820–1890), actor and playwright; reared by a Huguenot family in Dublin, but actually an illegitimate son of the scientist Dr Dionysius *Lardner. Educated in Dublin and London, he became an actor under the name 'Lee Moreton'. The success of his comedy *London Assurance at Covent Garden in 1841 led, in the following four years, to twenty-two plays being produced on the London stage. After marrying a rich French widow in 1845 he went to Paris. When his wife died he returned to London in 1848, where profligate spending soon led to bank-ruptcy. Boucicault began a second car-eer as an actor, and met his future wife, Agnes Robertson. When she went to America in 1853 to exploit her London success, he went with her. His success in the USA with The *Colleen Bawn (1860), made him decide to return to London. In 1872 he returned to America, tour-ing all the larger cities in the USA and Canada. He spent his last years as the impoverished director of an acting-school in New York. He was one of the most prolific playwrights of the 19th cent., writing some 150 plays. His greatest achievement lay in melo-drama. Plays such as The Poor of New York (1857), The *Octoroon (1859), The Colleen Bawn (1860), Omoo (1864), *Arrah-na-Pogue (1864/5), The Long Strike (1866), Flying Scud (1866), After Dark (1868), Belle Lamar (1874), and The *Shaughraun (1875) are masterpieces of the genre. Although he spent most of his life abroad, Boucicault saw himself as an Irishman: 'Nature did me that honour,' he replied when questioned on this point. Although he exploited the stereotype of the *stage-Irishman many of his plays show an awareness of Irish conditions and problems.

Bourke, Angela (1952–), fiction-writer; born in Dublin, and educated at UCD and Brest, then lectured at UCD. By Salt Water (1996) was a volume of stor-ies; The Burning of Bridget Cleary (1999) a study of a case of suspected witchcraft in Tipperary.

Bourke, P[atrick] J. (1883–1932), actor-manager and playwright. Born in Dublin, orphaned at 12, he attached himself to the Queen's Theatre. In polit-ical melodramas such as The Northern Insurgents (1912), For Ireland's Liberty (1914), and For the Land She Loved (1915) he focused on the patriotic heroism of Irish men and women. He wrote and produced one of the earliest full-length films made in Ireland, Ireland a Nation (1913).

Bourke, Ulick J. (Canon) (1829–1887), language activist. Born in Castlebar, Co. Mayo, he was educated at St Jarlath's, Tuam, before going to Maynooth. While still a student he compiled a College Irish Grammar (1858). He contributed a series to The *Nation on 'Easy Lessons or Self-Instruction in Irish', and was founding chairman of the *Society for the Preser-vation of the Irish Language in 1876. He left to establish the *Gaelic Union with David Comyn (1880) and to launch *Irisleabhar na Gaedhilge.

Bowen, Elizabeth [Dorothea Cole] (1899–1973), writer of fiction; born in Dublin into an Anglo-Irish fam-ily. The first years of her life were div-ided between Dublin, where her father was a barrister, and Bowen's Court in Co. Cork. The history of the family was recounted in Bowen's Court (1942). In 1921, after a brief spell as an art student in London, she became engaged to a lieutenant, but she did not marry him. Her first two novels, The *Hotel (1927) and The *Last September (1929), portray romantic engagements. In 1923, she published Encounters, a collection of stories, and married Alan Cameron. The stories collected in Ann Lee's (1926) and Joining Charles (1929) were followed by Friends and Relations (1931), a novel deal-ing with English middle-class life, and To the North (1932), which explores pas-sions underlying the social façade. The Cat Jumps (1934), Look at all Those Roses (1941), and The *Demon Lover (1945), con-tain short stories, a form which she felt allowed for extremes of experience. The effects of a disrupted upbringing explored in the novel The *House in Paris (1935), are more profoundly developed in The *Death of the Heart (1938). The Heat of the Day (1949) draws on her experience in London during the war. Three more novels were published: A

World of Love (1955), set in Ireland; *The Little Girls* (1964), dealing with the reopening of relationships; and the grotesque *Eva Trout* (1969). A volume of stories, *A Day in the Dark*, appeared in 1965. Bowen spent the last years of her life in Hythe, Kent. Her distinctive, highly wrought style, deals with innocence, betrayal, and the fears beneath the veneer of respectability. See Hermione Lee, *Elizabeth Bowen: An Estimation* (1981).

Boyce, John (pseudonym 'Paul Peppergrass') (1810–1864), novelist; born in Co. Donegal, he was ordained at Maynooth in 1837. He moved to America around 1845 and wrote comic novels including *Shandy M'Guire, or Tricks upon Travellers* (1848), *The Spaewife* (1853), and *Mary Lee, or Yankee in Ireland* (1864).

Boycott, Captain [Charles Cunningham] (1832–1897), a retired English soldier who acted as agent to Lord Erne in Mayo from 1873, and was the object of a form of 'moral Coventry' advocated by the *Land League and *Parnell.

Boyd, Henry (?1756–1832), clergyman and translator. Born in Dromore, Co. Antrim, and educated at TCD, he published a translation of Ariosto's *Orlando Furioso* (1785) and of *The Divina Commedia* of Dante (3 vols., 1802). *The Triumph of Petrarch* (1807) is another verse translation.

Boyd, John (1912–), playwright. Born in Belfast into a working-class Protestant family, he was educated at Royal Belfast Academical Institution, QUB, and TCD, after which he became a teacher. He co-founded and edited the magazine *Lagan* in 1943. In 1948 he joined BBC Northern Ireland as a producer. He became literary adviser to the *Lyric Theatre and editor of its journal, *Threshold*, in 1971. Boyd's drama explores sectarian division and the roots of conflict in Northern Ireland. *The Assassin* (1969) was presented at the Gaiety Theatre in Dublin. *The Flats* (1971) deals with the contemporary *Troubles, while *The Street* (1977) is autobiographical. *Out of My Class* (1985) and *The Middle of My Journey* (1990) are autobiographies. See *Collected Plays* (2 vols., 1981–2).

Boyd, Thomas (1867–1927), poet. Born in Carlingford, Co. Louth, he contributed poetry to *The *United Irishman. *Poems* (1908) makes use of Gaelic *folklore.

Boylan, Clare (1948–), journalist and novelist; born and educated in Dublin. *A Nail in the Head* (1983) was a short-story collection. *Holy Pictures* (1983) relates hilarious events in the life of Nan Cantwell. *Black Babies* (1988) is based on an imaginary result of missionary activity. *Home Rule* (1992) traces the family life of Nan Cantwell's grandparents.

Boylan, Henry (1912–), biographer; born in Drogheda, Co. Louth. He had a long career in public service. His *Dictionary of Irish Biography* (1978, rev. 1998) is the standard reference work. He wrote a life of Wolfe *Tone (1981), and studies of Gaelic writers.

Boyle, Francis, see *weaver poets.

Boyle, John, 5th Earl of Orrery (1707–1762). Born in England and educated at Westminster and Oxford, he edited the *Dramatic Works* (1739) of Roger *Boyle, his grandfather, and translated Pliny's *Letters* (1751). His *Remarks on the Life and Writings of Dr. Jonathan *Swift* (1751), accuses Swift of misanthropy.

Boyle, Patrick (1905–1982), short-story writer and novelist. Born in Ballymoney, Co. Antrim, he worked for the Ulster Bank in Donegal and Wexford.

He began writing in his forties. A collection of stories, *At Night All Cats Are Grey* (1966), was followed by his novel, *Like Any Other Man* (1966), an account of the ruinous love affair of a hard-drinking bank manager. Other collections are *All Looks Yellow to the Jaundiced Eye* (1969) and *A View from Calvary* (1976).

Boyle, Richard, 1st Earl of Cork (1566–1643), colonist and statesman. Born in Canterbury, he arrived in Dublin in 1588 and acquired the estates of Sir Walter Ralegh in Youghal. He was Lord Justice of Ireland in 1627 and Lord High Treasurer of England in 1631. His *Remembrances* (ed. Alexander B. Grosart, 5 vols., 1886) contain defences of his use of office.

Boyle, Robert (1627–1691), scientist; a son of Richard *Boyle, Earl of Cork. Born in Lismore, Co. Waterford, he was a founder-member of the Dublin Philosophical Society (later *RDS), best remembered for 'Boyle's Law', regarding the volume of gases under pressure. His writings include *The Sceptical Chymist* (1661) and *Occasional Reflections* (1665). He studied Scripture in the ancient languages and funded William *Bedell's Irish Bible.

Boyle, Roger, Lord Broghill, 1st Earl of Orrery (1621–1679), soldier and dramatic poet. Born in Lismore, Co. Waterford, son of Richard *Boyle, Earl of Cork. He was educated at TCD and served under *Cromwell in Ireland. Boyle is credited with the first heroic verse play in English, *Altemera, or The General* (printed 1702) performed in Dublin, October 1662. His other tragedies include *Mustapha* (1668), *The Black Prince* (1669), and *Herod* (1694). An early section of his long romance, *Parthenissa* (1665), was published at Waterford in 1654.

Boyle, William (1853–1923), playwright. Born in Dromiskin, Co. Louth, and educated in Dundalk, he worked in the customs service. Although he wrote stories, gathered in *A Kish of Brogues* (1899), Boyle is best remembered for his plays *The *Building Fund* (1905), *The Eloquent Dempsey* (1906), and *The Mineral Workers* (1906) at the *Abbey Theatre. His plays deal with the impact of modern economic life on Catholic values. He ceased writing for the Abbey out of disgust at *Synge's *Playboy of the Western World* (1907), but returned with *Family Failing* in 1912.

Boyne, Battle of the (1 July 1690), the best-remembered battle of the *Williamite War, involving a Jacobite army of about 25,000 French and Irish Catholics, and a Williamite army of 36,000 English, Dutch, Danes, Huguenots, and Irish Protestants. When a section of the Williamite army forced a crossing at Rosnaree, *James II moved the bulk of his troops to his left to meet them. The main Williamite army then fought its way across the river at Oldbridge, forcing the Jacobites to retreat or risk encirclement. Since the main part of the Jacobite army never engaged the enemy, losses were relatively light. Those killed included the Revd George *Walker and the Duke of Schomberg. Defeat broke the nerve of James II, who fled to Dublin ahead of his troops. From the mid-1790s the anniversary of the Boyne, now an aggressively Protestant festival, became the central ritual of the *Orange Order.

Boyne Water, The (1826), a panoramic novel by John *Banim dramatizing major events of the *Williamite War in Ireland. A bond of ecumenical accord between the Catholic McDonnells and Protestant Evelyns is disrupted by the sectarian forces of Irish history.

Bradshaw, Henry (1831–1886),

Cambridge University Librarian, the 'father of modern bibliography'. Born at Milecross, Co. Down, and educated at Eton and Cambridge, he taught at St Columba's College, Co. Dublin, before becoming Assistant Librarian in Cambridge, 1856, and Librarian, 1867–86. There he reformed the early printed books and manuscripts department. His collection of Irish books was catalogued by C. E. Sayle (3 vols., 1916). Bradshaw's example led to the pioneer work of Ernest Reginald McClintock *Dix and the Irish Bibliographical Society. The Henry Bradshaw Society was established in 1890 to publish ecclesiastical texts.

Brady, Nicholas (1659–1726), poet. Born in Bandon, Co. Cork. With Nahum *Tate, he published a *New Version of the Psalms of David* (1695), and produced a verse translation of *The Aeneid of Virgil* (4 vols., 1716) and a verse tragedy, *The Rape* (1692).

Brave Irishman, The; or Captain O'Blunder (1743; published 1754), a farce by Thomas *Sheridan dealing with the courtship of Lucy Tradewell, a London merchant's daughter, by a military Irishman of frank and honest disposition. O'Blunder is strongly marked by *stage-Irish characteristics. The central character provided a model for Charles *Macklin, John *O'Keeffe, and Richard *Cumberland.

Breathnach, Diarmuid (1930–), biographer and encyclopaedist; born in Kiltimon, Co. Wicklow, he was educated at UCD and became a librarian in Kilkenny, then a sound archivist and chief librarian at *RTÉ, 1974–86. His major achievement is the compilation, with Máire Ní Mhurchú, of *Beathaisnéis*, a five-volume dictionary of modern Gaelic culture (1986–97).

Breathnach, Pádraic (1942–), writer of fiction. Born in Moycullen, Co.

Galway, he was educated at UCG, after which he worked as a teacher before becoming lecturer at Mary Immaculate College, Limerick. His short story collections include: *Bean Aonair agus Scéalta Eile* (1974), *Buicéad Poitin agus Scéalta Eile* (1978), *An Lánúin agus Scéalta Eile* (1979), *Ar na Tamhnacha* (1987), *An Pincín agus Scéalta Eile* (1996), amongst others. *Gróga Cloch* (1990) and *As na Cúlacha* (1998) were novels, the latter a ferocious depiction of male carnality.

Brehon laws, see *law in Gaelic Ireland.

Brendan, St (*fl.* 580). Born probably near Tralee, Co. Kerry, he founded a monastery at Clonfert, Co. Kerry. He is reputed to have made many voyages into the Atlantic. The Latin *Navigatio Sancti Brendani* is a Christianized version of the imramm or voyage tale [see *tale-types].

Brennan, Rory (1945–), poet; born in Westport, Co. Mayo, and educated at TCD, he taught abroad before becoming director of *Poetry Ireland 1982–89. Collections include: *The Sea on Fire* (1979), *The Walking Wounded* (1985), and *The Old in Rapallo* (1997).

Brew, Margaret (?1850–?), novelist. Born in Co. Clare, probably the daughter of a landowner, she published *The *Burtons of Dunroe* (1880) and *Chronicles of Castle Cloyne* (1886), both seeking social accommodation between the religions and classes.

Brian Bóroime (Boru) (941–1014), King of Ireland. Born probably near Killaloe, Co. Clare, he became King of Munster in 987, dominating the Viking cities of Limerick and Waterford and the monastic towns Cork and Lismore. By 996 he ruled the southern half of Ireland. He described himself in the *Book of Armagh* in 1002 as 'Emperor of the

Irish', and by 1011 he was King of Ireland, shattering the authority of the Uí Néill in the north. In 1014 the Dubliners built up a defensive alliance against him including Sigurd, Earl of Orkney, Brodir of Man, and troops from the Hebrides. Brian faced the Viking confederates and the Leinstermen at *Clontarf on Good Friday; his opponents were routed, although Brian was hacked to death in his hut by fleeing Vikings. He was buried in Armagh with great ceremony. Clontarf was celebrated in Irish literature in *Cogadh Gaedhel re Gallaibh.

Brian Westby (1934), a novel by Forrest *Reid in which the ageing writer Martin Linton returns to Northern Ireland to recuperate from illness.

Bricriu, see *Fled Bricrenn.

Bride for the Unicorn, A (1933), a play by Denis *Johnston first staged at the *Gate Theatre. Based on Jason's quest for the Golden Fleece, the play centres on the central character Jay's pursuit of his ideal of love and beauty.

Bright Temptation, The (1932), a prose romance by Austin *Clarke set at the time of the *Vikings. Aidan, a student at Cluanmore (for *Clonmacnoise), strays from his monastic cell and encounters many misfortunes, but is rescued by the mysterious Ethna.

Brigit, St, a national patron saint. Although her cult is attached to the church at Kildare, she is Brigantia, goddess and patron of the Brigantes, overlords of much of northern England at the time of the Roman conquest (AD 43), who settled in Leinster. There is a Latin life by *Cogitosus and another in Irish. Her feast fell on 1 February, or Imbolg [see *festivals].

Brislech Mór Maige Murthemne, see Aided Chon Chulainn.

Brittaine, George (?1790–1847), Church of Ireland rector of Kilcormack and author of anti-Catholic novels. In The Election (1838) a Catholic supporter of the landed gentry is murdered by his co-religionists. Irish Priests and English Landlords (1830), Confessions of Honor Delany (1830), Hyacinth O'Gara (1830), and Irishmen and Women (1831) were in the same vein.

broadsheets (or broadsides), single-leaf texts of songs sold at public events such as markets and hiring fairs. The printing and sale of broadsheets was first introduced into Ireland from England and Scotland in the 17th cent. The songs dealt with a variety of subjects: love, politics, crime, carousal, and emigration. They were distributed by strolling singers. The form declined in the 20th cent.

Brock, Lynn, see Alexander *McAllister.

Broderick, John (1927–1989), novelist; born and educated in Athlone, where he ran the substantial family bakery. From The Pilgrimage (1961) he wrote a series of Balzacian studies of depressing life in the Irish midlands. In the first Julia Glynn has love affairs with the family doctor and then with a house-servant while living with a crippled husband. The Waking of Willie Ryan (1965) concerns a homosexual who has been committed to an institution by his family in connivance with a priest. Other works include: The Fugitives (1962), An Apology for Roses (1973), and London Irish (1979). The *Trial of Father Dillingham (1975) is set in Dublin, and concerns a group of migrants from the midlands whose urbanity is tested by the death of one of them. The Flood (1991) involves an attempt to sell water-logged land to an unsuspecting Englishman.

Brontë [Ó Pronntaigh], Revd Patrick (1777–1861), poet and father of the Brontës; born near Loughbrickland, Co. Down. After working as a black-smith, he taught at Glascar and was ordained in 1806. He became curate of Haworth in 1820. His poems and stories are didactic idylls. *The Maid of Killarney* (1818) is a tale of love between an Eng-lishman and an Irish Catholic peasant girl. His literary works were collected by V. Horsfall Turner in *Bronteana* (1898).

Brook Kerith, The (1916), a historical novel by George *Moore retelling the life of Jesus from a sceptical standpoint. Instead of dying on the cross, Jesus goes into a coma and is brought back to life by Joseph of Arimathea who takes him to a community of Essenes, where he finds peace. Years later, Paul visits the Essenes and meets the man whose resurrection he has made the basis of his teaching.

Brooke, Charlotte (?1740–1793), translator and anthologist. Born in Ran-tavan, Co. Cavan, daughter of Henry *Brooke, she grew up in Kildare and was educated by her father, who encouraged her study of Irish. She con-tributed translations of Irish poetry anonymously to *Historical Memoirs of the Irish Bards* (1786), a compilation by her antiquarian friend Joseph Cooper *Walker. *Reliques of Irish Poetry* (1789) asserts the merit and antiquity of Irish poetry, arguing that Irish verse is the 'elder sister' to the British. It contains heroic poems, elegies, and songs, each section having its own introduction and notes. The original poems are grouped together at the end. Besides an edition of her father's poetry in 1792, she also issued *The School for Christians* (1791).

Brooke, Henry (?1703–1783), novelist.

Born in Co. Cavan, he was educated at TCD. His philosophical poem *Universal Beauty* (1735) was followed by a transla-tion of Books I–III of Tasso's *Gerusalemme Liberata* (1738). In 1739 his play *Gustavus Vasa: The Deliverer of His Country* was banned by the Lord Chamberlain for its alleged attack on the Prime Minister, Robert Walpole. Under the title *The Pat-riot* it was produced in 1744 in Dublin. Brooke's later dramatic works include *Betrayer of His Country* (1742), *The Earl of Essex* (1750), and *Anthony and Cleopatra* (1778). His political writings began with *The Farmer's Six Letters to the Protestants of Ireland* (1745), warning his co-religionists of the Jacobite threat. How-ever, *The Tryal of the Cause of the Roman Catholics* (1761) argued for an alleviation of the *Penal Laws. Brooke is best remembered for *The *Fool of Quality* (1765–70), a novel of sentiment, which he followed with the less successful *Juliet Grenville* (1774). Charlotte *Brooke, his only surviving child, cared for him in his dotage.

Brooke, Stopford Augustus (1832–1916), man of letters. Born in Glendowan, Co. Donegal, and educated at TCD. *A Treasury of Irish Poetry in the Eng-lish Tongue* (1900), was edited with his son-in-law T. W. *Rolleston.

Brophy, Kevin (1943–   ), born in Co. Mayo, and educated at UCG and Bretton Hall, Wakefield, he taught for a number of years before working as a publisher. *Walking the Line* (1994) was a memoir of childhood, *Almost Heaven* (1997) a novel, and *In the Company of Wolves* (1999) another autobiography.

Brown, Christy (1932–1981), novel-ist; born with cerebral paralysis to a working-class family in Crumlin, Co. Dublin, he was taught reading by his mother and produced the auto-biographical *My Left Foot* (1954). *Down All the Days* (1970), a novel, treats of the same material. Later novels are: *A Shadow on Summer* (1973), *Wild Grow the Lilies* (1976), and *A Promising Career* (1982). His poetry was collected as *Softly to My Wake* (1971) and *Of Snails and Skylarks* (1978).

Brown, Stephen [James Meredith] (1881–1962), bibliographer; born in Co. Down and ordained a Jesuit in 1914. *Ireland in Fiction* (1919) contains summaries of nearly 2,000 Irish books. *Studies in Life, By and Large* (1942) contains reflective essays. The manuscript for a sequel to his great survey, covering prose works from 1918 to 1960, was completed by Desmond *Clarke and issued in 1985.

Brown, Terence (1944–), critic; born at Loping in southern China, the son of missionary parents, he was educated at Sullivan Upper School, Holywood, Magee University College, and at TCD where he became Fellow in 1976 then Professor in 1993. He published *Louis MacNeice: Sceptical Vision* (1978), followed by *Northern Voices* (1975), *Ireland: A Social and Cultural History 1922–79* (1981), *Ireland's Literature* (1988), and *The Life of W. B. Yeats: A Critical Biography* (1999); he edited Derek *Mahon's *Journalism* (1996) and a volume on *Celticism* (1996) among others.

Browne, Frances ('The Blind Poetess of Donegal') (1816–1879). Born in Stranorlar, Co. Donegal, she lived in London from 1847. Her fiction and children's stories include *Granny's Wonderful Chair and the Stories It Told* (1856). In *The Star of Atteghei* (1844) and *Pictures and Songs from Home* (1856), the recurrent theme of her poetry is an exile's homecoming. *My Share in the World* (1862) is an autobiography.

Bruidhean Chaorthainn (*Hostel of Rowan*), a bruidhean or hostel tale of the *Fionn cycle. Fionn and his warrior-

band are enticed by enchantment to a magical hostel by the *Viking king. Immobilized, they sound the Dord Fiann which brings help from Diarmaid [see *Tóraigheacht Dhiarmada agus Ghráinne].

Brug na Bóinne, see *New Grange.

Bryans, Robin, see Robert *Harbinson.

Buchanan, George (1904–1989), novelist and poet. Born in Kilwaughter, Co. Antrim, and educated at Campbell College, Belfast, he became a journalist. In the Second World War he served in the RAF. His first novel, *A London Story* (1935), compares the careers of two brothers. *Rose Forbes* (1937) and *The Soldier and the Girl* (1940) are studies of Irish women seeking fulfilment. *The Green Seacoast* (1959), an autobiographical work, covers the period of the *Easter Rising. In collections such as *Conversation with Strangers* (1959) and *Inside Traffic* (1976), his poetry deals with urban experience. *The Politics of Culture* (1977) is one of several essay collections.

Buckley, William (*fl.* 1905), writer of fiction. Born in Cork, he wrote for *The United Irishman*. His earliest novel, *Croppies Lie Down* (1903), is a painstakingly realistic narrative of the *United Irishmen's Rebellion. *Cambia Carty* (1907) is a collection of stories set in Cork city and county.

Buckstone, John [Baldwin] (1802–1875), English actor-manager who specialized in *stage-Irish roles; he also wrote melodramas and comedies for the Haymarket Theatre. In *The Boyne Water, or the Relief of Londonderry* (1831), George *Walker's daughter Oonagh revenges the death of her father. *The Green Bushes* (1845) dramatizes the escape of an Irish Jacobite to

Mississippi. *The Irish Lion* (1838) is a satirizing farce in which a loquacious Irish tailor is mistaken for Thomas *Moore.

Building Fund, The (1905), a comedy by William *Boyle first staged at the *Abbey Theatre. It tells how Shan Grogan and his niece are outwitted in their attempt to prevent his mother's money from going to the priest's building fund.

Buile Shuibne (*Frenzy of Sweeney*). Generally regarded as a 12th-cent. text, it is preserved in three manuscripts, the earliest of which can be dated to between 1671 and 1674. The events of *Buile Shuibne* follow on from the battle of Mag Rath (Moira) [see *Cath Maige Rath]. Driven mad by the din of battle, because of a curse by a cleric named Rónán, Suibne takes to the wilderness, where he spends many years naked, living in tree-tops, bemoaning his fate, celebrating nature in haunting lyrical verse, intermittently recovering his sanity, and finally settling at Teach Moling [St Mullins] in Co. Carlow. The mood of the story is penitential, the theme concerns transitional states. It continues to inspire Irish writers, notably Flann *O'Brien in *At Swim-Two-Birds (1939), Seamus *Heaney in *Sweeney Astray* (1983), and Cathal *Ó Searcaigh.

Bulfin, William (1861–1910), author of *Rambles in Eirinn* (1907), a popular work based on a cycle tour of Ireland in 1902. Born in Derrinlough, Co. Offaly, Bulfin became editor-proprietor of *The Southern Cross* in Argentina. He also published *Tales of the Pampas* (1900).

Bullock, Shan F[adh] (1865–1935), novelist. Born in Crom, Co. Fermanagh, he was educated in Farra School, Co. Westmeath, before going to London where he worked as a civil servant. His books deal chiefly with the farming community around Lough Erne. *By Thrasna River* (1895) is a tale of the hardship of life on smallholdings. *The *Red-Leaguers* (1904) depicts the consequences of a *Fenian rising. In *Dan the Dollar* (1906) the hero returns from America and sets his family up in a neighbouring *big house. *The *Loughsiders* (1924) also centres on the theme of the returned exile. Other works include *Robert Thorne* (1907), and *Thomas Andrews, Shipbuilder* (1912), about the architect of the *Titanic. Mors et Vita* (1923) is a collection of poems on the death of his wife.

Bunbury, Selina (1802–1882), fiction and travel writer. Born in Co. Louth, she began contributing to journals when her father became bankrupt. Her early writings, *A Visit to My Birthplace* (1821) and *Tales of My Country* (1833), are informed by patriotism and good humour. *Coombe Abbey* (1844) deals with a Protestant Irishman's brush with the Guy Fawkes plot. Other historical novels are *The Star of the Court* (1844), *Sir Guy D'Esterre* (1858), and *Florence Manvers* (1865). Her travel books include *The Pyrenees* (1845) and *Russia After the War* (1857).

Bunting, Edward (1773–1843), organist and collector of Irish music. Born in Armagh, he moved to Drogheda in 1782. He was made apprentice organist in Belfast at 11, and lived with the family of Henry Joy *McCracken. When the Belfast Harp Festival was organized in 1792, Bunting transcribed the airs from the harpers. In 1793 he began a series of collecting trips through Ulster and Connaught. His *General Collection of The Ancient Music of Ireland* (1796) inspired Thomas *Moore's *Irish Melodies*. An enlarged edition of the *General Collection* appeared in 1809. The *Ancient Music of Ireland* (1840) contained many more airs, and included specimens gathered by George *Petrie and translations by Samuel *Ferguson.

Burdy, Revd Samuel (1754–1820), poet. Born in Dromore, Co. Down, and educated at TCD, he was rector of Cullybackey, Co. Antrim. *Ardglass, or the Ruined Castles* (1802), contains a long topographical poem. He also wrote a *History of Ireland from the Earliest Times* (1817).

Burk, John Daly (?1775–1808), *United Irishman and dramatist who emigrated to America after expulsion from TCD in 1796. In 1797 he wrote *Bunker Hill, or the Death of General Warren* (1797), a patriotic verse play for Americans. In *Female Patriotism, or the Death of Joan d'Arc* (1798), democracy is praised. *Bethlam Gabor* (1807) is a prose melodrama set in Transylvania. He wrote a *History of the Late War in Ireland* (1799) and a *History of Virginia* (1804–16).

Burke, Edmund (1729–1797), political philosopher; born at Arran Quay, Dublin, the son of a Protestant lawyer and a Catholic mother, Mary Nagle from Co. Cork. He spent some years in Co. Cork with his mother's people, then joined the Quaker School in Ballitore, Co. Kildare, before going to TCD. He studied law at the Middle Temple in London. *A Vindication of Natural Society* (1756) was a defence of the established social order. In 1757 he married Jane Nugent, a Catholic, and in the same year published *A Philosophical Enquiry into the Origin of our Ideas of the *Sublime and Beautiful*, his treatise on aesthetics. In 1758 he began to edit the newly-established *Annual Register*, a yearly digest of politics, history, and the arts. In 1765 Burke became private secretary to Lord Rockingham, the Prime Minister, and was returned as MP for Wendover, throwing himself into Commons activity. *Thoughts on the Cause of the Present Discontents* (1770) grew out of his anger at the failure of the Rockingham ministry

to control George III's interventionist approach to Parliament. In 1773 Burke spent a month in Paris; there he encountered Diderot, one of the French *philosophes* whom he would later attack in his *Reflections on the Revolution in France*, and also met Louis XV, the Dauphin, and the Dauphine Marie Antoinette at Versailles. In April 1774, by which time he was the Rockingham spokesman on American affairs, he delivered his *Speech on American Taxation* in the Commons, arguing vehemently against the imposition of a tea tax. In this year he also became MP for Bristol. Around this time he became a close friend of Charles James Fox. He invested in the East India Company and began to take an interest in Indian affairs. Burke was the driving force behind a Commons select committee on India, whose Ninth Report (1782) gave a detailed account of mismanagement and corruption in the East India Company. He attacked Warren Hastings, Governor-General of Bengal, whose impeachment was to occupy him on and off from 1786 to 1795, when Hastings was finally acquitted. On the centenary of the Glorious Revolution (4 November 1788) Dr Richard Price, a Dissenting minister, gave a speech in London welcoming the events unfolding in France, Burke read the speech in early 1789 and immediately began writing his *Reflections. A powerful defence of English constitutional liberty, it developed and expanded the central tenets of his political thought. Burke's *Appeal from the Old to the New Whigs* (1791) warned against the tyranny of government by democratic majority. Fearful that revolutionary principles would find a ready audience in Ireland, Burke supported the Catholic Committee in Dublin then campaigning for relief measures [see *Catholic Emancipation]. His *Letter to Sir Hercules Langrishe* (1792) argued the necessity of representation for Catholics. *Letters on a Regicide Peace*

(1795/6) urged Britain to defend the established order in Europe. In a *Letter to a Noble Lord* (1796) he defended himself against an insult in the House of Lords regarding his civil-list pension, offering a dignified appraisal of his own career in the service of constitutional freedom. Although dying of stomach cancer, he continued to attack French expansionism and to excoriate the Protestant ascendancy in the Dublin Parliament for their intransigence on the Catholic question. Burke was the architect of modern British conservative thought, the leading principles of which he shaped in his reflections upon the great questions of his time. See Paul Langford (ed.), *The Writings and Speeches of Edmund Burke* (1981–   ); and Conor Cruise O'Brien, *The Great Melody: A Thematic Biography and Commented Anthology of Edmund Burke* (1992).

Burke, Thomas (also de Burgos) (?1710–1776), historian of the Dominican Order in Ireland. He was born in Dublin and ordained in Rome, 1726, becoming Bishop of Ossory in 1759. In 1762 he issued *Hibernia Dominicana*, published in Kilkenny with a fictitious Cologne imprint. Burke's other works include *Promptuarium Morale* (1731), *Propria Sanctorum Hiberniae* (1751), and *A Catechism, Moral and Controversial* (1752).

Burke, Thomas Nicholas (Revd) (1830–1883), Dominican priest and preacher, known as 'Father Tom Burke'; born in Galway, the son of a baker, and educated in Italy. His course of lectures in America during 1872 were published as *Ireland's Case Stated* (1873). A collection called *Lectures on Faith and Fatherland* (1874) challenges the anti-Catholic view of Irish history.

Burke's Landed Gentry of Ireland (1st edn. 1899), a genealogical dictionary of Irish landowning families, published by the company established by John Burke (1787–1848), compiler of Burke's *Peerage* (1826). After a fourth edition in 1958 the work was reissued as *Burke's Irish Family Records* (1976).

Burkhead, Henry (*fl.* 1645), author of *Cola's Fury, or Lirenda's Misery* (1645), a play printed in Kilkenny and dealing with events of the Irish *Rebellion of 1641 from an English standpoint.

Burnell, Henry (*fl.* 1640), author of *Landgartha* (1639), a tragicomedy in verse produced at *Werburgh Street Theatre. Based on material from Saxo Grammaticus, the prologue and epilogue are spoken by an Irish Amazon. Burnell was of a Leinster Anglo-Norman family, and a member of the *Confederation of Kilkenny (1642).

Burton, Sir Richard Francis (1821–1890), explorer and philologist; born in Tuam, Co. Galway, and educated at Oxford. After joining the Indian Army in 1842, Burton explored Arabia, Africa, and Russia. His travel books include *Personal Narrative of a Pilgrimage to El-Medinah and Meccah* (1855–6). An interest in orientalism led to translations of the *Kama Sutra* (1883) and *The Arabian Nights* (1885–8).

Burtons of Dunroe, The (1880), a novel by Margaret *Brew dealing with religious differences in Co. Limerick before *Catholic Emancipation, *concerns a love-match between a Catholic peasant girl and the son of a Protestant landlord.

Bushe, Paddy (1948–   ), poet; born in Dublin and educated at UCD he worked as a teacher until 1990. *Poems with Amergin* (1989) was followed by *Digging Towards the Light* (1994), *To Make the Stone Sing* (1996), and *Hopkins on Skellig Michael* (2000).

Butcher, Samuel [Henry] (1850–1910), author of a prose translation of the *Odyssey* (1879) with Andrew Lang. Born in Dublin, son of the Bishop of Meath, he was educated at Cambridge. His works of classical scholarship include an edition of Demosthenes' *Speeches* (1881), an essay on *Greek Genius* (1893), and a critical translation of *Aristotle's Poetics* (1895).

Butler, Hubert [Marshal] (1900–1990), man of letters. Born in Maidenhall, Bennetsbridge, Co. Kilkenny, and educated at Charterhouse and Oxford, he worked as a teacher and travelled in Asia and America. His criticism of Catholic policy on mixed marriages aroused antipathy in Ireland. In the 1980s he campaigned for nuclear disarmament. A growing appreciation of his distinction as an essayist led to the publication of several collections, *Escape from the Anthill* (1985), *The Children of Drancy* (1988), and *Grandmother and Wolfe Tone* (1990).

Butler, James, see Duke of *Ormond.

Butler, Sarah (d. ?1735), author of *Irish Tales, or Instructive Histories for the Happy Conduct of Life* (1716). She was probably of the Butler family of Kilkenny [see Duke of *Ormond]. Her only known work is among the earliest examples of Irish romantic fiction, and includes a historical tale concerning the Battle of *Clontarf.

Butler, Sir William Francis (1838–1910), soldier and author. Born at Suirville in Co. Tipperary, he was educated in Tullaby, Co. Offaly, before joining an infantry regiment in 1858. Besides biographies of General Gordon (1889) and Sir Charles Napier (1890), he issued accounts of his Canadian adventures in *The Great Lone Land* (1872) and *The Wild North Land* (1873). *Red Cloud* (1882) is a novel about the Sioux Indians.

Butt, Isaac (1813–1879), author and politician. Born in Stranorlar, Co. Donegal, he was educated at Raphoe and TCD, where he was one of the founders of the *Dublin University Magazine*. He published translations of the *Georgics* of Virgil and the *Fasti* of Ovid in 1833 and 1834. The conservativism that inspired his resistance to *O'Connell's Repeal movement was modified by the events of the *Famine. His novel, *The Gap of Barnesmore* (1848), set in 1688, makes a plea for a united Irish nation.

Byrne, Donn (pseudonym of Brian Oswald Donn-Byrne) (1889–1928), novelist. Born in New York but brought up in Armagh and Antrim. His stories and novels include *Stranger's Banquet* (1919), *The Changeling and Other Stories* (1923), *Blind Raftery* (1924), *O'Malley of Shanganagh* (1925), *Hangman's House* (1925), *Destiny Bay* (1928), and *Field of Honour* (1929). His Irish fiction typically combines elements of Gaelic and Anglo-Irish tradition in dramatic plots set against scenic backgrounds. The cosmopolitan settings of New York and the south of France in works such as *The Golden Goat* (1930) allowed a freer moral perspective. Working as a writer in America, his view of Ireland became increasingly sentimental, leading him to condemn rural electrification schemes. He died at Courtmacsherry, Co. Cork. *The Rock Whence I Was Hewn* (1929) gives a view of Ireland.

Byrne, Seamus (1904–1968), playwright. Born in Dublin and educated at UCD, he practised law before becoming a political activist, which led to a two-year prison sentence in 1940 for *IRA membership. His *Design for a Headstone* (1950), a controversial *Abbey production on hunger-strikers, set in Mountjoy Prison, was followed by *Innocent Bystander* (1951).

C

Caddell, Cecilia Mary (?1813–1877), novelist; born in Co. Meath. An invalid, her fiction includes *Blind Agnes* (1856) and *Nellie Netterville* (1867), both set in *Cromwellian times.

Cadenus and Vanessa (1762), a poem by Jonathan *Swift probably composed during 1713. 'Cadenus' is a Latin anagram for his new post as Dean, and 'Vanessa' a pet-name for Esther Vanhomrigh (1688–1723), the daughter of the wealthy widow of a Dublin merchant, who had moved her family to London. It describes the love and friendship between the Dean and the spirited young woman.

Caesar and Cleopatra: *A History* (1899), one of the *Three Plays for Puritans* by George Bernard *Shaw, concerning Caesar's sojourn in Egypt during the winter of 48–47BC.

Caffyn, Kathleen Mannington, see *IOTA.

Cailleach Bhéarra (Hag of Beare), a female divinity in Irish and Scottish Gaelic literature and oral tradition. The original pagan conception interacts with the more Christian sense of cailleach ('nun') in the 9th-cent. poem 'Lament of the Old Woman of Beare'. She is represented as an ancient nun bemoaning her past youth, but a connection with the goddess of sovereignty is also vestigially present.

Cáin Adamnáin (*Law of Adamnán*), also called *lex innocentium* (law of the innocents), was promulgated by *Adamnán, ninth abbot of Iona, at a synod held at Birr in 697. It deals with war crimes against women, children, and clerics.

Caisleáin Óir (1924), a novel by Séamus *Ó Grianna ('Máire'), set in the Donegal *Gaeltacht and telling how the love between Séimidh Phádraig Dubh and Babaí Mháirtin grows cold over time.

Caithréim Chellacháin Chaisil (*Victorious Career of Cellachán of Cashel*), a tale of the *historical cycle written in Munster between 1127 and 1134, when Cormac Mac Cárthaig was King of Munster. It glorifies the *Eoganacht kings and shows their ancestor Cellachán as defender of Ireland against the *Vikings.

Caithréim Chellaig (*Triumph of Cellach*), otherwise *Betha Chellaig* (Life of Cellach), a tale loosely linked to the *historical cycle, written probably in the 12th cent. Cellach, a monk at *Clonmacnoise, accedes to his father's wish that he become king of Connacht, but he is driven out by Guaire mac Colmáin and forced to take refuge in the woods, before being assassinated.

Caithréim Thoirdhealbhaigh (*Triumph of Turlough*) (?1365), a prose text written by Seán, son of the poet Ruaidhri Mac Craith (*fl.* 1317). It deals with the fierce warfare that followed the English confiscation of Ó Briain territories, and the triumph of Toirdhealbhach Ó Briain, who won them back.

Call My Brother Back, see Michael *MacLaverty.

Callanan, Jeremiah J. (1795–1829), poet and translator. Born in Ballinhassig, Co. Cork, he was educated at Cobh, then at Maynooth [see *universities], which he left without taking orders. He taught in the school kept by William *Maginn's father in Cork, and joined the antiquarian circle that included Thomas Crofton *Croker and John *Windele (1801–65). In 1828 *Blackwood's Magazine* published 'The Outlaw of Loch Lene', a loose adaptation of a love song. *The Recluse of Inchydoney* (1830) is a narrative and psychological poem dealing with a Byronic hero who has fled the city. His health damaged by tuberculosis, he took a post as tutor to a Cork family in Lisbon, where he died.

Campbell, Joseph (Seosamh Mac-Cathmaoil) (1879–1944), poet; born and educated in Belfast. He collaborated with Herbert Hughes in setting words to folk melodies in *Songs of Uladh* (1904), a collection which contains 'My Lagan Love'. Campbell was associated with the *Ulster Literary Theatre, for which he wrote *The Little Cowherd of Slainge* (May 1905). With Bulmer *Hobson he edited two issues of *Uladh*, in 1904–05. In London he published *The Rushlight* (1906), *The Gilly of Christ* (1907), and *The Mountainy Singer* (1909), acted as secretary to the Irish Literary Society [see *literary revival], and assisted Eleanor *Hull with the Irish Texts Society. A mystical strain in his sensibility found expression in *Irishry* (1913), and *Earth of Cualann* (1917), written after he had settled in Co. Wicklow in 1912. He took the anti-Treaty side in the *Civil War and was interned for eighteen months. He moved to New York where he founded the School of Irish Studies in 1925, lecturing at Fordham University before returning to Wicklow.

Campbell, Michael (1924–1984), journalist and novelist. Born in Dublin and educated at TCD, he became *Irish Times* correspondent in London. After *Peter Perry* (1956), set in shabby-genteel Dublin art circles, and *Mary, This London* (1959), a fantasy with Irish characters,

he wrote *Lord Dismiss Us* (1967), narrating events involving a homosexual attachment and the suicide of a schoolmaster. His brother was the columnist Patrick *Campbell.

Campbell, Patrick, 3rd Baron Glenavy (1913–1980), Dublin-born journalist, broadcaster, and columnist. He enjoyed great popularity as the author of comic sketches, and as 'Quidnunc', in the *Irish Times*.

Campbell, Thomas, see *weaver poets.

Campbell, Thomas (1733–1795), clergyman and author. Born in Glack, Co. Tyrone, and educated at TCD. *A Philosophical Survey of the South of Ireland* (1776), in forty-five letters, purports to be the record of an Englishman's tour, and argues for political union. *A Diary of a Visit to England in 1755* (1854) was discovered in Sydney, Australia, where his brother Charles had emigrated in 1810. It describes meetings with Johnson, *Goldsmith, and *Burke.

Campion, John Thomas (1814–1890), physician and author. Born in Co. Kilkenny, he contributed fiction to *The *Nation* and other nationalist papers. His historical novels include *Alice* (1862), about crusaders in 14th-cent. Kilkenny, and *The Last Struggles of the Irish Sea Smugglers* (1869), set in Wicklow.

Candida (1897), a play [see *Plays Pleasant . . .] by George Bernard *Shaw, written in 1894 and partly conceived as a reversal of the portrayal of sex relations in Ibsen's *A Doll's House* (1879), showing that 'in the real typical doll's house it is the man who is the doll'.

Candle for the Proud, see *Stand and Give Challenge.

Candle of Vision, The, see George
*Russell.

**Canning, A[lfred] S[tratford]
G[eorge]** (1832–1916), landlord and
author. His novels *Kilsorrell Castle* (1863)
and *Kinkora* (1864) deal with agrarian
crime, while *Heir and No Heir* (1890),
based on the disinheritance of George
*Canning the Elder, depicts the reli-
giously divided community of 'Dalragh'
(Garvagh, Co. Derry).

Canning, George (1730–1771), lawyer and poet. Born in Garvagh, Co.
Derry, and educated at TCD, he went to
London in 1757, having been disinherited, and wrote modernized translations of classical writings including
Horace's First Satire (1762). A founder of
The Anti-Jacobin Review and a leading
contributor to *The Quarterly Review*, he
wrote comical poems ridiculing republican philosophy. The *Poetical Works*
appeared in 1823 and the *Speeches* in
1828.

Cannon, Moya (1956–   ), poet; born
in Dunfanaghy, Co. Donegal, and educated in Donegal, at UCD, and at
Cambridge. She worked as a teacher in
the Gaelscoil in Inchicore, Dublin, and
as editor of *Poetry Ireland* (1995).
She was writer-in-residence in Trent
University, Ontario. Her collections
include *Oar* (1990) and *The Parchment
Boat* (1998).

Caoilte mac Rónáin, a warrior of the
*Fionn cycle. In folk tradition he is born
in the otherworld [see *sídh]. In *Acallam na Senórach* he survives into the time
of St *Patrick, to whom he recites the
lore of Fionn.

caoineadh (keen, keening), a sung
lament for the dead performed during
the wake and funeral, and occasionally
afterwards. Professional keeners often
performed at funerals. The keen is a

survival of funerary ritual of pagan
heroic tradition reflected in the
themes in praise of a man's physical
prowess or generosity. Eibhlín Dubh
*Ní Chonaill's caoineadh for Art
O'Leary records a version of a famous
keen.

Caoineadh Airt Uí Laoghaire, see
Eibhlín Dubh *Ní Chonaill.

***Captain Brassbound's Conver-
sion:*** *An Adventure* (1900), one of the
Three Plays for Puritans by George Bernard *Shaw. Lady Cicely Wayneflete
and her brother-in-law, the judge Sir
Henry Hallam, are escorted on an
expedition into the wilds of Morocco by
Brassbound, bent on revenge for a
wrongdoing in the past. Lady Cicely dis-
arms the surly Brassbound, and mocks
his vindictiveness, giving him a
renewed sense of purpose.

Captain with the Whiskers, The
(1960), a novel by Benedict *Kiely, drawing heavily on the oral tradition of Co.
Tyrone and dedicated to the memory of
his father.

Captive and the Free, The (1959), a
posthumously published novel by Joyce
*Cary. Walter Preedy, evangelist and
faith-healer, is patronized by Kate
Rideout, while Hooper, the editor of
the *Argus* newspaper which she con-
trols, is running stories about Preedy's
nefarious activities, but his plotting
fails.

Carbery, Ethna (pseudonym of Anna
MacManus, née Johnson) (1866–1902),
poet and short-story writer; born
in Ballymena, Co. Antrim. A frequent
contributor to The *Nation, she founded
The *Shan Van Vocht with Alice
*Milligan in 1896. Carbery's patriotic
poetry in The *Four Winds of Ireland*
(1902)—which includes the ballad
'Roddy McCorley'—is moving but

conventional. Her fiction was collected as *The Passionate Hearts* (1903), and *In the Celtic Past* (1904).

Cards of the Gambler, The (1953), a novel by Benedict *Kiely in which a *folklore-type narrative is juxtaposed with a realistic one to tell the same story.

Carey, Matthew (1760–1839), author of *Vindiciae Hibernicae* (1819), a refutation of English versions of Irish history, especially regarding the *Rebellion of 1641. He edited the *Pennsylvania Herald* and published the first US atlas.

Carleton, William (1794–1869), novelist; born to a family of Irish-speaking farmers in Prillisk, Co. Tyrone. His family was evicted in 1813 and Carleton joined the Ribbonmen [see *secret societies] for a while. Some time before 1818 he left Tyrone, earning a living as a teacher before arriving in Dublin, where he met the Revd Caesar *Otway, writer and anti-catholic controversialist, in 1828. Under his influence he joined the Church of Ireland. The first version of 'The *Lough Derg Pilgrim' appeared in Otway's *Christian Examiner* in 1828, followed later that year by 'The Broken Oath' and the serialized novella, *Father Butler. Traits and Stories of the Irish Peasantry* (1830) were critical accounts of rural life and customs followed by a second series in 1833. In 1839 he published his first novel, *Fardorougha the Miser* (serialized in the *Dublin University Magazine*, 1837–8). In addition to rewriting and editing his earlier works during 1840–5, Carleton published four novels in 1845: *Valentine M'Clutchy*, *Art Maguire*, *Rody the Rover*, and *Parra Sastha*—the last three written for the 'Library of Ireland' series promoted by The *Nation. Carleton responded to the *Famine with three novels: The *Black Prophet* (1847), The *Emigrants of Ahadarra*

(1848), and The *Tithe Proctor* (1849). All of Carleton's longer fiction of the 1840s shows the influence of the didactic tradition in which he first began to write in the 1820s. *Art Maguire* warns against the danger of alcohol, *Parra Sastha* encourages hard work and thrift, and *Rody the Rover* shows the evils of the Ribbon lodges. In 1855 he published *Willy Reilly and his Dear Colleen Bawn*, which ran to over thirty editions. He continued to write: *The Black Baronet* (1858); *The Evil Eye, or The Black Spectre* (1860); and *The Double Prophecy, or Trials of the Heart* (1862). *Redmond Count O'Hanlon, the Irish Rapparee* and *The Silver Acre and Other Tales* (a collection of short fiction from the 1850s) also appeared in 1862, followed by a diminishing trickle of short stories throughout the 1860s. He spent the years before his death working on his unfinished *Autobiography*, published along with a 'Further Account of his Life and Writings' by D. J. *O'Donoghue as *The *Life of William Carleton* in 1896. Living at a time when factional boundaries were clearly demarcated, Carleton wrote for the Unionist *Dublin University Magazine*, the nationalist *The Nation* and *Irish Felon*; the anti-Catholic *Christian Examiner*; and the pro-Catholic *Duffy's Hibernian Magazine*. Carleton's bilingualism, his familiarity with the culture of rural Catholic Ireland (towards which he often adopted a condescending tone), and his community feeling make him one of the first writers in 19th-cent. Ireland to embody in his career, language, and narratives the tensions inherent in *Anglo-Irish literature. See Benedict Kiely, *Poor Scholar* (1948).

Carlyle, Thomas (1795–1881), the Scottish man of letters best known as the author of *Sartor Resartus* (1833) and *On Heroes and Hero Worship* (1841), visited Ireland during the *Famine, in 1846, and again in 1849. Appalled by the scenes of human misery he witnessed, he characterized the people as irrational and disorderly in *Reminiscences of My Irish Journey* (1882). He also gives a caustic account of several Irish notables including Cardinal John *MacHale and Charles Gavan *Duffy. Carlyle's style was a model for Irish authors including John *Mitchel.

Carnduff, Thomas (1886–1956), poet and playwright. Born in Belfast, he was employed in the Belfast shipyards, and saw action in the First World War. Following the publication of his *Songs from the Shipyard* (1924), he went on to write plays for the *Abbey Theatre and the *Ulster Literary Theatre. *Workers* (1932) deals with sectarianism in the shipyard, and *Castlereagh* (1934) is a historical drama about the *United Irishmen. His poetry was reissued as *Poverty Street* (1993).

Carney, James (1914–1989), Gaelic scholar. Born in Portlaoise and educated by the Christian Brothers at UCD, and at Bonn, where he studied under Rudolf *Thurneysen. He joined the School of Celtic Studies in the *DIAS in 1941, and edited *Poems on the O'Reillys* (1950). His understanding of early Irish poetry is reflected in his *Early Irish Poetry* (1965), and in the translations in *Mediaeval Irish Lyrics* (1967).

Carolan, Turlough, see Toirdhealbhach *Ó Cearbhalláin.

Carr, Marina (1964–), playwright; born in Dublin, and brought up near Banagher in Co. Offaly, she was educated at UCD. Her plays include *Low in the Dark* (1989), *Ullaloo* (1991), *The Mai* (1994), *Portia Coughlan* (1996), and *By the Bog of Cats* (1998). Her writing, energetic and surprising, brings the speech of the midlands onto the stage with poetic force.

Carroll, Paul Vincent (1900–1968), playwright. Born in Dundalk, Co. Louth, he was educated at St Patrick's College, Drumcondra. In 1920 he moved to Glasgow, where he taught and began writing. In 1930 *The Watched Pot* was produced by the Peacock [see *Abbey Theatre], followed by *Things That Are Caesar's* (1932), *The Coggerers* (1937), and *Shadow and Substance* (1937), which concerns a cultured parish priest's encounter with bigotry and with the mysteries of faith. *The White Steed* (1939) was a commentary on the decay of rural life. His other plays include *The Strings, My Lord, Are False* (1942), *The Wise Have Not Spoken* (1944), *The Devil Came from Dublin* (1951), and *Green Cars Go East* (1951).

Carson, Ciaran (1948–), poet; born in Belfast, he spoke Irish until he was 4. After graduation from QUB he worked as a teacher, a civil servant and an Arts Council administrator. *The New Estate* (1976) contains adaptations of early Irish nature lyrics to modern times. *The Irish for No* (1987) marked a new departure, bringing to poetry the urgency of traditional music and story-telling. *Belfast Confetti* (1989) develops the themes and methods of the previous volume. *First Language* (1993) reveals a poet concerned with the roots of language and of conflict. Form and energy combine in other collections including *Opera et Cetera* (1996) and *The Twelfth of Never* (1998). *Last Night's Fun* (1996) is an account of the world of Irish traditional music, *The Star Factory* (1997) evokes Belfast and memory, and *Fishing for Amber* (1999) is a poetic assembly of lore and wisdom.

Carson, Edward (1854–1935), Unionist. Born in Dublin, he was educated at Portarlington School and TCD. After a successful legal career in Ireland, he was elected a Liberal Unionist MP for TCD. In 1895 he defended the Marquess of Queensberry in the libel case brought by Oscar *Wilde. In 1911 Carson became leader of the Irish Unionist Council campaigning against Home Rule [see *Irish Parliamentary Party]. Although he hoped to defeat Home Rule he had to settle for partition in 1922.

Carsuel, Seon (John Carswell) (?1525–1572), devotional writer. Born near Oban in Argyle, he was educated at St Andrews University and took holy orders *c.* 1550. When the Scottish Church reformed in the 1560s Carsuel became a superintendent of the Argyle region. His *Foirm na nUrrnuidheadh* (Edinburgh, 1567) is the first printed book in Gaelic. It is a translation of the *Book of Common Order* (1562) of the reformed Scottish Presbyterian Church, itself based upon John Knox's *Form of Prayers* (Geneva, 1556).

Carthaginians (1988), a play by Frank *McGuinness, first staged at the Peacock Theatre [see *Abbey Theatre] and written in testimony to 'Bloody Sunday' in Derry, 30 January 1972. Set in a cemetery, the play presents three men and three women holding a kind of vigil, all in some way devastated by failure or despair.

Carve (or Carew, orig. Ó Corráin), Thomas (1590–1672), military chronicler. Born in Co. Tipperary, he served as chaplain during the Thirty Years War in Germany, writing an account of campaigns there in *Itinerarium* (3 vols., 1639–46; repr. 1859). His *Lyra, seu Anacephalaeosis Hibernica* (1651) gives an account of Ireland from a royalist standpoint.

Carville, Daragh (1969–), playwright; born in Armagh he was educated at Kent University and QUB; *Language Roulette* (1996) dealt with intimacies of violence in the aftermath of the 1994 *IRA ceasefire. This was followed by *Dumped* (1997) and *Observatory*

(1999) which opened at the Peacock Theatre [see *Abbey].

Cary, [Arthur] Joyce [Lunel] (1888–1957), novelist; born in Derry into an Anglo-Irish family which settled in Ulster during the 17th-cent. plantation. Cary spent his childhood in London, where his father worked as a civil engineer, returning for holidays to the Inishowen peninsula. Cary was educated at Clifton and Trinity College, Oxford. In 1912 he served in Montenegro with the Red Cross and as a Second Lieutenant in the Cameroons. In 1917 he was appointed Assistant District Officer in the Colonial Service, in Nigeria. Leaving the Service in 1920, he settled in Oxford. *Aissa Saved* (1932) was the first of four novels about Africa, to be followed by *An American Visitor* (1933), *The *African Witch* (1936), and *Mister Johnson* (1939). *Castle Corner* (1938) grew out of his concern with change at the turn of the century. *Charley Is My Darling* (1940) and *A *House of Children* (1941) are two novels about children, the latter drawing on his recollections of Donegal. The first ('Gulley Jimson') trilogy—*Herself Surprised* (1941), *To Be a Pilgrim* (1942), and *The *Horse's Mouth* (1944) explores the conflict between imagination and responsiblity. *The Moonlight* (1946) is a reply to Tolstoy's *The Kreutzer Sonata*. *A *Fearful Joy* (1949) deals with female courage and vitality. In the second trilogy, *Prisoner of Grace* (1952), *Except the Lord* (1953), and *Not Honour More* (1955), he studies the destructive use of power. In 1949 Cary declined a CBE. In 1956 he prepared the Clark Lectures, *Art and Reality* (1958). A novel, *The *Captive and the Free* (1959), and a collection of short stories, *Spring Song* (1960), were published posthumously. See Barbara Fisher, *Joyce Cary: The Writer and his Theme* (1980).

Casadh an tSúgain (1901), a one-act play by Douglas *Hyde. Based on a scenario by W. B. *Yeats, it was produced by the Irish Literary Theatre [see *Abbey Theatre] with Hyde in the leading role of Hanrahan the poet.

Casement, Roger (1864–1916), human rights pioneer and Irish republican. Born in Sandycove, Co. Dublin, he was educated at Ballymena Academy and spent much of his youth at the family home in Ballycastle, Co. Antrim. After entering the British consular service he was sent to the Belgian Congo. His humanitarian work was acknowledged with a knighthood in 1911, by which date he was committed to nationalist politics. In 1913 he became treasurer of the *Irish Volunteers and helped to plan the Howth gun-running. He travelled to Germany to recruit among Irish prisoners of war for an invasion planned to coincide with the Easter Rising. He landed on Banna Strand in Kerry on 21 April 1916 and was arrested almost immediately, while The Aud, carrying guns, was scuttled. He was executed at Pentonville on 3 August 1916. Pleas for leniency were foiled by revelations of homosexual contacts with young men and boys in a diary circulated by the government. Irish nationalists long continued to insist that the diaries were forgeries.

Casey, John Keegan (pseudonym 'Leo') (1846–1870), a contributor to The *Nation from the age of 16, and author of 'The Rising of the Moon', a famous *ballad about the 1798 Rebellion [see *United Irishmen]. He was born in Mullingar, Co. Westmeath, the son of the Gurteen schoolmaster, and died shortly after his release from prison for involvement with the *Fenian movement.

Casey, Juanita (1925–), fiction-writer and poet. Born in England, the daughter of an Irish tinker, she was adopted and afterwards became horse-master at a circus. Her fiction deals with elemental forces embodied by woman and animals, notably in The Horse of Selene (1971). Hath the Rain a Father? (1966) is a collection of stories and The Circus (1974) is a second novel. Eternity Smith (1985) is a collection of poems.

Casey, Kevin (1940–), novelist; born in Kells, Co. Meath, and educated at Blackrock College, Dublin. The Sinner's Bell (1968) gives an oppressive account of a failed marriage in Meath. Other novels are A Sense of Survival (1979) and Dreams of Revenge (1977).

Casey, Philip (1950–), poet and novelist; born in Dublin and educated there, his collections include Those Distant Summers (1980), After Thunder (1985), and The Year of the Knife (1991). Novels are The Fabulists (1994) and The Water Star (1999).

Castle Corner (1938), a novel by Joyce *Cary, a study of the British Empire in Ireland, England, and Africa at a turning-point in its fortunes.

Castle Rackrent (1800), Maria *Edgeworth's first novel and the first regional novel in English, set in Ireland 'before the year 1782', to coincide with the legislative independence of the *Irish Parliament. Thady Quirk, an old steward, narrates the eccentricities and excesses of three generations of land-owning Rackrents. Thady's son Jason gains possession of the estate by loans and litigation. Castle Rackrent is the seminal example of the *big house novel.

Castlehaven, Earl of, see James *Touchet.

Castlereagh, Viscount (Robert Stewart) (1769–1822), politician and statesman. Born in Co. Down, he was educated at Armagh and Cambridge and became MP for Co. Down from 1790. In 1797 he became chief secretary of Ireland. His role in securing the votes of MPs through unparalleled use of the patronage system led to his reputation as the chief architect of the Union.

Cath Almaine (The Battle of Allen), an early Middle Irish saga of the *historical cycle composed some time after AD 950, and based on a battle fought in AD 722 between the northern Uí Néill and the men of Leinster at the Hill of Allen, Co. Kildare.

Cath Finntrágha (Battle of Ventry), a tale of the *Fionn cycle, dating from the 12th cent. It features *Fionn mac Cumhaill in his role as protector of Ireland against foreign invasion. Dáiri Donn gathers a force from all the countries of Europe in order to retrieve the wife and daughter of Bolcán, King of France. The invaders are defeated after Fionn slays Dáiri Donn and Ógarmach, a Greek amazon.

Cath Maige Mucrama (Battle of Mag Mucrama), an Old Irish saga concerning a battle fought on a plain to the southwest of Athenry, Co. Galway. It is preserved in the 12th-cent. *Book of Leinster. Lugaid mac Con of west Munster has gone into exile following a previous defeat. Intent on vengeance, he returns with a great army and defeats the forces of Art, King of *Tara, and Eogan, King of Munster.

Cath Maige Rath (Battle of Moira), a tale of the *historical cycle, surviving in a 12th-cent. redaction, about a battle which took place in AD 637 near the village of Moira in Co. Down. It deals with the dynastic struggle between Domnall, High King of *Tara, and Congal Claen of Ulster. The din of battle drives Suibne mad [see *Buile Shuibne]. The tale is continued in *Fled Dúin na nGéd.

Cath Maige Tuired (Battle of Mag Tuired), a saga of the *mythological cycle dealing with the defeat of the malevolent Fomoiri by the gods of the Irish, known as the Tuatha Dé Danann [see Irish *mythology] at Moytirra in Co. Sligo (near Lough Arrow).

catha, see *tale-types.

Cathleen Ni Houlihan, one of the names for Ireland conceived of as a feminine entity adopted by the *Jacobite poets of the 18th cent. Other names were Síle Ní Ghadhra, Róisín Dubh [see *'My Dark Rosaleen' and *folksong], the Sean Bhean Bhocht, Móirín Ní Cheallacháin, and Gráinne Mhaol. 'Caitlín Ní Uallacháin' is a Jacobite poem by Liam Dall *Ó hIfearnáin which identifies her with the sovereignty of Ireland [see Irish *mythology and *kingship] and the Blessed Virgin. In Cathleen Ní Houlihan, written by W. B. *Yeats in collaboration with Lady *Gregory and set in Killala during the Rebellion of the *United Irishmen, Michael Gillane is preparing to be married when Cathleen arrives at the house and inspires him to join the French invading army. Maud *Gonne played Cathleen in 1902 in the Irish Literary Theatre [see *Abbey Theatre].

Catholic Emancipation, a campaign of mass agitation led by Daniel *O'Connell in the 1820s radicalizing the cause earlier represented by the Catholic Committee. Relief Acts between 1778 and 1793 had removed most of the *Penal Laws; however, Catholics were still excluded from the highest civil and military offices. The effectiveness of popular mobilization was demonstrated in the general election of 1826, when tenant farmers defied their landlords to vote for pro-Emancipation candidates. In July 1828 O'Connell, though unable to take his seat, decisively defeated a government candidate in a by-election for Co. Clare. This threat to the legitimacy of the political system persuaded government to introduce a Relief Act (April 1829) admitting Catholics to Parliament and higher office.

Catholic University, see *universities.

Catholicism emerged as a distinctive force in Ireland during the late 16th and 17th cents., when it became clear that the imposition of the new Anglican State Church had failed, and that the Counter-Reformation had put down roots among the majority population. Irish Catholics were politically impotent at the beginning of the 18th cent. because of the *Penal Laws. An adversarial relationship with the State created an essentially domestic Church, deprived of the public dimension of Continental Catholicism. In a cultural milieu where social and religious behaviour was largely regulated by custom, the central religious events were communal occasions such as the wake, pattern (a celebration of a local patron saint's feastday), and station (when Mass was said in a house for which neighbours gathered). In the aftermath of the French Revolution the British and Vatican administrations moved to neutralize the threat of a Jacobinized Irish Catholic population. Catholic Relief Acts were passed in 1792 and 1793 and Maynooth College was opened in 1795. Daniel *O'Connell channelled the national question into a Catholic stream. The rapid politicization of Irish Catholics paved the way for Catholic Emancipation in 1829. Catholicism would henceforth be a dominant force

within Irish nationalist culture. Throughout the 19th cent. Irish Catholicism became more assertive and more Roman in character, as the institutional Church eclipsed its vernacular predecessor. The development of a heroic historiography of Irish Catholic resistance also permitted the Church to see itself as the historical, psychic, and societal core of Irish experience. With the emergence of the southern *Irish State, the Catholic Church was accorded a 'special position' in the 1937 Constitution (a clause removed by referendum in 1972). Irish Catholicism increasingly became a target for oppositional intellectuals in the 1960s and 1970s, yet it remained resistant to modernizing influences in some respects.

Catholics (1972), a novel by Brian *Moore set in a post-Vatican IV future in which the Catholic Church has abandoned its central beliefs and rituals in favour of *rapprochement* with other faiths.

Cattle Raid of Cooley, see *Táin Bó Cuailnge.

Caulfield, James, see Earl of *Charlemont.

Céitinn, Seathrún, see Geoffrey *Keating.

Céle Dé ('serving companion of God', anglicized Culdee), the name taken by reformists in the Irish Church in the 8th and 9th cents. who brought the austerity of the hermit's life into the religious community.

Celibates (1895), a collection of three stories by George *Moore dealing with celibacy, repression, and art.

Celtic languages, the westernmost branch of the *Indo-European family, located in historical times in western and southern Germany, Austria, Switzerland, Northern Italy, Spain, France, and Belgium, and on the islands of Britain and Ireland. The languages in question are: from ancient times, Celtiberian in Spain and Gaulish in France and northern Italy; Gaelic, first attested in the 5th-century *ogam inscriptions and surviving today as *Irish, Scottish Gaelic, and (until recently) Manx; British, first attested in ogam inscriptions of the 5th and 6th cents., and surviving today as Welsh and Breton, the latter spreading from southern Britain to the Armorican peninsula in the 5th and 6th cents. Two northern varieties of British, Pictish and Cumbrian, died out in the early Middle Ages, while Cornish survived until the 18th cent. The Celtic languages are most closely related to the Italic group of languages and somewhat more remotely to the Germanic. The Celtic languages are frequently classified into q-Celtic and p-Celtic, according to whether they retained the Indo-European sound 'q' or changed it to 'p'. The q-Celtic languages are Celtiberian and Gaelic. All the others are p-Celtic. For the past 2,000 years the Celtic languages have been under pressure from the Germanic and Latin languages. In Britain and Ireland the languages survived to modern times but in an ever-decreasing geographical area.

Celtic Society, see *Irish Archaeological Society.

Celtic Twilight, The (1893), a collection of supernatural writings by W. B. *Yeats, based on his own researches and fieldwork in *folklore. Most are stories collected in Co. Galway, often with Lady *Gregory's help, together with Sligo material from Mary Battle. The second edition of 1902 was enlarged. The final poem, originally named 'The Celtic Twilight', gave its name to the volume

and to a school of writing produced under Yeats's influence.

Celticism, see *translation from Irish.

Celts, a grouping of *Indo-European peoples of diverse ethnic origin recognized as sharing a common culture, reflected in their social and political institutions, their religious observances, and their languages. From around 1000 to 100 BC they spread out from their original territory, probably that area of present-day central Europe in which the border of southern Germany meets that of the Czech Republic and Austria, ranging eventually from Britain and Ireland to Spain, Transylvania, Galatia, and Italy. At c.500 BC, the beginning of the second period of the Iron Age, the La Tène period—so named after a site discovered in the 19th cent. at Lake Neuchâtel in Switzerland—the Celts begin to enter the written record in the works of Greek historians. The oldest archaeological evidence relating to them comes from Hallstadt, Austria, and dates to c.700 BC. Celtic peoples had settled in Britain from the 5th cent. BC. From about the 3rd cent. BC it is reasonable to refer to a Celtic presence in Ireland. Of the pre-Celtic language or languages of Ireland nothing is known. The Romans did not annex Ireland, with the consequence that, until the invasion of the *Vikings in the 9th cent., Celtic civilization and culture survived intact in Ireland. Celtic society, as with most Indo-European societies, was patriarchal. Its religion [see Irish *mythology] associated deities with rivers, wells, and trees. The oak was sacred, and there were animal-gods, such as Taruos in Gaul (Irish tarbh), and the mare Epona [Irish ech, reflecting the p/q differentiation—see *Celtic languages]. They believed in an afterlife, which was why they showed such disregard for death in battle. Fasting against an enemy, a widespread Indo-European custom, was sometimes used to obtain redress of a wrong.

Censorship of Publications Act (1929). The Act created a Board of Censors of the *Irish State, and was used to ban all literature which made explicit references to human sexuality, as well as contraceptive methods. The effect was to restrict the realistic examination of Irish society by its writers. By 1940 the list of banned books included almost all the serious Irish writers of the period, as well as those of other countries. In 1967 a Bill was passed allowing for the unbanning of books after twelve years; gradually censorship relaxed in the 1970s and 1980s.

Cent[i]livre, Susannah, [née Freeman] (?1667–1723), playwright, probably born in Co. Tyrone, where her parents settled. In 1707 she married a French chef whom she had met while performing in *The Perjur'd Husband* (1700), her first play, at the Windsor Court. Amongst her plays and farces were *The Busy Body* (1710), *The Wonder! or A Woman Keeps a Secret* (1714), and *A Bold Stroke for A Wife* (1718). Her only Irish character is the servant Teague in *A Wife Well-Managed* (1715).

Chaigneau, William (1709–1781), novelist. Born in Ireland of a Huguenot family, he is remembered for his single novel, *The History of Jack Connor* (1752; rev. edn. 1753). The hero travels to Dublin before leaving Ireland to seek his fortune.

Chamber Music, see James *Joyce.

Charabanc (1983–95), a touring theatre company founded by the actresses Marie Jones, Eleanor Meth-ven, Carol Scanlon Moore, and others with a view to staging plays that primarily dealt with community issues and women's experience in Belfast. Most of the plays up to 1990 were written by Marie Jones, following the successful debut of *Lay Up Your Ends* (with Martin *Lynch), on the theme of a mill-workers' strike in 1911. Plays such as *Oul Delf and False Teeth* (1984), *Now You're Talking* (1985), *Gold on the Streets* (1986), *Somewhere over the Balcony* (1988), and *The Hamster Wheel* (1990) confront the divided communities of *Northern Ireland.

Charlemont, Lord (James Caulfield) (1728–1799), politician. Born in Dublin, he became the principal supporter of patriot causes in the *Irish Parliament during the 1780s. In 1780 he accepted command of the *Irish Volunteers and figured as a leading figure at the Dungannon Convention, 1782.

Charles O'Malley (1841), a comic military novel by Charles *Lever. O'Malley is a carefree British sub-altern of the Napoleonic period who gets into scrapes and out of them along with a set of colourful *stage-Irish characters.

Charley is My Darling (1940), a novel by Joyce *Cary, loosely based on boyhood experiences in Moville, Co. Donegal. Charley Brown, a Cockney evacuated during the Second World War, leads a gang of youngsters in Devon. The name alludes to the 'Bonnie Prince'.

Charwoman's Daughter, The (1912), a novel by James *Stephens, first published serially in *The *Irish Review*. Mary and her mother compensate for the poverty of the Dublin tenements by daydreaming.

Cherry, Andrew (1762–1812), dramatist; born in Limerick. He travelled with a company of actors through Ireland. His opera *The Outcast* (1796) was produced in Drury Lane. Six of his fourteen plays were published, of which *The Soldier's Daughter* (1804) was a witty comedy about competing lovers. *Spanish Dollars; or, The Priest of the Parish* (1806) is set on the Irish coast,

Chesson, Nora Hopper, see Nora *Hopper.

Chetwood, William Rufus (?1700–1766), a London bookseller who served as Thomas *Sheridan's stage-manager at *Smock Alley after 1742, touring in Kilkenny and other towns in 1748. His *General History of the Stage in London and Dublin* (1749) is a source of Irish theatrical history. Irish works include a *Tour Through Ireland* (1748), and *Kilkenny* (1748), a poem. He wrote imaginary voyages, *Captain Falconer* (1724) and *Captain Vaughan* (1736); and a novel, *The Female Traveller* (1742).

Cheyney, Peter (1896–1951), crime writer; born Reginald Evelyn Peter Southouse-Cheyney in Co. Clare and educated in London, where he ran literary and detective agencies after wartime service. Beginning with *This Man Is Dangerous* (1936) and ending with *Ladies Won't Wait* (1951), Cheyney wrote more than fifty novels dealing with the streetwise sleuthing of Lemmy Caution and Slim Callaghan.

Child in the House, A (1955), a novel by Janet *McNeill. Henry and Maud Acheson are a childless Protestant couple who, like the Belfast terrace they live in, are in decline. Into their routine lives comes Elizabeth, who informs on her con-man father, hoping that God will save him.

Childers, [Robert] Erskine (1870–1922), novelist and politician. Born in London and educated at Cambridge, he fought in the Boer War in 1899, basing *In the Ranks of the City Imperial Volunteers* (1900) on it. *The Riddle of the Sands* (1903) is a fictional account of German preparations to invade England. He used his yacht *Asgard* to ship in German arms for the *Irish Volunteers in 1914. He acted as secretary to the Treaty negotiations [see *Anglo-Irish War] but sided with Eamon *de Valera. He was sentenced to death for possession of a revolver and executed. His son, Erskine Childers (1905–74), became fourth President of Ireland.

Children of the Dead End (1914), a novel by Patrick *MacGill. Subtitled *Autobiography of a Navvy*, it traces episodically the life of Dermod Flynn as a child in Donegal, a farm-hand in Co. Tyrone, a railway and construction-site labourer in Scotland, and a reporter on a London daily.

Christian Examiner and Church of Ireland Magazine, The (1825–1869). Founded by Revd Caesar *Otway and Joseph Henderson Singer, its principal aim was defence of the Church of Ireland. Besides its proselytizing efforts, it printed William *Carleton's first stories of the Irish peasantry and Otway's own accounts of his tours around Ireland.

chronicles, Anglo-Irish, a term for the body of political writings about Ireland written in English during the Tudor and Stuart periods and concerned with justifications for the expropriation of the country by the English Crown, its administration by Crown agents, and the recalcitrance of the Irish in the face of the supposed benefits of that regime. While often presented as history and topography based on personal observations in the country, the chronicles commonly recycled prejudices and misconceptions first circulated by *Giraldus Cambrensis. His role as the originator of the stereotypical view dominating the chronicles was applauded by John Hooker in his contribution to Holinshed's *Chronicles* (1577), and later condemned in the leading work of *Gaelic historiography, Geoffrey *Keating's *Foras Feasa ar Éirinn* (1613–34). Works such as Edmund Campion's *Two Bokes of the History of Ireland* (?1570), Richard Beacon's *Solon his Follie* (1594), Edmund *Spenser's *A *View of the Present State of Ireland* (written about 1596), Sir John *Davies's *A Discovery of the True Causes Why Ireland Was Never Entirely Subdued* (1612), Barnaby Rich's *A New Description of Ireland* (1617), and Fynes Moryson's *Itinerary* (1617) are pervaded by comparisons between the Irish and uncivilized races in other historical and geographical contexts, whether the barbarians of classical antiquity, the savage American 'Indians' of the New World, or the Britons before the Roman invasion. In the chronicles Ireland is commonly split into highly differentiated geopolitical regions. The civility of town life in the Pale [see *Irish State] and the agricultural wealth of heavily colonized Munster were starkly contrasted with the dank woods and impassable bogs where lurked the Irish rebels. The dangers of such regions are described in works such as William Camden's *Britannia* (1586). Many of the ethnographic themes and xenophobic caricatures sketched crudely in these writings were later refined into comedy by Anglo-Irish writers from Maria *Edgeworth to Charles *Lever. Their racist verdict on Gaelic Ireland before and after the Norman invasion was challenged by historiographers in the native tradition such as Philip *O'Sullivan Beare, Keating, and Roderick *O'Flaherty.

Chronicon Scotorum, a set of annals, ranging from the earliest times to 1135, copied by Dubhaltach *Mac Fhir Bhisigh in a paper manuscript now in TCD.

Ciarán, saint and patron of Clonmacnoise, of Saigir in Ossory, and over thirty other early Irish churches. Probably a non-historical figure, he appears to be a Christianized version of an ancestral deity of the Ciarraige (from *ciar*, tanned) who were settled in northeast Connacht and south Munster. The *Book of the Dun Cow* was written on the hide of a brown cow said to have followed the saint to Clonmacnoise.

Cin Dromma Snechtai or **Lebor Dromma Snechtai** (*Book of Drumsnat*), a lost Irish *manuscript compilation, which pre-dated the *Book of the Dun Cow* and the *Book of Leinster*, both of which refer to it.

Cináed úa hArtacáin (d. 975), poet. Called the chief poet of Ireland in an obituary in the Irish *annals. His extant poetry, mainly of the *dinnshenchas type, is of considerable literary and philological importance.

Citizen of the World, The (1762), a series of over 100 loosely-linked essays in letter form, written by Oliver *Goldsmith under the pseudonym of 'Lien Chi Altangi', first printed in *The Public Ledger* (1760–1). Lien Chi purports to be a philosophically-minded visitor to England whose letters home describe the manners of the country.

Civil War (1922–1923), the, a period of hostilities between the Army of the *Irish State and the Republican wing of the *IRA, following the rejection of the Treaty concluding the *Anglo-Irish War by Eamon *de Valera and others on 7 January 1922. On 13 April 1922 Rory O'Connor occupied the Four Courts in Dublin with a contingent of the IRA and remained there until 28 June. After

O'Connor surrendered, Liam Lynch, Liam Mellows, and Ernie *O'Malley began to organize the Republican IRA in southern Ireland. In the course of the fighting some 2,000 lives were lost before de Valera ceased hostilities. Michael *Collins was killed in an ambush in Co. Cork in August 1922. The war left a legacy of bitterness in the divided communities of the southern counties. The political parties Fine Gael (formerly Cumann na nGaedhael) and Fianna Fáil emerged from the divided loyalties of that time.

Claidheamh Soluis, An [*The Sword of Light*] (1899–1930), the bilingual organ of the *Gaelic League, and successor to *Fáinne an Lae* established the previous year. Under the editorship of Eoin *MacNeill, it aimed to provide material of general interest and sought to carry forward Douglas *Hyde's policy of developing a distinctively Gaelic culture for a modern Ireland. In 1903–9, when Patrick *Pearse was editor, he made the journal into a vehicle for contemporary literature in Irish.

Clancy Name, The (1908), a one-act play by Lennox *Robinson. First staged at the *Abbey Theatre, it established Robinson's reputation as a realist. John Clancy has killed a neighbour, but his intention of confessing to the police horrifies his mother.

Clarke, Austin [Augustine Joseph] (1896–1974), poet, playwright, and novelist. Born in Dublin, and educated by the Jesuits, and at UCD where he studied under Douglas *Hyde and Thomas *MacDonagh. *The Vengeance of Fionn* (1917), a narrative poem, brought immediate recognition. He fell unhappily in love with the playwright Geraldine *Cummins, and suffered a mental collapse. On New Year's Eve 1920 he and Cummins married in a registry office, and he lost his post at

UCD, apparently because of the civil marriage. In 1922 Clarke left for London and worked as a book-reviewer for fifteen years. His interest in Irish saga continued with *The Cattle Drive in Connaught* (1925), which tells of the disputes that lead to *Táin Bó Cuailnge, but his growing fascination with medieval Ireland is reflected in *The Son of Learning* (performed 1927, possibly written earlier), a play based upon the 12th-cent. *Aislinge Meic Conglinne. In *Pilgrimage and Other Poems* (1929), he turned to the drama of racial conscience which was to become the dominant theme of his work. The *Bright Temptation* (1932), first of his three romances of medieval Ireland, interweaves motifs from Irish tales, a device that culminates in the ingenuity of The *Sun Dances at Easter* (1952); but The *Singing-Men at Cashel* (1936) gives a portrayal of a conscience-stricken mind. In 1938 he was the subject of an offensive caricature in Samuel *Beckett's *Murphy, where his experiments with Gaelic prosody and his sexual repression are mocked in the figure of Austin Ticklepenny. In 1937 Clarke returned to Ireland with his wife Nora Walker, settling at Bridge House, Templeogue. As he had failed in a divorce action against Geraldine Cummins his marital position was irregular, and he suffered another nervous breakdown. The sombre poems of *Night and Morning* (1938) suggest the psychological impasse he had reached. Clarke began a prolonged silence as a poet, not broken until *Ancient Lights* (1955). During the 1940s he devoted himself to verse drama. With Robert Farren [*Ó Faracháin] he established the *Lyric Theatre Company. Among the more successful of his own plays are *The Flame* (1930) and *As the Crow Flies* (1943), for radio. The poetry written after 1955 showed a renewed energy. In protest against social injustices in contemporary Ireland, he added a satiric dimension to his quarrel with Irish Catholicism, attacking specific instances of clerical and state abuse. *Later Poems* (1961) greatly extended his reputation. Several substantial collections followed, including *Flight to Africa* (1963) and the sequence *Mnemosyne Lay in Dust* (1966), a long poem dealing with his period in St Patrick's Hospital. He wrote prolifically into his 70s, returning to mythological subjects in his last poems. 'The Healing of Mis' and *Tiresias* (1971) are exuberantly sexual narratives. He wrote two volumes of autobiography, *Twice Round the Black Church* (1962) and *A *Penny in the Clouds* (1968). See, Maurice Harmon, *Austin Clarke: A Critical Introduction* (1990).

Clarke, Desmond (1907–1979), bibliographer. Born in Co. Mayo, he served for many years as RDS Librarian, and edited *An Leabharlann*, 1956–66. Clarke's biographies include *The Ingenious Mr. *Edgeworth* (1965). He completed the second part of *Ireland in Fiction* (1985), which continued the valuable work of Stephen *Brown.

Clarkin, Seán (1941–), poet; born in New Ross, Co. Wexford, and educated in Rome, UCC, and TCD. He worked as a teacher and issued *Without Frenzy* (1974).

classical literature in Irish translation dates from the Middle Irish period, though there is evidence that Latin authors were being read in Ireland as early as the 6th cent. The earliest of the extant translations is *Scéla Alaxandair* (10th cent.), followed by *Togail Troí* (10th or 11th cent.). In the 12th cent. the Aeneid was translated into prose as *Imtheachta Aeniasa*, Lucan's *De Bello Civili* as *In Cath Catharda*, and Statius' *Thebaid* as *Togail na Tebe*. Of these *Merugud Uilix maic Leirtis* makes the *Odyssey* look like one of the Irish *Immrama* [see also *tale-types]. All the translations are anonymous but it may be assumed that the translators were members of monastic communities.

'Clay', a story in James *Joyce's *Dubliners* (1914), written in 1905. It centres on Maria, a marginalized woman in a society dominated by family and religion.

Clayton, Robert (1695–1758), theologian; born in Dublin and educated at Westminster and at TCD. His *Essay on Spirit* (1750) sets out his Arianism, and develops an imaginative theory of spirits which was used by Charles *Johnstone for his novel *Chrysal* (1760–5). His rationalism became increasingly evident in later works such as *A Defence of An Essay on Spirit* (1752) and *A Vindication of the Old and New Testaments* (3 vols., 1752–7).

Cleeve, Brian (1921–), novelist and bio-bibliographer. Born in Essex to a Limerick family, he ran away to sea in 1938, serving in the merchant navy and in counter-intelligence during the Second World War. He settled in Dublin and worked as a journalist. His first novel was *The Far Hills* (1952), followed by *Portrait of My City* (1953), *Assignment to Vengeance* (1961), a thriller, *Death of a Painted Lady* (1962) set in a seedy modern Dublin, *Dark Blood, Dark Tower* (1966), and *The Sudan Goat* (1966), among others. He compiled a *Dictionary of Irish Writers* (3 vols., 1967–71; rev. edn., with Anne Brady, 1985) and returned to fiction with *A Woman of Fortune* (1993).

Clifton, Harry (1952–), poet; born in Dublin and educated at UCD, after which he was an aid administrator in Thailand (1980–8). His first publication was the pamphlet *Null Beauty* (1976), followed by *The Walls of Carthage* (1977), *Office of the Salt Merchant* (1979), *Comparative Lives* (1982), *The Liberal Cage* (1989), and *Night Train Through the Brenner* (1994). *On the Spine of Italy* (1999) is a memoir, and *Berkeley's Telephone* (2000) a set of fictions.

Clive, Kitty [Catherine] (1711–1785), actress and playwright; daughter of a Kilkenny lawyer who moved to London. She wrote four farces, including *The Rehearsal* (1753) and *The Faithful Irishwoman* (1765).

Clonmacnoise (Cluain mac Nóis), the most significant monastic foundation [see *monasticism] of the Celtic Church on Irish soil, said to have been established in the mid-6th cent. by St *Ciarán. The monastery and its famous school were much patronized by the kings of the northern part of Ireland. The monastery was pillaged by the *Vikings and the Irish at different phases of its history. *Manuscripts thought to have originated at Clonmacnoise include the *Book of the Dun Cow; the *Annals of Tigernach; and the *Annals of Clonmacnoise.

Clontarf, Battle of, fought on Good Friday 23 April 1014 between the forces of *Brian Bóroime, King of Munster, and the Leinstermen with their *Viking allies, on the inner north shore of Dublin Bay.

Coady, Michael (1939–), poet. Born in Carrick-On-Suir, Co. Tipperary, he was educated at St Patrick's, Drumcondra, then at UCG and UCC. His collections include *Two for a Woman, Three for a Man* (1980), *Oven Lane* (1987), and *All Souls* (1997), a compendium of prose, poetry, memoir, and translation.

Cobbe, Frances Power (1822–1904), social reformer; born Co. Kildare. Her works include *Friendless Girls* (1861), *Broken Lives* (1864), and *The Hopes of the Human Race Hereafter and Here* (1874).

Cochrane, Ian (1942–), novelist. Born near Ballycastle, Co. Antrim, he was educated locally before emigrating to England as a teenager. His first novel, *Streak of Madness* (1973), was followed by *Gone in the Head* (1974), *Jesus on a Stock* (1975), and *F for Ferg* (1980) dealing with Cochrane's native Ulster, while *Ladybird in a Loony Bin* (1978) and *The Slipstream* (1983) have a London setting.

Cock-a-doodle Dandy (1949), a play by Sean *O'Casey, in which a magic Cock appears in the paralysed world of Nyadnanave and forces the characters to choose between repression or liberation.

Cock and Anchor, The (1845), Joseph Sheridan *Le Fanu's first novel, subtitled *A Chronicle of Old Dublin City* and reissued as *Morley Court* (1873). Set in Dublin at the start of the 18th cent., it is the story of Mary Ashwoode whose love for Edmond O'Connor is opposed by her unscrupulous family.

Code (or Cody), Henry Brereton (?–?1830); songwriter and dramatist. He edited the government paper *The Warder* and wrote the anti-Napoleonic play, *The Russian Sacrifice; or, The Burning of Moscow* (1813). He was pilloried by Thomas *Furlong in *The Plagues of Ireland* (1834). He wrote 'The Sprig of Shillelagh', and was credited with 'Donnybrook Fair'. Other plays were *The Patriot* (1810), and *Spanish Patriots a Thousand Years Ago* (1812).

Coffey, Brian (1905–1995), poet; born in Dublin, where his father was first President of UCD, he was educated at Clongowes Wood and at UCD. *Poems* (1930), published jointly with Denis *Devlin, was followed by *Three Poems* (1933), and *Third Person* (1938). From 1947 to 1952 he taught philosophy at St Louis, Missouri, before returning to teach mathematics in London. Michael *Smith's New Writers' Press published *Selected Poems* (1971). The 1970s and 1980s saw him develop his mixture of intellect, integrity, and emotional directness. *Advent* (1975, repr. 1986), *The Big*

Laugh (1980), *Death of Hektor* (1980, repr. 1982), and *Chanterelles* (1985) revealed his variety.

Coffey, Charles (?1700–1745), author of comic operas. Born in Dublin, he wrote music and librettos for adaptations of English and French plays. His first piece, *The Beggar's Wedding* (1729), borrowed from John Gay's famous opera but also made use of the songs 'Lillibulero' and 'Eileen Aroon' ('Eibhlín a Rúin'). He took the play to Drury Lane, where he later had success with *The Devil to Pay, or The Wives Metamorphos'd* (1731). Other plays were *The Female Parson* (1730) and *The Boarding School* (1733).

Cogadh Gaedhel re Gallaibh (*c*.1100–10), an account of the *Vikings in Ireland written in the reign of Muirchertach Ó Briain (1086–1119), with some later additions. It gives an account of Viking attacks on Ireland drawn from the *annals; the rest is a high-flown account of the triumphs of *Brian Bóroime over the Vikings, culminating in a heroic narrative of the Battle of *Clontarf.

Cogitosus, Leinster author of a Latin life of St *Brigit.

Coimín, Mícheál (Michael Comyn) (1688–1760), poet; born in Kilcorcoran, near Milltown Malbay, Co. Clare. He seems to have led a rumbustious life, three of his poems dealing with the abduction of one Harriet Stackpoole in which he was the culprit. *Laoi Oisín ar Thír na nÓg*, a longer poem in the amhrán metre [see Irish *metrics], describes *Oisín's adventures in the otherworld. *Eachtra Thoirdhealbhaigh Mhic Stairn* is a prose romance.

Colgan, John (Seán Mac Colgáin) (?1592–1658), hagiographer. Born near Carndonagh, Co. Donegal, he entered the Franciscan Order at St Anthony's College in Louvain about 1618, before going to Germany. Returning to Louvain he became closely involved in 1635 in the Franciscan scheme of compiling a series of publications on the ecclesiastical history of Ireland. Fr. Hugh Ward (d. ?1634) [see *Mac an Bhaird] and Fr. Patrick Fleming (d. 1631) had already done most of the groundwork, but Colgan undertook the task of editing the collections of *manuscript material in Louvain. In 1645 Colgan published *Acta Sanctorum Veteris et Maioris Scotiae seu Hiberniae, Sanctorum Insulae*, on the saints whose feast-days fell in the period 1 January–30 March. The lives of *Patrick, *Brigit, and *Colum Cille formed the subject of a second substantial volume, *Triadis Thaumaturgae* (1647). He was put in charge of the Franciscan colleges at Louvain, Prague, and Viehen, but he completed a study of Duns Scotus, *Tractatus de vita, scriptis Johannis Scoti* (1655), claiming Scotus as Irish. Colgan's work drew attention to the scholarship and piety of the early centuries of Christianity in Ireland, and to the richness and detail of Irish ecclesiastical records.

Colleen Bawn, The; or *The Bride of Garryowen* (1860), a popular melodrama by Dion *Boucicault based on Gerald *Griffin's novel *The *Collegians* (1829). In Boucicault's version the plot is given a happy ending: Myles-na-Goppaleen foils Danny Mann's murder attempt, and Hardress Cregan accepts the peasant girl as his bride.

Collegians, The (1829), Gerald *Griffin's best-known novel. Based on a notorious murder committed in Co. Limerick, it tells the story of Eily O'Connor, a beautiful but untutored country girl who is murdered at the instigation of her gentleman lover, Hardress Cregan, by his servant Danny Mann. Hardress and his friend Kyrle

Daly are the 'collegians' of the title, both being students at TCD. Rejected by the heiress Anne Chute, Hardress marries Eily but soon regrets this misalliance.

Collins, Michael (1890–1922), revolutionary. Born in Clonakilty, Co. Cork, to a farming family, he joined the IRB [see *Fenian movement] while an office worker in London. Released from internment after fighting in the *Easter Rising, he became Director of Intelligence for the *IRA. Reluctantly joining the Irish delegation in the Treaty negotiations, Collins supported the resulting settlement. When the *Civil War began he took command of the Free State forces [see *Irish State], and was killed in an ambush at Béal na Bláth.

Collins, Michael (1964–), short-story writer and novelist; born and educated in Limerick, before moving to America as a university teacher. He has issued a starkly violent short-story collection, *The Meat Eaters* (1992), and a first-person novel, *The Life and Times of a Tea-Boy* (1994).

Collis, John Stewart (1900–1984), ecologist and author. Born in Dublin, and educated in Co. Wicklow and Rugby, he wrote a number of books recognizing human dependence on nature, among them *Forward to Nature* (1927) and *The Worm Forgives the Plough* (1973). *Bound upon a Course* (1971) is an autobiography, while *Living with a Stranger* (1978) meditates on psychophysical union. Robert Collis, a twin brother (d. 1975), practised as a paediatrician in Dublin. He was instrumental in liberating the talent of Christy *Brown.

Colloquy of the Ancients, see *Acallam na Senórach.*

Colmán mac Lénéni (530– *c.*606), religious poet. Born probably in Co. Cork, he is regarded as the founder of the church at Cluain Uama (Cloyne). The surviving verse has been dated to the period 565–604, and is among the earliest examples of Irish writing in the Latin alphabet.

Colour of Blood, The (1987), a thriller by Brian *Moore, pitting a rational Christianity against nationalist-Catholic fanaticism. Cardinal Bem, Primate of a Soviet-bloc country, has made a concordat with the government, thereby earning the distrust of religious extremists. Facing the assassin's gun while administering communion, he accepts death and the will of God.

Coloured Dome, The (1932), a novel by Francis *Stuart. Gerry Delea, an *IRA sympathizer, meets Tully McCoolagh, an IRA godfather who is really a woman. They give themselves up at Mountjoy prison, as part of a deal with the authorities, where they share a cell and have sex. They are pardoned, but the experience of the night cannot be recaptured.

Colum, Mary (née Catherine Gunning Maguire) (1887–1957), literary journalist and critic. Born in Dublin and educated at UCD, she married Padraic *Colum in 1912. Moving to America with him, she shared closely in his literary life. *Life and the Dream* (1928) is an autobiographical account of the *literary revival. *From These Roots* (1937) contains essays on modern literature. Her memoir of James *Joyce was edited by her husband and issued as *Our Friend James Joyce* (1958).

Colum, Padraic (1881–1972), playwright, novelist, and *folklorist; born in Longford and educated at Glasthule. *The Saxon Shillin'* was rejected by the Irish National Theatre Society [see *Abbey

Theatre] as anti-recruiting propaganda. He had his first success in 1903 when *Broken Soil* (revised as *The Fiddler's House*, 1907) was produced by the Society, followed by *The *Land* (1905) and *Thomas Muskerry* (1910). In 1912 Colum married Mary Maguire [*Colum], leaving Ireland with her in 1914 for America, where he remained for most of his long life. His further dramatic works include *Mogu the Wanderer* (1917), a romantic fairytale, and the Strindbergian *Balloon* (1929). His early work established the genre of realist folk drama which featured prominently in the Abbey Theatre's repertoire. A gift for dramatic lyrics was evident in a first collection, *Wild Earth* (1907). The speakers in these, such as 'The Old Woman of the Roads', are marginalized people of rural Ireland. 'She Moved Through the Fair' successfully recreated *folksong. The first of his two novels, *Castle Conquer* (1923) is about the arrest and trial of Francis Gillick for an agrarian murder. *The Flying Swans* (1957) is a richly textured work involving themes of expulsion and return. In 1924 Colum was officially invited to record Hawaiian folklore, producing *At the Gateways of the Day* (1924) and *The Bright Islands* (1925). His children's books, including *A Boy in Éirinn* (1913), *The King of Ireland's Son* (1916), *Adventures of Odysseus* (1918), and *Orpheus* (1930), consist of versions of the epics and stories of the world. *Our Friend James Joyce* (1958), based on his wife's account of their acquaintance with *Joyce, is written in a spirit of fidelity to the writer's character and talk. His books on Ireland include *My Irish Year* (1912), *The Road Round Ireland* (1926), and *The Big Tree*, a short-story collection illustrated by Jack B. *Yeats (1935).

Colum Cille [Columba] (?521–597),

one of the three patron saints of Ireland, the others being *Patrick and *Brigit. Born in Gartan, Co. Donegal, he was baptized Crimthann and given the name Colum Cille ('dove of the church') by an angel. Educated at monasteries in Moville and Clonard, he founded churches in Derry, Swords, Durrow, and Kells. A dispute over the ownership of a Psalter was settled by Domnall, the High King, whose judgment went against Colum Cille. Sailing to *Iona with twelve others, he founded a monastery which became an ecclesiastical centre in Scotland, Northern Britain, and Ireland. In 575 he attended the convention of Druim Ceat, when he intervened on behalf of the *bardic order. At his death he was buried on Iona. The poem *Amra Choluim Cille* (*Eulogy of Colum Cille*) was written shortly after his death. *Vita Columbae*, a Latin life, was written a century later by *Adamnán. He became the supposed authority for many prophecies. Many traditional stories about the saint are narrated in Maghnus *Ó Domhnaill's 16th-cent. life, and he is described in John *Colgan's *Triadis Thaumaturgae* (1647).

Columba, St see *Colum Cille.

Columbanus, St (?543–615), ecclesi-

astic and missionary. Born in Leinster, he was educated at the monastery of Bangor, and from there set out on his *peregrination *c.*590. In Gaul he founded monasteries in Luxeuil and Fontaine. After much journeying, his final monastic foundation was Bobbio in Lombardy. His surviving Latin writings include letters to Popes Gregory and Boniface III and IV and sermons.

Comhairle Mhic Clámha (*Advice of MacClave*), an 18th-cent. satire on

boorish priests, most probably by Eoghan *Ó Donnghaile, a parish priest in Armagh, in 1704. The MacClave of the title is almost certainly John MacClave of Aughnamullen, Co. Monaghan, who gave evidence against St Oliver *Plunkett at his trial in 1681.

Comhar (1942–), a monthly literary journal founded by An Comhchaidreamh, the University Association of Irish-speakers. It set out to 'give guidance to the nation on the issues of the time'.

Communication Cord, The (1982), a comedy by Brian *Friel, set in a restored cottage in 'Ballybeg', Co. Donegal. In a farcical reprise of the themes of *Translations, the play satirizes modern Irish attitudes towards national tradition.

Compendium of Lovers, A (1990), a novel by Francis *Stuart, continuing the technique of merging fact and fiction which distinguishes his later work. Joel Simpson, an ageing writer, and his lover Abby become involved with a group of pioneering scientists who hold all life to be composed of stardust.

Compert Con Culainn (*Conception of Cú Chulainn*), a tale of the *Ulster cycle [see also *tale-types], telling how Dechtine, the daughter—perhaps the sister—of *Conchobor, bears a son whom she names Sétantae, later called *Cú Chulainn.

Compert Conchobuir (*Conception of Conchobor*), a tale of the *Ulster cycle concerning the birth of *Conchobor mac Nessa, the ruler of the Ulaid. Ness is out of doors one day when the *druid Cathbad declares that a man conceived on that day will be ruler of Ireland. She has sex with him, at her own request, and carries Conchobor for three years and three months.

comperta, see *tale-types.

Comyn, David (Daithí Coimín) (1854–1907), language activist. Born in Co. Clare, he helped found the Society for the Preservation of the Irish Language in 1876, leaving it to form the *Gaelic Union. In 1882 he founded *The Gaelic Journal* (*Irisleabhar na Gaedhilge).

Conall Cernach, warrior of the *Ulster cycle, protector of Ulster during the boyhood of *Cú Chulainn, who wins from Conall the hero's portion in *Fled Bricrenn. At Cú Chulainn's death Conall kills his adversaries as described in *Dergruathar Chonaill Chernaig (Red Rout of Conall Cernach)*. In *Scéla Mucce meic Da Thó, Conall takes the hero's portion; and in *Togail Bruidne Da Derga he defends King Conaire against his attackers. Three red-headed men kill him in revenge for Cú Roí mac Daire.

Conall Corc, common ancestor of the main branches of the *Eoganacht, according to the *genealogies, and hero of some of their early origin legends.

Conan Maol mac Mórna (Conán the bald), a warrior of the *Fionn cycle. *Acallam na Senórach depicts him as spiteful and belligerent. He is a coward in some tales and a buffoon in others such as *Bruidhean Chaorthainn.

Concanen, Matthew (1701–1749), poet and journalist. He published in Dublin *A Match of Football, or The Irish Champions* (1721), a mock-heroic poem, as well as *Poems upon Several Occasions* (1722). He moved to London. *A Supplement to the Profound* (1728) earned him a place in Pope's *The Dunciad*. His *Miscellaneous Poems* (1724) was the first collection of works by Irish authors. *Wexford Wells* (1721) is a comic opera, and he adapted Richard Brome's *The Jovial Crew* in 1731.

Conchobor mac Nessa, ruler of the Ulaid (men of Ulster) during the period of the *Ulster cycle, whose life is made to coincide with that of Christ in his death-tale, *Aided Chonchobuir*. After the death of his father Cathbad the *druid, his mother Ness accepts Fergus mac Roich as husband on condition that he relinquish his claim to the kingship to her son for a year, which Conchobor then retains on account of his wisdom and hospitality.

Confederation of Kilkenny (1642–1650), more properly the Confederate Catholics of Ireland, an assembly and executive body created by Catholic leaders following the *Rebellion of 1641.

Confessions of a Young Man (1888), George *Moore's account of his formative years in Paris, when trying to become an artist, and in London afterwards, deciding to be a writer.

Confessions of Harry Lorrequer, The (1839), Charles *Lever's first novel. Set in Napoleonic times, it is about a cheerful army subaltern who demonstrates a naïve but good-natured resourcefulness in picaresque adventures around Ireland and Europe.

Conformists, The (1829), a novel by John *Banim dealing with the fortunes of a Catholic family, the Darcys, under the *Penal Laws.

Congal (1872), a long narrative poem by Samuel *Ferguson, based on *The Banquet of Dun na nGédh and the Battle of Magh Rath* (1842), tales from the *historical cycle, edited by John *O'Donovan. Congal Claen, a pagan king of Ulster, declares war on the Christian High King Domnal when he is seated at his host's left hand at a banquet and served insulting food. Sweeny goes mad in the tumult [see *Buile Shuibne]. Congal is fatally wounded with a blow struck by the idiot Cuanna.

Conlon, Evelyn (1952–), writer of fiction; born in Rockcurry, Co.

Monaghan, she was educated at St. Patrick's College, Maynooth after travelling in Australia and Asia. An early story was published in the Attic Press's *Wildish Things* (1983), and *My Head is Opening* (1987) was a first collection. The Attic Press also issued her novel *Stars in the Daytime* (1989). Further publications include the story collection *Taking Scarlet as a Real Colour* (1993) and the novel *A Glassful of Letters* (1998).

Conn Cétchathach (Conn of the Hundred Battles), legendary pre-Christian king of *Tara, assigned to the 2nd cent. AD by later *annalists and *Gaelic historiographers. Ireland was divided between Conn and Eogan Mór of Munster into two political moieties demarcated by Escair Riada, a glacial esker extending east–west from Dublin to Clarinbridge, Co. Galway. Eogan, also known as Mug Nuadat (devotee of the god Nuadu), was killed at the Battle of Mag Léna in 177; but the southern half, called Leth Moga (Mog's Half) long remained under the control of his dynasty, the Eoganacht, centred at Cashel. The northern moiety, called Leth Cuinn (Conn's Half), was dominated in early medieval times by the Uí Néill, descendants of *Niall Noígíallach (Niall of the Nine Hostages) and ultimately of Conn himself.

Connaughton, Shane (1946–), actor, scriptwriter, and novelist. Born in Co. Cavan, he joined *RTÉ as an actor and came to general notice as co-author of the screen-play of Christy *Brown's *My Left Foot* (1987). His novels, *Border Station* (1989) and *Run of the Country* (1991), concern the life of a policeman and his family, the latter being a rite-of-passage story of a rebellious son tangling with the *IRA.

Connell, F. Norrys, see Conal Holmes O'Connell *O'Riordan.

Connell, Vivian (1905–1981), playwright, novelist; born in Cork, and self-educated. He wrote the plays *Throng o' Scarlet* (1941) and *The Nineteenth Hole of Europe* (1943), before embarking on novels that include *The Chinese Room* (1943), a wartime best-seller dealing with sexual freedom. *The Golden Sleep* (1948) has an autobiographical hero, while *The Hounds of Cloneen* (1951) is an extra-marital romp in the fox-hunting circles of Cobh, Co. Cork.

Connellan, Owen (1800–1869), Irish scribe and translator; born in Sligo, he transcribed the *Book of Lecan* and the *Book of Ballymote* during his twenty years of employment at the *RIA. He was appointed to the chair of Irish at Queen's College, Cork [see *universities in Ireland]. His edition and translation of *Imtheacht na Tromdháimhe* [see *Dallán Forgaill] appeared as *The Proceedings of the Great Bardic Institution* (1860).

Conner, [Patrick] Rearden (1907–1991), novelist. Born and educated in Cork, he went to London as a landscape gardener. *Shake Hands with the Devil* (1933) tells the story of an *IRA commander, Lenihan, who loses his humanity. *The Sword of Love* (1938) and *The Singing Stone* (1951) characterize village life as passionate and murderous. *Men Must Live* (1937) compares the idealism of the militants with an unromantic Irish hero. *A Plain Tale from the Bogs* (1937) is an autobiography.

Connolly, James (1868–1916), socialist and patriot. Born to Irish parents in an Edinburgh slum, he left school at 11 and worked in a variety of jobs before enlisting in the army. He came to Dublin in 1896, founded the Irish Socialist Republican Party in 1898, and edited *The Workers' Republic* until 1903. He went to America and worked with the labour movement there. On his return to Dublin in 1910 he organized the Socialist Party of Ireland. In 1913 he established the Citizen Army in order to protect worker's rights during the Lock-Out Strike. At the outbreak of the First World War he opposed attempts to introduce military conscription in Ireland. In 1916 he was appointed commander of the Republican forces in Dublin, acting from headquarters at the GPO [see *Easter Rising]. Though badly wounded in the fighting, he was sentenced to death by a British court martial and executed strapped in a chair on 12 May. *Labour in Irish History* (1910), the most influential of his writings, interprets early Irish society as socialist.

Connor, Elizabeth, see Una *Troy.

Connradh na Gaeilge, see *Gaelic League.

Conn's Half [of Ireland], see *political divisions.

Conry, Florence, see Flaithrí *Ó Maolchonaire.

Contention of the Bards, see *Iomarbhágh na bhFileadh.

Conversations in Ebury Street (1924), a collection of articles by George *Moore, reworked and fashioned into a trenchant statement of his artistic opinions, including praise for Anne Brontë and disdain for Tolstoy and Dickens.

Conyers, Dorothea (née Blood-Smyth) (1871–1949), born in Fedamore, Co. Limerick; author of more than forty sporting novels and collections, including *The Thorn Bit* (1900), *The Conversion of Con Cregan* (1909), *Sporting Reminiscences* (1919), *Hounds of the Sea* (1927), *Whoopee* (1932), and *Kicking Foxes* (1948).

Conyngham, D[avid] P[ower]
(1825–1883), novelist and historian of
the Irish Brigade in the American Civil
War. Born in Killenaule, Co. Tipperary,
he served as aide-de-camp to General
Sherman in Georgia. *The Irish Brigade and
Its Campaigns* (1866) gives an account of
Thomas *Meagher and other Irish
officers in the war. Conyngham's
novels include *Frank O'Donnell* (1861), *The
O'Mahoney* (1879), and *Rose Parnell* (1905).

Coogan, Tim Pat (1935–), bio-
grapher, historian, and journalist. Born
in Dublin, he was educated at Blackrock
College, leaving to work on *The Evening
Press* in 1954, eventually becoming edi-
tor of *The Irish Press* 1968–87. Books
include *Ireland Since the Rising* (1966), *The
IRA* (1970), *Ireland: A Personal View* (1975),
On the Blanket (1980), *Disillusioned Decades*
(1987), *Michael *Collins* (1990), **De
Valera: Long Fellow, Long Shadow* (1993),
The Troubles (1995), and *Wherever Green is
Worn* (1999), the latter a history of the
Irish diaspora.

Cooke, Emma (1934–), novelist. Born
in Portarlington, Co. Laois, and educated at Alexandra College, Dublin. A
first collection of stories, *Female Forms*
(1981), contrasts the cultural outlooks of
Irish-American and English visitors with
those of native Irish people. Her novels,
A Single Sensation (1982), *Eva's Apple*
(1985), and **Wedlocked* (1994), reflect
sexual opportunism and domestic
violence in middle-class Ireland.

Cooke, Henry (1788–1868), ultra-
Protestant apologist. Born near Magh-
era, Co. Derry, he was educated at
Glasgow University. He united the
Church of Ireland and the Presbyterian
Church against 'Romanism' in the
Hillsborough Meeting of 1835.

Corkery, Daniel (1878–1964), man of
letters. Born in Cork to a family of
craftsman carpenters and active trade
unionists, he was educated by the Presentation Brothers and at St Patrick's
College, Dublin. He taught at a Christian Brothers National School in Cork
for more than twenty years. With Terence *MacSwiney and other members
of the *Gaelic League he founded the
Cork Dramatic Society in 1908. His play
King and Hermit (1909) dramatizes a
conflict between civil authority and the
spirit. *A Munster Twilight* (1916) was a
collection of short stories drawing on
his familiarity with the west Cork
*Gaeltacht to illustrate the persistence
of Gaelic culture. Cork city is the setting for his novel *The *Threshold of Quiet*
(1917), a gloomy meditation on Irish
Catholic discontent. The play, *The Yellow
Bittern* (1917), centres on the dying
Cathal Buí *Mac Giolla Gunna and
deals with the relative merits of the
Gaelic poets of Munster and Ulster.
From 1901 Corkery had been a frequent contributor to D. P. *Moran's
Leader newspaper, sharing Moran's
brand of 'Irish-Ireland' nationalism. *The
Labour Leader* (1920) was performed at
the *Abbey Theatre; the theme is a
Cork dockers' strike in which the lead-
er Davro (modelled on Patrick Pearse)
calls for militant action. *The Hounds of
Banba* (1920), a collection of stories,
reflected Corkery's republicanism. In
The Hidden Ireland (1924) he described
the lives, work, and social conditions of
writers such as Aodhagán *Ó Rathaille,
Eoghan Rua *Ó Súilleabháin, and Brian
*Merriman, giving an account also
of the *aisling, a form of vision-
poem especially favoured by Munster
*Jacobite poets.

Corkery completed an MA at UCC in
1931, becoming Professor of English
there. In the same year he published his
thesis as *Synge and Anglo-Irish Literature*.
With the appearance of the work on
Synge, Corkery's conception of Irish
society and Irish writing came under
attack, and was long to remain a target

for revisionist critiques of Irish-Ireland ideology. Corkery's last collection of stories, *Earth Out of Earth* (1939), showed him returning to urban settings in a mood of sympathy and tolerance. He could be doctrinaire, but his best work reveals an understanding of rural and urban life in Ireland, a sympathy for the oppressed, together with an appreciation of their longing for freedom. See Patrick Maume, *Life That Is Exile: Daniel Corkery and the Search for Irish-Ireland* (1993).

Cormac mac Airt, grandson of *Conn Cétchathach, traditionally regarded as a great law-giver and patron of a golden age in pre-Christian Ireland while King at *Tara during the latter part of the 3rd cent. AD. Medieval Irish literature depicts him as an ideal king and an exemplar of fír flathemon ('truth of a ruler'), the quality of royal justice that secures peace and plenty, reflected in the attribution of the maxims on kingship in *Tecosca Cormaic to him. He is said to have convinced himself of Christianity through his own reason.

Cormac mac Cuilennáin (*fl.* 905), a saintly King of Munster, scholar, and the reputed author of *Sanas Chormaic* (*Cormac's Glossary*) and the *Psalter of Cashel*, a lost text. He reigned AD 901–8 at Cashel, inaugurating a time of peace and plenty but also taking hostages from the Connachta and, according to the *Annals of Inisfallen*, from the Uí Néill. After his death he came to be regarded as a saint. He is said to have married *Gormfhlaith, daughter of the High King Flann Sinna, only to divorce her to enter the Church.

Costello, Louisa Stuart (1799–1870), miniaturist and writer. The daughter of an Irish army officer and probably born in Ireland, she was taken to France by her mother in 1814. Her precocious poetry (e.g. *The Maid of

Cypress Isle, 1815) was approved by Thomas *Moore. She later issued translations of French poetry, which also features in her historical novels such as *The Queen's Poisoner* (1841). *Clara Fane* (1843) deals with the contemporary experiences of a governess. Her travel works include *A Tour to and from Venice* (1846).

Coulter, John (1888–1980), playwright. Born in Belfast and educated at the Art School, he taught in Belfast, and Dublin. He went to Canada, where he became a dramatist. *Conchobar* (1917) was based on the *Ulster cycle, as was the *Deirdre of the Sorrows* (1944). *The House in the Quiet Glen* (1925) is a matchmaking comedy. In *The Drums Are Out* (1948), for the *Abbey Theatre, an Ulster policeman's daughter marries an *IRA man. *Turf Smoke in Manhattan* (1949) is a novel adapted from his play *Holy Manhattan* (1941). His major Canadian work is a group of plays about Louis Riel, the doomed leader of the Metis Indians. *In My Day* (1980) is a theatrical memoir.

'Counterparts', a short story in James *Joyce's *Dubliners* (1914), written in 1905. Farrington, an inefficient copy-clerk in a law office, is bullied by his immediate superior, Mr Alleyne. Returning home drunk to find his wife out at the chapel, he takes out his resentment on his son.

Countess Cathleen, The (1899), a play by W. B. *Yeats, written for Maud *Gonne and published in 1892. First performed by the Irish Literary Theatre [see *Abbey Theatre] in the Antient Concert Rooms, Dublin, it shared the bill with Edward *Martyn's *The *Heather Field*, both plays addressing the conflict between spiritual and material values.

Country Dressmaker, The (1907), a play by George *Fitzmaurice, first staged at the *Abbey Theatre. Julia Shea, the dressmaker of the title, has waited ten years for her lover, Pats Connor, to return from America. When he does she turns him down, but he finally wins her back. It deploys a harsh and angry realism.

Country Girls, The (1960), the first novel by Edna *O'Brien in the trilogy that tells the story of Caithleen Brady and Baba (Brigid) Brennan, the others being *The *Girl with Green Eyes* (1962) and *Girls in Their Married Bliss* (1964). After years of disaffection at their convent school Baba contrives their expulsion for obscenity and they go to Dublin, Caithleen to be a shop assistant, Baba to do a secretarial course.

Cousins, James H[enry Sproull] (1873–1956), poet and playwright. Born in Belfast, he published a collection of lyrical and historical poems (*Ben Madighan*, 1894) before moving in 1897 to Dublin, where he wrote several plays for the Irish National Theatre [see *Abbey Theatre] including *The Racing Lug* (1902). Through meeting with George *Russell he formed the theosophical convictions that he held throughout a lifetime and expressed in numerous poetry collections, beginning with *The Voice of One* (1900). Yeats disliked him intensely, and in 1913 he set out for India with his wife Margaret. In Madras, he made a lasting impact with his teaching and his books, including *A Wandering Harp* (1932) and *The Hound of Uladh* (1942). *We Two Together* (1950) is an autobiography that he wrote with his wife.

Cox, Watty [Walter] (?1770–1837), gunsmith and political pamphleteer; born in Co. Westmeath. He founded *The Irish Magazine, or Monthly Asylum for Neglected Biography*, 1807-15, an antigovernment journal. In about 1816 he went to America, where he edited *The Exile*, 1817–18, also writing *The Snuff-Box* (1820) and a *Sketch of the Catholic Church in New York* (1819).

Coyle, Kathleen (1886–1952), novelist; brought up in Donegal, she lived in Paris and New York with her husband Charles Maher. She wrote realistic works including *Youth in the Saddle* (1927) and *A Flock of Birds* (1930), a study of family life during the *Troubles.

Coyne, Joseph Stirling (1803–1868), dramatist and comic journalist. Born in Birr, Co. Offaly, he produced a succession of farces at the Theatre Royal, Dublin, of which *The Phrenologist* (1835) was the first. He launched *Punch* with Mark Lemon and Henry Mayhew in 1841. *The Queer Subject* (1837) was followed by several full-length plays, but his speciality remained curtain-raisers, such as *How to Settle an Account with Your Laundress* (1847) is the best example and *Box and Cox Married and Settled!* (1852). *The Hope of the Family* (1853) was a three-act comedy. Others are *Irish Assurance and Yankee Modesty* (1857), *Paddy the Piper* (1857), and *The Bashful Irishman* (1857).

Craig, Maurice James (1919–), poet and architectural historian. Born in Belfast and educated at Cambridge, he wrote *The Volunteer Earl* (1948), a life of *Charlemont. Poetry collections include *Black Swans* (1941) and *Some Way for Reason* (1948). Along with *Dublin 1660–1860* (1952), his architectural studies include *Classic Irish Houses of the Middle Size* (1976), *Architecture of Ireland from the Earliest Times to 1880* (1982), and a life of James Gandon. He has also written on *Irish Bookbindings 1600–1800* (1954).

Crane Bag, The (1977–1985; 18 numbers in 9 volumes), a cultural and political journal founded by Mark Hederman and Richard *Kearney. The journal revealed a proliferation of ideas based on modern European thought as much as on traditional sources of intellectual life in Ireland.

Craoibhín Aoibhinn, An, see Douglas *Hyde.

Crawford, Julia (?1800–?1855), poet and composer. Little is known about the author of the much-anthologized poem 'Kathleen Mavourneen' except that she was the daughter of a British soldier and naturalist, born in Co. Cavan. She produced a volume of *Irish Songs* (1840).

Cré na Cille (*Churchyard Clay*) (1948) a novel by Máirtín *Ó Cadhain, dealing with Caitríona Pháidín, a recently deceased Irish matriarch whose history is revealed through conversations with others lying in the graveyard as each new arrival relates the progress of events above ground. It emerges that her life's passion was the besting of her sister Neil. The novel depicts the unpleasant side of Irish rural life. It is unflinchingly honest, very funny, and fiercely eloquent.

Creagh, Richard (?1525–1585), priest and Archbishop of Armagh, and author of manuscript treatises on the Irish language (*De Lingua Hibernica*) and lives of the Irish saints.

Críth Gablach, see *law in Gaelic Ireland.

Critic, The, or a *Tragedy Rehearsed* (1779), a comedy by Richard Brinsley *Sheridan based on a burlesque by George Villiers Buckingham (*The Rehearsal*). It concerns the production of a play called *The Spanish Armada*, in which two foolish critics, Dangle and Sneer, are invited to the rehearsal by the author, Mr Puff, who considers the play less important than good advertising.

Crock of Gold, The (1912), a novel by James *Stephens concerning the quests undertaken by the Philosopher, the Thin Woman of Inis Magrath (his wife), and Caitilin Ní Murrachu, during which they meet with the gods Pan and Angus Og. These encounters bring about Caitilin's sexual awakening and lead the Philosopher and his wife to a more balanced view of life. There is much comedy involving talking animals, bungling policemen, and leprechauns.

Crofts, Freeman Wills (1879–1957), crime writer. Born in Dublin, he became a railway engineer in Northern Ireland. His chief creation is Inspector French, the meticulous English policeman whose cases, such as *The Cask* (1920), *Man Overboard* (1936), and *The Affair at Little Woking* (1943), extend to over thirty novels and collections. He also wrote on real-life crime and Scripture.

Crohoore of the Bill-Hook (1825), a novel by Michael *Banim, the first and most popular of the *Tales by the O'Hara Family* (first series), presenting a bloody story of *secret societies, agrarian crime, and superstition, set in Co. Kilkenny towards the end of the *Penal era. Crohoore, a suspected murderer, is transformed from folk devil to hero, finally emerging as the symbol of an oppressed people.

Croker, Mrs B[ithia] M[ary] (née Shephard) (1850–1920), romantic novelist. Born in Co. Roscommon, she was educated in Cheshire before marrying an army officer. Her early novels, such as *Proper Pride* (1883) and *Pretty Miss Neville* (1883), depict Anglo-India. In *The Kingdom of Kerry* (1896) she surveys the down-at-the heel Anglo-Irish *ascendancy. *Beyond the Pale* (1897) and *Lismoyle* (1914) are further Irish novels.

Croker, John Wilson (1780–1857), author and politician; born in Galway, or possibly Waterford, educated at TCD. In 1804 he published anonymously *Familiar Epistles on the Present State of the Irish Stage. An Intercepted Letter from Canton* (1804) is a prose satire on contemporary Dublin. *The State of Ireland Past and Present* (1808) grudgingly advocated *Catholic Emancipation. A regular contributor to the *Quarterly Review* he became notorious for scathing reviews of Keats and Lady *Morgan. Barely remembered for his own work, Croker figured as a model of reaction in several novels including *Thackeray's *Vanity Fair*, Disraeli's *Coningsby*, and Lady Morgan's *Florence MacCarthy* (1818).

Croker, Thomas Crofton (1798–1854), *folklorist. Born in Cork, the son of a British officer, he was educated locally. Early antiquarian interests took him rambling through Munster. His first publication was an article in the *Morning Post* (1815) describing a *caoineadh heard in Gougane Barra in 1813. In 1818 John Wilson *Croker arranged an Admiralty clerkship for him in London. A tour in 1821 informed *Researches in the South of Ireland, Illustrative of the Scenery, Architectural Remains, and the Manners and Superstitions of the Peasantry* (1824). *Fairy Legends and Traditions of the South of Ireland* (1825) is regarded as the first significant collection of Irish folk narrative. Collections of folk songs were *Popular Songs of Ireland* (1839), *Historical Songs of Ireland* (1841), and *The Keen in the South of Ireland* (1844).

Croly, George (1780–1860), clergyman and author. Born in Dublin, educated at TCD, he was a leading contributor of stories to *Blackwood's Magazine. Salathiel the Immortal* (1829) is on the theme of the Wandering Jew. *Marston* (1846) is a first-person novel set in the French Revolution. He wrote a verse tragedy, *Cataline* (1822). Croly's other writings include lives of George IV (1830) and Edmund *Burke (1840), as well as a work on *Irish Eloquence* (1852) illustrated by the speeches of John Philpot *Curran. His theological writings such as *Popery and the Popish Question* (1825) are specimens of angry eloquence.

Crommelin, Mary de la Cherois (1850–1930), novelist; born at Carrowdore Castle, Co. Down, to a Huguenot family. An early woman-member of the Royal Geographical Society, she reported her travels in *Over the Andes to Chile* (1898) and other books, and wrote more than thirty novels, among them *Orange Lily* (1879), *Black Abbey* (1880), *Devil-May-Care* (1899), and *The Golden Bow* (1899).

Cromwell, Oliver (1599–1658), opposition MP under Charles I and Parliament's leading military commander in the Civil War. He ruled Britain and Ireland as Lord Protector from the end of 1653 until his death. In Ireland he is remembered mainly for the period August 1649–May 1650, when he took charge of the Parliamentary army and presided over the capture of Drogheda (11 September 1649) and Wexford (11 October 1649), each followed by the massacre of the garrison and its inhabitants. The period 1649–58 saw the suppression of Catholic resistance [see *Rebellion of 1641], the execution, transportation, or imprisonment of substantial numbers of Catholic clergy, and the wholesale confiscation of Catholic lands [see *plantations]. Gaelic poets of Cromwell's time saw him as directly responsible for the destruction of the traditional social order.

Cromwell (1983), a long poem sequence by Brendan *Kennelly which sets the figure of Oliver *Cromwell, as he appears in *folklore, history, and Irish racial hatred, against the character of Buffún, a version of the Irish upstarts from *Pairlement Chlainne Tomáis.

Crone, Anne (1915–1972), novelist; born in Dublin, educated at Oxford. The title-character of her first novel, Bridie Steen (1948), is an orphan of mixed parentage. Her other novels, This Pleasant Lea (1952) and My Heart and I (1955), are also set in rural Ulster.

Crone, John S. (1858–1945), physician, bibliographer and biographer; born in Belfast, and educated at QUB. His Concise Dictionary of Irish Biography (1928) remained the standard reference work for years.

Cronin, Anthony (1928–), poet and novelist. Born in Wexford and educated at UCD, he was part of the Dublin literary scene which he chronicled in Dead As Doornails (1976). In 1980 he became cultural adviser to the Taoiseach Charles J. Haughey and created Aos Dána, an affiliation of artists set up in 1983. A comic novel, The Life of Riley (1964), deals with Irish literary Bohemia in the 1940s. Identity Papers (1979) concerns the career of a young man who re-enacts Richard *Pigott's treachery until he finds that he is not his descendant. Cronin's poetry, collected in 1973 and again in 1982, is modernist and acerbic though rooted in ordinary experience. R.M.S. Titanic (1967) deals with human and technological crisis. The End of the Modern World (1989) is a sonnet suite dealing with history, sexuality, and decadence. Relationships (1994) is a reflective collection dealing with conscience, while The Minotaur (1999) confronts human violence and love. Criticism includes A Question of Modernity (1966) and Heritage Now (1982). No Laughing Matter (1989) is a biography of Flann

*O'Brien, and The Last Modernist (1997) of *Beckett.

Croppy, The (1828), a novel by Michael *Banim about the Rebellion of 1798 [see *United Irishmen] in Wexford.

crosántacht, a Gaelic literary form mixing verse and prose. In use from the late Classical Irish to the Early Modern period [see *Irish language], and associated with the crosáns, semi-ritual comic entertainers of medieval times. Some thirty examples of crosántacht survive, among them two epithalamia by Dáibhí *Ó Bruadair ('Iomdha scéimh ar chur na cluana' and 'Cuirfead cluain ar chrobhaing').

Cross, Eric (1905–1980), born in Newry, and best known as the memorialist of The Tailor and Ansty (1942), a work of living *folklore featuring Tim Buckley, an irreverent *seanchaí from Gougane Barra, Co. Cork, with his irrepressibly contrary wife and collaborator Antsy (Anastasia).

Crottie, Julia M. (1853–?1930), fiction writer; born in Lismore, Co. Waterford, and educated by the Presentation nuns. She published several collections of stories about spiritual paralysis in rural Ireland, among them Neighbours (1900) and Innisdoyle Neighbours (1920). The Lost Land (1902) describes the extinction of Republican idealism.

Crow Street Theatre, Dublin (1758–1820), erected by Spranger *Barry and Henry Woodward on the site of a music-hall in 1758, it became the *Theatre Royal when Barry acquired the patent of Master of Revels in 1759. Thomas *Sheridan, manager of *Smock Alley, opposed Crow Street in A Humble Appeal to the Public (1758) on the grounds that Dublin could not support two competing companies. In 1767 Barry leased Crow Street to his Smock Alley competitor, Henry *Mossop. At Mossop's failure in 1770 Crow Street was taken by William Dawson. In 1776 Dawson surrendered the lease to Thomas Ryder, who ran both theatres before surrendering Smock Alley to Richard Daly in 1779. In 1786 Daly acquired the Crow Street lease together with the patent of Master of Revels. In 1788 Daly reopened the extensively refurbished Crow Street Theatre Royal. In 1796 Frederick Jones obtained the patent. In the ensuing years, the fortunes of the theatre often flagged. In 1820 Henry Harris, proprietor of Covent Garden, acquired the patent and the management of Crow Street. After a season at the Rotunda Assembly Rooms in 1820, he removed the Theatre Royal to Hawkins Street where a new building was constructed.

Crowe, Eyre Evans (1799–1868); novelist. Born of Irish parents near Southampton, he attended TCD. Crowe's Irish fiction consists of two collections, *Today in Ireland* (1825) and *Yesterday in Ireland* (1829), respectively containing an account of agrarian violence sympathetic to the Catholic peasantry and a vivid tale of the *United Irishmen's Rebellion of 1798. His other fiction includes the novels *Vittoria Colonna* (1825) and *Charles Delmer* (1853).

Cruiskeen Lawn, see Flann *O'Brien.

Crystal and Fox (1968), a play by Brian *Friel, and the most enigmatic of a quartet which he described as a 'four-part catechism of love', with *Philadelphia, Here I Come!*, The *Loves of Cass Maguire*, and *Lovers*. The play is dominated by the dangerous character of Fox Melarkey, whose impatience with life's imperfection brings ruin on him and all around him.

Cú Chulainn, hero of the *Ulster cycle and the central figure of *Táin Bó Cuailnge*, where his heroic deeds and supernatural powers play a dominant part in the narrative. He is also a figure of recurrent interest for later Irish and Anglo-Irish writers. The story of his origin as given in *Compert Chon Culainn (Birth of Cú Chulainn)* relates that he was fathered by the god Lug [see Irish *mythology] on Deichtine, and brought up as Sétanta. His boyhood deeds (macgnímartha), narrated by Fergus in *Táin Bó Cuailnge*, mark him out as destined to become a famous if short-lived warrior. According to Fergus he received his name when Sétanta, being late for a feast at the house of Culann the smith, is attacked by the hound guarding the enclosure and kills it. The smith complains of his loss, and Sétanta undertakes to act as his guard-dog, at which the *druid Cathbad renames him Cú Chulainn (the hound of Culann). In *Tochmarc Emire* he courts and wins Emer despite the opposition of her father, Forgall Manach. This tale also recounts his training in arms in Scotland by the amazon Scáthach, and his coupling with her opponent Aífe, after he has defeated her in combat. *Aided Oenfhir Aífe relates how their son Connle later comes to Ireland, where he is slain by his father. In *Fled Bricrenn Cú Chulainn takes the hero's portion, surpassing *Conall Cernach, another hero of the Ulaid. *Serglige Chon Culainn tells how he is torn between his earthly love for Emer (or Eithne in Gubai, according to another version) and Fand from the otherworld. In *Aided Chon Culainn, Cú Chulainn's death tale, Lugaid, the son of Cú Roí whom he has slain, comes against him with other enemies. He breaks a *geis by eating the flesh of a dog, and at the end, while dying of his wounds, straps himself to a pillar-stone so that he can fight to the last.

Cú Roí mac Dáire, see *Fled Bricrenn.*

Cuala Press, The (1908–1987), formed after the *Dun Emer Press separated from Evelyn Gleeson's Dun Emer Industries, moved to Churchtown, Dundrum, and was renamed after the barony in which the house was sited.

Cúan úa Lothcháin (d. 1024), poet. Apparently born in Tethba, which formed part of the midland kingdom of Mide, Cúan acted as propagandist for Máel Sechnaill (d. 1022), King of *Tara and principal rival of *Brian Bóroime.

Cuanduine trilogy, the, a series of satirical novels by Eimar *O'Duffy comprising *King Goshawk and the Birds* (1926), *The Spacious Adventures of the Man in the Street* (1928), and *Asses in Clover* (1933). In the first of these, the Philosopher of Stoneybatter recruits Cuchulainn in Tír na nÓg [see *sidh] to do battle with King Goshawk, an international magnate. *The Spacious Adventures of the Man in the Street* (1928) deals with the Swiftian voyage of Aloysius O'Kennedy to a planet where the 'Ratheans' enjoy uninhibited sex, but suffer from a corresponding guilt about food. In *Asses in Clover* (1933) Cuanduine saves the world from the rapacity of Goshawk.

Cuchulain cycle, the, a cycle of plays by W. B. *Yeats based on the legendary Irish figure *Cú Chulainn. In *On Baile's Strand* (1904), Cuchulain swears loyalty to *Conchubor, King of Ulster, and is forbidden by him to befriend an unknown young man sent by Aífe, a woman who has trained the young stranger in warfare and sent him to kill Cuchulain. After learning that the youth he has killed was his own son by Aífe, Cuchulain dies fighting the waves. In *The Green Helmet* (1910; formerly *The Golden Helmet*, 1908) Cuchulain makes a sacrificial gesture in offering himself to the Red Man to kill. In *At the Hawk's Well* (1916) Cuchulain, as a young man, pursues the well's guardian and in doing so embraces his heroic destiny. In *The Only Jealousy of Emer* (published 1919) Emer renounces Cuchulain in order to save him from Fand, the woman of the *sídh, while Eithne Inguba, Cuchulain's young mistress, wins him back to life and to herself. In *The Death of Cuchulain* (published 1939) the Morrigu, a crow-headed goddess, gets Eithne Inguba to falsify a message from Emer so that Cuchulain is wounded six times, tied to a stake by Aífe, and killed by the Blind Man.

Cuchulain of Muirthemne (1902), a version by Lady *Gregory of *Táin Bó Cuailnge from the *Ulster cycle. Working from translations by Standish Hayes *O'Grady, and others, as well as from the original texts, Lady Gregory produced a continuous narrative written in Kiltartanese, her literary rendering of Galway *Hiberno-English.

Cúirt an Mheán-Oíche (*The Midnight Court*), a long poem by Brian *Merriman written about 1780 in Feakle, Co. Clare, using accentual metre [see Irish *metrics]. A monstrous female envoy from the fairies appears to the unmarried poet in a dream, summoning him to the court of Queen Aoibheall to answer charges of wasting his manhood when women are dying for love. He listens to complaints on subjects such as the celibacy of the clergy and marriages between old and young for purely economic reasons. At last Aoibheall pronounces judgment on the poet, who awakens as he is being severely chastised by the women of the court. *Cúirt an Mheán-Oíche* draws on the European courtly love tradition and its bawdier offshoots. These elements are subsumed into the framework of the native *aisling genre. The first translation was made by Denis Woulfe (Donnchadh Ulf) in the 1820s, and there have been more than half-a-dozen others, the best-known being Frank *O'Connor's (1945).

cúirt éigse (court of poetry). Courts of poetry were common in Munster in the 18th cent. A well-known cúirt was held at Carrignavar, Co. Cork, in the time of Seán *Ó Murchadha na Ráithíneach; and at Croom, Co. Limerick, another was presided over by Seán *Ó Tuama 'an Ghrinn' (of the Merriment) for the poets of the Maigue. At a cúirt new poems were read aloud and discussed. A *barántas (warrant) sometimes summoned the cúirt. The cúirt was revived in Galway by Fred *Johnston in the 1980s.

Culdees, see *Céle Dé.

Cumberland, Richard (1732–1811), the English author of successful sentimental dramas; son of the Bishop of Clonfert, Co. Galway. He wrote *The West Indian* (1771) while staying with his father to escape debts in London. The play includes a *stage-Irish character in Major O'Flagherty.

Cummins, Geraldine [Dorothy] (1890–1969), playwright and novelist; born in Cork and educated at home. Between 1913 and 1917 she wrote two *Abbey plays with her close friend Suzanne *Day, with whom she also founded the Munster Women's Franchise League in company with Edith *Somerville. She also wrote two novels, *The Land They Loved* (1919) and *Fires of Beltaine* (1936). In 1920 Cummins married Austin *Clarke, but they separated

after ten unhappy days. She had an absorbing interest in psychical research and issued numerous books composed by automatic writing. These include *The Childhood of Jesus* (1937) and *After Pentecost* (1944).

Cúndún, Pádraig Phiarais (1777–1857), poet; born near Ballymacoda, Co. Cork, where he farmed before emigrating to the USA in about 1826. His early songs and poems reflect contemporary events. Seven years after emigrating he began writing letters containing poems and songs to his friends back home, which were copied and circulated in manuscript.

Cunningham, John (1729–1773), playwright. Born in Dublin, he began by writing songs, and then produced *Love in a Mist* (1747), a farce. Cunningham went to England as an actor, and published *Poems Chiefly Pastoral* (1766).

Curious Street, A (1984), a novel by Desmond *Hogan. Alan Mulvanney is writing a novel about *Cromwell. He has an affair with Eileen Connolly, unconsummated because of his homosexuality, and she becomes a prostitute in England before marrying a businessman. Her son Jeremy is in the British Army serving in Belfast amid the *Troubles when he reads of Mulvanney's suicide.

Curran, Henry Grattan (1800–1876), poet and novelist. Born in Dublin, the natural son of John Philpot *Curran, he became a barrister. His poetry includes 'The Wearing of the Green'. He wrote topical novels including *Confessions of a Whitefoot* (1884).

Curran, John Philpot (1750–1817), barrister and orator. Born in Newmarket, Co. Cork, he was educated in TCD and the Middle Temple. As an MP in the *Irish Parliament (1783–97) he spoke in favour of *Catholic Emancipation, resigning in disgust at the corrupt measures used to pass the Act of *Union. He defended several *United Irishmen. In the aftermath of the 1803 rising of Robert *Emmet—to whom his daughter Sarah (*Curran) was secretly engaged—he defended some of the accused, though not Emmet himself. A lyric, 'The Deserter's Meditation' has been much anthologized. His speeches have been reprinted frequently.

Curran, Sarah (?1780–1808), daughter of John Philpot *Curran, fiancée of Robert *Emmet, and subject of Thomas *Moore's romantic lyric 'She Is Far from the Land'.

Curry, John (?1710–1780), physician and historian. Born in Dublin, educated in Paris and Reims, he practised medicine in Dublin, and founded the Catholic Committee [see *Catholic Emancipation] in 1756 with others. His *Review of the Civil Wars in Ireland* (1775) was an attempt to refute the theory of a Catholic massacre of Protestants in the *Rebellion of 1641.

Curtayne, Alice (1901–1981), author and critic; born in Tralee, Co. Kerry, and educated in England and in Italy. After *Catherine of Siena* (1929) she wrote several works of nationalist history including a life of Patrick *Sarsfield (1934). The novel *House of Cards* (1940) concerns an Irish girl who marries an Italian industrialist.

Curtin, Jeremiah (1838–1906), folklorist. Born in Detroit to Irish parents, he grew up in Milwaukee. He attended Milwaukee University, then Harvard, where he was taught by the folklorist F. J. Child. He worked at the Bureau of Ethnology (later the Smithsonian Institute) in Washington, 1883–91, and visited Ireland many times, collecting *folklore. *Myths and Folklore of Ireland* (1890) was amongst the first accurate collections of folk material. *Tales of the Fairies and Ghost World* (1893) and *Hero Tales of Ireland* (1894) followed.

Curtin, Michael (1942–), novelist; born in Limerick, and educated by the Christian Brothers, after which he worked at various jobs. His first novel *The Self-Made Man* (1980) was followed by *The Replay* (1981), *The League Against Christmas* (1989), *The Plastic Tomato-Cutter* (1991), and *The Cove Shivering Club* (1996).

Curtis, Edmund (1881–1943), historian. Born in Lancashire of Irish parents, he was working in a factory at 15 when published poems attracted support for his education. After degrees at Oxford and his first book, *The Normans in Lower Italy* (1912), he was appointed Professor of History at TCD in 1914. His works include *A History of Medieval Ireland* (1923), *Richard II in Ireland 1394–96* (1927), and *A History of Ireland* (1938).

Curtis, Tony (1955–), poet; born in Dublin, educated by the Christian Brothers and at Essex University. Collections include *The Shifting Stones* (1986), *Behind the Green Curtain* (1988), *This Far North* (1994), and *Three Songs of Home* (1998). Sometime editor of *Poetry Ireland.

Cusack, Cyril (1910–1993), actor and playwright. Born in Kenya, son of an Irish member of the police, he was educated at UCD. In 1932 he abandoned law to join the *Abbey Theatre. He had a stage triumph as Conn in a revival of The *Shaughraun at the Abbey in 1968. *Tar Éis an Aifrinn* (1942) was his first play. He published poetry: *Times Pieces* (1970) and *Between the Acts* (1992).

Cusack, Margaret Anne (Sister Mary, the 'Nun of Kenmare') (1829–

1899). Born in Dublin, she became an Anglican nun in London but converted to *Catholicism in 1858 and joined the Poor Clares. Besides a *History of Ireland* (1876) she wrote two novels, *Ned Rusheen* (1871), a murder mystery, and *Tim O'Halloran's Choice* (1877), a tale of 'soupers' and faithful Catholics in the *Famine. *The Nun of Kenmare* (1889) and *The Story of My Life* (1893) are mainly attacks on bishops with whom she quarrelled.

Cusack, Michael, see *GAA.

Cusack, Ralph (1912–1965), novelist. Born in Dublin, he trained as a painter in the south of France. In *Cadenza* (1958), his sole literary work, the narrator travels on an imaginary excursion through remembered places in Scotland, France, and Ireland.

cycle of the Kings, see *historical cycle.

Cyphers (1975–), magazine of poetry, fiction, and reviews, which publishes work in Irish and English.

D

Da (1973), a semi-autobiographical play by Hugh *Leonard. Set in Dublin, it takes the form of a ghost story in which the title character takes his foster-son Charlie back to a Dalkey childhood.

Dagda, see *mythological cycle.

Daiken, Leslie (1912–1964), socialist journalist and poet. Born Yodaiken in Dublin, he lived in London, edited *Irish Front* with Charles *Donnelly, and issued anthologies, such as *Goodbye, Twilight* (1936), containing working-class political poetry. *Go, the Irish* (1944) is a short miscellany of Irish writers in England or in the forces which includes a leading contribution from Sean *O'Casey. Daiken's own collections were *The Signature of All Things* (1944) and *The Lullaby Book* (1957).

Dalkey Archive, The (1964), a novel by Flann *O'Brien, set in the south Co. Dublin suburban town. The mainstays of the plot are the idiosyncratic scientist De Selby, who plans to destroy humanity, and a publican called James Joyce, who denounces the works imputed to him.

Dallán Forgaill (*fl.* 600), early poet known to legend and possible author of the *Amra Choluim Cille*, he was chief of the *bardic poets of Ireland. According to the tradition preserved in *Tromdámh Guaire* (also known as *Imtheacht na Tromdáimhe, Proceedings of the Great Bardic Assembly*), he formulated the rights of hospitality of the bardic order. Those claims were later advanced at the court of King Guaire of Connacht by his successor, Senchán Torpéist.

D'Alton, John (1792–1867), antiquar-ian and poet; born in Bessville, Co. Westmeath, and educated at TCD. *Dermid, or Erin in the Days of Boroimhe* (1814) was a romance in twelve cantos. He also wrote translations for *Hardiman's *Irish Minstrelsy* (1831). His *History of Ireland from the Earliest Period to 1245* (2 vols., 1845) won an *RIA prize.

D'Alton, Louis Lynch (1900–1951), playwright and novelist. Born in Dublin the son of a touring actor-manager, D'Alton worked as a civil servant. *The Man in the Cloak* (1937), staged at the *Abbey Theatre, depicted James Clarence *Mangan's mercurial temperament. Both *Tomorrow Never Comes* (1939) and *The Spanish Soldier* (1940) are psychological studies. *The Money Doesn't Matter* (1941) marks the beginning of a concentration on contemporary Irish life. *Lovers' Meeting* (1941) is about matchmaking. In the comedy *The Devil a Saint Would Be* (1951) the theme is selfish piety. D'Alton also wrote the novels *Death Is So Fair* (1936), and *Rags and Sticks* (1938).

Daly, Ita (1945–), fiction-writer; born in Drumshanbo, Co. Leitrim, and educated at UCD she was a teacher until 1980, when she published her first short-story collection, *The Lady With the Red Shoes*, followed by the novels *Ellen* (1986), *A Singular Attraction* (1987), *Dangerous Fictions* (1989), *All Fall Down* (1992), and *Unholy Ghosts* (1996). *Candy on the Dart* (1989) and *Candy and Sharon Olé* (1991) are children's books.

Daly, Pádraig J[ohn] (1943–), poet and Augustinian friar. He was born in Dungarvan, Co. Waterford, and educated at UCD, and at the Gregorian University in Rome. His first collection,

Nowhere But in Praise (1978), was followed by *This Day's Importance* (1981), *A Celibate Affair* (1984), *Out of Silence* (1993), and *The Voice of the Hare* (1997). *Libretto* (1999) is a translation from the Italian of Eduardo Sanguinetti.

dán díreach, see Irish *metrics.

Dana (May 1904–April 1905), a short-lived monthly magazine edited by John *Eglinton and Frederick *Ryan, sharply critical of the role of *Catholicism in Irish society.

Danaher, Kevin (Caoimhín Ó Danachair) (1903–   ), folklorist. Born Athea, Co. Limerick, he began to collect *folklore in 1934, when a student at UCD. After studies at the Universities of Berlin and Leipzig and a period as captain in the Irish Army, he was employed as a full-time ethnologist with the *Irish Folklore Commission from 1945, becoming lecturer in folk life at UCD. His numerous publications include *In Ireland Long Ago* (1962), *The Year in Ireland* (1972), *Ireland's Vernacular Architecture* (1975), *A Bibliography of Irish Ethnology and Folk Tradition* (1978), and *That's How It Was* (1984).

Dancing at Lughnasa (1990), a play by Brian *Friel, set in August 1936, the action taking place in the home of the Mundy family where five unmarried sisters, living near the village of 'Ballybeg', Co. Donegal, eke out a rural existence on the brink of emigration.

Danes, see *Viking invasion.

Daniel[l], William (Uilliam Ó Domhnaill) (*c.*1570–1628), Archbishop of Tuam and translator of The New Testament [see *Bible in Irish]. Born in Kilkenny, he was among the first students to enter TCD. He assumed responsibility for the translation project which *Elizabeth I had encouraged. Assisted

by Domhnall Óg Ó hUiginn of Galway (d. 1602), he saw *Tiomna Nuadha* (1603) through the press. He went on to make a translation of Cranmer's *Book of Common Prayer*, *Leabhar na nUrnaightheadh gComhcoidchiond* (1609).

dánta grádha, a term used to describe the surviving examples of a body of love poetry employing looser forms of classical metres [see Irish *metrics] from around the middle of the 14th to the 17th cent. Although mainly anonymous, it is evident that many of the poems were composed by men with bardic training [see *bardic poetry], while others were written by aristocratic amateurs. Many are dramatic lyrics in which a social situation is evoked. A poem by Niall Mór Mac Muireadhaigh, 'Soraidh slán don oidhche aréir', evokes a world of secret signs. In 'A bhean lán do stuaim', attributed to Geoffrey *Keating, an ageing man draws attention to his greying hair and ebbing manhood.

Danu, see *mythological cycle.

'Dark Rosaleen, My' (1846), a poem by James Clarence *Mangan, based on a translation of 'Róisín Dubh' by Samuel *Ferguson which appeared in *The *Nation.

Dark, The (1965), a semi-autobiographical novel of boyhood by John *McGahern dealing with the schooldays of an unnamed character who is living with his widower father.

Dark Tower, The: *A Radio Parable Play* (1946), a verse play by Louis *MacNeice. The central character, Roland, is being prepared for his journey across sea and desert by Tutor, Blind Peter, and Sergeant-Trumpeter, while other voices try, in vain, to deflect him from the Quest.

Darley, George (1795–1846), poet, critic, and mathematician. Born in Dublin, he was educated at TCD. After publishing in London *The Errors of Ecstasie* (1822), he issued, as 'Guy Penseval', *The Labours of Idleness; or Seven Nights' Entertainments* (1826), prose tales interspersed with verse. *Sylvia, or the May Queen* (1827), published under his own name, is a lyrical drama. Darley turned to popular mathematics, writing text books such as *Popular Algebra* and *Familiar Astronomy* between 1826 and 1830. *Nepenthe* (1835), his most significant work, was privately printed on coarse paper in broken typefaces. *Thomas à Beckett* (1840) and *Ethelstan* (1841) were dramatic chronicles.

Daunt, William Joseph O'Neill (1807–1894), historian and novelist. Born in Tullamore, Co. Offaly, he converted to *Catholicism in 1827. As MP for Mallow he was a supporter of the *Repeal Association. He wrote political works including *A Catechism of the History of Ireland* (1844), *Ireland Since the Union* (1888), and *Personal Memoirs of the Late Daniel *O'Connell* (1848). Among Irish novels written under the pseudonym 'Denis Ignatius Moriarty' were *Hugh Talbot* (1846), *Innisfoyle Abbey* (1840), *Saints and Sinners* (1843), and *The Gentleman in Debt* (1851).

Dave (1927), a late miracle play by Lady *Gregory, in which Dave, a poor serving-lad, is blamed by an older fellow-servant for his own misdeeds and dishonesty.

Davies, Sir John (1569–1626), lawyer, poet, and Anglo-Irish *chronicler. Born in Wiltshire, he was appointed Attorney-General for Ireland in 1603. As a poet he is best remembered for *Orchestra* (1596) and *Nosce Teipsum* (1599). In his chief work on Ireland, *A Discovery of the True Causes Why Ireland was Never Entirely Subdued until the Beginning of His Majesty's Reign* (1612), written from his experiences as president of the Ulster Plantation, he argued for a vigorous policy of anglicization.

Davis, Francis (1810–1885), poet. He was brought up in Hillsborough, Co. Antrim, though he later pretended to have come from Cork. He contributed poems to The *Nation as 'the Belfast Man' in the early 1840s. He worked as a weaver but was later employed at QUB. His poems were collected as *Earlier and Later Leaves, an Autumn Gathering* (1878).

Davis, Thomas Osborne (1814–1845), poet and patriot. Born in Mallow, Co. Cork, the son of an army surgeon, he was educated at TCD and called to the Bar in 1838. In an address of 1839 to the TCD Historical Society, he announced 'Gentlemen, you have a country!' Having joined Daniel *O'Connell's *Repeal Association in 1841, he founded *The Nation* with the other *Young Irelanders, Charles Gavan *Duffy and John Blake Dillon in 1842. Tensions between O'Connell and Young Ireland increased after a meeting chaired by Davis in May 1845 on the issue of non-denominational university education. Davis died of scarlatina that September. In numerous essays, and poems for *The Nation*, he attempted to launch a national literature. Among Davis's finest ballads are 'The Lament for Owen Roe O'Neill', 'Clare's Dragoons', 'A Nation Once Again', 'The West's Asleep', and 'My Grave'. Acknowledged by Patrick *Pearse as part of the testament of Irish nationalism, his political writings include a powerful advocacy of Irish in 'Our National Language', *The Nation* (1 Apr. 1843).

Davitt, Michael (1846–1906), political organizer; born in Straide, Co. Mayo, the son of a tenant farmer, who emigrated to Lancashire after being evicted in 1851. He joined the *Fenians in 1865 and in 1870 was jailed for gun-running. In America he worked out the New Departure with John Devoy, linking the campaign for land reform with that for independence. On returning to Ireland he founded the *Land League in 1879 with Parnell as President. *Leaves from a Prison Diary* (1884) was followed by *The Boer Fight for Freedom* (1902), *Within the Pale* (1903), and *The Fall of Feudalism in Ireland* (1904).

Davitt, Michael (1950–), poet. Born in Cork, he was educated at the North Monastery and at UCC, where he founded the poetry broadsheet and journal *Innti* in 1970. He was a central figure in a new movement in Gaelic poetry in the early 1970s. At *RTÉ he worked as a producer from 1988. *Gleann ar Ghleann* (1982) was a first collection, followed by *Bligeard Sráide* (1983), *An Tost a Scagadh* (1993), and *Scuais* (1998). He became a friend of Seán *Ó Ríordáin, to whose metaphysical wit he gave a sharp vernacular edge; and he was also influenced by the American Beat poets.

Dawe, Gerald [Chartres] (1952–), poet. Born in Belfast, he was educated at NUU and UCG; he worked as a lecturer at TCD from 1988. Amongst his collections are *Sheltering Places* (1978), *The Lundys Letter* (1985), *Sunday School* (1991), *Heart of Hearts* (1995), and *The Visible World* (2000). *How's the Poetry Going?* (1991), *A Real Life Elsewhere* (1993), *False Faces* (1994), *Against Piety* (1995) and *Stray Dogs and Dark Horses* (1999) are collections of essays. He founded *Krino in 1985.

Dawning, The, see *The *Old Jest.*

Day, Suzanne R[ouvier] (1890–1964), playwright and novelist. Born in Cork, she began writing plays for the *Abbey Theatre with her friend Geraldine *Cummins, with whom she produced *Broken Faith* (1913) and *Fox and Geese* (1917). In 1916 she published a novel, *The Amazing Philanthropists*, and went to France as a nurse at the Front, an experience that formed the basis of *Round About Bar-le-Duc* (1918).

Day-Lewis, C[ecil] (1904–1972), poet; born in Ballintubbert, Co. Laois, he was educated at Sherborne and Oxford. His first collections, *Beechen Vigil* (1925) and *Country Comets* (1928), reveal the strong influence of *Yeats. At Oxford he met W. H. Auden; and he, Auden, Stephen Spender, and Louis *MacNeice became the left-wing 'MacSpaunday poets'. Beginning with *Transitional Poem* (1929), a political vein runs through his collections of the 1930s: *From Feathers to Iron* (1931), *The Magnetic Mountain* (1933), *A Time to Dance* (1935), *Noah and the Waters* (1936), and *Overtures to Death* (1938). In 1935 he published the first of a series of popular detective novels under the pseudonym 'Nicholas Blake'. A conflict between sexual and parental love finds expression in *World Over All* (1943), *Poems 1943–47* (1948), *An Italian Visit* (1953), and *Pegasus* (1957). From 1951 to 1956 he was Professor of Poetry at Oxford, and was Poet Laureate from 1968. *The Buried Day* (1960) is an autobiography. His final collection, *The Whispering Roots* (1970), explores his own identity.

'Dead, The', the final story in James *Joyce's *Dubliners* (1914), written in 1907. Gabriel Conroy and his wife Gretta attend his aunt's annual Epiphany Night party. Gabriel, a literary journalist, is worried and self-conscious while his wife remembers a boy who died of love for her.

Deane, John F. (1943–), poet. Born on Achill Island, Co. Mayo, he was educated at Mungret College in Limerick, then at UCD. After training for the priesthood he became a teacher, 1967–79, then a writer, and founded Poetry Ireland, the National Poetry Society, in

1979 [see *Poetry Ireland*]. He is also the founder of Dedalus Press. His collections include *Stalking After Time* (1977), *High Sacrifice* (1981), *Winter in Meath* (1985), *Road with Cypress and Star* (1988), *The Stylized City: New and Selected Poems* (1991), *Walking on Water* (1994), and *Upon Foreign Soil* (1999). *Free Range* (1994) is a volume of short stories, *One Man's Place* (1994) a novel. The novel *In the Name of the Wolf* (1999) mixes Gothic and thriller elements in a study of suffering and victimage set on Achill.

Deane, Seamus (1940–), poet, scholar and novelist; born in Derry and educated at QUB and Cambridge, he taught at UCD, where he was Professor of Modern English and American Literature, before moving to the University of Notre Dame in 1993. *Gradual Wars* (1972), a first collection of poetry, introduces themes relating to personal and cultural continuity in a society divided along sectarian lines. These issues form the core of *Rumours* (1977) and *History Lessons* (1983). He became a Director of *Field Day and wrote two pamphlets: *Civilians and Barbarians* (1983) and *Heroic Styles: The Tradition of an Idea* (1984). *Celtic Revivals: Essays in Modern Irish Literature* (1984), *A Short History of Irish Literature* (1986), and the enigmatic *Strange Country* (1997) are critical works offering readings of Irish literary history as tracked by colonial tension and division. *French Revolution and Enlightenment in England, 1789–1832* (1988) was followed by the *Field Day Anthology of Irish Literature* (1991) which he edited. *Reading in the Dark* (1996) was an allusive and disturbing novel of the *Troubles.

Death and Nightingales (1992), a novel by Eugene *McCabe, set in Co. Fermanagh in the 1880s against the background of the *Land League agitation and the assassination of Lord Frederick Cavendish by the *Invincibles in Phoenix Park. After her mother dies in a gruesome accident, Elizabeth lives alone with her father Billy Winters, who molests her, knowing that she was actually fathered by another man.

Death of [. . .], see *Aided [. . .].

Death of the Heart, The (1938), a novel by Elizabeth *Bowen. When 16-year-old orphan Portia comes to London to stay with her half-brother Thomas and his sophisticated wife Anna, her naïvety exposes the sterility of their marriage.

De Bhailís, Colm (1796–1906), a major poet in the *folklore of Connemara; born in Leitir Mealláin, he worked as a stonemason. His songs were published by the *Gaelic League as *Amhráin Chuilm de Bhailís* (1904).

De Bhaldraithe, Tomás (1916–), lexicographer and philologist; born in Limerick and educated at Belvedere College, UCD, where he became Professor of Modern Irish in 1960. His research on *dialects led to *The Irish of Cois Fhairrge, Co. Galway* (1945). His *English–Irish Dictionary* (1959) registered a vocabulary for the conditions of modern life.

De Blácam, Aodh (1890–1951), literary historian and novelist. Born in London, son of a Newry MP, he learnt Irish there and, moving to Ireland, became a prominent figure in nationalist politics. His fiction draws on Irish myth and history. His short-story collections and novels include *The Ship That Sailed Too Soon* (1919), *The Druid's Cave* (1921), and *Patsy the Codologist* (1922). *Holy Romans* (1920) is a semi-autobiographical tale. His poetry was published as *Dornán Dán* (1917) and *Songs and Satires* (1920). *Gaelic Literature Surveyed* (1921) is a critical evaluation of Gaelic literature.

De Blaghd, Earnán, see Ernest *Blythe.

De Brún, Monsignor Pádraig (1889–1960), scholar and translator. Born in Grangemockler, Co. Tipperary, he was educated at UCD, Paris, Göttingen, and Rome, and was ordained in 1913. He was Professor of Mathematics at Maynooth 1914–45, then President of UCG. He published numerous translations of classical and European authors including Sophocles' *Antigone* (1926) and *Oedipus Rex* (1928), Racine's *Athalie* (1930), and Corneille's *Polyeucte* (1932). A long poem of repentance, *Miserere* (1971), was posthumously edited by his niece Máire *Mhac an tSaoi, who also confirmed his authorship of a translation of Homer's *Odyssey*, *An Odaisé* (1990).

De Búrca, Séamus (1912–), playwright; born Dublin, son of P. J. *Bourke. His dramatic works include *The End of Mrs. Oblong* (1968), a play with numerous Dublin characters.

December Bride (1951), a novel by Sam Hanna *Bell dealing with the hard life of a Presbyterian community in the Ards Peninsula in the early 20th cent. Sarah Gomartin and her mother are employed as servants on an isolated farm by Andrew Echlin and his sons, Hamilton and Frank. When Andrew dies, Sarah has affairs with both sons.

De Divisione Naturae, see *Eriugena.

Deevy, Teresa (1894–1963), playwright; born in Waterford and educated at the Ursuline Convent, UCD, and UCC. An ear disease rendered her totally deaf before she graduated. After her first play, *The Reapers* (1930), Deevy wrote a number of others for the *Abbey Theatre. In *The King of Spain's Daughter* (1935), Annie Kinsella learns to love her sensible husband. *Katie Roche* (1936) marries an older man and is only reconciled to him after she has discovered herself to be an illegitimate offspring of

a mysterious traveller called Reuben. In *Temporal Powers* (1932) a peasant couple find stolen money and get in trouble with their betters. *Wife to James Whelan* was rejected by the Abbey in 1937. Deevy wrote mostly for radio thereafter, returning to the Abbey with *Light Falling* (1948).

De Fréine, Celia (1948–), poet and dramatist; born in Newtownards, Co. Down, she was educated at UCD and Lancaster. She worked as a civil servant, theatre director, and teacher. Her plays include *The Midnight Court* (1982), *The Courting of Emer* (1985), *Diarmuid agus Gráinne* (1986, in Irish), and *Two Girls in Silk Kimonos* (1991). She has worked as a scriptwriter for Telefís na Gaeilge.

De híde, Dubhglas, see Douglas *Hyde.

Deirdre, see *Longes mac nUislenn.

Deirdre of the Sorrows (1910), a play by J. M. *Synge based on *Longes mac nUislenn. Begun in 1907 and still being reworked at his death, it substitutes psychological motivation for the *geis of the original and brings Deirdre to the centre of the narrative, while retaining much of the starkness of the earliest telling in the *Book of Leinster.

Delacour, Revd James (1709–1781), poet. Born in Blarney, Co. Cork, and educated at TCD, he wrote sonnets and longer poems including *The Prospect of Poetry* (1733).

Delanty, Greg (1958–), poet. Born in Cork and educated at UCC, he lectured at St Michael's College, Vermont. *Cast in the Fire* (1986), a first collection, was followed by *Southward* (1992), *American Wake* (1994), and *The Hellbox* (1998). Cork city is evoked with affection, providing a backdrop for love poems, elegies, and meditations. *Leper's Walk*

(2000) extends his reach in form and content. Translations of Aristophanes and Euripides appeared in 1999.

Delany, Mary (née Granville, earlier Mrs Pendarves) (1700–1788), letter-writer and wife of Patrick *Delany. Born in Wiltshire and brought up by her uncle at Longleat House, she was widowed in 1724. In 1743 she accepted Delany's marriage proposal and returned to Ireland. Her Irish letters provide a lively account of *big house society. She was a correspondent of Jonathan *Swift, who wrote to her of his growing isolation.

Delany, Patrick (?1685–1768), clergyman and early biographer of *Swift. Born probably in Dublin, he entered TCD as a sizar and became a Fellow. In *Revelations Examined with Candour* (3 vols., 1732–63) and *Reflections upon Polygamy* (1738), Delany defended polygamy. Following the death of his first wife, Delany married in 1743 a Mrs Pendarves [see Mary *Delany], whose connections secured him the deanery of Down. Thereafter he spent half his time in England. His *Observations upon Lord Orrery's Life and Writings of Dr. Jonathan Swift* (1754), printed pseudonymously ('J.R.'), comes from one who knew Swift.

Delargy, James H., see Séamus *Ó Duilearga.

Delaune, Thomas (?1635–1685), a Cork-born Catholic turned Baptist. He wrote *A Plea for the Non-Conformist* (1683) and *A Narrative of the Sufferings of T. D.* (1684).

Deliverer, The (1911), a play by Lady *Gregory and an allegory of the way that *Parnell was treated by the Irish people under the guise of the story of Moses in Egypt.

Dé Luain (1966), a novel by Eoghan *Ó

Tuairisc commemorating the 1916 *Easter Rising. An account of the twelve hours leading up to the Proclamation of the Irish Republic [see *Irish State], as well as a psychological study of the leaders of the rebellion.

Demi-Gods, The (1914), a novel by James *Stephens, in which two tinkers, Patsy MacCann and his daughter Mary, travel across the west of Ireland in search of food and are joined by three angelic beings, Finaun, Caeltia, and Art.

Demon Lover, The (1945), a collection of short stories by Elizabeth *Bowen, some of them with Irish themes. In the title-story a woman returns to her evacuated London home and finds a letter from a lover killed in the previous war.

Denham, Sir John (1615–1669), soldier and poet. Born in Dublin, he became English Surveyor-General at the Restoration. His first work was a Turkish tragedy called *The Sophy* (1641). *Cooper's Hill* (1643), his best-known work, was accepted as a model of style by Dryden and Pope. His version of the second book of Virgil's *Aeneid* was published as *The Destruction of Troy* (1656), with a preface on translation.

'Denis O'Shaughnessy Going to Maynooth' (1831), a novella by William *Carleton, first serialized in *The *Christian Examiner* and then included in *Traits and Stories of the Irish Peasantry* (2nd ser., 1833). Denis Senior trains his son in pedantry and bombast to prepare him for the Catholic priesthood. By bribing Dr Finnerty, the parish priest, Denis Senior ensures that his son is selected by the bishop for Maynooth, which he eventually leaves.

Denman, Peter (1948–   ), poet and scholar; born in Guernsey, he was educated at Clongowes, UCC, and Keele, before becoming lecturer at St. Patrick's College, Maynooth. He published *Samuel Ferguson* (1990), and edited **Poetry Ireland* 1992–93. Collections include *The Poet's Manual* (1991) and *Sour Grapes*, and he co-translated Seán **Ó Tuama's verse for *Death in the Land of Youth* (1997).

Denvir, John (1834–1916), journalist and author, born in Bushmills, Co. Antrim. He emigrated to Liverpool and edited *The *United Irishman*, and *The Nationalist*. *The Irish in Britain* (1892, 1894) is a survey of demographic patterns. His fiction includes the novels *The Brandons* (1903) and *Olaf the Dane* (1908). *The Life Story of an Old Rebel* (1910) was autobiography.

Deoraíocht (*Exile*) (1910), a novel by Pádraic **Ó Conaire, it tells the story of Micheál Ó Maoláin, an Irish exile in London. Badly mutilated as a result of an accident, he spends his compensation foolishly and becomes a circus freak.

De Paor, Louis (1961–), poet; born in Cork and educated at UCC, he lectured in Cork before working on Australian radio in Melbourne, 1995–96. Pádraig **Ó Snodaigh published his first volume, *Próca Solais is Luatha* (1988), followed by *30 Dán* (1992), *Gobán Cré is Cloch* (1996), *Seo Siúd agus Uile* (1996), and *Corcach agus Dánta Eile* (1999). *Coiscéim na hAoise Seo* (1991) was an anthology of modern verse edited with Seán **Ó Tuama, while *Faoin mBlaoisc Bheag Sin* was a study of Máirtín Ó Cadhain's stories. As a poet De Paor is learned, allusive, combining passion with the workings of a philosophical mind, sharpened by sceptical empiricism.

Depositions of 1643, see **Rebellion of 1641.

De Profundis (1905), the accepted title of a long, accusatory letter written by Oscar **Wilde in Reading Gaol in January–March 1897, and addressed to Lord Alfred Douglas, with whom he had the homosexual affair that led to his trial and imprisonment.

Dermody, Thomas (1775–1802), child prodigy and poet. Born in Ennis, Co. Clare, he ran away to Dublin, where he gained the support of Robert **Owenson. *Poems* (1789), was followed by a political pamphlet, *The Rights of Justice, or Rational Liberty* (1793). In England he published *Poems, Moral and Descriptive* (1800) and *The Histrionade; or, Theatric Tribunal* (1802).

Derrick[e] John (*fl.* 1581), an English engraver who accompanied Sir Henry Sidney on campaigns against Hugh **O' Neill in the 1570s. His detailed woodcuts in *The Image of Irelande with A Discovery of Woodkarne* (1581) depict contemporary scenes in camp and battle, and record contemporary Irish customs, dress and methods of warfare.

Dervorgilla (1907), a play by Lady **Gregory, set in the period of the **Norman invasion. Dervorgilla has betrayed her husband, O'Rourke of Breffney, by living with Diarmaid MacMorrough, who brings the Normans to Ireland. Dervorgilla, twenty years after these events, devotes herself to prayer.

Deserted Village, The (1770), a poem by Oliver **Goldsmith, it laments the forcible clearance of an imaginary village, based on his own childhood at Lissoy, Co. Westmeath, by a landowner keen to improve his estate.

Destruction of Da Derga's Hostel, The, see **Togail Bruidne Da Derga*.

De Valera, Eamon (1882–1975), revolutionary and politician, born in New York, of Hispanic and Irish parentage. When he was 2 he was sent home to Co. Limerick, where he went to the

Christian Brothers school at Charleville (Ráth Luirc), then Blackrock College, Co. Dublin, and the Royal University [see *universities]. He joined the *Gaelic League in 1908 and the *Irish Volunteers in 1913, and came to prominence in the 1916 *Easter Rising when he commanded the forces at Boland's Bakery in south Dublin. He escaped execution when political opinion swung against the shootings of May 1916. On his release from prison in 1917 he became President of *Sinn Féin, MP for East Clare, and the leader of Irish Republicanism. He did not lead the Sinn Féin delegation in the 1921 Treaty negotiations leading to the foundation of a Free State [see *Anglo-Irish War], and opposed the Treaty. In 1927 he compromised with the Free State when he led his newly-formed Fianna Fáil into the Dáil. Having won the 1932 election, de Valera proceeded with a Republican agenda, including an economic war with Britain, and a new Constitution in 1937 which recognized the 'special position' of the Roman Catholic Church [see *Catholicism], and claimed territorial rights to Northern Ireland. During the Second World War he held to a policy of neutrality. He was Taoiseach until 1948, thereafter serving two further terms, 1951–4 and 1957–9, and was President 1959–73. The impact of de Valera's personality on modern Ireland has been greater than that of any other statesman. See Tim Pat *Coogan, *De Valera* (1993).

De Valois, Dame Ninette [orig. Edris Stannis] (1898–), dancer and choreographer; born in Blessington, Co. Wicklow, she was a soloist with Sergei Diaghilev's Ballets Russes in 1923. She established a ballet school at the *Abbey Theatre in 1927, with Yeats's encouragement; and mounted ballet programmes from 1928 to 1933, as well as dancing in Yeats's plays. In 1931 she founded the Vic-Wells Ballet Company in London and the Sadler's Wells School. The company eventually became the Royal Ballet in 1956 and she was made a Dame of the British Empire in 1957.

De Vere, Aubrey (1814–1902), poet, son of Sir Aubrey *de Vere; born at Curragh Chase, Co. Limerick, and educated there and at TCD. During the *Famine of 1845–8 he assisted his elder brother, Sir Stephen de Vere (1812–1904), in relief schemes. These experiences informed the writing of *English Misrule and Irish Misdeeds* (1848). In 1851 he was received into the Catholic Church. *May Carols or Ancilla Domini* (1857) was a serial poem on Mary as 'religión itself in its essence', while *Legends of the Saxon Saints* (1879), and *Legends of St. Patrick* (1889), memorialized early Christianity. In 1856, at Cardinal *Newman's invitation, he delivered a series of lectures on literature at the Catholic University [see *universities] in Dublin. De Vere's most accomplished poem, *Inisfail* (published with *The Sisters* in 1861 and separately in 1862), attributes a spiritual mission to the country. *The Foray of Queen Maeve* (1882) celebrates the simplicity of the ancient Irish heroes. Amongst his other publications were *Picturesque Sketches of Greece and Turkey* (1850) and *Recollections* (1897), the latter containing portraits of his many friends.

De Vere [Hunt], Sir Aubrey (1788–1846), verse dramatist. He was educated at Harrow but spent his life at Curragh Chase, Co. Limerick. His verse dramas are *Julian the Apostate* (1822), *The Duke of Mercia* (printed with *Lamentations of Ireland*, 1823), and *Mary Tudor* (1847). Poetry included *Sonnets* (1847).

Devil's Disciple, The (1897), one of the *Three Plays for Puritans* by George Bernard *Shaw, set in Puritan New

Hampshire during the American War of Independence. Richard Dudgeon rebels against the Puritanism of his mother and his society and declares himself 'the Devil's Disciple'.

Devlin, Anne (1951–), playwright; born in Belfast and educated there before moving to Birmingham. Plays include *Ourselves Alone* (1985), *The Way-Paver* (1986), and *After Easter* (1994).

Devlin, Denis (1908–1959), poet. Born in Greenock, Scotland, to an Irish family that returned to Dublin in 1918, he was educated at Belvedere College and UCD. His first book, *Poems* (1930), was shared with Brian *Coffey. He taught English at UCD, resigning in 1935 to enter the Department of Foreign Affairs. *Intercessions* (1937) was published by George *Reavey's Europa Press. In 1946 he published *Lough Derg and Other Poems*. *The Heavenly Foreigner* (1967, ed. Brian Coffey) was a vindication of Christ's presence in the world. In 1950 he was appointed plenipotentiary to Italy and Ambassador in 1958. See James C.C. Mays (ed.), *Collected Poems* (1989).

Devlin, Polly (1944–), writer of fiction and memoirs; born Ardboe, Co. Tyrone, she became a journalist after education in Ireland, moving to London and writing high-profile interviews. *All of Us There* (1983) evokes a northern Catholic childhood; *Dora, or the Shifts of the Heart* (1990) is a novel; and *The Far Side of the Lough: Stories from an Irish Childhood* (1993) evocatively returns to her native Tyrone.

dialects of Irish. Before the 16th cent. the forms of written Irish display little variation which can be correlated with differences of region or of class. There was universal adherence in writing to a well-defined norm. The fully developed standard found in the earliest texts was already non-regional in character and was maintained by an educated class. Deviations occur increasingly from the 16th cent., but few fully localized texts, showing sufficient diagnostic features for a more detailed dialectology, occur before the 18th. From this period some fully localized records are, however, available. The most striking of these is *The *Book of the Dean of Lismore*, a 16th-cent. Perthshire text in Scots orthography. On the Isle of Man, a new orthography expressing the local dialect was developed in the 17th cent. By the end of the 18th cent. Gaelic Scotland had fully developed its own modification of traditional orthography. Knowledge of dialectal variation must primarily depend on what has been recorded of the spoken language over the last century in the Highlands, Ireland, and Man. Two large-scale dialectological surveys have been carried out: Heinrich Wagner's *Linguistic Atlas and Survey of Irish Dialects* in four volumes (1958–69) and Kenneth Jackson's *Linguistic Survey of Scottish Gaelic* (1993).

Diarmaid, see *Tóraigheacht Dhiarmada agus Ghráinne*.

DIAS (Dublin Institute for Advanced Studies) (1940–) comprises a School of Celtic Studies, a School of Theoretical Physics, and a School of Cosmic Physics, added in 1947, each governed by a separate board. The School of Celtic Studies was conceived as a scholarly agency for the publication of *manuscript records in Irish and of Irish-language studies, continuing the work initiated by Kuno *Meyer's School of Irish Learning (1903).

dictionaries of Irish developed from early glossaries such as *Sanas Chormaic, c.* AD 900 [see *Cormac mac Cuileannáin]. The first printed dictionary, Mícheál *Ó

Cléirigh's *Focloir no Sanasan Nua* (1643), was monolingual. All later dictionaries have been bilingual. Conchubhar Ó Beaglaoich and Aodh Buidhe *Mac Cruitín compiled the first English-Irish dictionary of 1732. John O'Brien's *Focalóir-Gaoidhilge-Sax-Bhéarla* (1768) contains many historical articles under place, family, and personal names. Edward *O'Reilly's Irish–English dictionary of 1817 includes Scottish Gaelic words from Shaw's Gaelic dictionary of 1780 and ghostwords from Tadhg *Ó Neachtáin's manuscript dictionary of 1739. In more modern times, the introduction of Irish into public administration and the running of all-Irish schools in post-Treaty Ireland [see *Anglo-Irish War] would scarcely have been possible without O'Neill Lane's English–Irish and Pádraig *Ó Duinnín's Irish–English dictionaries of 1916 and 1927. *The Dictionary of the Irish Language* (1913–76), produced under the auspices of the *RIA, is based mainly on Old and Middle Irish materials. Tomás *de Bhaldraithe's *English–Irish Dictionary* (1959) provided Irish equivalents for English words and phrases in common use. Niall *Ó Dónaill's *Foclóir Gaeilge–Béarla* (1977) presented the vocabulary of modern Irish usage with English meanings.

Dicuil (?765–?), astronomer, grammarian, and mathematician. Born possibly in Ireland or in the Hebrides, he seems to have been a monk on Iona [see *Colum Cille]. He wrote a *Liber de Astronomia*; a summary of the grammarian Priscian, *De Questionibus Decim Artis Grammatice*; *De Prima Syllaba*; and *Liber de Mensura Orbis*, a work of geography.

Dillon, Eilís (1920–1994), novelist and children's author. Born in Galway and educated at Sligo, she trained as a cellist, and married Cormac Ó Cuilleanáin, Professor of Irish at Cork. After his death she married the critic Vivian *Mercier. Her numerous children's novels are admirable for their gripping plots. They include *The Island of Horses* (1956), *The Singing Cave* (1969), and *The Island of Ghosts* (1989). In her historical novels *Across the Bitter Sea* (1973) and its sequel *Blood Relations* (1977), Dillon examines upheavals in personal relationships against the background of revolutionary events in Ireland from the mid-19th cent. *Inside Ireland* (1982) is an autobiography. Eilean *Ní Chuilleanáin is her daughter.

Dillon, Myles (1900–1972), philologist and Gaelic scholar. Born in Dublin, a son of the *Irish Parliamentary Party MP John Dillon (1851–1927), he was educated at Belvedere College, UCD, Berlin, Bonn, Heidelberg, and Paris. He lectured at TCD, UCD, Wisconsin University, the University of Chicago, and Edinburgh University, before returning to the School of Celtic Studies in the *DIAS. He wrote an account of the *historical cycle (*The Cycles of the Kings*, 1946) and a survey of *Early Irish Literature* (1948).

Dillon, Wentworth (4th Earl of Roscommon) (1633–1685), poet and translator; born in Dublin and educated at the University of Caen. His poetry reflects his concerns with the relation between culture and nationality. His *Essay on Translated Verse* (1684) argued the case for liberating poetry from the constraint of rhyme. He translated Horace's *Art of Poetry* (1680).

Dinneen, Patrick, see Pádraig *Ó Duinnín.

dinnshenchas (lore of prominent places), a term used generally to refer to toponymic lore preserved in early Irish literature, and more specifically to denote the large corpus of this lore which was assembled in the 11th or 12th cent. known as *Dinnshenchas Érenn (The Dinnshenchas of Ireland)*. Three forms of *Dinnshenchas Érenn* are found in the *manuscripts: a metrical collection in the 12th-cent. *Book of Leinster*; a collection in prose which is also in the *Book of Leinster* as well as two 16th-cent. manuscripts; and a collection in prose and verse which is found in many manuscripts from the 14th-16th cents. The bulk of the material seems to have been composed in the *bardic schools between the 9th and 12th cents. Place-names are explained by reference to legends which are linked to them by means of pseudo-etymological techniques, where sometimes fictitious stories are adduced to explain the existing names, with the result that some of these legends are only to be found in the *Dinnshenchas*, where they serve their explanatory purpose. It was part of the body of knowledge medieval Irish poets were expected to master.

Dobbs, Francis (1750–1811), dramatist and politician; born in Lisburn, Co. Antrim, and educated at TCD, where he wrote the verse tragedy, *The *Patriot King, or the Irish Chief* (1773). *A Summary of Universal History* (9 vols., 1800), sets out his interpretation of scriptural prophecy. Other works include *Modern Matrimony* (1773), a longer poem, and *Poems* (1788).

Doctor Copernicus (1976), the first of a tetralogy by John *Banville about the relation between scientific and imaginative perception. It traces the mentality and achievements of the austere but determined scientist who proposes the idea of a heliocentric universe and then sets out to illustrate his theory through systematic calculation.

Doctor's Dilemma, The: *A Tragedy* (1906), a high-spirited satire on the medical profession by George Bernard *Shaw. Sir Colenso Ridgeon, having discovered a cure for tuberculosis, has to choose between Dubedat, a bigamist and untrustworthy in money matters, and the dull but honest Blenkinsop. Ridgeon's decision to take on Blenkinsop is tainted by the fact that he has become infatuated with Dubedat's wife.

Dodwell, Henry (1641–1711), classicist. Born in Dublin, he was educated at TCD and later became Camden Professor of History at Oxford. Besides his major work, *An Account of the Lesser Geographers* (3 vols., 1698–1712), he wrote *De Veteribus Graecorum Romanorum Cyclis* (1701–7), and *Annals of Thucydides* (1702) in conjunction with John Hudson.

Doggett, Thomas (1660–1721), playwright. Born in Castle St., Dublin, he moved to London after acting at *Smock Alley. *The Country Wake* (1696) was one of several comedies.

Doheny, Michael (1805–1863), poet and *Young Irelander. Born in Brookhill near Fethard, Co. Tipperary, he qualified as a lawyer. He wrote as 'Eiranach' in *The *Nation, producing 'A Cushla Gal Mo Chree', and the patriotic 'The Shan Van Vocht'. After 1848 he escaped to practise law in America, co-founding the *Fenians. *The Felon's Track, or History of the Attempted Outbreak in Ireland*, appeared in New York in 1849.

Dolmen Press, the (1951–1987), founded by Liam Miller (1923–1987), an architect by training, and his wife Josephine. Their first publication was *Travelling Tinkers* by Sigerson Clifford. At the outset its productions were amateurish with uneven press-work, but Dolmen was to become known as the producer of some of the world's most finely designed books, as well as publishers of many Irish poets and play-wrights.

Donaghy, John Lyle (sometimes Lyle Donaghy) (1902–1947), poet. Born in Larne, Co. Antrim, educated at TCD, afterwards becoming a teacher. His verse in collections such as *At Dawn over Aherlow* (1926), *The Flute over the Valley* (1931), and *The Blackbird* (1933) presents quietistic images of nature. *Wilderness Sings* (1942) embraces chaos in form and emotion.

Donleavy, J[ohn] P[atrick] (1926–), novelist. Born in Brooklyn, New York, he studied at TCD after the Second World War, meeting fellow-American Gainor Crist, the original of Sebastian Dangerfield, hero of his best-selling first novel, *The Ginger Man* (1955), a story of high jinks in Bohemian Dublin. *A Singular Country* (1989) contains personal impressions, while *The History of The Ginger Man* (1994) is an autobiography.

Donlevy, Andrew (?1694–?1761), religious writer. Born probably in Sligo, he went to the Irish College in Paris in 1710, where he studied law. He published *An Teagasg Críosduidhe do reir ceasada agus freagartha* (1742), a Catholic Catechism.

Donnelly, Charles [Patrick] (1914–1937), poet. Born near Dungannon, Co. Tyrone, he was educated at UCD but left without taking a degree. In 1937 he was killed in action with the Abe Lincoln Battalion at the Battle of Jarama in the Spanish Civil War. Donnelly's surviving literary work consists of essays, short stories, and poems. Some later work has been lost, but 'Heroic Heart' and 'The Tolerance of Crows' rank amongst the best poems of the Spanish Civil War.

Donoghue, Denis (1928–), critic; born in Tullow, Co. Carlow, he was educated at UCD where he became Professor of English and American Literature, then assumed the Henry James Chair of English and American Letters in New York University. Amongst his works are *The Ordinary Universe: Soundings in Modern Literature* (1968); *Jonathan Swift* (1971); *Yeats* (1971); *Thieves of Fire* (1973); *Warrenpoint* (1991), a memoir; *We Irish* (1991), essays; and *The Practice of Reading* (1998).

Donoghue, Emma (1969–), novelist; born in Dublin, educated at UCD and Cambridge. Her novels, which deal with women's sexuality, include *Stir-Fry* (1994), and *Hood* (1995). *Kissing the Witch* (1997) is a volume of stories. *What Sappho Would Have Said* (1997) is a poetry anthology; while *We Are Michael Field* (1998) is a literary biography.

Donovan, Gerard (1959–), poet; born in Wexford, he was educated at UCG and at John Hopkins University in America, teaching English there and elsewhere. Collections include *Columbus Rides Again* (1992) and *Kings and Bicycles* (1995).

Donovan, Katie (1962–), poet; born in Wexford, educated at TCD and Berkeley 1980–86; journalist with the *Irish Times*. Published poetry collections include *Watermelon Man* (1993) and *Entering the Maze* (1997), and she edited, with others, the anthologies *Ireland's Women* (1994) and *Dublines* (1996).

Dopping, Anthony (1643–1697), Anglo-Irish statesman. Born in Dublin and educated at TCD, he served as chaplain to the Duke of *Ormond at the Restoration. *Modus Tenendi Parliamenta in Hibernia* (1692) includes a condemnation of the terms of the Treaty of Limerick.

Dorcey, Mary (1950–), poet and writer of fiction; born in Dublin, and educated there and at the Open and Paris VII Universities, she taught for a time before becoming a researcher in women's studies at TCD in 1997. Poetry includes *Kindling* (1982), *Moving into the*

Space Cleared by Our Mothers (1991), and *The River that Carries Me* (1995). Fiction includes *A Noise from the Woodshed* (1989), stories, and the novel *Biography of Desire* (1997).

Dorgan, Theo (1953-), poet. Born in Cork, he was educated at UCC before becoming director of *Poetry Ireland/Éigse Éireann*. He published *The Ordinary House of Love* (1990), a collection of clear meditative lyrics, and edited, with Gene Lambert *The Great Book of Ireland* (1991), a vellum manuscript containing autograph writings by contemporary Irish authors and illustrations by Irish artists. *Revising the Rising* (1991), edited with Máirín Ní Dhonnchadha, was a collection of essays evaluating nationalist tradition, *Rosa Mundi* (1995) returned to the celebration of love; the TV series *Hidden Treasures* (1998) evoked country ways with scrupulous affection.

Double Cross (1986), a play in two parts by Thomas *Kilroy first produced by *Field Day in Derry. Set during and shortly after the Second World War, it is based on the lives of Brendan Bracken (1901-58), Churchill's Minister of Information during the war, and William Joyce (1906-46), who made propaganda broadcasts in English from Nazi Germany.

Douglas, James (1929-), dramatist. Born in Bray, Co. Wicklow, he contributed to many *RTÉ serials, among them *The Riordans*, a long-running agricultural series, and *Tolka Row*, which had a working-class urban setting. He wrote radio and television plays, including *The Bomb* (1962), and *Too Short a Summer* (1973). His stage plays include *North City Traffic Straight Ahead* (1961), *The Savages* (1970), and *What Is the Stars?* (1970).

Dowden, Edward (1843-1913), critic; born in Cork and educated at TCD, where he was appointed Professor in 1867, the first Chair of English Literature. Though primarily a Shakespeare scholar who established his reputation with *Shakespere, His Mind and Art* (1875), he also wrote a *Life of Shelley* (1886). He opposed *Home Rule and the Irish *literary revival.

Dowling, Richard (1846-1898), novelist; born in Clonmel, Co. Tipperary, and educated in Limerick before working on The *Nation and editing *Ireland's Eye*. He published numerous books, including *The Mystery of Killard* (1879), a romance. Other novels are *Sweet Inisfail* (1882) and *Old Corcoran's Money* (1897).

Downey, Edmund (1856-1937), publisher and novelist. Born in Waterford, he worked with London publishers before establishing a company in 1894 which published Irish authors. His own fiction includes *Through Green Glasses* (1887), *Green as Grass* (1892), *Merchant of Killogue* (1894), and *Clashmore* (1903).

Dowsley, Revd W[illiam] G[eorge] (1871-1947), novelist. Born in Clonmel, Co. Tipperary, and educated at the Royal University [see *universities], he was ordained in Bristol in 1901. He wrote some novels taking a nationalist view of Irish history. *Travelling Men* (1925) is set in Clonmel in 1801; *Far Away Cows Have Long Horns* (1931) in Ireland and South Africa.

Doyle, James Warren ('JKL') (1786-1834), Catholic bishop and diplomatist; born in Co. Wexford, and educated at Coimbra in Portugal. During the Peninsular War he acted as intermediary between the Portuguese and Arthur Wellesley, later Duke of *Wellington. Returning to Ireland, he became Bishop of Kildare and Leighlin in 1819. As 'JKL' he wrote trenchant works including *A Vindication of the Principles and Rights of the Irish Catholics* (1824) and *Letters on the State of Ireland* (1824-5).

Doyle, Lynn C. (pseudonym of Leslie Alexander Montgomery) (1873–1961), comic writer. Born in Downpatrick, Co. Down, he was a bank manager in Dundalk. He wrote some plays for the *Ulster Literary Theatre, notably *Love and the Land* (1927), and produced a series of humorous *Hiberno-English stories set in a fictional townland named after Slieve Gullion. Among these are *Ballygullion* (1908), *Mr Wildridge of the Bank* (1916), *Me and Mr. Murphy* (1930), *The Shake of the Bag* (1939), *A Bowl of Broth* (1945), and *The Ballygullion Bus* (1957), a compendium. *An Ulster Childhood* (1921) is autobiographical.

Doyle, Roddy (1958–), novelist. Born in Dublin, he was educated at UCD before working in Kilbarrack (the 'Barrytown' of his fiction) as a teacher, 1979–93. His first novel, *The Commitments* (1989), reflected Dublin working-class life. *The Snapper* (1990) continued the saga of the Rabbitte family. *The Van* (1991) explores the enterprise culture of the marginalized working-class suburbs. *Paddy Clarke Ha Ha Ha* (1993) centres on the impressions of a 10-year-old boy as he reacts to the breakdown of his parents' marriage. *The Woman Who Walked into Doors* (1996) deals with domestic violence, returning to the issues and raw energy of the television series *Family* (1994). *A Star Called Henry* (1999) goes back to the period of the *Anglo-Irish War. Doyle's plays, *Brownbread* (1987) and *War* (1989), were followed by *Family*.

Dracula (1897), Bram *Stoker's novel, combining the 15th-cent. Walachian tyrant Vlad Dracul with the vampire of European folklore. The narrative is made up of journals, letters, newspaper cuttings, and phonograph recordings, beginning with Jonathan Harker's account of a journey to Transylvania on behalf of his law firm to meet the mysterious Count Dracula. Most of the action takes place in England, whither the Count travels surreptitiously.

Drama at Inish (1933), a comedy by Lennox *Robinson. First staged at the *Abbey Theatre, it deals with the visit of a travelling troupe of actors to an Irish seaside resort.

Drama in Muslin, A (1886), a novel by George *Moore narrating the experiences of Alice and Olive Barton, daughters of a Catholic *big house family in Co. Galway, who attend the debutantes' ball at Dublin Castle. Olive dismisses her admirer at home in order to become the beauty of the season. Alice commences a frugal existence in London with her doctor husband.

Drapier's Letters, The (1724–1725), a series of seven pamphlets written by Jonathan *Swift under the guise of the 'Drapier', a Dublin shopkeeper, in order to protest at England's treatment of Ireland as a 'depending Kingdom'. This famous controversy began with an economic and legal dispute over the grant of a patent to William Wood, an English entrepreneur, to mint halfpence for Ireland. During 1724 Swift published five pamphlets on the issue: *A Letter to the Shopkeepers*, *A Letter to Mr Harding*, *Some Observations upon a Report*, *A Letter to the Whole People of Ireland*, and *A Letter to Lord Viscount *Molesworth*. A sixth pamphlet, *A Letter to the Lord Chancellor Middleton*, was written in that year, but withheld for legal reasons. In 1725 a final pamphlet, *An Humble Address to both Houses of Parliament*, was shelved when the Government withdrew Wood's patent.

Dream (1986), a novel by David *McCart-Martin dealing with the origins of the *Troubles in *Northern Ireland. It embraces the period between

1899 and the Second World War, and seeks to measure the human cost of warfare whether on a European scale or in Northern Ireland.

Dream of Fair to Middling Women

(1992), Samuel *Beckett's first novel. Written in Paris in 1932, it was rejected at the time, and Beckett used parts of it in *More Pricks than Kicks*. The novel narrates the love affairs of Belacqua in Europe and Dublin while documenting his obsession with the relationship between mind and body.

Dreaming Dust, The

(1940), Denis *Johnston's play about Jonathan *Swift, set in St Patrick's Cathedral.

Dreaming of the Bones, The

(performed 1931), a play by W. B. *Yeats, first published in 1919, modelled on the Pound–Fenollosa translation of a Japanese Noh play, *Nishikigi*. The ghostly lovers Dermot MacMurrough [see *Norman invasion] and Dervorgilla, whose adultery brought the Normans into Ireland, are refused absolution by a young Republican on the run who has fought in the *Easter Rising.

Drennan, William (1754–1820), *United Irishman and poet. He was born in Belfast, studied medicine in Glasgow and Edinburgh, and practised in Belfast, Dublin, and Newry. A radical address to the *Irish Volunteers issued in 1792 led to his trial in 1794 at which he was successfully defended by John Philpot *Curran. He did not take part in the Rebellion of 1798 but wrote a celebrated patriotic *ballad, 'The Wake of William Orr', on Orr's execution in 1797. He founded the Belfast Academical Institution with others in 1814. His literary writings were collected as *Fugitive Pieces in Verse and Prose* (1815), while a collection including poems by his sons William (1802–73) and John Swanwick

(1809–93) appeared in 1859 as *Glendalloch*.

Druid Theatre, the, a theatrical company founded in Galway in 1975 by Garry Hynes, Mick Lally, and Marie Mullen.

druids, a learned class among the *Celts of Gaul, Britain, and Ireland. The name has been derived from the *Indo-European particle dru- with the second element coming from the Indo-European root wid-, 'to know'; but most linguists regard the word as being cognate with the Greek word for 'oak', a tree with which the druids are constantly associated in early sources. Most of our knowledge about the druids of Gaul and Britain is derived from classical authors. The greater part of the earliest commentaries, chiefly those by Strabo, Diodorus Siculus, and Caesar, can be shown to be based on the lost writings of Posidonius. Strabo and Diodorus Siculus divide the learned classes of Gaul into three, Strabo designating them druids, vates [corresponding to Irish filid], and bards. Although druidesses are mentioned in later classical sources and in early Irish literature, there is no evidence for their existence in the early period. Their main functions would seem to have been those of philosopher, judge, and teacher. While reference is made to their role as teachers they most often appear as wizards, with the power to influence the elements and to predict the future.

Druim Ceat (or Druim Ceit), at Mullagh, near Derry, the site of the Convention of AD 575 where it was agreed that the Irish Dál Riata, who had territories in Scotland, owed military service in Ireland. *Colum Cille intervened in the debate, and is also said to have taken the side of the *bardic caste, who had become so importunate that the patience of their patrons was exhausted.

Drummond, William Hamilton (1778–1865), poet and theologian. Born in Larne, Co. Antrim, and educated at Glasgow University, he graduated DD in Aberdeen (1810), settling in Dublin, where he ministered. Among his early publications were *Juvenile Poems* (1795) and *Hibernia* (1797), later followed by *The Battle of Trafalgar* (1806), also verse, and a metrical translation of the *First Book of Lucretius* (1808). An interest in natural history was reflected in *The Giant's Causeway* (1811). He energetically defended Unitarianism in *The Doctrine of the Trinity* (1827). He contributed verse translations of Irish poetry to *Hardiman's *Irish Minstrelsy* (1831), which won grudging praise from Samuel *Ferguson, and issued *Ancient Irish Minstrelsy* (1852), containing verse translations of poems from the *Fionn cycle.

Drums of Father Ned, The: A *Mickrocosm of Ireland* (1958), a utopian play by Sean *O'Casey about a tóstal (festival of music and arts) being organized in a fictitious Irish town, suggested by events in Wexford.

Drums Under the Windows, see *Autobiographies* [Sean O'Casey].

duanaire (family poem-book), a collection of poems made for enjoyment or professional use in Gaelic Ireland. The earliest example of a duanaire is the 14th-cent. *manuscript *Leabhar Mhéig Shamhradháin* (*Book of MacGovern*), compiled mainly by Ruaidhrí Ó Cianáin. Other vellum poem-books were compiled for families such as the Roches, the O'Reillys, and the O'Donnells. Amongst other poem-books are the 16th-cent. Scottish *Book of the Dean of Lismore*, *Duanaire Finn*, and the *Book of the O'Conor Don*.

Duanaire Finn (*Poem-Book of Fionn*), a compilation of late medieval Irish poems from the *Fionn cycle written by Aodh Ó Dochartaigh in Ostend in 1627 for the use of Somhairle Mac Domhnaill, an officer in the Spanish army in the Netherlands.

Dublin Drama League, the (1919–1929), founded by Lennox *Robinson, Ernest Boyd, James *Stephens, and W. B. *Yeats in October 1918, to introduce experimental drama to Dublin audiences. The League used the *Abbey Theatre on Sunday and Monday evenings. The first season opened with Srgjan Tucic's *The Liberators* on 17 February.

Dublin Institute of Advanced Studies, see *DIAS.

Dublin Magazine, The (2 series, 1923–1925 and 1926–1958), a literary magazine edited by Seumas *O'Sullivan, first as a monthly and then a quarterly. Until the appearance of *The *Bell it was the chief literary magazine of Ireland. With the consent of O'Sullivan's widow, the name was later assumed by another journal, formerly called *The Dubliner* (1961–4), and edited by Bruce Arnold and others, 1965–9.

Dublin Penny Journal, The, see George *Petrie.

Dublin Rising, 1916, see *Easter Rising.

Dublin University [TCD], see *universities.

Dublin University Magazine, The (1833–1877), a monthly journal of literature and ideas founded by a group of young Unionist conservatives at or linked with TCD after the passage of *Catholic Emancipation and the Reform Bill. Amongst the founders were John *Anster, Isaac *Butt, Samuel *Ferguson, and Caesar *Otway. It was first edited by Stanford, followed by Butt (1834–8), Charles *Lever (1842–5), and Joseph Sheridan *Le Fanu (1861–9), who was also proprietor, and others. Amongst its contributors were the editors themselves—Lever's *The *Confessions of Harry Lorrequer* was serialized 1837–40—and the major writers of Victorian Ireland: *Carleton, *Ferguson, *Mangan, *O'Donovan, and Sir William *Wilde. Strongly anti-liberal in its views from the start, the journal never deviated from boldly asserting Protestant Unionist convictions.

Dubliners (1914), a collection of fifteen short stories by James *Joyce dealing with the moribund lives of a cast of mostly lower-middle-class characters through pointedly undramatic events chosen to illustrate the crippling effects of family, religion, and nationality. Joyce conceived the idea of a thematically integrated volume, and he continued writing stories in the same 'vivisective' spirit after leaving Ireland in October 1904. In December 1905 he sent twelve stories to the English publisher Grant Richards, but in 1906 Richards repudiated his contract. The collection was rejected by English and Irish publishers, but in 1913 Richards approached Joyce again, and *Dubliners* finally appeared in 1914. In letters to Richards during 1906, Joyce described the governing idea of the collection: 'My intention was to write a chapter of the moral history of my country and I chose Dublin for the scene because that city seemed to me the centre of paralysis.'

Dudley-Edwards, Ruth (1944–), novelist and historian; born in Dublin she was educated at UCD. *The Triumph of Failure* (1977) was an authoritative if critical life of Pádraig *Pearse, followed by a life of James *Connolly (1981), and a history of the *Orange Order, *The*

Faithful Tribe (1999). She also writes crime fiction, which includes *Clubbed to Death* (1992), *Ten Lords A-Leaping* (1995), and *Murder in the Cathedral* (1996).

Duenna, The (1775), a comic opera by Richard Brinsley *Sheridan. Don Jerome, an irascible father, obstinately decides that his daughter Louisa will marry the unpleasant Isaac, a wealthy Jew, though she loves Antonio. The Duenna, Louisa's chaperone, acts as an intermediary between Louisa and Antonio. Isaac is tricked into marrying her, inadvertently bringing the young lovers together.

Dufferin, Lady, see Helen *Blackwood.

Dufferin, Lord, see Frederick *Blackwood.

Duffet, Henry (*fl.* 1676), Irish-born London milliner and author of farces including *The Mock Tempest* (1675) and *Psyche Debauch'd* (1678), parodies of plays by John Dryden and Thomas *Shadwell.

Duffy, Bernard (1882–1952), comic playwright. Born in Carrickmacross, Co. Monaghan, he was educated at TCD, qualifying in law in 1907. His one-act rural comedies were popular at the *Abbey Theatre. In 1916 four of his plays were staged, of which *Fraternity* satirizes the Ancient Order of Hibernians and *The Old Lady* demonstrates how an Irish mother out-manœuvres a chorus-girl. *The Piper of Tavran* (1921) was a one-act folk drama. *Cupboard Love* (1931) was a three-act comedy. Duffy also wrote two novels, *Oriel* (1918) and *The Rocky Road* (1929).

Duffy, Charles Gavan (Sir) (1816–1903), politician, statesman, and author. Born in Co. Monaghan, he was educated at Belfast Academical Institution, 1839–40. He worked on newspapers in Dublin and on *The Belfast Vindicator* before commencing to edit *The *Nation*, which he founded with Thomas *Davis and John Blake Dillon in 1842. In 1843 he issued *The *Spirit of the Nation*, and then edited a further volume called *The Ballad Poetry of Ireland* (1845). In 1844 he sided with William Smith *O'Brien and other *Young Irelanders when the Repeal Association split over Daniel *O'Connell's pacificist principles. In 1850 he founded the Tenant League with others [see *Land League]. He emigrated to Australia in 1855, practised law, and became Prime Minister of Victoria, 1871. He retired to France in 1880 but served as first President of the Irish Literary Society in London [see *literary revival], 1892.

Duffy, James (1809–1871), publisher; born in Co. Monaghan and educated in a *hedge school. He started publishing in Dublin with a chapbook of 'prophecies' called *Boney's Oraculum*, and launched a Popular Sixpenny Library of books tailored to the needs of Irish Catholics, such as *A Pocket Missal* (1838). Charles Gavan *Duffy asked him to take on the reprintings of the *ballad anthology *The *Spirit of the Nation* in 1843. The link with *Young Ireland led to a Library of Ireland series on topics such as Hugh *O'Neill, the Ulster *plantation, and the *United Irishmen. Duffy produced a succession of journals combining literature, politics, and religion: the *Irish Catholic Magazine* (1847–8), the *Fireside Magazine* (1850–4), and the *Hibernian Magazine* (1860–4).

Dun Emer Press, the (1902–1908), founded by Elizabeth Corbet Yeats ('Lollie') and Susan Mary Yeats ('Lily') in the hope of reviving the art of bookprinting. It was later renamed the *Cuala Press.

Dunkin, William (?1709–1765), poet.

Born Dublin, educated at TCD, he was a member of *Swift's literary circle. His *Murphaeid* (1734) deals with the pretensions of a college porter. Collections of his works appeared in 1769–70 and 1774. He is a poet of considerable energy and intelligence.

Dunne, [Christopher] Lee (1934–), novelist. Born in Dublin, he wrote his early fiction while working as a taxi-driver in London. *Goodbye to the Hill* (1965), a lively evocation of working-class life in Dublin, was followed by *A Bed in the Sticks* (1968), *Does Your Mother?* (1970), *Paddy Maguire Is Dead* (1972) and *Ringleader* (1980).

Dunne, Seán (1956–1995), poet. Born in Waterford, he was educated at UCC, before working as a journalist. Collections include *Against the Storm* (1985) and *The Sheltered Nest* (1992). *In My Father's House* (1991) is an autobiographical memoir.

Dunsany, Edward Lord (John Moreton Drax Plunkett, 18th Baron) (1878–1957), dramatist and writer of fiction. Born in London into a Norman-Irish family, he was educated at Eton and Sandhurst, succeeding to the title in 1899. Dunsany created an Eastern fantasy-world in *The Gods of Pegana* (1905). In *Time and the Gods* (1906), *The Sword of Welleran* (1908), *A Dreamer's Tales* (1910), *A Book of Wonder* (1912), and *Tales of Wonder* (1916) he elaborated his mythological world further. Dunsany's first two plays, *The Glittering Gate* (1909) and *King Argimenes and the Unknown Warrior* (1911), were written for the *Abbey Theatre. At the outbreak of the First World War Dunsany joined the Royal Inniskilling Fusiliers and saw action with the 10th (Irish) Division. *Tales of War* (1918) is a collection of stories reflecting his wartime experience in France. Later writings were the yarns told by a highly imaginative sponger, beginning with *The Travel Tales of Mr. Joseph Jorkens* (1931) and concluding with *Jorkens Borrows Another Whiskey* (1954). He helped Francis *Ledwidge find a publisher for *Songs of the Fields*.

Dunton, John (1659–1733), an English bookseller who gives accounts of Ireland after the Restoration in *The Dublin Scuffle* (1699) and *Conversations in Ireland* (1699). He criticizes theatre customs at *Smock Alley from a puritanical standpoint.

Durcan, Paul (1944–   ), poet. Born in Dublin into a legal family with roots in Co. Mayo and related to John MacBride and Maud *Gonne, he was educated at UCC. With the publication of a first collection with Brian *Lynch (*Endsville*, 1967), followed by a first solo collection, *O Westport in the Light of Asia Minor* (1975), he gained a reputation as a witty iconoclast. Among subsequent poetry collections were *Teresa's Bar* (1976), *Sam's Cross* (1978), *Jesus, Break His Fall* (1980), *Ark of the North* (1982), *Jumping the Train Tracks with Angela* (1983), *The Berlin Wall Cafe* (1985), *Going Home to Russia* (1987), *Daddy, Daddy* (1990), *A Snail in her Prime* (1993), *Christmas Day* (1996), and *Greetings to Our Friends in Brazil* (1999). The commitment to the idea of love that lies at the core of his vision is served by a talent for bizarre scenarios. His characteristic tone is a mixture of colloquial intimacy and mocking incantation.

Dutch Interior (1940), a novel by Frank *O'Connor dealing with the interconnecting lives of a group of young men and women in Cork who are frustrated by constraints of family, duty, religion, and most of all poverty.

E

eachtra, echtra, see *tale-types.

Eachtra Bhodaigh an Chóta Lachtna (*Adventure of the Churl of the Grey Coat*), a 16th- or 17th-cent. tale of the *Fionn cycle, in which the Fianna defend Ireland against invaders and receive assistance from the otherworld [see *sídh]. Caol an Iarainn, the son of the King of Thessaly, agrees not to invade Ireland if someone can beat him in a race. The repulsive Churl competes against Caol. They race from Sliabh Luachra in Cork to Howth, and the Churl wins easily. He decapitates Caol and replaces his head backwards.

Eachtra Ghiolla an Amaráin (*Adventures of a Luckless Fellow*), a lengthy poem by Donncha Ruadh *Mac Conmara describing his possibly imaginary emigration to Newfoundland and written about 1750. The goddess Aoibheall of Craig Liath [see *Cúirt an Mheán-Oíche] appears to the poet when he is seasick, and takes him to Acheron.

Eachtra Mhic na Míochomhairle, see *Siabhradh Mhic na Míochomhairle.

Eachtra Thoirdhealbhaigh Mhic Stairn, see Mícheál *Coimín.

Early, Biddy (?1798–1874), famous folk healer. Born at Faha, near Kilanena, Co. Clare, she lived most of her life at Kilbarron, where she died. She accepted gifts rather than money from her patients. Her power was believed to derive from the fairies [*sídh].

early Irish lyrics, highly prized by readers of medieval Irish literature, they often survived by the merest chance. The earliest extant personal poetry in the vernacular dates from the 9th cent. These lyrics often idealize religious life and asceticism; their monotheistic view of creation intensified enjoyment of the beauty of the world, and heightened awareness and acceptance of the transience of human life. Some of the best short lyrics are found in unique copies in the marginalia of religious manuscripts. The famous poem on the monk and his pet cat, 'Pangur Bán', survives in a fragmentary manuscript now in the monastery of St Paul in Unterdrauberg, Austria. With few exceptions, the names of the authors of the early Irish lyrics have not survived.

Easter Rising, the (1916), occurred between Easter Monday, 24 April, and Saturday 29 April, when about 1,800 members of the *Irish Volunteers and the Irish Citizen Army occupied various prominent buildings in central Dublin. Their headquarters was established at the General Post Office in O'Connell St., where Patrick *Pearse read out a proclamation establishing the Provisional Government of the Irish Republic. Besides Pearse, the signatories were Thomas Clarke, Seán MacDiarmada, Thomas MacDonagh, Éamonn Ceannt, James *Connolly, and Joseph *Plunkett—all members of the Military Council of the IRB [see *Fenian movement]. Following an abortive attempt to take Dublin Castle, the main events of the Rising centred on the positions taken up by the insurgents, notably at the GPO (occupied by the main body under Pearse, Connolly, Clarke, and MacDiarmada), the Four Courts (under Edward Daly and Sean Heuston), the College of Surgeons on St Stephen's

Green (under Michael Mallin and Countess *Markievicz), Jacob's Factory (under MacDonagh and Major John Mac-Bride), the South Dublin Union (under Ceannt and Cathal Brugha), and Boland's Mill (under Eamon *de Valera). The countermanding of the rallying call to Volunteers throughout the country by Commander-in-Chief Eoin *MacNeill in the *Sunday Independent* (23 April) restricted outbreaks in the rest of Ireland to isolated places, notably at Ashbourne in Co. Meath. The insurgents' capitulation was effected with the signatures of Pearse, Connolly, and MacDonagh, following the bombardment of the GPO by the gunboat *Helga* in the Liffey. During the week of hostilities 500 people were killed and 2,500 wounded. Of the 90 prisoners sentenced to death in secret court martial, 15 were executed by firing squad between 3 and 12 May. Of signatories and leaders, Eamon de Valera and Markievicz were reprieved on account of their nationality and their gender respectively. After the harsh measures taken against the insurgents the Republican separatism of *Sinn Féin began to eclipse the constitutional nationalism of the Irish Parliamentary Party.

Echtra Airt meic Cuinn (*Adventure of Art Son of Conn*), a story of the echtra *tale-type on the theme of *kingship, involving *Conn Cétchathach, Bécuma Cneisgel, a woman of the *sídh, and a blight remedied by blood sacrifice at *Tara.

Echtra Brain maic Febail, see *Immram Brain maic Febail.*

Echtra Chonlai (*Adventure of Conlae*), one of the earliest examples of the echtra *tale-type. Conlae, son of *Conn Cétchathach, is visited by a woman from the world of the *sídh, where there is perpetual peace. When she invites Conlae to join her, his father

summons a *druid who casts a spell that repels her. Torn between love of his people and love for the woman, Conlae finally leaps into her crystal boat and they leave together.

Echtra Chormaic i dTír Tairngiri (*Adventure of Cormac in the Land of Promise*). Manannán mac Lir of the *sídh visits *Cormac mac Airt at *Tara, bearing a silver branch with three golden apples. Cormac grants the visitor three requests. Manannán asks for Cormac's wife and two children, whom he takes with him to the Land of Promise. Cormac follows them there and witnesses the threefold nature of truth.

Echtra Fergusa maic Léti (*Adventure of Fergus son of Léite*), an early Irish saga, dealing with a dispute between Fergus, a prehistoric King of Ulster, and the King of *Tara. When it is settled Fergus dives into Loch Rudraige and encounters a sea-monster from which he flees but later defeats.

Echtra Láegairi (*Adventure of Laegaire*), a 9th-cent. tale of the echtra *tale-type in which Laegaire, with the help of the *sídh, wins back his wife in the otherworld. Laegaire stays in the world of the sídh, where he marries.

Echtra mac nEchach Muigmedóin (*Adventure of the Sons of Echu Muigmedóin*), a 12th-cent. tale of the *historical cycle dealing with the right of the Uí Néill to the kingship of *Tara. *Niall Noígíallach, the ancestor of the Uí Néill, is reared in exile by the poet Tórna. When he returns to Tara he surpasses his brothers in feats of valour, thus securing the *kingship.

Echtra Nerai (*Adventure of Nerae*), a story of the echtra *tale-type, set at Cruachan in Connacht during *Samhain [see *sídh]. Nerae goes searching for a drink at the request of a dead man who has been hanged, and whom he carries on his back. Nerae witnesses the destruction of Cruachan by the fairy host in a vision, and follows them into the mound.

Edgeworth, Maria (1767–1849), novelist. The third child of Richard Lovell *Edgeworth, she was born at Black Bourton near Reading and educated there and in London, moving with her father to the family estate at Edgeworthstown, Co. Longford, in 1782. She taught the children of his later marriages, sharing his progressive ideas on education. Her early writings, encouraged by him, led to The Parent's Assistant (1796), a series of children's stories in the didactic manner. This was followed by Practical Education (2 vols., 1798), a joint work recommending learning through recreation. Her children's series was continued in Early Lessons (1801), Moral Tales (1801), concluding with Harry and Lucy (1825). In 1800 Maria published *Castle Rackrent, the earliest regional novel in English. Belinda (1810) is a satiric novel in which the wicked Lady Delacour is reformed. Essay on Irish Bulls (1802) was written with her father, Popular Tales and The Modern Griselda (both 1805) without him. After a period in Paris she composed Tales of Fashionable Life, the first series (1809) containing *Ennui (vol. I); Almeria, Madame de Fleury, and The Dun (vol. II); and Manœuvring (vol. III). The second series, also three volumes, contained Vivian, Emilie de Coulanges, and The *Absentee (1812). *Ormond (1817) is a novel innovative in its exploration of the effect of reading on the hero. She edited and completed her father's Memoirs (1820). In later years she was largely occupied with rectifying her brother's mismanagement of the Edgeworthstown estate, and in relieving victims of the *Famine. Of her later novels, Harrington (1817) reflects the lack of her father's enthusiastic

encouragement, while Helen (1834) presents a depressing view of the prospects for Irish society. Her last work, Orlandino (1848), was written for the Poor Relief Fund. See Marilyn Butler, Maria Edgeworth (1972).

Edgeworth, Richard Lovell (1744–1817), improving landlord and author; born in Bath, and educated at TCD and Oxford. In England he was part of a circle of progressives including Humphry Davy and Josiah Wedgwood. Throughout his life he worked on mechanical and engineering problems, constructing a turnip-cutter and a velocipede, as well as devising methods of reclaiming bogs. He returned to Ireland in 1782, settling at the family estate in Edgeworthstown, Co. Longford. Married four times, he had twenty-two children of whom Maria *Edgeworth was the eldest daughter. A liberal in politics, he disparaged the *Orange Order. As an MP he voted twice against the *Union, not because he disagreed with it but because he despised the corrupt methods used to pass it. Interested in education, he collaborated with his daughter in Practical Education (2 vols., 1798) and Essays on Professional Education (1809), as well as the Essay on Irish Bulls (1802). He also wrote an Essay on the Construction of Roads and Carriages (1813). Maria completed the Memoirs of Richard Lovell Edgeworth (1820) after his death.

Egan, Desmond (1936–   ), poet and publisher. Born in Athlone, Co. Westmeath, and educated at St Patrick's College, Maynooth, he taught until 1987. He founded the Goldsmith Press in 1972, and edited Era, an occasional literary magazine, from 1974. His poetry collections include Midland (1972), Leaves (1974), Siege! (1976), Athlone? (1980), Seeing Double (1983), Collected Poems (1983, 1984), Poems for Peace

(1986), *A Song for my Father* (1989), *Peninsula* (1992), and *Famine* (1997). *The Death of Metaphor* (1990) is a collection of prose essays and meditations.

Egan, Pierce (1772–1849), author of burlesques and sports guides, probably born in Ireland. His first work, *The Mistress of Royalty* (1814), was a satire on the Prince Regent. He set a trend in popular writing with his slangy *Life in London, or The Day and Night Scenes of Jerry Hawthorn, Corinthian Bob, and Bob Logic* (1820–1), later issued as *Pierce Egan's Life in London and Sporting Guide* (1824). In 1821 Egan published *Real Life in Ireland, or the Day and Night Scenes, roving rambles, sprees, blunders, bodderation and blarney of Brian Boru, Esq., and his elegant friend Sir Shawn O'Dogherty . . . by a Real Paddy* (1821), an extreme exercise in *stage-Irish caricature.

Egerton, George (pseudonym of Mary Chavelita Bright, née Dunne) (1859–1945), writer of fiction. Born in Melbourne, Australia, she was educated in Ireland, training as a nurse in London before running away to Norway with Henry Higginson. Returning to England, she married Clairmonte Egerton, then the literary agent Reginald Golding Bright. She made her reputation with *Keynotes* (1893), a volume of stories with a dust-jacket by Aubrey Beardsley, followed by the collections *Discords* (1894), *Symphonies* (1897), and *Fantasias* (1898), all characterized by a view of marriage as 'legal prostitution'.

Eglinton, John (pseudonym of William Kirkpatrick Magee) (1868–1961), literary controversialist and editor of *Dana. He was born in Dublin, educated at TCD, and worked at the National Library of Ireland, 1895–1921. In 'The De-Davisisation of Irish Literature' (1902), he defended *Anglo-Irish literature against cultural nationalists. He

attacked nationalist ideology in the collections *Bards and Saints* (1906) and *Anglo-Irish Essays* (1917). His *Irish Literary Portraits* (1935) contains retrospective verdicts on the figures of the *literary revival. He published *A Memoir of AE* (1935).

Éigse (1939–), a bilingual academic journal of Irish language and literature established at UCD with Gerard *Murphy as founding editor.

Éire, see *Ériu.

Éire-Ireland (1966–), a journal of Irish studies, established by the Irish American Cultural Institute at St Paul, Minnesota, under the editorship of Eóin McKiernan.

Elizabeth I, Queen of England (1533–1603), the daughter of Henry VIII by his second wife Anne Boleyn. When her father died in 1547 her half-brother Edward, then 10 years old, acceded to the throne. He was followed in 1553 by Elizabeth's Catholic half-sister Mary, daughter of Catherine of Aragon. Mary, aided by her husband, Philip of Spain, osught to restore the Catholic faith. When Mary Tudor—known in English history as 'Bloody Mary' because of her persecution of Protestants—died in 1558, Elizabeth became Queen, to popular jubilation. She led England back to the Reformation, and became head of both Church and State. Elizabeth was excommunicated by Pope Pius V in 1570. She determined to proceed with the Reformation in Ireland [see *Protestantism] through the artful exploitation of contending claimants to traditional Gaelic lordships. In 1580 a force of Spanish and Italians, sent to assist the rebellion in Munster led by James Fitzmaurice Fitzgerald, entrenched themselves at Smerwick in Kerry (Port del Oro), but were ruthlessly put to the sword by Arthur, Lord Grey de Wilton, to whom Edmund *Spenser acted as secretary. Elizabeth then sought to pacify Munster by means of *plantation. When in 1588 the Armada foundered off the western and northern coasts of Ireland Hugh *O'Neill lent assistance to survivors, and throughout the 1590s he moved towards outright rebellion against the English Crown. Elizabeth sent her favourite, Robert Devereux, Earl of Essex, to subdue O'Neill, but Essex made a truce and then returned to England without permission. Charles Blount, Lord Mountjoy, succeeded Essex as Elizabeth's commander in Ireland, defeating O'Neill and a Spanish force at the Battle of *Kinsale in December 1601. The *Flight of the Earls from Lough Swilly in 1607 completed the Elizabethan conquest of Ireland. In 1592 she provided a charter for TCD [see *universities in Ireland] as part of her effort to spread the Reformation. She also subsidized the preparation of an Irish fount for the printing of Protestant devotional writing in Irish. Although some *bardic poets adventitiously praised Elizabeth on her accession and after, as the new century progressed she was increasingly demonized in Gaelic *political poetry. This hostility was built upon in the *Jacobite poetry and *folklore of the 18th cent. and after, Henry VIII and Elizabeth I featuring as creatures lost in sensuality and error.

Ellis (or Eyles), Hercules (?1810–1879), anthologist and poet. Born in Dublin and educated at TCD, he issued *The Songs of Ireland* (1849) and *Romances and Ballads of Ireland* (1850).

Ellmann, Richard (1918–1987); literary scholar and biographer. Born in Michigan, and educated at Yale and TCD, where he completed doctoral work on W. B. *Yeats leading directly to the publication of *Yeats: The Man and the Masks* (1948, rev. 1979), to be followed in 1954 by *The Identity of Yeats* (1954). His magisterial life of James *Joyce (1959, rev. 1982) established a new standard for Irish literary biography. *Oscar *Wilde* (1988) gave expression to Ellmann's interpretation of his subject as an essentially modern spirit. He was Goldsmith Professor of English Literature at Oxford from 1970 until his death.

Emain Macha, the capital of the Ulaid (Ulstermen) in early Irish writing. Pseudo-historical tradition assigns its foundation to the 7th cent. BC and its collapse to about the 4th cent. AD, when the Ulaid dynasty was driven into the east of the province. The legendary site is identified with Navan Fort, a large earthwork approximately 2 miles west of Armagh, which Macha [see Irish *mythology] marked out with her breast-pin (eo-muin), having won the sovereignty of Ireland. A series of round houses, presumably associated with the regional aristocracy, gave way in the 1st cent. BC to the erection of a massive circular temple or hall. This was subsequently buried under a stone cairn and covered with an earthen mound. The literary associations of Emain Macha centre on its pivotal position as the capital of the Ulaid in the *Ulster cycle, like Camelot in the Arthurian tales. The site had achieved the status of a national monument by the Middle Ages. It was visited by *Brian Bóroime in 1005.

Emancipation, Catholic, see *Catholic Emancipation.

Emigrants of Ahadarra, The: *A Tale of Irish Life* (1848), a novel by William *Carleton. The plot concerns Bryan M'Mahon's love for Kathleen Cavanagh, who rejects him because he is suspected of apostasy. Her pious suspicions arise from an intrigue engineered by the profligate Hycy Burke who wants Kathleen for himself. Hycy's deceit is revealed to the returning absentee landlord, and he is sent abroad, whereas the M'Mahons had looked the more likely emigrants.

Emily's Shoes (1992), a novel by Dermot *Bolger which tells how Michael MacMahon, whose father is dead, is traumatized when his mother also dies. He is taken care of by his aunt Emily, who wears red shoes to the funeral, which he fetishizes.

Emmet, Robert (1778–1803), revolutionary, born at St Stephen's Green, Dublin. He was a prominent member of the Historical Society at TCD, and a student member of the *United Irishmen. In the year following the United Irishmen's Rebellion of 1798, a warrant was issued for his arrest but not enforced. In France he met his brother Thomas Addis Emmet and planned with him another rising. On 23 May 1803 Emmet led an abortive attack on Dublin Castle and the brutal killing of Lord Chief Justice Lord Kilwarden. Emmet went into hiding, and was apprehended at Harold's Cross by Major Sirr. He was convicted of treason, hanged, and beheaded. The literary myth of Robert Emmet begins with his dock speech, variously reported. His relationship with Sarah *Curran was romantically celebrated by Thomas Moore.

'Encounter, An', a story in James *Joyce's *Dubliners (1914), written in 1905. Three schoolboys plan a day of 'miching' (truancy), inspired by comic-book adventures, but only the narrator and Mahoney appear at the rendezvous. They are approached by a man who interrogates them about their girlfriends, who then masturbates.

Endgame (1957), a play by Samuel *Beckett, produced in French in London and first performed in the author's English translation in New York, 1958. Hamm, blind and paralysed, is cared for by his still mobile servant Clov. Hamm's parents, the legless Nagg and Nell, live in dustbins. Outside their room everything seems dead.

Enemy Within, The (1962), a play by Brian *Friel, dealing with the conflict St Columba (*Colum Cille) experiences in exile on the island of Iona between his religious calling and the worldly demands of family and home.

Ennis, John (1944–), poet. Born in Coralstown, Co. Westmeath, he was educated at UCC, UCD, and Maynooth before teaching in Waterford Institute of Technology. His first collection, Night on Hibernia (1976), revealed narrative speed and intellectual concentration. His interests and range seek expression in longer poems such as 'Orpheus' in Dolmen Hill (1977) or Arboretum (1990), which describes his marriage of idealism and reality. Other collections include In a Green Shade (1991), Down in the Deeper Helicon (1995) and Telling the Bees (1995).

Ennui (1809), a novel by Maria *Edgeworth, set in 1798, the year of the United *Irishmen Rebellion. Lord Glenthorn, a bored aristocrat, leaves fashionable London society for his Irish estate. He discovers that he is not the rightful holder of the Glenthorn title and surrenders it to Christy Donoghue. Donoghue burns the castle down with a bedside candle, dying in the blaze. Lord Glenthorn resumes his position and responsibility.

Enright, Anne (1962–), writer of fiction; born in Dublin and educated at TCD and at Vancouver, she worked as a producer at *RTÉ before issuing her first collection The Portable Virgin (1991), followed by the novel The Wig my Father Wore (1995).

Envoy (1949–51), a monthly review of literature and art, filling the place vacated by The *Bell. Founded and edited by John Ryan (1925–1992) with Valentin *Iremonger as poetry editor, it saw itself as a link between Irish and European writing.

Eóganacht, a Munster dynasty of the early historic period with branches also in Connacht. The eponym of the Eóganacht is Eógan Már, represented in the *genealogies as their remote ancestor, but the dynasties generally regarded as Eóganacht all descend from the later figure, *Conall Corc, the founder of Cashel [see *political divisions]. By 972 the kingship of Munster had passed to a new dynasty, Dál Cais, ruled first by Mathgamain (d. 976) and then by his brother, *Brian Bóroime.

epiphany, a term used by James *Joyce—and widely adopted since—to describe a sudden manifestation when the significance of some social or psychological experience is made clear. In particular, the term refers to some seventy records of such moments of perception written down by Joyce between 1901 and 1904.

Érainn, an early people recorded by Ptolemy, and located in the south of Ireland.

Ériu (Mod. Ir. Éire), goddess among the Tuatha Dé Danann [see Irish *mythology], who serves as eponym for Ireland. In *Lebor Gabála Érenn it is related that she and her sisters, Banba and Fótla (whose names are also traditionally used for Ireland), married the Milesian invaders Mac Gréine, Mac Cécht, and Mac Cuill.

Eriugena, John Scottus (?820–?880), theologian. Born in Ireland—hence 'Ériu-gena' and 'Scottus' [see *Irish language]—he was at the Court of Charles II (the Bald) (823–77), near Laon in France from about 845, where he taught grammar, dialectics, and Greek. He became involved in disputes over the Eucharist and predestination, writing a treatise, De Predestinatione, in 851. Charles commissioned Eriugena, whom he especially valued for his knowledge of Greek, to translate the work of Pseudo-Dionysius the Areopagite, a Christian Neoplatonist honoured in France as St Denis, from Greek into Latin. Between 862 and 866 he wrote his principal work, De Divisione Naturae or Periphyseon, a dialogue in five books, attempting to reconcile Neoplatonic ideas of emanation with Christian teachings on the Creation.

Ervine, St John [Greer], born John Irvine (1883–1971), dramatist and novelist. The son of deaf-mutes in east Belfast, he moved to London, joining the Fabian Society out of admiration for George Bernard *Shaw. His first play, Mixed Marriage (1911), a study of bigotry in his native city, was produced at the *Abbey Theatre after a meeting with W. B. *Yeats, and in 1915 he became manager of the theatre. During his time there he directed his own play, John Ferguson (1915), a study in Presbyterian rectitude, before his conflict with the company caused him to join the Dublin Fusiliers. He lost a leg from wounds in France and settled in Devon. Throughout the 1920s he wrote ephemeral West End comedies such as Anthony and Anna (1926) and The First Mrs. Fraser (1926). Of his realistic Belfast fiction one novel, The Foolish Lovers (1920), tells of a young man's affair with a policeman's wife, while another, The Wayward Man (1927), deals with low-life experience in New York. The plays Boyd's Shop (1936) and Friends and Relations (1941) present a warmer picture of his province.

Essay on Irish Bulls, see Richard *Edgeworth.

Essay towards a New Theory of Vision, An (1709), George *Berkeley's first major work propounds the view that the proper objects of sight are not material objects but light and colour.

Esther Waters (1894), a novel by George *Moore concerning a Plymouth Sister whose stepfather drives her from home into service. At Woodview, a famous racing stable, she enjoys the support of her mistress, but becomes pregnant by William Latch, a fellow servant. She finds employment as a wet-nurse. Esther manages to raise her child. Latch comes back into her life and she goes to live with him. When Latch dies Esther returns to Woodview.

Étaín, see *Tochmarc Étaíne.

Eureka Street (1996), a novel by Robert McLiam *Wilson, set in the pre-ceasefire Belfast of the *Troubles, it tells of the adventures of Chuckie Lurgan, entrepreneur of the war-zone. Acidly comic, it registers the human cost of violence.

Eva Trout (1969), Elizabeth *Bowen's last novel, on the theme of innocence and corruption. After an orphaned childhood and an irregular upbringing, Eva forms an attachment to her boarding-school teacher, acquires a deaf-mute child by illegal means, and trails around America. The child kills Eva with a revolver left in the luggage.

Evans, E[myr] E[styn] (1905–1989), geographer. Born in Shrewsbury and educated at the University of Wales, Aberystwyth. He was appointed lecturer at QUB in 1928 and founded the Institute of Irish Studies there in 1968. In *The Personality of Ireland: Habitat, Heritage and History* (1973) Evans took Irish historians to task for ignoring social and cultural history, and especially the evidence of the environment, in their narratives. He regarded the northern landscape as a 'common ground' where natives and settlers had interacted. His publications include *Irish Heritage* (1942), *Irish Folkways* (1957), *Prehistory and Early Christian Ireland* (1966).

'Eveline', a story in James *Joyce's *Dubliners* (1914). A girl keeping house for her father meets a sailor who asks her to leave Ireland with him. She agrees to go, but her courage fails her at the moment of departure.

Evelyn Innes (1898), the first of a pair of novels by George *Moore which tell the story of an opera singer, taking for theme the relationship between sensuality and religious feeling. In the sequel, *Sister Teresa* (1901), Evelyn leaves the convent to look after her father, but returns when he dies to help the nuns pay convent debts with recitals in the chapel.

Except the Lord (1953), a novel by Joyce *Cary in the second trilogy, the others being *Prisoner of Grace* (1952) and *Not Honour More* (1955). Chester Nimmo recounts his impoverished childhood and early manhood in dissenting West Country England. Years later, Nimmo resumes his political career, encouraged by Mary Latter (see *Prisoner of Grace*).

Exile of the Sons of Uisliu, see *Longes mac nUislenn.

Exiles (1918), a play by James *Joyce, set among the Dublin intelligentsia and written in the manner of Gerhart Hauptmann. The plot concerns the return of Richard Rowan with his wife Bertha after his admirer and correspondent Beatrice Justice has persuaded her cousin Robert Hand, his former friend and now a noted journalist, to secure the Chair in Modern Languages for him in UCD.

Expugnatio Hibernica, see *Giraldus Cambrensis.

Factory Girls (1982), Frank *McGuinness's first play, staged at the Peacock [see *Abbey Theatre] and based on the experiences of the playwright's mother in a Donegal shirt factory.

Fagan, James Bernard (1873–1933), playwright. Born in Belfast, he was educated at Clongowes Wood and TCD, then joined the theatrical companies of Sir Frank Benson and Max Beerbohm. He enjoyed success with a Pepysian comedy, *And So to Bed* (1926), as also with *The Improper Duchess* (1931).

Fahy, Francis A[rthur] (1854–1935), song-writer; born near Kinvara, Co. Galway. A contributor to *The *Nation*, *United Ireland*, and the *Shamrock*, his popular pieces include 'Little Mary Cassidy' and 'The Ould Plaid Shawl'. He was a founding member of the Southwark Irish Literary Club (1883). See *Irish Songs and Poems* (1887), and *The Ould Plaid Shawl and Other Songs*.

Faillandia (1985), a novel by Francis *Stuart. Following his wife's death, Gideon Spokane returns to Faillandia with his lover Kathy. The State is politically and spiritually bankrupt, with both political parties pandering to the Church. Gideon and his friends establish a subversive magazine offering alternative views of life, literature, and religion.

Fáinne an Lae, see An *Claidheamh Soluis.

fairies, see *sídh.

Fairy Tales and Traditions of the South of Ireland, see Thomas Crofton *Croker.

Faith Healer (1979), a play by Brian *Friel consisting of four long monologues spoken by three characters: Frank Hardy, an itinerant Irish faith healer; his wife Grace; and their Cockney manager Teddy. Each tells of a precarious existence spent travelling throughout Ireland, Scotland, and Wales, ending with an account of Frank's violent death at the hands of local farmers in Ballybeg, Co. Donegal.

Falconer, Edmund (pseudonym of Edmund O'Rourke) (1814–1879), poet, playwright, and theatre manager. Born in Dublin, he wrote the libretto *The Rose of Castile* (1858) for Michael *Balfe's opera company. He also published longer poems including *Man's Mission* (1852), *The Bequest of My Boyhood* (1863), and *O'Ruark's Bride: The Blood Speck in the Emerald* (1865), while *The Cagot* (1856) was one of several full-length verse plays. His *Peep o'Day or Savourneen Deelish* (1861), based on Banim's *John Doe* (1825), gives a sentimental treatment to the theme of *secret societies. *Eileen Oge, or the Hour Before Dawn* (1871) is a melodrama.

Fallon, Padraic (1905–1974), poet. Born in Athenry, Co. Galway, he was educated in Roscrea, before joining the Customs and Excise Department. In 1939 he was posted to Wexford and remained there until retirement in 1970. He published little in his lifetime. Apart from Austin *Clarke, whose sensuality he shares, he was amongst the few writers in English to engage seriously with Gaelic literary tradition during the 1940s and 1950s. His exuberant verse plays *Diarmuid and Grania* (1950) and *The Vision of Mac Conglinne* (1953), broadcast on Radio Éireann [see *RTÉ], successfully dramatize Gaelic material. Like Clarke, Fallon experimented with the use of Irish *metrical patterns. He made a special study of Antoine *Raiftearaí, wrote a series of poems about him, and brilliantly translated 'Mary Hynes'. The devotional strain in his work is blended with eroticism in poems such as 'Assumption' and 'The Poems of Love'.

Fallon, Peter (1951–), poet and publisher. Born in Germany to Irish parents who moved to Co. Meath in 1957, he was educated at TCD. He founded the Gallery Press in 1970, which became a major poetry imprint, and issued *Among the Walls* (1971), *Coincidence of Flesh* (1973), *The First Affair* (1974), *Victims* (1978), *Winter Work* (1983), *The Men and Weather* (1987), *Eye to Eye* (1992), amongst others.

False Delicacy (1768), a comedy by Hugh *Kelly. Lord Winworth loves Lady Betty Lambton, who loves him in return but is too delicate to admit it. On the rebound he seeks Miss Marchmont; she accepts because she thinks Lady Betty wants her to.

Famine, the ('the Great Hunger') (1845–1848), a national disaster caused by the devastation of the potato crop by the fungus *phythopthera infestans*, reducing yields to two-thirds of normal levels in 1845 and to about one-fifth in 1846. The 1847 crop was healthy but only one-tenth of the pre-famine acreage had been planted, while the fungus reappeared in 1848. Failure on this scale wiped out the main food supply of well over half the population, pushed up the price of other foods, and caused the collapse of a tillage economy based on the intensive use of labour paid for with small plots of potato ground. Sir Robert Peel's Tory administration was able to respond effectively to the partial failure of 1845

by importing maize ('Indian meal') for sale at controlled prices. The Whig Government that took office in June 1846 sought to meet the much greater losses of the next year with public works, replaced from Spring 1847 by the distribution of free food from soup kitchens; but these measures proved wholly inadequate. Best estimates are that around one million people died, mainly from typhus and other diseases, while over a million emigrated between 1845 and 1851. To later nationalists, the Famine was proof of the failure of the Act of *Union. John *Mitchel's *The Last Conquest of Ireland (Perhaps)* (1861) accused government not only of indifference to Irish misery but of actively pursuing a genocidal policy. The Famine is a central component of the historical self-awareness of the Irish people and a recurrent theme on which William *Carleton, Patrick *Kavanagh, Liam *O'Flaherty, Walter *Macken, and others have all founded works in English. Writings in Irish memoirs reflecting the experience of the Famine include Peadar *Ó Laoghaire, *Mó Scéal Féin* (1915).

Famine (1937), a historical novel by Liam *O'Flaherty dealing with the Great *Famine. The older Kilmartins live in the Black Valley and follow custom and tradition, but when the young couple, Martin and his wife Mary, take over the running of the house and farm, the domestic conflict is played out against the growing ravages of potato blight.

Fand, see *Serglige Con Culainn.

Fardorougha the Miser, or *The Convicts of Lisnamona* (1839), William *Carleton's first novel. Fardorougha's son, Connor O'Donovan, and Una O'Brien are deeply in love, provoking the jealousy of Bartle Flanagan, a Ribbonman who implicates Connor in an agrarian crime [see *secret societies]. To his parents' great distress, Connor is transported to a penal colony.

Farquhar, George (?1677–1707), dramatist. Born near Derry, he attended TCD from 1694. Encouraged by Robert *Wilkes, he left for London, taking with him the text of his first play, *Love and a Bottle (1698), which was produced at Drury Lane. His next, The Constant Couple (1699), ran for fifty-three nights, and led to a sequel, Sir Harry Wildair (1701). In the interim he produced The Inconstant (1699). The *Twin Rivals (1702) was the last of his plays to première at Drury Lane. In 1704 he joined the army, and went on duty as a recruiting officer in the Shrewsbury region. From October 1704 to July 1705 he was in Ireland recruiting in Kildare and Dublin. The *Recruiting Officer (1706) was not successful, and Farquhar was reduced to borrowing from Wilkes while writing The *Beaux' Stratagem (1707).

Farrell, Bernard (1939–), playwright. Born in Sandycove, Co. Dublin, he was educated by the Christian Brothers at Monkstown Park and worked as a clerk until a first play, I Do Not Like Thee Doctor Fell (1979), dealing with encounter groups, was staged at the *Abbey Theatre. His subsequent work includes Canaries (1980), about holidays abroad; All in Favour Said No! (1981), concerned with strike action; Petty Sessions (1983) and All the Way Back (1985), about unemployment; as well as Say Cheese (1987), The Last Apache Reunion (1993), Stella by Starlight (1996), and Kevin's Bed (1998). A popular dramatist, his themes reflect the values of a suburban society wary of idealism.

Farrell, M. J., see Molly *Keane.

Farrell, Michael (1899–1962), novelist. Born in Carlow, he studied medicine at UCD but spent some time in prison during the *Anglo-Irish War for possession of illegal documents. He went to the Belgian Congo, returning to Ireland in the early 1930s, abandoning medical studies for broadcasting. He became the amateur drama correspondent for The *Bell. He is remembered for a novel, *Thy Tears Might Cease (1963), a long work which attained mythic status in Dublin literary circles during composition and was edited by Monk *Gibbon after his death.

Farren, Robert, see Roibeárd *Ó Faracháin.

Farrington, Conor (1928–), playwright; born in Dublin and educated at TCD. He worked with an English touring company until he joined the Radio Éireann [see *RTÉ] repertory company in 1955. Among early radio plays were Death of Don Juan (1951) and The Good Shepherd (1961). His stage plays include The Last P.M. (1964), and Aaron Thy Brother (1969), a historical verse drama based on the *Emmet rebellion. The Lifted Staff (1991) was the first in a cycle of three historical plays on the *Norman invasion.

Fatal Revenge, The, or The Family of Montorio (1807), the first novel by Charles Robert *Maturin, published in three volumes under the pseudonym 'Dennis Jasper Murphy'. Set in late 17th-cent. Italy, it tells how Orazio dedicates himself to vengeance against his usurping brother, the Count of Montorio.

Fate of the Children of Lir, see *Three Sorrows of Storytelling.

Fate of the Children of Tuireann, see *Three Sorrows of Storytelling.

Fate of the Children of Uisneach, see *Longes mac nUislenn and *Three Sorrows of Storytelling.

Father Butler (1828), a polemical novella by William *Carleton. Originally published pseudonymously in Caesar *Otway's *Christian Examiner* (Aug.-Dec. 1828), it tells of a young man who is forced into the priesthood by superstitious parents after being cured of an illness by the sinister 'Father A—'.

Father Connell (1840), a novel by Michael *Banim, offering an idealistic portrait of an Irish country priest. Venerable, saintly, and kind, Father Connell's concern centres on an orphan, Neddy Fennell, whose high spirits seem to frustrate his hopes for him.

Father Prout, see Francis Sylvester *Mahony.

Father Ralph (1913), an autobiographical novel by Gerald *O'Donovan about a priest's self-discovery and his growing disillusionment with his role. Fr. Ralph leaves the priesthood in order to find his religion, and is rejected by his mother.

Faulkner, George (1699–1775), printer and publisher. Born in Dublin, he served a printer's apprenticeship, then formed a bookselling partnership with James Hoey (d. 1774) in 1726, and started *Faulkner's Dublin Journal* two years after. He was soon adopted by Swift as his printer; the first edition of his works went through the press in 1735. In 1744 he issued an ambitious and successful *Universal History* in seven-volume folio, by which time Swift was praising him as 'the Prince of Dublin Printers'. He published the attack on Swift by Lord Orrery [John *Boyle] in 1751, and was heavily criticized for doing so. In 1758 he became involved with Charles *O'Conor the Elder and John *Curry in the campaign for Catholic Relief [see *Catholic Emancipation]. Faulkner's monument is the edition of Swift's *Works* issued in twenty octavo volumes in 1772.

Faustus Kelly, a play by Myles na Gopaleen [Flann *O'Brien] first produced at the *Abbey Theatre in 1943. Kelly, chairman of an unspecified Urban District Council, makes a pact with the Devil in the local by-election.

Fay, Frank (1871–1931), actor. Born in Dublin, he was a member of his younger brother W.G. *Fay's National Dramatic Society which merged with the Irish Literary Theatre to become the Irish National Theatre Society, the originating body of the *Abbey. Fay was an excellent tragic actor with a superb speaking voice. With his brother he left the Abbey in 1908, after which he worked in America and in England.

Fay, W[illiam] G[eorge] (1872–1947), actor. Born in Dublin and educated at Belvedere College, he became an electrician and an amateur actor and director, forming the Irish National Dramatic Company in 1902 with the aim of producing plays in Irish and English. Attracting the attention of W. B. *Yeats, the company produced *Cathleen Ni Houlihan* in 1902 before joining forces with the Irish Literary Theatre in 1903 to become the Irish National Theatre Society with Yeats as President [see *Abbey Theatre]. Fay established himself as a comic actor of genius, playing Christy Mahon in The *Playboy of the Western World* and Martin in The *Well of the Saints*. As director and stage-manager he suffered the disapproval of Miss *Horniman for his nationalist attitudes, and left the Abbey in 1908 with his brother Frank [*Fay] to produce Irish plays in America.

Fearful Joy, A (1949), a novel by Joyce *Cary, dealing with the affairs and marriages of Tabitha Baskett and her children between the 1890s and the Second World War.

Feast of Bricriu, The, see *Fled Bricrenn*.

Feast of Lupercal, The (1957), a novel by Brian *Moore set in religiously polarized 1950s Belfast. Diarmuid Devine, a Catholic teacher in his old school, is disastrously jolted out of his slide into middle-aged bachelorhood by an overheard comment on his sexual primness.

Feasta (1948–), an Irish-language monthly founded under the auspices of the *Gaelic League, reflecting the renewal of literary cultural activity among Irish-speakers which took place in the late 1930s.

Feiritéar, Piaras (?–1653), poet and soldier of Hiberno-Norman stock. In the *Rebellion of 1641 he was entrusted with arms and ammunition by Lord Kerry and empowered to raise 600 men. He shifted allegiance to Finín Mac Cárrthaigh and the Gaelic interest, however, capturing Tralee Castle in 1642 and holding it until 1652. He was arrested at Castlemaine and hanged in Killarney. As a poet, Feirtéar used both syllabic and accentual amhrán metres [see Irish *metrics]. His love poetry draws upon the courtly love traditions of Europe.

Feis Tighe Chonáin (*Feast at Conán's House*), a late medieval tale in the *Fionn cycle of the *bruidhean type. When Fionn and his warrior band (fian) are hunting in the south-west of Ireland, he and Diorraing are separated from them at nightfall. They are given hospitality for the night in the fairy fort [see *sídh] of Conán, whose daughter Fionn asks for in marriage, and wins.

Félire Oengusso, see *martyrologies.

Fenian cycle, see *Fionn cycle.

Fenian movement, the, a secret revolutionary organization more properly known as the Irish Republican Brotherhood (IRB), and established by James *Stephens in 1858, with an American counterpart in the Fenian Brotherhood founded by John *O'Mahony, who borrowed the name of the warrior troop in the *Fionn cycle. The movement adopted the pledge-bound format of the *secret societies, adding a cellular structure with a Supreme Council and a Head Centre. Its weekly organ, *The Irish People*, was edited by John *O'Leary and Charles Joseph *Kickham from 1861 to its suppression in 1865. The Fenian Rising eventually mounted on 5 March 1867, following Stephens's deposition, was easily suppressed. In 1879 *Parnell and a section of the IRB leadership agreed on a programme of joint action known as the New Departure. In about 1907 the Irish branch of the movement was revived by Thomas Clarke, one of the *Easter 1916 signatories, who planned the Rising with Patrick *Pearse and others. Thereafter the IRB continued as a secret organization within *Sinn Féin and the *IRA. Under the influence of Michael *Collins the Supreme Council supported the Anglo-Irish Treaty [see *Anglo-Irish War].

Ferguson, Sir Samuel (1810–1886), poet and scholar. Born in Belfast, he attended the Belfast Academical Institution and TCD. In 1833 he contributed 'A Dialogue Between the Head and Heart of an Irish Protestant' to the newly founded *Dublin University Magazine*, a classic statement of divided loyalties. In 1834 he contributed to the *Dublin University Magazine* a series of four review articles on *Hardiman's *Irish Minstrelsy* (1831), attacking the editor for scholarly sedition, and making his own vivid verse translations of poems such as 'Cashel of Munster' and 'Uileacan Dubh Ó'. 'The Fairy Thorn' was published in *Blackwood's* in 1834; also in that year he began publishing a series of historical fictions called *Hibernian Nights' Entertainments* in the *Dublin University Magazine*. In 1838 he contributed to *Blackwood's* 'Father Tom and the Pope', a burlesque on Irish *Catholicism. By 1845, when he published 'The Vengeance of the Welshman of Tirawley', a longer poem based on a feud in medieval Co. Mayo, he had established a reputation as an antiquarian and scholar. In Dublin he formed literary friendships with William *Carleton, George *Petrie, James Clarence *Mangan, John *O'Donovan, Eugene *O'Curry, and in particular Thomas *Davis, at whose death in 1845 he wrote a formal elegy. He was a founding member of the Protestant Repeal Association in 1848, and in that year he married Mary Catherine Guinness of the brewing family. Throughout the 1850s he worked on his epic poem *Congal* (1872). *Lays of the Western Gael and Other Poems* (1864), Ferguson's first collection of poems, contained many of his best-known pieces. Ferguson became QC in 1859 and Deputy Keeper of the Public Records of Ireland in 1867, and was knighted in 1878. *Poems* (1880) collects his shorter pieces written since 1864. *Shakespeare Breviates* (1882) were adaptations of Shakespeare for drawing-room performance. Ferguson's *Ogham Inspirations in Ireland, Wales, and Scotland* (1887) was published posthumously. See Peter Denman, *Samuel Ferguson: The Literary Achievement* (1990).

festivals. The Celtic year is divided into two seasons: winter, beginning at *Samhain, and celebrated on 1 November; and summer, beginning at Bealtaine (*Beltaine) or Cétshamhain, and celebrated on 1 May. These halves are further divided by the quarter-days marking spring and autumn: Imbolg, Christianized as St *Brigit's day and celebrated on 1 February; and Lúnasa (*Lughnasa), celebrated on 1 August.

Fetches, The (1825), the first contribution by John *Banim to *Tales by the O'Hara Family* (1st series). It is a morbid story concerning Irish *folkloric belief in the 'Fetch' or supernatural double, which is said to appear as an omen of impending death.

Fiacc, Padraic (pseudonym of Patrick Joseph O'Connor) (1924–), poet, born in Belfast. His family emigrated to New York, where he was educated at St Joseph's Seminary, and he returned to Belfast in 1946. His first collection of poems, *Woe to the Boy* (1957), was followed by *By the Black Stream* (1969) and *Odour of Blood* (1973). *The Wearing of the Black* (1974) was a controversial anthology; further collections were *Nights in the Bad Place* (1977), *The Selected Padraic Fiacc* (1979), and *Missa Terribilis* (1986).

Fianna (fian, fianaighecht, fiannaíocht), see *Fionn cycle and *Fionn mac Cumhaill.

Fiche Bliain ag Fás (*Twenty Years A-Growing*) (1933), an autobiography by Muiris *Ó Súilleabháin, conveying the daily life of the Great Blasket Island with remarkable freshness and immediacy.

Field Day, a theatrical company founded in Derry in 1980 by the playwright Brian *Friel and the actor Stephen Rea with the intention of establishing the city as a theatrical centre; and an associated literary movement which set out to redefine Irish cultural identity in the last quarter of the 20th cent. They were soon joined on the board of Field Day by Seamus *Deane, David Hammond (the film-maker), Seamus *Heaney, and Tom *Paulin. Field Day offered to writers and readers a 'fifth province of the mind' in which potential identities for Ireland could be explored outside the constraints of existing traditions. It first produced Friel's *Translations in 1980 in Derry. In 1982 Friel's The *Communication Cord farcically re-interrogated many of the issues of Translations. In 1986 Tom *Kilroy's *Double Cross dealt with Irish identity as refracted through the characters of Brendan Bracken (the Irish-born secretary to Winston Churchill) and William Joyce, 'Lord Haw-Haw' (the pro-German wartime broadcaster). Kilroy soon afterwards became a director of Field Day. Friel's *Making History (1988) explored how historians can be prisoners of their own narratives. In 1990 Seamus Heaney provided a version of Sophocles' Philoctetes as The Cure at Troy. Tom Kilroy's The Madam MacAdam Travelling Show (1992) was a comic study of the nature of playing. A Field Day pamphlet series was inaugurated in 1983. Tom Paulin's A New Look at the Language Question proposed the recognition of *Hiberno-English as an authentic language system. Heaney's Open Letter was a verse protest against his recent inclusion in a collection of 'British' poetry; and Deane's Civilians and Barbarians explored the destructive simplifications implicit in those terms. Thereafter, pamphlets continued to be published in groups of three. The largest of its critical undertakings was the publication of the three-volume Field Day Anthology of Irish Writing (1991), edited by Deane, presenting Irish writing in Irish, Latin, and English from earliest times. Field Day publications continued into the new century in collaboration with Cork University Press.

Field, The (1965), a play by John B. *Keane. First staged at the Olympia Theatre, it tells the story of 'the Bull' McCabe, a Kerry farmer who murders a rival over the auction of a field.

Figgis, Darrell (pseudonym 'Michael Ireland') (1882–1925), author and statesman. Born in Dublin and brought up in India, he was involved with Erskine *Childers in the Howth gun-running in 1914 and later became a member of Dáil Éireann [see *Irish State] in 1918. Besides writings such as The Historic Case for Irish Independence (1920), he published poetry such as A Vision of Life (1909), an *Abbey play (Queen Tara, 1913), and five novels, including The House of Success (1921) and The Return of the Hero (1923). He is Ompleby in Eimar *O'Duffy's The Wasted Land (1919).

file, see *áes dána.

Finbar, St (Fionnbar, 'white head'; otherwise Finnian), patron saint of Cork though historically connected with Moville church on the Ards peninsula and the nearby monastery of Bangor, Co. Down. Although he is unlikely to have visited Cork, his cult developed there and prominent religious sites in the county such as Gougane Barra are also associated with him.

fine, a word for family or kin in early Irish society, recognized in the laws as a male descent group whose members had common rights and reciprocal obligations. It did not signify a 'tribe'. There were four kin-groups: gelfhine, descendants of a common grandfather, first cousins and closer; derbfhine, descendants of a common great-grandfather, second cousins and closer (including the gelfhine); iarfine, descendants of a common great-great-grandfather, third cousins or closer (including gelfhine and derbfhine); and indfhine, descendants of a common great-great-great-grandfather, fourth cousins or closer (including the three others). The derbfhine was the maximal lineage: only four generations could be alive together. A man lived within his gelfhine.

Fingal Rónáin (*Rónán's Slaying of a Kinsman*), a saga of the *historical cycle in early Middle Irish. It tells how Rónán mac Aeda, King of Leinster kills his beloved only son, Máel-Fhothartaig.

Finn and His Companions (1892), a volume of four stories from the *Fionn cycle adapted for children by Standish James *O'Grady.

Finnegans Wake (1939), a novel by James *Joyce written in a highly innovative 'dream-language' combining multilingual puns with the stream-of-consciousness technique developed in *Ulysses*. The title is taken from an Irish-American ballad about Tim Finnegan, a drunken hod-carrier who dies in a fall from his ladder and is revived by a splash of whiskey at his wake. It also suggests that *Fionn mac Cumhaill will return to be punished once more for his recurrent sins. The structure of the work is largely governed by Giambattista Vico's division of human history into three ages (divine, heroic, and human), to which Joyce added a section called the 'Ricorso', or return. It also systematically reflects Giordano Bruno's theory that everything in nature is realized through interaction with its opposite. The central figures of the *Wake* are Humphrey Chimpden Earwicker (HCE), Anna Livia Plurabelle (ALP), Shem the Penman, Shaun the Post, and Issy—respectively the parents, sons, and daughter living at the Mullingar Inn in Chapelizod, Co. Dublin. In a sense, however, these are not characters at all but aspects of the Dublin landscape, with the Hill of Howth and the River Liffey serving as underlying symbols for male and female in a world of flux. Other recurrent characters are the four old men, collectively called Mamalujo and modelled on the four evangelists and also an apostolic group of twelve who feature as

clients in the pub, or members of a jury. The narrating voice of individual sections can generally be identified with one or other member of this polymorphous cast. In 'Shem the Penman', the autobiographical section of the work, Joyce describes the work as an 'epical forged cheque' made up of 'once current puns, quashed quotatoes, messes of mottage'. The narrative line of *Finnegans Wake* consists of a series of situations relating to the sexual life of the Earwicker family. HCE perpetrates a sexual misdemeanour in the Phoenix Park. ALP defends him in a letter written by Shem and carried by Shaun. The 'litter' is retrieved by a hen scratching in the midden. The boys endlessly contend for Issy's favours. HCE grows old and impotent, is buried, and revives. Aged ALP prepares to return as her daughter Issy to catch his eye again; and the book ends with an unfinished phrase (' . . . along the') flowing into the first words of the first paragraph ('riverrun . . . '). *Book I*. 'The Fall' retells the story of Tim Finnegan against mythical and historical backgrounds ranging from the Tower of Babel to the Wall Street Crash. *Book II*. 'The Mime of Mick, Nick and the Maggies' is a matinée performance in 'the Feenicht's Playhouse' based on children's games and full of Dublin theatrical lore. In 'Night-lessons' the children are at their homework studying a classroom textbook to which Shem and Shaun add rubrics in the margins. 'Scene in the Pub' features two television plays: 'The Norwegian Captain' is a love-story concerning a hunchback sailor and the daughter of a ship's chandler; the other, 'How Buckley Shot the Russian General' is based on a Crimean story told by Joyce's father. In 'Mamalujo' the romance of Tristan and Isolde is narrated by the four old men in the guise of seagulls hovering above the lovers' boat. *Book III*. 'The Four Watches of Shaun' describes the passage of Shaun the Post along the

Liffey in a barrel. Shaun's censorious attitude combines freely with a prurient interest in sexual matters. The 'Yawn' chapter is a seance or an inquisition. Lying at the centre of Ireland at the Hill of Uisneach in Co. Westmeath, Shaun reveals a treasure-trove of Irish culture whose contents are transmitted in a radio broadcast involving a welter of voices. *Book IV*. The 'Ricorso' is a triptych with St Kevin and St Patrick in the side positions and St Laurence O'Toole at the centre. Anna Livia's letter defending HCE is given its fullest statement. The *Wake* ends with her soliloquy. Joyce began *Finnegans Wake* in autumn 1922 by accumulating material in a notebook known as Buffalo Notebook. Many episodes appeared as separate publications between 1924 and 1932, during which time the book was known as 'Work in Progress' and its final title kept a secret. Joyce frequently compared the *Wake* to another complex Irish literary production, the *Book of Kells*. If *Finnegans Wake* is about creation on a theological scale, its characteristic amalgam of sadness and laughter marks it as a comic masterpiece.

See Samuel *Beckett et al., Our Exagmination round His Factification for an Incamination of Work in Progress* (1929); and John Bishop, *Joyce's Book of the Dark* (1986).

Fionn cycle (Fíanaigecht or Fiannaíocht) or the Ossianic cycle, a body of stories centred on the exploits of the mythical hero *Fionn mac Cumhaill, his son *Oisín (whence 'Ossianic'), and other famous members of the fian (warrior-band) of Fionn, collectively known as the Fianna, who hunt, fight, conduct raids, and live an open-air nomadic life. This set of literary conventions reflects a feature of early Irish society in that such bands of warriors did live outside the structures of that society while retaining links with it. One of the characteristics of the cycle is its frequent celebration of the beauty of nature, and birdsong, mountain, river, and seashore are frequently evoked. The Fionn cycle developed in Munster and Leinster and may reflect a desire on the part of medieval story-tellers and scribes in these areas to develop a counterbalance to the *Ulster cycle. However the tales spread throughout Ireland and Scotland. By the 12th cent. the literary shaping of a very old tradition of oral Fionn tales was firmly established and took one of its most impressive forms in *Acallam na Senórach*, a compendious gathering of Fionn stories and poems uniting pagan and Christian elements, though not without strain. The cycle is set in the 3rd cent. AD, but, in the tradition, a number of the Fianna survive into Christian Ireland, providing the theme of the *Acallam*. Here St *Patrick welcomes and blesses the recital of Fionn lore by *Caoilte, but in the *lays that developed from the 12th cent. onwards exchanges between Oisín and Patrick become more acrimonious, the saint's dogma being countered by defiance. James *Macpherson based his Ossianic pieces on these lays. Prose tales developed too, such as *Eachtra Bhodaigh an Chóta Lachtna, *Bruidhean Chaorthainn, *Cath Finntrágha, and *Feís Tighe Chonáin. In these stories the Fianna retain their roles as protectors of Ireland; Fionn's divinatory powers are in evidence; and there is a marked responsiveness to natural beauty.

Fionn mac Cumhaill, hero of the *Fionn or Ossianic cycle of tales, leader of a band of warriors (fian) under the High King *Cormac mac Airt. Fionn's troop, known as the Fianna, assumed pre-eminence in Irish storytelling tradition, and accounts of their exploits came to be known as Fianaigecht or Fiannaíocht. As a member and leader of a fian, a band of nomadic hunters and warriors, Fionn was to some extent an outlaw; yet he was also a poet, diviner, and sage. His father, Cumhall, was a leader of the Tara fian in the service of *Conn Cétchathach, High King of Ireland, while his mother was Muirne (or Muireann), daughter of a *druid, so that his parentage combined warrior and visionary elements. As well as being endowed with physical courage, Fionn possesses a gift of special insight which he can summon by biting his finger. Thereafter he finds himself inspired with imbas (great knowledge) whenever he puts the damaged finger into his mouth. By chewing his thumb to the marrow—an activity known as teinm laída (chewing the pith)—or by putting it under his déad feasa (tooth of knowledge) he can attain the state of wisdom. When Cormac mac Airt becomes King, Fionn serves him and protects Ireland from foreign invasion, as narrated in *Cath Finntrágha. Noted members of Fionn's warrior-band were Caoilte mac Rónáin, and *Conán mac Mórna the buffoon. Fionn had his headquarters at the Hill of Allen in Co. Kildare (Almu or Almha). In the main tale of the Fionn cycle, *Tóraigheacht Dhiarmada agus Ghráinne, Fionn appears as a vindictive and jealous older man, initially threatened by the youthful Diarmuid but eventually getting Gráinne back. According to Aided Finn (Death of Fionn), Fionn is killed by the five sons of Urgriu after he has been weakened in combat. In folk tradition he is still alive and ready to help Ireland in times of need. Fionn ('bright', 'fair') has been seen as a variation on Lug, a divinity of the Tuatha Dé Danann; he is also associated through his name with light, and linked to Welsh Gwynn, as well as with the Celtic origins of Vienna. See Joseph Falahy Nagy, The Wisdom of the Outlaw (1985).

Fionn mac Cumhaill, pseudonym of Maghnas *Mac Cumhaill.

Fir Bolg, see *mythological cycle and *Lebor Gabála Érenn.

First Love (in French as Premier Amour, 1970; in English, 1973), a story by Samuel *Beckett. Written in French in 1946, it was not published until much later, being based on an affair with a woman still living at the time.

Fís Adamnáin (Vision of Adamnán), a saga of the vision *tale-type. It relates a journey to heaven and hell supposedly made by *Adamnán, Abbot of Iona (d. 704).

Fitzgerald, Barbara (née Gregg) (1911–1982), novelist. Born in Cork, she lived much in Africa. We Are Besieged (1946), a *big house novel dealing with the burning-out of an Anglo-Irish family, was followed by Footprint upon Water (1983—but written in 1955).

Fitzgerald, Desmond (?1888–1947), revolutionary and playwright; born in London, he was a poet in his early manhood, before joining the IRB (see *IRA) in Co. Kerry. He fought in the GPO during the *Easter Rising for which he was imprisoned. On his release in 1918 he rejoined the struggle for independence in the *Anglo-Irish war, and supported the *Treaty side in 1922. He served in politics until 1943. A play The Saints (1919) was produced at the *Abbey Theatre, and he also wrote political philosophy. His son, Garrett *Fitzgerald became Taoiseach 1981–82 and then 1982–87.

Fitzgerald, Lord Edward (1763–1798), revolutionary. A son of the first Duke of Leinster, he saw military service during the Anglo-American War. A member of the *United Irishmen, he was one of the delegates in the negotiations with the French authorities to enlist their support. He died in June 1798 of wounds received while resisting arrest.

Fitzgerald, Garret (1926–), statesman and author; born in Dublin into a political and literary family, he was educated at Belvedere College and at UCD. He worked in a managerial role with Aer Lingus, then as an economic consultant; he became Chairman of the Irish Council of the European Movement in 1959 and in that year also became a lecturer in economics at UCD. A member of the Irish Senate 1965–69, he became a member of the Dáil (see *Irish State) in 1969, then Minister for Foreign Affairs, 1973–77, and led his party Fine Gael 1977–87. He was Taoiseach 1981–82 and 1982–87. In the latter period he negotiated the Anglo-Irish Agreement, signed with the British government in 1985. His published works include: *Planning in Ireland* (1969), *Towards a New Ireland* (1972), *The Israeli-Palestinian Issue* (1990), and *All in a Life* (1991), an autobiography.

Fitzgerald, Gerald, 8th Earl of Kildare, see *Gearóid Iarla Mac Gearailt.

Fitzgerald, Percy Hetherington (occasional pseudonym 'Gilbert Dyce') (1834–1925), sculptor and man of letters. Born in Co. Louth, he was educated at Stoneyhurst, and practised law before settling as a man of letters in London. His numerous works included popular lives of Charles Lamb, David Garrick, and the Kembles. He issued many novels, of which the first, *Mildrington The Barrister* (1863), was serialized in the *Dublin University Magazine*. His best-known was *Bella Donna* (1864).

Fitzmaurice, Gabriel (1952–), poet; born in Moyvane, Co. Kerry, educated there and at Mary Immaculate College, Limerick. He worked as a teacher in Moyvane from 1975. Poetry collections include: *Rain Song* (1984), *Nocht* (in Irish, 1989), *Dancing Through* (1990), *The Father's Part* (1992), *Ag Síobshúil chun an Rince* (1995), and *Giolla na nAmhrán* (1998). Poetry for children includes: *The Moving Stair* (1993) and *Nach Iontach Mar Atá* (1994). *The Flowering Tree* (1991) was an anthology of Gaelic poetry with translations, co-edited with Declan *Kiberd.

Fitzmaurice, George (1877–1963), playwright; born near Listowel, Co. Kerry, the son of a clergyman, and the tenth of twelve children. After working in a bank he joined the Land Commission and lived in Dublin in increasingly eccentric isolation. His earliest works were short stories, collected as *The Crows of Mephistopheles* in 1970. His first staged play, *The *Country Dressmaker*, attracted comparisons with *Synge and Lady *Gregory when it appeared at the *Abbey in 1907. His originality was confirmed with *The *Pie-Dish* (1908) and *The *Magic Glasses* (1913), plays combining peasant realism, satire, symbolism, and fantasy. *The Dandy Dolls* was rejected by W. B. *Yeats in 1913 but published in *Five Plays* (1914), which also includes *The Moonlighters*, a melodrama written with John *Guinan. Only one more of his plays reached the Abbey stage, '*Twixt the Giltinans and the Carmodys* (1923).

Fitzpatrick, W[illiam] J[ohn] (1830–1895), biographer. Born in Dublin and educated at Clongowes Wood, he became Honorary Professor of History to the RHA, 1876. Fitzpatrick wrote about the informers in the Rebellion of 1798 [see *United Irishmen] in books such as *Lord Edward *Fitzgerald and his Betrayers* (1869). His *Secret Service Under Pitt* (1892) was based on government payment records. Other works include studies of Charles *Lever (1879) and Lady *Morgan (1860), and an edition of Daniel *O'Connell's *Correspondence* (1888).

Flanagan, Thomas (1923–), Irish-American critic and novelist. Born in Connecticut and educated at Amherst and Columbia, he was Professor in the University of California at Berkeley and New York State University. In 1958 he published *The Irish Novelists 1800–1850*, for many years the standard work. In 1979 he issued a novel, *The Year of the French*, dealing with the events of the French invasion at Killala. *The Tenants of Time* (1988) reconstructs the social and political conditions linking the Fenian Rising of 1867 to the Land War of the 1880s. In 1994 Flanagan added a third volume to his historical series *At the End of the Hunt*, set in the *Troubles, 1919–23.

Flannery, James (1936–), writer, singer, and man of the theatre; born in Hartford, Connecticut, he was educated at Yale and at TCD before teaching at Ottawa, Rhode Island, and Emory Universities. His *W.B. Yeats and the Idea of a Theatre* (1976) expounded *Yeats's dramatic theory and analysed his practice. He was Director of the Yeats International Theatre Festival at the *Abbey Theatre 1989–93, directing fourteen of Yeats's plays himself during that time. *Dear Harp of My Country* (1997) was a study with recordings of his own renditions of them of the Irish melodies of Thomas *Moore, sung in a faithful and dramatic manner.

Flann mac Lonáin (?–896), poet, described in the *Annals of the Four Masters* as the 'Virgil of the Irish race', born probably in the east Clare/west Tipperary area. A distinguished poet in his own day, his verse was cited as an exemplar in metrical tracts.

Flann Mainistrech (Flann of Monasterboice) (?–1056), a poet and historian described in the *Annals of Ulster* as the 'supreme exponent of Latin learning and professor of historical lore in Ireland'. He was head of the school at *Monasterboice in Co. Louth, where his son was to become Abbot. Flann was one

of what Eoin *MacNeill called the Irish synthetic historians, who grafted Irish *genealogy and historical lore to the Christian teaching on world history. His surviving poems deal with the destruction of Troy, the Túatha Dé Danann [see *mythology], and the kings of *Tara.

Flecknoe, Richard (?–1678), poet and playwright. Said to have been born in Ireland and a Jesuit, he was the butt of an anti-Catholic lampoon by Andrew Marvell ('Flecknoe, An English Priest at Rome', *c.*1645) and later figured as the 'Monarch of Dullness' in Dryden's satire on Thomas *Shadwell (*MacFlecknoe*, 1682). His *Ariadne* (1654) appears to have been the first English opera. Flecknoe made a journey from Lisbon to Brazil, 1646–50, and afterwards wrote *A Relation of Ten Years Travels in Europe, Asia, Africa, and America* (1656).

Fled Bricrenn (*Feast of Bricriu*), a tale of the *Ulster cycle concerning the mischief-maker Bricriu Nemthenga (Poison-Tongue). Bricriu invites the Ulster heroes to a feast and maliciously exploits the convention, attested for the Continental *Celts by Posidonius, that the choicest portion is given to the greatest hero. He promises it in turn to *Cú Chulainn, Lóegaire Buadach, and *Conall Cernach, and creates a parallel contention among their wives. A churl delivers a bizarre challenge: he will allow one of the heroes to behead him on condition that the roles be reversed on the following night. Loegaire and Conall accept but renege when their turn arrives. Cú Chulainn, however, offers his head to the giant, who spares him and proclaims him victor.

Fled Dúin na nGéd (*Feast of Dún na nGéd*), a tale of the *historical cycle, recounting the background to the battle fought at Moira, Co. Down, in AD 637. The Ulster king Congal Claen revolts against Domnall, the Uí Néill king at *Tara, having been insulted at a feast at Dún na nGéd. Samuel *Ferguson's *Congal* (1872) is based on John *O'Donovan's 1842 edition of the tale and its sequel *Cath Maige Rath*.

Flight of the Earls. On 14 September 1607 Hugh *O'Neill, Earl of Tyrone, Rory O'Donnell, Earl of Tyrconnell, son of the dead Red Hugh *O'Donnell, and Cúchonnacht Maguire of Fermanagh, son of Hugh [see Eochaidh *Ó hEódhasa] set sail for Europe from Rathmullen, on Lough Swilly, Co. Donegal. Although both O'Neill and O'Donnell were installed as Earls at their submission in 1603, they suffered continuing harassment from the English authorities and their Irish rivals. In early October they arrived in France, proceeding to *Louvain and thence to Rome. Their journey across Europe was chronicled by Tadhg *Ó Cianáin.

Flood, Henry (1732–1791), politician; born in Kilkenny and educated at TCD and at Oxford. Flood entered the Irish Commons in 1761 and quickly established himself as an accomplished orator. He withdrew to a Westminster seat after 1783 and accepted a sinecure in 1775 where his career languished.

Florence Macarthy (1818), a novel by Lady *Morgan, addressing the contemporary state of Irish social and political culture. While the heroine is wooed by a kidnapped heir, the tyrannical Crawley family of land agents exercises despotic power over the neighbourhood, backed by a private army.

Flower, Robin [Ernest William] (1881–1946), Gaelic scholar. Brought up in Leeds and educated there and at Oxford, he became Deputy Keeper of Manuscripts at the British Museum in 1929, having issued *Catalogue of Irish Manuscripts in the British Museum* (vols. i and ii, 1926; vol. iii, 1953), bringing to completion the work of Standish Hayes *O'Grady. Flower formed a strong connection with the Blasket Islands and encouraged Irish speakers there to record their memories and folklore. Besides collecting Peig Sayers' stories, he issued a translation of Tomás *Ó Criomhthain's *An t*Oileánach* as *The Islandman* (1929). *The Western Island or The Great Blasket* (1945) is a memoir.

Flowering Cross, The (1950), a novel by Francis *Stuart. Mistakenly accused of being a communist agitator, Louis Clancy, a Canadian sculptor who has survived the horrors of war in Germany, is held in the prison of a French mining town. There he is drawn to a blind girl, Alyse, to whom he returns after betraying her, full of remorse and hope.

folklore. A very rich body of folklore survives in Ireland, owing to the country's position on the western periphery of Europe, an innately conservative element in Irish tradition, and the importance which that tradition attaches to oral narration. Irish folk narrative may be divided into the following categories: native hero-tales of mythical or literary origin; adaptations of international folk-tales; oral legends which purport to describe occurrences in ordinary life; and numerous minor forms such as verse anecdotes and accounts of personal experiences. The hero-tales and longer types of international folk-tale are told quite formally and are found almost exclusively in Irish. Shorter or more conversational genres, such as ghost and fairy legends and a wide variety of humorous lore, flourish to an equal extent in Irish and English. Folk renditions of stories from the *Ulster cycle

have their sources in *manuscript
retellings from the post-medieval
period. The most popular of these have
been accounts of the youthful deeds of
*Cú Chulainn and of Deirdre (see
*Longes mac nUislenn). Folklore concern-
ing *Fionn mac Cumhaill is very common. The international wonder-tale,
telling of events in a world long past,
was the dominant genre in the repertoire of the Irish story-teller. Hundreds
of versions of these wonder-tales have
been collected in Ireland, such as the
story of the dragon-slayer who rescues
a princess and upstages a dishonest
rival. There were many forms of short
oral legends, involving accounts of
marvellous events interrupting normal
life; or occurrences with a supernatural
origin, such as the lore of rivers which
claim their victims once a year. The
rich fairy lore of Ireland [see *sídh] is
the subject of many oral legends. Stories about Christ followed European
tradition, for the most part; and
legends concerning saints derived from
Irish and European medieval literature,
and from local devotion. The lore of the
saints *Patrick, *Brigit, and *Colum
Cille was widespread. *Cormac mac
Airt, *Brian Bóroime, and more recent
figures such as Oliver *Cromwell and
Daniel *O'Connell figure in the
legends, while more localized lore concerns warriors, outlaws, tyrants,
sportsmen, clergymen, and individuals
such as Biddy *Early, the healer from
Co. Clare. Especially popular were stories about poets, such as Eoghan Rua *Ó
Súilleabháin; and humorous anecdotes
regarding a variety of learned individuals, such as Jonathan *Swift or
John Philpot *Curran. Much folklore
gathered about *festivals, such as
*Lughnasa, *Samhain, and Easter. The
collection of Irish folklore began in the
early 19th cent. Thomas Crofton
*Croker's anthologies were based on
material gathered in Munster. Patrick
*Kennedy's collections had a more

accurate style and greater precision.
The American-Irish anthropologist and
linguist Jeremiah *Curtin scrupulously
collected a wide variety of narrative
from native Irish speakers. W. B.
*Yeats and Lady *Gregory collected
and published material from *Hiberno-
English narration. William *Larminie
and Douglas *Hyde presented the original Irish of their informants as well
as reliable translations. Séamus *Ó
Duilearga and his colleagues in the
*Irish Folklore Commission brought
high standards of linguistic accuracy to
the field of study. See Seán *Ó Súilleabháin, A Handbook of Irish Folklore
(1942).

folksong in English, see *ballads in
Ireland.

folksong in Irish comprises a body
of material very great in extent and
impressive in quality. Singing and
story-telling were the most common
forms of entertainment in Gaelic culture, and singers were praised for their
skills of delivery and interpretation; for
their powers of ornamentation in the
style known as *sean-nós; and for their
ability to involve the listeners in the
mood and atmosphere of the song.
That dramatic elements were significant in performance is suggested by
the traditional form of request: 'abair
amhrán', 'say a song'. The folksongs of
the Irish are amongst the richest folk
legacies in Western Europe, combining
as they do music and poetry of great
antiquity. The *Irish language, unlike
*Hiberno-English, did not on the whole
accommodate itself to the *ballad.
Such narrative as there is, is often
uncertain, and emphasis is placed
instead on emotion and situation. As in
other folk traditions, by far the most
common type of folksong in Irish concerns love. In many a male persona
is entranced by the beauty of the girl
he loves (e.g. 'An Chúilfhionn', 'Bean

Dubh an Ghleanna'). He often implores the girl to go away with him, leaving the family who oppose him (e.g. 'Uileacán Dubh O'). In other songs it is the girl who proclaims her love, and sometimes she is deserted (e.g. 'Domhnall Óg', 'An Droighneán Donn'), or married to an old man (e.g. 'An Seanduine Dóite'). 'Róisín Dubh', originally a love-song, was later given a political slant, so that by the time James Clarence *Mangan translated it as 'My *Dark Rosaleen' the female figure had become a symbol of nationhood. In this way the love conventions of heightened emotion were often transposed to patriotic verse (e.g. 'Droimeann Donn Dílis'). Another class of songs deals with specific historical occurrences. Thus 'Cill Chais' laments the destruction of the Butlers' seat at Kilcash, near Clonmel, Co. Tipperary. 'Seán Ó Duibhir an Ghleanna' is a song remembering the dispossession of a Gaelic landowner in 17th-cent. Munster. Religious songs concerning Christ's passion or the sufferings of the Virgin Mary are common. There are songs on local tragedies such as drownings and accidents, and from the 18th cent. onwards an increasing number deal with failed uprisings, hangings, transportation, and emigration. There are satiric songs mocking meanness and tyranny, songs in praise of drink and drinkers, while other pieces celebrate heroic feats of valour or of sport. Macaronic songs, in Irish and English, are frequent; they deal humorously with a variety of subjects and the English is quaintly ornamented to match the often inflated poetic style of the Irish. See Hugh Shields, *A Short Bibliography of Irish Folk Song* (1985).

Fomoire [Fomorians], see *mythological cycle and *Lebor Gabála Érenn.

Fool of Quality, The; *or the History of Henry Earl of Moreland* (1765–70),

by Henry *Brooke. His was the first extended treatment of childhood education in English fiction, dealing with the raising of the hero to be a good landlord. A blend of sensibility and religion with humour reminiscent of *Tristram Shandy*, it was admired by John Wesley, who produced his own abridgement.

Foras Feasa ar Éirinn (*Groundwork of Knowledge of Ireland*), the most influential of all works of *Gaelic historiography, written by Geoffrey *Keating between c.1618 and 1634. Keating's account of the history of Ireland from earliest times down to the coming of the *Normans and the death of Rory O'Connor in 1198 draws upon the *annals, medieval Irish synthetic history as in *Lebor Gabála*, and the lore of the *Ulster, *Fionn, *mythological, and *historical cycles. Mixing legend and history, he provides a coherent narrative based upon traditional materials. His intention was to vindicate Gaelic society against the ignorance of Tudor historians such as *Spenser and *Stanyhurst [see *Anglo-Irish chronicles]. His clarity of style and story-telling ability are everywhere in evidence. A Latin translation was published at St Malo by John *Lynch in 1660, while an English version was issued in 1723 by Dermod *O'Connor.

Fortunes of Colonel Torlogh O'Brien, The (1847), a novel by Joseph Sheridan *Le Fanu, first serialized anonymously in the *Dublin University Magazine*. It is set in the period of the *Williamite Wars and tells the story of Grace, daughter of the planter Hugh Willoughby, who is in love with Torlogh O'Brien, a Catholic.

Foster, Roy [Robert Fitzroy] (1949–); historian and man of letters. Born in Waterford and educated there and at TCD. He lectured at London

University, becoming Carroll Professor of Irish History at Oxford in 1991. Besides his *Modern Ireland* (1988), summarizing the tendency of historical revisionism, he published the first volume of the authorized biography of W.B. *Yeats in 1997.

Four Masters, see *Annals of the Four Masters*.

Fox, George (1809–?1880), poet; born in Belfast and educated at TCD. Fox's only known work is 'The County of Mayo', a much-anthologized translation of a 17th-cent. Irish original by Thomas Flavell on the theme of exile.

Francis, M[ary] E. (pseudonym of Mrs Francis Blundell) (1859–1930), novelist. Born in Killiney Co. Dublin, and educated in Brussels. After her husband's death she wrote fifty novels, some set in Ireland and some in Lancashire. *The Story of Dan* (1894) and *The Story of Molly Dunne* (1913) are among her Irish novels. *Molly's Fortune* (1889–90) tells a tale of cosmopolitan adventure. *Dark Rosaleen* (1915) is a tragic story of mixed marriage in north-west Ireland. *Miss Erin* (1898) argues the necessity of Irish rebellion against English social convention.

Francis, Sir Philip (1740–1818), author of the *Junius Letters*. Born in Dublin and educated at TCD, he wrote the brilliant series of invectives against the Duke of Grafton's Ministry which appeared under the name 'Junius' in *The Public Advertiser* (21 Jan. 1769–21 Jan. 1772; printed 1812) while working in the War Office. In 1773 Francis went to India and on his return assisted Edmund *Burke in his effort to impeach Hastings.

Free State, see *Irish State.

Freedom of the City, The (1973), a play by Brian *Friel. Although set in 1970, it recalls Bloody Sunday in Derry, 1972, and the ensuing Widgery Report. When an unauthorized civil-rights march is dispersed three demonstrators take refuge in the Mayor's Parlour in Derry's Guildhall. When they leave the building with hands above their heads they are shot dead by British soldiers. Parallel to this, a tribunal examines the events and exonerates the security forces.

Freeman's Journal, The (1763–1923), a political newspaper founded by Charles Lucas (1713–1771), an apothecary and politician who set out to win privileges for the Protestant guilds of 'freemen'. Notable contributors to *The Freeman's Journal* included Henry *Grattan. In the time of Daniel *O'Connell, the paper broadcast the policies of Irish nationalism under the editorship of Michael Staunton (1788–1870). *The Freeman* supported John *Redmond in the reconstituted Irish Parliamentary Party under William Brayden's editorship (1892–1916). The paper supported the Treaty Party [see *Anglo-Irish War] and its premises were destroyed by the *IRA in a raid of March 1922.

French, [William] Percy (1854–1920), writer of *ballads. Born in Cloonyquin, Co. Roscommon, he was educated at Foyle College and TCD where he qualified as a civil engineer. He became a surveyor of drains in Co. Cavan. When he was laid off in 1887 he became editor of the comic journal *The Jarvey*. He then turned to musical comedy, co-authoring *The Knights of the Road* (1888). This venture launched him as a song-writer and performer of his own works. These include *The First Lord Liftinant and Other Tales* (1890) and *The Irish Girl* (1918), a comic opera. His songs, such as 'Are Ye Right There Michael' and 'Come Back, Paddy Reilly', have charm, because of their use of *Hiberno-English, and a satiric edge.

Friel, Brian (1929–), dramatist; born in Omagh, Co. Tyrone, and educated at St Columb's College, Derry, Maynooth (which he left after two years), and St Joseph's College, Belfast. He worked as a teacher in Derry until 1960. In 1967 he moved to Donegal, first to Muff and in 1982 to Greencastle. Two collections of short stories, *The Saucer of Larks* (1962) and *The Gold in the Sea* (1966), display a strong sense of place. *The *Enemy Within*, produced by the *Abbey Theatre in 1962, revealed his command as a dramatist. *Philadelphia, Here I Come!* (1964) confronted traditional Irish subject-matter in a stimulating and original form. A series of related plays explored the theme of love, *The *Loves of Cass McGuire* (1966), *Lovers* (1967), and *Crystal and Fox* (1968). They were followed by *The Mundy Scheme* (1969), a political satire, and *The Gentle Island* (1971), whose ironic title masks a violent confrontation between myth and reality. In the early 1970s the *Troubles in the North of Ireland drew Friel into an artistic response, resulting in two contrasting plays, *The *Freedom of the City* (1973), a direct reaction to contemporary events, and *Volunteers* (1975), a more symbolic treatment of Irish history. In *Living Quarters* (1977) he turned to the family unit in dissolution, a theme given a historical dimension in *Aristocrats* (1979). The four monologues used in *Faith Healer* (1979) testify to his search for a dramatic technique that can marry content and form. With the foundation of *Field Day Theatre Company in 1980 Friel's career took a new turn. The first production was his own *Translations* (1980), a play about the mapping of Ireland by the Ordnance Survey in the 1830s which became a landmark in the debate over historical revisionism. There followed two more

Field Day productions of Friel plays: Chekhov's *Three Sisters* (1981), and *The *Communication Cord* (1982), a sister play to *Translations*. Friel's next play for Field Day, *Making History* (1988), showed him relating questions of myth and history to cultural and ideological debate. With *Dancing at Lughnasa* (1990) a new play by Friel was premièred by the Abbey for the first time since 1979. In content this play represents a return to an autobiographical strand in his work. In *Wonderful Tennessee* (1993) three couples confront their own and each other's failures against a backdrop of nature with hints of ritual and mystery. *Molly Sweeney* (1994), at the *Gate *Theatre, returns to the dramatic structure of *Faith Healer*, where different voices offer their constructions of events. *Give Me Your Answer, Do!* (1997) returns to the familial tensions of *Aristocrats*, save that here the realm of imagination is pitted against necessity. The play emits a strange aloof calm and radiance. Friel's work explores the tensions between tradition and change in individuals and in society. His plays investigate the inner spaces that shape the belief and passion which determine outer actions. See Alan Peacock (ed.), *The Achievement of Brian Friel* (1992).

Froude, J[ames] A[nthony] (1818–1894), English historian and author of *The English in Ireland in the Eighteenth Century* (1872–4), in which he argued that the Irish are an inferior people. *The Two Chiefs of Dunboy* (1889) is a novel set in Cork in the 1770s, illustrating his notion of the struggle between English order and the barbarous Irish.

Fudge Family &c., see Thomas *Moore.

Furlong, Thomas (1794–1827), poet. Born in Ballylough, Co. Wexford, the

son of a small farmer, he was educated at a *hedge-school and apprenticed to a Dublin grocer in 1809. An
elegy on the death of his employer, Mr
Hart, brought him to the attention of
Jameson the distiller, who supported
him. In 1819 he published *The Misan-
thrope* at his own expense. It was followed by *The Plagues of Ireland* (1824), a
satire on government hacks and place-
men such as Henry *Code, advocating
rebellion. James *Hardiman asked him
to work up literal versions of Gaelic
poems and songs into verse for his *Irish
Minstrelsy* (1831). *The Doom of Derenzie*
(1829) was a romantic narrative poem
featuring witchcraft, abduction, and
hanging.

G

GAA (Gaelic Athletic Association) (1884–), a national sporting movement established on 1 November 1884 by Michael Cusack, Maurice Davin, John Wyse-Power, J. K. Bracken, and others, with the aim of promoting traditional Irish games such as hurling and Gaelic football. Born in Carron, Co. Clare, Cusack (1847–1906) ran a business college. Underlying the success of the GAA was its connection with *Fenianism. The Association created an Irish version of the new-style spectator sports emerging contemporaneously elsewhere in Europe.

Gaelic historiography, a term used to describe the historical writings in Latin or in Irish composed in the 17th cent. to defend the Gaelic order against charges of barbarism and superstition made in the Anglo-Irish *chronicles. Such writings were usually compiled at or in relation to the centres of Irish learning on the Continent, which had been established by clerical exiles driven abroad. In the most eminent cases—Geoffrey *Keating and Mícheál *Ó Cléirigh—the compilations were made in Ireland in an attempt to record information then being scattered. The dedication of the historians ensured the survival of many sources that would otherwise have perished. Besides *Louvain, Irish colleges with manuscript libraries of some extent sprang up in Paris, Douai, Rouen, Bordeaux, Salamanca, Lisbon, Seville, and Rome. The chief texts to emerge from the 17th-cent. project in Gaelic historiography are Geoffrey Keating, *Foras Feasa ar Éirinn (written 1618–34); Philip *O'Sullivan Beare, Historiae Catholicae Iberniae Compendium (Lisbon, 1621); Mícheál Ó Cléirigh, with others, *Annals of the Four Masters (written 1632–6); John *Colgan, Acta Sanctorum Hiberniae (1645); John *Lynch, Cambrensis Eversus (1662); and Roderick *O'Flaherty, *Ogygia (1685). These compilers saw themselves as pitted against the English historians of Ireland including: *Giraldus Cambrensis, *Spenser, *Stanyhurst, and *Davies.

Gaelic Journal, The, see *Irisleabhar na Gaedhilge.

Gaelic League, the (Connradh na Gaeilge), was founded at 9 Lower O'Connell St., Dublin, on 31 July 1893, with the purpose of keeping the Irish language spoken in Ireland at a time when census returns indicated that the number of native Irish-speakers was in rapid decline as a consequence of high emigration and the abandonment of the language in favour of English. The founding members were Douglas *Hyde (President), Eoin *MacNeill (Secretary), Fr. William Hayden, SJ, Thomas O'Neill *Russell, Charles P. Bushe, Pádraig Ó Briain, Mártan Ó Ceallaigh, Patrick Hogan, James Cogan, and Thomas W. Ellerkerr. In seeking to revive Irish as a living language the Gaelic League followed the aims of its immediate precursors, the *Society for the Preservation of the Irish Language of 1876 and the *Gaelic Union of 1880. While insisting from the outset on its non-sectarian and non-political character, the League's vision was broadly nationalist, building on the ideas promoted by Hyde in his lecture 'On the Necessity for De-Anglicizing Ireland' to the National Literary Society [see *literary revival] in 1892. The Gaelic League broke new ground in establishing itself as a popular movement based on a branch structure throughout the country. An important part in the dissemination of League ideas was played by the timirí (messengers), whose visits were often followed by the múinteoir taistil (travelling teacher). Administrative skills developed by the *Land League and the Gaelic Athletic Association (*GAA) supplied a significant input to the new organization, while opportunities for social mixing between young men and women offered a widely attested stimulus to new membership. By 1908 there were almost 600 branches, chiefly in English-speaking areas. However, the League's foothold in the *Gaeltacht areas was negligible. The activities of the branches included Irish-language classes and social gatherings where Irish music and dancing were promoted. The League also produced a weekly newspaper—originally Fáinne an Lae, followed by An *Claidheamh Soluis, among whose editors were MacNeill and Patrick *Pearse. A publishing house was established in 1900, and already by 1909 some 150 books had appeared under the Connradh na Gaeilge imprint. The list of authors included virtually every major writer involved in the creation of a modern literature in Irish, among them Pearse, Pádraic *Ó Conaire, P. S. *Ó Duinnín, and An tAth. Peadar *Ó Laoghaire. As time went by many of the more ardent Gaelic Leaguers became increasingly impatient with the non-political stance of the leadership. Hyde tried in vain to keep the League a broad cultural movement clear of political involvement, but a vote in favour of committing the organization to 'a free, Gaelic-speaking Ireland', at the 1915 Ard Fheis (annual conference), drove him to resign as President. Numerous Leaguers went on to participate in the *Easter Rising in 1916. The educational policy of the new State was deeply coloured by Gaelic League ideas, while the special

status given to Irish in the 1937 Constitution was consistent with the League's primary objective. See Proinsias Mac Aonghusa, Ar Son na Gaeilge: Conradh na Gaeilge 1893–1993: Stair Sheanchais (1993).

Gaelic Society of Dublin, the, founded on 19 January 1807, with the aim of improving the general understanding of the literature and antiquities of Gaelic Ireland. The first secretary of the Society was Theophilus O'Flanagan (1764–1814), a native Irish-speaker from Co. Clare who had been educated at TCD, and who had assisted Charlotte *Brooke in compiling Reliques of Irish Poetry (1789). He edited the Society's only volume, The Transactions of the Gaelic Society (1808).

Gaelic Union, the (Aondacht na Gaeilge), founded in March 1880 by a group of Irish-language activists and scholars who had previously been members of the *Society for the Preservation of the Irish Language, including David *Comyn, Thomas O'Neill *Russell, and Canon Ulick *Bourke. Dissatisfied with what they judged to be the lack of dynamic popular impact of the former society, the Gaelic Union founder-members wished to implement practical measures that would arrest the decline of Irish as a living vernacular. It published a bilingual journal, *Irisleabhar na Gaedhilge, which was influential in laying the basis for a new literature in Irish.

Gaeltacht, the name given to the Irish-speaking districts in Ireland. It is estimated that in 1851 there were such communities in perhaps twenty-three of the thirty-two counties of Ireland when the number of Irish-speakers in the country was about one and a half million. By 1891, though there were still nearly three-quarters of a million native

Irish-speakers in the country, Irish was in full retreat to the Atlantic seaboard. While the *Gaelic League sought to arrest and reverse the language change from Irish to English throughout the country, the extent and population of the Gaeltacht areas continued to decline. In 1925 the Irish Free State established a Commission which recommended making competence in Irish obligatory for all senior civil servants dealing with the people of the Gaeltacht, together with economic development (based on indigenous resources), improved educational opportunities, and the planned resettlement of Gaeltacht families. A small new Gaeltacht was 'planted' in Co. Meath in the 1930s and has survived. But the Gaeltacht has continued to contract since the 1920s. In 1972 the Gaeltacht was provided with its own radio station, Radio na Gaeltachta. Cooperative and community projects and renewed vitality in aspects of popular culture (notably *sean-nós singing) may be seen as countersigns to the main story of decline. The 1980s and 1990s provided evidence of a new confidence in their indigenous culture and language among sections of Gaeltacht youth.

Gallagher, James (Séamus Ó Gallchóir) (?1680–1751), author of sermons in Irish. Born in the diocese of Kilmore, he was educated in Paris and Rome, returning to become Catholic Bishop of Raphoe from 1725, and of Kildare, 1737–51. His *Sixteen Sermons in An Easy and Familiar Stile* (1735), with facing translations, was one of the very few books published in Irish in the time of the *Penal Laws.

Gallery Press, see Peter *Fallon.

Gallivan, Gerald P. (1920–), playwright. Born in Limerick, he moved to England before returning to work at Shannon Airport. He wrote over twenty-five stage plays and many scripts for radio and television. From *Decision at Easter* (1959), to radio works on Gladstone (*The Final Mission*, 1991), and the siege of Limerick (*Prophecy*, 1992), he explores Irish political history. Among his best-known plays are: *Mourn the Ivy Leaf* (1960) about Parnell, *The Stepping Stone* (1963), *The Dáil Debate* (1971), and *Dev* (1977).

Galvin, Patrick (?1927–), poet and dramatist; born in Cork. When he left school at about 11 he worked at a variety of jobs. Two somewhat fictionalized autobiographies, *Song of a Poor Boy* (1989) and *Song for a Raggy Boy* (1991), reveal a Cork city slum culture of immense vitality. Galvin went to Belfast in 1943 and joined the RAF. His first collection of poems, *Heart of Grace* (1959), was followed by *Christ in London* (1960), and these two volumes show him adapting the narrative energy of *Hiberno-English *ballads to the urban 1950s. *The Woodburners* (1973) marks a turn to a more reflective mode. Early plays, *And Him Stretched* (1960) and *Cry the Believers* (1963), were produced in London, and *Boy in the Smoke* (1965) was a television play. He was awarded a Leverhulme Fellowship in 1973 attached to the *Lyric Theatre, Belfast, writing plays on political and sexual divisions, among them *Nightfall to Belfast* (1973), *The Last Burning* (1974), and *We Do It for Love* (1976). *Folk Tales for the General* (1989), poems, was followed by *New and Selected Poems* (1996), ed, by Greg *Delanty and Robert *Welch.

Gamble, Dr John (?1770–1831), army surgeon and author. Born in Strabane, Co. Tyrone, he served in the army in Holland but returned to Ulster with an eye infection, and took to touring Ireland collecting historical traditions. Using this material he wrote novels such as *Sarsfield* (1814), *Howard* (1815),

Northern Irish Tales (1818), and *Charlton* (1827), set in the 17th and 18th cents.

Gaol Gate, The (1906), a play by Lady *Gregory. Two country women, mother and wife of Denis Cahel, come to the gates of Galway Gaol, believing that he has turned informer. The gatekeeper tells them that he has been hanged the day before. Grief and shame give way to triumph at his self-sacrifice.

Gate Theatre, founded by Hilton Edwards and Mícheál *Mac Liammóir to present world drama and experimental productions. On 14 October 1928 the Dublin Gate Theatre Studio presented Ibsen's *Peer Gynt* at the Peacock Theatre attached to the *Abbey Theatre. The company opened at the Gate Theatre, attached to the Rotunda Hospital, with Goethe's *Faust* in February 1930. Plays by *Shaw, *Sheridan, and Shakespeare followed, and work by new Irish playwrights, including Mac Liammóir and Denis *Johnston. From 1936 the theatre was shared equally with Longford Productions, run by Edward, Lord *Longford and his wife Christine. On Longford's death in 1961, his wife restored the theatre completely to the partners. It entered a new phase in the 1990s under Michael Colgan.

Gearnon, Antoine (?1610–?1670), theologian. Born possibly in Co. Louth, he studied at St Anthony's College, *Louvain, and was ordained a Franciscan priest in 1635. He worked in Ireland from 1639 to 1644 before returning to St Anthony's, where he compiled *Parrthas an Anma (Soul's Paradise)* (1645), a catechism and prayer-book conveying the Catholic teachings of the Council of Trent.

Gearóid iarla (Gerald Fitzgerald, 4th Earl of Desmond) (1338–1398), poet. As justiciar of Ireland, 1367–9, Gearóid carried out a policy of integration with native Irish families. He introduced the French conventions of courtly love into Irish poetry [see *dánta grádha]. Thirty of his poems are preserved in the *Book of Fermoy*.

Gébler, Carlo (1954–), novelist; born in Dublin, and educated at Bedales School and York University after which he went to the National Film and Television School. After working as a scriptwriter and producer he turned to writing full-time. Novels include *The Eleventh Summer* (1985), *August in July* (1986), *Malachy and His Family* (1990), *The Cure* (1995), and *How to Murder a Man* (1998). Plays include *Dance of Death* (1998), a version of Strindberg.

geis (pl. gessi, geasa), usually translated 'taboo', is a ritual prohibition, a supernaturally sanctioned injunction to forego or perform certain actions. In Irish heroic literature the vast majority of gessi can be understood as defining, sustaining, or challenging the status or honorific prerogatives of prominent characters, particularly with regard to conduct in emotionally charged spheres of social life such as warfare, feasting, and sexual behaviour. Such gessi play a central role in some of the principal early Irish tales, among them *Longes mac nUislenn* and *Aided Oenfhir Aife*. *Togail Bruidne Da Derga* is constructed around the successive fated violations of his gessi by the King, Conaire.

genealogy (Latin, peritia; Irish, senchas, coimgne), a major source for the history of early and medieval Ireland. The principal genealogical *manuscripts are found in the *Book of Glendalough* (1125–30), the *Book of Leinster* (c.1150–65), the *Book of Ballymote* (c.1400), the *Book of Lecan* (1397–1418), and Dubaltach *Mac Fir Bhisigh's *Great Book of Genealogies* (c.1650–64). These and other manuscripts preserve the largest corpus of pre-1200 genealogy for any

European country, containing the names and descents of about 20,000 individuals from the prehistoric/mythological period, proto-historical times, and the historical period beginning about AD 550. The genealogies were compiled within the framework of an origin myth which traces all the Irish back to a fabulous Míl Espáine (Miles Hispaniae) and back from him to Japhet, Noah, and Adam, thus incorporating them in the history of salvation. The tradition found its fullest expression in the 12th-cent. *Lebor Gabála Érenn*.

General John Regan (1913), a novel by George A. *Birmingham, satirizing Irish small-town life. The story deals with the consequences of a returning American's practical joke in persuading the towns-people of Ballymoy to erect a statue to an imaginary local hero supposed to have played a part in the liberation of Bolivia.

Geneva: *Another Political Extravaganza* (1938), a play by George Bernard *Shaw. Begonia Brown, a Cockney secretary, brings about a crisis at the International Court of Justice at The Hague when she refers to it a number of accusations against European leaders.

Gentleman, Francis (1728–1784), actor and play-wright. Born in York St., Dublin, he appeared in Thomas *Southerne's *Oroonoko*, before going on to write for the stage in England. His tragic works include *Sejanus* (1751) and *The Sultan of Love and Fame* (1770); his comedies *The Modish Wife* (1773) and *The Tobacconist* (1771).

Geoffrey Austin: Student (1895), Canon Patrick *Sheehan's first novel, warning of the dangers of college education for talented young people when unaccompanied by religious training. In *The Triumph of Failure* (1899), a sequel, Austin drifts from one poorly-paid job

in Dublin to another while his friend Charles Travers sets about organizing a religious revival. Travers's career comes to a humiliating end when he is tried on trumped-up charges.

Geoghegan, Arthur Gerald (1810–1889), poet. Born in Dublin, he wrote verse for *The *Nation*, and published *The Monks of Kilcrea* (1853), a poem on Irish history.

Ghost Hunter and His Family, The (1833), a novel by Michael *Banim. Set in Kilkenny, it concerns the Brady family, based on that of the author's mother.

Ghosts (1993), a novel by John Banville, sequel to *The *Book of Evidence*. Released from prison after serving ten years for murder, Freddie Montgomery is sharing a house on an island off the west of Ireland with Professor Kreutznaet, and a motley crew of charlatans and criminals.

Giacomo Joyce, see James *Joyce.

Giall, An (1958), the original Irish version of Brendan *Behan's play *The *Hostage*. Commissioned by Gael-Linn, it is more dramatically coherent than *The Hostage*, and written in a combination of comic, lyric, and tragic styles.

Gibbings, Robert (1889–1958), artist, book-designer, and travel writer. Born in Cork, he was educated at UCC and served at Gallipoli. He came under the influence of the artist Eric Gill, running the Golden Cockerel Press from 1924 to 1933. Besides a series of books on rivers including *Sweet Thames Run Softly* (1940) and *Lovely is the Lee* (1945), he wrote about the South Seas in *Coconut Island* (1936).

Gibbon, [William] Monk (1896–1987), man of letters; born in Dublin and educated at St Columba's College and Oxford, he served in the First World War. *Inglorious Soldier* (1968) tells of his war experiences. His poetry, in collections such as *For Daws to Peck At* (1929) and *Seventeen Sonnets* (1932), reflects his admiration for English Georgian verse. *The Seals* (1935) is a narrative of a hunting expedition in the west of Ireland. *Mount Ida* (1948) recreates tentative love affairs of schoolteaching days, while *The Pupil* (1981) confesses his platonic love for a schoolgirl.

Gigli Concert, The (1983), a play by Thomas *Murphy dealing with the English dynamatologist J. P. W. King, a quack psychiatrist. He is visited by the Irish Man, a property developer with a wish to sing like Gigli. King comes to share the Man's obsession.

Gilbert, Sir John (1829–1898), antiquarian; born in Dublin, and educated in Bath. Author of a *History of the Viceroys of Ireland* (1865) and a *History of the City of Dublin* (3 vols., 1854–9), which is a standard reference work. Gilbert established the Dublin Records Office.

Gilbert, Lady, see Rosa *Mulholland.

Gilbert, Stephen (1912–   ), novelist; born in Newcastle, Co. Down, the son of a Belfast merchant. A protégé of Forrest *Reid, his fantasy novels show Reid's influence. *The Landslide* (1943) is set in a world of talking dragons. *Monkeyface* (1948) is the story of an apeboy brought from a jungle paradise to Belfast. *The Burnaby Experiments* (1952) describes an experiment in psychic translocation. *Ratman's Notebooks* (1968) is about a misfit who develops a power over rats as a child. *Bombardier* (1944) is an account of an AA battery in the Second World War.

Gilla Na Naem úa Duinn (?–1160), poet and historian of the monastery on Inchcleraun (Inis Clothrann) in Lough Ree. His best-known poem, 'Éire iarthar talman torthig', is a summary of the contents of the *dinnshenchas in the *Book of Ballymote*.

Giraldus [de Barry] Cambrensis (?1146–?1220), an Anglo-Norman prelate who visited Ireland as secretary to Prince John in 1184, and wrote two books about the country. Born in Pembrokeshire of Welsh nobility, his *Expugnatio Hibernica* (1189), or *The Conquest of Ireland*, describes events leading up to Henry II's invasion in 1169. Giraldus criticizes the colonists for disobedience to the Crown, and accuses them of forsaking their own culture. *Topographia Hibernica* (1188), or *The Topography and History of Ireland* provides portraits of the land and people.

Girl with Green Eyes, The (1964), originally issued as *The Lonely Girl* (1962), a novel by Edna *O'Brien. Set in Dublin, it concerns Caithleen and Baba, the heroines of *The *Country Girls* (1960) and *Girls in Their Married Bliss* (1964). Caithleen falls in love but her alcoholic father brings her back to the west of Ireland. The novel ends with the girls living in London.

Glenanaar (1905), a novel by Canon Patrick *Sheehan, set in Doneraile and based on the 1829 conspiracy trials in which Daniel *O'Connell successfully defended peasants accused of agrarian crimes.

Glendalough (Gleann Dá Loch), a monastic community initiated by St Kevin (d. 618). He led—according to tradition—a hermit's life near the lakes which lie in the Wicklow Hills. His reputation attracted followers, leading to the foundation of several ecclesiastical buildings. Beside the often illustrated round tower, celebrated features of the site include St Kevin's Well, St

Kevin's House, and St Kevin's Bed, each associated with legendary aspects of the saint's life. The *Book of Glendalough* is held to have been compiled there at the beginning of the 12th cent.

Glenmornan (1919), a novel by Patrick *MacGill recounting in fictional form his return to Donegal shortly before the First World War. Disillusioned by life as a journalist in England, Doalty Gallagher returns hopefully to his mother's smallholding in Glenties. He works hard and woos Sheila Dermod, a local girl; but when the parish priest denounces his newspaper articles about the locality from the altar he is ostracized, even by Sheila and his mother.

glossaries survive from the Old and Middle Irish periods, and comprise lists of words elucidated by a combination of explanatory *glosses, etymological analysis, and quotation. The most compendious glossary is *Sanas Chormaic* [see *Cormac mac Cuileannáin].

glosses, remarks and additions written between the lines and in the margins of medieval *manuscripts containing, usually, Latin texts which they explain, either in Latin or in the vernacular. The most important collections of glosses compiled by early Irish commentators can be found in manuscripts presently kept in Würzburg, Milan, and St Gallen. They are a major source for our knowledge of Old Irish.

gnomic writing, a feature of Old Irish literature in which traditional wisdom is expressed in proverbial, pithy, and self-contained forms of which the *triad is the best-known.

Gobán Saor, a mythical craftsman in Irish medieval literature and *folklore.

Gógan, Liam S. (1891–1979), poet.

Born in Dublin, he was educated at UCD. He was assistant keeper of antiquities at the National Museum of Ireland from 1914. He was interned after the *Easter Rising, and re-employed at the Museum in 1922, becoming Keeper 1936–56. His verse draws on Irish *bardic poetry and early modernists such as Théophile Gautier. Volumes were *Nua-Dhánta* (1919), *Dánta agus Duanóga* (1929), *Dánta an Lae Indiu* (1936), *Dánta Eile* (1946), *Dánta agus Duanta* (1952), and *Duanaire a Sé* (1966).

Gogarty, Oliver St John (1878–1957), writer and surgeon. Born in Dublin, he was educated at Stoneyhurst, the Royal University [see *universities], and TCD, where he studied medicine and established his reputation as a wit. He, R. S. Chenevix Trench, and James *Joyce, with whom he had a short-lived friendship, figure as Mulligan, Haines, and Stephen Dedalus in *Ulysses*. Gogarty married in 1906, and in 1907 undertook postgraduate study in otolaryngology in Vienna. He became a well-known figure in Dublin's literary and cultural life. His first work to come before the public was *Blight: The Tragedy of Dublin* (with Joseph O'Connor, 1917), the first 'slum play' to be staged at the *Abbey Theatre. He supported the Free State [see *Civil War] and was kidnapped by Republicans, from whom he escaped by swimming the Liffey, a feat commemorated in his first substantial collection of poetry, *An Offering of Swans* (1923). A further collection was *Wild Apples* (1928). When he became a Senator (1922–6) he had his house, 'Renvyle', in Connemara burned down by Republicans. In 1937, after losing a libel action arising from his autobiography *As I Was Going Down Sackville Street*, he moved to London and then to America in 1939, where he finally abandoned medicine. *I Follow St Patrick* (1938) and *It Isn't This Time of Year at All!*

(1954) were further volumes of auto-biography. *Tumbling in the Hay* (1939) is a comic work describing a night in Holles Street Hospital. In New York he wrote the novels *Going Native* (1940), *Mad Grandeur* (1941), *Mr. Petunia* (1945), and issued his *Collected Poems* (1951). See Ulick *O'Connor, *Oliver St John Gogarty* (1963).

Golden Cuckoo, The (1939), a play by Denis *Johnston. Mr Dotheright, a freelance writer of obituaries, is caught up in a farcical situation in which he is given an assignment by a newspaper editor, who refuses payment because the subject is still alive. In protest Dotheright occupies the post office in a parody of the *Easter Rising.

Goldsmith, Oliver (1728–1774) man of letters; born in Pallas, Co. Longford, though the family moved to Lissoy, near Ballymahon, Co. Westmeath. His college career at TCD involved painful humiliations and he was frequently in disciplinary trouble. In 1752 he studied medicine at Edinburgh, visited the Highlands the year after, and then set off on a Continental tour, making his way by flute-playing and singing. Returning destitute to London in 1756, he acted, practised medicine, and corrected proofs. He met Ralph Griffiths, editor of the *Monthly Review*, and began contributing to his journal. His *An Inquiry into Present State of Polite Learning* (1759) called for an unaffected style and temper. He became editor of a weekly journal, *The Bee*, writing most of the eight numbers himself. In 1760–1 the series of Chinese letters later published as *The *Citizen of the World* (1762) appeared in John Newbery's *Public Ledger*. About this time he met Samuel Johnson, and in 1763 he was a founding member of the Club that met in the Turk's Head in Soho. *A History of England* (1764) in the form of a letter-series from a nobleman to his son was a popular success. *The Traveller, or a Prospect of Society* (1764), begun during his European wanderings, shows Goldsmith praising the 'sympathetic mind' which tries to see the good in all. In 1764 Johnson, intervening to save Goldsmith from arrest over debt, sold the manuscript of *The *Vicar of Wakefield* (1766). Its mixture of sentiment and irony won Goldsmith many admirers. In 1767 Goldsmith's *The *Good-Natur'd Man* was produced. In this comedy Goldsmith turned back towards the humour of *Farquhar, whom he greatly admired. His *Roman History* (1769) was followed by a *History of England* (1771), and from around 1767 he laboured at a *History of the Earth and Animated Nature* (1774). In 1770 *The Deserted Village* appeared. The poem mixes memories of childhood around Ballymahon with criticism of the enclosures taking place in the English countryside. The second of his plays, *She Stoops to Conquer* (1773), is a free-wheeling comedy consummately realizing the preference for 'laughing' over 'weeping' comedy outlined in his essay in the *London Magazine* for the same year. *Retaliation* (1774) light-heartedly takes revenge on friends, including Edmund *Burke, who had teased him. From letters to his friend Bob Bryanston, it is evident that Ireland was close to Goldsmith's heart. His standpoint on the country finds its most direct expression in 'A Description of the Manner and Customs of the Native Irish' (1759), and in his 'History of Carolan, the Last Irish Bard' (1760), both of which are deficient in accurate information about Gaelic language and culture. Goldsmith's Irishness is ultimately conveyed in the calm but ironic perspective he offers on English life and manners. See A. Lytton Sells, *Oliver Goldsmith* (1974).

Goll mac Mórna, enemy of *Fionn mac Cumhaill in the *Fionn cycle. His name (meaning 'one-eyed') links him with Balor of the Fomoiri [see *Cath Maige Tuired*].

Gonne, Maud (later Gonne Mac-Bride) (1866–1953), revolutionary. Born in Aldershot and educated in France, she arrived in Ireland when her father was posted to Dublin in 1882, shortly meeting the *Fenian John *O'Leary, and through him in 1889 W. B. *Yeats. While recovering from tubercular haemorrhage in France she met Lucien Millevoye, a Boulangist intent on regaining Alsace-Lorraine from Germany, with whom she had two children, the second of which was Iseult (b. 1895)—conceived on the grave of the first for spiritual reasons—who was to marry Francis *Stuart. Yeats proposed to her for the first time in 1891 and wrote *The *Countess Cathleen* for her the year after. The relationship with Millevoye ended in 1899, by which date she was deeply involved in Yeats's life and work. During this period and later she insisted on keeping their relationship non-physical, preferring to regard it as a 'spiritual union'. In Dublin she founded Inghinidhe na hÉireann ('Daughters of Ireland') in 1900, and later launched *Bean na hÉireann* (1908), a journal advocating militancy and feminism. In 1902 she memorably personified the spirit of Ireland in the title-role of *Cathleen Ni Houlihan*. Her marriage of 1903 to Major John MacBride, former commander of the *Irish Brigade in the Boer War, disturbed Yeats, but he continued to write poetry about her. Her son Seán (Nobel Peace Prize winner in 1974) was born in 1904, but the marriage ended in divorce. She was living in France when MacBride was executed in the aftermath of the *Easter Rising. On rejecting the Anglo-Irish Treaty in 1922 [see *Anglo-Irish War], she worked for Republican prisoners and their families, and was herself imprisoned in 1923. *A Servant of the*

Queen (1938) is an autobiography, concentrating on her 'shining days', 1890–1900.

Good Behaviour (1981), a novel by Molly *Keane exploring the moral and economic decline of the Anglo-Irish *ascendancy. Opening with the death of Mrs St Charles, whose middle-aged daughter Aroon is the narrator, it takes the form of a prolonged flashback to childhood and adolescence.

Goodby, John (1958–), poet and critic; born in Birmingham, and educated at Hull and Leeds Universities after which he taught at Leeds, UCC, and Swansea. His collections include *A Birmingham Yank* (1998) and *In Ballast to the White Sea* (2000); his critical work has ranged across modern Irish, English, and Welsh poetry. *From Stillness into History* (2000), is a comprehensive study of Irish poetry since 1950, covering many often-neglected figures.

Good-Natur'd Man, The (1768), a comedy by Oliver *Goldsmith. When the open-hearted young Honeywood gives away to others the money owing to his friends his uncle, Sir William, has him arrested for debt to teach him a lesson. Eventually Honeywood marries Miss Richland, having learnt the price of seeking the good opinion of acquaintances to the neglect of real friends.

Gore-Booth, Eva [Selena] (1870–1926), poet; born at Lissadell, Co. Sligo, and sister of Countess *Markievicz. After moving to Manchester she worked in the women's movement, sharing a lifelong commitment to feminism with Esther Roper. Her early poems were admired by W. B. *Yeats and anthologized by George *Russell. Her verse plays include: *The Buried Life of Deirdre* (1905), and *The Triumph of Maeve*.

Gormfhlaith, the name of two famous and much-married queens. The first was the daughter of the High King Flann Sinna (d. 916) and wife of three kings in succession: *Cormac mac Cuilennáin (d. 908); his foster-brother and conqueror Cerball (d. 909), King of Leinster; and Niall Glúndub (d. 919), High King of Ireland. The second (d. 1030) was daughter of Murchad (d. 972), King of Leinster. Her first husband was Amlaíb Cuarán (d. 981), King of Dublin; her next was Máel Sechnaill (d. 1022), High King of Ireland; and her third was *Brian Bóroime, King of Ireland.

'Grace', a story in James *Joyce's *Dubliners* (1914), written in 1905. Mr Kernan, a commercial traveller, falls drunkenly down the steps of the lavatory in a pub. At home in bed he is visited by friends who involve him in a plan to change his ways at a religious retreat.

Graham, Revd John (1776–1844), poet. Born in Co. Longford, and educated at TCD. He contributed poetry and prose as 'Apprentice Boy' to *The Warder*. He wrote a number of longer poems, such as *God's Revenge against Rebellion* (1820), *The King's Vision* (1822), and *Harcourt's Vision* (1823).

Gráinne, see *Tóraigheacht Dhiarmada agus Ghráinne*.

Grammatica Celtica (1853), by Johann Kasper *Zeuss, inaugurated the modern study of Celtic linguistics, firmly establishing *Irish and the other *Celtic languages as part of the *Indo-European family.

grammatical tracts, *manuscript compilations of linguistic learning used in the *bardic schools from the 12th to the 17th cent. They reflect the codification and consolidation of the literary language which accompanied the emergence of the learned bardic families [see *bardic poetry], and the creation of a new caste of hereditary scholars when the monastic schools went into decline.

Grand, Sarah [Frances Elizabeth McFall] (née Clarke) (1854–1943), novelist. Born in Ulster, she married an army surgeon at 16, separating from him after the commercial success of a first novel, *Ideala* (1888). *The Heavenly Twins* (1893), a series of interconnected tales, deals with marital abuse. *The Beth Book: A Study in the Life of a Woman of Genius* (1897) is autobiographical, and contains lengthy passages on women's rights. Other novels include *The Domestic Experiment* (1891), *The Modern Man and Maid* (1898), *Emotional Moments* (1903), and *The Winged Victory* (1916).

Grania (1892), a novel by Emily *Lawless set on the Aran Islands. The heroine is a vivacious young woman living with her dying sister, whose father has left them wealthy. Grania falls in love with Murdough Blake, who deserts her when she needs his help. She drowns during a storm while trying to row to Inishmore to bring a priest to her sister's bedside.

Granuaile, see Grace *O'Malley.

Grattan, Henry (1746–1820), politician. Born in Dublin, he was educated at TCD and entered the *Irish Parliament in 1775. His rousing speech on legislative independence on 16 April 1782 became a touchstone of Anglo-Irish oratory. After the Union, which he vigorously opposed, he sat at Westminster campaigning for *Catholic Emancipation.

Graves, Alfred Perceval (1846–1931), poet and anthologist; born in Dublin, son of Charles Graves (1812–99), a clergyman and mathematician who was Archbishop of Limerick from 1866.

Graduating from TCD, Graves joined the department of education and became a school inspector 1875–1910. His prolific verse writings were mostly genteel and humorous lyrics. Many are set to Irish airs and were issued in collections such as *Irish Songs and Ballads* (1880) and *Songs of Old Ireland* (1882). His best-known piece was 'Father O'Flynn', first published in 1875. *To Return to All That* (1930), an autobiography, corrects the account of family history given by his son, the poet Robert Graves (1895–1985) in *Goodbye to All That* (1929).

Graves, Clotilde Inez Mary (pseudonym 'Richard Dahen') (1864–1932), dramatist and fiction-writer; born in Buttevant, Co. Cork, a cousin of Alfred P. *Graves. Her play *Nitocris* (1887) appeared at Drury Lane, while *The Lover's Battle* (1902), based on Alexander Pope's *The Rape of the Lock*, was among others performed in London and New York. Her successful *The Doctor Dop* (1910) was one of nearly twenty novels and story collections issued under her pseudonym, among which *A Well-Meaning Woman* (1894) and *Between Two Thieves* (1914) addressed serious social issues.

Graves of Kilmorna, The: *A Story of '67* (1915), Canon Patrick *Sheehan's posthumously published novel, vindicating the spirit of the *Fenians and accusing the *Land League of fostering materialism.

Greacen, Robert (1920–   ), poet. Born in Derry, he was educated at TCD. He published *The Bird* (1941) followed by the collections *One Recent Evening* (1944) and *The Undying Day* (1948). From 1948 he worked as a teacher in London. He wrote studies of the novelist C. P. Snow (1952) and the playwright Noel Coward (1953). *Even Without Irene* (1969) was an autobiographical memoir written after the death of his wife, Patricia Hutchins.

He did not return to poetry until *A Garland for Captain Fox* (1975), followed by *Young Mr Gibbon* (1979) and *A Bright Mask* (1985), a volume of new and selected poems, and *Carnival at the River* (1991). *Collected Poems* (1995) was followed by *Protestant Without a Horse* (1997). *Brief Encounters* (1991) is a memoir of literary life; *The Sash my Father Wore* (1997) autobiography.

Great Hunger, The (1942), a longer poem in fourteen parts by Patrick *Kavanagh, realistically documenting the life of an Irish farmer whilst opening symbolic perspectives on its subject. The mute frustration of its central figure, Patrick Maguire, is representative of the despair experienced in a land where human and spiritual values are betrayed by rural materialism masquerading as morality.

Great Push, The (1916), a first-person novel by Patrick *MacGill recounting his experience as stretcher-bearer with the London Irish Rifles in the First World War. The loosely connected narrative describes the fates of Felan, Gilhooley, and some others who go over the top at the battle of Loos, September 1915.

Greek learning, see *classical literature in Irish.

Green, Alice [Sophia] Stopford (1847–1929), historian. Born Kells, Co. Meath, she was educated at the College of Science, Dublin. Moving to London in 1874, she married the historian John Richard Green, whose *Conquest of England* (1883) she completed posthumously. Addressing Irish history in *The Making of Ireland and Its Undoing* (1908) and *Irish Nationality* (1911), she opposed the notion that the Anglo-*Normans brought civilization to Ireland. Her last major work, *A History of the Irish State to 1014* (1925), reflects her nationalist viewpoint.

Green, F[rederick] L[aurence]
(1902–1953), English-born novelist who
settled in Belfast in 1932, and achieved
success with *Odd Man Out* (1945), a novel
dealing with the flight through Belfast
of a wounded *IRA man, Johnny
McQueen. It became an atmospheric
film by Carol Reed (1947), with James
Mason in the lead role. His other novels
include *On the Night of the Fire* (1939);
Music in the Park (1942); *Mist on the Water*
(1948), *Julius Penton: Magician* (1951), and
Ambush for a Hunter (1952).

Green Fool, The (1938), an autobiographical novel by Patrick *Kavanagh, describing his youth and struggles
as a poorly-educated cobbler and small
farmer trying to become a writer.

Green Helmet, The (1910), a play by
W.B. *Yeats, first performed in a prose
version under the title *The Golden Helmet*
at the *Abbey Theatre in 1908. Based on
*Fled Bricrenn, it tells how a Red Man
from the otherworld challenges the
warriors of Ulster to take off his head.

Gregory, Lady (née [Isabella] Augusta
Persse) (1852–1932), dramatist, folklorist, and translator. Born in Roxborough,
Co. Galway, she was educated privately.
In 1880 she married Sir William
Gregory of Coole Park, former Governor
of Ceylon, and after the birth of their
only child Robert in 1881 they wintered
in Egypt, where they supported the
nationalist Arabi Bey, the subject of her
first publication, *Arabi and His Household*
(1882). She and Wilfrid Scawen *Blunt,
with whom she had an affair, campaigned to prevent Arabi's execution.
While involved with Blunt she wrote a
love-sequence called 'A Woman's Sonnets', published anonymously in Blunt's
*Love Lyrics and Songs of Proteus with the Love
Sonnets of Proteus* (1892). After her husband's death in 1892, she edited his
Autobiography (1894). The following year
she met W. B. *Yeats for the first time,

and in 1897 he stayed with her at Coole,
beginning a creative friendship that
lasted for life. Under his influence her
interest in Irish *folklore revived, and
she began to study Irish mythology, taking her research into the field. From
1897 she and Yeats spent much time
collecting folklore around Coole and
further afield. Also in 1897, she, Yeats,
and Edward *Martyn conceived the idea
of establishing a National Theatre [see
*Abbey Theatre]. Coole became a haven
for many of the writers of the *literary
revival, most of whom carved their initials on the autograph tree still standing
in the gardens. In 1898 she edited *Mr.
Gregory's Letter-Box* containing the political correspondence of her husband's
grandfather. She prepared a translation
of 'An Pósaidh Gléigeal' by *Raiftearaí
for 'Dust Hath Closed Helen's Eye',
Yeats's 1899 essay on the poet. She
assisted Yeats in writing *Cathleen Ní
Houlihan* and The *Pot of Broth; and by
now she was developing her idiomatic
literary style, known as 'Kiltartanese',
after the townland of that name.
Cuchulain of Muirthemne (1902) translated the tales of the *Ulster cycle, and
shaped *Táin Bó Cuailnge* and its pre-
tales, such as *Longes mac nUislenn, into a
coherent narrative. *Poets and Dreamers*
(1903) contains translations of
Raiftearaí, as well as reminiscences of
the poet taken down from local people.
Gods and Fighting Men (1904) translated
the main tales from the *mythological
and *Fionn cycles. *A Book of Saints and
Wonders* (1906) gathered together lore
relating to St *Brigit, St *Patrick, St
*Colum Cille, as well as incidental stor-
ies of the early Church. Her first original
play, *Twenty Five*, was produced in 1903
with Yeats's *The Hour-Glass*. On the opening night of the Abbey *Spreading the
News* was staged with Yeats's *On Baile's
Strand* [see *Cuchulain cycle]. Recognizing the need to balance the poetic
intensity of much of the Abbey programme with more realistic scenes, she

set out as a comic dramatist. She provided a Kiltartan Molière in *The Doctor in Spite of Himself* (1906), *The Rogueries of Scapin* (1908), *The Miser* (1909), and *The Would-Be Gentleman* (1923). *Kincora (1905) was a 'folk history' play, a form she returned to with *The *White Cockade* (1905), *The Canavans* (1906), *Dervorgilla* (1907), *The *Deliverer* (1911), and *Grania* (1911), each dealing with crucial moments of conflict in Ireland's past. The sheer volume of administration and creative work she undertook in these years on behalf of the Abbey and the literary revival is impressive. She continued to write comedy in *Halvey* (1906), *The *Image* (1909), and *Damer's Gold* (1912). She prepared *The Kiltartan History Book* (1909), *The Kiltartan Wonder Book* (1910), and *Irish Folk History Plays* (1912) for publication. *The *Rising of the Moon*, a play with a strongly revolutionary theme was written with Douglas *Hyde and produced in 1907, the year which also saw the production of *The Workhouse Ward* under its earlier title *The Poorhouse*. *Our Irish Theatre* (1913) is the history of the Abbey Theatre from her viewpoint, and while it underestimated the work of the *Fay brothers, it is revealing about the extent of her creative influence, especially on Yeats and on *Synge. In 1915 *Shanwalla*, a ghost play, was produced; in that year her nephew Hugh Lane was drowned when the *Lusitania* was sunk by a German U-boat. She campaigned for the return of his collection of paintings from London. *The Kiltartan Poetry Book* (1918), a collection of translations from the Irish, was followed by *Visions and Beliefs in the West of Ireland* (2 vols., 1920) which represented the fruits of more than twenty years of shared fieldwork and thought with W. B. Yeats. *An *Old Woman Remembers* (1923), a nationalist historical monologue, was recited by Sara *Allgood at the Abbey. Her last plays were *Sancha's Master* (1927) and

*Dave (1927). In *Coole* (1931) she recorded the history of her house. Coole Park was sold to the Forestry Commission in 1927, with Lady Gregory receiving a life tenancy, but it was demolished for no good reason in 1941. Lady Gregory became entirely committed to the cultural nationalism of the literary revival. She saw the decline of the Irish language as one of the great cultural landslides of 19th-cent. Ireland, the other being the *Famine. She wrote for her own people in Kiltartan, believing, with Yeats, that art which was not rooted in people's lives was shallow. Her great labour and artistic vision are celebrated in two of Yeats's finest poems, 'Coole Park, 1929' and 'Coole Park and Ballylee, 1931', written during her last illness from breast cancer. The *Collected Works* is published in the Coole Edition (1970–), general editors Colin *Smythe and T. R. *Henn, and includes her autobiography, *Seventy Years* (1974), and *Journals* (1978 and 1987). See Ann *Saddlemyer and Colin Smythe (eds.), *Lady Gregory: Fifty Years After* (1987).

Grene, Nicholas (1947–), critic; born in Chicago, Illinois, where his parents taught at the University of Chicago, and educated in the Belfast Royal Academy, TCD, and Cambridge, he taught at Liverpool and TCD where he was elected to the Edward *Dowden Chair of English in 1999. His work includes studies of *Shaw* (1984), *Synge* (1985), and *The Politics of Irish Drama* (1999). He has also written on comedy in Shakespeare, Jonson, and Moliere (1985) and on *Shakespeare's Tragic Imagination* (1996).

Grennan, Eamon (1941–), poet. Born in Dublin and educated at UCD and Harvard, he taught at Vassar College. His collections, *Wildly for Days* (1983), *What Light There Is* (1987), *As If It Matters* (1991), and *So it Goes* (1995) reveal a poet with a strong visual sense.

Leopardi (1995) is a volume of translations.

Grierson, Constantia (née Phillips) (?1705–1733), poet and editor. Born at Graiguenamanagh, Co. Kilkenny, she was apprenticed at 14 to train in midwifery but acquired considerable learning in Latin, Greek, and Hebrew through self-education. She married the King's Printer in Ireland, George Grierson, and worked on his classical editions of Terence (1727) and Tacitus (1730). Poems in praise of friends are collected in *Poems by Eminent Ladies* (1755). She was a friend of *Swift.

Griffin, Gerald (1803–1840), novelist and poet. Born and educated in Limerick, he left Ireland in 1823 with the ambition of becoming a dramatist but *The Tragedy of Aguire*, was rejected by William *Macready. *Gisippus* (1842) was produced by Macready after his death. Impressed by the success of *Tales by the O'Hara Family* (1825) by his friend John *Banim, he abandoned drama and produced *Holland-Tide* (1827), a set of regional stories. In 1829 he published *The *Collegians*, a tale of crime and punishment which draws heavily on his familiarity with Irish Catholic society. Later novels include *The *Rivals* and *Tracy's Ambition* (both 1829) and *The Duke of Monmouth* (1836). He also published further sets of stories: *Tales of the Munster Festivals* (1827), *Tales of My Neighbourhood* (1835), and the posthumous *Talis Qualis, or Tales of the Jury Room* (1842). Griffin's fiction provides portraits of peasant types with colourful and convincing idiom, accounts of the irresponsible Irish squirearchy, and didactic portrayals of Catholic families. Always moralistic in tendency, he became convinced of the futility of writing, burned his manuscripts (including *Aguire*) and joined the Christian Brothers in 1838 taking the name Brother Joseph. In 1839 he was transferred to the North Monastery in Cork, where he achieved as a religious the serenity which had eluded him before. See John Cronin, *Gerald Griffin: A Critical Biography* (1978).

Griffith, Arthur (1872–1922), political activist. Born in Dublin and educated by the Christian Brothers, he trained as a printer, and joined the *Gaelic League before going to South Africa in 1896. On his return in 1898 he supported the Boers and began editing *The *United Irishman* for William *Rooney—with whom he also founded Cumann na nGaedhael, a nationalist organization that subsequently amalgamated with other groups to create *Sinn Féin in 1905. Griffith's initial strategy was to persuade the *Irish Parliamentary Party to withdraw from Westminster and create an Irish government in Dublin. His political prospects were dim until the *Easter Rising in 1916, called at once the Sinn Féin Rebellion although it took him entirely by surprise. In the aftermath he was interned by the Government. In October 1917 he resigned the Presidency of Sinn Féin in favour of Eamon *de Valera. He headed the Irish delegation to London that negotiated the Treaty in December 1921, and resolutely defended the outcome in the subsequent Dáil debate. He was elected President of Dáil Éireann in January 1922, but died during the opening stages of the *Civil War. As editor of the newspaper *Sinn Fein* (1906–14) Griffith advanced an equation between the human soul and the soul of the nation. Besides contributions by Patrick *Pearse and other militants, his papers gave space to George *Russell, Frank *Fay, Maud *Gonne, and W. B. *Yeats.

Griffith, Elizabeth (?1720–1793), born in Wales, prolific playwright and novelist. Her *The Platonic Wife* (1765) contains an Irish servant who is rewarded for loyalty with the means to return to Ireland. She married Richard *Griffith.

Griffith, Richard (?1704–1788), playwright. Born in Dublin and educated at TCD. His works include *The Triumvirate* (1764), a bawdy novel, and *Variety* (1782), a comedy performed at Drury Lane. Griffith collaborated successfully with his wife Elizabeth in *A Series of Genuine Letters between Henry and Frances* (1757), a novel derived from their amorous correspondence. Two sequels, *Delicate Distress* (1769) by 'Frances' and *The Gordian Knot* (1770) by 'Henry', were written independently. A son, Richard (d. 1820), was a member of the *Irish Parliament, while his son, Sir Richard Griffith (1784–1878), devised 'Griffith's valuation', the system adopted for rating agricultural property. On 'Henry' and 'Frances', see *Escape from the Anthill* (1985) by Hubert *Butler, who inherited their house at Bennetsbridge.

Grimshaw, Beatrice (?1870–1953), traveller and novelist. Born in Cloona, Co. Antrim, and educated in Belfast, she worked as a sports writer and social editor in Dublin before moving to London. An inveterate traveller, she settled for a time in New Guinea. She issued numerous travel books including *In the Strange South Seas* (1907) and *From Fiji to the Cannibal Islands* (1917), but also produced more than thirty novels and story collections set in exotic places, among which are *Vaiti of the Islands* (1916), *Conn of the Coral Seas* (1922), and *South Sea Sarah* (1940).

Groves, Revd Edward (?–?1850), playwright and author of *The Warden of Galway*, based on the story of Walter Lynch, who was compelled to pass sentence of death on his own son. Groves also wrote *Alomprah, or The Hunter of Burma, The O'Donoghue of the Lakes*, and *The Donagh*, all published in 1832.

Guests of the Nation (1931), a collection of short stories by Frank *O'Connor, dealing with the *Anglo-Irish and *Civil Wars in a style of poetic realism modelled on Turgenev and George *Moore.

Guinan, John (1874–1945), playwright. Born in Ballindown near Birr, Co. Offaly, he worked as a civil servant. Besides short stories he wrote realist plays for the *Abbey. These were *The Cuckoo's Nest* (1913), *The Plough Lifters* (1916), *Black Oliver* (1927), and *The Rune of Healing* (1931).

Guinan, Fr. Joseph (1863–1932), novelist. Born in Co. Offaly and educated at Maynooth, he worked in Liverpool before becoming Canon in Dromod, Co. Longford in 1920. He wrote novels from a strongly Catholic standpoint, proclaiming the bond between priests and people. Among them are: *Scenes and Sketches in an Irish Parish, or Priest and People at Doon* (1903); *The Island Parish* (1908); *The Soggarth Aroon* (1905), his best-known work; *The Moores of Glynn* (1907); *The Curate of Kilcloon* (1913); and *The Patriots* (1928).

Guinness, Bryan Walter, Lord Moyne (1905–1992), man of letters. Born in Dublin into the brewing family, educated at Eton and Oxford. His plays include *The Fragrant Concubine* (1938); amongst his collection of verse are *Reflexions* (1947), *The Rose in the Tree* (1964), and *The Clock* (1973). His novels include *Singing out of Tune* (1933), and *The Giant's Eye* (1964). *Potpourri* (1982) is a memoir.

Gulley Jimson trilogy, see *Herself Surprised*, The *Horse's Mouth*, and *To Be a Pilgrim*.

Gulliver's Travels (1726), a prose satire by Jonathan *Swift. Written in Ireland and carried by Swift to London, it was published pseudonymously. The purportedly autobiographical narrative is conducted by Lemuel Gulliver, a ship's surgeon, who tells of his voyages to Lilliput, Brobdingnag, Laputa, and the country of the Houyhnhnms. Intended as a political satire addressed to the contemporary English audience, it also allowed Swift to elaborate his views on the relation between reason and civilization. Gulliver travels first to Lilliput, where the diminutive inhabitants refer to their visitor as the 'Man-Mountain'. In Brobdingnag the perspective is reversed: Gulliver is diminutive and the Brobdingnagians gigantic. On his next journey he visits the flying island Laputa and neighbouring Lagado and Luggnagg. Laputa's inhabitants are obsessed with astronomical speculations involving mathematics and music which Gulliver finds incomprehensible. On his last voyage Gulliver visits the land of the horses, or Houyhnhnms, who live by the dictates of reason and whose language is the 'perfection of nature'. Having listened to Gulliver's account of European politics in general they decide that he is a Yahoo, the vilest form of life in their country.

Gúm, An (The Scheme), established in 1925 by Ernest *Blythe, Minister for Finance in the *Irish Free State, to ensure the supply of textbooks and reading matter which the policy of reviving the Irish language required. Translations into Irish, which formed an important part of this project, were mostly from English, although there were also a number from other European languages. Publication was slow and the quality of the published work varied greatly. However, it provided necessary financial support for Irish-language writers, and it also published original writing by such authors as Tomás *Ó Criomhthain, Seosamh *Mac Grianna, and Máirtín *Ó Cadhain. It continues to function as a state publishing agency.

Gwynn, Stephen [Lucius] (1864–1950), man of letters. He was brought up mostly in Donegal and went to Oxford before setting up in London as a writer. Up to 1901 he published works on English topics only, and then began reporting developments at the Irish Literary Theatre [see *Abbey Theatre] for *Fortnightly Review*. He also wrote Irish verse (*A Lay of Ossian and St. Patrick*, 1903), fiction set in Donegal (*The Old Knowledge*, 1901: *The Glade in the Forest*, 1907), a historical novel (*John Maxwell's Marriage*, 1903), and a reconstruction of Robert *Emmet's rising (1909). *Irish Literature and Drama in the English Language* (1920), an extended survey, charts the tradition of *Anglo-Irish literature. Gwynn wrote numerous biographies including those of Thomas *Moore (1904), *Swift (1933), *Goldsmith (1935), and *Grattan (1939).

gyre, a symbol and concept in W. B. *Yeats's later writing and thought. The gyre is a circling movement beginning at the tip of a cone and expanding to the broad end; it then reverses and contracts back, changing the direction of spin, or pern, as it does so. Yeats thought of reality as two such cones interpenetrating one another.

H

Hackett, Francis (1883–1962), novelist. Born in Kilkenny and educated at Clongowes Wood, he emigrated to America and worked on various papers. He later moved to France, then Ireland, leaving when his Clongowes novel *The Green Lion* (1936) was banned. *The Senator's Last Night* (1939) portrays the kind of plutocratic quasi-fascist he despised. *The Green Lion* criticized the celibacy of his teachers.

Hag of Beare, see *Cailleach Bhéarra.

hagiography, see *saints' lives.

Haicéad, Pádraigín (?–1654), poet. Born probably near Cashel, Co. Tipperary, he was a protégé of the Butlers of Kilcash. He is said to have studied at the Dominican convents of Coleraine and Limerick. Around 1628 he went to St Anthony's College in *Louvain. He returned to Ireland some time in the late 1630s and became Prior in Cashel. 'Éirghe mo dhúithche le Dia', written in 1641, is a piece of propaganda, calling for outright rebellion. When the *Confederation of Kilkenny split in 1646 the Dominicans took sides against those seeking a compromise. Haicéad excoriated these 'traitors' in 'Músgail do mhisneach, a Bhanbha'. His poetry of these years reflects his despairing and outraged state of mind, and complains of indifference towards him and his talents. He returned to Louvain. His tragic and isolated later years there were occupied in controversy over the rotation of the headship of his college. In spite of the combativeness of his professional life, he was humorous and amiable in his personal relationships, the Butler family having a particular place in his affections.

Hail and Farwell, a three-volume comic autobiography by George *Moore. Comprising *Ave* (1911), *Salve* (1912), and *Vale* (1914), it tells the story of his involvement in the *literary revival from 1901 to 1911, though covering some events before and after. The narrative includes a retrospective appraisal of his early life and family, his struggle with Catholic dogmatism, and his championing of the *Gaelic League. The accounts of friendships formed and dissolved are woven together in an impressionistic style, uniting an inner monologue with an informal chronicle of events.

'Half Sir, The' (1827), one of three stories in Gerald *Griffin's *Tales of the Munster Festivals*. Eugene Hamond, a young man of humble birth, is reared and educated by a wealthy relative. He falls in love with well-to-do Emily Bury, but his self-consciousness leads to many difficulties.

Haliday, William (1788–1812), translator and grammarian. A Dublin-born solicitor, he published *Uraicecht na Gaedhilge* (1808), a grammar of Irish, and the first volume of a translation of *Foras Feasa ar Éirinn* by Geoffrey *Keating in 1811.

Hall, Anna Maria (Mrs S. C. Hall, née Fielding) (1800–1881), novelist. She was born in Dublin and grew up in Bannow, Co. Wexford, before leaving for London in 1815. She married the journalist Samuel Carter *Hall in 1824, thereafter collaborating with him on many works, including *Ireland, Its Scenery, Character, &c.* (1842). Her Wexford childhood provided background for her *Sketches of Irish Character* (1829). In works such as *Lights* *and Shadows of Irish Life* (1838) and *Stories of the Irish Peasantry* (1840) Mrs Hall sought to improve English understanding of Ireland. In *The *Whiteboy* (1845) she shows various ways by which Anglo-Irish relations might be improved.

Hall, Samuel Carter (1800–1889), editor and journalist. The son of an English army officer, he was born near Waterford and settled in London in 1821, where he joined *The Literary Observer*. In 1824 he married Anna Maria Fielding (*Hall), whose early stories he published and with whom he collaborated in writing *Ireland, Its Scenery, Character, &c.* (1842) and *A Week at Killarney* (1843). In 1826 he founded *The Amulet*, which he edited until 1837. For his pioneering work as editor of the *Art Union Monthly Journal* (later *The Art Journal*) from 1839 he was awarded a civil-list pension.

Halloran, Revd Laurence H[ynes] (1766–1831), poet; born in Ireland and educated at TCD. He wrote a poem on *The Battle of Trafalgar* (1806). Later he settled in Capetown and was dismissed from a teaching position for *Cap-Abilities, or South African Characteristics* (1811). Other verse includes *The Female Volunteer, or The Dawning of Peace* (1801) and *Lachrymae Hibernicae, or the Genius of Erin's Complaint* (1805).

Halpine, Charles Graham ('Private Myles O'Reilly') (1829–1868), comic poet. Born in Oldcastle, Co. Meath, he was a *Young Irelander who worked briefly in London before emigrating to America, becoming proprietor of *The New York Citizen*. Collections included *Lyrics by the Letter H* (1854); *The Patriot Brothers* and *Mountcashel's Brigade* were historical novels.

Hamilton, [Count] Anthony (?1646–1720), soldier and author. Born

in Roscrea, Co. Tipperary, he was Governor of Limerick in 1685, and fought at the *Boyne (1690). At the end of the *Williamite War he went to France, and at the Restoration returned to London. He produced elegant stories, translated as *Fairy Tales and Romances* (1846), and a version of Pope's *An Essay on Man* in French alexandrines.

Hamilton, Edwin (1849–1919), dramatist; educated at TCD, he went on to write waggish plays including *Rhampsinitus* (1873), *Ballymuckbeg* (1892), and *Turko the Terrible* (1871), a pantomime adapted to local conditions from a London piece.

Hamilton, Hugo (1953–), novelist; born in Dun Laoghaire, he trained as a journalist before publishing *Surrogate City* (1990), followed by *The Last Shot* (1991), *The Love Test* (1994), *Dublin Where the Palm Trees Grow* (1996), and *Headbanger* (1997).

Hamilton, William Rowan (1805–1865), polymath; born in Dublin and educated at TCD, he is best remembered for his mathematical theory of quaternions. In 1822, while still an undergraduate, he was appointed superintendent of Dunsink Observatory and Professor of Astronomy at TCD. Besides classical and European languages, he studied Arabic and Sanskrit. He accompanied William Wordsworth on his tour of Ireland. He wrote some notable philosophical sonnets.

Handy Andy (1842), a *stage-Irish novel by Samuel *Lover dealing with aspects of Irish life in a light-hearted way. The episodic plot centres on the title-character, a blundering servant.

Hangman's House (1925), a novel by Donn *Byrne. Connaught, daughter of Lord Chief Justice O'Brien of Glenmalure ('Jimmy the Hangman'), is loved by Dermot MacDermot, but her dying father persuades her to marry John D'Arcy, who proves cruel and deceitful. The novel portrays a vestigial Gaelic aristocracy, and is studded with comic and sentimental episodes.

Hanley, Gerald (1916–1992), novelist and travel writer. Born in Cork, the brother of James *Hanley, he joined the British army at the outbreak of the Second World War. His first novel, *Monsoon Victory* (1946), describes service in Burma. *The Consul at Sunset* (1951) depicts the twilight of empire. *The Year of the Lion* (1953) and *Drinkers of Darkness* (1955) are based on African experiences. *The Journey Homeward* (1961) was about the turmoil of Indian and Pakistani Independence, as was *Noble Descents* (1982). Hanley introduces matters of conscience into novels of action.

Hanley, James (1901–1985), novelist and playwright. Brother of Gerald *Hanley, he was born to a poor family in Dublin and, like the protagonist of his novel *Boy* (1931), he went to sea at 13, serving in the Canadian navy during the war and later as a merchant seaman. His literary output was prodigious, comprising nearly thirty novels, sixteen volumes of short stories, six plays, and seven volumes of other writings including an autobiography, *Broken Water* (1937). He wrote accurately about seafaring, and about a Liverpool Irish family in *The Furys* (1935), *The Secret Journey* (1936), *Our Time Is Gone* (1940), *Winter Journey* (1950), and *An End and Beginning* (1958). *No Directions* (1943) is an evocation of London during the Blitz. Plays include *Say Nothing* (1962) and *The Inner Journey* (1965).

Hannay, James Owen, see George *Birmingham.

Happy Days (1961), a play by Samuel *Beckett. Winnie, a woman in her 50s, is buried to her waist in a mound of sand and talks constantly to her husband Willie, sitting nearby, who remains largely silent.

Harbinson, Robert (pseudonym of Robert Harbinson Bryans) (1928–), autobiographer and travel writer; born in East Belfast and educated at Enniskillen. After working as a cabin-boy in Belfast Lough he became an evangelical preacher in London, Canada, and the wider world. The autobiographical series *No Surrender: An Ulster Childhood* (1960), *Song of Erne* (1960), *Up Spake the Cabin Boy* (1961), and *The Protégé* (1963) explores the culture of low-church Protestantism. *Tattoo Lily* (1961) and *The Far World* (1962) are story collections.

Hard Life, The (1961) a novel by Flann *O'Brien. Two orphans, Manus and his brother Finbarr (the narrator), are brought up in turn-of-the-century Dublin by Mr Collopy, a relative, whose mind is fixed on a project to institute public lavatories for women.

Hardiman, James (1782–1855), scholar. Born in Westport, Co. Mayo, he grew up in Galway and studied for the priesthood but did not proceed, owing to blindness in one eye. He worked in the Public Record Office in Dublin from 1811 until he returned to Galway in about 1830. In 1848 he was appointed Librarian at Queen's College, Galway [see *universities]. Hardiman's *History of the Town and County of Galway* (1820) lists inhabitants during the period of the *Rebellion of 1641. His *Irish Minstrelsy, or Bardic Remains of Ireland* (2 vols., 1831) is an anthology of Irish poetry from all periods, the contents ranging from relics attributed to mythological figures such as Tórna Éigeas to the contemporary Gaelic poet Antoine *Raiftearaí, whom he knew. The object of the work was to attest the antiquity of Irish poetry and to show that it possessed a dignity equal to the classical literatures of Greece and Rome. He also edited Roderick *O'Flaherty's *Chorographical Description of West or h-Iar Connaught* (1846). In *Irish Minstrelsy*, Hardiman enlisted a team of assistants including Thomas *Furlong, John *D'Alton, Edward Lawson, Henry Grattan *Curran, and William Hamilton *Drummond to render his prose translations in verse.

Harding, Michael (1953–), playwright and novelist; born in Cavan, he was educated there and at Maynooth, working as a teacher until 1985 when he became a full-time writer. *Priest* (1988) and *The Trouble with Sara Gullion* were novels, followed by *Strawboys* (1987), *Una Pooka* (1989), *Misogynist* (1990), *Hubert Murray's Widow* (1993), *Sour Grapes* (1997) and *Amazing Grace* (1998), all staged at the *Abbey Theatre. The plays deal in fractured relationships and identities and mostly have the *Troubles as a looming threat or dire presence.

Harley 913, a 14th-cent. Irish manuscript held in the British Library, containing writings in *Hiberno-English, Latin, and Norman French, among them *The *Land of Cokaygne*. Internal evidence indicates that the manuscript was written at the Franciscan monastery at Kildare.

Harmon, Maurice (1930–), critic and biographer; born in Balbriggan, Co. Dublin, he was educated at UCD and Harvard, teaching at Lewis Clarke College in Portland, Oregon, then Notre Dame, and UCD, where he became Professor. His work includes a *Select Bibliography for the Study of Anglo-Irish Literature and its Backgrounds* (1977); studies of Richard *Murphy (1978), Sean *O'Faolain (1984), Austin *Clarke (1989);

and a biography of O'Faolain (1995). *No Author Better Served* (1998) was an edition of the correspondence between Samuel *Beckett and Alan Schneider.

Harper's Turn, The (1982), a prose collection by Tom *MacIntyre, containing oblique fictions and enigmatic pieces.

Harris, Frank [christened James Thomas] (1856–1931), editor and autobiographer. Born in Galway, and educated at Armagh, he ran away to America in his early teens and worked at various occupations across the country. He moved to London, and by 1886 was editing the *Fortnightly Review*. In 1894 he took over the *Saturday Review*. In 1895 George Bernard *Shaw became his drama critic, and Oscar *Wilde dedicated *An Ideal Husband* to him. He wrote novels and plays, but made a mark with *The Man Shakespeare* (1909) and *Shakespeare and His Loves* (1910). His biography of *Oscar Wilde* (1916) incensed Boseyites and Wilde's defenders equally. *My Life and Loves* (1923–30) is an unabashed and unreliable account of his sexual exploits.

Harris, Walter (1686–1761), Anglo-Irish historian, and editor of the works of Sir James *Ware. Educated in Dublin and employed as administrator to the Bishop of Meath, he prepared *The Whole Works of Sir James Ware* in two volumes (1739 and 1746). His *History and Antiquities of the City of Dublin* (1766) was a pioneering work of research.

Harte, Jack (1944–), writer of fiction; born in Killeenduff, near Easkey, Co. Sligo, he was educated at UCD while working as a teacher, before becoming Principal of Lucan Community College. *Murphy in the Underworld* (1986), short stories, was followed by *Homage* (1992), a novella, and *Birds and Other Tails* (1996).

Hartigan, Anne, [Le Marquand]
(1937–   ), poet and playwright; born in
Reading, she was educated at the university there and became a visual artist.
She turned to writing in the 1980s, producing poetry collections such as *Long
Tongue* (1982), *Now is a Moveable Feast*
(1991), and *Immortal Sins* (1993); and the
plays *Beds* (1982), *La Corbiere* (1989), and
Jersey Lilies (1996).

Hartley, May (née Laffan) (?1850–
1916), novelist. Born in Dublin, she
married an English scientist teaching at
the Royal University [see *universities].
Flitters, Tatters and the Counsellor (1879)
were realistic studies of the lives of
slum children. *Hogan M.P.* (1876) charts
the rise and fall of an unscrupulous
nationalist; *The Honourable Miss Ferrard*
(1877) recounts the courtship of an
impoverished girl; *Ismay's Children* (1877)
explores the malignant influence of
*Fenianism; and *Christy Carew* (1880)
describes the heartlessness of Catholic
policy on mixed marriages.

Hartnett, Michael [Mícheál Ó hArt-
néide] (1941–1999), poet. Born in
Croom, Co. Limerick, and educated
locally, he moved to Dublin in 1963
where he co-edited the magazine *Arena*
with James *Liddy. He lived in Madrid
and London, then returned to Dublin
before moving to Newcastle West, Co.
Limerick, in 1974. *Anatomy of a Cliché*
(1968), a book of love-poems, draws
upon the wit of the *dánta grádha while
allowing feeling images of surprising
freshness. Translation was for Hartnett
a means of studying the techniques of
poetic language, as in *The Hag of Beare*
(1969), a version of one of the most con-
densed examples of the *early Irish
lyrics. *Gipsy Ballads* (1973) contained versions of Lorca. *A Farewell to English* (1975)
marked the end of a long apprenticeship in Irish. *Cúlú Íde/The Retreat of Ita
Cagney* (1975) shows him exulting in the
emotional spaciousness that Irish

opened up for him, a freedom further
exploited in *Adharca Broic* (1978) and *An
Phurgóid* (1983). *Do Nuala: Foidhne Chrainn*
(1984), a dark collection dedicated to
Nuala *Ní Dhomhnaill, confronts self-
doubt. The first volume of *Collected
Poems* (1984) contains a selection of his
work in English; a second volume contains translations, including versions of
his own poems in Irish (1986). *Inchicore
Haíku* (1985) marked a return to English,
while *An Lia Nocht* (1985) strips the psyche bare. A new phase announced itself
in *Poems to Younger Women* (1989) and *The
Killing of Dreams* (1992). Translations
continued with *An Damh-Mhac* (1987),
from the Hungarian of Ferenc Juhász;
selections from Daibhí *Ó Bruadair
(1985) and Nuala Ní Domhnaill (1986);
and versions of Pádraigín *Haicéad
(1993), *Ó Rathaille (1998) reflecting his
identification with Gaelic Ireland.

Haughey, Charles J. (1925–   ), politician; he was born in Castlebar, Co.
Mayo, and educated by the Christian
Brothers and at UCD, spending periods
of time with relatives in Swatragh, Co.
Derry. Marrying Maureen Lemass,
daughter of the Fianna Fáil Taoiseach
Seán Lemass, he joined the party, and
entered the Dáil in 1957. He became
Minister for Justice in 1961, and subsequently held Ministries in Agriculture
and Finance. He led Fianna Fáil 1979–
92, and became Taoiseach in 1979, a
position he held intermittently until
1992, when he resigned. His significant
legacy to Irish literary culture was the
Aos Dána scheme for the support of
writers and artists he established with
Anthony *Cronin in the 1980s.

Havard, William (1710–1778), actor-
playwright. Born in Dublin the son of a
vintner, he abandoned surgery for acting and appeared in London theatres
from 1730. After the success of *Scander-
beg* (1732) his manager was in the habit
of locking him in a room to grind out

verse plays. *Charles I* (1737) is a tear-jerker in which the king goes nobly forth to meet a death that only makes him more divine, while Cromwell wonders out loud if history will condemn him as a regicide. The doomed hero of *Regulus* (1774) is an advice-dispensing Roman reminiscent of Polonius.

Haverty, Anne (1959–), novelist and poet; born in Holycross, Co. Tipperary, she was educated at TCD and the Sorbonne, before working as a journalist on the *Irish Times* and elsewhere. A biography of *Constance Markievicz: An Independent Life* (1989) was followed by *Elegant Times* (1995), a history of the Brown Thomas store in Dublin. A compelling study of the compulsion and excitement of love issues in the novel *One Day as a Tiger* (1997), while *The Beauty of the Moon* (1999) is a collection of poems. *The Far Side of a Kiss* (2000) is a further novel.

Hayes, Maurice (1927–), civil servant and author; born in Killough, Co. Down, he was educated at QUB before becoming town-clerk of Downpatrick and eventually Ombudsman for Northern Ireland. He acted as adviser to and author of a number of commissions and reports, including an inquiry into electoral areas in 1992, and the 1999 investigation into the Royal Ulster Constabulary. *Sweet Killough Let Go Your Anchor* (1994) is an evocation of a Catholic childhood; *Minority Verdict: Experiences of a Catholic Public Servant* (1995) is a professional memoir; and *Black Puddings with Slim* (1996) returns to early boyhood and youth.

Hayes, Richard (Risteárd de Hae) (1902–1976), bibliographer. Born in Co. Limerick and educated at Clongowes Wood and TCD, he joined the National Library in 1923, becoming Librarian in 1940. Hayes produced extensive bibliographies of Irish writing in Irish and in

English. The first of these, with Brighid Ní Dhonnchadha, is the three-volume series *Clár Litridheacht na Nua-Ghaedhilge, 1850–1936* (1938–40), and the second a vast enterprise in two parts: *Manuscript Sources for the History of Irish Civilisation:* (11 vols., 1965) and *Sources for the History of Irish Civilisation: Articles in Irish Periodicals* (9 vols., 1970).

Hayward, Harold Richard (1892–1964), poet and topographical writer; born in Larne, and educated there, he worked for a firm in Liverpool before returning to Belfast where he joined the *Ulster Literary Theatre. *Poems* (1917) was followed by *Love in Ulster and Other Poems* (1922); *Sugarhouse Entry* (1936) was a novel of rural Ulster. He collected, recorded, and composed many ballads; perhaps the best-known is 'The Humour is on Me Now', his own composition, recorded with the singer Delia Murphy in 1942. From the late 1930s he embarked on the topographical series of books, illustrated by Raymond Piper and J. H. Craig, for which he is best-known. Amongst these are: *In Praise of Ulster* (1938), *Where the River Shannon Flows* (1940), *In the Kingdom of Kerry* (1946), and *Munster and the City of Cork* (1964). He died in a road accident near Ballymena.

Head, Richard (?1637–?1686), playwright and book-seller, born in Carrickfergus. A play called *Hic et Ubique, or the Humours of Dublin* (1663) concerns the exploits of English adventurers in Ireland. Head was part-author of *The English Rogue* (1665), a scabrous narrative written in the tradition of Spanish picaresque novellas. His other writings include *Proteus Redivivus, or the Art of Wheedling or Insinuation* (1675).

Healy, Dermot (1947–), poet and writer of fiction. Born in Finea, Co. Westmeath, he worked in the theatre for a time, then lived in Sligo. *Banished*

Misfortune (1982) was a collection of stories, followed by the novel Fighting with Shadows (1984), set in the border area of Fermanagh, and the script for the film Our Boys (1988). The Ballyconnell Colours (1992) is a collection of poems, as was What the Hammer (1998). A Goat's Song (1994) is a novel dealing with the tragic consequences of love between a Catholic and a Protestant in Co. Donegal. It was followed by The Bend for Home (1996), a memoir, and Sudden Times (1999), a further novel.

Heaney, Seamus [Justin] (1939–), poet. Born in Co. Derry, he was educated at St Columb's College and QUB. He taught for a year and then became a lecturer at QUB. His first collection, Death of a Naturalist (1966), is rooted in childhood experiences of life in rural Co. Derry. Door into the Dark (1969) shows a willingness to go beyond the familiar into the unknown. Wintering Out (1972) deals with exposure and endurance in poems that are circumspect about the re-emergent civil and sectarian conflict of the Northern Ireland *Troubles. Relaxing his former grip on the physical world, the poet now works through more nebulous intimations in his search for symbols adequate to the conflict. In 1972 Heaney moved from Belfast to Glanmore, Co. Wicklow, working for a time as a freelance writer and then at Carysfort College in Co. Dublin. North (1975) was his most controversial volume. The poetry involves a profound ambivalence of feeling, recognizing on the one hand the grounds for 'civilized outrage' at atrocity and on the other the impulse towards 'intimate revenge'. In Field Work (1979) a new voice is heard, and there is a movement outwards into the light. A central sequence entitled 'Glanmore Sonnets' contains mature love-poems that reflect a rueful awakening to life's tangled issues. A selection of Heaney's critical writings (Preoccupations: Selected Prose 1968–1978) appeared in 1980. The following year he accepted a post as Visiting Professor at Harvard where, in 1984, he was elected Boylston Professor of Rhetoric and Poetry. 1982 saw the publication of a children's poetry anthology, The Rattle Bag, co-edited with Ted Hughes. In 1983 Sweeney Astray, Heaney's translation of the Middle Irish romance *Buile Shuibne, was published by *Field Day, the Derry theatre company of which he had been a Director since its formation in 1980. The centrepiece of Heaney's next collection, Station Island (1984), is the title-poem, set at *Lough Derg, a traditional site of pilgrimage. The poem dramatizes a series of dream encounters with literary ghosts and dead figures from his personal history. The Haw Lantern (1987) is coloured by a newly-political language, conditioned by Heaney's admiration for Eastern European poets such as Zbigniew Herbert and Czeslaw Milosz. The T.S. Eliot Memorial Lectures at Canterbury in 1986 were published as The Government of the Tongue (1988)—a title which underlines Heaney's conviction that poetry is a form of responsible language. The Cure at Troy (1990), a play based on Sophocles' Philoctetes, and first performed by Field Day, dramatizes questions of personal conscience, duty, and loyalty to the tribe. In 1989 he was elected to the Chair of Poetry at Oxford. Seeing Things (1991) attests to a continued attentiveness to everyday reality, but also shows a concern with a metaphysical vision. This book evinces a buoyant confidence and a relaxed visionary quality. In 1993 he issued The Midnight Verdict, a verse translation of extracts from Brian *Merriman's *Cúirt an Mheán-Oíche bracketed by versions from Ovid's Metamorphosis, a juxtaposition allowing him to present a view of gender conflict. The Redress of Poetry (1995), was collected in Oxford Lectures, and in that year he was awarded the Nobel prize for literature. In The Spirit

Level (1997) a tough allegiance is evoked, while the poetry seeks to reconcile deep divisions. *Beowulf* (1999) is a deeply-felt version of the Anglo-Saxon warrior-epic. See Bernard O'Donoghue, *Seamus Heaney and the Language of Poetry* (1994).

Hearn, [Patricio] Lafcadio (1850–1904), orientalist and philosopher; born on Lefkas, one of the Ionian Islands (hence his name), to an Irish navy surgeon father and a local mother. He worked as a journalist, then moved to Japan in 1890, where he taught at the Imperial University, 1896–1903. Hearn admired the unity of Japanese life and culture. He married a Japanese and took the name Yakumo Koizumi. Amongst his books are *Glimpses of Unfamiliar Japan* (1894), and *Japan: An Attempt at Interpretation* (1904).

Heartbreak House: *A Fantasia in the Russian Manner on English Themes* (1920), a play by George Bernard *Shaw written in 1916–17. The play is set in the ship-like house of the retired sea captain Shotover, an eccentric, rum-drinking weapons inventor, who has two 'demon daughters': Hesione and Ariadne. The main plot concerns the fortunes of Ellie Dunn, who progresses from disillusionment to realism. The inhabitants of Heartbreak House represent a society on the brink of apocalyptic doom, unable to control the ship of state but playing furtive and childish games.

Hector, Annie (née French; pseudonym 'Mrs Alexander') (1825–1902), novelist. Born in Dublin, she moved to Liverpool, then London. In 1845 she became a magazine writer with encouragement from Mrs [Anna Maria] *Hall, issuing her first novel, *Look Before You Leap*, in 1865. *The Wooing of O't* (1873) was a three-decker tale of an orphaned middle-class London girl who refuses an English lord, but accepts his

impoverished cousin. *Kitty Costello* (1904) is the story of a naïve Irish girl come to England.

hedge schools, run on a fee-paying basis by private schoolmasters, provided the main means of education for the rural Catholic population in the 18th and early 19th cents. under the *Penal Laws and for some decades after *Catholic Emancipation. The growth of the hedge schools is attributed to the act of 1695 that forbade Catholics to run or teach in schools. Schoolmastering provided a livelihood for many Gaelic poets and scribes, such as Eoghan Rua *Ó Súilleabháin, Donncha Rua *Mac Conmara, and Mícheál Óg *Ó Longáin, who were no longer able to look to aristocratic patronage.

Héloïse and Abelard (1925), a novel by George *Moore drawing upon Peter Abelard's *Historia Calamitatum*, and retelling the story of the 12th-cent. lovers. Fulbert, Canon of Notre Dame, discovers that his niece Héloïse knows Latin and invites her to live with him. When Abelard, a famous controversialist, becomes Héloïse's tutor they fall in love; she becomes pregnant, and they flee to Brittany. Héloïse retires to a convent, Abelard to a monastery.

Henn, T[homas] R[ice] (1901–1974), scholar; born in Sligo he was educated in Fermoy and at St. Catharine's College, Cambridge, where he was Senior Tutor, 1945–47, and President, 1951–61. He served in the British army in the Second World War, rising to the rank of Brigadier. *The Lonely Tower* (1950) was a study of W. B. *Yeats; he edited J. M. *Synge in 1963, and embarked on the Coole edition of Lady *Gregory with Colin *Smythe towards the end of his life.

Herbert, William (1553–93), an undertaker for the Munster Plantation [see *plantation] who lived in Ireland as a colonist from 1587 to 1590. He is chiefly notable for his Latin treatise, *Croftus Sive De Hibernia Liber* (1591). He insists that Irish character and customs be stamped out.

Herne's Egg, The (published 1938), a verse play by W. B. *Yeats, remotely based on Samuel *Ferguson's epic *Congal* (1872) and telling how Congal steals eggs from a heron's nest and dies at the hands of a fool, as forewarned by Attracta, priestess of the Herne.

Herself Surprised (1941), a novel by Joyce *Cary, first of the Gulley Jimson trilogy, the others being The *Horse's Mouth* and *To Be a Pilgrim*. Sara, married to the wealthy Matt Monday, tolerates sexual advances from Hickson, who gets Jimson to paint nude studies of her. The novel portrays Sara's dangerous but loving readiness to adapt to life's surprises.

Hesperi-Neso-Graphia, *or A Description of the Western Isle* (1716), by W. M., later identified, perhaps correctly, with William Moffet, a schoolmaster. In the style of Farewell's The *Irish Hudibras*, it caricatures native Irish culture as barbaric and deranged.

Hewitt, John (1907–1987), poet; born in Belfast and educated at Methodist College and QUB. From 1930 he worked at the Belfast Museum and Art Gallery until he took up a position as Director of the Herbert Art Gallery in Coventry, 1957–72. His return to Belfast on retirement in 1972 marked the beginning of a period of intense poetic activity. In the 1940s his poetry had been strongly influenced by the notion of Ulster regionalism, and his anthology *Rhyming Weavers and Other Country Poets of Antrim and Down* (1974), reflects an interest in the dialect verse of the Protestant radicals [see *weaver poets]. His later poetry, too, is much concerned with exploring the Scots, English, and

Irish elements that make up his concept of Ulster identity. 'The Colony' elaborates a parallel between a Roman colony and *plantation Ireland. He is responsive to nature and expresses sympathy with the imaginative world of the Irish Catholics. As a poetry of the nonconformist conscience, Hewitt's work reflects his belief in progress, independence of mind, and rationalism. Hewitt's volumes of poetry include: *Conacre* (1943), *The Day of the Corncrake: Poems of the Nine Glens* (1969), *Out of My Time* (1974), *Time Enough* (1976), *The Rain Dance* (1978), *Mosaic* (1981), *Loose Ends* (1983) and *Freehold* (1986). He was awarded honorary degrees from NUU and QUB in 1974 and 1983 respectively. The *Collected Poems* was edited by Frank *Ormsby in 1992.

Hibernian Nights' Entertainments, The, a series of historical fictions by Samuel *Ferguson, published in *Blackwood's Edinburgh Magazine* ('The Return of Claneboy', 1833; and 'Shane O'Neill's Last Amour', 1834) and in the *Dublin University Magazine* ('The Death of the Children of Usnach', 1834; 'The Captive of Killeshin', 'The Rebellion of Silken Thomas', and 'Corby Mac Gillmore', 1835; 'Rosabel of Ross', 1836). The tales are supposedly told by the poet Turlogh Buy O'Hagan, imprisoned with Henry and Art O'Neill in Dublin Castle before the rising of 1594–1603 [see Hugh *O'Neill].

Hiberno-English, the term applied to those varieties of English which were and are spoken, and sometimes written, in Ireland. These varieties are also sometimes referred to as Anglo-Irish or Irish-English. They are distinct from other varieties of English in that they have their own grammatical structures, vocabularies, sound systems, pronunciations, and patterns of intonation. The most significant varieties are the Northern and the Southern: roughly speaking, those to the north or the south of a line drawn from Bundoran in the west to Dundalk in the east. The dialect of parts of the north and east of Ulster is also, and perhaps more appropriately, termed Ulster Scots. Modern Hiberno-English derives from the *plantations of the 16th and 17th cents. Parts of the north and east of Ulster were settled by lowland Scots (giving rise to Ulster Scots) and the rest of Ulster, Leinster, and Munster were settled by regional dialect speakers of English, many of whom are likely to have come from the north of England. From its introduction Modern Hiberno-English was at a remove from the English of England, and remained conservative by comparison. However, it was in almost continuous contact with Irish, so that the influence of that language was considerable and pervasive. As Modern Hiberno-English progressively superseded Irish it often added (at least temporarily) further elements from that language, but it also lay upon a deep substratum of Irish, which is exposed in the English speech of natural bilinguals. Hiberno-English, like other regional varieties of English, is in general a spoken rather than a literary language. In the late 17th and 18th cents. a number of Irish-born dramatists achieved success in England with plays that made use of the *stage-Irishman and his speech to point to the follies and cruelties of English society. Among these plays are George *Farquhar's The *Twin Rivals (1702) and The *Beaux' Stratagem (1707), and Thomas *Sheridan's The Brave Irishman (1773). The exaggeration of the characteristics of Hiberno-English is seen in its most extended form in Dion *Boucicault's The *Shaughraun (1874). Although the stage-Irishman and his language survived into the 20th cent., a new realism in the portrayal of the Irish and their language emerged in the *literary revival, notably in the work of *Lady Gregory and

*Synge. Synge's approach is developed to a degree in the Dublin plays of Sean *O'Casey. Modern Irish drama is free to handle any subject-matter and any kind of character and will use the appropriate language, whether Hiberno-English or not. Billy *Roche's and Marina *Carr's plays in the 1990s addressed contemporary issues and used an energetic version of Hiberno-English. In prose fiction, Hiberno-English is generally used only when reporting the speech of peasants. An early example is Maria *Edgeworth's *Castle Rackrent (1800), the whole of which is narrated by a southern Hiberno-English speaker. More convincing, perhaps, is the representation of northern Hiberno-English in the works of William *Carleton. A significant creative departure is the Molly Bloom soliloquy in *Joyce's *Ulysses (1922), while in *Finnegans Wake (1939) Hiberno-English is used as a major component in the conglomeration of linguistic forms that combine to produce a new language for prose fiction. See Diarmuid Ó Muirithe, The English Language in Ireland (1977).

Hidden Ireland, The, see Daniel *Corkery.

Hiffernan, Paul (1719–1777), journalist and playwright. Born in Co. Dublin, he studied at Montpellier for the priesthood and returned to Dublin about 1747. His works include The Self Enamour'd, or the Ladies' Doctor (1750), The Hiberniad (1754), The Earl of Warwick (1764), The Philosophic Whim (1774), and The Wishes of a Free People (1761), a dramatic poem. Hiffernan made scurrilous attacks on David Garrick and others, notably in the *Bickerstaffe affair.

Higgins, Aidan [Charles] (1927–   ), fiction writer. Born in Celbridge, Co. Kildare, he was educated at Clongowes Wood. He lived in South Africa (1958–60), and spent extended periods in

Germany and Spain. *Felo de Se* (1960) was a volume of stories exploring inanition. Higgin's best-known novel was *Langrishe, Go Down* (1966). *Images of Africa* (1971) is a diary of his South African sojourn. *Balcony of Europe* (1972) is an analysis of late 20th-cent. tedium. The autobiographical improvisations of *Scenes from a Receding Past* (1977) have an arresting rhythm and structure, as does *Bornholm Night-Ferry* (1983). *Lions of the Grunewald* (1993), a novel, revisits cosmopolitan settings.

Higgins, F[rederick] R[obert] (1896–1941), poet. Born in Foxford, Co. Mayo, he grew up in Co. Meath. He worked as a clerk in a building firm, then in the Clerical Workers' Union. In 1915 he and Austin *Clarke became friends, encouraging each other in their enthusiasm for *folklore, Gaelic literature, and the art of the early Irish Church [see *monasticism]. *Island Blood* (1925) was followed by *The Dark Breed* (1927), and these early volumes show him adapting the images and directness of *Hyde's *Love Songs of Connacht*. He revels in the opportunities for musical effect offered by imitating Gaelic metres, as Austin Clarke was doing at the same time. In *Arable Holdings* (1933) and *The Gap of Brightness* (1940) the style is barer and the verse has a rough energy. A one-act play, *A Deuce of Jacks*, was produced at the *Abbey in that year, and in 1936 he was made a director, and later manager of the theatre.

Higgins, Rita Ann (1955–), poet. Born in Galway and educated there, she worked at various jobs, married, and had two children before publishing her first book, *Goddess on the Mervue Bus* (1986), which revealed an urgent and sardonic voice. Other collections include *Witch in the Bushes* (1988), *Goddess and Witch* (1989), *Philomena's Revenge* (1992), *Higher Purchase* (1996) and *Sunny Side Plucked* (1996); while *Face Licker Come Home* (1991) and *God-of-the-Hatch-Man* (1993) are plays.

High Consistory, The (1981), a novel by Francis *Stuart. In a plane crash on a flight from Paris to Ireland, the diaries and memoirs of Simon Grimes, the artist-hero of the novel, are mixed together, and the narrative follows the accidental re-ordering of these documents with much shuttling back and forth in time.

Hinkson, Katherine, see Katharine *Tynan.

Hinkson, Pamela (1900–1982), novelist, born in London, the daughter of Katharine *Tynan. She was educated privately, and travelled in Europe for the British Ministry of Information. Her staple output was girls' school fiction. However, *End of All Dreams* (1923), her first novel, together with *The Deeply Rooted* (1935) and *The Lonely Bride* (1951), are about Irish *big house families in decline. *The Ladies of the Road* (1932) tells of an English and an Irish country house. *Indian Harvest* (1941) is based on her Indian experience.

historical cycle, a group of early Irish tales composed between the 9th and 12th cents., and so designated because they deal with persons and events of the early historical period from the 6th to the 8th cents. Often concerned with kingship, dynastic conflicts, and battles, these tales are sometimes also referred to as the king cycle. A number of the tales deal with specific events of historical record. Among these are *Cath Maige Rath* and *Cath Almaine*, recounting events in battles which took place in AD 637 and 722 respectively. The famous *Buile Shuibne* moves beyond immediate historicity to incorporate mythic and religious concerns. A further 12th-cent. development was the writing of pseudo-historical tracts such as *Cogadh Gaedhel re Gallaibh* and *Caithréim Chellacháin Chaisil*. These purport to describe the period of the *Viking wars but, in fact, rewrite history as dynastic propaganda.

Historical Memoirs of the Irish Bards, see Joseph Cooper *Walker.

historiography, Gaelic, see *Gaelic historiography.

History of Ireland: *The Heroic Period* (1878), the first volume of a series of legendary histories by Standish James *O'Grady which mixes material about the pre-Celts, the *Celts, and *kingship with narratives dealing with the Milesian invasion [see *Lebor Gabála], the defeat of the Tuatha Dé Danann [see *mythology], *Fionn mac Cumhaill, and *Cú Chulainn, whose heroism provides the main focus of the book.

Hitchcock, Robert (?-1809), a Drury Lane prompter who moved to *Smock Alley about 1781 and wrote *An Historical View of the Irish Stage* (2 vols., 1788, 1794). The first full account of the subject, it is rich in anecdotes about dramatists, managers, and actors between 1637 to 1787. He wrote a number of comedies such as *The Coquette* (1777).

Hobhouse, Violet (née McNeill) (1864-1902), novelist. Born in Co. Antrim, she wrote some poetry and two novels, *An Unknown Quantity* (1898) and *Warp and Weft* (1899), the latter concerned with changes in the linen-producing communities of Ulster.

Hobson, Bulmer (1883-1969), Gaelic enthusiast and Republican activist. Born in Belfast, he was educated at Friends School, Lisburn. He joined the *Gaelic League in 1901, and co-founded Fianna Éireann in 1903. As Vice-President of *Sinn Féin in 1907, Hobson introduced the organization to the USA. He left

Sinn Féin and started and edited *Irish Freedom* in 1910, and organized the Howth gun-running in 1914. Hobson informed Eoin *MacNeill of the plans for the *Easter Rising, which led to MacNeill's countermanding order. He later became a civil servant under the Free State [see *Irish State]. Hobson's autobiography was *Ireland: Yesterday and Tomorrow* (1968).

Hoey, Frances Sarah (née Johnston) (1830-1908), novelist, born in Dublin. Daughter of a clerk, she married in 1846 and was soon widowed, then went to London. In 1858 she married John Cashel Hoey, formerly manager of *The *Nation. She produced many novels including: *A House of Cards* (1868), *A Golden Sorrow* (1872), and *Kate Cronin's Dowry* (1877).

Hogan, Desmond (1950-), fiction writer. Born in Ballinasloe, Co. Galway, he was educated at UCD. *A Short Walk to the Sea* (1975) was staged at the Peacock [see *Abbey Theatre] after which he published *The Ikon Maker* (1976), an atmospheric novel in which a young artist rediscovers an intimacy with his mother. *The Leaves on Grey* (1980) and *A *Curious Street* (1984) reveal a novelist who explores personal consciousness and national and community histories. *A New Shirt* (1986), a novel, and the story collections *The Mourning Thief* (1987), *Lebanon Lodge* (1988), and *A Link with the River* (1989) show Hogan anatomizing his own fictional world of the western midlands. *A Farewell to Prague* (1995) continues an odyssey of exploration into personal, sexual, and cultural histories.

Hogan, Edmund, SJ (1831-1917), toponymic author and Irish revivalist. Born in Great Island, Co. Cork, and educated in Rome, he was Todd Professor of Celtic at the *RIA and Professor of Irish language and history at UCD. Among many works, he translated the *Ulster cycle saga *Cath Ruis na Ríg for Bóinn* (*Battle of Rosanaree*) (1892), wrote on *Distinguished Irishmen of the Sixteenth Century* (1894) and also on *The Irish Wolfhound* (1897). His *Onomasticon Goedelicum* (1910) deals with Gaelic tribes and *place-names.

Hogan, James, see Augustus *Young.

Hogan, Robert (1930–1999), scholar; born in Boonville, Missouri, he was educated at the University of Missouri and taught at Delaware and elsewhere. *After the Irish Renaissance* (1968) was a history of Irish theatre after Sean *O'Casey. With Michael J. O'Neill he edited selections from the diaries of Joseph *Holloway; and with James Kilroy and others he provided a documentary history of the Irish theatre from 1899 to 1926 in six volumes (1975–1992). His *Macmillan Dictionary of Irish Literature* (1979) was expanded in 1996.

Hole in the Head, A (1977), a novel by Francis *Stuart exploring the workings of the neurological system in an attempt to understand the source of creativity. The writer Barnaby Shane is under treatment for a nervous breakdown. His recovery is complete only when Emily Brontë, his muse, disappears from his hallucinations and he is able to distinguish a frontier between the inner and outer worlds.

Holland-Tide (1827), Gerald *Griffin's first book is a set of regional tales consisting of a novella, 'The Aylmers of Bally-Aylmer', and six shorter stories such as 'The Brown Man', a grim narration that combines folk tale with Gothic horror.

Holloway, Joseph (1861–1944), Dublin-born architect and theatrical enthusiast. He remodelled the

Mechanics' Hall as the *Abbey Theatre for Miss *Horniman and W. B. *Yeats, and attended Dublin theatres with such regularity for fifty years that he left a journal of more than 200 volumes, now held in the National Library of Ireland. He also edited the section on Irish plays and playwrights in Stephen *Brown's *A Guide to Books on Ireland* (1912).

Holy Ireland (1935), a novel by Norah *Hoult. Set in turn-of-the-century Dublin, it tells the story of an intelligent and spirited girl, Margaret, driven to marry an English Protestant turned Irish theosophist by the bullying pietism of her father.

Home Rule, see *Irish Parliamentary Party.

Hone, Joseph [Maunsell] (1882–1959), biographer. Born in Dublin, he was educated at Wellington and Cambridge. He was a director of *Maunsel and Co. *A Study of W. B. Yeats* (1915) was followed by lives of *Berkeley (1932), George *Moore (1938), and *Yeats (1942).

Honest Ulsterman, The (1968–), a literary magazine founded by James *Simmons in Portrush, Co. Antrim, while teaching at the NUU. It was subsequently edited by Michael Foley and Frank *Ormsby, 1969–72; Ormsby alone, 1972–84; Ormsby with Robert Johnstone, 1984–9; then by Johnstone with Ruth Hooley; and latterly by Tom Clyde and Frank *Sewell.

Hope, Jemmy (?1765–1846), weaver and revolutionary. Born in Templemore, Co. Antrim, he joined the *United Irishmen in 1795, and took part in the Battle of Antrim in 1798. Escaping to Dublin, he lived in hiding with his family until the amnesty of 1806, when he returned to Belfast.

Hopper, Nora [Jane] (1871–1906), poet. Born in Exeter, daughter of an Irish officer in the British army, she published poetry in the *Celtic Twilight mode including *Ballads in Prose* (1894), *Under Quicken Boughs* (1896), *Songs of the Morning* (1900), *Aquamarines* (1902), and *Dirge for Aoine and Other Poems* (1906).

Horniman, Annie E[lizabeth Fredericka] (1860–1937), founding patron of the *Abbey Theatre. An English tea-merchant heiress, she was educated at the Slade School of Art and met W. B. *Yeats through the Order of the Golden Dawn in London. She began subsidizing the Irish National Theatre Society in 1903, purchasing for it the disused theatre in Abbey Street in 1904. She commenced paying professional salaries in 1905, but strongly opposed a policy of nationalist plays, leading to a rift with the management and members of the company. The final break occurred when the theatre remained open during the period of mourning for Edward VII in 1910. She sold out to the directors on favourable terms. Her subsequent work in Manchester, continuing until 1917, contributed greatly to the English repertory theatre movement.

Horse's Mouth, The (1944), a novel by Joyce *Cary, third and most exuberant of the first trilogy, the others being *Herself Surprised* (1941) and *To Be a Pilgrim* (1942). Gulley Jimson, a fiery 60-year old painter, is just out of prison. He persuades his ex-mistress Sara Monday (whose story is told in *Herself Surprised*) to relinquish her claim on early canvases. Rent by rage and violence, but equally by energy and delight (the 'horse's mouth'), Jimson is addicted to quotations from William Blake, while Adolf Hitler, a distant but fearsome presence in the novel, represents demonic freedom from restraints.

Hostage, The (1958), a three-act play by Brendan *Behan, directed by Joan Littlewood for the Theatre Workshop in London. The play is set in a Dublin brothel managed by Pat, a former *IRA member, and his 'consort' Meg. The plot concerns the taking of a British soldier, Leslie, as a hostage brought to Dublin from Northern Ireland to forestall the execution of an IRA man in Belfast. Behan allowed Littlewood to turn his rendering of the tragedy *An *Giall* into a bawdy musical-hall piece.

Hotel, The (1927), first novel by Elizabeth *Bowen, set against the background of the Italian riviera, where a motley collection of English people on holiday engage in a variety of encounters.

Hoult, Norah (1898–1984), novelist. Born in Dublin, she was educated in the north of England. She worked mostly as a journalist in London, visiting Ireland in 1931–7 and America in 1937–9. As a writer of short stories she dealt mostly with themes of prostitution, alcoholism, and bad marriages in collections such as *Poor Women* (1930) and *Cocktail Bar* (1957). *Holy Ireland* (1935) describes the impact of the paternalistic narrow-mindedness of Patrick O'Neill on his family at the turn of the century. *Coming from the Fair* (1937), a sequel, deals with the family's disintegration after his death in 1903. *Father and Daughter* (1958) and *Husband and Wife* (1959) narrate the experiences of the Mallory family of actors travelling in the Irish midlands.

House by the Churchyard, The (1863), a novel by Joseph Sheridan *Le Fanu, first serialized in the *Dublin University Magazine, it is narrated by Charles Cresseron (a Le Fanu family name) and set in the 18th cent. at Chapelizod, outside Dublin. The central incident is the attack on an army doctor, Sturk, whose skull is smashed by a mysterious assailant, after Sturk recognizes Paul Dangerfield as a murderer.

House in Paris, The (1935), a novel by Elizabeth *Bowen, centring on the brief affair, as seen in retrospect, between Karen Michaelis and Max Ebhart while the former is engaged to Ray Forrestier and the latter to Karen's friend Naomi Fisher. The affair and Max's suicide are seen to be spitefully engineered by Naomi's mother.

House of Children, A (1941), a novel by Joyce *Cary, set on the Inishowen peninsula, Co. Donegal (Annish), and based upon Cary's own childhood experiences in the 1890s. Evelyn and his brother Harry, whose mother has recently died, are being looked after by their aunt. They play with cousins and local children in a world of freedom where the young are left to their own devices.

House of Gold, The (1929), a novel by Liam *O'Flaherty set in 'Barra' (Galway), covering one frantic day in the lives of four characters whose fate is suggested by a three-part division into Passion, Disintegration, and Nemesis. Ramon Mor Costello is ruined by Nora, who is both angel and devil.

How It Is (in French as Comment c'est, 1961; in English 1964), a novel by Samuel *Beckett. In fragmentary sentences forming unpunctuated paragraphs, a disembodied voice tells of his progress crawling through a void towards someone called Pim; of time spent torturing him; and of the period that follows the encounter.

How Many Miles to Babylon? (1974), a novel by Jennifer *Johnston, dealing with the friendship between Alex Moore, a young Anglo-Irishman, and Jerry Crowe, a Catholic stable-boy.

Years later the two serve in the First World War in France.

How to Settle Accounts with Your Laundress (1847), a romantic farce by Joseph Stirling *Coyne. Wittington Widgett, a tailor, is engaged to Mary the Laundress, but her 'hymeneal' determination unnerves him. After much farcical distraction Widgett falls into the arms of his fiancée.

Howard, Gorges Edmund (1715–1786), poet and dramatist. Born in Coleraine, Co. Derry, he wrote several verse tragedies including the patriotic; The Siege of Tamor (1774). Miscellaneous Works in Verse and Prose appeared in 1782.

Huddleston, Robert, see *weaver poets.

Hull, Eleanor (1860–1935), Gaelic scholar and translator. Born in Manchester, she was educated at Alexandra College, Dublin, and was encouraged in Irish studies by Standish Hayes *O'Grady. In 1898 she issued an account of the *Cú Chulainn saga and with others established the year after the Irish Texts Society, aiming to publish the manuscript materials and records of Irish literature and *folklore. Her other publications include Pagan Ireland (1904), Early Christian Ireland (1904), A Textbook of Irish Literature (2 vols., 1906), and The Poem Book of the Gael (1912). Among her verse translations of Irish poetry is 'Be Thou My Vision, O Lord of My Heart', which appears in the Canterbury Hymn Book.

Hungerford, Margaret Wolfe (née Hamilton) (1855–1897), romantic novelist. Born in Cork, she wrote some thirty light novels such as Molly Bawn (1878), A Little Irish Girl (1891), The Red House Mystery (1893), and The Hoyden (1894). Lady Verner's Flight (1893) is about the abuse of a wife.

Hurrish: *A Study* (1886), a novel by Emily *Lawless set in Co. Clare during the Land War [see *Land League]. Hurrish (Horatio) O'Brien, a prosperous small farmer, accidentally kills Matt Brady, a resentful neighbour who has attacked him. When he is acquitted of murder, Brady's brother wounds him fatally in revenge.

Hutcheson, Francis (1694–1746), philosopher; born near Saintfield, Co. Down, he was educated at Glasgow University, where he was elected to the Chair of Moral Philosophy. His major works include: *Inquiry into the Original of our Ideas of Beauty and Virtue* (1725), *An Essay on the Passions with Illustrations on the Moral Sense* (1728), and *A Short Introduction to Moral Philosophy* (1747). Hutcheson's moral philosophy greatly influenced contemporaries such as his own pupil Adam Smith, while David Hume sent *A Treatise of Human Nature* to him for comment. His work formed an important link between Locke and Scottish rationalist thought. Much of his ethical thinking is directed against self-interest as the overriding motive, and he is credited with laying the foundation of classical utilitarianism with the doctrine of 'the greatest happiness for the greatest numbers'. At Glasgow, Hutcheson was part of the 'New Light' theological group, with strong links with the non-subscribing Presbyterian movement represented in Ireland by John *Abernethy, Robert *Molesworth, and others. His ideas had considerable influence on the liberal tradition in Ulster and on his friend Thomas Drennan, father of William *Drennan, the *United Irishman.

Hutchinson, Francis (1660–1739), historian. Born in Causington, Derbyshire, and educated at Cambridge, he became Vicar of Hoxne in Suffolk. *An Historical Essay Concerning Witchcraft* (1718) reflects his experiences of such cases. On his appointment as Bishop of Down and Connor in 1720 he went to live in Lisburn. To speed up conversion on Rathlin Island he sponsored the publication of *The Church Catechism in Irish* in 1722. His *A Defence of the Antient Historians, with a particular Application of it to the History of Ireland and Great Britain* (1734) reveals his familiarity with Irish *mythology.

Hutchinson, Pearse (1927–) poet. Born in Glasgow to Irish parents, he was brought back to Dublin in 1932, and educated at UCD. His first book was a volume of translations from the Catalan of Josep Carner, *Poems* (1962). *Dolmen Press issued his collection, *Tongue Without Hands* (1963). His next volume, *Faoistin Bhacach* (1968), was in Irish, allowing a different emotional register from English. *Expansions* (1969) contains much outraged social comment. *Watching the Morning Grow* (1972) relates the form of poetry to change. *The Frost Is All Over* (1975) was followed by *Climbing the Light* (1985). *Le Cead na Gréine* (1989), Hutchinson's second collection in Irish, reveals a poetry charged with pity. *The Soul that Kissed the Body* (1990) is a selection of his Irish poems translated by the poet himself. *Barnsley Main Seam* (1997) remains open, thoughtful, and loving.

Hutton, Seán (1940–), poet. Born in Dublin, he had his primary education in Hacketstown, Co. Carlow, then attended UCD and Hull University. He worked as a teacher in Bridlington, Yorkshire, 1969–88, then for the British Association for Irish Studies. Amongst his collections are *Go Cathair Na Traoi* (1980), *Gáirdín Mo Sheanuncail* (1983), *Seachrán Ruairí* (1986), and *Na Grása* (1993). The title-poem of *Seachrán Ruairí* follows a walk round Dublin made by Roger *Casement which he recorded in *The Black Diaries* (1959).

Hy Brasil, see *sídh.

Hyacinth Halvey (1906), a play by Lady *Gregory, in which Hyacinth, the new sanitary inspector, arrives in Cloon. Unable to discourage the locals in their desire to see him as an exemplary character, his efforts to blacken himself farcically redound to his credit.

Hyde, Douglas (1860–1949), scholar, cultural activist, and first President of Ireland, 1938–45. Born at Frenchpark, Co. Roscommon, and educated at home, he learned Irish from James Hart, and at TCD, where he joined the *Society for the Preservation of the Irish Language, the Young Ireland Society where he met W. B. *Yeats. He studied law, winning several college prizes in literature and oratory while beginning to publish original poems in Irish under the pseudonym 'An Craoibhín Aoibhinn' ('The Pleasant Little Branch'). In 1888 Yeats included three folk-tales translated by him in *Fairy and Folk Tales of the Irish Peasantry*, where notice is given of Hyde's forthcoming *Leabhar Sgéaluigheachta* (1889), a collection of stories and rhymes in Irish made by him from living speakers. *Beside the Fire* (1890) reprinted the three tales along with others and provided facing-page translations in an adaptation of *Hiberno-English usage. In 1890 Hyde began publishing in *The *Nation* a series of 'The Songs of Connacht' with commentary and translations. He spent a year teaching at the University of New Brunswick, Canada, before becoming President of the newly formed National Literary Society [see *literary revival] on his return in 1891. His inaugural address to the Society, 'On the Necessity for De-Anglicizing Ireland', on 25 November 1892 argued for the preservation and revival of all that was best in Irish language and culture. In October 1893 he married Annette Kurtz. When the *Gaelic League was founded by Eoin *MacNeill,

Thomas O'Neill *Russell, and others in July 1893, Hyde became its President, resigning his office in the National Literary Society. His determination to keep the League out of political involvements held sway until the rise of the *Irish Volunteer movement, when the League's constitution was changed at the Dundalk Ard Fheis (AGM) of 1915 to declare the aim of achieving a free, Gaelic-speaking Ireland. Hyde resigned immediately. His *Love Songs of Connacht* (1893) collected the series of poems published in the *Nation* in 1890 and continued in the *Weekly Freeman*, 1892–3. Publication in book form allowed the opportunity of recasting a number of them into English verse, reproducing the rhymes and metres of the originals in the manner initiated by Edward *Walsh. Hyde's commentary for these songs describes the Gaelic world out of which they come, while the literal translations carry into English the directness of the originals. *The Story of Early Gaelic Literature* (1895), a first attempt at a literary history of a complex body of material, was followed by the magisterial *A Literary History of Ireland* (1899). A more popular contribution to the language revival was *Casadh an tSúgáin*, a play written by Hyde from a scenario by Yeats and performed by the Gaelic League Amateur Dramatic Society at the Gaiety Theatre in 1901, with Hyde playing the lead part of Red Hanrahan. In 1905 Hyde became Professor of Modern Irish at UCD, and in the following year he went on a fund-raising tour of the USA (described in *Mo Thuras go hAmerice*, 1937), where he raised money for the Gaelic League. *Religious Songs of Connacht* (1905–6) collected, translated, and provided commentary upon Connacht religious folklore. *Songs Ascribed To Raftery* (1907), which had also appeared in serial form in newspapers, was an edition of the poet's works [see Antoine *Raiftearaí], with a commentary on his life. Other volumes of folklore were

Legends of Saints and Sinners (1916) and *Sgéalta Thomáis Uí Chathasaigh* (1939). Hyde served as an Irish Free State Senator [see *Irish State], 1925–6. He was elected President of Ireland in 1938. *Mise agus an Connradh* (1937) is an account of his management of the Gaelic League. See Janet and Gareth Dunleavy, *Douglas Hyde: A Maker of Modern Ireland* (1991).

Hyde, H[arford] Montgomery (1907–1989), biographer. Born in Belfast and educated at QUB and Oxford, he served as an Intelligence Officer in the Second World War. Thereafter he wrote up a great number of case histories, notably *The Trials of Oscar Wilde* (1948) and *The Trial of Sir Roger Casement* (1960). He wrote a life of Edward *Carson (1953), and two studies of Oscar *Wilde (1963 and 1976).

I Knock at the Door, see *Auto-biographies* [Sean O'Casey].

Iberno-Celtic Society, the, founded on 28 January 1818 to preserve and publish ancient Irish literature, reflecting the antiquarian interests of sections of the *ascendancy. It published one volume, the *Transactions*, comprising Edward *O'Reilly's *Irish Writers* (1820).

Ideal Husband, An (1895), a comedy by Oscar *Wilde in which a wife defends her marriage against the machinations of Mrs Cheveley, who is blackmailing her husband, Sir Robert Chiltern, over his past involvement with the shady financier Baron Arnheim.

Ideas of Good and Evil (1903), a volume of early essays by W. B. *Yeats. 'The Autumn of the Body' is written in a mannered and allusive style. 'The Symbolism of Poetry' proposes that symbols call down disembodied powers. 'The Philosophy of Shelley's Poetry' deals exclusively with that poet's symbols, while 'Magic' is a profession of faith. In 'At Stratford-on-Avon' Yeats presents Shakespeare as a poet writing out of collective knowledge.

Image, The (1909), a tragi-comedy by Lady *Gregory, dealing with the hopes and disillusionment of a village community when two whales are washed ashore.

Imbolg, see *festivals.

Immram Brain maic Febail (*Voyage of Bran Son of Febal*), one of the earliest of the immrama or voyage tales [see *tale-types], possibly written in the 8th cent. Besides the typical immram feature of sea travel to strange islands, it also displays elements of the echtra tale-type concerning excursions to the other-world [see *sídh]. A woman of the sídh describes to Bran the beauties of her island paradise. Bran departs with a crew and meets the sea-god Manannán mac Lir [see Irish *mythology]. Reaching their destination, Bran and his companions stay for many years, although it seems only a year. When they finally return home, one of the crew turns to ashes. Bran relates the story of his voyage, writes it down in *ogam, and sails away again.

Immram Curaig Máele Dúin (*Voyage of Máel Dúin's Boat*), an immram or voyage tale [see *tale-types], dating from the 8th or 9th cent. Máel Dúin learns of the murder of his father by marauders and embarks on a sea voyage to avenge him. He sees many wonders and faces great dangers. Máel Dúin himself undergoes a transformation and is reconciled with the murderers.

Immram Snédgusa ocus Maic Riagla (*Voyage of Snédgus and Mac Riagla*), an immram or voyage tale [see *tale-types] dating from the 10th cent. Snédgus and Mac Riagla, two monks from the monastery of Iona [see *Colum Cille] undertake a sea pilgrimage for the love of God, in the course of which they come upon many islands in the ocean, similar to those of the other voyage tales.

Immram Ua Corra (*Voyage of the Uí Chorra*), an immram or voyage tale [see *tale-types] dating from the 11th cent. Conall Derg Ua Corra and his wife make a pact with the devil in order to secure an heir. Three boys are born on the same night. When they grow up they kill clerics and burn churches, but they repent and embark on a voyage of pilgrimage.

Importance of Being Earnest, The

(1895), a play by Oscar *Wilde. Jack Worthing and Algernon Moncrieff both pretend to be called Ernest in order to secure the affections of Gwendolen Fairfax and Cecily Cardew. The girls are led to think first that they are engaged to the same man and then that neither is really Ernest. The ensuing confusions are resolved when it is discovered that Jack was indeed so named. The play derives force from a brilliant fabric of epigram and paradox.

Importance of Being Oscar, The

(1960), a one-man entertainment written and performed by Mícheál *MacLiammóir. It consists of excerpts from the writings of Oscar *Wilde linked by a sympathetic commentary, the actor taking the part both of characters and their author.

Imtheacht na Tromdáimhe, see

*Dallán Forgaill.

In a Glass Darkly (1872), a collection

of five stories by Joseph Sheridan *Le Fanu. 'Green Tea' tells of a clergyman driven to suicide by a persistent apparition. Both 'The Familiar' and 'Mr. Justice Harbottle' tell of hauntings. 'The Room in the Dragon Volant' is a novella-length mystery based on the use of a drug that causes a death-like trance, while 'Carmilla' is a vampire story. The stories are loosely linked as case histories narrated by Martin Hesselius, a German physician.

In the Shadow of the Glen (1903),

a play by J. M. *Synge. Nora Burke is married to an old farmer in Co. Wicklow who shams death to catch her making marriage plans with a young man. A Tramp offers her his company on the roads and she leaves with him.

In Wicklow and West Kerry (1910),

a travel-book by J. M. *Synge, consisting of 'In Wicklow', 'In West Kerry', 'In the Congested Districts', and 'Under Ether'.

inauguration, originally the ἱερος γάμος (sacred marriage), a symbolic mating of the new king with the goddess of the kingdom [see *kingship]. Scholars claim that the most famous of these inaugural fertility rites was the Feis Temro (feast of *Tara), at which the new king married the goddess *Medb [see also *Lia Fáil]. The last instance of this event occurred in AD c.560. These rites were tenaciously recalled, with traditional rhetoric, in medieval Irish literature as metaphors of kingship, but by then the clergy had thoroughly christianized inauguration.

Indo-European, the term used to refer to the family of languages which were originally spoken throughout much of Eurasia west of the Urals and also in the Indian subcontinent, with an outlying branch in Chinese Turkestan. The language from which all these languages are descended, called proto-Indo-European, can be reconstructed by historical and comparative linguistics. It was probably spoken in the Pontic-Caspian region of southern Russia in about 3000 BC. The earliest attested subgroups of the Indo-European language family are Anatolian, Hellenic, Indic, and Iranian. The other major subgroups are: *Celtic, Italic, Germanic, Baltic, Slavonic, Albanian, Armenian, and Tocharian.

Informer, The (1925), a novel by Liam

*O'Flaherty set in Dublin shortly after the *Civil War. Gypo Nolan, a mindless brute, informs on a fellow-revolutionary and thereafter is pursued by members of the 'Organization'. He escapes from a kangaroo court, but is betrayed by his mistress. He dies riddled with bullets.

Inglis, Brian (1916–1991), journalist and author. Born in Malahide, Co. Dublin, he was educated at TCD and Oxford, and joined *The Irish Times*. During the Second World War he served in the RAF. His many books, latterly devoted to medicine and psychic phenomena, include *Freedom of the Press in Ireland* (1954), *The Story of Ireland* (1956) and *Roger *Casement* (1973). *West Briton* (1966) was an autobiography.

Ingram, John Kells (1823–1907), author of 'The Memory of the Dead', a celebrated ballad of the *United Irishmen's Rebellion ('Who fears to speak of 'Ninety-eight . . . '), which appeared in *The *Nation* in April 1843. Born in Co. Donegal, he was educated in Newry, before going to TCD, where he became Professor of Oratory and of Greek, as well as founding editor of *Hermethena* in 1874.

Inishfallen, Fare Thee Well, see *Autobiographies* [Sean O'Casey].

Inniu, an Irish-language newspaper. Appearing first as *Indiu* and conceived as a daily paper, it was published weekly between 1943 and 1984. It was founded by Ciarán *Ó Nualláin and Proinsias Mac an Bheatha. Ó Nualláin remained as editor until 1979, when he was succeeded by Tarlach *Ó hUid. This well-produced paper was succeeded by *Anois* in 1984.

Innti, an Irish-language magazine containing verse, critical essays and reviews. It was founded in March 1970 as a poetry broadsheet by students of UCC, and was resurrected as a journal in 1980 by Michael *Davitt, one of the founder-editors. The magazine helped to draw attention to the work of a group of young poets associated with the

University, among them Nuala *Ní Dhomhnaill, Liam *Ó Muirthile, and Gabriel *Rosenstock. Frequently referred to as 'the *Innti* group', what they had in common was a commitment to a renewal of Irish-language poetry invigorated from a variety of sources, among them jazz and contemporary popular culture.

Insurrection (1950), Liam *O'Flaherty's last published novel. Set in Dublin during the *Easter Rising, it traces the transformation of Bartly Madden from Connemara labourer to heroic freedom fighter.

Insurrection in Dublin, The (1916), a descriptive essay by James *Stephens giving an eye-witness account of his day-to-day impressions of the *Easter Rising 1916 in the form of diary entries.

Intelligent Woman's Guide to Socialism and Capitalism, The (1928), a treatise by George Bernard *Shaw. Begun in response to a request for a few ideas about socialism, it grew into one of Shaw's principal essays on politics. He advocates equality of income as the proper goal of socialism.

Interpreters, The (1922), a novel by George *Russell set in a future when the materialistic investigation of nature has been exhausted, and scientists have traced all phenomena back to the three primal manifestations of deity: mind, substance, and energy.

Invincibles, the (1882), a *Fenian splinter group established with the plan of assassinating British government officials. On 6 May the Chief Secretary, Lord Frederick Cavendish, and the Under-Secretary of State, Thomas *Burke, were attacked with surgical knives and stabbed to death as they walked in the Phoenix Park, Dublin. Joe Brady, Tim Kelly, and Michael Kavanagh were arrested and hanged on the evidence of James Carey, who turned Queen's evidence.

Iomarbhágh na bhFileadh (*Contention of the Bards*), the title given to a dispute in verse concerning the rival historical claims to supremacy in Ireland of the descendants of the mythical Éibhear mac Míleadh, representing the southern half of Ireland, and those of Éireamhón mac Míleadh, representing the northern half. Much of the Contention occurred probably between 1607 and 1614 and was instigated by Tadhg mac Dáire *Mac Bruaideadha, ollam [see *áes dána] to the O'Briens (Ó Briain), Earls of Thomond. He was answered by another historian, Lughaidh *Ó Cléirigh of Co. Donegal. As the dispute gathered momentum it was joined, on the northern side, by two members of the legal family [see *law in Gaelic Ireland] of *Mac Aodhagáin, and by a Franciscan, Roibeard Mac Artúir (his name being used, perhaps, as a cover for Flaithrí *Ó Maoilchonaire).

Iona, an Irish monastery established by St *Colum Cille in 563 on an island in the Hebrides. After Colum Cille the post of abbot was always filled by members of his *fine, the Cenél Conaill, of whom *Adamnán, his biographer, is the most celebrated. By his day Iona was established as the head of the Celtic Church.

Íosagán agus Sgéalta Eile (1907), a collection of four short stories of children by Pádraic Mac Piarais (Patrick *Pearse). With their frank adoption of the form and technique of the modern short story they counteract the conservative tendency of other writers espousing traditional Irish *folklore models.

Iota (Kathleen Mannington, née Caffyn) (?1855–1926), novelist. Born in Co. Tipperary, she trained as a nurse before marrying Stephen Mannington, a surgeon and author. Her first novel, *A Yellow Aster* (1894), was on love and marriage. A number of New Woman novels followed, arguing for female liberation. The heroines of several of her books, such as *Poor Max* (1898) and *Anne Mauleverer* (1899), are spiritually-minded horsewomen given to opinions considered disgraceful by some reviewers.

IRA (Irish Republican Army), the name given to the national force that fought the *Anglo-Irish War, 1919–21, often known as the *Troubles, and later perpetuated by other militant groups regarding themselves as its successors in the struggle to secure an Irish Republic in thirty-two counties of Ireland. During the *Civil War the name was retained by the Republicans, referred to as 'Irregulars'. Only a small minority of the IRA continued operations after the main body, led by Eamon *de Valera, entered constitutional politics in 1927. From the 1930s to the 1960s the organization engaged in a campaign of violence in *Northern Ireland and Great Britain. Stringent measures in the North and de Valera's use of internment in the Republic resulted in the apparent termination of the movement in 1957. Under pressure of the events of the Northern Troubles of 1967–72, however, the IRA re-emerged to defend nationalist communities under sectarian attack. It soon took the form of a 'liberation' army fighting in the name of the Irish Republic and claimed the 'national right to self-determination' as its mandate for attacks on the army and police, on Unionists, and later on Catholics co-operating with security forces. When the Marxist-orientated Official IRA declared a unilateral cease-fire in 1972, the chiefly Ulster membership reformed itself as the Provisional IRA ('Provos'), with Sinn Féin as its political wing. By the 1990s its campaign of bombing and assassination, together with reprisals by Protestant paramilitaries (UDA, UVF, and UFF) and the activities of the security forces, had caused over 3,000 deaths in Ulster and elsewhere. After protracted talks between Sinn Féin and the leader of the Socialist and Democratic Labour Party (SDLP), John Hume, the IRA declared a ceasefire in August 1994. In February, 1996 the ceasefire ended, after political inaction, with bombs in London, Manchester, and Northern Ireland. In 1997, after a new Labour government was elected in Britain, the IRA renewed the ceasefire, and work began towards the Good Friday Agreement of 1998. Despite continuing political stalemate, the IRA guns remained silent into 2000.

Iremonger, Valentin (1918–1991), poet. Born in Dublin, he was educated at Coláiste Mhuire before joining the Department of Foreign Affairs, becoming ambassador to Sweden, Norway, and Finland (1964–73), Luxembourg (1973–79), then Portugal until retirement in 1980. The magazine, *Envoy* (1949–51), issued his first collection, *Reservations* (1950). After a long interval he published *Horan's Field and Other Reservations* (1972), followed by *Sandymount, Dublin* (1988), a final selection.

Irish Agricultural Organisation Society, see Horace *Plunkett.

Irish Archaeological Society, the. Founded in 1840, its principal objective was the publication of scholarly material on Irish antiquities. A key figure in the foundation and work of the Society was William Elliot Hudson (1796–1853), who also supported the Celtic Society, founded in 1845. Both societies merged in 1853 to form the Irish Archaeological and Celtic Society.

Irish Book Lover, The (1909–1957), a quarterly review of Irish literature and bibliography established by John Smyth *Crone. Its thirty-two volumes included authoritative bibliographies relating to Irish printing and publication at home and abroad, studies, biographies, notes and queries, and obituaries of Irish writers.

Irish Brigade (1692–1791), the, a corps in the French service that originated with the 5,000 or 6,000 men brought to France during the *Williamite War in exchange for troops sent to assist *James II in Ireland. A further 12,000 men who left Ireland under terms of the Treaty of Limerick initially formed a separate force under James II's authority, but were absorbed into the French army from 1697. Irish soldiers of this sort were known as the *Wild Geese, and such regiments, reinforced by further recruits from Ireland, were referred to as the Irish Brigade. In July 1791 separate national groupings within the French Republican army were abolished.

Irish bulls, see *stage-Irishman.

Irish Citizen Army, see *Easter Rising 1916.

Irish Cousin, An (1899), the first book by *Somerville and Ross, the former using the pseudonym 'Geilles Herring'. The novel was a study of *ascendancy society under pressure, interspersed with comic scenes anticipating the stories in *Some Experiences of an Irish R. M.

Irish Folklore Commission, the (An Coimisiún Béaloideasa Éireann), established in 1935 under the directorship of Séamus *Ó Duilearga, Professor of Folklore at UCD, a classified archive of Irish *folklore materials gathered under the direction of Seán *Ó Súilleabháin and Kevin *Danaher. It is the largest such holding in the world.

Irish Free State, see *Irish State.

Irish Homestead, The (1895–1923),
a weekly journal founded by Sir
Horace *Plunkett as the organ for
his Irish Agricultural Organisation
Society (IAOS). Its editors included T. P.
Gill, 1895–7, and George *Russell,
1905–23.

Irish Hudibras, The; *or the Fingallian
Prince* (1689), by James Farewell according to the copy in the British Library,
though nothing else is known about
him. In this parody of Virgil's *Aeneid*,
Book VI, Aeneas' descent into Hades is
transposed to Fingal in north Co.
Dublin, allowing the author to
denigrate Irish habits of dress,
behaviour, and speech. The caricature
of *Hiberno-English usage provides an
early example of *stage-Irish linguistic
stereotyping.

Irish language. Irish is a member of
the Celtic family of languages and,
before it split in recent centuries into
Modern Irish, Scottish Gaelic, and
Manx, was the sole attested representative of a distinct branch known to historical linguists as Goidelic [see *Celtic
languages and *Indo-European]. The
language is frequently referred to as
Gaelic, and the recent dialectal
divergence of Irish is sometimes recognized by differentiating the three main
dialects as Irish Gaelic, Scottish Gaelic,
and Manx Gaelic. The earliest Celtic
settlements in Ireland may reasonably
be associated with the beginnings of
the Iron Age, around 500 BC. The descendants of these Celtic settlers, com-
mingled with the descendants of earlier
inhabitants of the island, make their
first appearance in history almost 1,000
years later as one of the barbarian
peoples who were encroaching on the
British province of the declining
Roman Empire. These adventurers
were by then a linguistically and

culturally unified Goidelic-speaking
society, and were known to other
peoples in the region as Scoti. The
Anglo-Norman powers became involved
in the Irish-speaking world, first in Scotland and then in Ireland a century later
[see *Norman invasion]. In doing so,
they initiated a political process by
which gradually, over 400 years, the
Irish-speaking regions lost their
autonomy and became a denigrated
periphery within London's sphere of
influence. In Scotland, the south and
east became fairly rapidly English-
speaking; and by the 14th cent. the use
of Irish had receded to the Galloway
area in the south-west and to the Highlands in the north; it then held its position for about three centuries in Galloway, and until the 20th cent. in the
Highlands and Isles. In Ireland, though
substantial communities of Norman
French and English-speakers were
introduced during the early phases of
Anglo-Norman expansion, the Irish
language retained its dominance and,
by the late 15th cent., was again the
language of all sections of Irish society.
The Irish language then came under
renewed pressure in Ireland. The Tudor
and Stuart suppressions and population resettlements (1534–1610), the
Cromwellian settlement (1654), the
*Williamite War (1689–91), and finally
the enactment of the *Penal Laws (1695)
had the cumulative effect of eliminat-
ing the Irish-speaking aristocracy and
learned classes and of destroying their
institutions. As a result of these developments, by the 18th cent. Irish was,
with few exceptions, the language of
the disenfranchised and the dispossessed. In Galloway it was in terminal
decline. It remained the language of the
great mass of the population throughout the Highlands, Ireland, and Man,
and continued to be used extensively in
literature, religion, and local community affairs. Irish speakers included
the poorest classes and, though they

increased in number in the late 18th cent. and in the first decades of the 19th, reaching over four million, they were unprotected against the calamities which were to befall them repeatedly as the 19th cent. progressed. They were decimated by recurring famine, the most devastating period being 1845–8 [see the *Famine], and by the large-scale emigration which followed. According to the 1851 census of population, the first to include a question on language, the total number of Irish-speakers (including Irish-English bilinguals) had been reduced to 1,524,286, or just below a quarter of the population of Ireland. There are two reasons why, 100 years later, Irish still survives. Firstly, the rate of language shift slowed as it encountered around the western seaboard the densely populated areas, officially at the time called 'congested districts', in which communities were almost autonomous in their subsistence economies and had little access to competence in English. These are the areas, known collectively by the term *Gaeltacht, where an Irish-speaking tradition has continued. Secondly, towards the end of the 19th cent., there emerged a vigorous Irish-language restoration movement [see *Gaelic League]. The latter contributed significantly to a renewal of the idea of political separatism. As a consequence, Irish was designated as the 'national language' in the constitution of the Irish State in 1922.

Irish Literary Society, see *literary revival.

Irish Literary Theatre, see *Abbey Theatre.

Irish Magazine, see Walter *Cox.

Irish Melodies, see Thomas *Moore.

Irish metrics, see Irish *metrics.

Irish Minstrelsy, see James *Hardiman.

Irish Monthly, The (1873–1954; 83 vols.), a religious journal edited by Fr. Matthew *Russell. It serialized novels by Catholic authors such as Margaret *Brew and M. E. *Francis in the 1880s and 1890s. Before and during the *literary revival it carried writings by Oscar *Wilde, W. B. *Yeats, and others.

Irish National Dramatic Society, see *Abbey Theatre.

Irish Parliament, the (1692–1800). While building on a parliamentary tradition in Ireland that stretched back to 1264, the Irish Parliament in the years following the *Williamite victory of 1690–1 represented only the Protestant community, since Catholics were excluded by the *Penal Laws. Restrictions on its autonomy were relaxed in 1782 following a show of force from the *Irish Volunteers. The social and political prestige of the Anglo-Irish *ascendancy was at its highest in this period. A series of constitutional crises, in conjunction with the inability of Parliament to reform its representation to include Catholics, brought about the Irish Parliament's final abolition by the Act of *Union in 1801.

Irish Parliamentary Party, the, a title normally used to describe Irish nationalist representation at Westminster of the period between the leadership of Isaac *Butt in the 1870s to its effectual destruction by *Sinn Féin at the general election of 1918. Under *Parnell it was honed as a disciplined grouping in Parliament. The political objective of the Party was Home Rule, the term for the Repeal of the Union and the establishment of a separate Irish Parliament in Dublin. In 1890 the

Irish Party split as a result of the Parnell scandal, but reunited under John *Redmond in the following decade.

Irish R.M., see Some *Experiences of an Irish R.M.

Irish Sketch Book, The, see William Makepeace *Thackeray.

Irish State, the (1922–). The modern political entity that governs three-quarters of the island has a short history but a long pedigree, tracing its origins to a distinct Irish nation from the earliest times. After the Act of *Union of 1800 a separatist movement began to emerge, originating with the struggle for *Catholic Emancipation led by Daniel *O'Connell, nurtured by the Repeal Association, radicalized by *Young Ireland, and galvanized by the catastrophic experience of the *Famine. Crucially, the Gaelic concept of the sovereignty of Ireland [see Irish *mythology] was conflated with the modern idea of nationhood, while the insular character of the territory suggested a corresponding natural political unity. An Irish Republic was proclaimed by Patrick *Pearse at the outset of the *Easter Rising, and following the landslide victory of *Sinn Féin candidates in the general election of 1918, a separatist Irish parliament (Dáil Éireann) was established in Dublin in 1919, on behalf of which the *IRA fought the *Anglo-Irish War. The Anglo-Irish Treaty of December 1921 created an Irish Free State of twenty-six counties, the Better Government of Ireland Act of 1920 having already established the six northern counties as the state of *Northern Ireland, thus institutionalizing the partition of the island. The newly formed Free State was defined by its Constitution as a dominion of the British Commonwealth. A new Constitution of 1937, largely drawn up by Eamon *de Valera, contained a more explicit declaration of sovereignty and removed the king from internal affairs. The State, now called Éire or Ireland, remained associated for purposes of external relations with the Commonwealth. Impatience with this compromise led a coalition government under J. A. Costello to declare a Republic with effect from 18 April 1949. The creation under the 1937 Constitution of a popularly elected non-executive Presidency provided a Head of State. The administrative structure and legal system was built round British precedent and practice, as was the Civil Service. However, a conservative Catholic ethos was established involving *censorship and an embargo on divorce legislation. Irish neutrality during the Second World War increased the cultural and economic isolationism of the country. Later, free-trade policies with investment incentives under the Whitaker plan for economic development, implemented by Seán Lemass in 1958, in conjunction with United Nations membership in 1955 and membership of the European Economic Community in 1973, resulted in wider political affiliations with associated benefits and disadvantages. *Rapprochement* with Northern Ireland, the object of anti-partition propaganda throughout the history of the State, became a matter of constructive policy with the signing of a series of bilateral accords with the British Government from the Sunningdale Agreement (1973), to the Good Friday Agreement (1998).

Irish Statesman, The (1923–1930), a journal edited by George *Russell for Sir Horace *Plunkett. Russell merged it with The *Irish Homestead, the organ of the agricultural co-operative movement, which he was then editing.

Irish University Review (1970–), an interdisciplinary journal of Irish studies. Taking over from *University Review*, edited by Lorna Reynolds (1955–68), it was first edited by Maurice *Harmon at UCD then Christopher Murray, and Anthony Roche.

Irish Volunteers, the (1782). A force developing from a tradition of local defence in 18th-cent. Ireland, it emerged in response to invasion fears at the height of the American War of Independence in 1778. Mainly Protestant in its membership, it assisted Henry *Grattan in his campaign for legislative autonomy [see *Irish Parliament].

Irish Volunteers, the (1913), a paramilitary organization, formed in November 1913 and inspired by the formation of the *Ulster Volunteer Force in the previous January to prevent, militarily, the imposition of Home Rule on Ulster. The Irish Volunteers were organized by a steering committee headed by Eoin *MacNeill and Patrick *Pearse, representing all shades of nationalist opinion, and were reluctantly supported by John *Redmond. After the outbreak of war in 1914, the organization split on Redmond's call for enlistment in the British army with the anti-Redmondites providing the force [see *IRA] that would carry out the *Easter Rising.

Irish Writing (1946–57), a quarterly literary magazine published in Cork and edited by David *Marcus and Terence Smith, 1946–54, and later by Seán J. White, 1954–7.

Irisleabhar na Gaedhilge (*The Gaelic Journal*), a bilingual magazine founded under the auspices of the Gaelic Union [see *Gaelic League] in 1882, continuing publication until 1909.

Irisleabhar Mhá Nuad (1898–), founded as the magazine of the League

of St Columba at Maynooth [see *universities]. Its period of influence as a critical journal began when, from 1966 onwards, successive issues were devoted entirely to critical consideration of aspects of Irish-language literature. This development was influenced by Breandán *Ó Doibhlin's interests in French new criticism.

Irvine, Alexander (1862–1941), novelist; born in Antrim town, his much-loved work, *My Lady of the Chimney Corner* (1913), deals with the sanctity of his mother, Anna Gilmore. Two sequels, *The Souls of Poor Folk* (1921) and *Anna's Wishing Chair* (1937), reflect her gift of story-telling. *From the Bottom Up* (1914) and *A Fighting Parson* (1930) are autobiographies relating his own troubled adolescence and young manhood. In 1903 he completed an extramural theology degree at Yale, and helped to organize the American labour movement. In the First World War he served as a padre (an experience recorded in *God and Tommy Atkins*, 1918).

Irvine, John (1903–1964), poet. Born in Belfast, he issued collections from small presses in Belfast and Dublin, among them *A Voice in the Dark* (1932), *Wind From the South* (1936), *The Quiet Stream* (1944), and *Lost Sanctuary* (1954). Other collections were *Willow Leaves* (1941), containing poems in the manner of early Chinese poets, and *The Fountain of Hellas* (1943), a volume of translations from the Greek.

Irwin, Thomas Caulfield (1823–1892), poet; born in Warrenpoint, Co. Down, and educated at home. When family circumstances declined he moved to Dublin; he began contributing to *The *Nation* from 1853. His collections include *Versicles* (1856), *Irish Poems and Legends* (1869), *Pictures and Songs* (1880), and *Sonnets on the Poetry and Problems of*

Life (1881). His verse is marked by a striking accuracy in describing nature and an atmosphere of contentment and acceptance. Irwin later became mentally unstable, at one time threatening to shoot his next-door neighbour John *O'Donovan.

Islandman, The, see *An t**Oileánach.

'Ivy Day in the Committee Room', a story in James *Joyce's *Dubliners* (1914). A group of hired canvassers are gathered in the office of a nationalist candidate in the municipal elections on the anniversary of *Parnell's death. Mr O'Connor, Mr Henchy, and Mr Hynes conduct most of the backbiting conversation which makes up the substance of the story.

Jackman, Isaac (?1732–?1831), dramatist. Born in Dublin, he went to London as an author of comic operas, and became editor of *The Morning Post*, 1786–95. His earliest play, *All the World's a Stage* (1777), was revived frequently. *The Milesian* (1777) concerns a Captain Cornelius O'Gollagher. In *The Divorce* (1781) a *stage-Irish adventurer begins teaching Gaelic instead of French to the lady he is wooing. *Hero and Leander* (1787) was a classical burlesque, while *The Man of Parts* (1795) is English social comedy.

Jackson, Revd William (?1737–1795), journalist and *United Irishman. Born and educated in Dublin, he moved to London and became secretary to Elizabeth Chudleigh, the bigamous Duchess of Kingston. He is remembered for his suicide while being tried in Dublin for treason. The documents taken from him incriminated Wolfe *Tone. In London Jackson was at different times editor of *The Public Ledger* and *The Morning Post* (with Isaac *Jackman).

Jacob, Rosamund (1888–1960), novelist; born in Waterford to a Quaker family, she was educated at Newtown. She wrote a history of *The Rise of the United Irishmen* (1927), and a novel about the wife of Henry Joy *McCracken, *The Rebel's Wife* (1957). Other historical novels were *Callaghan* (1921) and *The Troubled House* (1928); *The Raven's Glen* (1980) was a children's story.

Jacobite poetry. The underlying values of Gaelic political poetry for most of the 18th cent. can be identified as Jacobite; and the main poets of the period can be classified as Jacobite poets, i.e. poets who championed the cause of *James II (in Latin *Jacobus*, hence Jacobite) and his descendants. Underpinning all Jacobite thinking was traditional social theory, which claimed that a divinely ordained and rightful hierarchical order had been ruptured in 1688 [see *Williamite War] and could be restored only by the return of the true king. Return and restoration were common elements both in Jacobite propaganda and in the traditional Irish ideology of kingship [see Irish *mythology]. A particularly potent theme was the foretelling of the restoration of the rightful king by an indigenous prophet. This prophecy was frequently presented in the *aisling, a stylized and ornate poetic genre in which the poet, wandering forth by river, glen, mountain, or sea, accosts a beautiful woman who, revealing herself to be Ireland, delivers her message that right will be restored when the true king returns. The many practitioners of this form included Aodhagán *Ó Rathaille, Eoghan Rua *Ó Súilleabháin, and Seán Clárach *Mac Dómhnaill.

Jacobite-Williamite War, see *Williamite War.

Jail Journal, see John *Mitchel.

James II (1633–1701), who succeeded his brother Charles II in February 1685, was England's last Catholic monarch, having converted from the Church of England in 1672. Although he was initially unwilling to alarm Protestant opinion unduly, James's Irish policy was increasingly influenced by Richard Talbot, Earl of Tyrconnell, who became Lord Deputy in 1686 and created the virtual Catholic monopoly of places in the judiciary, the army, and central and local government that is celebrated in the poetry of Dáibhí *Ó Bruadair. On 5 November 1688 William of Orange, Dutch husband to James's Protestant daughter Mary, invaded England to secure it for the Protestant interest. James fled to France. From there Louis XIV sent him to Ireland, where Tyrconnell retained control. In a Parliament of May-July 1689, James disappointed his Irish supporters by opposing bills asserting the independence of the Irish Parliament. Disillusionment was completed by his flight from Ireland following the Battle of the *Boyne.

Jameson, Anna Brownell (née Murphy) (1794–1860), author. Born in Dublin, she served as a governess in several aristocratic households. Following the success of her first book, *Diary of an Ennuyée* (originally *A Lady's Diary*, 1826), she produced several studies, including her much-admired *Shakespeare's Heroines* (originally *Characteristics of Women*, 1832), as well as essays on art such as *Memoirs of the Early Italian Painters* (1845).

Jeffares, A[lexander] N[orman] (1920–   ), scholar. Born in Dublin, he was educated at TCD and Oxford, before teaching at Groningen University in Holland, and at Edinburgh, Adelaide, Leeds and Stirling Universities. *W. B. Yeats: Man and Poet* (1949) was the first of many works devoted to the poet. In 1968 he founded IASIL, the International Association for the Study of Irish Literatures, an organization which has played a major role in developing understanding of the achievements of Irish writers in the English language from the 17th cent. His editorial and scholarly work did much to reveal the full range of Irish literature in the English language. His poems are collected in *Brought Up in Dublin* and *Brought Up to Leave* (both 1987).

Jenkinson, Biddy (a pseudonym), an Irish-language poet who preserves privacy and refuses to be translated, as a gesture signifying that everything in Irish cannot be 'harvested and stored' without loss in English. Her collections *Báisteadh Gintlí* (1987), *Uiscí Beatha* (1988), and *Dán na hUidhre* (1991) seek to recreate a sense of the sacral world of nature and women's role in sustaining it. Her poetic manifesto appeared as a letter to the editor in the *Irish University Review* (Spring/Summer 1991).

Jephson, Robert (1736–1803), playwright. Born to an Anglo-Irish family in Mallow, Co. Cork, he served in the army and settled in London, associating there with Edmund *Burke and others. *The Count of Narbonne* (1781), a successful stage version of his friend Horace Walpole's *Castle of Otranto*, played in London and Dublin. His farce *The Hotel, or the Servant with Two Masters* (1784) first appeared at *Smock Alley, while Robert *Owenson opened his Irish National Theatre with *The Carmelite* (1784). Among other plays were *Braganza* (1775), a tragedy, and *Two Strings to Your Bow* (1791), a farce. His *Roman Portraits* (1794) was in heroic verse.

JKL, see James Warren *Doyle.

John Bull's Other Island (1904), a play by George Bernard *Shaw about the differences between England and Ireland, but subverting the sentimental stereotypes of the *stage-Irishman and the hard-headed Englishman. The action concerns a jovial and effective Englishman, Broadbent, and his acerbic Irish partner, Larry Doyle. In Roscullen in Ireland Broadbent is the subject of much merriment amongst the villagers, but he carries all before him with his conquest of Nora O'Reilly, his selection for the parliamentary seat, and his plans to turn the village into a Garden City with tourist attractions. His relentless materialism and Doyle's bitterness are countered by the spiritual visions of Keegan, a defrocked priest.

John Doe, or The Peep o'Day (1825), a novel by John *Banim. Included in the *Tales by the O'Hara Family (Ist series), it attempts to give an account of the underlying causes of agrarian violence while making conciliatory gestures towards contemporary British public opinion. A young English officer leads his command into the mountains of Tipperary in search of 'John Doe', the leader of a *secret society.

Johnson, Lionel (1867–1902), poet. Born in Broadstairs in Kent, the son of an Irish army officer, he was educated at New College, Oxford. In 1891 he converted to Catholicism, and when he joined the Rhymers Club in London he was attracted to the *literary revival and Irish nationalism. He visited Dublin in 1893 and the following year published Poems, followed by Ireland and Other Poems (1894). He identified deeply with the heroic mythology of the Irish movement. His death was caused by a fall from a bar-stool. The *Dun Emer Press issued Twenty One Poems (1904), selected by Yeats, who memorialized him.

Johnston, Anna Isabel, see Ethna *Carbery.

Johnston, [William] Denis (1901–1984), playwright. Born in Dublin into a legal family, he was educated at St Andrew's College, Cambridge, and Harvard Law School, after which he worked as a barrister in Dublin and involved himself in theatre activities, taking an active part in the *Dublin Drama League, where he met Shelagh Richards, whom he married in 1928. In that year he submitted Rhapsody in Green to the *Abbey Theatre, but the typescript was returned to Johnston with 'The Old Lady Says "No" ' written

on it, a reference to Lady *Gregory. The play was produced at the *Gate Theatre in 1929 using this remark as its title. The *Moon in the Yellow River (1931), produced at the Abbey, concentrates on hostilities between Republicans and Free Staters after the *Civil War. In 1931 he joined the Board of the Gate, which staged A *Bride for the Unicorn (1933), a play with a complex symbolism. He joined the BBC in Belfast in 1938, moving to London to work in television. The *Golden Cuckoo (1939) attacks the blindness of the legal system. He became a war correspondent for the BBC in 1942, and he witnessed the relief of Buchenwald. These experiences are recorded in Nine Rivers From Jordan (1953), an enigmatic autobiography. He divorced Richards in 1945 and married Betty Chancellor. The following year he was appointed Director of Programmes at the BBC, but he resigned and went to New York to work as a freelance author and director. *Strange Occurrence on Ireland's Eye (1956) was a reworking of Blind Man's Buff (1936), and in it Johnston returns to question the nature of justice in society. The *Scythe and the Sunset (1958) is a dramatic response to *O'Casey's The *Plough and the Stars. Johnston retired to Guernsey in 1967, then to Dublin in 1969. In the years following he worked on The Brazen Horn (1976), a philosophical treatise which tries to disentangle his theories about time.

Johnston, Fred (1951–), poet and novelist. Born in Belfast and educated at St Malachy's College, he became a journalist. In the 1970s he was co-founder with Neil *Jordan and Peter Sheridan of the Irish Writers' Co-Operative before settling in Galway, where he established Cúirt, a literary festival. Life and Death in the Midlands (1979) was a first collection, followed by A Scarce Light (1987), Song at the Edge of the World (1989), Measuring Angles (1993), Browne

(1993), a long poem, and *True North* (1997). *Picturing a Girl in a Spanish Hat* (1979) was a novel; *Keeping The Night Watch* (1998) a volume of stories. In the 1980s and 1990s Johnston was a stringent and thoughtful reviewer of poetry. His own verse unites reflection and feeling and carries a personal charge while avoiding sentiment.

Johnston, Jennifer [Prudence] (1930–), novelist. Born in Dublin, the daughter of Denis *Johnston and the actress and director Shelagh Richards (1903–1985), she was educated at TCD. Married with four children, then divorced and remarried, she settled near Derry in the 1970s. Johnston began as a novelist with *The Captains and the Kings* (1972) and *The Gates* (1973— although written first), dealing with the isolation of *ascendancy families in 20th-cent. Ireland. *How Many Miles to Babylon?* (1974) examines a friendship between an Anglo-Irish officer and a soldier, both serving in the trenches of the First World War. *Shadows on Our Skin* (1977) explores an ultimately tragic relationship between a Catholic school-boy and his Protestant teacher in modern Derry. She returned to the ascendancy setting with *The *Old Jest* (1979), an account of a quest for personal integrity in the face of divided sympathies. *The Christmas Tree* (1981) is the story of Constance Keating, who meets her end on her own terms. Both *The Railway Station Man* (1984) and *Fool's Sanctuary* (1987) play variations on the theme of private worlds of love destroyed by violence. *The Invisible Worm* (1991) is a story of hidden intimacy. *Two Moons* (1998) was a further novel.

Johnston, Myrtle (1909–), novelist; born in Dublin, and educated privately at Magheramena Castle. Her father was private secretary to the Lord Lieutenant, Lord Aberdeen. The family moved to Bournemouth in 1921. She published

Hanging Johnny (1927), about an executioner, followed by *Relentless* (1930), *The Maiden* (1930), and *A Robin Redbreast in a Cage* (1950), amongst others.

Johnston, William (1829–1902), novelist. Born in Downpatrick, he was educated at TCD. His election as an independent MP for South Belfast in 1868 threatened the major parties with a show of popular loyalism. He issued numerous pamphlets with titles such as *Protestant Work to be Done* (1853) and *The Nunnery Question* (1854). His political and sectarian fears are luridly dramatized in novels such as *Nightshade* (1857) and *Under Which King?* (1872).

Johnstone, Charles (?1719–?1800), novelist. Born in Carrigogunnel, Co. Limerick, and educated at TCD, he practised law though handicapped by deafness, and in 1782 went to India to follow a career as a journalist. Johnstone's best-known novel, *Chrysal* (1760–5), is narrated by the spirit of gold in a guinea coin and set in various countries where it circulates. *Arsaces* (1774), a much admired Oriental tale, is a thinly veiled allegory of the worst effects of colonialism in America. *Anthony Varnish* (1781) and *John Juniper* (1786), also attributed to Johnstone, use Irish characters and locations.

Jones, Frederick, see *Crow Street Theatre.

Jones, Henry (1721–1770), poet and dramatist. Born near Drogheda, Co. Louth, he became a brick-layer but gained the patronage of the Viceroy, Lord Chesterfield. His poetry includes *Poems on Several Occasions* (1749), *The Relief, or Day-Thoughts* (1754), *The Invention of Letters* (1755), and *Vectis, or The Isle of Wight* (1766), one of several topographical poems. His sentimental tragedy, *Earl of Essex* (1753), was successful, as was the *Cave of Idra*, revised for

publication as *The Heroine of the Cave* by
Paul *Hiffernan (1775).

Jordan, John (1930–1988), poet and
critic. Born in Dublin, he was educated
at UCD, and lectured there 1956–69. In
1962 he refounded *Poetry Ireland*. His
first book of poems was *Patrician Stations*
(1971). Later collections were *A Raft from
Flotsam* (1975) and *With Whom Did I Share
the Crystal* (1980). *Yarns* (1977) was a series of stories. His *Collected Poems* (1991)
were edited by Hugh McFadden.

Jordan, Neil (1950–   ), writer of fiction and filmmaker; born in Sligo and
educated at UCD. His first collection,
Night in Tunisia (1976), reveals an anti-
traditionalist outlook. *The Past* (1980) is a
novel exploring repression in society
and family. *The Dream of a Beast* (1983)
articulates a preoccupation with the
problem of personal freedom. His success as an author-director has tended to
overshadow his achievement as a
writer. His first film, *Angel* (1982), dealt
with the *Troubles. In *Mona Lisa* (1986)
he successfully reworked the urban
crime thriller. Two American films, *High
Spirits* (1988) and *We're No Angels* (1990),
were comedies. Jordan returned to more
personal film-making with *The Miracle*
(1991) and *The Crying Game* (1992), an
exploration of shifting political and
sexual identities. Jordan returned to fiction with a novel, *Sunrise with Sea Monster*
(1995). *Michael Collins* (1997) was a film
treatment of the *Collins myth.

Journal of Irish Literature, (1972–
1994), a magazine edited by Robert
*Hogan at The University of Delaware,
publishing works by contemporary
Irish writers, as well as reprints of
writers from the past.

Journal to Stella, see *Stella.

**Joyce, James [Augustine Aloy-
sius]** (1882–1941), novelist; born in

Rathgar, Dublin, to May and John Stanislaus Joyce, the latter, figuring in his
son's books as Simon Dedalus. Joyce
went to Clongowes Wood, entered the
Royal University at St Stephen's Green
[see *universities] on a scholarship, and
there studied languages together with
courses in mathematics and philosophy. He began to write prose
sketches in 1900 with the composition
of *epiphanies, short writings in the
form either of dramatic vignettes or
prose-poems. These short notations
were first circulated by him in manuscript, but later used to indicate
moments of heightened perception in
the novels from *Stephen Hero to
*Ulysses. A broadside against the Irish
Literary Theatre [*Abbey Theatre],
attacking W. B. *Yeats and the other
leaders of the dramatic movement for
'surrender[ing]' to the popular will',
appeared as 'The Day of the Rabble-
ment' (1901). On completion of his
degree, Joyce met and felt himself
rebuffed by leaders of the Irish *literary revival. His antipathy to Patrick
*Pearse soon took the form of a satir-
ical sketch of an Irish-language class
given by a Mr Hughes in *Stephen
Hero*—the novel where, in 1904, he set
about marshalling his arguments
against simplistic views of Irishness,
sexuality, and politics. After first
enrolling at the medical school of the
Royal University, he left Dublin for
Paris on 1 December 1902 with a view
to training there instead, but
encountered difficulties over entrance
qualifications. He returned for Christmas, but left again on 23 January 1903,
to be recalled by a telegram in August
informing him of his mother's impending death. Back in Dublin he embarked
on a period of dissipation with Oliver St
John *Gogarty, but continued the literary notices for the *Daily Express* which he
had begun to write in 1902. He briefly
stayed with Gogarty at the Martello
Tower in Sandycove, 9–15 September

1904, quitting in a spirit of mutual distrust which was never entirely overcome. Three stories of what was to be the *Dubliners (1914) collection were invited by George *Russell and appeared in The *Irish Homestead (Aug.-Dec. 1904). In June 1904 he met Nora Barnacle, a girl from Galway who was working as a chambermaid. His love for her opened a source of ordinary human feeling upon which he drew at all stages of his career, basing Molly Bloom and Anna Livia Plurabelle in Ulysses and Finnegans Wake on her vitality. In October 1904 Joyce left Dublin with Nora for a teaching post in Trieste, where he remained for ten years. From there, he sent twelve stories of Dubliners to the London publisher Grant Richards, but it was not to appear until 1914. With Joyce's encouragement, his brother Stanislaus joined them in 1905 and became an economic mainstay for the family. He left the Berlitz School in 1907, taking with him some private pupils who provided better rates of payment. In 1909 he undertook to open a Dublin cinema, the Volta (the first in Ireland), for a Triestino company. Owing to his choosing Italian rather than American films, the audience rapidly fell off. In 1913 Yeats alerted Ezra Pound to Joyce's talent, and when Joyce sent him the first chapter of his autobiographical novel in its revised form Pound found a publisher for it: A Portrait of the Artist as a Young Man first appeared serially in The Egoist (2 Feb. 1914-1 Sept. 1915) and then in book form in New York (1916), an Egoist Press edition following in London (1917). Meanwhile, Joyce had reopened negotiations with the publisher Grant Richards, and Dubliners was issued in London on 15 June 1914. Joyce now began to receive financial support through Pound's advocacy, notably from Miss Harriet Shaw Weaver (co-editor of The Egoist with Dora Marsden). Improved finances and Pound's critical support gave Joyce the confidence to

commence a novel which he had contemplated as a final story for Dubliners. He began writing Ulysses with the 'Calypso' episode on 1 March 1914, and had completed the first three chapters ('Telemachiad') by early 1915. The First World War compelled Joyce to move to Zürich, arriving 30 June 1915. There he continued with Ulysses. Joyce returned at the cessation of hostilities to Trieste (mid-October 1919) before moving to Paris (8 July 1920) on Pound's advice. There he soon met Sylvia Beach, who offered to bring out Ulysses under her Shakespeare & Company bookshop imprint, with the help of Adrienne Monnier. The book appeared in time for Joyce's 40th birthday, 2 February 1922. With the production of his play *Exiles in 1919, Joyce fulfilled an early ambition to write for the theatre. Exiles, a study of jealousy, was begun in 1913, when he was urging Nora towards infidelities (which she resisted) in a spirit of emotional inquiry. During the autumn of 1922 he began to compile notes for a new book, incorporating unused material from Ulysses. During that year he studied Sir Edward Sullivan's 1920 Studio edition of the *Book of Kells, drawing his friends' attention to the Irishness of its densely patterned illuminations. On 10 March 1923 he wrote a draft of the first episode, 'King Roderick O'Conor'. The ensuing labour of 'Work in Progress'—as the book was known before publication—took seventeen years, during which Joyce experienced physical, mental, and emotional trials. Sections of Finnegans Wake were published in avant-garde magazines including Transatlantic Review (Apr. 1924), Criterion (July 1925), Navire d'argent (Oct. 1925), and transition (Apr. 1927–Apr./May 1938). Episodes and combinations of episodes were published as Anna Livia Plurabelle (1928); Tales Told by Shem and Shaun (1929) ; and Haveth Childers Everywhere (1930). Finnegans Wake was completed on 13

November 1938 and published on Joyce's 57th birthday, on 2 February 1939. The outbreak of the Second World War caused the Joyces to move to Gérand-le-Puy, the town near Vichy where Maria Jolas (editor of *transition* with her husband Eugene) kept a bilingual school attended by Joyce's grandson Stephen (b. 1932). In December 1940, the family entered Switzerland with special visas—all except Lucia, his son, who was by then in a sanatorium. Joyce died after an apparently successful operation for an ulcerated duodenum on 13 January. See Michael Groden *et al.* (eds.), *The James Joyce Archive* (63 vols., 1977–9) and Richard *Ellmann, *James Joyce* (1959; rev. 1982).

Joyce, John Robert (1951–), novelist and children's writer; born in Weymouth, Dorset, and educated in Swansea and East Anglia universities, he researched marine biology at UCC, subsequently working for the Fisheries Board. *Virtually Maria* (1998) and *A Matter of Time* (1999) are thrillers; *Captain Cockle and the Pond* (1997) a children's tale.

Joyce, P[atrick] W[eston] (1827–1914), linguist and geographer. Born in Ballyorgan, Co. Limerick, and educated at local *hedge schools and TCD. He joined the *Society for the Preservation of the Irish Language. *The Origin and History of Irish Names of Places* (3 vols., 1869–70), was followed by *Ancient Irish Music* (1873), a collection of airs; *Old Celtic Romances* (1879); *A Social History of Ancient Ireland* (2 vols., 1907), revealing impressively detailed knowledge of early Irish culture; and his study of *Hiberno-English, *English as We Speak it in Ireland* (1910).

Joyce, Robert Dwyer (1830–1883), poet. Born in Glenosheen, Co. Limerick, the brother of Patrick Weston *Joyce,

he was educated at Queen's College, Cork [see *universities], where he studied medicine. Before leaving for America in 1866, he published *Ballads, Romances and Songs* (1861), later extended in *Ballads of Irish Chivalry* (1872). His longer poems, such as *Deirdre* (1876) and *Blanaid* (1879), retell stories from the *Ulster cycle.

Joyce, Stanislaus (1884–1955), brother of James *Joyce and a model for the stolid Shaun-type in *Finnegans Wake*. He was born and educated in Dublin but fled poverty to Trieste, where he joined the Joyce household. There he worked as a teacher and university professor, supporting the growing family of the profligate novelist. When James became more and more involved in 'Work in Progress' [see *Finnegans Wake], his admiration cooled and finally turned to indignation. He came to notice with the publication of *Recollections of James Joyce* (1950), followed by *My Brother's Keeper* (1957).

Joyce, Trevor (1947–), poet; born in Dublin, he was educated at UCD, later moving to UCC as a computer scientist. His collections include *Sole Glum Trek* (1967), *Watches* (1969), *Pentahedron* (1972), *The Poem of Sweeney Peregrinus* (1976), and *stone floods* (1995).

Judge, Michael (1921–), dramatist; born in Dublin and educated at UCD. He was one of the first Irish television writers and his work includes *The Chair* (1963), *Don't Ever Talk to Clocks* (1964), *The Fiend at My Elbow* (1965), *No Trumpets Sounding* (1967), and *Whose Child?* (1979). Judge's first stage play was an adaptation of *The Chair* (1963). In 1966 *Death Is For Heroes* was staged by the *Abbey Theatre, and it was followed by *Please Smash the Glass Gently* (1972), *A Matter of Grave Importance* and *Someone to Talk To* (both 1973), and *And Then Came Jonathan* (1980).

Judith Hearne, see The *Lonely Passion of Judith Hearne.*

Juno and the Paycock (1924), a play by Sean *O'Casey first produced at the *Abbey Theatre, with Barry Fitzgerald (1888–1961) and F. J. *McCormick as the 'Captain' and Joxer. Set in a Dublin tenement during the *Civil War, it concerns the misfortunes of the Boyle family. Charley Bentham, schoolmaster and lawyer's apprentice, brings news of a will by which Boyle is to inherit a legacy. Two months later Bentham has fled to England, leaving Mary pregnant, and the will has proved to be defective. The terrified son Johnny is taken out by two Republican Irregulars [see *IRA] and shot. Juno, the 'paycock's' wife, tries in vain to hold a ruined family together.

K

Kane, Sir Robert John (1809–1890), scientist. Born in Dublin and educated at TCD, he became President of the *RIA in 1877. Kane founded the *Dublin Journal of Medical Science* in 1832, and established a Museum of Science and Industry on St Stephen's Green in 1846. His *Industrial Resources of Ireland* (1844) was adopted as an economic justification for Irish independence by *Young Ireland.

Kavanagh, Julia (1824–1877), novelist and biographer. Born in Thurles, Co. Tipperary, after 1844 she issued more than twenty novels, including tales of provincial life in France such as *Madeleine* (1848) and *Sílvia* (1870). In *Nathalie* (1850) a young woman who is dying of tuberculosis persuades her sister to accept her death in a spirit of pious joy.

Kavanagh, Patrick [Joseph] (1904–1967), poet and novelist. Born the son of a cobbler and farmer in the parish of Inniskeen in Co. Monaghan, he left school at 13. *Ploughman and Other Poems* (1936) was followed by a commissioned autobiography, *The *Green Fool* (1938). In 1939 Kavanagh moved to Dublin, which was to become his permanent home. From the mid-1930s his brief lyric poems, which had tended to be vaguely rural, were more sharply realized. In *The *Great Hunger* (1942) he emerged as an anti-pastoral yet visionary poet. It was followed by his most sociologically ambitious poem, the posthumously-published *Lough Derg* (1971), a narrative commentary on a Lough Derg pilgrimage. Kavanagh's second collection of poems was *Soul for Sale* (1947). An autobiographical novel with a farmer-poet hero, *Tarry Flynn*

(1948), went through numerous redraftings throughout the 1940s. In 1952 he edited the short-lived *Kavanagh's Weekly*. His literary criticism, often intemperate, was cruelly dismissive of his fellow Irish writers. He advocated that literature should record the writer's affectionate response to ordinary phenomena and commonplace happenings. He substituted 'parochialism', the evocation of a particular place, for the cult of Irishness, and in *Envoy he stressed the importance of 'personality'—individuality rather than ethnicity—in art. In March 1955 Kavanagh was operated on for lung cancer. Restoration to health was followed by a spate of rapturous lyrics collected in *Come Dance with Kitty Stobling* (1960). His *Collected Poems* was published in 1964 and his *Collected Prose* in 1967.

Kavanagh, Rose (1859–1891), poet; born in Killadray, Co. Tyrone, she was educated at the Loreto Convent in Omagh and the Dublin School of Art. She published as 'Ruby' in *The Shamrock* and The *Nation poems and tales of Ulster life. She nursed Charles J. *Kickham in his latter years and died herself of T.B. Her poetry was gathered by Matthew Russell in 1909.

Kavanagh's Weekly (April–July 1952; thirteen issues), a journal of literature and politics edited by Patrick *Kavanagh, who contributed most of the articles and some poems, using a variety of pseudonyms. It was published, designed, and distributed by his brother Peter Kavanagh.

Keane, John B[rendan] (1928–), playwright. Born in Listowel, he was educated by the Christian Brothers before going to Northampton, where he worked at various jobs and began to write. He returned to Listowel in 1954 and began managing a public house. His first play, *Sive (1959), performed by the Listowel Drama Group, was then staged by the Southern Theatre Group, giving him a firm base in Cork when the *Abbey Theatre rejected his work. Keane turned out stage successes all through the 1960s. His plays are set in the life of Co. Kerry, combining melodrama with realism. In some of them Keane manifests a strong social conscience, as in the musical Many Young Men of Twenty (1961) and Hut 42 (1962), both concerned with emigration. The *Field (1965), probably his best play, depicts an obsession with the land. Big Maggie (1969) heralds a new emancipation in Irish society. Keane's nondramatic writings included The Streets and Other Poems (1961), and a series of fictional letters beginning with Letters of a Successful T.D. (1967), as well as short stories (Death Be Not Proud, 1976; Stories from a Kerry Fireside, 1980; and The Ram of God, 1991). The *Bodhrán Makers (1986) concentrated his humour and independence into a best-selling novel; Durango (1992) continued in this mode. During the 1980s his plays were in new demand at the Abbey and elsewhere.

Keane, Molly [Marry Nesta] (née Skrine) (1904–1996), novelist and playwright. Born in Co. Kildare, her mother being Moira *O'Neill, she was educated privately. The Knight of the Cheerful Countenance (1926), a first novel, was published under the pseudonym 'M. J. Farrell' (being the name on a public house), as were her next ten. She resumed writing under her own name in the late 1970s after a lapse of twenty years. Her fiction is set typically in a *big house ambience. Among her novels are: Young Entry (1928), *Taking

Chances (1929), and Mad Puppetstown (1931)—which is, like *Two Days in Aragon (1941), set against the background of the *Troubles, 1919–21. In Devoted ladies (1934) Keane attempts to give a detached view through the perspective of an American heroine. Loving Without Tears (1951) and Treasure Hunt (1952) have the character of drawing-room comedies, the latter being based on one of the plays which Keane wrote in association with John Perry. Others are Spring Meeting (1938) and Ducks and Drakes (1941). The first novel to appear under her own name was the black comedy *Good Behaviour (1981), followed by Time After Time (1983), which puts the Anglo-Irish gentry face to face with the savagery of modern history. Loving and Giving (1988) narrates the life and death of a heroine haunted by memories.

Kearney, Colbert (1945–   ), novelist and critic; born in Dublin he was educated at UCD and King's College, Cambridge, before becoming lecturer then Professor of English at UCC. The Writings of Brendan Behan (1977) was a critical study; The Consequence (1993) a novel mingling art with life; The Glamour of Grammar (2000) a further work of criticism.

Kearney, Peadar (1883–1942), songwriter and author of 'The Soldier's Song' in 1911. Born off Dorset St., Dublin, and educated by the Christian Brothers, he trained as a house-painter and worked behind the scenes at the *Abbey Theatre from 1911 until 1916, when he participated in the *Easter Rising. His patriotic song later became the national anthem of the *Irish state. He was uncle to Brendan *Behan.

Kearney, Richard (1954–   ), novelist and philosopher; born in Cork and educated at Glenstal, UCD, and Paris; he became Professor of Philosophy at UCD in 1992. With others he edited *The *Crane Bog*, an influential journal in the 1970s and 1980s devoted to cultural philosophy. There followed a series of edited volumes on Irish intellectual history, including *The Irish Mind* (1984), and studies in narrative and the imagination. *Angel of Patrick's Hill* (1991) was a volume of poems, followed by the novels *Sam's Fall* (1995) and *Walking at Sea Level* (1997).

Keating, Geoffrey (Seathrún Céitinn) (*c.*1580–*c.*1644), Irish historian and poet of Anglo-Norman extraction, born in Burges (Buiríos) near Cahir, in Co. Tipperary. He was ordained in Ireland before leaving in 1603 for education at Bordeaux and Reims. In France he collected the material for *Eochair-sciath an Aifrinn*, a prose work in defence of the Mass written in 1610–13. On returning to Ireland he occupied a parish at Tubrid in his native part of Co. Tipperary. According to tradition, he was driven into hiding in 1618 or 1619, and is said to have planned *Foras Feasa ar Éirinn*, the foremost work of *Gaelic historiography, while living in a cave in the Galtee Mountains. In the 1620s he exhaustively examined all the historical manuscripts and materials he could find. The entire work seems to have been complete in 1634. Although *Foras Feasa ar Éirinn* is often seen as a synthetic compilation of Gaelic historiography and the final statement of a doomed people, Keating himself conceived it as a grounding for an emergent composite Catholic nation of Ireland. *Trí Biorghaoithe an Bháis* (*Three Shafts of Death*) is a typical 17th-cent. tract reflecting the post-Tridentine obsession with death. He also wrote *Saltair Mhuire*, a brief treatise on the rosary, which exemplifies the Marian emphasis of Counter-Reformation *Catholicism. Keating was a considerable poet. 'Óm sceól ar ardmhagh Fáil' combines personal anguish and historical trauma. 'A bhean lán de stuaim' is a love-poem renouncing the flesh with irony and regret.

Keegan, John (1809–1849), poet. Born in Co. Laois, and educated in a *hedge school, he contributed to *The *Nation. Keegan's tales mainly treat of *folklore themes such as the *banshee, while his verses increasingly registered the horror of *Famine.

Keenan, Brian (1950–), memoirist; born in Belfast, he left school at 15 and worked as an apprentice engineer before going to NUU where he studied English and wrote an MA thesis on the poetry of Padraic *Fiacc (1985). In 1985 he accepted a post in the American University of Beirut, was taken hostage by Shi'ite fundamentalists, and held for over four years. *An Evil Cradling* (1992) recounts his experiences and simultaneously charts the growth of a soul.

keen, see *caoineadh.

Kell, Richard (1927–), poet. Born in Youghal, Co. Cork, he attended TCD. His collections include *Control Tower* (1962), *Differences* (1969), and *Heartwood* (1978).

Kelleher, D[aniel] L[aurence] (1883–1958), playwright and man of letters. Born in Cork and educated at UCC, he was associated in his early career with the group of dramatists known as the 'Cork Realists' [see *Abbey Theatre]. *Stephen Grey* (1910) was produced at the Abbey in 1910, and thereafter he wrote *A Contrary Election* (1910). His travel sketches reflect his varied career, and include *Paris, Its Glamour and Life* (1914), *Lake Geneva* (1914), *The Glamour of Dublin* (1918, as 'D. L. Kay'), *The Glamour of Cork* (1919), *Round Italy* (1923), and *Great Days with O'Connell* (1929). His poetry includes *Cork's Own Town* (1920), *Poems Twelve a Penny* (1911) and *Twelve Poems* (1923).

Kelly, Hugh (1739–1777), dramatist; born in Killarney, Co. Kerry. He moved to London in 1760 and took a succession of jobs before becoming editor of the *Court Magazine* then John Newbury's *Public Ledger* in 1768. *Thespis* (1766), a satirical poem on the actors at Drury Lane, earned him the favour of David Garrick, whom he adulated. This led to the production of his great success, **False Delicacy* (1768), which appeared at Drury Lane. The plays from Kelly's hand that followed are concerned with fashionable English life and love intrigues, all written in the sentimental mode. Other pieces were *Clementina* (1771), a tragedy; *A School for Wives* (1773), a comedy; and *The Romance of an Hour* (1774). *The Man of Reason* (1776) failed, and proved his last attempt.

Kelly, John (1942–), scholar; born in Abingdon, England, he was educated at TCD and Cambridge, where he studied under T. R. *Henn. His major work is the impeccable edition of W. B. *Yeats's *Letters*, which he began in 1974, issuing the first volume in 1986, with succeeding volumes thereafter. The whole will run to twelve volumes.

Kelly, Mary Anne (1825–1910), the poet 'Eva' of *The *Nation*. She was born at Headford, Co. Galway, and married Kevin Izod O'Doherty (1823–1905), co-editor of *The Irish Tribune* with Richard d'Alton *Williams. Her collected *Poems* appeared in San Francisco (1877) and Dublin (1907).

Kelly, Michael (1764–1826), tenor and composer. Born in Dublin, he first appeared at *Smock Alley and became principal tenor at the Vienna Opera, 1783–7, where he sang in the first production of Mozart's *The Marriage of Figaro*. A two-volume set of *Reminiscences* (1826) is ghost-written by Theodore Hooker.

Kelly, Rita (1953–), poet. Born in Galway, she was educated at the Convent of Mercy in Ballinasloe. In 1972 she married the poet Eoghan *Ó Tuairisc, who had written little since the death of his first wife in 1965. They went to live at an isolated lock house in Mageney, Co. Carlow, where together they wrote *Dialann sa Díseart* (1981), a collection of lyric meditations on nature. After her husband's death in 1982 she published *An Bealach Éadóigh* (1984), poems, *The Whispering Arch and Other Stories* (1986), and *Farewell/Beir Beannacht* (1990), poems in Irish and English. *Frau Luther* (1984) was a play.

Kellys and the O'Kellys, The, see Anthony *Trollope.

Kennedy, Patrick (pseudonym 'Harry Whitney') (1801–1873), folklorist. Born in Co. Wexford, he moved to Dublin, opening a bookshop in Anglesea Place. He wrote anecdotes and *folklore for *The *Dublin University Magazine* and published, as Harry Whitney, *Legends of Mount Leinster* (1855), followed by *Fictions of Our Forefathers* (1859), *Legendary Fictions of the Irish Celts* (1866), *The Banks of the Boro* (1867), and *Evenings in the Duffrey* (1870).

Kennedy, William (1799–1847), poet and diplomat; born in Dublin and educated in Belfast and in Scotland. He wrote some poetry, a historical verse drama, *The Siege of Antwerp* (1838), and *The Republic of Texas* (1841), an account of the State where he was British Consul, 1841–7.

Kennelly, Brendan (1936–), poet, dramatist, and novelist. Born in Ballylongford, Co. Kerry, he was educated at TCD and the University of Leeds. He became Professor at TCD in 1973. His first collections, *Cast a Cold Eye* (1959) and *The Rain, The Moon* (1961), were co-published with Rudi Holzapfel.

My Dark Fathers (1964) revealed a new, distinctive voice articulating the hurt bequeathed by history. The long poem sequences *Cromwell* (1983), *The *Book of Judas* (1991), and *Poetry my Arse* (1995) are investigations into the shifting and troubled passions that work in two arenas of hate and anger: Ireland's relation with England, and modern Ireland's relation with herself. He wrote two novels, *The Crooked Cross* (1963) and *The Florentines* (1967), the latter reflecting experiences of student life in Leeds. His versions of classical texts, *Antigone* (1986) and *Medea* (1988), written in the wake of a broken marriage, project a scorching feminism. *The Trojan Women* (1993) examines the aftermath of war. *A Drinking Cup* (1970) and *Mary* (1987) contain translations from Irish. Amongst his other poetry collections are *Good Souls to Survive* (1967), *Dream of a Black Fox* (1968), *Love Cry* (1972), *A Kind of Trust* (1975), *A Small Light* (1979), *Moloney Up and At It* (1984), and *The Man Made of Rain* (1998), the latter written in recovery from a heart attack. He edited *The Penguin Book of Irish Verse* (1970, rev. 1981).

Kenner, [William] Hugh (1923–), critic; born in Peterborough, Ontario, Canada, he was educated there and at Toronto and Yale Universities. He taught in many universities, including the University of California (Santa Barbara), the John Hopkins, Baltimore, and the University of Georgia (Athens). He is a leading critic of modernism and a powerful and sensitive exponent of the work of Irish writers in books such as *Dublin's Joyce* (1956), *Samuel Beckett* (1961), *Joyce's Voices* (1978), *Ulysses* (1982), and *A Colder Eye: The Modern Irish Writers* (1983). His distinctive edgy style unites learning with an imaginative engagement with the varied worlds his writers create. He has also written on art and mathematics.

Kepler (1981), the second novel in John *Banville's tetralogy about the scientific imagination, is set in Reformation Europe, where the young astronomer seeks to develop and authenticate the heliocentric theory through precise mathematical formulae.

Kettle, Thomas (Tom) (1880–1916), economist and poet. Born in Co. Dublin, Kettle became Nationalist MP for East Tyrone in 1906, and Professor of Economics at UCD in 1909. Kettle established a Peace Committee with Horace *Plunkett in the 1913 Lock-Out [see James *Larkin]. After the 1916 *Easter Rising he volunteered for service in France, and died at Ginchy on the Somme. A gifted political speaker, he edited a selection of Irish oratory in 1914. His political essays are collected in *The Open Secret of Ireland* (1912), *The Day's Burden* (1910), and *The Ways of War* (1917). His poetry was issued as *Poems and Parodies* (1912).

Kiberd, Declan (1951–), critic; born in Dublin, educated at Belgrove School, Clontarf (where he was taught by John *McGahern), at TCD, and at Linacre College, Oxford where his research on *Synge and the Irish Language* (1973) was supervised by Richard *Ellmann. He was Professor of Anglo-Irish Literature and Drama at UCD from 1997. He has published *Men and Feminism in Modern Literature* (1985), *Idir Dhá Chultúr* (1993), and *Inventing Ireland* (1995). His literary scholarship is grounded on a deep familiarity with literature in Irish and in English.

Kickham, Charles J[oseph] (1828–1882), novelist and political activist; born at Cnoceenagaw near Mullinahone, Co. Tipperary, nephew of John *O'Mahony, co-founder of the *Fenians in the USA. Despite permanent damage to his hearing and sight sustained in an accident with gunpowder at 16, he helped to establish a Confederate Club in Mullinahone and later was an active member of the Tenant League [see Charles Gavan *Duffy], contributing to *The *Nation*. He joined the *Fenians about 1860 and wrote extensively for the organization's paper, *The Irish People*. Arrested with James *Stephens in 1865 he was sentenced to fourteen years' imprisonment for treason felony. Before his release in the amnesty of 1869 he wrote *Sally Cavanagh* (1869). *Knocknagow* is perhaps the most influential novel in the Irish nationalist tradition. Kickham's awareness of the transatlantic dimension of Irish nationhood led him to include American episodes: thus Ned Shea in *Sally Cavanagh* and Tom Dwyer in *For the Old Land* (1886; completed by William *O'Brien) are both wounded in the Civil War.

Kiely, Benedict (1919–), novelist and critic; born in Dromore, Co. Tyrone, and educated at UCD. He worked as a journalist, 1945–64, taught at several American universities, 1964–8, and followed a career as an author and broadcaster in Dublin. *Poor Scholar: A Study of the Works and Days of William *Carleton* (1947) discerned the basis of that novelist's fiction in bilingual Co. Tyrone. His book *Modern Irish Fiction* (1950) addressed the achievement of contemporary Irish writers. His early novels deal with small-town life at the time of Kiely's upbringing. *Land Without Stars* (1946) tells the story of two brothers, rivals for the same woman. *Call for a Miracle* (1950) is an urban novel, dealing with a complex pattern of sexual relationships in Dublin. *In a Harbour Green* (1949) depicts the west of Ireland. Three subsequent novels (*The *Cards of the Gambler*, 1953; *The *Captain with the Whiskers*, 1960; *Dogs Enjoy the Morning*, 1968) merge strands of reality and fantasy. *There Was an Ancient House* (1955) presents a disillusioned view of life in a Jesuit novitiate. The later novels

Proxopera (1977) and *Nothing Happens in Carmincross* (1985) reproach the violence of extremists. Short-story collections include *A Journey to the Seven Streams* (1963), *A Ball of Malt and Madam Butterfly* (1973), and *A Cow in the House* (1978). *Drink to the Bird* (1992) is an expansive memoir.

Kilkenny, Confederation of, see *Confederation of Kilkenny.

Kilkenny, Statutes of, see *Statutes of Kilkenny.

Kilroy, Thomas (1934–), novelist and playwright. Born in Callan, Co. Kilkenny, he graduated from UCD and became Professor of English at UCG, 1978–89. Kilroy served as play editor at the *Abbey in 1977 and was appointed a director of *Field Day in 1988. The Abbey play *The Death and Resurrection of Mr. Roche* (1969), deals with the hard-drinking life of 'the lads' in Dublin's flatlands. The novel *The *Big Chapel* (1971) explores the sectarian tensions in the 19th cent. *Tea and Sex and Shakespeare*, a comedy about the writer as anti-hero, appeared at the Abbey in 1976. *Talbot's Box* (1979), deals with the Dublin working-class ascetic Matt Talbot as a symbol of victimage. His version of *The Seagull* (1981) transposes Chekhov's play to the west of Ireland. A radio play on Brendan Bracken for the BBC in 1986 led to a Field Day production of *Double Cross* (1986), in which the wartime careers of Bracken and William Joyce ('Lord Haw-Haw') are contrasted. In 1991 Field Day staged his 'farce', *Madam MacAdam's Travelling Theatre*, set during the Emergency, 1939–45. *The Secret Fall of Constance Wilde* (1997), at the Abbey, explored the damaged personalities of Oscar *Wilde and his wife.

Kincora (1905, rev. 1909), a 'folk-history' play by Lady *Gregory giving an account of the Battle of *Clontarf, where *Brian Bóroime defeated the Danes [see *Viking invasion]. The play takes liberties with history in order to depict a complex of human relationships behind the famous battle.

King, Edward, Viscount Kingsborough (1795–1837), bibliophile; born in Co. Cork and educated in Oxford, he edited the *Antiquities of Mexico* in vellum and colour plates (9 vols., 1830–48) at a personal expense of £32,000.

King, Richard Ashe (1839–1932), novelist. Born Ennis, Co. Clare, he was educated at TCD; in the 1880s he moved to London. Novels include *Love the Debt* (1882); *The Wearing of the Green* (1884), dealing sympathetically with the *Land League; *A Coquette's Conquest* (1887); *Bell Barry* (1891); and *A Geraldine* (1893). He wrote a study of *Swift (1875), and a life of Oliver *Goldsmith (1910).

King, William (1650–1729), theologian and Archbishop of Dublin. Born in Antrim and educated at TCD, he became Dean of St Patrick's Cathedral. He was made Bishop of Derry after the Battle of the *Boyne and translated to the see of Dublin in 1703. A friend and correspondent of Jonathan *Swift, he privately encouraged The *Drapier's Letters. In *The State of the Protestants of Ireland under the Late King James's Government* (1691) he gave a damning account of the short-lived administration of Richard Talbot, Earl of Tyrconnell [see *James II]. When Bishop of Derry, he addressed the Presbyterians in *A Discourse Concerning the Inventions of Men in the Worship of God* (1694). His theological treatise, *De Origine Mali* (1702), became the subject of a debate that involved Leibniz. The English translation by Edward Law (*An Essay on the Origin of Evil*, 1731) became the standard edition. In *Divine Predestination and Foreknowledge* (1709) King defended the doctrine of free will.

king cycle, see *historical cycle.

King Goshawk and the Birds, see *Cuandine trilogy.

King Oedipus (1926; published 1928), a version of Sophocles' *Oedipus Rex* made by W. B. *Yeats for the *Abbey Theatre. Having first contemplated the project in 1903, Yeats finished it in 1926 at the promptings of his wife.

King of Friday's Men, The (1948), a three-act play by M. J. *Molloy. Set in the west of Ireland in 1787, it deals with the custom of 'tally women', that is, the landlord's sexual rights over his tenantry.

kingship. The law texts [see *law in Gaelic Ireland] of the 7th and 8th cents. list four ascending grades of kings: rí tuaithe, king of a local community or petty king of which there were according to some (unlikely) estimates eighty or so at any time; ruirí (great king), over-king of a number of petty kings; rí ruirech, king of over-kings, equated with rí cóicid (king of a province); and ard-rí, high king, regularly equated with the king of *Tara, usually the most prestigious king in Ireland. By the 8th cent. the petty kings were being reduced to local nobility, and by the 10th cent. the kings of provinces were the real power-holders. The males in royal dynasties were polygamous, their branches multiplied rapidly, and succession to kingship was determined not by primogeniture (or filiogeniture) but by power-play (often violent and nearly always disruptive). The sagas and the *Audacht Morainn, a late 7th-cent. advice to a prince, preserve the native ideology concerning kingship. A true prince will have fír flathemon ('the prince's truth'), he will be righteous, of impeccable character, from a high ancestry, and capable of heroic action, and his rule will bring many benefits. He carries a sacral aura, and his *inauguration is the holy marriage of king and goddess that makes land, sea, people, and animals fertile.

King's Threshold, The (1903), a play by W. B. *Yeats, in which the poet Seanchan goes on hunger-strike against the king Guaire.

Kinsale, Battle of, where Hugh *O'Neill and Red Hugh *O'Donnell were defeated by Lord Deputy Mountjoy on 24 December 1601 in the decisive battle of the Nine Years War (1594–1603). A long-promised Spanish expeditionary force finally reached Ireland in September 1601 but disembarked at Kinsale in Munster, which the Crown had already reduced to submission. The Spanish force of 3,500 under Don Juan del Aquila was besieged by Mountjoy. The forces of O'Neill and O'Donnell trapped Mountjoy between the Irish and Spanish armies. A dawn attack by the Irish went disastrously wrong and they were routed.

Kinsella, Thomas (1928–), poet and translator; born in Dublin and educated at UCD. Working as a civil servant, in the early 1950s he began to write poetry. In 1965 he became writer in residence at the University of Southern Illinois. Five years later he took up the position of Professor of English at Temple University, Philadelphia. In 1955 he married Eleanor Walsh and his first collection, *Poems* (1956), was issued as a wedding gift. *Another September* (1958) deals centrally with the precariousness of human relationships and the sustaining force of personal love. *Downstream* (1962) contains a number of longer pieces, amongst them the title-poem which investigates the problem of evil and corruption. *Wormwood* (1966) describes an enduring marriage. *Nightwalker and Other Poems* (1968) takes

themes of alienation and suffering into a European context. In *Davis, Mangan, Ferguson? Tradition and the Irish Writer* (1970) he characterized Irish tradition as deeply divided, offering the writer no alternative to forging his or her own identity. For Kinsella this involved studies in Old Irish literature, culminating in his translation of *Táin Bó Cuailnge*, published superbly by Dolmen as *The Táin* (1969). Kinsella's poetry now turned downward into the psyche, towards origin, myth, and individuation, reflecting an interest in Jungian psychology. *Notes from the Land of the Dead* (1972) confronts fragmentation and absurdity with meticulous self-scrutiny. *Butcher's Dozen* (1972) reacts with outrage to the Widgery Report and its almost total exoneration of the British Paratroop Regiment from culpability for the shooting of thirteen civilians on Bloody Sunday (Derry, 30 January 1972). This volume was the first of the series to appear under his own Peppercanister imprint which issued poems and sequences, later gathered for trade editions. *A Selected Life* (1972) and *Vertical Man* (1973) are poems celebrating the composer Seán *Ó Riada, while *The Good Fight* (1973) commemorates John F. Kennedy. These were reprinted in *Fifteen Dead* (1976) and *Song of the Night* (1978). In Peppercanister issues such as *Songs of the Psyche* (1985), *Out of Ireland: A Metaphysical Love Sequence* (1987), and *St Catherine's Clock* (1987) Kinsella shows himself equal to the troubled realities of spiritual life in the late 20th cent. The Peppercanister sequences continued under the auspices of John F. *Deane's Dedalus Press with *Fifteen Poems from Centre City* (1990), *Madonna and Other Poems* (1991), and other editions, including *Godhead* (1999). Working with Seán *Ó Tuama, Kinsella produced *An Duanaire: Poems of the Dispossessed, 1600–1900* (1981), an anthology of Irish verse written after the defeat at *Kinsale. He also edited *The New Oxford Book of Irish Verse*

(1986), translating many of the Gaelic poems. *Collected Poems* appeared in 1995.

kinship, see *fine.

Klaxon, see A. J. *Leventhal.

Knife, The (1930), a novel by Peadar *O'Donnell. Set in east Donegal, 1916–23, it deals with the impact of the *Anglo-Irish and *Civil Wars on a rural community.

Knocknagow, or the Homes of Tipperary (1879), a nationalist novel by Charles *Kickham which shows how a rotten land system was rendering all classes on the land vulnerable to eviction and ruin at the whim of cruel and unscrupulous landlords, pointing the moral with an evocation of the traditional culture that was facing extinction at the time. An English visitor, Lowe, nephew of the landlord, stays as guest with the Kearneys, who introduce him to the homes of Tipperary.

Knowles, J[ames] S[heridan] (1784–1862), playwright. Born in Cork, second cousin to R. B. *Sheridan, he studied medicine but joined Andrew *Cherry's touring company and played in Waterford, where his *Poems on Various Subjects* and an early dramatic piece, *Leo or the Gypsy,* were printed in 1810. In the next few years his plays *Brian Boroimhe* (1811) and *Caius Gracchus* (1815) were staged in Belfast, and *Virginius* (1820) in Glasgow. In 1825 he premièred in London with *The Fatal Dowry,* an adaptation from Philip Massinger. *William Tell* (1825) established him as the most popular dramatist of the period, offering patriotic passions in blank verse. *The Hunchback* (1832) and *The Love Chase* (1837) were successful pieces. In 1844 he abandoned theatre and became a Baptist preacher. He wrote two novels, *Fortescue* (1846) and *George Lovell* (1847). His son Richard Brinsley Knowles (1820–1882), a journalist who converted to Catholicism in 1849, wrote a comedy, some Irish fiction, and a privately printed biography of his father.

Krapp's Last Tape (1958), a one-act play by Samuel *Beckett in which the title-character, a writer on his 69th birthday, listens to a tape-recording he had made on his 39th birthday.

La Tène culture, see *Celts.

Lady Windermere's Fan (1892), a melodrama set in London high society and Oscar *Wilde's first theatrical success. The lady of the title is a young woman with ideals, in contrast to Mrs Erlynne, who left society after a liaison of which Lady Windermere had been the fruit, and who now attempts to blackmail Lord Windermere.

Lake, The (1905), a novel by George *Moore, originally planned as a story for inclusion in The *Untilled Field. When Rose Leicester, the young schoolmistress of Garranard, becomes pregnant, Fr. Oliver Gogarty denounces her from the pulpit. After her departure he comes to realize that he is in love with her and decides to leave for America.

Lallah Rookh (1817), a long poem by Thomas *Moore comprising a series of oriental tales in verse interspersed with linking passages in prose told to the princess Lallah Rookh, as she travels from Delhi to Kashmir to be married. A ghostly parallel is suggested between Gheber and Catholic, Iran and Erin.

Lalor, James Fintan (1807–1849), *Young Irelander and land-reformer. Born in Tenakill, Co. Laois, he was educated at home and at Carlow. Small and sickly, Lalor was the most radical Irish political thinker of his period. In 1845 he founded the Tenant League with Michael *Doheny and planned an unsuccessful no-rent campaign in Co. Tipperary. In a series of letters to The *Nation during 1847 he formulated a revolutionary programme of peasant proprietorship through rent strike and joint resistance to eviction. After the arrest of John *Mitchel and the suppression of The *United Irishman he moved to Dublin to edit The Irish Felon, until his own arrest after the Rising of July 1848.

Lament for Art O'Leary, see Eibhlín Dubh *Ni Chonaill.

Land (1946), a historical novel by Liam *O'Flaherty dealing with the *Land War and *boycotting. Two major forces oppose one another in the Irish countryside, the *Fenians and the landlords; in between, vacillating and unreliable, are the people.

Land, The (1905), a play by Padraic *Colum dealing with the condition of the Irish peasantry after the *Wyndham Land Act of 1903. Murtagh Cosgar, who has bought his farm under the provisions of the Act, disapproves of his son Matt's love for Ellen Douras, the daughter of a farmer who has not. Matt overcomes his father's resistance to modern love-matches, but Ellen declares that she wants her freedom.

Land Acts, see *Wyndham Land Act.

Land League, the, founded in Dublin on 21 October 1879 by Charles Stewart *Parnell, Michael *Davitt, and Andrew Kettle (father of Thomas *Kettle), in response to agricultural depression and landlordism. It attracted widespread support from townspeople and the Catholic clergy, as well as farmers. Its historic slogan, 'The Land for the People', was interpreted as The Three Fs: 'fair rent, free sale, and fixity of tenure', already promulgated by the Tenant League of 1850 [see Charles Gavan *Duffy]. A centrepiece of the New

Departure policy of *Fenian–Parnellite co-operation for self-government and land reform, the League was a constitutional movement, though it triggered a sporadically violent Land War. Its celebrated tactic was the boycott, so called from its use against Capt. Charles *Boycott, a land agent who refused to concede rent reductions.

Land of [Youth, etc.], see *sídh.

Land of Cokaygne, The, a *Hiberno-English goliardic poem, preserved in a 14th-cent. manuscript known as *Harley 913 in the British Library, which also contains the hymn of a Friar *Michael of Kildare, indicating a possible association with that town. This poem describes a country of great comfort and abundance where there are two religious communities of abbots and nuns.

Land of Spices, The (1941), a novel by Kate *O'Brien, set in an Irish convent of a French order, telling how the Reverend Mother embraced religious life because of the shock she suffered on discovering that her father was homosexual.

Landleaguers, The (1883), an unfinished novel by Anthony *Trollope, written during a late visit to Ireland in response to the Land War [see *Land League] and particularly the Phoenix Park Murders perpetrated by the *Invincibles.

Lane, Denny (1818–1895), poet and *Young Irelander. Born in Cork, he contributed poems to The *Nation. His best-known song is 'Carrig Dhoun'. He was briefly imprisoned after 1848, later becoming a railway proprietor and a director of the Cork Gas Co.

Lane, Sir Hugh (1875–1915), founder of the Municipal Gallery of Modern Art,

Dublin. Born in Ballybrack, Co. Cork, he was a nephew of Lady *Gregory. A successful art dealer, in 1908 he lent a group of Impressionist paintings, chiefly French, to form the nucleus of the Municipal Gallery. When a 'Bridge of Sighs' designed by Sir Edward Lutyens to span the Liffey was rejected in 1913 by a City Council that disapproved of the paintings, he removed them to London. An unwitnessed codicil to his will stipulated that they should return to Dublin if a permanent home were allocated to them. The sinking of the *Lusitania*, in which he drowned in May 1915, led to the paintings being retained in London. The former house of the Earl of *Charlemont in Dublin was purchased for the Municipal Gallery in 1929, and the Lane Pictures are regularly displayed there since 1960.

Lane, Temple (pseudonym of Mary Isabel Leslie) (1899–1978), novelist. Born in Dublin, she was raised in Co. Tipperary, educated in England, and at TCD. Her fifteen novels, from *Burnt Bridges* (1925) to *My Bonny's Away* (1947), address questions of growth and maturity in young women. *Friday's Well* (1943) tells how Anna Prendergast hides an American airman in the cellar of the family farmhouse. The possibility of reconciliation between landlords and tenants is illustrated in *House of My Pilgrimage* (1941).

Langrishe, Go Down (1966), a *big house novel by Aidan *Higgins. Set in the late 1930s in rural Co. Kildare, the novel describes the bored lives of three spinster Langrishe sisters in Springfield House, their decaying home. The story concerns an affair between Imogen Langrishe and Otto Beck, a German student writing a doctorate in Celtic Studies.

Lanigan, John, DD (1758–1828), author of *An Ecclesiastical History of Ireland*

(4 vols., 1822). Born in Cashel, Co. Tipperary, he was ordained in Rome and taught Hebrew and Divinity at Pavia University. In 1799 he was employed at the RDS as librarian, and later joined Edward *O'Reilly and others in founding the *Gaelic Society of Dublin.

Laoide, Seosamh (Lloyd, Joseph Henry) (1865–1939), folklorist and editor. Born in Dublin, he was educated at TCD, and became joint treasurer of the *Gaelic League in 1893. He was appointed editor of the *Gaelic Journal* [see *Irisleabhar na Gaedhilge] from 1899 and oversaw the publication of 200 Irish titles between 1902 and 1915.

laoithe [sing. laoi], see *lays.

Lardner, Dionysius (1793–1859), a science writer, he was the natural father of Dion *Boucicault. Born in Dublin and educated at TCD, he lectured in science at London University from 1827. He edited the *Cabinet Encyclopaedia* (1829–49) and the *Edinburgh Cabinet Library* (1830–2).

Larkin, James (1874–1947), labour leader. Born in Liverpool of Irish parents, he left school at 13 for an engineering apprenticeship. An active socialist from 1893, he became an organizer for the Dock Labourers and was sent to Ireland in 1907. He defected to form the Irish Transport and General Workers' Union (ITGWU) in 1908. He was also founder-editor of the *Irish Worker* (1911–15), the most famous Irish labour paper. Employers combined in 1913 to lock out all Larkinites in Dublin. In 1923 he split from mainstream Labour to lead the Worker's Union of Ireland and the Irish Workers' League, a communist party. 'Big Jim' is remembered especially for his heroic leadership during the lockout, the inspiration for books and plays by Sean *O'Casey and James *Plunkett.

Larminie, William (1849–1900), poet and folklorist. Born in Castlebar, Co. Mayo, he was educated at TCD before entering the India Office in London. *Fand and Other Poems* (1892) made use of Gaelic assonance. He had some knowledge of the Irish language: his *West Irish Folk Tales and Romances* (1898) were, in part at least, based on fieldwork among native speakers. *Glanlua and Other Poems* (1899) was a further collection.

Last Baron of Crana, The (1826), a novel by John *Banim. Written as a sequel to The *Boyne Water* (1826), it concerns the fate of two Catholic families in the early *Penal years following the Treaty of Limerick [see *Williamite War]. The plot tells how Miles Prendergast, a liberal Williamite, tries to shelter the son of his dead Jacobite opponent, Sir Redmond O'Burke, on his northern Irish estate.

Last September, The (1929), a novel by Elizabeth *Bowen. Set in the Naylors' *big house, Danielstown, Co. Tipperary, it explores their niece Lois Farquahar's emotional and sexual awakening against the background of the *Troubles in 1920.

Latin learning, see *classical literature in Irish.

L'Attaque (1962), a historical novel in Irish by Eoghan *Ó Tuairisc. Set in Co. Mayo, it chronicles the part played by a small band of *United Irishmen from Co. Leitrim in the military campaign following the arrival of the French forces under General Humbert in Killala in 1798.

Laudabiliter (papal bull), see Anglo-Irish *chronicles.

Laurence Bloomfield in Ireland (1864), a verse-novel about the Land War [see *Land League] by William

*Allingham. Bloomfield, an idealistic young landlord who has been travelling abroad, returns to his estate at Lisnamoy. An inclusive canvas—with hovels, *big house, round tower and lake, violent peasantry and feckless *ascendancy, flashy Catholic chapel and trim Protestant church—the settings of the poem encapsulate Allingham's vision of mid-19th-cent. Ireland.

Laverty, Maura (née Kelly) (1907–1967), novelist. Born in Rathangan, Co. Kildare, she trained to teach at Brigadine Convent, Co. Carlow; she went to Spain in 1925 as a Catholic governess. Her adventures there are narrated as Delia's story in *No More than Human* (1944), while the early autobiographical novel *Never No More* (1942) recalls childhood. Besides her other novels, *Alone We Embark* (1943) and *Lift Up Your Gates* (1946), she wrote children's stories and scripts for *RTÉ.

Lavin, Mary (1912–1996), writer of fiction. Born in Massachusetts of Irish parents, she returned to Ireland at the age of 10 and lived for some time in Athenry, the Castle-rampart of many of her stories; she was educated at UCD. Her first stories, *Tales from Bective Bridge* (1943), were followed by, among others: *The Long Ago* (1944), *The Becker Wives* (1946), *A Single Lady* (1951), *The Patriot Son* (1956), *A Likely Story* (1957), *The Second-Best Children in the World* (1972), *A Memory* (1972), *The Shrine* (1977), and *A Family Likeness* (1985). Her stories often draw upon the abrupt transitions of speech, and make use of monologue to reveal character and situation. *The House in Clew Street* (1945), a novel, tells how a young man rebels against the restrictions of living with his two aunts, while *Mary O'Grady* (1950) describes an ordinary Dublin family with care and sympathy.

law in Gaelic Ireland. Native law tracts dealing in detail with a wide variety of topics such as contracts, theft, marriage, kinship, insanity, and so on, were in use in Ireland until the break-up of the Gaelic order. Though the date of origin is impossible to determine, a legal system (fénechas) based on early Celtic institutions was fully developed by the arrival of St *Patrick. Approximately fifty Old Irish law texts survive in copied versions—often incomplete— with many shorter fragments from intermediate *manuscripts now lost. Though the surviving manuscripts are mainly from the 14th to the 16th cents., linguistic evidence shows that the law texts themselves date from the 7th or 8th cents. AD. The largest collection of law texts, *Senchas Már* (*Great Tradition*), is thought to have been compiled at a school connected with a monastery in the north midlands during the 8th cent., while others would have been kept in similar schools elsewhere. After the *Norman invasion the legal system passed into the keeping of learned families, the most notable being the *Mac Aodhagáin family in Co. Galway, the Mac Fhlannchadha of Thomond, the Ó Breisléin of Fermanagh, and the *Ó Duibhdábhoireann in Co. Clare. The laws are often known as the Brehon laws (from Irish breitheamh, 'judge').

Lawless, Hon. Emily (1845–1913), novelist and poet. Born at Lyons Castle, Co. Kildare, daughter of Lord Cloncurry, she was brought up in England and the west of Ireland. Excepting *A Chelsea Householder* (1882) and *A Millionaire's Cousin* (1885), her novels are devoted to Irish subjects. Her first novel, *Hurrish* (1886), deals with agrarian crime during the Land War, while *Grania* (1892) takes the side of an Aran island girl against the males of her society. Her other novels are mostly historical. *With Essex in Ireland* (1890) is the 'diary' of an Englishman during Essex's campaign in Ireland. The title-character in *Maelcho*

(1894) is a *seanchaí who relates the grim events of the Desmond Rebellion, 1579–82. *With the Wild Geese* (1902) is a collection of lyrics relating to the *Irish brigades. *The Race of Castlebar* (1914), dealing with the *United Irishmen's Rebellion, was written in collaboration with Shan *Bullock. *Ireland* (1885) is part topography, part autobiography.

Lawrence, W[illiam] J. (1862–1940), theatrical historian and drama critic, born in Belfast. His general works on theatrical history include *The Physical Conditions of the Elizabethan Public Playhouse* (1927) and *Old Theatre Days and Ways* (1935). Among many Irish researches, he discovered the parentage of Dion *Boucicault and wrote lives of Michael *Balfe and the tragic actor Gustavus Vaughan Brooke (1818–67), while his 'Notebooks for a History of the Irish Stage', held at Cincinnati University, provide a unique record.

Lawson, John (1712–1759), rhetorician. Born in Dublin, he prepared the groundwork for the Anglo-Irish oratorical tradition in his lectures at TCD on the Philippics, published by George *Faulkner in 1758.

lays (laoithe; sing. laoi), sung narratives in verse which developed in the 12th cent. from the *Fionn cycle. They are collected in the 16th-cent. *Book of the Dean of Lismore* and in *Duanaire Finn* (1627).

Leabhar [. . .], see individual entries, also *Book of* [. . .] and *manuscripts.

Leabhar Bhaile an Mhóta, see *Book of Ballymote.*

Leabhar Breac (*Speckled Book*), a *manuscript compiled by Murchadh Ó Cuindlis, one of the scribes of the *Book of Lecan*, in 1408–11. Also known as *Leabur Mór Dúna Daidhri* (*Great Book of Duniry*), the manuscript was consulted by Mícheál *Ó Cléirigh in 1629. Mainly consisting of religious matter, the body of the manuscript was bought by the *RIA in 1789.

Leabhar Clainne Suibhne (*Book of Clan Sweeney*), a 16th cent. Donegal *manuscript in Irish. Containing religious material but with an interesting historical tract on Clann Suibhne, it is held in the *RIA Library as MS No. 475.

Leabhar Cloinne Aodha Buidhe, a poem-book [*duanaire] of the Clandeboye branch of the O'Neill family, drawn up by the Sligo scribe Ruairí Ó hUiginn in 1680 at the request of Cormac O'Neill. The Clandeboye O'Neills occupied land corresponding to latter-day south Antrim and north Down, known formerly as Cland Aodha Buidhe.

Leabhar Leacáin, see *Book of Lecan.

Leabhar Uí Dhubhagáin, see *Book of Uí Mhaine.*

Leadbeater, Mary (1758–1826), poet, and diarist. Born in Ballitore, Co. Kildare, granddaughter of the founder of a Quaker school. She published improving collections of anecdotes and 'biographies', among them, *Cottage Dialogues* (1811). Her *Collection of Lives of the Irish Peasantry* (1822) is compassionate. Her literary monument is, however, the journals she kept from 1766 to the end of her life, later edited by her niece Elizabeth as *The Leadbeater Papers* (2 vols., 1862) and subtitled *Annals of Ballitore.*

Leader, The, see D.P. *Moran.

Leamy, Edmund (1848–1904), author of fairy-tales. Born and educated in Waterford, he edited *United Ireland* in the 1890s, and published collections such as *Irish Fairy Tales* (1889) and *By the Barrow River* (1907).

Leared, Arthur (1822–1879), physician and traveller. Born in Wexford and educated at TCD, he wrote *Morocco and the Moors* (1876) and *A Visit to the Court of Morocco* (1879).

Le[a]th Cuinn, Le[a]th Moga, see *political divisions and *Conn Cétchathach.

Leavetaking, The (1977), a novel by John *McGahern dealing with the last day in post of the schoolteacher Patrick Moran, who has been dismissed for marrying an American divorcée in a registry office.

Lebor [. . .], see individual entries, also *Book of [. . .] and *manuscripts.

Lebor Gabála Érenn (*Book of Invasions*), a medieval chronicle recounting the legendary history of Ireland from the Creation to the 12th cent. This tradition originated in learned speculation concerning the descent of the Irish from Noah, which traced historical kings back to his Scythian descendants, probably through the etymological association of Latin Scotti with Scythae. The 'Milesians' (i.e. 'sons of Míl Espáine, soldier of Spain') are said to have conquered Ireland around the time of Alexander the Great. Other races such as the Fir Bolg [see *mythological cycle], Fir Domnann, and Gáiléoin, the deities of the Tuatha Dé Danann [see *mythology], and their monstrous enemies the Fomoire, the Britons, and the Picts, are traced back to previous invasions which give the text its name, while even earlier invasions are attributed to Cessair, Partholón, and Nemed.

Lebor Glinne Dá Loch, see *Book of Glendalough.

Lebor Leacáin, see *Book of Lecan.

Lebor na Cert, see *Book of Rights.

Lebor na hUidre, see *Book of the Dun Cow.

Lecky, W[illiam] E[dward] H[artpole] (1838–1903), historian. Born in Newton Park, Co. Dublin, and educated at TCD. After some poems and essays he issued anonymously *Leaders of Public Opinion in Ireland* (1861) which promoted a liberal, Unionist, *ascendancy view. His *History of England in the Eighteenth Century* (8 vols., 1878–90) refuted the 'anti-Irish calumnies' of J. A. *Froude's *The English in Ireland* (1872–4). The Irish sections were republished as *The History of Ireland in the Eighteenth Century* (5 vols., 1892–6). Chief among his later works were *Democracy and Liberty* (1896) and *The Map of Life* (1899).

Ledrede, Richard (?1275–1360), English-born Franciscan poet and Bishop of Ossory from 1316. In 1324 he presided over the trial of Dame Alice Kyteler of Kilkenny for witchcraft. Some sixty Latin hymns by him or recorded by him are preserved in the *Red Book of Ossory* in Kilkenny.

Ledwich, Edward (1738–1823), antiquarian. Born in Dublin and educated at TCD. His *Antiquities of Ireland* (1790) is written from the standpoint of the Anglo-Irish *chronicles and informed by suspicions that Charles *O'Conor the Elder and others were attempting to enhance the cultural appreciation of Gaelic Ireland as part of a campaign against the *Penal Laws. His disparaging view of the lives of the Irish saints was disputed in John *Lanigan's *Ecclesiastical History* (1822).

Ledwidge, Francis *(1891–1917), poet. Born in Slane, Co. Kildare, he worked locally as a labourer. He was active in the *Gaelic League. Lord *Dunsany organized the publication of *Songs of the Field* (1915). He joined up in Dunsany's regiment (Royal Enniskilling Fusiliers) in October 1914. He served as a corporal, saw action in Gallipoli, the Balkans, and France, and was killed at Ypres, 31 July 1917. Dunsany edited *The Complete Poems* (1919).

Le Fanu, Alicia (1791–?), author of *The Memoirs of the Life and Writings of Frances Sheridan* (1824), which comprises family anecdotes and a defence of R. B. *Sheridan. She also wrote a number of poems and romantic novels, such as *The Flowers, or A Sylphid Queen* (1809), and *Henry the Fourth of France* (4 vols., 1826).

Le Fanu, Joseph Sheridan (1814–1873), novelist. Born in Dublin, of Huguenot extraction, he was educated at home before entering TCD. A growing involvement in writing and publishing led to his becoming editor and/or proprietor of *The Warder*, The *Dublin Evening Packet*, the *Evening Mail*, and the *Dublin University Magazine*. Neither of Le Fanu's first two full-length narratives, *The *Cock and Anchor* (1845) and *The *Fortunes of Colonel Torlogh O'Brien* (1847), enjoyed success, and it was not until 1863 that he returned to novel-writing with *The *House by the Churchyard*. Eleven other novels quickly followed, most of them appearing first as serials in the *Dublin University Magazine*. These were *Wylder's Hand* (1864), *Uncle Silas* (1864), *Guy Deverell* (1865), *All in the Dark* (1866), *The Tenants of Malory* (1867), *A Lost Name* (1868), *Haunted Lives* (1868), *The Wyvern Mystery* (1869), *Checkmate* (1870), *The Rose and the Key* (1871), and *Willing to Die* (1873). He also published the story collections *Ghost Stories and Tales of Mystery* (1851), *Chronicles of Golden Friars* (1871), and *In a Glass Darkly* (1872). Le Fanu excelled in documenting stress-induced states of consciousness, looking out on a frightening world where the evidence of the senses and of the powers of reasoning are jeopardized. A. P. *Graves issued Le Fanu's *Poems* in 1896.

Leitch, Maurice (1933–), novelist. Born in Muckamore, Co. Antrim, he became a teacher and worked afterwards as a BBC producer in Belfast and London. Most of his novels, including *The *Liberty Lad* (1965), *Poor Lazarus* (1969), *Stamping Ground* (1975), and *Silver's City* (1981), and the novella *Chinese Whispers* (1987), are set in the south Antrim of his youth or Belfast. *Burning Bridges* (1989) is about a country-and-western singer. Albert Yarr in *Poor Lazarus* is naïve and idealistic, like Frank Glass in *The Liberty Lad*. *Silver's City* is about Protestant paramilitary activity. *Gilchrist* (1994) is a study of a corrupt Ulster Protestant evangelist.

Leland, Mary (1941–), novelist; born in Cork, she was educated at the South Presentation Convent before entering journalism with the *Cork Examiner*. Her novel *The Killeen* (1985) was followed by the stories in *The Little Galloway Girls* (1986), and a further novel, *Approaching Priests* (1991).

Leland, Thomas (1722–1785), historian. Born in Dublin and educated at TCD, where he was appointed Professor of Oratory in 1763. Leland's frequently reprinted translation of the *Orations of Demosthenes* (3 vols., 1754–70) provided a model for Anglo-Irish parliamentary speaking. His *Life of Philip of Macedon* (1758) was for many years the standard work. Following his attack on James *Macpherson's Ossianic poems in 1772, Charles *O'Conor supplied Leland with translations of Irish *annals in the hope that his forthcoming history would overturn the tradition of a widespread massacre of Protestants in the

*Rebellion of 1641. In the event, his *History of Ireland from the Invasion of Henry II* (3 vols., 1773) supported the version promulgated by Sir John *Temple and others [see Anglo-Irish *chronicles and *Gaelic historiography]. Leland's sole work of fiction, *Longsword, Earl of Salisbury* (1765), is an early historical novel.

Lendennie, Jessie (1946–), poet and publisher; born in Blytheville, Arkansas; educated in London. Founded in 1984 Salmon Publishing, a significant outlet for poetry in Galway and the west. Also published a collection of her own: *Daughter* (1988).

Leonard, Hugh (pseudonym of John Keyes Byrne) (1926–), dramatist. Born in Dublin to a single mother, he was adopted, brought up in Dalkey, Co. Dublin, and educated locally. In 1945 he joined the Civil Service (Land Commission) and remained there until 1959. After the *Abbey Theatre rejected *The Italian Road* in 1954 the author assumed the name of its hero in submitting another play, *The Big Birthday*, which the Abbey staged in 1956. He wrote the comedy *Madigan's Lock* (1958), after which he worked for Granada Television in Manchester. The success of *Stephen D* in Dublin in 1962 led to a production in London. After this he wrote numerous plays, such as *The Poker Session* (1964), *Mick and Mick* (1966), and *The *Patrick Pearse Motel* (1971). In 1973 Leonard turned to dramatic autobiography with *Da. Leonard mined this material again in the prose works *Home Before Night* (1979) and *Out After Dark* (1989), and in the play *A Life* (1980). *Summer*, first staged in 1974, is in the Chekhovian vein. He wrote a 1916 commemorative series comprising eight television dramatizations, *Insurrection* (1966).

Leslie, Sir Shane (1885–1971) (John Randolph; 3rd Baronet Glaslough), man of letters. Born at Castle Leslie, Co. Monaghan, he was educated at Eton and Cambridge, and became a Catholic in 1908. His writings include biography, memoirs and autobiographical novels, poetry, and studies of the Oxford Movement. He wrote *The Skull of Swift* (1928); and studies of *Lough Derg (1917). One of several novels, *Doomsland* (1923) traces Irish political events in 1910. His autobiographical novels are *The Oppidan* (1922), *The Cantab* (1926), and *The Anglo-Catholic* (1929). His autobiographies were *The Passing Chapter* (1934) and *The Film of Memory* (1938).

Letter to a Noble Lord, A (1796), a vindication of his own career by Edmund *Burke and a devastating attack on the Duke of Bedford, in the form of an open letter to him and another who had spoken against the civil pension granted to Burke in 1794.

Letter to Sir H. Langrishe, *Bart. MP, on the subject of the Roman Catholics of Ireland, A* (1972), a political tract by Edmund *Burke in the form of a letter to Sir Hercules Langrishe (1731–1811), MP in the Irish Parliament, on the justice of giving Catholics the vote. Langrishe had earlier supported relaxation of the *Penal Laws, and here Burke is seeking to influence him and other liberal-minded Anglo-Irish Protestants towards further reforms in favour of the Catholic majority in Ireland.

Letters on a Regicide Peace (I and II, 1796; III, 1797; IV in *Collected Works*, 1803–27), political tracts by Edmund *Burke in the form of a series of letters to an MP, written when William Pitt was negotiating terms of peace with France. Filled with the urgency and rage of a dying man, these letters set temperance aside to contemplate the horror of Jacobin France.

Letts, Winifred M. (1882–1972), poet and author of fiction; born in Co. Wexford and educated at Alexandra College. She wrote plays for the *Abbey: Eyes of the Blind* (1907) and *The Challenge* (1909). Her collection, *Songs of Leinster* (1913), was followed by *More Songs of Leinster* (1926). *Knockmaroon* (1933) is a reminiscence about grandparents.

Leventhal, A[braham] J. ('Con') (1896–1979), TCD lecturer and man of letters. Born in Dublin and educated at TCD, he helped to found a Zionist weekly paper. He backed the publication of the controversial magazine *Tomorrow* (1924). In 1932 he succeeded Samuel *Beckett as a lecturer in French at TCD.

Lever, Charles [James] (1806–1872), novelist. Born in Dublin, he was educated at TCD before travelling in Europe and Canada, 1822–7, returning to study medicine at the Royal College of Surgeons. In 1832 he was appointed dispensary doctor at Portstewart, Co. Derry, where he met William Hamilton *Maxwell, whose *Wild Sports of the West* (1932) inspired Lever's early military novels such as *Harry Lorrequer* (1839). Begun at Portstewart, this novel portrays the comic adventures of ebullient young subalterns of the Napoleonic period enjoying themselves in Ireland. The peasantry provide unthreatening rustic entertainment, and the world these young army men inhabit is virtually free of the menace of *secret societies, public hangings, and agrarian outrages. In 1839 he left for Brussels, where he practised. There he wrote *Charles O'Malley* (1841), serialized in the *Dublin University Magazine*, which he returned to edit, 1842–5; during his tenure as editor it published *Our Mess: Jack Hinton, the Guardsman* (1842–3), *Arthur O'Leary* (1843), and *Tails of the Trains* (1845). Lever left for Europe in 1845, settling in Florence in 1847. He

wrote the *O'Donoghue* (1845), *St Patrick's Eve* (1845), *The Knight of Gwynne* (1847), *Roland Cashel* (1850), and *The Martins of Cro' Martin* (1856), among others. He was appointed British Vice-Consul at Spezia in 1858, a year which also saw the publication of *Davenport Dunn*. In 1867 he was appointed Consul at Trieste. From *Tom Burke of 'Ours'* (1843) through to *Lord Kilgobbin* (1872), his last novel, Lever explores the ways in which characters respond to different loyalties.

Lewis, Cecil Day, see C[ecil] *Day-Lewis.

Lewis, C[live] S[taples] (1898–1963), scholar and man of letters. Born in Belfast he was educated at University College, Oxford, interrupting his studies there to serve in the First World War. After being wounded in 1918 he was discharged, published *Spirits in Bondage* (1919), and resumed his studies, becoming a Fellow in English at Magdalen in 1925. His rediscovery of the significance of orthodox Christianity in the modern world in 1929 was reflected in *The Pilgrim's Regress: An Allegorical Apology for Christianity, Reason and Romanticism* (1933). His belief that literature could strengthen moral awareness informed his *Allegory of Love* (1936), a study of courtly love. These concerns are also evident in his science fiction in the trilogy *Out of the Silent Planet* (1938), *Perelandra* (1943, later retitled *Voyage to Venus*) and *That Hideous Strength* (1945). *The Problem of Pain* (1940) established him as an exponent of belief. *The Screwtape Letters* (1942), advice from an experienced devil to a younger colleague on how to tempt sinners, was followed by *Mere Christianity* (1952); *Miracles* (1947); *The Four Loves* (1960); and *A Grief Observed* (1961), on the death of his wife, Joy Davidman, in 1960. The seven tales of the Narnia Chronicles for children began with *The Lion, the Witch, and the Wardrobe* (1950) and ended with *The Last Battle* (1956).

Other literary studies included *A Preface to Paradise Lost* (1942) and *The Discarded Image* (1964).

Lhuyd, (or Lloyd), Edward (?1660–1709), Celtic scholar. Born at Oswestry on the English-Welsh border, he was educated at Jesus College, Oxford. He was appointed Assistant Keeper of the Ashmolean Museum in 1687 and became Keeper in 1691. He acquired a competence in Welsh and Irish, making contact with John *Toland at Oxford, 1694–5. His *Lithophylacii Britannici Ichnografia* (1699) was a catalogue of British fossils. In 1699–70 he spent time in Ireland, researching its language and antiquities. He met Dubhaltach *Mac Fhir Bhisigh and collected some twenty-five *manuscripts. His labour in Celtic studies bore fruit in *Archaeologia Britannica* (1707). His manuscript collection, which included the *Book of Leinster* and the *Yellow Book of Lecan*, were bought by Sir Thomas Sebright in 1715 and presented to the Library of TCD by his son, Sir John, in 1786.

Lia Fáil (Stone of Destiny), a talisman of the Tuatha Dé Danann [see Irish *mythology]. It was reputed to shriek when a worthy candidate for the *kingship of *Tara touched it with the axle of his chariot. The historical Lia Fáil was probably an *inauguration site in the form of a flagstone rather than a phallic monument. Fergus Mór mac Eirc took Lia Fáil to Scotland. It is also held that it was carried to Scone then finally removed to Westminster Abbey in the 13th cent.

Liber Armachanus, see *Book of Armagh*.

Liberty Lad, The (1965), a novel by Maurice *Leitch. Set in Co. Antrim, it deals with the early adult years of Frank Glass, a teacher and the son of a linen worker who rejects the values exemplified by his father's refusing to join a trade union, and by his hostile attitude to Catholics.

Liddy, James (1934–   ), poet; born in Dublin and educated at UCD, and the King's Inns, he practised law in Dublin and then taught in America. His poetry expresses a discontent with orderly lives and humdrum routine, praising spontaneity and emotion. His chief collections are *Esau, My Kingdom for a Drink* (1962), *In a Blue Smoke* (1964), *Blue Mountain* (1968), *A Munster Song of Love and War* (1969), *Orpheus in the Ice Cream Parlour* (1975), *Comyn's Lay* (1979), *At the Grave of Father Sweetman* (1984) and *Art Is Not for Grown-Ups* (1990). A short novel, *Young Men Go Walking* (1986), is notable for its open celebration of homosexuality. His *Collected Poems* were issued in 1995.

Liddy, John (1954–   ), poet; born in Youghal, Co. Cork, educated in Limerick and at UCG. Subsequently worked for the British Council at Madrid as a librarian. He published *Boundaries* (1974), *The Angling Cot* (1991), *Song of the Empty Cage* (1997), and *Wine and Hope* (1999).

Life and Opinions of Tristram Shandy, The (1760–7), a fiction by Laurence *Sterne. Representing itself as an autobiography, and written with ludicrous fidelity to John Locke's *Essay Concerning Human Understanding* (1690), it emphasizes the role of arbitrary causes in experience, seeking an explanation of Tristram's character in the comical circumstances of his conception and the accident of his circumcision. The passage of multitudinous unrelated thoughts through the minds of the characters anticipates the stream-of-consciousness technique developed by James *Joyce.

Life of William Carleton, The (1896), composed of an autobiographical fragment together with a biographical commentary by Frances

*Hoey and D. J. *O'Donoghue. The autobiographical part, written towards the end of Carleton's life, recalls his childhood in rural Co. Tyrone and narrates a series of adventures in the manner of a picaresque novel.

Lisheen, or The Test of the Spirits (1907), a novel by Canon Patrick *Sheehan, set in Co. Kerry in the 1890s, recounting the experiences of a young landlord who lodges incognito with his tenants and witnesses their eviction at the hands of his own agent.

literary revival, a term used to describe the modern Irish literary movement, lasting from around 1890 and the fall of *Parnell to about 1922, a date marking the end of the *Anglo-Irish War and the publication of *Ulysses. As a movement it originated in the earlier cultural developments of the 19th cent.: the antiquarian studies of Sylvester *O'Halloran and Charlotte *Brooke culminating in the work of the Ordnance Survey co-ordinated by George *Petrie; and the idealistic popular balladry and fiction of the *Young Ireland movement expressed in the columns of The *Nation. In the early 1890s it seemed to W. B. *Yeats that the time was right for a new cultural movement in Irish society which would replace the political one for Home Rule [see *Irish Parliamentary Party]. He immersed himself in Irish legend and *folklore, and set about enthusing others. His Fairy and Folk Tales of the Irish Peasantry (1888) represented months of hard work, in which he was assisted by Douglas *Hyde, whose Beside the Fire (1890), an anthology of tales with facing translations, is the first authentic collection of folklore in Irish. In 1892 Yeats, T. W. *Rolleston, and Charles Gavan *Duffy set up the Irish Literary Society in London; in Dublin Yeats founded the National Literary Society in the same year, with

Hyde as first President. This cultural activity was carried forward by the foundation of the *Gaelic League in 1893, with Hyde again becoming its first President. Also in that year appeared his The Love Songs of Connacht. In the 1890s the new Irish writings of Yeats and others found ready acceptance among British readers, who were attracted to a culture not yet entirely modernized. In a world growing increasingly industrialized, the Celts and other so-called primitive peoples were thought to possess an instinctive understanding and knowledge, qualities reflected in Yeats's The *Celtic Twilight (1893, 2nd edn. 1902), which grew out of his recollections of Sligo and Howth and showed his respect for the intuitions of Irish country people. A formative book, it gave the movement a popular name. A desire to return to ancient truth is revealed in the title of George *Russell's Homeward: Songs by the Way (1894). Yeats met Edward Martyn, George Moore, Lady *Gregory, and *Synge in the 1890s and these friendships formed a dynamic set of relationships that determined the course of the revival for the next ten years or more and led to the founding of the *Abbey Theatre. Research into Gaelic language and literature, after a period of relative inactivity in the 1870s and 1880s, began to revive, in particular with Standish Hayes *O'Grady's Silva Gadelica (1892), a large anthology of stories from the various branches of classic Irish narrative (see *tale-types). George *Sigerson's Bards of the Gael and Gall (1897), an anthology of translated Irish verse from the earliest times, proclaimed the antiquity of Irish poetry. The Gaelic League sponsored editions of Irish writings, notably Aodhagán *Ó Rathaille and Eoghan Rua *Ó Suilleabháin. Patrick *Pearse became editor of the Gaelic League weekly An *Claidheamh Soluis, 1903–9, and argued for a modern literature in Irish. *Cú

Chulainn, the dominant fictional figure of the revival, and the embodiment of the heroic nationalism celebrated and criticized in many of its writings, was the subject of the second volume of Standish James *O'Grady's *History of Ireland: Cuculain and his Contemporaries* (1880) and of his novel *The Coming of Cuculain* (1895). Cú Chulainn entered Yeats's own poetry in 1892 with 'Cuchulain's Fight with the Sea'. However, the stories of the *Ulster and other cycles of Irish literature seemed to Yeats to be 'a wild anarchy of legends', so that when he and Lady Gregory joined forces she undertook to shape the Cú Chulainn stories into the coherent narrative of *Cuchulain of Muirthemne* (1902). Yeats drew upon this work for his *Cuchulain cycle of plays; and the hero was also a powerful symbol for Patrick Pearse. The union of aristocrat and peasant which Yeats and Lady Gregory tried to realize left out the Catholic middle classes, who became more vocal as the 20th cent. progressed. Catholic and Gaelic nationalism had a spokesman in D. P. *Moran, the editor of *The Leader* (founded 1900), which tended to regard the revival as a dalliance of the remnants of an outmoded Anglo-Irish *ascendancy. Synge's *The *Playboy of the Western World* (1907) was received as an insult. *Joyce stood aside from the revival, his hero Stephen Dedalus in *A *Portrait of the Artist as a Young Man* (1916) escaping the nets of nationalism, family, and religion. At the Abbey Theatre the management were frequently in disagreement with the actors, who regularly expressed views favouring a more overtly nationalist policy. The *Easter Rising (1916) had amongst its leaders writers who had been influenced by cultural nationalism, but who were ready to act out in reality some of its images. Yeats was later to ask, 'Did that play of mine send out | Certain men the English shot?', referring to *Cathleen Ni Houlihan (1902), a play which had Maud *Gonne in the title-role, embodying nationalist intensity. With Joyce's *Ulysses* (1922) and Yeats's 'Nineteen Hundred and Nineteen' (published 1922) the revival draws to a close. Against nationalist fixity Joyce sets the broad humanity of Leopold Bloom, Jew, citizen of the world, and good man; and Stephen Dedalus, the artist. Yeat's poem, written in the aftermath of the Rising and in the midst of the Anglo-Irish War, declares that 'no work can stand'. The revival helped to create an image of a pastoral, mythic, unmodernized Ireland that influenced subsequent writers and artists. Some, like Austin *Clarke and F. R. *Higgins, continued to exploit the image of an idealized west in poems and novels based on folklore and myth. Others openly mocked the ethos of the revival, as in Samuel *Beckett's dismissal of it as 'Cuchulainoid'. In the 1980s *Field Day reopened the issues of the revival, sometimes calling for the abandonment of its myths, but more often questioning its premisses to test their value for late 20th-cent. Irish society. See George J. Watson, *Irish Identity and the Literary Revival* (1979).

'Little Cloud, A', a story in James *Joyce's *Dubliners* (1914), written in 1906. Little Chandler is going to meet his former friend Ignatius Gallaher, now a London journalist. In a fashionable eating-house, Gallaher regales him with stories of sexual licence and Chandler confesses meekly to his marriage. Returning home, he feels resentment and loses his temper when the baby starts to cry.

Living Quarters (1977), a play by Brian *Friel, subtitled *After Hippolytus* and based on Euripides. When Commandant Frank Butler returns to 'Ballybeg' from distinguished service with the United Nations, his public role as hero is tested in the private world of home and family.

Lloyd, John (Seán Lúid) (1741–1786), Limerick-born itinerant schoolteacher and bilingual author. He wrote a *Short Tour, or Impartial Description of Clare* (1780).

Lombard, Peter (?1560–1625), churchman and Irish historian. Born in Waterford to an *Old English family and educated at *Louvain he was ordained in 1594. In December 1600 he completed *De Regno Hiberniae Commentarius* (Louvain, 1632), a work on 'the island of Saints', promoting Hugh *O'Neill. Lombard was made Archbishop of Armagh and Primate of All Ireland in June 1601, but remained in Rome, where he was to be joined by O'Neill, and where he died.

Lomnochtán, An (*The Nude*) (1977), a novel by Eoghan *Ó Tuairisc. The book depicts events in the life of a young child growing up in an Irish midland town during and after the *Civil War. The style involves a distinctive use of language in the attempt to depict an English-speaking environment through Irish.

London Assurance (1841), a comedy by Dion *Boucicault (as 'Lee Moreton'). Although it exploits the traditional dichotomies of comedy—female versus male, town versus country, youth versus old age—it provides an unconventional plot as well as highly original characters, especially Lady Gay Spanker, the fox-hunting virago. The true virtues of a gentleman triumph over mere London assurance.

London Vertigo, The (1992), an adaptation by Brian *Friel of Charles *Macklin's 18th-cent. farce *The *True Born Irishman* (1762).

Londonderry, 3rd Marquis of, see Charles William *Stewart.

Lonely Passion of Judith Hearne, The (1955), a Belfast novel by Brian *Moore, exploring the mental anguish of an ageing spinster living on a small annuity after the death of the aunt who exploited her as a housekeeper, and who is now living in a boarding-house along with several other Catholics.

Longes mac nUislenn (*Exile of the Sons of Uisliu*), the tragic story of Deirdre (Derdriu) and the sons of Uisliu from the *Ulster cycle. Preserved in the *Book of Leinster* and the *Yellow Book of Lecan*, it is known as one of the *Three Sorrows of Storytelling. When Fedlimid, ollam [see *áes dána] to Conchobor, gives a drunken feast at his house, the child his wife is bearing is born. The *druid Cathbad names her as Deirdre and foretells that she will cause destruction. Conchobor decrees that she be brought up in secret. Years later, Deirdre accosts Noisi at *Emain Macha, and when he tries to remind her of the prophecy she mocks him. Noisi and his brothers flee with Deirdre. They eventually agree to return, but the men are slaughtered. Deirdre lives on in joyless subjection to Conchobor. When he plans to give her to an accomplice in his treachery, she smashes her head against a rock.

Longford, Lady (née Christine Trew) (1900–1980), novelist and playwright. Born in Somerset and educated at Oxford, she married Edward Pakenham, Lord *Longford, in 1925, and participated with him in the running of the *Gate Theatre and Longford Productions. Her earliest novel, *Making Conversation* (1931), was a clever study of English silliness, and *Mr. Jiggins of Jigginstown* (1933) soon applied the same principle to the Anglo-Irish, while *Printed Cotton* (1935) depicts the Dublin art world. *The United Brothers* (1942) is a study of the *United Irishmen.

Longford, Lord (Edward Arthur Henry Pakenham; 6th Earl) (1902–1961), playwright and director of the *Gate Theatre from 1931, and founder of Longford Productions in 1936. His first play, *The Melians* (1931), reflected Irish politics in an ancient Greek setting. He dramatized Sheridan *Le Fanu's *Carmilla* (1932) and, in 1933, translated two plays from Aeschylus' Oresteian Trilogy (*Agamemnon* and *Drink Offering*). *Yahoo* (1933) is about Jonathan *Swift, and *Ascendancy* (1935) a melodrama of the decline of the Anglo-Irish aristocracy. His own company produced *Armlet of Jade* (1936), a translation of Molière's *Tartuffe* (1938), and *The Vineyard* (1943).

Longford, Lord (Frank Pakenham; 7th Earl) (1905–); author and social reformer. Brother of Edward *Longford, born and educated in England, he became a socialist and a Catholic and campaigned against capital punishment, prison conditions, and pornography, becoming Lord Privy Seal in 1966. His study of the Anglo-Irish *War in *Peace By Ordeal* (1935) gained him the reputation of a Republican. His many volumes of autobiographical writings, which include *Born to Believe* (1953), *The Grain of Wheat* (1974), and *Avowed Intent* (1994), reflect a busy public life.

Longley, Edna (1940–), critic; born in Dublin, she was educated at TCD where she met her husband Michael *Longley. She lectured at QUB, where she became Professor of English. She edited Edward Thomas's prose and poetry (1971 and 1973); her criticism includes *Poetry in the Wars* (1986), *Louis MacNeice* (1988), *The Living Stream* (1994) and *Poetry and Posterity* (2000). A close reader of poetry, she tests its insights against the brute world of politics and anger.

Longley, Michael (1939–), poet. Born in Belfast to English parents, he read classics at TCD. He joined the Northern Ireland Arts Council, serving as Director of Combined Arts from 1970 until retirement in 1991. A first volume, *No Continuing City* (1969), revealed a complex talent. *An Exploded View* (1973), includes the re-emergence of the *Troubles in its range. *Man Lying on a Wall* (1976) shows Longley's feeling for nature and his naturalist's eye at work. *The Echo Gate* (1979) includes versions of the Latin love elegy. *Gorse Fires* (1991) shows him transmuting the lyric mode into a vehicle of moral awareness. *The Ghost Orchid* (1995), *Broken Dishes* (1998) and *The Weather in Japan* (2000) reveal an enigmatic openness and a moral energy. *Tuppenny Stung* (1994) is a short volume of autobiography.

Lord Kilgobbin (1872), Charles *Lever's last novel. Set in the Bog of Allen, it juxtaposes political antagonists against a background of gloom, poverty, and decay. The static qualities of conservative old Ireland are embodied in Mathew Kearney, Lord Kilgobbin. His son Dick is a snob, and the daughter Kate has to bear the responsibilities the men neglect.

loricae (breastplates), a term applied to a genre of charms or prayers found in Irish and British Latin, Irish, Welsh, Anglo-Saxon, and Icelandic, and derived from the Pauline conception of the Christian life as an armed struggle. The earliest lorica is ascribed to Laidcenn mac Buith Bannaig of Clonfert-Mulloe, who died in 661. Somewhat later is the well-known St *Patrick's Breastplate, which has no historical connection with the saint.

Lough Derg, a religious site of pilgrimage associated with St *Patrick's legendary fast of forty days on Oiléan na Naomh, a lake-island in south-east Co.

Donegal. It has been revered as a holy place throughout Europe from the 12th cent. Station Island continues to be a site for penitential exercises annually between June and August. Beginning with its use by William *Carleton in *Traits and Stories of the Irish Peasantry* (1830), the Lough Derg pilgrimage has become established as a modern Irish literary theme for the examination of self and society in works by W. B. *Yeats, Denis *Devlin, Patrick *Kavanagh, Sean *O'Faolain, and Seamus *Heaney.

'Lough Derg Pilgrim, The' (1828), William *Carleton's first published work. Originally entitled 'A Pilgrimage to Patrick's Purgatory' and written with the encouragement of Caesar *Otway, who published it in his *Christian Examiner*, it appeared with *Father Butler* in 1829. It tells of the author's adventures as a pilgrim; initially mistaken for a priest, he is robbed of his clothes and money by a confidence trickster.

Loughsiders, The (1924), a novel by Shan *Bullock set in a community of Fermanagh farmers. Returning from America, Richard Jebb woos Rachel Nixon, but she turns him down because he unromantically negotiates her dowry with her father.

Louvain University [or Leuven], founded in what is now Belgium, in the provincial capital of Brabant, in 1425, it was a major centre for the Counter-Reformation in the 16th cent. Among the scholars of the Irish Counter-Reformation who studied at Louvain are Richard *Creagh and Peter *Lombard. In 1606 Philip III of Spain established the Franciscan College of St Anthony of Padua. Aodh *Mac Aingil was appointed first Professor of Philosophy and Theology, and made Guardian in May 1616. The Franciscans set up their own printing press at St Anthony's and produced Mac Aingil's Sgathán Shacramuinte na

hAithridhe (Mirror of the Sacrament of Confession, 1618). Aodh Mac an Bhaird (1593–1635), who became Guardian in 1626, co-ordinated a research project at Louvain which aimed to collect the ecclesiastical, hagiographical, and political records of Ireland. Mícheál *Ó Cléirigh acted as a field-worker in Ireland, and John *Colgan took over the work at Louvain at Mac an Bhaird's death, and published Acta Sanctorum Hiberniae (1645) and Trias Thaumaturga (1647), based on the work undertaken in Ireland by Ó Cléirigh and others. The *Annals of the Four Masters were also a product of this initiative. St Anthony's was suppressed during the French Revolution.

Love à la Mode (1759), a comedy by Charles *Macklin, first performed at Drury Lane Theatre, London. Charlotte Goodchild, an heiress, is courted by four lovers: Squire Groom, Archy MacSarcasm, Beau Mordecai, and Sir Callaghan O'Brallaghan, a voluble, *stage-Irish character, who wins her.

Love and a Bottle (1698), the earliest play by George *Farquhar, first produced at Drury Lane Theatre, London. Roebuck, an Irish gentleman, lacks a livelihood and debates between soldiering, highway robbery, and fortune-hunting. After some adventures he marries Leanthe and leaves his wild life.

love poetry, see *dánta grádha and *folksong in Irish.

Lover, Samuel (1797–1868), novelist, painter and song-writer. Born in Dublin, he displayed precocious abilities at an early age. He began writing tales loosely based on *folklore for Dublin magazines, later gathered as Legends and Stories of Ireland (2 vols., 1831 and 1834). He moved to London in 1833, where he found success as a society painter and author of songs, such as the *stage-Irish '*Rory O'More', which he worked up into a novel and play in 1837. *Handy Andy: A Tale of Irish Life (1842) was serialized in Bentley's Miscellany, which he founded with Charles Dickens and others. He toured his one-man show to the USA and then produced Paddy's Portfolio (1848), a new entertainment based on his experiences abroad.

Lovers (1967), a play in two parts by Brian *Friel, 'Winners' and 'Losers', both exploring the tragedy of personal love in conflict with the institutions of family, marriage, and religion.

Loves of Cass McGuire, The, a play by Brian *Friel first presented in New York in 1966. The title-character returns from New York where she has worked as a waitress for many years. Her brashness and drinking habits offend and she is put into a rest-home. Cass directly addresses the audience, which serves as her link with reality.

Lucas, Charles, see The *Freeman's Journal.

Luck of Barry Lyndon, The (1844), a novel by William Makepeace *Thackeray, set in the late 18th cent. and centred on the career of Redmond Barry, an Irish adventurer who progresses from common soldier to English aristocrat by marrying the Countess of Lyndon. Barry narrates the history of his progress, blissfully unaware of the chasm between his self-aggrandisement and the brutality of his nature.

Lug, see *mythological cycle.

Lughnasa (Lúnasa) [see also *festivals], the day marking the beginning of autumn, identified with 1 August in the Julian calendar. A survival of the ancient harvest festival, it is named after the god Lug, as noted in the 9th-

cent. Sanas Chormaic [see *Cormac mac Cuilennáin and *glossaries].

Luke Delmege (1901), a novel of clerical life by Canon Patrick *Sheehan. A proudly intellectual curate, returning from mission work in England, at first fails to adapt to life back in rural Ireland but finally undergoes a painful process of self-recognition.

Lyceum, The (1887–94), a monthly journal for history, politics, and literature, edited in Dublin by Fr. Thomas Finlay, 1887–8, and William Magennis, 1887–94, and later resumed by Fr. Finlay as The *New Ireland Review (1894–1911).

Lynch, Brian (1945–), poet; born in Dublin, and educated at UCD he worked as a journalist and Government press officer. Collections include Perpetual Star (1981), Beds of Down (1983), Paul Celan: 65 Poems (translations, 1985), and An Angry Heart (1998). He scripted Love and Rage (1999), a feature film.

Lynch, Hannah (1862–1904), novelist. Born in Dublin, she joined the Ladies' *Land League and continued William *O'Brien's paper United Ireland (suppressed 1881) in France. The majority of her novels, such as An Odd Experiment (1897), deal with aspects of the New Woman, while others such as The Prince of the Glades (1891) are stories of the Fenian movement. Autobiography of a Child (1899) recounts the experiences of an abused girl dictated in Dublin to the author.

Lynch, John (?1599–?1673), historian. Born in Galway, he was a pupil of Dubhaltach *Mac Fhir Bhisigh. He studied in France, returning to Ireland on his ordination in 1622, taught classics and was made Archdeacon of Tuam, but fled back to France when Galway surrendered to the Parliamentary army in 1652. He probably settled at St Malo. In 1660 he made a Latin translation of *Keating's *Foras Feasa ar Éirinn. His *Cambrensis Eversus* (1662) drew upon Keating and 17th-cent. *Gaelic historiography to refute the charges of the Anglo-Irish. *chronicles. His *Alithinologia* and *Supplementum Alithinologiae* (1659 and 1667) advocated conciliation between the *Old English and the native Irish.

Lynch, Liam (1937–1992), novelist and playwright; born in Dublin, he lived in Cork and Limerick as a child. His plays include *Do Thrushes Sing in Birmingham?* (*Abbey, 1963), and *Soldier* (Peacock, 1969), the latter a powerful evocation of the damage of war and emotional privation. His novels *Shell, Sea Shell* (1984), and *Tenebrae: A Passion* (1985) reveal a storyteller attuned to the sadness and despair of the Ireland in which he came to maturity. His style is exacting, clear, and scrupulous.

Lynch, Martin (1950–), playwright. Born in Belfast, he left school at 15 and worked as a cloth-cutter until 1969. His plays include *They're Taking the Barricades Down* (1979) and *What About Your Ma, Is Your Da Still Workin'?* (1981). As resident playwright at the *Lyric Theatre he wrote *Dockers* (1981) and *The Interrogation of Ambrose Fogarty* (1982). While writer in residence at UUC (1985-8) he wrote *My Minstrel Boy* (1985), and *Welcome to Bladonmore Road* (1988). Later work includes *Rinty* (1990) and, for community drama groups, *The Stone Chair* (1989) and *Moths* (1992).

Lynch, Patricia (1898–1972), children's writer; born in Cork, she was educated in Bruges. She became a journalist in the women's movement, and during the *Easter Rising Sylvia Pankhurst sent her to Dublin to report the insurrection. Settling in Dublin, she married the socialist author R[ichard] M[ichael] Fox in 1922 and became a prolific writer of children's best-sellers. *The Turf Cutter's Donkey* (1935) began a series in which the Irish landscape is lovingly evoked. Another series, on Brogeen the leprechaun, began with *Brogeen of the Stepping Stones* (1947).

Lynch, Patrick (1757–c.1820), polymath schoolmaster, born in Quin, Co. Clare. His grammar of English was printed as *The Pentaglot Preceptor* (1796), followed by *An Introduction to the Knowledge of the Irish Language* (1815), and an introduction to *Practical Astronomy* (1817), in mnemonic verse.

Lynd, Robert [Wilson] (1879–1949), essayist. Born in Belfast and educated at QUB, he went to London and joined the *Daily News* in 1908. *Rambles in Ireland* (1912) was illustrated by Jack B. *Yeats. *Ireland a Nation* (1919) is an essay in nationalist historiography. *Dr Johnson and his Company* (1929) was a success.

Lyons, F[rancis] S[teward] L[eland] (1923–1983), historian. Born in Derry and educated at TCD. He taught at the University of Kent before becoming Provost of TCD in 1974. His authoritative survey *Ireland Since the Famine* (1971) was preceded by books on the *Irish Parliamentary Party (1951) and the fall of *Parnell (1960), as well as biographies of John Dillon (1968) and Parnell (1977). *Culture and Anarchy in Ireland 1890–1939* (1979) is an essay on divergent traditions.

Lyric Players Theatre, The (1951–), founded in their home in Belfast by Mary O'Malley and her husband Pearse for the performance of Irish plays, initially focusing on the verse drama of *Yeats and Austin *Clarke, and influenced by the latter's *Lyric Theatre Company in Dublin. *Threshold*, a journal associated with the theatre, was founded in 1957. In 1968 the Lyric Theatre, funded from various sources, opened at its site at Ridgeway Street.

Lyric Theatre Company, Dublin (1944–51), founded by Austin *Clarke with Roibeárd *Ó Faracháin as the theatrical offshoot of the Dublin Verse Speaking Society (1940). The company appeared bi-annually at the Abbey with verse plays including revivals and premières of works by W. B. *Yeats, Clarke, and others.

Lysaght, Edward (1887–1986), see Edward *MacLysaght.

Mac Ádhaimh, Roibeárd (Robert S. McAdam) (1808–1895), scholar and patron. Born in Belfast, he was educated at the Royal Belfast Academical Institution. He worked in his father's business and became co-founder of the Ulster Gaelic Society (*Cuideachta Gaeilge Uladh*) in 1833. Mac Ádhaimh sponsored traditional Irish scholars, including Aodh *Mac Dómhnaill and Art *Mac Bionaid, who collected and transcribed *manuscripts for him. He ran the Soho Iron Foundry.

Mac Aingil, Aodh (or Mac Cathmhaoil) (1571–1626), poet and divine; born in Downpatrick and educated on the Isle of Man before Hugh *O'Neill engaged him as a tutor. In 1600 he went to Salamanca, where he joined the Franciscan Order. In 1607 he began lecturing at St Anthony's College in *Louvain, and became Guardian in 1609. His *Sgáthán Shacramuinte na hAithridhe* (*Mirror of the Sacrament of Confession*) (1618), printed on the Franciscans' press at Louvain, explains the sacrament of Penance in simple and direct Irish. His *Scoti Commentaria* (2 vols., Antwerp, 1620) is an extended commentary on the works of the philosopher Duns Scotus. The *Apologiam Apologiae pro Johanne Duns-Scoto* (Paris, 1623) defends Scotus from attacks by the Dominicans and the Jansenists. This volume and his editions of Scotus, among them *Quaestiones in Metaphysicam* (Venice, 1625), reveal him as deeply involved in the doctrinal debates of the Counter-Reformation. Mac Aingil was a gifted poet. In 1623 he moved to Rome, joined the Irish Franciscan College of St Isidore on its foundation in 1625, and was appointed Archbishop of Armagh in 1626.

Mac a Liondáin (or Mac Giólla Fhiondáin), Pádraig (*c.* 1665–1773), poet. He was born in Creggan in south Armagh and, like Art *Mac Cumhaigh, he is buried in Creggan graveyard. He was acquainted with Séamus Dall *Mac Cuarta and Toirdhealbhach *Ó Cearbhalláin [Carolan]. He wrote poetry that is elegant and formal, reflecting the repertoire of a traditional *bardic poet. He was also known as a harper.

MacAlister, R[obert] A[lexander] S[tewart] (1870–1950), archaeologist; born and educated in Dublin, where he held a Chair at UCD, 1909–43. His Irish archaeological studies, such as *Ireland in Pre-Celtic Times* (1921), *Archaeology of Ireland* (1927), *Tara: A Pagan Sanctuary* (1931), and *Ancient Ireland* (1935, rev. 1944) were marred by idiosyncratic theories. He edited *Lebor Gabála* for the Irish Texts Society (vols. i–iv, 1938–41; vol. v, 1956), and also the *Book of Uí Mhaine* (1942). *The Secret Languages of Ireland* (1937) provided examples of Shelta, the language of the Irish tinkers.

McAllister, Alexander [pseudonyms 'Anthony P. Wharton' and 'Lynn Brock'] (1877–1944), playwright and novelist. Born in Dublin, and educated at the Royal University [see *universities], he became chief secretary at NUI, and wrote the plays *Irene Wycherly* (1906) and *At the Barn* (1912). After the First World War, in which he served, he wrote a series of detective stories beginning with *The Deductions of Colonel Gore* (1925), followed by *The Two of Diamonds* (1926), a serious novel.

Mac Amhlaigh, Dónal (1926–1989), writer of fiction. Born near Galway, after army service he emigrated to

England, settled in Northampton, and spent the rest of his life working as a labourer while writing largely autobiographical works in Irish. *Dialann Deoraí* (1960), translated by Valentin *Iremonger as *An Irish Navvy* (1964), was followed by *Saol Saighdiúra* (1962), an account of his years in the Irish army. *Diarmaid Ó Dónaill* (1965) is the story of a young man coming of age in the 1940s. He published two collections of short stories, *Sweeney agus Scéalta Eile* (1970) and *Beoir Bhaile* (1981). *Schnitzer Ó Sé* (1974) is a satire on Irish literary life. The novel *Deoraithe* (1986) deals with emigrant life in Britain in the 1950s.

Mac an Bhaird family, one of the learned families of late medieval Ireland [see *bardic poetry]. They originated in Co. Galway and remained prominent there until the 17th cent. when a Donegal branch acquired greater fame. Some family members were notable churchmen, in particular Hugh Ward (Aodh Mac an Bhaird) (d. 1635), Professor of Theology at *Louvain from 1616. The most distinguished members of the family are Eoghan Ruadh mac Uilliam Óig [*Mac an Bhaird], and Fearghal Óg mac Fearghail [*Mac an Bhaird].

Mac an Bhaird, Diarmaid (*fl.* 1670), poet. One of the last fully trained *bardic poets, he was a son of Laoiseach Mac an Bhaird and a member of the learned family. He lived probably in Co. Monaghan, although he had associations with Clandeboye, in present-day south Antrim and north Down, as shown by a poem he addressed to Cormac Ó Néill of the Clandeboye O'Neills [see *Leabhar Cloinne Aodha Buidhe]. He was involved in a poetic contention with Eoghan *Ó Donnghaile from Tyrone as to who had the right to use the Red Hand of Ulster as an emblem.

Mac an Bhaird, Eoghan Ruadh, the name of at least three poets of the

Mac an Bhaird learned family, the best-known being Eoghan Ruadh mac Uilliam Óig (?1570–?1630), born in Co. Donegal, and poet to the Ó Domhnaills. He wrote 'Rob soruidh t'eachtra, a Aodh Ruaidh' on Red Hugh *O'Donnell's journey to Spain in 1602, asking God to protect his patron. In Rome Eoghan Ruadh wrote 'A bhean fuair faill ar an bhfeart', a moving elegy on the dead O'Donnells. *Mangan derived his 'O Woman of the Piercing Wail' from a translation of this poem furnished by Eugene *O'Curry. He is said to have composed much religious verse.

Mac an Bhaird, Fearghal Óg (*fl.* 1600), poet; member of the Donegal branch of the learned family. He visited Scotland and enjoyed the patronage of James VI. Red Hugh *O'Donnell accorded him high status, and in 1602 Fearghal Óg wrote the lament 'Teasda Éire san Easbáinn', describing Ireland as an infertile waste after her prince's death. When James VI ascended the English throne in 1603 Fearghal Óg wrote an inaugural poem, 'Trí coróna i gcairt Shéamais', celebrating the new king's claims to three crowns. Some time after writing an elegy on Aodh Óg Ó Domhnaill of Ramelton, Co. Donegal, in 1616, Fearghal Óg went to *Louvain, where he lived in poverty.

Mac an Leagha, Uilliam (*fl.* 1450), a member of a learned family of north Roscommon. It is highly probable that three Early Modern Irish translations from English, *Stair Ercail* (*History of Hercules*), *Betha Mhuire Eigiptachdha* (*Life of Mary of Egypt*), and the Irish version of Guy de Warwick, are his [see *translation into Irish].

Mac Anna, Ferdia (1955–), novelist; born in Dublin and educated at TCD, his novels include *The Last of the High Kings* (1991), *The Ship Inspector* (1994), and *Cartoon City* (1999). He edited *The Penguin*

Book of Irish Comic Writing (1996) and also wrote Bald Head: A Cancer Story (1988).

Mac Anna, Tomás (1926–), theatre director and playwright; born in Dundalk, he was educated at the College of Art in Dublin, worked as a customs officer 1945–47, and then at the *Abbey Theatre as a producer of Gaelic plays, subsequently becoming Artistic Adviser to the Board in 1966, then Artistic Director 1972–79 and 1984–85. His work as an innovative stage director was crucial in modernizing the Abbey style after its re-opening in 1966. He co-wrote the Irish pantomimes for years. Amongst his original plays are Winter Wedding (1956), Dear Edward (1973), Scéal Scéalaí (1977), and Glittering Spears (1983), a drama-documentary on O'Casey's The Silver Tassie.

Mac Annaidh, Séamas (1961–), novelist. Born in Enniskillen, he was educated at NUU, after which he ran a folk-rock group, the Fermanagh Blackbirds. His novel Cuaifeach Mo Londubh Buí (1983), the first of a trilogy, is an experimental fiction. In Mo Dhá Mhící (1986), the anti-hero Mící Mac Crosáin [see *crosántacht] rejects all rules or categories that would limit the play of understanding. Rubble na Mickies (1990) concludes the trilogy by drawing strands from the previous novels into a tangled skein. Féirín, Scéalta agus Eile (1992) is a collection of short stories. An Deireadh (1997) is a fiction in the thriller mode, but darkened by enigma. Colún Deataigh (1999) is a translation from the Italian of Andrea Camilleri, while Fermanagh Books, Writers, and Newspapers of the 19th Cent. (1999) is a bibliography.

Mac Aodhagáin (Mac Egan), a learned family of Connacht, who provided the hereditary lawyers [see áes dána] to the O'Conors and later to the Norman-Irish de Burghs. The earliest extant Irish *law manuscript, In Senchas Már, written before 1350, came from the Mac Aodhagáin school at Duniry (Dún Daighre), near Loughrea, Co. Galway. The family maintained another centre of learning at Park, near Tuam, Co. Galway. Rory O'More (d. 1652), a leader of the 1641 *Rebellion, hoped that an Irish centre of learning with a printing press be established before Flann Mac Aodhagáin, one of the most learned men of his day, died.

Macardle, Dorothy (1899–1958), author and novelist. Born in Dundalk and educated at UCD, she taught at Alexandra College to her arrest for Republican activities in 1922. She was a supporter of Eamon *de Valera, to whom she bequeathed the royalties of The Irish Republic (1937), her history of the *Anglo-Irish War. Earth-Bound (1922), a story collection written in prison, was followed by the novels The Seed was Kind (1940), Uneasy Freehold (1942), and Fantastic Summer (1946), dealing with women's lives and the influence of the supernatural.

McArdle, John (1938–), writer of fiction and playwright. Born near Castleblayney, Co. Monaghan, he was educated at St Patrick's College, Drumcondra, before becoming a teacher. He wrote the script for the film The Kinkisha (1978). The title story of his collection It's Handy When People Don't Die (1981) was made into a film (1982). Celebration (1989) was a play for the National Youth Theatre; while Something's in the Way (1996) and Not a Quiet Night In (1997) were further plays. He scripted the film Angela Mooney Dies Again (1998).

McAughtry, Sam (1923–), writer of fiction. Born in Belfast and educated at St Barnabas', he left school at 14 and served in the RAF. On leaving the armed forces he worked as a labourer, then civil servant, later becoming a Senator of the Irish government. *The Sinking of The Kenbane Head* (1977), an auto-biography, was followed by *Play It Again Sam* (1978), *Blind Spot* (1979), and *Sam McAughtry's Belfast* (1981), a collection of sketches. *McAughtry's War* (1985) and *Hillman Street High Roller* (1994) are auto-biography and autobiographical fiction; *Down in the Free State* (1987) a travel book; and *Touch and Go* (1993) a novel.

McAuley, James J. (1936–), poet; born in Dublin and educated there, his collections include *Observations* (1960), *A New Address* (1965), *Recital* (1975), and *Coming and Going* (1989).

Mac Bionaid (Bennett), Art (1793–1879), poet and scholar. Born in Bal-lykeel, near Forkhill in south Armagh, and a stonemason by trade, he tran-scribed manuscripts for Roibeard *Mac Ádhaimh in Belfast. He wrote occa-sional verse in traditional modes. About twenty of his manuscripts survive.

McBreen, Joan (1944–), poet; born in Sligo and educated there and as a Froebel teacher in Dublin. A teacher for many years, she began publishing in the 1980s, issuing *The Wind Beyond the Wall* (1990) and *A Walled Garden in Moylough* (1995), and editing *The White Page* (1999), an anthology of women's poetry.

MacBride, Maud Gonne, see Maud *Gonne.

Mac Bruaideadha, a learned family who resided near Inchiquin, Co. Clare. They were poets to the O'Briens [Uí Bhriain], barons of Inchiquin and Earls of Thomond. Leading members of Clann Bruaideadha were Diarmuid mac Con-chobhair (d. 1563) and Tadhg mac Dáire [*Mac Bruaideadha] (d.?1652).

Mac Bruaideadha, Tadhg mac Dáire (?1570–?1652), poet. Born to a learned family in Co. Clare, he became ollam [see *áes dána] to Donnchadh Ó

Briain, 4th Earl of Thomond. In *c.* 1616 Tadhg instigated the bardic dispute known as *Iomarbhágh na bhFileadh in which he asserted the superiority of the O'Briens over the O'Neills and, with it, of southern over northern learning. According to tradition, Tadhg was killed by a Cromwellian soldier who was granted his Dunogan lands and threw him from a cliff-top.

McCabe, Cathal (1963–), poet; born in Newry, and educated at York University and Oxford, he taught at universities in Poland, before becoming British Council literature consultant in Warsaw. Collections include *A Letter from Łódz* (1996) and *Epithalamium* (1998).

McCabe, Eugene (1930–), play-wright and writer of fiction. Born in Glasgow, where his family lived until he was 9, he was educated at Castleknock School, Co. Dublin, and UCC. In 1955 he took over the management of the fam-ily farm near Clones. His play *King of the Castle* (1964) tells the story of a childless couple on a farm, and how the husband arranges to have his wife made preg-nant by another man. A trilogy for tele-vision called *Victims* (1976) dealt with the horror of sectarian violence. The novel *Victims*, corresponding to *Siege* in the trilogy, appeared in the same year, followed by *Heritage and Other Stories* (1978). Films scripted by McCabe for RTÉ include *Gale Day* (1979) and *Winter Music* (1981). After a non-writing period he published *Death and Nightingales* (1992), a powerful historical novel, followed by *Tales from The Poorhouse* (1999).

McCabe, Patrick (1955–), novelist. Born in Clones, Co. Monaghan, he worked as a teacher and in a touring dance band. He wrote *Music on Clinton Street* (1986), *Carn* (1989), and then *The Butcher Boy* (1992). The narrative conveys the inner life of Francie Brady, a socially deprived adolescent whose father is alcoholic and whose mother commits suicide. A stage version, *Frank Pig Says Hello*, was produced by Co-Motion Theatre (1992). *A Mother's Love Is a Blessing* (1994) was a TV drama. *The Dead School* (1995) is written in an urgent prose which breaks into sharp psychological vignettes to reveal the breakdown of a primary teacher. *Breakfast on Pluto* (1998) deals with a transvestite homosexual prostitute, who gets snarled up in the 1970s *Troubles in Ireland and England, while *Mondo Desperado* (1999) is a serial novel in the pulp-fiction genre.

McCall, Patrick Joseph (1861–1919), author of ballads. He was born in Dublin and educated at the Catholic University [see *universities], and later owned a pub. He was a founding member of the National Literary Society [see *literary revival]. *The Fenian Nights' Entertainments* (1897) contained Irish sagas comically retold. His best-known ballad, 'Boula-vogue', was written for the 1798 centenary. His poetry appeared as *Irish Nóinins* (1894), *Pulse of the Bards* (1904), *Songs of Erin* (1911), and *Irish Fireside Songs* (1911).

Mac Cana, Proinsias (1926–), Celtic scholar. Born in Belfast, he studied Celtic languages at QUB and later at the Sorbonne. He joined *DIAS, and then became Professor of Welsh at UCD in 1963. He was appointed to the Chair of Early Irish in 1971. His work includes *Scéalaíocht na Ríthe* with Tomás Ó Floinn (1956); commentaries on the second branch of the *Mabinogion*, *Branwen Daughter of Lir* (1958), and on the collection as a whole, *The Mabinogi* (1977, 1992); *The Learned Tales of Medieval Ireland* (1980); and *Celtic Mythology* (1970).

McCann, Colum (1965–), novelist; born in Dublin, he worked at a variety of jobs before publishing the stories in *Fishing the Sloe Black River* (1994). *Song Dogs* (1995) was a novel, and *We Fell Like Snow* (1997) was based on the Irish and black builders of the New York subway. *This Side of Brightness* (1998) was a further novel.

McCann, John (1905–1980), playwright and politician. Born in Dublin he became a journalist. *The Dreamer* (1930) was staged at the Peacock [see *Abbey]. He was elected to Dáil Éireann [see *Irish State] in 1939 and served as Lord Mayor of Dublin, 1946–7. In the 1950s he had a popular success with his comedy *Twenty Years A-Wooing* (1954). He quickly followed this with *Blood Is Thicker than Water* (1955) and *Early and Often* (1956). *Give Me a Bed of Roses* (1957), *I Know Where I'm Going* (1959), *Put a Beggar on Horseback* (1961), and *A Jew Called Sammy* (1962), were other plays.

MacCann, Michael Joseph (1824–1883), poet and journalist. Born in Galway, he taught for a time at St Jarlath's, Tuam. His famous poem, 'The Clan Connel War Song', usually known as 'O'Donnell Aboo', appeared in *The *Nation*, 28 January 1843.

McCart-Martin (formerly Martin), [William] David (1937–1996), novelist. Born in Belfast, he became an apprentice electrician, and served in the RN Fleet Air Arm, 1955–62, before attending Keele University, after which he joined the Ulster Polytechnic (later UUJ). *The Task* (1975) was the first of four novels investigating the roots of violent conflict in *Northern Ireland. *The Ceremony of Innocence* (1977) confronts the psychological aftermath of Ulster's sectarian divisions in an episodic narrative. *The Road to Ballyshannon* (1981) moves back in time to the period of the *Civil War to chronicle the escape of two Republicans from a prison ship in Belfast Lough. *Dream* (1986) moves the focus further back to embrace a period extending from the end of the *Land League agitations to the Second World War.

MacCarthy, Catherine Phil
(1954–), poet; born in Limerick, and
educated at UCC and TCD, she lectured
at Waterford Institute of Technology
from 1978. Collections include *This Hour
of the Tide* (1994) and *The Blue Globe* (1998).

MacCarthy, Denis Florence (1817–
1882), poet and translator. Born in Dublin he was educated at Maynooth and
King's Inns, later becoming Professor of
English at the Catholic University [see
*universities]. His poetry was gathered
as *Ballads, Lyrics and Poems* (1850), *Under-
Glimpses* (1857), and *The Bell-Founder*
(1857). *Poets and Dramatists* (1846), his
work of Irish biography, claimed many
writers previously regarded as English.
He translated five plays by Calderon
(1853). *Shelley's Early Life* (1872) deals
largely with the poet's Irish visit of
1812.

MacCarthy, J[ohn] Bernard (1888–
1979), playwright; born in Crosshaven,
Co. Cork, where he worked as a
postman. Four plays, *Kinship* (1914), *The
Supplanter* (1914), *Crusaders* (1918), and
Garranbraher (1923), were produced at
the *Abbey Theatre; some twenty
others were printed for amateur companies. His material was the ethical
dilemmas of rural and seaboard life,
rendered in his 'Cork realist' style. His
many short stories, such as *Annie All-
Alone* (1931) and *A Disgrace to the Parish*
[with] *The Quiet One* (1927), were
published by the Catholic Truth Society.
He wrote three novels, *Covert* (1925),
Possessions (1926), and *Exile's Bread* (1927).

McCarthy, Justin (1830–1912), novelist and anthologist. Born in Cork, he
started work on newspapers there and
moved to England, becoming editor of
The Morning Star in 1864. In 1879 he was
elected MP for Longford, but led the
anti-Parnellites out of Committee Room
15 [see Charles Stewart *Parnell]. *A
History of Our Own Times* (5 vols., 1879)

was a work of contemporary history.
McCarthy wrote nearly twenty novels,
three of them with Mrs Campbell Praed,
including *The Right Honourable* (1886).
Many were written to influence British
attitudes towards Ireland. In *A Fair Saxon*
(1873), the Fenians are criticized. *Mono-
nia* (1901), set in *Young Ireland times,
is more nationalistic in tone. McCarthy
edited a ten-volume anthology *Irish Literature* (1904) with Maurice Egan
Maguire.

McCarthy, Justin Huntly (1860–
1939), novelist; born and educated in
London. Like his father, Justin
*McCarthy, he became an Irish nation-
alist MP, 1884–92. He travelled widely.
His novels include *A London Legend*
(1895), *The Flower of France* (1900), *The God
of Love* (1909), and *Truth—and the Other
Thing* (1924). *The Illustrious O'Hagan*
(1906), *The O'Flynn* (1910), and *The King
Over the Water* (1911) are historical
romances contradicting English stereotypes of the Irish. The *Young Ireland
movement is the subject of *Lilly Lass*
(1889).

MacCarthy, Thomas (1954–),
poet. Born in Cappoquin, Co. Waterford,
he was educated at UCC. *The First Convention* (1978) was followed by *The Sorrow
Garden* (1981), and these collections
revealed a thoughtful elegiac mode
appraising the political colorations of
southern Ireland. *The Non-Aligned Story-
teller* (1984) engages strenuously with
the tedium of post-war Ireland. *Seven
Winters in Paris* (1989) deals with the joy
and trouble of parenthood in a time of
menace. *The Lost Province* (1996) is a complex response to the peace process in
*Northern Ireland in the 1990s. *Without
Power* (1990) and *Aysa and Christine* (1993)
are novels dealing with loyalty to the
ideals of Fianna Fáil [see *Irish State].

Mac Cathmaoil, Seosamh, see
Joseph *Campbell.

MacCawell, Hugh, see Aodh *Mac Aingil.

Mac Cóil, Liam (1952–), novelist; born in Dublin, he was educated at Blackrock College, UCD, and TCD. He worked as an editor for An *Gúm, and as a lexicographer. His first novel, *An Dochtúir Áthas* (1994), won recognition, and was followed by *An Claíomh Solais* (1998).

Mac Conmara, Donncha Rua, (1715–1810), poet; probably a native of Cratloe in Clare. He spent some years in the early 1740s in the Sliabh gCua district of Waterford and in Imokilly in East Cork. Between 1745 and 1755 he may have emigrated to Newfoundland. His best-known work is *Eachtra Ghiolla an Amaráin*, a possibly imaginary account of his emigrant's voyage to Newfoundland. His other poems include an elegy in Latin for his fellow poet Tadhg Gaelach *Ó Súilleabháin (d. 1795) and his song of repentance ('An Aithrighe').

Mac Con Midhe, a learned *bardic family settled around Ardstraw, Co. Tyrone, who were poets to the O'Gormleys, the O'Neills, the O'Donnells, and the O'Conors of Connacht between the 13th and the 16th cents.

Mac Con Midhe, Giolla Brighde (?1210–?1272), poet; born into the *Mac Con Midhe bardic family. His chief patrons were members of the O'Gormley family. He dedicated poems to members of the O'Donnell family and at least one to an O'Neill. Mac Con Midhe married and had children, all of whom died at an early age. His most famous poem, 'Deán oram trócaire, a Thríonnóid', beseeches heaven for a child to replace those he has lost, and concludes with a request to Brigit to intervene for him. It appears that there was another poet of the same name who lived earlier in the 13th cent.

McCormack, W[illiam] J[ohn] (1947–), poet (pseudonym 'Hugh Maxton') and critic. Born near Aughrim, Co. Wicklow, and educated at TCD, he taught English at NUU (now UUC), Leeds, and became Professor at Goldsmith's College in 1996. In poetry collections such as *Stones* (1970), *The Noise of the Fields* (1976), *Jubilee for Renegades* (1982), *At the Protestant Museum* (1985), and *The Engraved Passion: New and Selected Poems 1970–1991* (1992) lyricism achieves resonance and gravity of tone. As a critic he has focused on the complexities of *Anglo-Irish literary tradition in *Sheridan Le Fanu and Victorian Ireland* (1980); *Ascendancy and Tradition in Anglo-Irish History, 1789–1939* (1985); and *Dissolute Characters* (1993). *The Battle of the Books* (1986) appraises Irish cultural issues. A biography of Synge was published in 2000.

McCormick, F. J. (stage name of Peter Judge) (1889–1947), actor; born in Skerries, Co. Dublin. He joined the *Abbey in 1918, having worked in the Post Office, and played in the original productions of *O'Casey's Dublin plays, creating Joxer in *Juno and the Paycock* (1924). A veteran of 500 plays, he also appeared in films including Carol Reed's *Odd Man Out* (1947).

McCourt, Frank (1930–), born in New York into an Irish family, he returned to Limerick city as a child where he was educated before leaving for America. He worked in a variety of jobs before joining the U.S. army. As a demobbed GI he was entitled to free college education. He became a teacher and worked on Staten Island in New York until he retired in 1987. *Angela's Ashes* (1996), a memoir of a poverty-stricken childhood in Limerick, became a world best-seller; followed by '*Tis* (1999), an account of his life in America up to his first marriage.

McCracken, Henry Joy (1767–1798),

revolutionary. Born in Belfast, he was a successful factory owner at 22, and was a founding member of the *United Irishmen. In October 1796 he was arrested and imprisoned in Kilmainham Gaol, Dublin, but released a year after. As commander-in-chief of the Antrim contingent he led several thousand men in an attack on Antrim town in June 1798. After the battle, in which about 300 of his men died, McCracken retreated to the Slemish mountains. He was seized, convicted for treason, and publicly hanged at Belfast in July 1798.

Mac Craith, Aindrias ('An Mangaire Súgach' (The Merry Pedlar)) (?1708–1795), poet. Born probably near Kilmallock, Co. Limerick, he spent much of his life in Croom. Although he is remembered as a rake, he was a teacher of note and one of the two chief poets of the Maigue school ('filí na Máighe'), the other being Séan *Ó Tuama an Ghrinn. One of his best-known poems, 'Slán is ceád ón dtaobh so uaim' (1738), addressed to Ó Tuama, bids farewell to the locality he has had to leave on account of a sexual indiscretion. Other poems reflect his feelings about the Jacobite rebellion of 1745 [see *Jacobite poetry]. Although he and Ó Tuama habitually exchanged verse insults, Mac Craith wrote a glorious elegy for his friend in 1775.

Mac Cruitín, Aindrias (?1650–?1738), poet; born to a family of hereditary poets in Moyglass, near Milltown Malbay, Co. Clare, where he was educated and where he spent most of his life, teaching and working as a scribe. His best-known poem, composed in old age, describes the neglect into which his profession has fallen.

Mac Cruitín, Aodh Buidhe (Hugh MacCurtin) (?1680–1755), poet. Born in Kilmacreehy, Corcomroe, Co. Clare, he was educated in the *bardic tradition at

Moyglass by his cousin Aindrias Mac *Cruitín, and is said to have been tutor to the Stuart household in France. By about 1700 he had become a prominent member of Seán *Ó Neachtáin's circle of Gaelic scholars in Dublin. His *Discourse in Vindication of the Antiquity of Ireland* (1717) was the first history of Ireland in English to be written from the standpoint of native tradition. He wrote a grammar, *Elements of the Irish Language* (1728), followed by an *English-Irish Dictionary* (1732), compiled with Conor Begley.

Mac Cuarta, Séamus Dall (c.1650–1733), poet. Born, probably, in Omeath, Co. Louth, he seems to have lived all his life in that area. His loss of sight in youth gave rise to a tradition that he was endowed with the gift of poetry by the *sídh. He used the syllabic metres of *bardic poetry, but also the more recent amhrán measure [see Irish *metrics], and perfected the 'trí rainn agus amhrán' form in a series of occasional poems [see *Irish *metrics]. One of these, 'Tithe Chorr an Chait', is a brilliant mixture of contempt and rage at lack of generosity.

Mac Cumhaigh, Art (1738–1773), poet. Born the son of small farmers at Mounthill in the parish of Creggan, Co. Armagh, he worked locally as a labourer and as gardener. Of some twenty-five poems attributed to him more than half are in a metre (trí rainn agus amhrán) specially cultivated by the Ulster poets [see Irish *metrics]. Some of his poems were very popular, notably 'Úr-Chill an Chreagáin', an *aisling. In other aislingí, the conventions of *Jacobite poetry are modified by local loyalty to a branch of the O'Neills then in Creggan.

Mac Cumhaill, Maghnas (pseudonym Fionn 'Mac Cumhaill') (1885–1965), novelist; born in the Rosses, Co. Donegal, and educated for a period at

UCD, after which he emigrated to America, where he was a professional boxer. He drew on traditional story-telling for both theme and style in six novels, beginning with '*Sé Dia an Fear is Fearr* (1928), and of which *Na Rosa go Bráthach* (1939), a rambling tale set in 19th-cent. Ireland, is the best. *Maicín* (1946) and a further volume, *Gura Slán lem' Óige* (1974), are autobiographical.

Macdermots of Ballycloran, The (1847), the first novel of Anthony *Trollope. Set in Co. Leitrim, it deals with the tragic end of an old Catholic family, reduced to poverty like their own tenants.

Mac Domhnaill, Aodh (1802–1867) poet, philosopher, and scholar. Born in Lower Drumgill, Co. Meath, he taught for a time before proselytizing for the Home Mission under the aegis of the Irish Society as a Bible instructor. He moved to Belfast in 1842 as an assistant to Roibeárd *Mac Ádhaimh. While in Belfast Mac Domhnaill also wrote a treatise on natural philosophy. A poem, 'I mBéal Feirste cois cuain', celebrates the Gaelic learning of the Belfast scholars Samuel Bryson and Larry Duff.

Mac Domhnaill, Seán Clárach (1691–1754), poet. Born near Charleville, Co. Cork, and educated locally, he worked as a farmer, and was a teacher. In 1723, on the death of Philip, Duke of Orleans, he wrote a poem reproaching him for indifference towards Ireland. Other poems reveal his intense loyalty to the house of Stuart. 'Mo Ghille Mear' and 'Ag taisteal dom trí na críocha' are examples of his enthusiastic exhortation. He visited the proceedings of the Maigue poets in Croom, Co. Limerick, in 1735. He is known to have begun a translation of Homer.

MacDonagh, Donagh (1912–1968), poet and playwright. The son of Thomas *MacDonagh, he was educated at Belvedere College and UCD, and became a district justice. An abiding interest in *folklore is reflected in his drama and poetry. *Happy as Larry* (1946) was a *ballad opera. *Step-in-the-Hollow* (1957) is a farcical comedy.

MacDonagh, John (?–1961), play-wright and theatre/film director; born in Cloughjordan, Co. Tipperary. In 1914, with Edward *Martyn, Joseph Mary *Plunkett, and his brother Thomas *MacDonagh, he joined in founding the Irish Theatre. His first play, *Author! Author!* (1915), was a satire on *Abbey peasant drama. *Weeds* (1919) was a study of landlordism and land rights, after which he started working in film and in popular theatre. Amongst his films were *Willy Reilly and His Colleen Bawn* (*c.*1919), based on *Carleton's novel.

MacDonagh, Thomas (1878–1916), poet, dramatist, and revolutionary; born in Cloughjordan, Co. Tipperary, and educated at Rockwell College, he taught in Fermoy, Co. Cork, 1903–8. Of his poetry collections, *April and May and Other Verses* (1903) and *Through the Ivory Gate* (1903) were devoted to religious and Celtic themes. These were followed by *The Golden Joy* (1906) and *Songs of Myself* (1910). *Lyrical Poems* (1913) contains autobiographical pieces and trans-lations. In 1908 he became assistant head to Patrick *Pearse at St Enda's Col-lege. In the same year *Yeats was per-suaded to allow an *Abbey production of *When the Dawn Is Come* (1908), a '*Sinn Féin drama'. Set in the revolutionary future, it centres on a Catholic intel-lectual who behaves 'like one seeking death'. He wrote an MA thesis on *Thomas Campion and the Art of English Poetry* (published 1913). In 1911 he was appointed lecturer in English at UCD, and founded *The *Irish Review* with Pad-raic *Colum and others. His second play, *Metempsychosis* (1912), was a satire on theosophy. In 1912 he married Muriel Gifford. MacDonagh joined the *Irish Volunteers at its foundation in 1913, becoming Director of Training. For Edward Martyn's Irish Theatre he wrote *Pagans* (1915), a play in which the hero reflects his own increasing militancy. The essays which emerged from his reflections on Irish writing in English, were incorporated into *Literature in Ireland* (1916), published posthumously. In it MacDonagh sought to define the special character of *Anglo-Irish literature. In April 1916 MacDonagh was one of the signatories of the Proclamation of the Irish Republic, and took part in the *Easter Rising as commander of the Volunteers in Jacob's factory. With the other leaders he was condemned to death by a British court martial, and executed by firing squad on 3 May 1916. A poem by Francis *Ledwidge ('He shall not hear the bittern cry') is his literary epitaph.

McDONNELL, Randal [William] (1870–?1930), bibliophile and novelist. Born in Dublin and educated at TCD, he was for a time assistant librarian at Marsh's Library at St Patrick's Cathedral. His novels, such as *Kathleen Mavourneen* (1905), *When Cromwell Came to Drogheda* (1906), *My Sword for Patrick Sarsfield* (1907), and *Ardnaree* (1911), often use the device of editing supposedly contemporary accounts of 17th- or 18th-cent. events.

MacDonogh, Patrick (1902–1961), poet. Born in Blackrock, Co. Dublin, and educated at TCD. Early collections, *Flirtation* (1927) and *A Leaf in the Wind* (1929), express the pain of love. After a period of silence MacDonogh began publishing again in the 1940s, issuing *A Vestal Fire* (1941), *Over the Water and Other Poems* (1943), followed by *One Landscape Still* (1958). The work of this second phase shows him exploring private struggles

and fears in language which has developed a sardonic edge.

McDonogh, Steve (1949–), poet and publisher; born in Dublin, he was educated at Marlborough College and York University. He founded *Cosmos* magazine in 1968, and was Chair of the Irish Writers' Co-operative 1977–81. Moving to Dingle, Co. Kerry, he set up Brandon Publishing in 1982. Poetry includes *York Poems* (1972), *My Tribe* (1982), and *By Dingle Bay and Blasket Sound* (1991). His folklore and local history work includes *Green and Gold: The Wren Boys of Dingle* (1983), and *The Dingle Peninsula* (1993). *Open Book: One Publisher's War* (1999) is a memoir. He established Mount Eagle as a separate company in 1997, incorporating Brandon later that year.

MacEgan, learned family, see *Mac Aodhagáin.

MacÉil, Seán, see John *MacHale.

McEntee, Máire, see Máire *Mhac an tSaoi.

McFadden, Roy (1921–1999), poet; born in Belfast and educated at QUB, where he studied law before becoming a solicitor in Belfast. A first collection, *Swords and Ploughshares* (1943), was followed by *Flowers for a Lady* (1945). In 1948 he began editing, with Barbara Edwards, the periodical *Rann*, which sought to encourage new writing in Northern Ireland. In *The Hearts' Townland* (1947), *The Garryowen* (1971), *Verifications* (1977), *A Watching Brief* (1978), *Letters to the Hinterland* (1986), and *After Seymour's Funeral* (1990), personal concerns are linked to larger questions of identity. *Collective Poems* (1996) revealed a copious and lasting gift, and a steadiness of focus.

Mac Fheorais, Seán (1915–1984), poet. Born in Co. Kildare, he worked as a schoolteacher. His lyrical poems appeared in two collections: *Gearrcaigh na hOíche* (1954) and *Léargas—Dánta Fada* (1964).

Mac Fhir Bhisigh, Dubhaltach (?1600–1671), historian; born in Lackan, Co. Sligo, the last of the line in the Mac Fhir Bhisigh learned family. Educated at Lackan, he may also have studied in the *O'Davoren law school. His principal works are transcriptions of earlier materials. These include *Dúil Laithne* (1643); a fragmentary *Annals of Ireland* (1643); *Chronicon Scotorum* (*c.*1643); and a *Catalogue of Irish Bishops* (1665). His *Leabhar na nGenelach* (*Book of Genealogies*), was in progress in 1650 when he was at the College of St Nicholas in Galway, but he was still adding to it as late as 1664. Sir James *Ware employed him in Dublin, 1665–6, and based his writings partly on the result. Mac Fhir Bhisigh was fatally stabbed in an inn at Doonflinn, Co. Sligo, by a man called Crofton who was molesting the young girl in charge.

Mac Fhir Bhisigh, Giolla Íosa (*fl.* 1400), historian and ollam [see *áes dána] to Ó Dubhda of Tireragh (Tír Fhiachrach), Co. Sligo, and head of the learned family of that name. He wrote the genealogical tract entitled *Leabhar Fiachrach*.

Mac Gabhann, Micí (1865–1948), author of the autobiography *Rotha Mór an tSaoil* (1959), an account of a labourer's life in late 19th-cent. Ireland, Scotland, and America, told in a plain, direct style. Born in Cloughaneely, Co. Donegal, he began work as a spailpín (hired labourer) when he was 9. At 20 he emigrated to America, where he worked in the silver mines in Butte, Montana, before joining in the Klondyke gold rush. His son-in-law, the folklorist Seán Ó hEochaidh, persuaded him to dictate the autobiography.

Mac Gabhráin (Mac Shamhradháin), Aodh (Hugh McGauran) (*fl.* 1715), poet. Born in Glengoole, Co. Cavan, he was a member of the *Ó Neachtain circle of scholars in early 18th-cent. Dublin. 'Pléaráca na Ruarcach', a bacchanalian account of drinking and fighting in the O'Rourke household, is his best-known poem in consequence of being translated by Jonathan *Swift.

McGahern, John (1934–), fiction writer. Born in Dublin, he grew up in Cootehill, Co. Cavan, where his father was the local sergeant, and was educated at St Patrick's Training College and UCD. He taught in Clontarf, Co. Dublin, for a number of years and had his first success with *The Barracks* (1963). His second novel, *The *Dark* (1965), was banned under the *Censorship Act, and McGahern was dismissed from his teaching post. He moved to London, where he worked as a teacher and on building sites. He settled near Mohill in Co. Leitrim. Among his other novels are *The Leavetaking* (1974), *The Pornographer* (1979), and *Amongst Women* (1990). In addition he published collections of short stories: *Nightlines* (1970), *Getting Through* (1978), and *High Ground* (1985), while a play, *The Power of Darkness*, was produced by the *Abbey Theatre in 1991.

Mac Gearailt, Gearóid, see *Gearóid Iarla.

Mac Gearailt, Muiris mac Dáibhí Dhuibh, see *Mhic Gearailt.

Mac Gearailt, Piaras (1702–1795), poet. Born near Ballymacoda, Co. Cork. He converted to Protestantism to retain the family farm, and in his tortured poem 'A chogair, a charaid' he expresses remorse. His best-known poem is the rousing *Jacobite battlesong, 'Rosc Catha na Mumhan'.

McGee, Thomas D'Arcy (1825–1868), journalist and author; born in Carlingford, Co. Louth, and raised in Wexford, he emigrated to America aged 17. Returning to Ireland, he wrote for *The *Nation*, to which he contributed many poems. Escaping in disguise after the *Young Ireland Rising in 1848, he founded the New York *Nation* (1848). In 1862 he became Canadian Minister of Agriculture. He spoke against militant Republicanism on a visit to Wexford in 1865, and was assassinated in Ottawa after the *Fenian raid on Canada. Besides *Eva MacDonald* (1844), a novel about the *United Irishmen, he wrote *A Gallery of Irish Writers of the Seventeenth Century* (1846), *A Popular History of Ireland* (1862), and political memoirs.

Mac Geoghegan , Conall (Conall Mac Eochagáin) (*fl.* 1620–1640), historian and translator. He lived in what appear to have been reasonably prosperous circumstances in Lismoyny, Co. Westmeath. In 1627 he translated the *Annals of Clonmacnoise* into English, from an original now lost. In 1636 Mac Geoghegan made transcriptions from the *Book of Lecan* probably at the request of James *Ussher, who lent him the *manuscript.

MacGill, Patrick ('the Navvy Poet') (1891–1963), poet and novelist. Born in Maas, Co. Donegal, he grew up in Glenties, the 'Glenmornan' of his fiction. As eldest of eleven children in a poor farming family, he was sent to the hiring fair of Strabane at the age of 12, remitting most of his small wages to his parents. At 14 he left for Scotland to work in the potato-fields, then on the railways and construction sites, gaining the experience of itinerant labouring that formed the basis of his novels *Children of the Dead End* (1914), *The *Rat-Pit* (1915), and *Moleskin Joe* (1923). He began writing verse in his teens and a first collection, *Gleanings from a Navvy's Scrapbook* (1910), was printed at Derry. In 1913 he was taken on as a reporter on the *Daily Express* in London, but he returned to Donegal, where his anticlerical views incurred the wrath of the establishment, as he relates in *Glenmornan* (1919). In the First World War he saw active service as a stretcher-bearer. He documented the horrors of trench warfare and the resilience of ordinary soldiers in *The Amateur Army* (1915), *The *Great Push* (1916), and *The Red Horizon* (1916). In the ensuing years he wrote further books on navvy life and war, as well as tragic and comic novels of Irish rural life. After *Helen Spenser* (1937), a Donegal love-story, he wrote no more. His verse is cast in the form of traditional *folksong (*Songs of Donegal*, 1921), and works best when juxtaposed with the horror of modern war (*Soldier Songs*, 1917). In 1981 a MacGill Summer School was launched in Glenties.

McGinley, Patrick (1937–), novelist; born in Glencolumkille, Co. Donegal, and educated at UCG. He taught in Ireland before emigrating to England, where he became a publisher. McGinley's first novel, *Bogmail* (1978), was followed by six more in the space of ten years. Although *Goosefoot* (1982) and *Foxprints* (1983) both have urban settings, they convey hankerings for rural Ireland. McGinley's novels are mostly murder mysteries; however *The Lost Soldier's Song* (1994) concerns the fate of a young Republican at the hands of the *Black and Tans. In *Foggage* (1993) narrative economy and philosophical playfulness give the work an enigmatic quality.

Mac Giolla Ghunna, Cathal Buí (?1680–1756), poet; mostly associated with Co. Cavan in folk tradition, where he is perceived as a typical poetic rake. The poems ascribed to him reflect a wayward existence. In his best-known song, 'An Bonnán Buí', the poet laments a bittern he finds dead of thirst, and resolves to steer clear of abstinence in future.

Mac Giollarnáth, Seán (1880–1970), folklorist and naturalist. Born in Gurteen, Co. Galway, he entered the Civil Service in London and joined the *Gaelic League and the IRB [see *IRA] there. Back in Ireland in 1908, he edited *An Connachtach* and in 1909 replaced Patrick *Pearse as editor of *An *Claidheamh Soluis*. *Peadar Chois Fhairrge* (1934) and *Loinnir Mac Leabhair agus Sgéalta Gaiscídh Eile* (1936) consist of lore and stories collected by him. *Mo Dhúthaigh Fhiáin* (1949) is a study of fauna and their habitat.

McGlashan (or M'Glashan), James (?1800–1858), publisher. Born in Edinburgh, where he trained on *Blackwood's Magazine*, he worked for William Curry of Dublin from 1830, forming his own company at Curry's death in 1846. McGlashan was involved in setting up the *Dublin University Magazine* in 1833.

Macgnímhartha Finn, see *Fionn cycle.

MacGreevy, Thomas (1893–1967), poet. Born in Tarbert, Co. Kerry, he served as an artillery officer in the First World War, and entered TCD on his return. He worked as an art critic in Dublin and London, then moved to France, 1927–9. There he formed friendships with James *Joyce and Samuel *Beckett. In 1941 MacGreevy returned to Dublin and was appointed Director of the National Gallery in 1950. Besides numerous essays and articles, he wrote studies of *Jack B. Yeats* (1945), and *Nicolas Poussin* (1960). *Collected Poems* (1971) has a foreword by Beckett.

Mac Grianna, Seosamh (pseudonym 'Iolann Fionn') (1901–1990), novelist. He was born in Ranafast in the Donegal *Gaeltacht, and educated at St Patrick's College, Dublin. He joined the *IRA and was interned during the *Civil War. Before the publication of his first story collection, *An Grá agus An Ghruaim* (1929), he lived by temporary teaching. During 1933–53 he worked as a translator for An *Gúm. *Pádraig *Ó Conaire agus Aistí Eile* (1936) is a collection of critical essays; *An Bhreatain Bheag* (1937) and *Na Lochlannaigh* (1938) are travel books. A visit to Wales in the early 1930s is recorded in *Mo Bhealach Féin* (1940), a searching autobiographical essay. After his return to Donegal, a nervous disorder led to a long sojourn in the Letterkenny mental asylum, where he eventually died. *An Druma Mór* (1969), his last published work, deals with the sharing of a marching drum by *Orangemen and nationalists in a Donegal parish. He adopted the Mac form to distinguish himself from his brother Séamus *Ó Grianna ('Máire'), with whom he quarrelled.

McGuckian, Medbh (1950–), poet; born in Belfast and educated at QUB. She became a teacher before becoming writer in residence at QUB, 1986–9. In 1980 she published the pamphlets *Single Ladies* and *Portrait of Joanna*, followed by *The Flower Master* (1982), then *Venus and the Rain* (1984), *On Ballycastle Beach* (1988), *Marconi's Cottage* (1991), *Captain Lavender* (1994), and *Shelmalier* (1998). Her lyrical yet disturbing verse uses a taut and thoughtful language based on the patterns of intimate speech. Many of her poems have domestic settings, rendered magical and threatening as they explore issues of violence and identity. *The Grateful Muse* (2000) is an anthology of Irish Women's poetry.

McGuinness, Frank (1953–), playwright; born in Buncrana, Co. Donegal, educated at UCD. He began to write poetry and short stories in 1974. McGuinness taught at NUU, UCD, Maynooth, then UCD again. He started writing for the stage with *Factory Girls* (1982), which opened at the Peacock [see *Abbey Theatre]. His next play, *Friends*, was rejected by *Field Day but later reworked as *Carthaginians*, dealing with the impact of 'Bloody Sunday' in January 1972 on the people of Derry. *Observe the Sons of Ulster Marching Towards the Somme* (1985) was staged at the Abbey and presented a sympathetic view of loyalism. *Innocence* (1986) was performed at the *Gate; it dealt with the dynamics of the creative life in a portrait of the artist Caravaggio. Among his successful translations and versions of European plays are *Rosmersholm* (1987), at the English National Theatre, *Yerma* (1987), *Peer Gynt* (1988), *Three Sisters* (1990), and *The Threepenny Opera* (1991). The effect of his engagement with these classics can be seen in the contemporaneous original works, *Carthaginians* (Peacock 1988), *Mary and Lizzie* (Barbican 1989), and *The Breadman* (Gate 1990). *Someone Who'll Watch Over Me* (1992) was based on the experiences of Western hostages in Beirut, notably Brian *Keenan. McGuinness has also written for television the plays *Scout* (1987) and *The Hen House* (1989). *Bird Sanctuary* (1993) is a comedy of manners, and *Booterstown* (1994) was a first collection of poems. *Mutability* (1997) turned to Edmund *Spenser to explore colonial tensions; *Dolly West's Kitchen* (1999) is set in Donegal, during the Second World War.

Macha, see *Emain Macha.

MacHale, John (1791–1881), Archbishop of Tuam and translator; raised a native speaker in Tobbernavine, Tirawley, Co. Mayo, he was educated at Maynooth and ordained in 1814. He supported *O'Connell's *Repeal Movement, and criticized British administration. He was opposed to the increasing neglect of the Irish language. He wrote poetry in Irish, as well as devotional literature, and translated the *Pentateuch* (1861) and the *Iliad* (1844–71) into Irish, as well as Thomas *Moore's *Melodies* (1871).

McHenry, James (1785–1845), playwright and novelist. Born in Larne, Co. Antrim, and educated at TCD and Glasgow, where he qualified in medicine, he emigrated to Philadelphia. In 1842 he became American Consul at Derry. His poetry includes *Patrick* (1810), a narrative of the Rebellion of 1798 [see *United Irishmen], and *A Revolutionary Tale in 3 Cantos* (1823). His novels are *O'Halloran, or the Insurgent Chief* (1824) and *The Hearts of Steel* (1825), written from a Presbyterian standpoint.

McIlroy, Archibald (1860–1915), novelist. Born in Ballyclare, Co. Antrim, he left a job with the Ulster Bank to become an insurance agent, moved to Canada, and drowned on the *Lusitania*. His nostalgic collections of stories, *The Auld Meetin' House Green* (1898), *By Lone Craig Linnie Burn* (1900), *Burnside* (1908), *By the Ingle Nook* (1910) are written in Ulster-Scots [see *Hiberno-English]. *The Humour of Druid's Island* (1902) is set in Islandmagee, Co. Antrim. *A Banker's Love Story* (1901) tells the love-story of a friend.

MacIntyre, Tom (1931–), man of letters. Born in Cavan and educated at UCD, he taught at Ann Arbor, and elsewhere. *Dance the Dance* (1969), a volume of short stories, was followed by *The Charollais* (1969), a novel of fantasy. *Through the Bridewell Gate* (1971), recording the Arms Trial of 1970, was succeeded by versions of Irish poetry in *Blood Relations* (1972). His first play, *Eye-Winker, Tom Tinker* (1972), produced at the Peacock [see *Abbey Theatre], was a naturalistic piece. His interests in dance, film, and Polish theatre are reflected in the plays he wrote in the 1970s, *Jack Be Nimble* (1976), *Find the Lady* (1977), and *Doobally Back Way* (1979). *The Great Hunger* (1983, published 1988) relied heavily on the abilities of director Patrick Mason and actor Tom Hickey to translate *Kavanagh's poem into stage action. MacIntyre's subsequent plays were *The Bearded Lady* (1984); *Rise Up Lovely Sweeney* (1985); *Dance for Your Daddy* (1987); *Snow White* (1988); *Sheeps Milk on the Boil* (1994); and *Good Evening, Mr Collins* (1995), which continued his exploration of issues of identity by means of surrealistic imagery and fractured language. Their psychic material also informs his short stories in *The *Harper's Turn* (1982), *I Bailed Out* (1987), and *The Word for Yes: New and Selected Stories* (1992). *Kitty O'Shea* (Peacock 1990) marked a return to a more naturalistic style. *Fleur de Lit* (1991) is a volume of poems.

Macken, Walter [Augustine] (1915–1967), novelist and playwright; born in Galway, where he was educated. At 17 he joined An *Taibhdhearc, to which he returned in 1939, promoting Irish-language theatre for several years. He became more widely known when *Mungo's Mansion* was produced by the *Abbey Theatre in 1946. In this and its successors, *Vacant Possession* (1948) and *Home is the Hero* (1952), he represented the life of the Galway slums. The success of his novel, *Rain on the Wind* (1950), dealing with a Claddagh fisherman, encouraged him to devote himself to a writing career interrupted by occasional acting roles. His later plays eschewed simple realism: *Twilight of a Warrior* (1955), *Look in the Looking Glass* (1958), and *The Voices of Doolin* (1960). His novels include *Quench the Moon* (1948), *I Am Alone* (1949), *The Bogman* (1952), *Sunset on the Window Panes* (1954), *Sullivan* (1957), and *Brown Lord of the Mountain* (1967). He also published three collections of short stories. His best-known work is a sequence of three novels on the crises of Irish history: the *Cromwellian campaign (*Seek the Fair Land*, 1959), the *Famine (*The *Silent People*, 1962), and the *Anglo-Irish War (*The Scorching Wind*, 1964). Macken spent a brief period as artistic adviser and assistant manager of the Abbey shortly before his death.

MacKenna, John (1952–), fiction writer. Born in Castledermot, Co. Kildare, and educated at UCD, he worked as a producer in *RTÉ. In 1976 he published *The Occasional Optimist*, the first of a number of story-collections set in his native landscape. The novel *The Fallen* (1993) and *A Year of Our Lives* (1995) use the multiple narratives also employed in *Clare* (1994), a novel based on the life of the poet John Clare.

McKenna, Siobhán (1923–1986), actress. Born in West Belfast, she was educated in Galway and Monaghan. As a student at UCG (where her father was Professor of Mathematics from 1928) she acted in An *Taibhdhearc. In 1944 she joined the *Abbey company, playing in many of the Irish and English plays of the period. Her roles included G. B. *Shaw's *Saint Joan* at the *Gate Theatre in the 1950s, and Pegeen Mike in J. M. *Synge's The *Playboy of the Western World*, the latter also in a film of 1961. In a late appearance, she created the role of Mommo in Tom Murphy's *Bailegangaire* in 1986.

MacKenna, Stephen (1872–1934), translator of the *Enneads* of Plotinus; born in Liverpool of Irish parents, he worked as a bank clerk in Dublin. He took up journalism in London and, moving to Paris, shared a close friendship with J. M. *Synge. He returned to Dublin in 1907 and commenced writing for *The *Freeman's Journal*. In 1908 he published a translation from the first book of Plotinus' text ('On Beauty', I. 6). He moved to London in disillusionment after 1922, continuing his work on Plotinus. The *Enneads* (1917–30) is generally recognized as the finest English translation of any Greek classic.

McKenzie, Revd John (?1648–1696), a minister from Cookstown who served as chaplain in Revd George *Walker's regiment during the siege of Derry in 1689, and wrote an account of those events. McKenzie's *Narrative of the Siege of Londonderry in Ireland* (1690) is a more detailed account than Walker's.

Macklin [McLoughlin], Charles (?1697–1797), actor and playwright. Born probably in Culdaff, Co. Donegal, he moved in early life to Dublin, where he played the heroine in Thomas Otway's *Orphan*. After his success he ran away to act in London but was brought home. In 1725 he was engaged by the Lincoln's Inn Fields company, and from 1731 began appearing regularly in comic roles. In 1741 he achieved a sensational success with *The Merchant of Venice*, playing Shylock as a tragic villain. Macklin's championing of realistic delivery in place of a declamatory manner greatly influenced contemporaries, notably David Garrick. In 1744 he re-opened the Haymarket Theatre with Samuel Foote and others; among the productions his own plays, such as *King Henry VII* (1746) and *The Fortune Hunters* (1750), failed repeatedly. For many years he acted alternately in London and in Dublin, initially under Thomas *Sheridan at *Smock Alley, and later in the *Crow Street and Capel Street theatres also. Excepting the jingoistic *King Henry VII* (composed during the Jacobite Rebellion of 1745), his plays are comedies and farces, of which the most successful were *Love à la Mode* (1759) and *The Man of the World* (1781). These revolve around regional characters: a *stage-Irishman and a fortune-hunting Scot, a stereotypical Englishman and a Jew. Macklin had success in Dublin with *The *True Born Irishman* (1762), a satire on the snobbish affectations of English metropolitan manners.

MacLaverty, Bernard (1942–), fiction writer. Born in Belfast, he worked as a medical laboratory technician before taking a degree at QUB in 1974 and moving to Scotland. His story collections, *Secrets and Other Stories* (1977), *A Time to Dance* (1982), and *The Great Profundo* (1987), give accounts of the marginalized and eccentric. The novel, *Lamb* (1980), describes the tragic relationship between Michael Lamb, a member of the staff of a Borstal, and one of his young charges. *Cal* (1983) deals with the love affair between a young terrorist and the widow of his victim. *Walking the Dog* (1994) alternates short stories with shorter modernist pieces. *Grace Notes* (1997) was a further novel.

McLaverty, Michael [Francis] (1904–1992), fiction writer. Born in Carrickmacross, Co. Monaghan, he lived for a time on Rathlin Island, Co. Antrim, before moving to Belfast, where he was educated at QUB. A teacher and headmaster, he developed a distinctive style in precise, compassionate short stories mostly concerned with the young and the dispossessed. When his publishers asked for a longer work he produced a semi-autobiographical novel, *Call My Brother Back* (1939). The novel, *Lost Fields* (1941), explored the Belfast of McLaverty's childhood. *In This Thy Day* (1945), and his two short-story collections, *The White Mare* (1943) and *The Game Cock* (1947), indicate his growing concern with underlying tensions in Ulster life. Between 1948 and 1965 he produced the novels *The Three Brothers* (1948), *Truth in the Night* (1951), *School For Hope* (1954), *The Choice* (1958), and *The Brightening Day* (1965), each written in an unadorned style which presents the lives of ordinary people. The short stories written after 1948 were issued as *The Road to the Shore* (1976).

MacLeod, Fiona, see William *Sharp.

Mac Liammóir, Mícheál (1899–1978), actor, director, author. Born Alfred Willmore in Willesden, London (not Cork, as he claimed), he worked as a designer and illustrator for the *Dublin Drama League, and changed his name on joining the *Gaelic League. In 1928 he founded the Dublin *Gate Theatre with his partner Hilton Edwards (1903–82). Mac Liammóir acted over 300 roles. An *Taibhdhearc, in Galway, which he co-founded, opened in 1928 with his *Diarmuid agus Gráinne*, while an English translation was presented at the Gate later in the year. His thirteen plays include *The Ford of the Hurdles* (1929), *Easter 1916* (1930), *Where Stars Walk* (1940), *Dancing Shadows* (1941), *Ill Met by Moonlight* (1946; filmed 1956), and *Home for Christmas* (1950). *The Importance of Being Oscar* (1963), a one-man entertainment on Oscar *Wilde, gained him celebrity. His autobiographical accounts of theatrical life include *All for Hecuba* (1946), *Put Money in Thy Purse* (1950), and *Aisteoirí Faoi Dhá Sholas* (1956; translated as *Each Actor on his Ass*, 1961). *Theatre in Ireland* (1950 and 1964) is chronicle and commentary. *Enter a Goldfish* (1977) is an autobiographical novel. His poems were collected as *Bláth agus Taibhse* (1965).

Maclise, Daniel (1806–1870), historical painter. Born in Cork, he studied at the School of Art and the Royal Academy. His historical works include pictures from Shakespeare, and others based on English history in a commission for the Westminster Houses of Parliament. A series of engravings for *Fraser's Magazine* from 1830 captured likenesses of literary contemporaries such as William Wordsworth, Thomas *Moore, James Sheridan *Knowles, William *Maginn, and Francis *Mahony. Maclise's fantastic illustrations for T. Crofton *Croker's *Fairy Legends* (1826) and his satirical sketches in Mahony's *Reliques of Father Prout* (1836) were followed by picturesque scenes for John Barrow's *A Tour Around Ireland* (1836). He illustrated Moore's *Irish Melodies* (1845 ed.). His Irish masterpiece is *The Marriage of Strongbow and Aoife* (1854).

MacLysaght, Edward (1887–1986) (formerly Lysaght), historian and genealogist. Born on board ship to Australia, he was educated at Oxford and UCC. He was by turns farmer, publisher and director of *Maunsel & Co., prisoner during the *Anglo-Irish War, Free State Senator, and Chief Genealogical Officer in the National Library of Ireland, 1943–55. *Irish Life in the Seventeenth Century* (1939) is a well-researched social history. *Irish Families: Their Names, Arms and Origins* (4 vols., 1957–65) is a pioneering work of modern genealogy. His novel *The Gael* (1919) is a critique of Irish society. He wrote several books in Irish, including the novel *Cúrsaí Thomáis* (1927).

MacMahon, Bryan [Michael] (1909–1998), writer of fiction; born in Listowel, Co. Kerry, and educated at St Patrick's College before becoming a national schoolteacher and eventually headmaster in Listowel. Issued as *The Lion Tamer* (1948), his first stories reflect his appreciation of rural life. *Children of the Rainbow* (1952), an ambitious novel evoking the energy and colour of North Kerry, was followed by *The Red Petticoat* (1955), a further collection of stories. A play, *The Bugle in the Blood* (1949), was produced at the *Abbey Theatre, where *The Song of the Anvil* (1960) also appeared. *The Honey Spike* (staged at the Abbey in 1961), is based on his understanding of Irish tinkers and their way of life. It was rewritten as a novel in 1967. *The End of the World* (1976) and *The Sound of Hooves* (1985) are collections of psychologically complex stories underpinned by a sense of the power of nature to heal and to console. An autobiography, *The Master* (1992), was followed by a further short-story collection, *The Tallystick* (1994).

MacManus, Anna, see Ethna *Carbery.

MacManus, Francis (1909–1965), novelist and broadcaster. Born in Kilkenny and educated at St Patrick's College and at UCD, he taught before joining Radio Éireann [see *RTÉ] in 1948. He began writing with a trilogy comprising *Stand and Give Challenge* (1934), *Candle for the Proud* (1936), and *Men Withering* (1939), set in the *Penal days and concerning the life of the Gaelic poet Donncha Rua *Mac Conmara. He then turned to modern rural Ireland with a second trilogy, *This House Was Mine* (1937), *Flow On, Lovely River* (1941), and *Watergate* (1942), set in Co. Kilkenny. Other novels are *The Greatest of These* (1943), and *The Fire in the Dust* (1950), in which the sexuality of returning emigrants gives rise to scandal and tragedy. His other works include biographies of *Boccaccio* (1947) and *Colum Cille, (1963).

MacManus, Lily (1894–1941), novelist; born in Castlebar, Co. Mayo, she was educated at home and in Torquay, becoming an outspoken republican nationalist after the *Anglo-Irish War. Her novels reflect her firmly-held views and include *The Silk of the Kine* (1896), *In Sarsfield's Days: A Tale of the Siege* (1906), *Nuala* (1908), *The Professor in Erin* (1918). *White Light and Flame* (1929) is an autobiography.

MacManus, M[ichael] J. (1888–1951), novelist and man of letters. Born in Co. Leitrim and educated at London University, he became a journalist and returned to Ireland in 1916. From 1931 he acted as literary editor of *The Irish Press*. His popular historical writings

include *So This is Dublin* (1927) and *Irish Cavalcade* (1939). He also wrote two novels, *The Green Jackdaw* (1939) and *Rackrent Hall* (1941).

MacManus, Seamas (?1870–1960), man of letters; born near Mount-charles, Co. Donegal, and educated locally. His sketches based on local traditions at first appeared in news-papers, and then in *Shuilers from Healthy Hills* (1893), *The Humours of Donegal* (1898), and other books. In 1899 he emigrated to America. In 1901 he married the poet Anna Johnston ('Ethna *Carbery') who died the year after. The *Abbey Theatre staged his plays *The Townland of Tamney* (1904) and *The Hard-Hearted Man* (1905). *The Rocky Road to Dublin* (1938) is an autobiography.

Mac Mathúna, Séamus (1945–), scholar; born in Portadown, Co. Armagh, he was educated at St. Patrick's Academy, Dungannon, and at QUB before studying at Zürich and in Iceland. He lectured in Uppsala and at UCG before assuming the Chair of Irish at the NUU (later UUC) in 1980, where he became Director of the Centre for Irish and Celtic Studies. At Coleraine his department gained a reputation for excellence in teaching and research in the 1980s and 1990s, making a major contribution to the renewal of Gaelic cultural life in the north. Publications include editions of *Immraim Brain* (1985) and *Clann Ua gCorra* (1997). He is co-editor of the Collins Irish dictionaries (1995 and 1997), of *Miscellanea Celtica in Memoriam Heinrich Wagner* (1997), and of *Minority Languages in Scandinavia, Britain, and Ireland* (1998).

Mac Meanmain, Seán (1886–1962), short-story writer. Born in Iniskeel, Co. Donegal, a native speaker, he learnt to read and write in Irish from his parents. His collections include *Scéalta Goiridhe*

Geimhridh (1915), *Inné agus Inniu* (1929), and *Ó Chamhaoir go Clapsholas* (1940), as well as plays and historical pieces, all rooted in 19th-cent. Co. Donegal.

McNally, Leonard (1752–1820), dramatist and informer. Born in Dublin and educated at TCD. His first dramatic piece was *The Ruling Passion* (1777), a comic opera. Living in London—where he was called to the Bar in 1783—he produced well-made but derivative comedies, commencing with a satire of R. B. *Sheridan in *The Apotheosis of Punch* (1779) and continuing with *Tristram Shandy* (1783), adapted from *Sterne, and others such as *Fashionable Levities* (1785), *Richard Cœur de Lion* (1786), and *Critic Upon Critic* (1788). In 1792 he defended Napper Tandy, the *United Irishmen's agent in France, and later appeared for William *Jackson and Wolfe *Tone, but by 1794 he was in the pay of the Government. His play *Robin Hood* (1784) was playing in Dublin on the night in 1798 when Lord Edward *Fitzgerald was captured with his connivance. In 1803 he stood in for John Philpot *Curran as Robert *Emmet's barrister, but confided the case for the defence to the Government.

MacNamara, Brinsley (pseudonym of John Weldon) (1890–1963), novelist and playwright. Born in Delvin, Co. Westmeath, he joined the *Abbey Theatre as an actor in 1909 and took part in the American tour of 1911, remaining there to freelance until 1913, after which he settled in his home town to write his first novel, *The *Valley of the Squinting Windows* (1918). It caused an immediate furore, resulting in a *boycott of his father's school and ensuing litigation. In 1919 his first play, *The Rebellion in Ballycullen*, was produced by the Abbey. Three novels followed, all written in the spirit of disillusionment: *The Clanking of Chains* (1919) is the story of a disappointed nationalist; *In Clay and Bronze* (1920) records his own artistic growth; and *Mirror in the Dusk* (1921) paints a gloomy picture of rural life. In 1924 he succeeded James *Stephens as Registrar of the National Gallery of Ireland. His association with the Abbey continued with two comedies (*The Glorious Uncertainty*, 1923, and *Look at the Heffernans!*, 1926), and the complex and brooding *Margaret Gillan* (1933). A brief spell as a Director of the Theatre ended in his resignation over the 1935 production of *O'Casey's *The *Silver Tassie*. The *Various Lives of Marcus Igoe* (1929), his most innovative fiction, is a series of day-dreams and 'real' occurrences in the context of village life. There were two collections of short stories and sketches—*The Smiling Faces* (1929) and *Some Curious People* (1945); two further novels, *Return to Ebontheever* (1930) and *Michael Caravan* (1946); and a novella, *The Whole Story of the X.Y.Z.* (1951).

MacNamara, Gerald (pseudonym of Harry C. Morrow) (1865–1938), playwright. He was a member of the *Ulster Literary Theatre in Belfast. *Suzanne and the Sovereigns* (1907) burlesques Catholic-Protestant relations, while *The Mist That Does Be on the Bog* (1909) was a parody of Abbey peasant realism. His *Thompson in Tir na nÓg* (1918) concerns an *Orangeman transported to the Land of Youth when his gun explodes on the way to a sectarian affray.

McNamee, Eoin (1961–), novelist; born in Kilkeel, Co. Down, and educated at TCD, where he studied law. After graduation, he worked in New York before returning to Dublin. Dermot *Bolger published *The Last of Deeds* (1989) along with three short stories. His novel *Resurrection Man* (1994) deals with a series of sectarian killings perpetrated in Belfast by a gang of Protestant paramilitaries. It conveys the workings of ethnic hatred in the mind of the central character, Victor Kelly.

MacNeice, [Frederick] Louis (1907–1963), poet. Born in Belfast and brought up in Carrickfergus, Co. Antrim, where his father was Church of Ireland rector, he was educated at Marlborough public school and then Merton College, Oxford. He taught Classics at Birmingham University, 1929–36. MacNeice then taught at Bedford College, London, before joining the BBC in 1941, where he worked in the renowned Features Department run by Laurence Gilliam. During the 1930s MacNeice was a leading figure among the new generation of left-wing English poets—Stephen Spender, Cecil *Day-Lewis, and W. H. Auden (with whom he collaborated on *Letters from Iceland*, 1937). His first collection, *Blind Fireworks* (1929), explored a personal landscape, but the political concerns of the decade encroached more strongly in *Poems* (1935). *The Earth Compels* (1938) is a collection permeated by omens of war, while *Autumn Journal* (1939), a verse meditation in twenty-four sections, was occasioned by the Munich Crisis in September 1938 when the British Government attempted to appease Hitler. The collections which MacNeice published during the 1940s, *Plant and Phantom* (1941), *Springboard* (1944), and *Holes in the Sky* (1948), engage with the issues of personal and communal responsibility posed by war. In *Ten Burnt Offerings* (1952) and *Autumn Sequel* (1954), however, the scope widens as the mood relaxes. In *Visitations* (1957) he began to develop a concentrated 'parable-poem'. In *Solstices* (1961) and *The Burning Perch* (1963) his acute sense of mortality fuses with a darkly ironic outlook on contemporary society. MacNeice died of pneumonia after going down potholes in Yorkshire with BBC engineers. MacNeice's experience of and reaction against his Irish background led him to reject religious and secular orthodoxy, and to celebrate an 'incorrigibly plural' universe. At the same time he remained interested in questions of belief, reflecting his Ulster Protestant background in a continuing fascination with the Bible. *The Poetry of W. B. Yeats* (1941) was the first serious critical book on *Yeats. His moral realism has had a marked influence on later northern poets such as Seamus *Heaney, Michael *Longley, Derek *Mahon, and Paul *Muldoon, and on southern poets such as Brendan *Kennelly. Posthumous works include *The Strings Are False: An Unfinished Autobiography* (1965); and *Varieties of Parable*, Clark Lectures, 1963 (1965). See Jon Stallworthy, *Louis MacNeice* (1995).

MacNeill, Eoin (1867–1945), activist and historian. Born in Glenarm, Co. Antrim, he was a founder of the *Gaelic League with Douglas *Hyde and others, and became Professor of Early Irish History at UCD. Following the publication of his article 'The North Began' the *Irish Volunteers were founded on 25 November 1913, with MacNeill as Commander in Chief. On learning that an insurrection was planned by Patrick *Pearse and others for *Easter 1916, he countermanded their mobilization orders, thereby preventing a large-scale insurrection throughout the country. As well as expounding the idea of an earlier native *Irish State, his historical works, *Phases of Irish History* (1919) and *Celtic Ireland* (1921), developed scholarly method in medieval Irish history.

McNeill, Janet (1907–), novelist; born in Dublin and educated at St Andrews University, she moved to Northern Ireland to be near her ailing father. Employed as a secretary for the *Belfast Telegraph*, she did not begin writing until she had brought up a family of four. She began with radio drama. Encouraged to adapt the script of *A *Child in the House* as a novel (1955), she went on to write: *The Other Side of the Wall* (1956), *Tea at Four O'Clock* (1956), *A

Furnished Room (1958), *Search Party* (1959), **As Strangers Here* (1960), *The Early Harvest* (1962), *The *Maiden Dinosaur* (1964), *Talk to Me* (1965), and *The *Small Window* (1967). She focuses on a time of mid-life crisis which forces her protagonists to confront unfinished business from their past. Eight of the novels are set in Ulster, frequently exploring the psychoses of a waning Protestant middle class.

McNulty, Edward (1856–1943), playwright and novelist. Born in Co. Antrim, he was educated in Dublin. Besides plays for the *Abbey Theatre such as *The Lord Mayor* (1914), a study of corruption, and *The Courting of Mary Doyle* (1921), a comedy, he wrote novels about peasant life including *Misther O'Ryan* (1894), *Son of a Peasant* (1897), and *Mrs Mulligan's Millions* (1903).

Macpherson, James (1736–1796), poet and controversial translator; born in Kingussie and educated at Aberdeen and Edinburgh. After publishing *The Highlander* (1758), a heroic poem, he met the Celticist [see *translation from Irish] John Home and was encouraged to collect the Ossianic epic he described in conversation. *Fragments of Ancient Poetry, Collected in the Highlands of Scotland, and Translated from the Galic or Erse Language* (1760) was enthusiastically received. *Fingal, an Ancient Epic Poem, in Six Books* (1762) was followed by *Temora* (1763). Fingal is Macpherson's distortion of *Fionn Mac Cumail, and Temora his version of *Tara (Temair in Irish). He mixes up the *Fionn and *Ulster cycles, Cú Chulainn appearing as Cuthulinn, but the works of Ossian are based, as scholarship has shown, on lays of the Fionn cycle. These Ossianic pieces affected the development of the gloomy landscapes of Romanticism as well as influencing the ways in which the ancient history of the Celtic peoples was imagined as uniting sincerity and

wildness. The poems of Ossian were immensely popular all over Europe: Goethe quoted extracts in *The Sorrows of Young Werther* (1774), and Napoleon affected a certain style of speech which was known as *ossianer*. His influence on the style and atmosphere of Celticism was all-pervasive, in Ireland as much as anywhere else.

Mac Piarais, Padraic, see Patrick *Pearse.

MacReady, William (?1755–1829), actor and theatre manager. Born in Dublin, he appeared at *Smock Alley, and at Covent Garden. He wrote the comedies, *The Irishman in London, or The Happy African* (1792) and *The Bank Note, or Lessons for Ladies* (1795). His son, the celebrated tragic actor William Charles Macready (1793–1873), produced Gerald *Griffin's play *Gisippus* and others by John *Banim and George *Darley.

Mac Réamoinn, Seán (1921–), author and journalist; born in Birmingham, and educated at UCG. He joined the Department of External Affairs in 1944, and moved to Radio Éireann [see *RTÉ] in 1947, writing and producing programmes on literary and religious affairs. He was in Rome as special correspondent during the Second Vatican Council, 1962–5, an experience reflected in *Vaticáin II agus an Réabhlóid Cultúrtha* (1987). Appointed Controller of Radio Programmes, 1974, and Head of External Affairs, 1976, he served on the RTÉ Authority, 1973–6. Publications include *The Pleasures of Gaelic Poetry* (ed.) (1982); *The Synod on the Laity: An Outsider's Diary* (1987); and *Laylines* (1993).

Mac Síomóin, Tomás (1938–), poet; born in Dublin and educated at UCD, the Netherlands and Cornell. In 1973 he became a lecturer in applied biology in Dublin. A first collection,

Damhna Agus Dánta Eile (1974), was followed by *Codarsnaí* (1981), *Cré Agus Cláirseach* (1984), and *Scian* (1989). He edited *Comhar* 1988–95.

MacSwiney, Owen (also Swinny and Swiney) (1675–1754), actor and playwright. Born in Wexford, he moved to London and produced a satire on physicians, *Quacks* (1705), to be followed by an opera, *Camilla* (1707), and a tragedy, *Pyrrhus and Demetrius* (1709). In 1707 he leased the Haymarket Theatre and gave *Farquhar's The *Beaux' Stratagem* its successful première.

MacSwiney, Terence (1879–1920) revolutionary. Born in Cork, he was educated at the North Monastery, and UCC. He helped found the Celtic Literary Society in 1901, and with Daniel *Corkery established the Cork Dramatic Society in 1908, for which he wrote plays, among them *The Revolutionist* and *The Wooing of Emer*. He also wrote poems and edited a paper, *Fíanna Fáil*. In 1916 MacSwiney was to have been second-in-command of the *Easter Rising in Cork and Kerry, but obeyed Eoin *MacNeill's orders to disperse. When the Lord Mayor, Tomás MacCurtain, head of the Cork Brigade of the *IRA, was killed in March 1920, MacSwiney succeeded him in both positions. He was arrested in August, began a hunger strike, and was taken to Brixton Prison. His seventy-four-day fast and death focused world attention on the Irish struggle.

Mac Toirdhealbhaigh, Brian, see Padraig *Mac Giolla.

Madden, Aodhan (1954–), playwright; born in Dublin he was educated at Rathmines College before working as a journalist and a teacher. *Demons* (1980) was a collection of poems, followed by *The Midnight Door* (1984), *Sensations* (1986), and *Josephine in the Night* (1988),

all staged at the *Abbey Theatre. *Mad Angels of Paxenau Street* (1990) was a work of fiction, while *Night Train* (1999) and *Skerries* (1999) were scripts for feature films.

Madden, Deirdre (1960–), novelist. Born in Belfast, she was educated at TCD. Her first novel, *Hidden Symptoms* (1988), set in Belfast, deals with the impact of a young man's murder on his twin sister. *The Birds of the Innocent Wood* (1988) explores the distances between members of a family. *Remembering Light and Stone* (1992), set in Italy, deals with a young Irish girl's growing maturity. *Nothing is Black* (1994), concerned with the lives of women settled in Donegal, was followed by *One by One in the Darkness* (1996).

Madden, R[ichard] R[obert] (1798–1886), historian. Born in Dublin, he trained in medicine in Ireland and Paris, London, and Naples. An interest in the *United Irishmen led to a life of Robert *Emmet (1840) and then his chief work, *The Lives and Times of the United Irishmen* (7 vols., 1842–6; 4 vols., 1857–60), the last part of which C. P. *Meehan reissued as *Literary Remains of the United Irishmen* (1887) with Madden's poetry included. Madden also wrote on Cuban slavery (1840), the Egyptian nationalist Mohammed Ali (1841), the *Penal Laws (1847), and *Irish Periodical Literature* (2 vols., 1847). His essay on *Galileo and the Inquisition* (1863) repudiates the Protestant view. *The United Irishmen* long remained the main source of narratives about the 1798 Rebellion.

Madden, Samuel (1686–1765), playwright and economist. Born in Dublin and educated at TCD, he contributed to the anti-absentee campaign, chiefly with his *Reflections and Resolutions Proper for the Gentlemen of Ireland* (1732). A tragedy, *Themistocles, or Lover of his Country* (1729), was produced in London. With

Thomas *Prior and others he was a founder of the *RDS.

Máel Dúin (Maeldune), see *Immram Curaig Máele Dúin.

Máel Muire mac Céilechair (fl. 1090), thought to have been the principal scribe of the *Book of the Dun Cow.

Máel Muru (d. 887), poet, usually referred to as Máel Muru 'Othna', being a member of the monastery of Othain at Fahan, Co. Donegal. He was amongst the early poets and historians who produced various parts and recensions of *Lebor Gabála.

Maelísa úa Brolcháin (?-1086), poet and scholar of the Clann Brolcháin, a learned family which produced scholars and ecclesiastics up to the 18th cent. He was educated at the monastery of Both Chonais, Co. Donegal. He was an ecclesiastic at Armagh, and died in Lismore, Co. Waterford. His poems address devotional or didactic themes.

Maeve, see *Medb.

Magee, William Kirkpatrick, see John *Eglinton.

Magic Glasses, The (1913), a fantasy play by George *Fitzmaurice, first staged at the *Abbey Theatre. Jaymony Shanahan has taken to the loft. Mr Quille, an eloquent quack summoned by his parents, finds that Jaymony is secretly absorbed in the visions he sees in three sets of magic glasses.

Maginn, William (pseudonym 'Sir Morgan O'Doherty') (1793–1842), man of letters. Born in Cork, he was educated at TCD then taught in his father's school. He began contributing to *Blackwood's Magazine* and other journals in 1819, writing parodies of Thomas *Moore, amongst others. After visiting

William Blackwood in Edinburgh in 1821 he began writing the 'Noctes Ambrosianae' (1822–8), a series of whimsical dialogues. He knew J. J. *Callanan in Cork and recommended his translations to *Blackwood's*. He published *Whitehall, or The Days of George IV* (1827), a satirical extravaganza. Breaking with *Blackwood's* in 1828, he founded *Fraser's Magazine* in 1830, to which he contributed his 'Gallery of Literary Characters', complemented by the portraits of Daniel *Maclise. A cruel review, written while drunk, of Grantley Berkeley's novel *Berkeley Castle* led to a duel in 1836 from which both contestants emerged unscathed. His 'Homeric Ballads', versified episodes from the *Odyssey* told in brisk, headlong style, were for *Fraser's*. He retired to Walton-on-Thames, where he worked on *John Manesty, the Liverpool Merchant* (1844), a novel completed after his death by Charles Ollier. His friend *Thackeray portrayed him as Captain Shandon in *Pendennis* (1848–50).

Mahaffy, Sir John Pentland (1839–1919), classicist; born in Switzerland and educated at home in Donegal and at TCD, where he became Provost, 1914. A versatile scholar, Mahaffy translated Kuno Fischer's *Commentary on Kant* (1866) and issued *Kant's Critical Philosophy for English Readers* (1871) before turning to classical society, on which he published *Prolegomena to Ancient History* (1871), *Social Life in Greece from Homer to Menander* (1874), *Greek Antiquities* (1876), and the more informal *Rambles and Studies in Greece* (1876). He strenuously opposed the introduction of Irish to school syllabuses and, together with Professor Atkinson, became the *bête noire* of the *Gaelic League. A wit and conversationalist, Mahaffy issued *The Principles of the Art of Conversation* (1887) as a guide.

Mahon, Derek (1941–), poet. Born in Belfast, he grew up in Glengormley, and was educated at TCD. He worked as a teacher, and as a journalist. He was writer in residence in NUU, 1978–9, and TCD, 1988, and moved to New York. His work responds in a complex manner to a northern, Protestant, middle-class background. Without a community to which he can easily belong, Mahon in *Night Crossing* (1968), his first collection, is drawn to the forgotten and neglected. In *Lives* (1972) the central issue is the relation of self to the world, with the imagination coming under pressure. Rather than exploring the past, Mahon's poems often project into an apocalyptic future. In *The Snow-Party* (1975) form and chaos are held in delicate equipoise. *Poems: 1962–1978* (1979) was followed by *Courtyards in Delft* (1981), many of the poems in this volume reappearing in *The Hunt by Night* (1982). Meditations on war, human decay, lost innocence, and cultural decline are accompanied by a growing uncertainty. Mahon's recurring settings are desolate Northern landscapes, deserted beaches, and scenes of cosmic isolation. In *Antarctica* (1985), symbolic landscape is even more wasted and extreme. Mahon translated Gérard de Nerval's *The Chimeras* (1982); Molière's *School for Husbands as High Time* (1985), which was presented by *Field Day in 1984; Molière's *School for Wives* (1986); and *Selected Poems of Philippe Jaccottet* (1988). *The Hudson Letter* (1995) and *The Yellow Book* (1998) are volumes in which form relaxes into loose-rhyming couplets as social satire grows harsher. *Collected Poems* appeared in 1999.

Mahony, Francis Sylvester (pseudonym 'Fr. Prout') (1804–1866), humorous poet and journalist. Born in Cork, he was educated at Amiens, Paris, and Rome, before returning to teach at Clongowes, intending to become a Jesuit. Compelled to resign, he went to Italy and was ordained a secular priest. He was assigned to a parish in Cork, but left for London in 1834 after differences with his bishop. There he wrote for *Fraser's Magazine*, in which his fellow Corkman William *Maginn had an interest. Fraser, the publisher, issued *The Reliques of Father Prout* (1837), described as the late parish priest of Watergrasshill, Co. Cork. Fr. Prout was an actual parish priest who had died in 1830. Mahony adopts this persona to expatiate on a variety of topics, from 'Women and Wooden Shoes' to 'The Rogueries of Tom Moore'. He wrote for Dickens's *Bentley's Miscellany*. He settled in Paris in 1848.

Maiden Dinosaur, The (1964), a novel by Janet *McNeill, tracing the belated sexual awakening of Sarah Vincent, a middle-aged schoolmistress.

Máire, see Séamus *Ó Grianna.

Major Barbara (1905), a play by George Bernard *Shaw exploring themes of power and morality. Major Barbara is in charge of a Salvation Army shelter, which is under threat of closure. The only way the shelter can be saved is by donations from her father, Andrew Undershaft, a munitions manufacturer, and Sir Horace Bodger, a distiller.

Making History (1988), a play by Brian *Friel dramatizing the writing of Irish history as well as the historical events before and after the Battle of *Kinsale, 1601.

Malone, Edmund (1741–1812), Shakespeare scholar. Born in Dublin, he was educated at TCD and practised law on the Munster circuit until his father's death in 1777. In London he became a member of Dr Johnson's Literary Club and a close acquaintance of *Burke. He helped James Boswell with his *Life of Johnson* (1791). His first work on Shakespeare was *An Attempt to Ascertain in which Order the Plays were Written* (1778).

In 1780 he published *An Historical Account of the Rise of the English Stage*, dealing with the Elizabethan period, and soon after that an edition of Shakespeare (11 vols., 1790).

Malone Dies (in French as *Malone meurt*, 1953; in English, 1958), a novel by Samuel *Beckett, second in a trilogy that includes *Molloy* and The *Unnamable*. An invalid old man, awaiting death in conditions like those of a workhouse ward, gives an account of himself composed of memories and stories which help him to stave off suicide.

Man and Superman: *A Comedy and a Philosophy* (1905), a play by George Bernard *Shaw, written in 1901-2. The work includes a dream scene (sometimes performed separately under the title *Don Juan in Hell*) and an Epistle Dedicatory which constitute major expressions of Shaw's ideas about the Life Force and his creed of Creative Evolution. The character of Jack Tanner is conceived as that of a modern Don Juan who is the 'marked-down prey' rather than the pursuer in the hunt of sex, through which the Life Force operates.

Manannán mac Lir, see *mythological cycle.

Manchester Martyrs, the name given to William Philip Allen, Michael O'Brien, and Michael Larkin, hanged publicly at Salford Jail, 23 November 1867, for the murder of Sgt. Charles Brett. None of the three men, all active *Fenians, admitted firing the shot, and O'Brien claimed not to have been present.

Mangaire Súgach, An, see Aindrias *Mac Craith.

Mangan, James Clarence (1803-1849), poet and translator. Born in Dublin, he was educated in Saul's Court before working as a copy-clerk. In the 1820s he was publishing in local almanacs. In the early 1830s he contributed to the *Dublin Penny Journal*. During 1833 he met George *Petrie, John *O'Donovan and Eugene *O'Curry, scholars who were to supply him with versions of Irish poems on which he based his translations. Petrie employed him in the Ordnance Survey Office, 1833-9. His prose contributions to Dublin journals mix autobiographical fantasy, psychological self-scrutiny, and free-wheeling speculation. His wide reading ranged from contemporary German, French, and Spanish authors to Persian, Hungarian, and Icelandic poetry of all periods. From 1835 he regularly contributed to the *Dublin University Magazine* an 'Anthologia Germanica', comprising translations of modern German Poetry. A gloomy and introverted figure, he played the part of a poet in outlandish clothes, including a voluminous cloak, green spectacles, and pointed hat. In early life Mangan had been jilted, and he remained unmarried. In spite of his heavy abuse of alcohol he worked strenuously, and produced a large quantity of verse variously signed and initialled, or unsigned, or under pseudonyms such as 'The Man in the Cloak'. In 1837 he began for the *Dublin University Magazine* a series of Oriental translations entitled 'Literae Orientales', being versions of Persian, Turkish, and Arabic poems. In 1846 he wrote some of his finest poems and translations, spurred into creative activity by the worsening conditions in the country during the *Famine. Contributions to *The Nation* for that year included 'Siberia', 'Dark Rosaleen', and 'Sarsfield'. In 1847 he began in the *Dublin University Magazine* an *Anthologia Hibernica*, and started to work on translations of the *Jacobite poetry of Munster with John *O'Daly, posthumously published as *The Poets and Poetry of Munster* (1849).

Mangan composed about this time an *Autobiography* which gives a lurid and unreliable account of his early years. In the last year of his life he wrote for *The Irishman* a series of sketches of Charles *Maturin, Maria *Edgeworth, Gerald *Griffin, and others. Mangan was hospitalized on several occasions after May 1848, and fell victim in June 1849 to the cholera epidemic of the Famine years. He was taken to the Meath Hospital, where he died. See Ellen Shannon-Mangan, *Mangan: A Biography* (1996) and Jacques Chuto *et al.* (ed.), *Collected Poems*, 4 vols (1996–2000), and *Collected Prose* (2000).

Mangan Inheritance, The (1979), a novel by Brian *Moore. Jamie Mangan, a failed poet married to a successful actress whose fame has swamped his self-esteem, is deserted by her, and returns to his father's Canadian home where he learns that his family are supposedly descended from the Irish poet James Clarence *Mangan.

Mannin, Ethel (1900–1984), novelist. Born in London of Irish parents, she lived in Connemara for many years. Her earliest novels explored the lives of working-class women. Later she focused on anarchism and pacifism, basing *Red Rose* (1942) on the life of Emma Goldmann the Russian anarchist, while *The Blossoming Bough* (1943) takes its central character from Ireland to the Spanish Civil War via an affair in Paris and brings him patriotically home to Ireland and to his beloved actress-cousin Katherine O'Donal. In *Late Have I Loved Thee* (1948), a best-seller in Ireland, an Englishman converts to Catholicism following the death of his sister in a Continental climbing accident, and finally joins the Jesuits. After the death of her second husband in 1958 Mannin visited many countries, producing a travel or children's book during each trip. She wrote seven autobiographies between

Confessions and Impressions (1930) and *Young in the Twenties* (1971), revealing her hatred of hypocrisy and her gradual withdrawal from socialism. She was instrumental in securing Francis *Stuart's release from custody after the war, and was a close friend of Yeats's in his latter years. In 1954 she issued *Two Studies in Integrity* on the Irish writers Gerald *Griffin and Francis *Mahony.

Manning, Mary (1906–), novelist and playwright. Born in Dublin to an Anglo-Irish family she studied acting at the *Abbey Theatre. *Youth Is the Season —?* (1931) was a successful comedy. Her own novels, written in America, include *Mount Venus* (1938) and *Lovely People* (1953). *The Last Chronicles of Ballyfungus* (1978) are comic stories of Ireland.

manuscripts in Irish. Irish writings prior to the use of paper and print were written on vellum in a distinctive minuscule script which reflects 1,000 years of literary tradition. Extant examples, deriving from the end of the 11th to the end of the 16th cent. (though sometimes containing material copied from much earlier writings), are bound in codices or collections held at various libraries in Ireland and abroad. Besides the *annals, the chief of these are the *Book of Armagh; the *Book of Ballymote; the *Book of Fermoy; the *Book of Glendalough; the *Book of Lecan; the *Book of Leinster; the *Book of Lismore; the *Book of Rights; the *Book of the Dun Cow (Lebor na hUidre); the *Book of Uí Mhaine; *Leabhar Breac (Speckled Book or Book of Duniry), *Leabhar Clainne Suibhne; and the *Yellow Book of Lecan. The manuscripts are the source for all the major texts of Old and Middle Irish literature, such as sagas [see *tale-types], *dinnshenchas, *genealogies, *law tracts, and much other lore. The most important surviving manuscripts from the pre-Norman period are associated with centres of learning in Leinster such as

*Clonmacnoise and *Glendalough. See individual entries; and Francis John Byrne, *A Thousand Years of Irish Script* (1979).

manuscripts in Irish from 1700.
From the latter part of the 17th to the third quarter of the 19th cent., Irish literary tradition, with some few exceptions, continued to be transmitted in manuscript. Gaelic literature was preserved during this period in handwritten simple paper notebooks copied by professional scribes, who were often poets also. That there was a great deal of Irish literature circulating in this way is attested by Crofton *Croker, who remarked in the 1820s that every Munster village possessed its Gaelic manuscripts. When Edward *O'Reilly bought the manuscript library of the poet and scribe Muiris *Ó Gormáin in 1794 it amounted to five sackfuls. Amongst the poets who were also proficient scribes are Dáibhí *Ó Bruadair, Aodhagán *Ó Rathaille, Peadar *Ó Doirnín, and Art *Mac Bionaid. Latter-day scribal families were the *Ó Neachtains of Dublin, and the *Ó Longáins of Carrignavar, near Cork.

Marcus, David (1924–   ), literary editor and novelist. He was born in Cork and qualified at law. In 1946 he founded *Irish Writing* with Terence Smith. After the appearance of his first novel, *To Next Year in Jerusalem* (1954), he moved to London. In 1967 he founded 'New Irish Writing', the literary page of *The Irish Press* that ran till 1988. His late novels about Cork Jews, *A Land Not Theirs* (1986) and *A Land in Flames* (1988), were popular successes. He is married to the novelist Ita *Daly.

Markievicz, Countess Constance (née Gore-Booth) (1868–1927), revolutionary. Born in London to an Anglo-Irish *ascendancy family, she was educated at home in Lissadell, Co. Sligo, and at the Slade in London, after which she studied painting in Paris, meeting there the Polish Count Casimir Markievicz, whom she married after his wife's death in 1900. Back in Ireland she became involved in cultural and political activities. Condemned to death as an officer in James *Connolly's Citizens' Army during the *Easter Rising, she was reprieved on the grounds of her sex. She inspired two poems by W. B. *Yeats: 'On a Political Prisoner' and 'In Memory of Eva Gore-Booth and Countess Markievicz'.

Marshall, W[illiam] F[rederick] (1888–1959), poet and novelist. Born in Derebard, Co. Tyrone, and brought up in Sixmilecross where his father was a schoolmaster. He was a Presbyterian minister, spending his main years of ministry in Castlerock, near Coleraine. He was a recognized authority on Ulster dialect. *Ballads and Verses from Tyrone* (1929) contains his most popular verse.

Martin, [William] David, see David *MacCart-Martin.

Martin, James (1783–1860), poet; born in Oldcastle, Co. Meath, where he farmed. He wrote and published, mainly in nearby Kells or Cavan, some twenty volumes of narrative verse including *Translations from Ancient Irish Manuscripts* (1811), and *Reformation the Third, or the Apostate N-l-n and the Perverts of Athboy* (1838), satires from a Catholic nationalist viewpoint.

Martin, Mary Letitia (1815–1850), novelist. Born in Galway, she was the daughter of 'Humanity Dick' Martin from whom she inherited Ballinahinch Castle and a vast but worthless estate. She moved to Belgium with her husband Arthur Gonne Bell (who took her name) and wrote two novels. *St. Etienne* (1845) is set in the Vendée in

Napoleonic times, while *Julia Howard* (1850) concerns the daughter of an 18th-cent. Anglo-Irish landlord who acquires an estate from the ruined O'Connors and dies tragically. She died in childbirth shortly after reaching New York.

Martin, Violet, see Martin *Ross.

Martyn, Edward (1859–1923), playwright. Born in Co. Galway into a wealthy Catholic family exempted from the *Penal Laws by an Act in the reign of Queen Anne, he was educated in Oxford, but returned to Tulira, his ancestral home, and involved himself in every aspect of the *Irish literary revival. He became fluent in Gaelic, serving as President of *Sinn Féin, 1904–8; co-founded Feis Ceoil, the annual festival of traditional music; endowed the Palestrina choir in the pro-Cathedral, Dublin (of which John McCormack was a member); and led a crusade to improve the quality of ecclesiastical art in Ireland. With Lady *Gregory and *Yeats, Martyn co-founded the Irish Literary Theatre (1899). Martyn's The *Heather Field was produced with Yeats's The *Countess Cathleen in the first season in 1899, and his *Maeve* was performed the following year. In spite of his generous financial support during the first three years, aesthetic differences with Yeats, exacerbated by personality conflicts with his cousin *George Moore, caused him to break from the movement that eventually evolved into the *Abbey Theatre. See Robert Hogan and James Kilroy (eds.), *The Irish Literary Theatre, 1899–1901* (1975).

Martyr, The (1933), a novel by Líam *O'Flaherty set in Kerry during the last days of the *Civil War, attacking the nationalist cult of martyrdom.

martyrologies (félirí), calendars of saints' days and festivals, with a saint assigned to each day of the year other than the feast-days and festivals such as Christmas or Corpus Christi. Often, as in *Félire Oengusso* (*Calendar of Oengus*), there is a text for every day of the year. The earliest surviving martyrology, the *Martyrology of Tallaght*, composed *c.*830, was based on a version of a martyrology which entered Irish Church tradition through Iona, which itself drew upon martyrological learning that developed from the ecclesiology of St Jerome (*fl.* 400). *Félire Oengusso* was also composed at Tallaght by Oengus the *Céle Dé (client of God, Culdee), and reflects Tallaght's status as a centre of the Culdee reform movement. The *Martyrology of Gorman* was written in verse between 1166 and 1174 by Mael Muire ua Gormáin, abbot of an Augustinian monastery at Knock, Co. Louth, drawing upon the *Martyrology of Tallaght*. A martyrology recently discovered in Turin was also composed in the second half of the 12th cent. and shows signs of having been composed in the midlands. The *Psalter of Cashel* has been lost since the 17th cent. but its text, largely drawn from *Félire Oengusso*, can be partly restored by reference to extracts from it made by John *Colgan. The *Martyrology of Donegal* was written by Mícheál *Ó Cléirigh in 1630 and concerns itself exclusively, unlike all its predecessors, with Irish saints. See Eugene *O'Curry, *Lectures on the Manuscript Materials of Ancient Irish History* (1861).

Mason, Patrick (1951–), theatre director; born in London, he was educated at Downside and at the Central School of Speech and Drama in London, after which he lectured at Manchester University in Hugh *Hunt's department. He became resident director at the *Abbey in 1977, then Artistic Director 1994–99. In the 1980s and 1990s he was responsible for brave and adventurous staging and presided over the Abbey's imaginative and creative renewal, directing plays by Brian *Friel, Tom *MacIntyre, Thomas *Kilroy, Frank *McGuinness, and many others.

Mathew, Theobald (1790–1856), priest and Temperance reformer. Born in Co. Tipperary, he joined the Capuchin order after being expelled from Maynooth. His Temperance Movement (in fact a pledge of total abstinence) began in Cork in 1838 and spread rapidly through the southern half of Ireland: between 1838 and 1842 consumption of legally distilled spirits fell by over half.

Mathews, Aidan [Carl] (1956–), novelist and poet. Born in Dublin, educated at Gonzaga College, and TCD, he joined *RTÉ as a producer. A first collection, *Windfalls* (1977), was followed by *Minding Ruth* (1983). His plays include *Exit/ Entrance* (1990) and versions of *Antigone* and Lorca's *The House of Bernarda Alba*. *Adventures in a Bathyscope* (1988) are stories blending ordinary situations with metaphysical anxiety. *Muesli at Midnight* (1990) and *According to the Small Hours* (1998) are novels.

Maturin, Charles Robert (1780–1824), novelist. Born in Dublin of a Huguenot [see *Protestantism] family, educated at TCD and ordained in 1803, he was appointed curate at Loughrea in the west of Ireland, marrying Henrietta Kingsbury a year later. The time he spent in the west made a deep impression on his romantic imagination, and his memories of its landscape inspired much of his work, particularly *The *Milesian Chief* (1812). In 1805 he became curate of St Peter's parish, Aungier St., Dublin, where he remained until his death. Maturin himself financed publication of *The *Fatal Revenge* (1807) and *The *Wild Irish Boy* (1808) before a reversal of family fortunes forced him to turn his love of writing to commercial gain. His literary career, combined with his reputation for eccentricity, dandyism, and a love of dancing and theatre, prevented his preferment in the Church. *Women, or Pour et Contre* (1818) is a romantic story of a young man who chooses between a daughter and her mother without realizing that they are related. Maturin turned to the stage with *Bertram*, a tragedy which, with Edmund Kean in the title-role, was the season's hit at Drury Lane in 1816. Though the author visited London on the strength of it, his subsequent dramas, *Manuel* (1817) and *Osmyn the Renegade* (1819), did not succeed as well. With *Melmoth the Wanderer* (1820), a work of lasting interest, he returned to fiction. From the moment of its appearance its power was recognized. Shortly before his death Maturin produced *The *Albigenses* (1824), a novel planned as the first of a projected trilogy of historical romances. Neglected in Ireland, he did, however, find a readership in France, all of his novels being translated by 1825, with Baudelaire and Hugo declaring their admiration for his work, while Balzac produced a sequel, *Melmoth réconcilié* (1835), in his *Comédie humaine*. Oscar *Wilde, related to Maturin on his mother's side, adopted the pen-name 'Sebastian Melmoth' after his release from Reading Gaol. See Claude Fierobe, *Charles Robert Maturin: l'homme et l'œuvre* (1974).

Maude, Caitlín (1941–1982), poet and singer. Born in the Connemara *Gaeltacht at Casla, Co. Galway, and educated at UCG, she taught in Ireland and in London between 1962 and 1969. Her *sean-nós singing on *Caitlín* (1975), was electrifying in its lyric intensity. Her collected poems, *Dánta* (1984), posthumously edited by Ciarán Ó

Coigligh, deal with a range of subjects, and reveal a voice by turns direct and ironic but always passionate. She was active in the Gaelic civil-rights movement in the 1970s, and supported the Long Kesh hunger strikers, writing an elegy on the death of Bobby Sands (1954–81), 'I m'áit dhúchais ó thuaidh'.

Maunsel & Company (1905–1923), publishers and dramatic agents founded by George Roberts (1873–1953), a Belfast poet and actor at the *Abbey Theatre, Stephen *Gwynn, and Joseph Maunsel *Hone, being named after the latter, who invested £2,000 in the company and became its chairman. The imprint changed to George Roberts, 1917–20, and Maunsel & Roberts, 1920–3.

Maxton, Hugh, see W. J. *McCormack.

Maxwell, Revd W[illiam] H[amilton] (1792–1850), novelist and historian. Born in Newry, Co. Down, and educated at TCD, he became Church of Ireland vicar of Balla, Co. Mayo. A lifelong enthusiasm for military life, apparently frustrated by parental wishes, resulted in *Stories of Waterloo* (1829) and *The Bivouac* (1837) which earned him the name of father of the military novel. His world of irresponsible young men let loose in the playground of colonial Ireland set the tone for much of Anglo-Irish fiction, notably the 'rollicking' novels of Charles *Lever who did not scruple to plagiarize him. Maxwell fought back with diffuse three-volume works such as *Hector O'Halloran and His Man Mark Antony O'Toole* (1842), *Captain O'Sullivan, a Gentleman on Half-Pay* (1846), and *Luck is Everything, or The Adventures of Brian O'Linn* (1856). *Wild Sports of the West* (1832), his best-known work, is a compendium of hunting-and-fishing lore and melodramatic stories of the marriage-by-capture variety. Max-

well's disapproval of rebellion was signalled to the *Young Irelanders in a work extravagantly titled *The Irish Movements, Their Rise, Progress, and Certain Termination, with a few Broad Hints to Patriots and Pikemen* (1848).

Mayne, Rutherford, see Samuel *Waddell.

Maynooth [St Patrick's College], see *universities.

Mayor of Windgap, The (1834), a novel by Michael *Banim, combining morality tale with melodrama in an idyllic evocation of rural Ireland in a past age. Set in Co. Kilkenny in 1779, it tells a sensational story of stolen inheritance involving jealousy, revenge, and parricide, and featuring a mysterious villain who is in fact an ex-pirate.

Meagher, Thomas Francis (1823–1867), nationalist orator. Born in Waterford and educated at Clongowes Wood and Stonyhurst, he acquired the name of 'Meagher of the Sword' after a speech of 1846 in Conciliation Hall when he refused to stigmatize militant nationalism, leading to the withdrawal of the *Young Irelanders from *O'Connell's constitutional Repeal Association. Transported to Tasmania with a commuted sentence, he escaped to America in 1852. He was afterwards made Secretary of Montana Territory, but drowned while travelling on a Mississippi riverboat in obscure circumstances.

Medb [or Medbh], legendary queen who leads the Connachta (men of Connacht) against the Ulaid (men of Ulster) to seize the great bull of Cooley in *Táin Bó Cuailnge*. Her name (literally 'the intoxicating, or intoxicated one') links her to the drink consumed by a new king at his *inauguration, supposedly bestowed as a token of true *kingship by the goddess of sovereignty, who also sleeps with him.

Medbh, Máighréad (1959–), poet; born in Newcastle West, Co. Limerick, educated there and at UCC. She worked mainly as a performance poet for years, but published *The Making of a Pagan* (1990) and *Tenant* (1999).

Meehan, Fr. C[harles] P[atrick] ('Clericus' of *The *Nation* (1812–1890), historical writer and literary editor. Born in Dublin and ordained at Rome, he served for many years as curate of SS Michael and John Church in Dublin and is best remembered as the confessor of *Mangan, whose poems and prose he edited in the 1880s.

Meehan, Paula (1955–), poet. Born in Dublin, she was educated at the Central Model Girls' School, and at TCD, before working at a variety of jobs. Her collections include: *Return and No Blame* (1984), *Reading the Sky* (1986), *The Man Who Was Marked by Winter* (1991), *Pillow Talk* (1994) and *Mysteries of the Home* (1996), a selection. Plays include *Mrs Sweeney* (1997).

Meldon, Maurice (1926–1958), playwright. Born in Dundalk, he lived and worked in Dublin as a civil servant. *House Under Green Shadows* (1951), a political allegory and a moody examination of the declining days of an *Anglo-Irish family, was staged at the *Abbey Theatre. *Purple Path to the Poppy Field* (1958), was his last play before his tragic death in a road accident.

Melmoth the Wanderer (1820), Charles Robert *Maturin's most celebrated novel. This Gothic romance allowed Maturin to indulge his taste for extravagance and complicated plots, and his talent for powerful story-telling.

John Melmoth, a student in early 19th-cent. Dublin, provides the narrative framework for five interwoven tales linked by the evocation of an earlier Melmoth, the eponymous wanderer who has bargained away his soul in return for 150 years of power and knowledge on earth. Translated into French and adopted as a cult figure by French romantic writers, *Melmoth* also provided an alias for Oscar *Wilde in exile.

Memorial (1973), a novel by Francis *Stuart. Set against a background of the *Troubles in *Northern Ireland, it involves Fintan Francis Sugrue, an ageing writer prone to fantasizing; Herra, a neurotic young girl who reawakens him as a sexual being and an artist; and Liz Considine, an alcoholic governess hired as Herra's chaperone when the couple set up home, insulated from the world's disapproval in a remote country house.

Men Withering, see *Stand and Give Challenge*.

Mercier, Vivian (1919–1989), bilingual literary historian. Born in Clara, Co. Offaly, he was educated at Portora Royal School, Enniskillen, and at TCD. He completed doctoral work on *Realism in Irish Fiction* before taking up a succession of teaching posts in American universities. In 1974 he married his second wife, the novelist Eilís *Dillon. *The Irish Comic Tradition* (1962) argued for an imaginative bond between Anglo-Irish literature and its Gaelic antecedents. The impact of Irish texts in translation on W. B. *Yeats and other authors of the *literary revival provided the subject-matter of *Modern Irish Literature* (1994).

Merriman, Brian (?1745–1805), poet. Born in west Co. Clare, and generally believed to have been illegitimate, he settled with his mother and step-father near Lough Graney in Feakle, where his long poem *Cúirt an Mheán-Oíche was written in about 1780, reputedly while he was laid up with an injured foot during a prolonged engagement before marriage. In Feakle he ran a *hedge school and a small farm, winning *RDS prizes for flax-growing in 1797, before moving in about 1802 to Limerick city, where he started a school of mathematics, assisted by his daughter. Only two other slight pieces from his hand are known, suggesting that he regarded himself primarily as a man of practical affairs in spite of his aptitude in the traditional forms of Gaelic poetry [see Irish *metrics]. For fragmentary accounts of his life, see Liam Ó Murchú (ed.), *Cúirt an Mheon-Oíche* (1982). A Merriman Summer School has been conducted in his native country since 1967.

Merugud Uilix maic Leirtis (*Wanderings of Ulysses son of Laertes*), a retelling in late Middle Irish (*c.*1200) of the story of the *Odyssey*, but in a form which bears little resemblance to the original [see *classical literature].

metrics, Anglo-Irish. Compared with most native English speech patterns, *Hiberno-English speech has longer and swifter rhythmic runs, with a far higher proportion of unstressed to stressed syllables. This feature was reflected in the development of Anglo-Irish metrics and was first felt through the rhythms of *folksongs. Drawing on Irish music, Thomas *Moore transformed the metrics of the Anglo-Irish lyric, and in doing so deeply influenced the rhythms of the English Romantic lyric, already to some extent Celticized by Burns and Scott. J. J. *Callanan, *Ferguson, *Mangan, Edward *Walsh, and others extended the development of a new metrics, spun in the creative tension between Gaelic and English,

coming closer than Moore to the energy of the amhrán metric in Irish poetry. George *Sigerson's *Bards of the Gael and Gall* (1897) outlined a history of Gaelic prosody and adapted Irish metrics to Anglo-Irish literature in a systematic if mechanical way in his translations of Irish verse. Yeats mastered the varied possibilities of Anglo-Irish rhythm, and continuing experimentation has been evident in the work of Austin *Clarke, Roibeárd *Ó Faracháin, Thomas *Kinsella, and Eoghan *Ó Tuairisc. John *Montague's spare and exact style owes something to the bardic model, as does Seamus *Heaney's use of the terse quatrain. See Seán Lucy, 'Metre and Movement in Anglo-Irish Verse', *Irish University Review*, 8 (1978).

metrics, Irish, can be divided into two formal categories, accentual and syllabic. Early Irish accentual verse, often described as *rosc (or roscad), is characterized by having a regular number of stressed feet but an irregular number of syllables in the lines. Syllabic Irish verse developed out of the older accentual forms but is distinguished by an equal number of syllables in the lines, and regularity of stress only in the line-endings, where it occurs in meeting the requirement for rhyme between final stressed words. Syllabic verse is generally organized in four-line strophes, whereas the number of lines in a rosc passage is not fixed. A later type of accentual verse is known as amhrán. The amhrán or song metres have a richly assonated stanzaic form, and are also accentual. Broadly speaking, the extant corpus of rosc, syllabic verse, and amhrán suggests three successive periods in the history of Irish versification. Among the very earliest surviving poems in Irish is the accentual (or rosc) eulogy known as *Amra Choluim Cille, apparently composed soon after the death of *Colum Cille in 597.

While there is no syllabic verse in existence that may be dated earlier than AD 650, such metres (núa-chrutha, 'new forms') dominated for the next millennium. The bulk of Old and Middle Irish verse consists of two types of metre, deibhidhe and rannaigheacht, and deibhidhe is by far the more popular metre in the period of classical Modern Irish. The emergence of strict dán díreach (classical syllabic verse) and the new literary standard of Classical Modern Irish (AD c.1200–1650) was the result of a thorough and systematic investigation of both the literary and spoken forms of the language current in the 12th cent. Accentual verse finally re-emerges in *manuscripts at the end of the 17th cent., but references to earlier makers of amhrán, and the highly developed form in which it appears, attest to a long, unrecorded tradition. See Gerard Murphy, *Early Irish Metrics* (1961).

Meyer, Kuno (1858–1919), Celtic scholar. Born in Hamburg, he left school at 15 and spent two years in Edinburgh. During his sojourn in Scotland he encountered spoken Gaelic in Arran, after which he studied Celtic in Leipzig under Ernst Windisch. In 1896 he founded *Zeitschrift für Celtische Philologie*, which became a major influence on Celtic learning. Deploring the neglect of Irish by learned institutions in Dublin, he founded there in 1903 a School of Irish Learning to train students in scholarly method and philology. Under his directorship the school attracted distinguished students from Britain, Europe, and America such as Robin *Flower and Julius Pokorny, while visiting scholars such as Rudolf *Thurneysen gave prestigious summer courses. Meyer succeeded Windisch in the Chair of Celtic at Berlin in 1911. *Selections from Ancient Irish Poetry* (1911) was acclaimed for its editorial scholarship and the sensitivity of his translations. See Seán Ó Lúing, *Kuno Meyer 1858–1919* (1992).

Mhac an tsaoi , Máire (1922–), poet. The daughter of the politician and author Seán McEntee (d. 1984) and a niece of the scholar and translator Monsignor Pádraig *de Brún, she was born in Dublin but spent long periods in the Kerry *Gaeltacht during childhood. She was educated at UCD and the Sorbonne and worked in the *DIAS, editing *Dhá Sgéal Artúraíochta* (1946) and assisting with Tomás *de Bhaldraithe's *English-Irish Dictionary*, before joining the Department of External Affairs. Her work unites self-expression with technical sophistication, as in *Margadh na Saoire* (1956), where she uses traditional forms and rhythms to write modern love poetry. In *Codladh an Ghaiscígh* (1973) and *An Galar Dubhach* (1980), the writing becomes more thoughtful as she contemplates change. She has also issued *A Concise History of Ireland* (1972) with her husband, Conor Cruise *O'Brien.

Mhic Gearailt, Muiris mac Dáibhí Dhuibh (*fl.* 1600–1626), *bardic poet; probably born in Co. Kerry. His father Dáibhí Dubh Mac Gearailt was killed in the Desmond Rebellion at Aghaloe near Killarney in 1581. The son's most substantial work, 'Mór idir na haimsearaibh [Times differ greatly]'— contrasts former stability with present chaos after *Kinsale. The extant works were edited by Nicholas Williams in 1979.

Michael of Kildare, Friar (*fl.* 1300), author of a 'Hymn' to Jesus in a 14th-cent. manuscript (MS *Harley 913) which also contains *The *Land of Cokaygne*.

Michelburne, John (1647–1721), an English soldier who was joint Governor with Revd George *Walker during the siege of Derry in 1689, and sole Governor when Walker left for London after the relief in July. Michelburne's wife and seven children died in the siege. He published *The Siege of Londonderry* (1705), illustrating the piety and valour of the garrison.

Midnight Court, The, see *Cúirt an Mheán-Oíche*.

Milesian Chief, The (1812), a novel by Charles Robert *Maturin. Set in the west of Ireland at the turn of the century, it tells the story of Connal O'Morven, the grandson of an Irish chieftain who has been dispossessed by the English Lord Montclare, and now lives in servitude on the edge of his former lands.

Milligan, Alice (1866–1953), poet and dramatist. Born in Omagh, she was educated at Methodist College, Belfast, and London University, returning to lecture on Irish history for the *Gaelic League. She edited *The *Shan Van Vocht* (1896–9) with Ethna *Carbery, and wrote some early heroic plays for the Irish Literary Theatre [see *Abbey Theatre], *The Last of the Fianna* (1900) and *The Daughter of Donagh* (1902). Her poetry collection *Hero Lays* (1908) was seen as a clarion call to literary nationalism.

Milliken (or Millikin), Richard Alfred (1767–1815), author of the burlesque poem 'The Groves of Blarney'. Born in Castlemartyr, Co. Cork, he became a Dublin solicitor and published some poetry, fiction, and drama, including *The Slave of Surinam* (1810), a tale of cruelty, and *Darby in Arms* (1810), an Irish affray which played in Dublin. The poem for which he is remembered is a mock-idyll concerning the well-appointed estate of Lady Arabella Jeffreys, proprietor of Blarney Castle.

Millionairess, The (1936), a play by George Bernard *Shaw. The heiress Epifania Fitzfossenden leaves her husband Alastair, giving him her fortune, but she tires quickly of her lover, Adrian, and leaves him for an Egyptian doctor.

Mills, Billy (1954–), poet; born in Dublin and educated there and the Open University, he worked in Barcelona and Eastbourne teaching English. He returned to Ireland and settled in Limerick. He founded hardPressed Poetry with Catherine *Walsh. Amongst his publications are *Genesis and Home* (1985), *Triple Helix* (1987), *Letters from Barcelona* (1990), *Tiny Pieces* (1998), and *A Small Book of Songs* (1999).

Milne, [Charles] Ewart (1903–1987), poet. Born in Dublin and educated in Christ Church Grammar School, he ran away to sea and subsequently became a journalist. He rejected his Anglo-Irish background, and fought on the Republican side in Spain, 1937–41. His fourteen volumes of poetry show a restless variety. The early books, *Forty North Forty West* (1938) and *Listen Mangan* (1941), indicate the influence of *Yeats's high style. *Time Stopped* (1967) consists of a loosely-handled poem sequence with prose intermissions, dealing with his second wife's infidelity which he learnt of after her death in 1964.

Miriam Lucas (1912), a novel by Canon Patrick *Sheehan addressing socialist issues from a Catholic standpoint. The heroine, a Catholic, is forced off her estate by an unscrupulous guardian who compels her to join him in Dublin. Miriam espouses the cause of the workers in his transport company.

Mister Johnson (1939), a novel by Joyce *Cary set in northern Nigeria. Johnson, a black clerk in the district administration, is dismissed for misappropriation of funds and resorts to theft. Accidentally knifing the brutal English ex-serviceman who runs the government store, he is sentenced to be hanged, but the District Officer, Rudbeck, shoots Johnson at his own request.

Mitchel, John (1815–1875), journalist, revolutionary, and historian. Born in Dungiven, Co. Derry, son of a Trinitarian minister, he was educated in Newry and at TCD. In 1843 he began to write for The *Nation, developing a distinctive style of biting satire using a neo-biblical vocabulary and forceful rhetorical periods influenced by Thomas *Carlyle. In 1847 he became the editor. His militancy alienated many moderate nationalists, however, and he left to found The United Irishman. He was transported for treason-felony in May 1848. His Jail Journal, or Five Years in British Prisons (1854) was written in enforced isolation as he was being shipped to Van Diemen's Land (Tasmania). Its emotive identification of the individual and the nation made it a central text of Irish nationalism. In 1853 he escaped from Australia and settled in the USA. He reworked his journalism of the 1840s in The Last Conquest of Ireland (Perhaps) (1861) and The History of Ireland (1868), books that impute active malevolence to the English in Ireland, treating the *Famine as deliberate genocide. He was imprisoned in the late 1860s for articles supporting the use of slavery and the Southern States. See Malcolm Brown, The Politics of Irish Literature (1972).

Mitchell, Susan [Langstaff] (1866–1926), editor and poet. Born in Carrick-on-Shannon, Co. Leitrim, she was adopted by aunts in Dublin on the death of her father. In 1900 she stayed with the *Yeats family in London and found herself surrounded by participants in the *literary revival. Her witty observation of the literary scene bore fruit in

Aids to the Immortality of Certain Persons in Ireland Charitably Administered (1908), a collection of pasquinades in seemingly offhand but very well-made verses. Her short study of the novelist in George Moore (1916) probed his character and his self-portrayal of it.

Mo Bhealach Féin (1940), a fictionalized autobiography by Seosamh *Mac Grianna, defiantly setting the values of his native Donegal against the modern world.

Modest Proposal, A (1729), a pamphlet by Jonathan *Swift on Ireland, written during the summer of 1729. In form and tone it resembles a conventional philanthropic appeal to solve Ireland's economic crisis, but Swift's anonymous speaker suggests a barbarous plan, to cannibalize the nation's children. It is a masterpiece of rhetorical irony, a disturbing fiction which marks the end of Swift's pamphleteering role on national affairs after a decade of passionate involvement.

Moffat, William, see *Hesperi-Neso-Graphia.

Molloy (in French, 1951; in English, translated with Patrick Bowles, 1954), a novel by Samuel *Beckett, first of a trilogy that includes *Malone Dies and *The Unnamable. The title-character is in his mother's room, writing an account of how he got there which confusedly describes his setting off on a bicycle, before being arrested by a policeman and taken home by a Mrs Lousse. In the second part of the novel, a detective called Moran relates how he hunts for Molloy.

Molloy, Charles (1690–1767), dramatist; born in Dublin and educated in TCD before going to London where he studied law. He wrote three successful comedies, The Perplexed Couple (1715),

The Coquette (1718), and *The Half-Pay Officers* (1720).

Molloy, M[ichael] J[oseph] (1917–1994), playwright and farmer; born Milltown, Co. Galway, educated St Jarlath's College, Tuam. Preparations for the priesthood at St Columba's College, Derry, were terminated by ill health. His enthusiasm for drama stemmed from a childhood visit to the *Abbey, where his first work, *The Old Road*, was produced in 1943. The play involves a romantic plot, eccentric characters, and colourful language—all elements which recall the works of J. M. *Synge, whom he greatly admired. It focuses on the inevitability of emigration in the poverty-stricken west of Ireland, a theme to which Molloy returned in *The *Wood of the Whispering* (1953) and other works. *The Visiting House* (1946), a celebration of traditional Irish values on the verge of extinction, reveals Molloy's deep interest in story-telling. *The Paddy Pedlar* (1952), a macabre story about the contents of the pedlar's sack, also draws successfully on the folk imagination. *The *King of Friday's Men* (1948), is a tangled love-story and his best-known play, *Petticoat Loose* (1979), is likewise set in a historical period—1822—and deals with the Church's opposition to rural superstition. Molloy shows sympathetic insight into lives of desperate loneliness, and directs his anger against the authorities who permitted the depopulation of the west of Ireland.

Molyneux, William (1656–1698), scientist and political writer. Born in Dublin and educated at TCD and the Middle Temple, he was Surveyor-General and Chief Engineer during 1684–8 and again after 1691. A founder of the Dublin Philosophical Society (later *RDS), he published a translation of Descartes's *Meditations* (1680), but subsequently concentrated on optics and mathematics, publishing *Sciothericum Telescopicum* (1686) and *Dioptrica Nova* (1692). He corresponded with Locke from 1692 until his death, earning a mention in the second edition of the *Essay Concerning Human Understanding*. His most famous work, *The Case of Ireland's being Bound by Acts of Parliament in England, Stated* (1698), defends the autonomy of the *Irish Parliament by appealing to rights inherited from the Gaelic rulers of the Middle Ages, to the English ancestry of the contemporary Protestant population, and to natural rights. The *Case* became an influential statement of patriot claims, and was widely reprinted both in Ireland and America.

Monahan, Noel (1947–), poet; born in Dublin, he was educated at St Patrick's College and TCD and became a teacher until 1999. *Opposite Walls* (1991) was followed by *Snowfire* (1995), and *Curse of the Birds* (2000).

Monasterboice (Mainistir Bhuithe), a monastic foundation established by St Buithe in the 5th cent. Lying between Drogheda and Dundalk in Co. Louth, it is noted for its round tower and high crosses. In the 11th cent. the monastery was a centre of monastic learning under *Flann Mainistrech.

monasticism was the dominant form of ecclesiastical and scholarly life in Ireland from the 6th to the 12th cents., when the *bardic schools emerged, and remained central to Gaelic society until the 16th cent., when the Dissolution of the Monasteries associated with the English Reformation was extended by Crown authorities to Ireland. The foundations of the Norman period [see *Norman invasion], such as the Cistercian abbeys at Mellifont and Jerpoint, reflected the advent of Continental influence in Ireland. In the earlier period, the communities associated with the Celtic Church in Ireland were fully integrated with native Christian culture in its social and literary aspects. The main foundations were *Clonmacnoise, said to have been founded by St *Ciarán; *Iona, founded by St *Colum Cille; *Glendalough, founded by St Kevin; and *Monasterboice, founded by St Buithe. Most of the earliest churches of Ireland were either small communities living a religious life, or tiny churches where a single cleric served the immediate community. The 7th cent. saw the growth of monastic communities in which clergy led a communal life. Clustered around such communities were agricultural dependants, craftsmen, and traders, forming small monastic towns. Monastic churches, large and small, maintained schools and cultivated both the copying of books and writing of literature. By the 8th cent. copies of many books composed in Irish schools had reached monastic libraries in France, Germany, Switzerland, and Italy. The high level of intellectual activity in the Irish monasteries of this period is evident from the contemporary development of *law as a civic discipline. Legal tracts in Latin and Irish during the 7th, 8th, and 9th cents. reveal a close examination of biblical law, with some traces of Roman jurisprudence. In this environment Irish writing was adapted to the Latin alphabet. The saga literature of Ireland which has survived from earliest times owes its preservation to the monastic scriptoria.

Monks of the Screw (?1780–1795), a Dublin literary and social club which met in John Philpot *Curran's home, 'The Priory'. Monastic dress was worn.

Montague, John (1929–), poet. Born in Brooklyn, New York, and sent at the age of 4 to live with aunts in Garvaghey, Co. Tyrone, he was educated at St Patrick's College, Armagh, UCD, and Yale. He lived in Paris and taught at Berkeley and at UCC. His first four volumes of poetry—*Forms of Exile* (1958), *Poisoned Lands* (1961), *A Chosen Light* (1967), and *Tides* (1970)—examine personal experience, family, and community, expressing disaffection with a puritanical Ireland and demystifying the romantic myths of the past. In *The Rough Field* (1972) Montague adapts the panoramic but individualized technique of the American epic devised by Walt Whitman and William Carlos Williams in order to examine the disintegration of Ulster life. An elegiac tone recalling *Goldsmith's *The *Deserted Village* is mixed with bitterness and anger as the poet contemplates Ulster's colonial history. His perspective is nationalist, the poetry expressing an intensely personal realization of historical experience, but seeking also to discover a mythic dimension in Irish rural life. Composed of a series of lyrics, the poem ranges from the townland of Garvaghey (from the Irish garbhachadh, 'a rough field') to Paris and New York. *A Slow Dance* (1975) contains poems about nature as a healing power, but loss and death are never far away in the book's harsh vision of the dance of life and death. *The Great Cloak* (1978), a collection of love-poems, sheds the burden of history. *The Dead Kingdom* (1984) returns to *The Rough Field*'s concerns with family and politics. *Mount Eagle* (1989) confirms an achieved serenity. *Time in Armagh* (1993), *Border Sick Call* (1995), and *Smashing the Piano* (1999), bring a stoical composure and a humane perspective to bear on the traumas of personal and community history. Montague's characteristic short-lined verse, a modernist version of *bardic poetry, reflects the effort made to balance intensity and economy. Montague also published *Death of a Chieftain* (1964), a collection of nine stories; and *The Lost Notebook* (1987), a novella dealing with the loss of innocence. *The Figure in the Cave* (1990) collects reminiscences and literary essays.

Montgomery, Leslie A., see Lynn *Doyle.

Mooney, Martin (1964–), poet; born in Belfast, educated at QUB. *Grub* (1993) introduced his vernacular energy, also evident in *Bonfire Makers* (1995); these were followed by *Rasputin and his Children* (2000).

Moon in the Yellow River, The (1931), a play by Denis *Johnston dealing with the Irish response to modernization. Tausch, a German engineer, is appointed by the *Irish State to oversee the first hydro-electric scheme. Blake, a likeable revolutionary, tries to blow up the generator and is shot.

Moonlight, The (1946), a novel by Joyce *Cary. The Vann girls, Rose, Bessie, and Ella, worship their hypocritically Victorian father. While her sisters carry out his wishes, Ella looks after the ailing Rose, whom she hates. When Rose kills herself Ella commits suicide also, consumed by guilt.

Moore, Brian (1921–1999), novelist. Born in Belfast into a Catholic family, he did not follow his father and elder brother into medicine, and after leaving St Malachy's College in 1938 joined the Air Raid Precautions Unit in 1940, an experience reflected in *The Emperor of Ice-Cream* (1965). In 1943 he enlisted in the British Ministry of War Transport, working in North Africa and, later, as a port official with the Allied occupation forces in Naples and Marseilles. Moore emigrated to Canada in 1948 and took citizenship in 1953. His experiences as a new immigrant, when he took uncongenial work as a proof-reader, gave him material for *The Luck of Ginger Coffey* (1960). In 1951 he married Jacqueline Sirois; he moved to the USA in 1959, first to Long Island and New York, then to Malibu, California, where he lived with his second wife, Jean Denney,

whom he married in 1967. In addition to novels, he has written short stories and film scripts. *Judith Hearne* (1955), republished as *The *Lonely Passion of Judith Hearne* (1956), *The *Feast of Lupercal* (1957), and *The Emperor of Ice-Cream*, all novels set in Belfast, deal with the struggle to achieve personal autonomy in a narrowly religious and repressive society. The determinism of these first novels, in which individual identity is virtually overwhelmed by religious, social, and family pressures, is undercut in *An Answer From Limbo* (1962), *I Am Mary Dunne* (1968), and *Fergus* (1970). Set in North America, these works begin a reassessment, where responsibility for one's adult being cannot be deterministically apportioned to nurture. The quasi-fictional *The Revolution Script*, dealing with the kidnapping and murder of a Quebec politician, appeared in 1971 and the novella *Catholics* in 1972. The protagonist of *The *Mangan Inheritance* (1979) confronts the image of what he could become were he to repudiate traditional familial values and follow his fantasy of artistic self-fulfilment. *The Temptation of Eileen Hughes* (1981) was followed by three novels involving different attitudes to religious belief and authority, *Cold Heaven* (1983), the historical novel *Black Robe* (1985), set in 17th-cent. Canada, and *The *Colour of Blood* (1987), set in a Soviet bloc country. *Lies of Silence* (1990) and *No Other Life* (1993) embody Moore's concern with ethical questions in a political context. The first, a thriller set in the contemporary Ulster *Troubles, centres on the moral dilemma of a man forced to drive a bomb to a human target while his wife is held hostage. In *No Other Life*, a retired white missionary priest examines his role in the education and rise of a messianic Caribbean leader. The novel is loosely based on contemporary events in Haiti. In *The Statement* (1995) Moore explores the mentality and the combination of patriotism and compromise that lead a Nazi sympathizer in Vichy France to collaborate with brutality. *The Magician's Wife* (1997) is concerned with showing the human cost of sacrificing personal integrity for vanity and ambition. When he died Moore was working on a novel dealing with the poet Rimbaud's years in the desert, after relinquishing his art. See Jo O'Donoghue, *Brian Moore: A Critical Study* (1990).

Moore, F[rancis] F[frankfort]

(1855–1931), novelist. Although born in Limerick, he was raised and educated in Belfast, before moving to work in London, 1876–92. Throughout his career he issued a book or more each year, the early ones being mostly set in the South Seas (*Under Hatches*, 1888; *From the Bush to the Breakers*, 1893). He was most successful with *I Forbid the Banns* (1893), a play about sectarian division, and wrote 18th cent. studies such as *The Jessamy Bride* (1897), on Dr Johnson's circle. *The Truth About Ulster* (1914) illustrates the dangers of sectarianism in relation to social history. He died at Lewes in Suffolk.

Moore, George [Augustus] (1852–

1933), novelist. Born at Moore Hall, Ballyglass, Co. Mayo, he was the eldest son of George Henry Moore (d. 1870), Nationalist MP, Catholic landowner, racehorse trainer, and one-time friend of Maria *Edgeworth. Moore went briefly to Oscott College, a minor Catholic public school near Birmingham. Left unsupervised and largely in the company of stable-boys at Moore Hall, he nurtured the ambition of becoming a jockey. Spared a military career by his father's death, and heir to 12,000 acres, Moore left for Paris in 1873, determined to be a painter. Moore came to realize that he had little talent for painting and decided to write instead. He met Mallarmé, at whose suggestion he went to the Nouvelle Athènes in Montmartre, a café and a meeting-place for the

Impressionists and their friends. There he met Manet (who painted him three times), Degas, and others. Poor harvests and rent failures in the west of Ireland forced Moore to return to England in late 1879. Having begun as a poet he turned to prose and resolved to follow Zola's naturalistic experiments. His first novel, *A Modern Lover* (1883), dealt with the exploitation of women by an unscrupulous artist, and was banned by Mudie's commercial library. Undeterred, he brought out *A *Mummer's Wife* (1885) with Henry Vizetelly, Zola's publisher in English, using a one-volume format aimed at book-buyers rather than borrowers. The driving-force of *A *Drama in Muslin* (1886) is his awareness of various forms of social injustice in Ireland. At Moore Hall he found a changed and changing world. The age of deference was over; he half-feared, half-despised his tenants, and he recognized that landlords like himself had no future. He outraged nationalist opinion in *Parnell and His Island* (1887), a collection of bitterly satirical essays, mixing pity and contempt, with the latter making the stronger impression. In *The Confessions of a Young Man* (1888) he detached himself even further from the places, people, and ideals of his childhood and youth, striking instead the pose of an aesthete. Moore wrote articles on literature and art for a number of magazines, later collected as *Impressions and Opinions* (1889) and *Modern Painting* (1893). He published two unsuccessful novels, *Mike Fletcher* (1889) and *Vain Fortune* (1891), but with the publication of *Esther Waters* (1894) he established himself as a writer with a keen awareness of the vulnerability of women in society. He made no attempt to repeat his success. Instead he tried his hand as a playwright and continued to experiment with short fiction, as in *Celibates* (1895), a book of stories about people whom life has overcome. He embarked on two musical novels,

Evelyn Innes (1898) and *Sister Teresa* (1901). Around this time he first met Maud Burke, later Lady Cunard, for whom he was to have a deep and lasting affection. Edward *Martyn, his cousin and childhood friend, introduced him to W. B. *Yeats in 1897, when Moore became an unlikely ally in the attempt to establish an Irish national theatre [see *Abbey Theatre]. Moore had some experience with the Independent Theatre in London, and he helped Martyn with his play *The Tale of a Town* (later rewritten as *The *Bending of the Bough*, 1900). In 1901 he moved to Dublin and took a house in Upper Ely Place. However, Moore had little patience with Yeats's idea of heroic drama and they quarrelled. Though not an Irish-speaker himself, he threw himself behind the language movement, writing *The *Untilled Field* (1903) for translation into Irish, to be used by the *Gaelic League. This book forced him to analyse the state of Ireland, his motives in returning, and the chances of success for the *literary revival. In 1903, wishing to draw attention to the reactionary nature of Irish *Catholicism, he declared himself a Protestant in *The Irish Times*. However, *The *Lake* (1905) dealt earnestly with the subject of belief and religious conviction. Here Moore developed the 'melodic line', a self-consciously fluid rhythmic prose based on oral speech patterns, an effect not unlike the stream-of-consciousness technique pioneered in *Joyce's *Ulysses*. *Hail and Farewell*, his three-volume history of the revival, is his comic masterpiece. The account of family and childhood caused a breach with his brother Maurice which was never fully healed. After the first volume was published (*Ave*, 1911), he decided it would be tactless to stay on in Dublin and by the time the others appeared (*Salve*, 1912; *Vale*, 1914) he was again settled in London. Moore spent the remaining twenty-three years of his life at 121 Ebury St. In 1913 he travelled to the Holy Land to research the background for *The *Brook Kerith* (1916). Amongst his later works are: *A *Story Teller's Holiday* (1918), *Héloïse and Abelard* (1921), the conversational memoirs *Avowals* (1919), and *Conversations in Ebury Street* (1924). With the burning of Moore Hall in February 1923, Moore lost his last link with Ireland and declared it was not a country for a gentleman. While writing *Aphrodite in Aulis* he became ill with uraemia, but he continued working to the end. At his own request his ashes were buried on Castle Island in Lough Carra, across the lake from Moore Hall. See Richard Cave, *A Study of the Novels of George Moore* (1978).

Moore, Thomas (1779–1852), poet; born in Aungier St., Dublin, the son of a Catholic merchant. He was educated at TCD, where he befriended the *United Irishman Robert *Emmet. Moore's first book, a translation of the *Odes of Anacreon* (1800), appealed to the Prince of Wales, who agreed to have the volume dedicated to him. *The Poetical Works of the Late Thomas Little Esq.* (1801) purported to be a collection of verses by a youthful amatory poet who died at 21. Byron met him in 1811, and they became close friends. *Epistles, Odes, and Other Poems* (1806) reflect his experiences of the Caribbean and America. When Francis Jeffrey savaged the book in the *Edinburgh Review*, Moore challenged him to a duel, which was stopped in time. Moore's *Irish Melodies*, based on the airs recorded by Edward *Bunting, was first issued in two volumes in 1808 and ran to an additional eight volumes up to 1834. The early numbers evoke leaders of the 1798 Rebellion, in words and music full of sorrowing futility. Beneath the emotional pathos, there was often the veiled hint of sedition and a warning that violence would break out again in

Ireland if justice were not done to the Irish Catholics. *National Airs* (6 vols., 1818–28) were based on music from other *folksong traditions than the Irish. *Corruption and Intolerance* (1808), two long poems in harsh rhyming couplets, rage against the machinations employed to pass the Act of *Union and the intolerance in Anglo-Irish relations. *A Letter to the Roman Catholics of Dublin* (1810) argued for conciliation. From 1808 Moore participated in the Kilkenny theatre festival, and there he met Elizabeth Dyke, an actress whom he married in 1811 when she was 16. *Intercepted Letters, or The Two-Penny Post Bag* (1813), a collection of squibs and comic verse, met with success, its mockery of court vanity and anti-Catholic prejudice appealing to the liberal reformers who gathered at Holland House in London. *Lallah Rookh* (1817) was greeted with enthusiastic acclaim on publication, though some critics reverted to old charges of licentiousness and impiety. A trip to France inspired *The Fudge Family in Paris* (1818), a collection of verse letters to different correspondents, mocking British anti-Napoleonic policy of the time. Deeply in debt, Moore left for the financial asylum of the Continent with Lord John Russell, his future editor and later Prime Minister. In Venice Byron gave him the manuscript of his projected *Memoirs*. On his return to England he published *The Loves of the Angels* (1822), a poem which sought to describe the effects of original sin. *Fables for the Holy Alliance* (1823) attacked the post-Napoleonic *entente* between Russia and Austria. *Memoirs of Captain Rock, the Celebrated Irish Chieftain* (1824) was a history of Ireland from the standpoint of a Whiteboy [see *secret societies], which argued that English misrule begets Irish violence. On Byron's death in 1824 a dispute arose about the *Memoirs*. At the behest of Byron's widow and half-sister, these

were burnt in the London office of the publisher John Murray. Moore's *Memoirs of the Life of the Right Honourable Richard Brinsley Sheridan* (1825) did not spare the Prince Regent for his neglect of the dying *Sheridan. *Letters and Journals of Lord Byron, with Notices of his Life* (2 vols., 1830) was based on recollections of Byron. Thereafter, Moore began work on a *Life of Lord Edward Fitzgerald* (1831). In 1832 Gerald *Griffin and his brother William tried to persuade Moore to stand as an MP for Limerick as part of the *Repeal campaign, but he declined. Next he embarked upon a four-volume *History of Ireland* (1935–46), but his scholarship, minute and searching in its way, did not have the command of the professional. *The Poetical Works of Thomas Moore*, collected by himself, in ten volumes, was issued in 1841. *The Memoirs, Journal, and Correspondence* (1853–6) were edited by his friend Russell, and savaged by John Wilson *Croker, reviewing in *The Critical Quarterly*. His reputation declined swiftly after his death and his work has often been trivialized. See Terence de Vere White, *Tom Moore: The Irish Poet* (1977).

Moran, D[avid] P[atrick] (1869–1936), proprietor and editor of *The Leader* newspaper from 1900. He was born in Manor in Co. Waterford and educated at Castleknock College near Dublin before working as a journalist in London, where he was a member of the Irish Literary Society [see *literary revival]. He returned to Ireland in order to promote cultural and economic nationalism after the formation of the *Gaelic League, and wrote *The Philosophy of Irish-Ireland* (1905). There and in the columns of his paper, Moran developed a powerful vocabulary of disparagement, notably the terms 'shoneen', and 'West-Briton' which became widely current among supporters of *Sinn Féin and the *GAA. Moran looked towards an industrialized, Gaelic-speaking Ireland free of English influence.

More Pricks than Kicks (1934), a collection of short stories by Samuel *Beckett dealing with episodes in the life of Belacqua Shuah, a torpid TCD student of modern languages who is named after a slothful character in Dante's *Purgatorio*.

Morgan, Lady (née Sydney Owenson) (?1776–1859), novelist; born at sea, and educated at the Huguenot school in Clontarf, Co. Dublin. As a girl she accompanied her widower father, the actor-manager Robert *Owenson, on his theatrical tours of Ireland. Attracting attention first by her harp-playing, she published *Twelve Original Hibernian Melodies* (1805) which set English words to Irish tunes. Two early novels, *St Clair, or the Heiress of Desmond* (1803), an imitation of Goethe's *Sorrows of Young Werther*, and *The Novice of Dominick* (1805), were followed by *The *Wild Irish Girl* (1806), which launched her as a social celebrity. Becoming a member of the Marquis of Abercorn's household, she met and subsequently married (1812) Sir Charles Morgan, her patron's surgeon. Other novels were: *O'Donnel* (1814), *Florence Macarthy* (1818), and *The *O'Briens and the O'Flaherties* (1827). *France* (1817) and *Italy* (1821) dealt with travel, politics, and society. In 1837 she became the first female recipient of a literary pension. See Mary Campbell, *Lady Morgan: The Life and Times of Sydney Owenson* (1988).

Morrígan, see *mythological cycle.

Morrison, Danny (1953–), novelist; born in Belfast and educated there he was interned in Long Kesh in 1972. On his release in 1975 he edited Sinn Féin's *Republican News* and subsequently *An Phoblacht/Republican News*. He was director of publicity for Sinn Féin from

1979 to 1990 when he was arrested for involvement in *IRA activities and held for eight years. *West Belfast* (1989) was a novel of childhood and innocence against a *Troubles background; *On the Back of a Swallow* (1994) explores homosexual love; while *The Wrong Man* (1997) is a powerful evocation of betrayal, deceit, and guilt. *Then the Walls Came Down* (1999) is an autobiography based on prison journals and letters.

Morrison, Van [George Ivan] (1945–), musician. Born in Belfast, the son of a shipyard worker and part-time jazz musician, he was educated at Elm Grove and Orangefield schools before leaving in 1960. By 1964 he was touring with a band called The Monarchs in Germany, and in that year formed Them, whose single 'Gloria' entered the charts. In 1967 he went to the USA, where he produced the album *Blowin' Your Mind*, followed by many others, including *Astral Weeks* (1968), *Moondance* (1970), *Into the Music* (1979) *Beautiful Vision* (1982), *Poetic Champions Compose* (1987), *Irish Heartbeat* (1988), *Enlightenment* (1990), and *Too Long in Exile* (1993). Throughout his work he evokes the longing and hope of his Belfast childhood.

Morrow, Harry C., see Gerald *MacNamara.

Morrow, John (1930–), novelist. Born in Belfast, and educated there. His novels include *The Confessions of Proinsias O'Toole* (1977), a spicily colloquial picaresque novel set in the Belfast of the Northern *Troubles, and *The Essex Factor* (1982).

Moryson, Fynes, see Anglo-Irish *Chronicles.

'Mother, A', a story in James *Joyce's *Dubliners* (1914), written in 1905, in which Mrs Kearney relaunches her social aspirations in the atmosphere of the Irish *literary revival.

Moxley, Gina (1957–), playwright; born in Cork, she was educated at Crawford Municipal School of Art. Her first play, which made daring use of Cork *Hiberno-English, was *Danti-Dan* (1995) followed by *Dog House* (1997), and *Toupees and Snare Drums* (1998).

Mr. Gilhooley (1926), a novel by Liam *O'Flaherty portraying a middle-aged sensualist adrift in Dublin.

Mrs Warren's Profession (1902), a play [see *Plays Pleasant . . .] by George Bernard *Shaw dealing with prostitution.

Muircheartach mac Liacc (or Liag) (d. 1015), poet and chief ollam [see áes dána] to *Brian Bóroime, a life of whom tradition credits him with writing, as well as a chronology of the Munster wars in which his patron was involved.

Muirchú moccu Machthéní (fl. 700), author of a Latin Life of St *Patrick preserved in the *Book of Armagh and elsewhere, born probably near Armagh. Muirchú's Life depicts St Patrick as a heroic Christian figure subduing the pagan *druids at *Tara.

Muldoon, Paul (1955–), poet. Born in Eglish, Co. Armagh, raised near Moy, Co. Tyrone, and educated at St Patrick's College, Maghera, and QUB. He worked as a radio producer with BBC Ulster before moving on to teach at Princeton. In *New Weather* (1973) the exigencies of plot and even naming are resisted in a search for linguistic openness. In *Mules* (1977), he is 'in two minds', rejecting the polarities of life in *Northern Ireland. *Why Brownlee Left* (1980) and *Quoof* (1983) speculate on the nature of perception, while *Meeting the British* (1987) is 'all very Ovidian' in its transformation of the ordinary. *Madoc: A Mystery* (1990), based on Robert Southey's epic *Madoc* (1806), makes daring use of linguistic and cultural linkages. *The Annals of Chile* (1994) contains a long poem-sequence on childhood and adolescence, entitled 'Yarrow'. *Hay* (1998) is attentive to the tensions that underlie revolution and rebellion.

Mulholland, Rosa (Lady Gilbert) (1841–1921), novelist. She was born into a Belfast medical family and became the wife of Sir John *Gilbert. Her novels seek to advance a version of Irish Catholic life acceptable to Victorian sensibilities. An early success, *The Wild Birds of Killeevy* (1883), shows Irish people holding their own in international adventure. *Marcella Grace* (1886) sees the creation of a Catholic gentry as a solution to the Land War [see *Land League].

Mulkerns, Val[entine] (1925–), novelist and short-story writer, born in Dublin. Her first short stories appeared in the The *Bell in the early 1950s. *Antiquities* (1978) depicts three generations of the Mullen family. *An Idle Woman and Other Stories* (1980) deals with the private and public aspects of Irish society. *Very Like a Whale* (1986) charts the changes that a young man encounters when he returns to Dublin.

Mullen, Michael J. (1937–), novelist in English and Irish. Born in Castlebar, Co. Mayo, he was educated in the local national school, then at Mallow and Waterford Training College before becoming a teacher in 1958. His first novel, *Kelly* (1981), was followed by a series of fictions dealing with aspects of Irish history and cultural identity, among them *Festival of Fools* (1984), *The Hungry Land* (1986), *Rites of Inheritance* (1990), and *The House of Mirrors* (1992). Others, such as *Sea Wolves from the North* (1983) and *Scáth na nAingeal* (1997), are for children.

Mummer's Wife, A (1885), a novel by George *Moore, concerning men's victimization of women.

Mungo's Mansion (1946), a play by Walter *Macken, first produced by the *Abbey Theatre, and set in the Galway tenement home of Mungo King who resists a move to newer corporation housing.

Murdoch, [Jean] Iris (1919–1999), philosopher and novelist. Born in Dublin, of Anglo-Irish parents, she was brought up in London and educated at Badminton and Somerville College, Oxford. From 1948 to 1963 she was Fellow and Tutor in Philosophy at St Anne's College, Oxford. Only two of her novels are set in Ireland, *The *Unicorn* (1963) and *The *Red and the Green* (1965); nevertheless, Irish people appear more or less prominently in many of her works. Some of these Irish references are ironic or playful, occasionally using stereotypes of charm and irresponsibility, but the country also appears to fascinate her as a place of moral decisiveness. In *Under the Net* (1954) the hero's friend Finn retreats from the uncertainties of London to his home country. In *The Philosopher's Pupil* (1983) Emma is preoccupied with conflict in Ireland. Her early novels, *Under the Net, The Flight from the Enchanter* (1956), *The Sandcastle* (1957), *The Bell* (1958), *A Severed Head* (1961), and *An Unofficial Rose* (1962), deal with the discovery of freedom and purpose. Her next group of novels, *The Unicorn, The Italian Girl* (1964), *The Red and the Green*, and *The Time of the Angels* (1966), explore in a highly wrought manner questions of self-assertion, artistic creativity, issues of faith, and political conviction. *The Nice and the Good* (1968) belongs with the third phase of her work, which shows a more subtle discrimination of character and morality. Works of this period are *A Fairly Honourable Defeat*

(1970); *The *Black Prince* (1973); and the outstanding *The *Sea, The Sea* (1978). Her later works, *Nuns and Soldiers* (1980), *The Philosopher's Pupil, The Good Apprentice* (1985), *The Message to the Planet* (1989), and *The Green Knight* (1993) show a looser structure, continuing to investigate the problem of evil. Her philosophical works include *Sartre* (1953) and *Metaphysics as a Guide to Morals* (1992). See Peter J. Conradi, *Iris Murdoch: The Saint and the Artist* (1986).

Murphy (1938), a burlesque novel by Samuel *Beckett, set in London, in which an Irishman attempts to free himself from his attachments in a series of contrivances that parody the mind/body distinction in Cartesian philosophy.

Murphy, Arthur (1727–1805), actor and dramatist. Born in Cloonyquin, Co. Roscommon, the son of a merchant who died at sea, he was educated in France at St Omer Jesuit College, 1738–44, and spent two years clerking in Cork, 1747–9. He left Ireland and found employment with a banking house in London. During 1752–4 he launched and edited the *Gray's Inn Journal*. He qualified as a barrister at Lincoln's Inn and practised successfully until 1788, when deafness forced his retirement. In 1756 he wrote a Drury Lane farce called *The Apprentice* and earned £800 by it. This was followed by *An Englishman from Paris* (1756). *The Upholsterer, or What News?* (1757) was a farce on tradesmen meddling in politics. Murphy tried his hand at tragedy with *The Orphan of China* (1755). His later plays include *The Way to Keep Him* (1760), *The Citizen* (1761), and *Three Weeks After Marriage* (1776). He also attempted classical themes in *Zenobia* (1768) and *Arminius*, a pro-war play which secured him a royal pension in 1798. Murphy made little overt use of his Irish background, beyond a *stage-Irishman in *The Apprentice* who declaims

Othello in *Hiberno-English. His Latin scholarship found expression in translations such as the *Works of Sallust* (1793). See Richard B. Schwartz, *The Plays of Arthur Murphy* (4 vols., 1979).

Murphy, Dervla (1931–), travel writer; born in Lismore, Co. Waterford, where she remained until the death of her parents before setting out on an intrepid bicycle journey through Afghanistan to India. Her first book, *Full Tilt* (1965), was followed by *Tibetan Foothold* (1966), *In Ethiopa with a Mule* (1968), *On a Shoestring to Coorg* (1976), and *Where the Indus Is Young* (1977).

Murphy, Gerard (1900–1959), scholar; born in Co. Monaghan and educated at UCD where he became Professor of the History of Celtic Literature from 1918. He made a special study of the *Fionn cycle, publishing *Ossianic Lore and the Romantic Tales of Medieval Ireland* (1955) and editing volumes ii and iii of *Duanaire Finn*. He also edited and translated *Early Irish Lyrics* (1956).

Murphy, Gerry (1952–), poet; born in Cork and educated at UCC, worked as a lifeguard in the Mayfield Leisure Centre. He published *A Small Fat Boy Walking Backwards* (1985), followed by *Rio de la Plata and All That* (1993), *The Empty Quarter* (1995) and *Extracts from the Lost Log-Book of Christopher Columbus* (1999). His work, which is strange and comic at once, explores the risky limits of feeling and the sharp reversals of human relations.

Murphy, Hayden (1945–), editor and poet. Born in Dublin, and brought up there and in Limerick, he was educated at Blackrock College and TCD. During 1967–78 he edited, published, and personally distributed *Broadsheet*, which contained poetry and graphics. Among his publications are *Poems*

(1967), *Places of Glass* (1979), and *Exile's Journal* (1992).

Murphy, James (1839–1921), novelist. Born in Carlow, he was Professor of Mathematics at the Catholic University in Dublin [see *universities]. He wrote a number of novels and collections of stories from a nationalist standpoint including *Convict No. 25* (1883), *The Forge of Clohogue* (1885), *Hugh Roach the Ribbonman* (1887), and *The Shan Van Vocht* (1889).

Murphy, Richard (1927–), poet. Born in Milford House, Co. Galway, to an Anglo-Irish family, he spent part of his childhood in Ceylon (Sri Lanka) and the Bahamas, where his father was Governor General. He was educated at Canterbury School, Magdalen College Oxford (where he was taught by C. S. *Lewis), and at the Sorbonne. In 1959, after settling on Inishbofin Island, he bought and restored a boat of traditional design, and made her the subject of 'The Last Galway Hooker' in *Sailing to an Island* (1963). *The Battle of Aughrim* (1968) is a meditation on the final action of the *Williamite War. The next collection, *High Island* (1974), embodies a stoical acceptance of life's brutalities, tempered by a compassionate love for the inarticulate and the helpless. *The Price of Stone* (1985) examines the costs of vanity. *The Mirror Wall* (1989) uses exuberant Sri Lankan traditional art to focus Western fears. His *Collected Poems* appeared in 2000.

Murphy, Tom [Thomas] (1935–), playwright. Born in Tuam, Co. Galway, he was educated by the Christian Brothers before attending the technical school. He became a metalwork teacher at Mountbellew near Tuam. He acted locally and wrote the one-act play, *On the Outside* (1959), with Noel O'Donoghue, which dealt with class tensions. In 1960 Murphy sent *A Whistle in the Dark* to Ernest *Blythe at the *Abbey Theatre, who rejected it. It had a successful production in London. After *The Fooleen*, later retitled *A Crucial Week in the Life of a Grocer's Assistant*, was also rejected by the Abbey in 1961, Murphy emigrated to England. *Famine* (1968) dealt with the 'natural extravagance' of youth which wants to expand into love. *A Crucial Week in the Life of a Grocer's Assistant* (1969), part expressionist dream-play, part naturalism, balances the pull of excitement and emigration against the attractions of the known and familiar. Murphy returned to Ireland in 1970. *The Morning After Optimism* (1971), made use of a complex range of theatrical resources. In a forest of images James and Rosie, a pimp and his whore, encounter their better selves, the dream lovers Edmund and Anastasia. *The Sanctuary Lamp* (1975) features two outcasts, the Irish Francisco and the English Henry, who overturn a confession box in a church, finding refuge in friendship and fellow-feeling. In *The Blue Macushla* (1980) the night-club of the title is a false sanctuary, run by the corrupt Eddie O'Hara, who is involved in *IRA activities. *Conversations on a Homecoming* (1985) was produced by the *Druid Theatre in Galway, with which Murphy was writer in association, 1983–5. It is set in the White House, a run-down pub, where Michael's friends gather to celebrate his return from the USA. Music is central in *The *Gigli Concert* (1983), where it symbolizes an ideal perfection. *Bailegangaire* (1985) returns to a more naturalist form, but these two plays represent an affirmation of the human spirit in the face of adversity. *Too Late for Logic* (1989) returns to the exploration of family ties. *The Wake* (1998) deals with the return of an Irishwoman, now a whore in New York, to her native village, where havoc is let loose. Murphy is a playwright who explores individual and

community identity to reveal the great gulf that lies between the ideals projected by the founders of the *Irish State, and by the Catholic Church, and the actual conditions in which people live and their mental and emotional states. See Fintan O'Toole, *The Politics of Magic* (1987, rev. 1993).

Murray, Paul (1947–); poet. Born in Newcastle, Co. Down, and educated at St Malachy's College, Belfast, he entered the Dominicans in 1966, teaching in Tallaght, as well as at UCD and Rome. *Ritual Poems* (1971), *Rites and Meditations* (1982), and *The Absent Fountain* (1991) combine meditation and enthusiasm in the act of prayer. He has also written *The Mystical Debate* (1977) and *T. S. Eliot and Mysticism* (1991).

Murray, T[homas] C[ornelius] (1873–1959), playwright. Born in Macroom, Co. Cork, and educated locally and at St Patrick's College, Drumcondra, he taught in Cork before being appointed headmaster of the Inchicore Model Schools in Dublin, 1915–32. Murray's first play, *Wheel of Fortune* (1909), was staged at the Cork Little Theatre, which he founded with Daniel *Corkery and others. In 1910 its successor, *Birthright*, a tale of fratricide in rural Ireland, was produced successfully at the *Abbey, establishing a vogue for stark realism. *Maurice Harte* (1912) dramatizes the history of a young clerical student under pressure from ambitious parents who has no vocation. He observed Irish country life closely, capturing its values and its speech accurately and without sensationalism. The same clear-eyed realism is seen in his one-act plays, *Sovereign Love* (1913), and *Spring* (1918), as in his full-length plays, *Aftermath* (1922) and *Autumn Fire* (1925). The last-named is well-made, realistic, and moving. *Spring Horizon* (1937) is a short autobiographical novel of childhood during *Land League days.

My New Curate (1900), a novel by Canon Patrick *Sheehan. An old parish priest, Father Dan, tells of life and work in a rural parish in the west of Ireland, describing the process of mutual education he and his active new curate undergo.

Myles-na-Gopaleen (Myles of the Ponies), a minor character in Gerald *Griffin's novel The *Collegians (1829), later becoming a major figure with Dion *Boucicault's stage adaptation, The *Colleen Bawn (1860). The name was used later by Flann *O'Brien as a pseudonym.

mythological cycle, the. The division of medieval Irish literature into four cycles—mythological, *Ulster, *Fionn, and *historical or king—is a modern one. There is virtually no segment of medieval narrative that is without a mythological constituent or dimension: the Ulster tales may be characterized by heroic endeavour, but mythic themes play a large role in them; the historical tales offer a rich documentation of Celtic and Indo-European myth and ritual particularly in relation to *kingship; and the Fionn cycle, inextricably intertwined with the supernatural world of the *sídh (fairies), belongs more to the mythological than to the heroic frame of thought. However, the mythological cycle may be taken to refer to those tales which deal specifically with the gods of pagan Ireland. Of the tales normally considered part of the mythological cycle, by far the most important is *Cath Maige Tuired. Its central topic is the mythic battle between the divinities of pagan Ireland, the Tuatha Dé Danann, and that other mythological people, the Fomoiri [see *mythology], who continually threatened disruption of social

order and prosperity. Cath Maige Tuired is concerned with the arrival in Ireland of the Tuatha Dé Danann and their conquest of their predecessors, the Fir Bolg, which figure also in *Lebor Gabála. They take control of Ireland, but the Fir Bolg are permitted to retire to the province of Connacht. This is the battle in which Nuada Argetlám (Silver-Arm, the equivalent of Welsh Lludd Llaw Ereint), King of the Tuatha Dé, is said to have lost his arm, later replaced with one wrought in silver by the divine leech Dian Cécht. See Proinsias *Mac Cana, Celtic Mythology (1970).

mythology, Irish, the body of mythological narrative and verse which informed and reflected public and private belief and behaviour in pagan Ireland, not directly accessible to modern scrutiny, but reflected in the extant mythological literature that has survived in the *manuscripts of monastic scribes and redactors. The manuscript survivals are complemented by other comparable material: Welsh/British literature, classical comments on the Celts, and the iconography and epigraphy of Celtic and Romano-Celtic monuments in Britain and the Continent. The inevitably fragmentary nature of this material, and its inadequacy in reflecting pagan Celtic belief, accentuate the apparent heterogeneity and disorganization of the tradition and disguise its underlying consistency. The often complex and nuanced thematic structures that emerge from the extant texts indicate the existence in an earlier period of a coherent and organized mythological system. The god Lug is (sam)ildánach ('skilled in many arts together'), like his Gaulish counterpart, the 'inventor of all the arts' in Caesar's account. He gave his name to Lugdunum/Lyon. The youthful conqueror of malevolent oppressors, his feast was celebrated throughout the Celtic lands, and to some extent still is in Ireland and Brittany in the *Lughnasa festival. As the divine archetype of sacral *kingship he is closely associated with the goddesses identified with the integrity of the land under several aspects. Because of her validating function as goddess of sovereignty, she sometimes assumes an assertive persona which is variously reflected in the literary portrayals of *Medb, Macha [see *Emain Macha], and even the very human Deirdre [see *Longes mac nUislenn]. The sovereignty myth figured by the triad of *Ériu, Fódla, and Banba had at its core a ritual in which the new ruler accepted a drink from the goddess and subsequently mated with her. *Brigit ('the Exalted One') is patron of poetry, healing, and craftsmanship, equivalent in

name to Brigantí/Brigantia, tutelary deity of the British tribe of the Brigantes, and in function similar to the Gaulish goddess called 'Minerva' by Caesar. Boann, personification of the Boyne [see *New Grange], the sacred river with its own prolific mythology, has the Dagda for her husband and Mac ind Óc/Oengus for her son, forming a triune family abundantly attested in the rest of the Celtic world as well as in universal mythology. Kingship, the pivotal institution of early Irish society, has its own rich mythology woven into the legends of famous kings such as Conaire, *Cormac mac Airt, and *Niall Noígiallach, and embodying many reflexes of Indo-European ideology. See Alwyn and Brinley Rees, *Celtic Heritage* (1961).

Naboth's Vineyard (1891), a novel by *Somerville and Ross, and their only full-length treatment of Irish village life. A melodramatic plot involves the frustrated love of Harriet Donovan for the handsome Rick O'Grady whom she earlier rejected to marry John Donovan.

Nation, The (1842–8; 2nd series 1849–96), a weekly cultural and political journal founded by Thomas *Davis, John Blake Dillon, and Charles Gavan *Duffy on 15 October 1842. Until 29 July 1848, when it was suppressed, it spread the views of *Young Ireland amongst a wide section of the population, selling in excess of 10,000 copies per issue, and reaching an estimated readership of 250,000. Essays such as Davis's 'Nationality' and John *Mitchel's 'Letters to the Protestant Farmers, Labourers and Artisans of the North of Ireland' influenced Irish nationalism for many years. Largely through the retrospective judgements of W. B. *Yeats, The Nation is often thought of purely as the vehicle of strident balladeering [see *ballads]; in fact, it also explored many aspects of the Irish past, promoted the Irish language, and reviewed the work of *Carlyle, Tennyson, and John Stuart Mill, as well as publishing non-political verse and translations of poetry from a wide range of European languages. After Mitchel's deportation in May of 1848, Richard d'Alton *Williams and Kevin Izod O'Doherty began The Irish Tribune, which was joined by John Martin's Irish Felon, until both were suppressed along with The Nation in July 1848. In September 1849, the moderate wing of the original group—Gavan Duffy, Lady *Wilde, and A. M. *Sullivan—began publishing a 'second series' of The

Nation, which continued until 1896. The poetry and essays which appeared in The Nation were collected in book form. The most important such collection was The *Spirit of the Nation (1843), edited by Duffy.

National Literary Society, see *literary revival.

National University of Ireland, see *universities.

Navigatio Sancti Brendani Abbatis (*Voyage of St Brendan*), a Hiberno-Latin narrative of the immram *tale-type, composed possibly as early as the 8th and not later than the 10th cent. One of the most influential texts of the Middle Ages, it is contained in over 100 manuscript copies in Latin and was translated into most European vernaculars. With some followers St *Brendan sets out in a coracle; over seven years they visit many islands and have numerous adventures. Having reached the island of Saints they return to Ireland, where Brendan relates his adventures and dies shortly thereafter.

Neilson, Samuel (1761–1803), *United Irishman and founding editor of the *Northern Star; born in Ballyroney, Co. Down, the son of a Presbyterian minister. He proposed the formation of the revolutionary society to Henry Joy *McCracken in 1791, was imprisoned for sedition in 1796–8, and re-arrested in May 1798 having been wounded in an attempt to rescue Lord Edward *Fitzgerald from prison.

Neilson, William (1774–1821), grammarian and lexicographer; born in Rademon, Co. Down, where his father, a

Presbyterian minister, ran a school. He was educated locally, where he was taught Irish by Patrick *Lynch, and at Glasgow University. He was licensed in 1796 and became a minister in Dundalk. In 1798 he was seized by the authorities as he was about to preach at his father's church, but released when his sermon was shown to be free of *United Irishmen leanings. His *Introduction to the Irish Language* (1808), a grammar, also comprised a collection of words, phrases, and short dialogues, together with a selection from Irish *manuscripts, and is particularly valued for its record of the Irish dialect of Co. Down. At the Belfast Academical Institution he taught the future Gaelic patron Roibeárd *Mac Ádaimh.

Nepenthe (1835), a poem in two cantos by George *Darley set in Arabia. In his own account of it, the first canto was meant to show the ill effects of 'over-joy', the second those of melancholy, while a third canto, never completed, was intended to show contentment with 'the natural tone of human life' as the true Nepenthe or elixir.

New English, a term for settlers in Ireland after the *Protestant Reformation in England.

New Grange, megalithic passage tomb near the Boyne River in Co. Meath. Erected *c*.3300–2900 BC by a pre-Celtic people, it has a long passage, corbelled central chamber, decorated stones, and a roof box which permits the sun's rays to penetrate the length of the passage at the winter solstice. In early Irish literature the site is primarily depicted as the otherworld residence [see *sídh] of major figures of the Tuatha Dé Danann of the *mythological cycle. It was also regarded as the burial place of both the Tuatha Dé Danann and the High Kings of *Tara.

New Ireland Review, see *The *Lyceum.*

Newman, John Henry (Cardinal) (1801–1890), theologian and cultural philosopher. Born in London and educated at Trinity College, Oxford, he was a leading member of the Oxford Movement, which emphasized the Catholic tradition in the English Church. Convinced that the Church of Rome was the true inheritor of the apostolic succession, he converted in 1845. In 1852 he began his lectures in Dublin on *The Idea of a University* (published 1873) and was made Rector of the Catholic University of Ireland 1854–8 [see *universities].

Newmann, Joan (1942–), poet; born in Armagh, and educated at QUB, she published pamphlets, such as *Suffer Little Children* (1991), before issuing *Coming of Age* (1995), followed by *Thin Ice* (1998).

Ní Chonaill, Eibhlín Dubh (*c*.1743–*c*.1800), composer of the famous *Caoineadh Airt Uí Laoghaire*. Born in Derrynane, Co. Kerry, she was an aunt of Daniel *O'Connell. In 1767 she fell in love with Art Ó Laoghaire (1747–73) of Rathleigh near Macroom, recently returned from service in the Hungarian Hussars. They lived in Rathleigh in some affluence, but in 1773 when Abraham Morris, the Sheriff of Cork, and an enemy, offered £5 for a prize mare (as a Protestant was entitled to do under the *Penal Laws) Ó Laoghaire refused and went on the run. After a failed ambush on Morris at Millstreet he was shot at Carraig an Ime. According to the *Caoineadh*, his blood-drenched mare galloped to Rathleigh, where Eibhlín Dubh mounted her and rode back to Carraig an Ime, to declaim the first parts of the *Caoineadh* over her husband and drink his blood. The verses of the *Caoineadh*, written down many years later from oral tradition, are the most remarkable set of keening verses to have survived. See Seán *Ó Tuama (ed.), *Caoineadh Airt Uí Laoghaire* (1961).

Ní Chuilleanáin, Eiléan (1942–), poet; born in Cork into a Republican family. She was educated at UCC and Oxford before lecturing at TCD. *Acts and Monuments* (1972), her first collection, was followed by *Site of Ambush* (1975); *The Second Voyage* (1977), a volume of selected poems; *The Rose-Geranium* (1981); *The Magdalene Sermon* (1990); and *The Brazen Serpent* (1994).

Ní Dhomhnaill, Nuala (1952–), poet. Born in Lancashire to Irish physicians, she was sent back to the Irish-speaking area west of Ventry in Co. Kerry at the age of 5, and later attended UCC where she studied English and Irish, coming into contact with the *Innti* group. After her marriage to Dogan Leflef, a Turkish geologist, in 1973, she lived in Holland and in Turkey before they settled in Ireland. Her first collection, *An Dealg Droighin* (1981), was followed by *Féar Suaithinseach* (1984), and *Feis* (1991). The convergence in her work of Gaelic tradition with feminist and other contemporary perspectives attracted the interest of poets eager to make her better known in English, resulting in bilingual selections such as *The Astrakhan Cloak* (1991), with translations by Paul *Muldoon.

Ní Dhuibhne, Éilís (1954–), writer of fiction; born in Dublin, educated at UCD and Copenhagen, she worked as a folklore archivist at UCD 1979–81 and in 1984–5, and in the National Library. *Blood and Water* (1988) was a short-story collection, followed by others including *Eating Women is Not Recommended* (1991) and *The Inland Ice* (1997). Novels include *The Bray House* (1990) and *The Dancers Dancing* (1999). Works for children include *The Hiring Fair* (1993) and *Blueberry Sunday* (1994) written as 'Elizabeth O'Hara'.

Ní Ghráda, Máiréad (1896–1971), playwright; born in Co. Clare and educated at the Convent of Mercy, Ennis, and UCD. A member of Cumann na mBan, the women's division of the *Irish Volunteers, she was secretary to Ernest *Blythe during the period of the first Dáil Éireann. She published a collection of short stories, *An Bheirt Dearbhráthar agus Scéalta Eile* (1939), as well as a science fiction novel, *Mannán* (1940). Her plays include *An Uacht* (1935), *An Grá agus An Gárda* (1937), *Giolla an tSolais* (1954), *Úll Glas Oíche Shamhna* (1960), *Súgán Sneachta* (1962), *Stailc Ocrais* (1966), and *Breithiúnas* (1978). *An Triail* was one of the successes of the Dublin Theatre Festival of 1964.

Ní Laoghaire, Máire Bhuí (1774–?1849), poet; born in Túirín na nÉan in Uíbh Laoghaire (Iveleary), near Inchigeelagh, Co. Cork. In about 1792 she married Séamas de Búrca, a horse-trader from Skibbereen, and they bought a holding near Céim an Fhia (Keimaneigh), where they lived in some prosperity. She was illiterate, but her poems and songs were orally transmitted and survive in the *folklore of her locality. Her best-known poem is 'Cath Chéim an Fhia', which gives a graphic account of an affray between the Whiteboys [see *secret societies] and the local battalion of yeomanry in 1822.

Niall Noígiallach (Niall of the Nine Hostages), said to have been king at *Tara in the early 5th cent., and regarded as ancestor of all but two of the high kings (ard-rí; see *kingship) up to the Battle of *Clontarf, as well as the progenitor of the Uí Néill dynasty. His sobriquet comes from the hostages he took from each of the provinces of Ireland.

Ní Ghlinn, Áine (1955–), poet; born in Gould's Cross, Co. Tipperary, and educated at UCD, she worked as a teacher then journalist from 1987. Her collections include: *An Chéim Bhriste* (1994), *Deora Nár Caoineadh/ Unshed Tears* (1997), a bilingual volume, and *Gáirdín Pharthais* (1998). She has also written non-fiction for younger readers.

'Night That Larry Was Stretched, The', a much-anthologized anonymous 18th-cent. Dublin ballad which deals with the execution by hanging of a felon and his comical farewells, and written by an educated hand in *Hiberno-English cant.

Nine Rivers from Jordan (1953), an autobiographical account of Denis *Johnston's experiences as a BBC correspondent with the British army in North Africa and Europe during the Second World War.

'Ninety-Eight', see *United Irishmen.

Niníne Éces (*fl.* 700), poet; probably a member of the Uí Echdach, a kinship group [see *fine] known for learning, with territories south and west of Armagh, which produced numerous high-ranking ecclesiastics. Compositions attributed to him include 'Admuinemmar nóeb-Patraicc', a poem addressed to St *Patrick on which Tomás *Ó Flannghaile based his 'Dóchas Linn Naomh Pádraig'.

Noble Descents (1982), a fictional study of colonial tensions by Gerald *Hanley. Set in post-independence India of the early 1950s, it traces the interactions between a group of British expatriates, some American film executives, and the Maharajah and his relations.

Norman French Literature, see *Harley 913.

Norman invasion. The insular world of Gaelic Ireland was significantly breached with the arrival of the Anglo-Normans in the years following 1169. After the defeat of the Vikings at Clontarf in 1014, the government of the country became radically unstable, creating a situation in which the *Annals of the Four Masters* entry for the year 1145 can describe the country as 'a trembling sod'. The Norman invasion was precipitated, according to tradition, by Dermot MacMurrough (Diarmait Mac Murchadha), King of Leinster, in a struggle against the O'Neill, O'Brien, and O'Rourke families. In 1152 MacMurrough abducted Tiernan O'Rourke's wife Dervorgilla. In 1166, Roderick O'Conor, High King of Ireland, and O'Rourke attacked Diarmait, who retreated to Bristol and thence to Aquitaine, where he sought assistance from Henry II. Henry had already acquired authority to invade Ireland in a Papal Bull (*Laudabiliter*) secured by John of Salisbury from Adrian IV (the English Pope Nicholas Breakspear) in 1155. Basing himself in Bristol, Dermot gathered an army around the nucleus provided by Richard FitzGilbert de Clare, Earl of Pembroke (known as Strongbow in Irish tradition). After the initial incursion of a limited Norman party at Baginbun in Wexford in 1169, Strongbow arrived with 200 knights and 1,000 men-at-arms in 1170. The success of the mailed knights and their bowmen was immediate. When Dermot died in 1171 Strongbow assumed the office of King of Leinster. Henry II came to Ireland in order to secure the feudal loyalty of the Normans, and many Irish chieftains. Strongbow died in 1175, by which year Leinster and part of Munster were in Norman hands but Ulster and Connacht remained Gaelic. The appointment of Prince John as Lord of Ireland by his father in 1175 and his succession to the throne of England in 1199 initiated the second phase of the conquest. John made extensive grants in Gaelic territories to his Norman liege-lords, establishing the Butler, Fitzgerald, and de Burgh dynasties of Ireland. The penetration of Gaelic society by cultural forms associated with the Normans made a lasting alteration in the development of Irish culture, for instance in the *dánta grádha, the Irish lays [see *laoithe], and in the elaboration of native patterns of story-telling by the addition of romantic elements. There were, also, a number of literary productions in Norman French and in English (such as The *Land of Cokaygne); and English began to be used as the language of commerce and administration beyond the Pale. Extensive political and economic changes reflected the process of feudalization intrinsic to the Norman system of social administration and land use. Gaelic writers varied in the degree of their attachment to the Normans and their legacy, the closest point being reached in Geoffrey *Keating's *Foras Feasa ar Éirinn, a classic of *Gaelic historiography that characterizes his own Norman lineage as the 'Sean-Ghaill' ('Older Foreigners') in contradistinction to the 'Nua-Ghaill' or *New English, settled in the *plantation period.

Norsemen, see *Viking invasion.

Northern Ireland came into being shortly before the Anglo-Irish Treaty of December 1921 [see *Anglo-Irish War], which established a sovereign Irish Free State [see *Irish State] within the United Kingdom. The northern state owed its existence to the strongly-felt antipathy of Ulster Unionists to Home Rule legislation [see *Irish Parliamentary Party], which they identified with rule by a preponderantly Roman Catholic and economically underdeveloped population that had traditionally been the religious and racial enemy of northern Protestants since the 17th-cent. Ulster *plantation. On 28 September 1912,

almost half a million Northern Protestant men and women signed an Ulster Covenant vowing resistance to Home Rule under the leadership of Edward *Carson and the Unionist Council. Under the Better Government of Ireland Act of 1920 (with effect from 1 May 1921), Northern Ireland was equipped with a parliament at Stormont from 1932 on the outskirts of Belfast, constructed on the Westminster model and subject to the authority of the imperial parliament. Commonly—but erroneously—called Ulster or the Province, Northern Ireland had at the outset a clear two-thirds Protestant majority of which one-third was Church of Ireland and two-thirds Presbyterian. Together these dominated political life under a succession of conservative Unionist governments led by James Craig (Viscount Craigavon), 1921–40, J. M. Andrews, 1940–3, and Sir Basil Brooke (Lord Brookborough), 1943–63. Meanwhile Catholics found themselves systematically excluded from political office and discriminated against in matters of employment and housing. However, the extension of British post-war legislation in health and education began to bring the benefits of the Welfare State to all sections of the Northern population from 1947. This had the effect of creating the generation who formed the nationalist movements of the 1960s—notably the Northern Ireland Civil Rights Association, 1967; People's Democracy, 1968; and the Social Democratic Labour Party (SDLP). With the accession of Terence O'Neill to the premiership came the promise of liberalization in the North and friendly overtures towards the neighbouring Republic. An ultra-Protestant reaction in 1966 led to the formation of the new Ulster Volunteer Force (UVF). Revd Ian Paisley, Moderator of his own Free Presbyterian Church of Ulster and later founder of the Democratic Unionist Party in 1971, soon emerged as leader of the ultra-Protestants. Protestant violence at Burntollet during a Belfast-Derry march, abetted by the RUC (Royal Ulster Constabulary), led to the battle of the Bogside, and the introduction of the British army on 15 August 1969 at the request of the new premier, James Chichester-Clark (Lord Moyola). A reinvigorated *IRA emerged to defend the nationalist community and quickly took the offensive in a campaign of shootings and bombings. Internment was implemented disastrously on 9 August 1971—the intelligence lists were out of date and UVF paramilitaries were exempted. Thirteen civilian marchers were shot dead by British paratroopers on 'Bloody Sunday' in Derry on 30 January 1972, and direct rule by secretary of state was introduced in March of that year. The Sunningdale Agreement between Britain and Ireland (1973) established a power-sharing executive which was brought down by the Ulster Workers' Council strike of May 1974. A concerted policy of criminalization was levelled against the IRA by the Tory government of Margaret Thatcher (who narrowly escaped becoming one of the IRA's assassination victims). In November 1985 the Hillsborough Agreement confirmed that neither government would support unity without the clear and formal consent of the Northern majority. Talks between John Hume of the SDLP and Gerry *Adams of Sinn Féin in Autumn 1993, and a joint declaration by the Irish and British governments with the assent of the Official Unionists under James Molyneux, raised the possibility that peace might 'break out' in early 1994, confirmed by the IRA and Loyalist ceasefires later in the year. The IRA ended its ceasefire in 1996 with the bombing of Canary Wharf in London, and Sinn Féin were barred from the inter-party talks under the Chairman George Mitchell, a U.S. Senator. In 1997 Tony Blair was elected Prime Minister at Westminster and brought a fresh impetus to the process of peacemaking, along with Mo Mowlam, Secretary of State. In July 1997 the IRA renewed its ceasefire, Sinn Féin joined the talks, and signed up to the Mitchell principles, which were based on compromise and non-violence. In 1998 Mitchell, after exhausting and nail-biting negotiations involving both governments and all parties (apart from the Democratic Unionist Party) brokered the 'Good Friday Agreement', which put in place wide-ranging strategies of accommodation between Northern Ireland and the Republic, and between Ireland and Britain. In 1999 a devolved assembly was formed in Stormont, only to be revoked in 2000 when agreement could not be reached on the decommissioning of weapons.

Northern Iron, The (1907), a novel by George A. *Birmingham, set in Co. Antrim just before the *United Irishmen's Rebellion of 1798.

Northern Star (1984), the first of a trilogy of history plays by Stewart *Parker. Set in a 'continuous present', it conveys the 'night thoughts' of Henry Joy *McCracken after the failure of the 1798 Rebellion [see *United Irishmen] as a pastiche of Irish playwrights from *Farquhar, through *Boucicault to *Beckett.

Norton, Hon., Mrs Caroline (1808–1877), poet and novelist; born in London, granddaughter of Richard Brinsley *Sheridan. Of her poetry, 'The Arab's Farewell to His Steed' was best known. In *A Voice from the Factories* (1836) she looked at the abuse of women and children. Her novels, such as *Woman's Reward* (1836) and *Lost and Saved* (1865), reflect the unhappiness of her own marriage. She was the model for George Meredith's *Diana of the Crossways* (1885).

Not Honour More (1955), a novel by Joyce *Cary, third in the second trilogy, the others being *Prisoner of Grace* and *Except the Lord*. Jim Latter, a bluff soldier, is awaiting sentence for murdering his wife Nina, who had been solacing the ageing statesman Chester Nimmo, her ex-husband. His account of events during the General Strike in 1926, dictated in prison, is in a brutally direct style which reveals him as impulsive and uncompromising.

Not I (1972), a play by Samuel *Beckett, it consists of a monologue spoken by a Mouth which floats in the air eight feet above stage floor—the actor speaking through a hole in a black cloth.

Nowlans, The (1826), a novel by John *Banim in the *Tales by the O'Hara Family* (2nd series). A powerful and psychologically perceptive story of the temptation and fall of a young priest which results in personal tragedy followed by repentance.

Nugent, Robert Craggs (Viscount Clare and Earl Nugent) (1702–1788), poet and politician. Born in Carlanstown, Co. Westmeath, he was MP for Bristol, 1724, and St Mawes, Cornwall, 1774. His poetical works include discourses on *Justice* (1737), *Happiness* (1737), *Odes and Epistles* (1739), a poem on *Faith* (1774), and *The Genius of Ireland* (1775).

Nuinseann, Uilliam (William Nugent) (1550–1625), poet; brother of Christopher Nugent, 9th Baron of Delvin, Co. Westmeath, who prepared an Irish primer for Elizabeth I. He studied at Oxford, but after returning to Ireland he was suspected of treason and fled north, where he had the protection of the O'Neills and Maguires. 'Diombáidh triall ó thulchaibh Fáil', a poem of exile, collected by Charlotte *Brooke in *Reliques of Ancient Irish Poetry* (1789), is attributed to him.

Nutt, Alfred (1856–1910), publisher and Celticist [see *translation from Irish]. Born in London, he was educated in England and on the continent. In 1878 he succeeded his father as head of the family firm, through which he promoted works in *folklore and Celtic literature. He was also active in establishing the Irish Texts Society, whose productions he published.

Oak Leaves and Lavender: *or A World on Wallpaper* (1946), a play by Sean *O'Casey set in an English west-country manor house.

Ó Briain, Liam (1888–1974), revolutionary and language revivalist. He was born in Church St. in Dublin and educated by the Christian Brothers and at UCD where he lectured in French. He fought in the *Easter Rising, *Cuimhní Cinn* (1951) giving a lively account of those events. He translated into Irish works by Shakespeare, Molière, *Synge, and *Pearse for the *Taibhdhearc theatre in Galway.

O'Brian, Patrick (1914–2000), novelist; born in London as Richard Patrick Russ into a medical family, he later assumed the identity of a Gaelic-speaking Irishman, cloaking his education and training in deliberate obscurity. His novels suggest a military or naval intelligence career. The Jack Aubrey/Stephen Maturin series of sea-novels, set during the period of the Napoleonic wars, began with *Master and Commander* (1970), and include *Post Captain* (1972), *H.M.S. Surprise* (1973), *Desolation Island* (1979), *The Reverse of the Medal* (1986), *Clarissa Oakes* (1992) and *The Wine-Dark Sea* (1993). He wrote a biography of Picasso (1976), and short stories in *The Chian Wine* (1974) and other collections.

O'Brien, Attie (Frances Marcella) (1840–1883), novelist. Born into a Catholic gentry family in Co. Clare, she published four novels: *The Monk's Prophecy* (1882) and *The Caradassan Family* (1886) are romantic comedies; *Won by Worth* (1891) and *Through the Dark Night* (1897), however, have a markedly nationalist dimension.

O'Brien, Charlotte Grace (1845–1909), novelist. Born in Cahirmoyle, Co. Limerick, she spent part of her childhood on the Continent with her father William Smith *O'Brien and later lived in Ireland. Some of her early fiction, such as *Dominick's Trials* (1870), is sectarian, but her best novel, *Light and Shade* (1878), is conciliatory in outlook.

O'Brien, Conor Cruise (1917–), politician and man of letters. Born in Dublin to a nationalist family, he was educated at Sandford Park and TCD, where he wrote a doctorate on Charles Stewart *Parnell before joining the Department of External Affairs in 1944. In 1960 he went to the Congo as U.N. representative, and in that capacity undertook measures to prevent the secession of Katanga. His account is given in *To Katanga and Back* (1962). He subsequently accepted the Vice-Chancellorship of the University of Ghana, before entering Irish politics to serve as a Minister and spokesman on *Northern Ireland in the Coalition Government, 1973–7. As a critic O'Brien is centrally concerned with the 'unhealthy intersection' between politics and literature. *Maria Cross* (1952), published under the pseudonym 'Donat O'Donnell', was a study of a group of modern Catholic writers. *States of Ireland* (1972) is a statement on the *Troubles in Northern Ireland. The title-essay in *Passion and Cunning: Essays on Nationalism, Terrorism, and Revolution* (1988) examines the growth of W. B. *Yeats's political thought. His study of the Israeli-Palestinian conflict, *The Siege: A Saga of Israel and Zionism* (1986), argued against Arab nationalist thinking. *The Great Melody* (1992), a thematic biography and anthology on Edmund *Burke, argued for the influence of Catholicism on Burke's conservatism. *Ancestral Voices* (1994) is a study of the role of Catholic sectarianism in the Republican tradition. An autobiography, *My Life and Themes* (1998) is an evaluation of the ideas that shaped his life and writing. In the 1990s, as the peace-making process evolved in Northern Ireland, his political allegiances vacillated as events confounded his confident predictions. At one stage, in 1998, he shifted from Unionism to advocacy of a United Ireland in a matter of weeks.

O'Brien, Dillon (1817–82), novelist. Born in Tullabeg, Co. Roscommon, and educated there, he emigrated to the USA, working as a teacher among Native Americans before settling in St Paul, Minnesota. *The Dalys of Dalystown* (1866), a novel, is set in Ireland. It advocates a solution to Ireland's land question based on the virtues of a Catholic upper class. *Dead Broke* is concerned with the conflict between human values and the modern world.

O'Brien, Edna (1930–   ), novelist and short-story writer. Born in Tuamgraney, Co. Clare, she was educated in Loughrea, Co. Galway, and in Dublin. In 1951 she married Ernest Gébler and settled in London in 1959, but divorced in 1967. She achieved a literary sensation with her first three books, *The *Country Girls* (1960), *The Lonely Girl* (1962; reprinted as *The *Girl with Green Eyes*), and *Girls in Their Married Bliss* (1963), a socially and psychologically realistic series of novels dealing with young women coming to maturity in a puritan Ireland. *August Is a Wicked Month* (1964) is a study of a separated woman whose husband and son are killed while she has a holiday affair in France. *A Pagan Place* (1971) returns to the subject-matter of the trilogy. In *The High Road*

(1988) a waitress who falls in love with a woman is killed by her jealous husband. O'Brien's short story collections include *The Love Object* (1968), *A Scandalous Woman* (1974), and *Lantern Slides* (1988). *Time and Tide* (1992) deals with separation, custody, and loss, while *House of Splendid Isolation* (1994) concerns the relationship between an *IRA man on the run and the woman whose house he commandeers.

O'Brien, [Michael] Fitz-James [de Courcy] (1828–1862), fantasy-writer. Born in Co. Cork and raised in Castleconnell, Co. Limerick, he contributed poetry to *The *Nation. Moving to London at 21, he squandered a large inheritance. In New York after 1851, he wrote the stories of horror and imagination on which his place in literary history depends. They were collected in 1881.

O'Brien, Flann (pseudonym of Brian O'Nolan; Brian Ó Nualláin) (1911–1966), novelist and columnist, who also wrote as Myles na gCopaleen; born in Strabane, Co. Tyrone, the son of a Customs Officer. Having spoken Irish at home and learnt his English from books, he was educated by the Christian Brothers in Synge Street, Dublin, before proceeding to UCD. In 1935 he joined the Civil Service, rising to be principal officer for town planning. *At Swim-Two-Birds* (1939) was hailed critically but sold poorly. O'Nolan's next novel, *The *Third Policeman, went the round of publishers in 1940 and met with repeated rejections in wartime England, causing him such disappointment that he made no further attempts to have it published. (It appeared posthumously in 1967.) R.M. Smyllie, editor of *The Irish Times*, invited him to contribute a humorous column 'Cruiskeen Lawn', which ran in the paper from 1940 until his death. For the first year the column was mainly in Irish, but it drifted into

English and continued thus exclusively. Some of the material was simply humorous but much of it was satirically directed against politicians, bureaucrats, and mediocrities in office. A satirical Irish novel, An *Béal Bocht (1941), had a limited market until it appeared in English as The Poor Mouth (1964). In 1953 the Civil Service persuaded him to take voluntary retirement. A bleak period ended on reissue in 1960 of At Swim-Two-Birds which enjoyed tremendous success. O'Nolan soon produced The Hard Life (1961). Illness and work on a television series delayed completion of The *Dalkey Archive (1964). The publication of The Third Policeman (1967) revealed a genius capable of joining comedy and terror. See Anthony *Cronin, No Laughing Matter: The Life and Times of Flann O'Brien (1989).

O'Brien, Kate (1897–1974), novelist. Born in Limerick, the daughter of a horse-dealer, she was educated there at Laurel Hill Convent, and won a scholarship to UCD. A play, Distinguished Villa (1926), brought success at its first production in London with a three-month run. After *Without My Cloak (1931), the story of a Catholic family like her own, she turned to depicting the inner lives of young women reaching adulthood only to find themselves in conflict between their moral training and the call of sexual love. Confronted with the choice, the heroines of The Ante-Room (1934) and Mary Lavelle (1936) choose differently, Agnes in the former novel accepting abstinence while Mary in the latter embraces sexual initiation. The *Land of Spices (1941) is an examination of the spiritual development of a dedicated nun, as she recovers her capacity for love. O'Brien's next novel, *That Lady (1946), generally regarded as her best, gives a version of the conflict between Aña de Mendoza and

Philip II of Spain, and celebrates individual resistance to despotic power. The two subsequent novels, The Flower of May (1953) and As Music and Splendour (1958), show a falling-off in intensity, though the themes remain the same. She wrote two travel books, Farewell Spain (1937) and My Ireland (1962); a book of reminiscences, Presentation Parlour (1963), centred on the convent where two of her aunts were nuns; and a study of the Spanish saint, Teresa of Avila (1951). See Adele M. Dalsimer, Kate O'Brien (1990).

O'Brien, Kate Cruise (1948–1998), writer of fiction. Born in Dublin, the daughter of Conor Cruise *O'Brien, she was educated in Rathgar and at TCD. A Gift Horse (1978), a collection of short stories, was followed by The Homesick Garden (1991), a novel of troubled adolescence. She became literary editor of Poolbeg Press in 1993.

O'Brien, R[ichard] B[aptist] (1809–1885), novelist. Born in Carrick-on-Suir, Co. Tipperary, he became a priest and worked for a time in Nova Scotia, eventually becoming Dean of Limerick. He founded the Catholic Young Men's Society amd was a supporter of Home Rule [see *Irish Parliamentary Party]. O'Brien's novels advanced the anti-liberal, ultramontane Catholicism of Pius IX. Ailey Moore (1856) and The D'Altons of Crag (1882) envision a harmonious solution to the land question. Jack Hazlitt, A.M. (1875) is an ultramontane novel.

O'Brien, William (?1736–1815), actor-dramatist. Closely related to the O'Brien Earls of Thomond and Inchiquin, he appeared as Captain Brazen in *Farquhar's The *Recruiting Officer in 1758 and acted for some years. He wrote a farce, Cross Purposes (1772), and a comedy, The Duel (1772), both based on French models.

O'Brien, William (1852–1928), journalist, politician, and novelist; born Mallow, Co. Cork, educated Queen's College, Cork [see *universities]. He organized the Plan of Campaign to achieve controlled rents with John Dillon in 1886. He mediated between Parnellites and anti-Parnellites in 1890. His novel, *When We Were Boys* (1890), written in prison after his prosecution for organizing a rent strike in 1887, gives a vivid account of the *Fenian movement and its enemies. *A Queen of Men* (1898) is set in Galway and Clare Island in the time of Granuaile (Grace *O'Malley). His *Recollections* (1908) and *The Irish Revolution* (1928) are among many examinations of the events he was involved in.

O'Brien, William Smith (1803–1864), *Young Irelander. Born at Dromoland, Co. Clare, he was educated at Harrow and Cambridge before becoming Conservative MP for Ennis, 1825, and later for Co. Limerick, 1835. He joined Young Ireland but did not share the anti-landlord politics of John *Mitchel and James Fintan *Lalor. In October 1848, he lead the only significant action of the young Ireland rising, and fought off a contingent of policemen at the Widow McCormack's house in Ballingarry. The death sentence passed on him was commuted and he spent five years in Tasmania before going to America. His political testament is *Principles of Government or Meditations in Exile* (1856). There is a monument in O'Connell St., Dublin.

O'Briens and the O'Flahertys, The (1827), Lady *Morgan's final novel and her most complex examination of Irish problems. It is set in the late 18th cent. and deals with the history of two Irish families under the impact of the *Penal Laws.

Ó Broin, León (1902–1996), bilingual author. Born and educated in Dublin, he was called to the Bar in 1924 and served for many years from 1925 in various ministries, including the Department of Education, where he was active in setting up An *Gúm. He issued Irish story collections in 1923, 1924, and 1929, and later wrote a number of plays, besides translating works into Irish. His historical and biographical works include *The Unfortunate Mr. Robert *Emmet* (1958) and *Fenian Fever* (1971). *The Chief Secretary* (1969) is a study of Augustine Birrell. *Just Like Yesterday* is an autobiography (1985).

Ó Bruadair, Dáibhí (?1625–1698), poet. Born in the area around Carrigtwohill in eastern Co. Cork, he received training at a *bardic school. The body of his work almost uniquely provides a native Irish perspective on the social upheavals of the turbulent period between the *Rebellion of 1641 and its bitter sequel in *Cromwell's campaign in Ireland, to the devastation of Catholic hopes with the Treaty of Limerick [see *Williamite War]. In one of Ó Bruadair's earliest poems, 'Adoramus Te Christe', written about 1648 and beginning 'Adhraim thú, a thaidhbhse ár gcrú', he dedicates his literary powers to the praise of the Lord. In much of his subsequent writings he addressed the transformation of Irish society in the 17th cent., and especially the changing fortunes of aristocratic Gaelic families. 'Créacht do dháil mé', a poem dated at 1652, pours scorn on the Cromwellian upstarts who are taking over Irish lands in the new *plantation and settlement, attacking their affectations, mincing speech, and close-cropped hair. In 1660 he removed to west Co. Limerick and wrote 'Iomdha scéimh ar chur na cluana', an epithalamium on the marriage of Una Bourke of Cahirmoyle, whose parents, John Bourke and Anna Ní Urthuile, became his patrons and remained supporters of the Jacobite cause. Ó

Bruadair seems to have enjoyed the support of several Jacobite households other than the Bourkes up to 1674, when he complains in 'Is bearnadh suain' that kindness and generosity have disappeared from his life. The new élite have, he claims, infected the manners and mores of even the Gaelic nobility, who now coldly disregard his grief-stricken pleas. At around this time also he wrote the cynical 'Is mairg nach bhfuil im dhubhthuata', ironically wishing he were an uneducated lout who might fare better in the new economic order. In 1680 he described his circumstances—living penniless in the 'Corner of a Churchyard in a Cottage . . . well-contented with his Stock, which is only a little Dog, a Cat, and a Cock'. At around this time he wrote 'D'aithle na bhfileadh n-uasal', expressing his sorrow at the decay of Irish learning as books and manuscripts lie rotting in forgotten corners. 'Suim Purgadóra bhFear nÉireann' is a verse chronicle of the years 1641–84, from the 'betrayal' of Charles I to the Popish Plot. At the succession of *James II, Catholic and Jacobite hopes revived with a proclamation of religious freedom for Catholics. These developments are joyously recounted in a poem of 1687, 'Caithréim an Dara Séamuis'. In December 1688 he records his disgust at the Glorious Revolution, which installed William of Orange as King of England and Ireland. From the date when James landed in Ireland in the following year to Ó Bruadair's death, his poetry reflects the fortunes of the Jacobite cause with an immediacy of response that is as complex as it is agitated. 'Caithréim Phádraig Sáirséal' triumphantly recalls *Sarsfield's victory when he spiked William's artillery in a daring military exploit at Ballyneety, Co. Limerick. His famous poem 'An Longbhriseadh' (The Shipwreck) describes the country's situation after the departure of the *Wild Geese. It would

appear that little or no assistance was coming from any quarter, and that his erstwhile patrons were themselves reduced to poverty, but in 'Geadh scannail le daoinibh' (c.1693) he tells us that Anna Ní Urthuile has nevertheless given him the mantle off her own back. Ó Bruadair is unremitting in his view that utter calamity has overtaken Ireland, and he is certain that a great part of the blame must be laid on his own countrymen for their deceit and ungodliness. See John C. Mac Erlean, SJ (ed.), *Duanaire Dháibhidh Uí Bhruadair* (3 vols., 1910–17).

Ó Buachalla, Breandán (1936–), scholar; born in Cork and educated at St. Nessan's Christian Brothers school, and at UCC, where he read Celtic Studies. He taught at QUB before studying philology and linguistics under Julius *Pokorny at Munich, then at UCD, where be became Professor of Modern Irish Language and Literature in 1978. His books include: *Clár Lamhscríbhinní Gaeilge sa Leabharlann Phoiblí i mBéal Feirste* (1962), and *I mBéal Feirste Cois Cuain* (1968), a study of Gaelic culture in late 18th century and 19th century Belfast. He edited the poems of Peadar *Ó Doirnín (1969) and *Nua-Dhuaraire* (I and II, 1972 and 1976), anthologies of poetry in Irish. *Aisling Ghéar* (1996) is a comprehensive literary history of one of the great forms of Gaelic poetry since 1600.

Observe the Sons of Ulster Marching Towards the Somme (1985), a play by Frank *McGuinness about a group of *Ulster Volunteers in the First World War, dealing with the friendships, feelings, and beliefs of a group of eight Protestant soldiers up to the moment when they enter the Battle of the Somme.

Ó Cadhain, Máirtín (1906–1970), novelist and short-story writer. Born in Cois

Fharraige, in the Connemara *Gaeltacht, to a family of well-known story-tellers, Ó Cadhain was educated at the local national school in Spiddal and qualified as a teacher at Saint Patrick's College in 1926. He joined the *IRA, eventually becoming a recruiting officer and a member of the Army Council. He also became involved in Gaeltacht issues. He was a lifelong, often controversial, language-rights activist, declaring that 'the Irish language is my life essence'. *Idir Shugradh agus Dáiríre* (1939) was a volume of stories based on the life of his own community. Because of his republican activities, Ó Cadhain spent most of the war years (1939–45) in the Curragh Internment Camp. His novel *Cré na Cille* (1948) is a major work of modern Irish literature. It is a commentary on the foibles and futile preoccupations of men and women in Ó Cadhain's Gaeltacht community. In the collections *An Braon Broghach* (1948) and *Cois Caoláire* (1953) he integrates traditional content and modernist forms. After internment Ó Cadhain was appointed to the Government Translation Service. His final three collections, *An tSraith ar Lár* (1967), *An tSraith Dhá Tógail* (1970), and the posthumously published *An tSraith Tógtha* (1977), introduce the dehumanized, deracinated, and nameless people of the modern urban wasteland. In 1956 Ó Cadhain was appointed Junior Lecturer in Irish at TCD and he became Professor of Irish in 1969. *Athnuachan* (1995) was published after lying in typescript since 1951, when it won the *Oireachtas prize. Ó Cadhain did not wish to publish it in his lifetime, because the central character, Beartla Mór, a hypochondriac old man obsessed with death, was based upon his uncle. It is a work as commanding as *Cré na Cille*, comic, grotesque, and tragic by turns. *Caiscín* (1998) collects his articles for *The Irish Times* published 1953–56. He is difficult to read in Irish

because of an allusive style based not only on the rich heritage of his local dialect and its folk inheritance but also on the full range of the literary tradition. See Louis *de Paor, *Faoin mBlaoisc Bheag Sin* (1992).

Ó Caiside, Tomás (*fl.* 1750), poet. Born probably in Roscommon and ordained an Augustinian friar, he seems to have been defrocked on account of a love affair with a young girl who may have been the one addressed in 'Máire Bhéil Átha hAmhnais', the *folksong attributed to him.

Ó Caoimh, Eoghan (?1655–1726), scholar and poet. Born into a bardic family in Co. Cork, he married Eilionóir de Nógla (Nagle) in 1680 and spent some years first in Co. Kerry, and then near Cork, where he copied *manuscripts. Following the deaths of his wife in 1707 and his son Art in 1709, he was ordained in 1717, becoming parish priest at Doneraile, whence he conducted a sharp correspondence with Seán Clárach *Mac Domhnaill.

Ó Caomhánaigh, Seán Óg [Mac Murchadha] (1885–1946), folklorist and novelist, also known as 'Seán an Chóta'. Born in Co. Kerry, he was educated there and at St Patrick's College, Drumcondra. He emigrated to America, working for some years in the Mid-West, experiences which are reflected in *Fánaí* (1927), an amalgam of American dime novel and Irish folklore, in which the hero, a farm labourer, wins the hand of a rich woman.

O'Casey, Sean (1880–1964) playwright; born in Dublin into a Protestant working-class family and christened John Casey. The known facts of his early life are few, but O'Casey started work at 14. He was employed in a variety of manual jobs, and lived with his mother. He joined James *Larkin's

Irish Transport and General Workers' Union, becoming Secretary of its political wing, the *Irish Citizen Army. He took part in the Lock-Out Strike of 1913, but left in 1914 when James *Connolly moved it closer to the revolutionary position of Patrick *Pearse. He wrote The Story of the Irish Citizen Army (1919). A number of his plays were rejected by the *Abbey Theatre before The *Shadow of a Gunman was produced in 1923, revealing his critical attitude towards Irish nationalism. This theme was pursued with theatrical brilliance in the two plays which followed, *Juno and the Paycock (1924) and The *Plough and the Stars (1926). Juno and the Paycock, though dealing with the violence of the *Civil War, had enough charm in the characters of Captain Boyle and Joxer his parasite to lighten its darker sides, but The Plough and the Stars, set at the time of the 1916 *Easter Rising (its title referring to the Citizen Army emblem) caused deep offence. There was a riot in the theatre, and *Yeats railed against those who had 'disgraced themselves again', proclaiming the author as the new Synge. The *Silver Tassie (1928), dealing with the horror of the First World War, was an attempt to break away from realism. After its rejection by Yeats and the Abbey it had a London production, where it met with a lukewarm response. Disillusioned with the Abbey, and at odds with the ethos of the new *Irish State, O'Casey now settled in England where he had met and married Eileen Carey Reynolds in 1927. I Knock at the Door, the first volume of Autobiographies, appeared in 1939, subsequent volumes continuing to 1954. In 1940 the O'Caseys moved to Totnes in Devon. Throughout these years O'Casey retained his conviction, formed in his years with Larkin's Union, that communism would provide a solution to the problems of poverty and injustice, views reflected in the plays The *Star Turns Red (1940), *Red Roses for Me (1942), *Purple Dust (1945), and *Oak Leaves and Lavender, each of which has a worker-hero. The later experimental works, *Cock-a-Doodle Dandy (1949), The *Bishop's Bonfire (1955), and The *Drums of Father Ned (1959), have a generalized Irish setting and are allegories based upon a Utopian vision of human transformation. In Behind the Green Curtains (1962, published 1961) he attacks Ireland directly, but there is a kind of reconciliation in The Moon Shines on Kylenamoe (published 1961), a one-act play. See David Krause, Sean O'Casey: The Man and his Work (1975 ed.); and Heinz Kosok, O'Casey the Dramatist (1985).

Ó Catháin, Liam (1896–1969), novelist; born in Dunacummin, Emly, Co. Tipperary, into a farming family, he wrote a trilogy of novels on the life of the poet Liam Dall Ó hIfearnáin: Ceart na Sua (1964), Ceart na Bua (1968), and Ceart na hUaighe (1986).

Ó Ceallaigh, Uaitéar, see *Stair an Bhíobla.

Ó Cearbhalláin, Toirdhealbhach (Turlough Carolan) (1670–1738), harper, and poet. Born near Nobber, Co. Meath, he grew up in Ballyfarnan, Co. Roscommon. When he was left blind by smallpox at 18, he was trained as a harper. At some point he married a Mary Maguire from Fermanagh and settled at Mohill, Co. Leitrim, fathering seven children. He was buried at Kilronan in Roscommon after a wake lasting four days. Ó Cearbhalláin enjoyed the social status traditionally accorded to the harper in Gaelic society, but was on equally familiar terms with patrons of native and planter stock. His music, comprising mostly songs, dance-tunes, laments, and some religious pieces, draws upon native tradition but was also influenced by European composers such as Vivaldi and Corelli. Numerous Anglo-Irish writers including *Goldsmith, J. C. *Walker, and George *Petrie wrote about him, usually emphasizing the pathetic side of his career as the last exemplar of a lost culture. His best-known pieces include 'Gracey Nugent', 'Mabel O'Kelly', and 'Carolan's Concerto'.

Ó Cearnaigh, Seán (John Kearney) (?1542–?1587), translator. Born in Leyney, Co. Sligo, he was educated in Cambridge. In 1571 he published in Dublin *Aibidil Gaoidheilge & Caiticiosma* (*Gaelic Alphabet & Catechism*), the first book in Irish printed in Ireland.

Ó Céileachair, Donncha (1918–1960), writer of fiction; born in the Cork *Gaeltacht to a literary family. His best-known work is a collection of short stories, *Bullaí Mhártain* (1955), which he wrote with his sister Síle, showing a fusion of folk material and style with a modern manner and sensibility.

Ó Cianáin, Tadhg (*fl.* 1600), author of a chronicle of the *Flight of the Earls. His narrative is written in journal form and records in brisk style the stages of Hugh *O'Neill and Red Hugh *O'Donnell's journey from Donegal to Rome between September 1607 and April 1608. A lost manuscript in his hand containing hagiographical material was used by Mícheál *Ó Cléirigh in 1627.

Ó Cléirigh a learned family of Donegal, poet-historians and scribes to the O'Donnells, including the poet Cúchoigríche (*fl.* 1603) and Lughaidh *Ó Cléirigh, poet and author of *Beatha Aodha Ruaidh Uí Dhomhnaill.

Ó Cléirigh, Lughaidh (?1580–?1640), poet and historian, and member of the Donegal learned family. His father Maccon (d. 1595 in Thomond) was chief

historian to Ó Domhnaill, and his brothers Cúchoigcríche [see *Annals of the Four Masters] and Maccon Meirgeach were also poets. He is best known as the author of *Beatha Aodha Ruaidh Uí Dhomhnaill, a heroic life of Red Hugh *O'Donnell, completed some time before 1616. With Tadhg mac Dáire *Mac Bruaideadha of Thomond, from whom he is said to have received instruction, he began the *Contention of the Bards* (*Iomarbhágh na bhFileadh*), in which he challenged Mac Bruaideadha's assertions that the southern poets were better than their northern counterparts.

Ó Cléirigh, Mícheál (?1590–1643), annalist, and chief compiler of the *Annals of the Four Masters. Born in Kilbarron, near Ballyshannon, Co. Donegal, into the *Ó Cléirigh learned family, his baptismal name was Tadhg, but when he was professed in *Louvain as a Franciscan lay brother, he took the name of Mícheál. He was trained as a scholar in the family tradition, and when Aodh *Mac an Bhaird in Louvain was co-ordinating the research there and in Ireland which led to John *Colgan's *Acta Sanctorum Hiberniae* (1645) and other publications, he sent Ó Cléirigh home in 1626 to gather *manuscript material and to check dates and sources with living Irish scholars. He was based in the Franciscan friary at Bundrowes, Co. Donegal, but for eleven years he travelled the country, visiting friaries, convents, and lay learned schools, transcribing and checking, and sending fresh copies back to Louvain. For the *Réim Ríoghraídhe* (*Succession of the Kings*) (completed November 1630), he had the assistance of three lay scholars: Fear Feasa *Ó Maoilchonaire from Co. Roscommon, Cuchoigríche Ó Cléirigh, his cousin from Co. Donegal, and Cuchoigríche *Ó Duibhgeannáin from Co. Leitrim. These three, along with Ó Cléirigh, were called the 'Four Masters' by Colgan in his preface to *Acta Sanctorum Hiberniae*, in recognition of the fact that they undertook the great bulk of the work leading to the *Annals of the Four Masters*. In undertaking the *Annals* Ó Cléirigh was greatly extending his original brief. They began work at Bundrowse in January 1632 and finished on 10 August 1636. In 1637 Ó Cléirigh returned to Louvain, where he prepared his Irish lexicon, *Foclóir nó Sanasán Nua* (*A New Vocabulary or Glossary*) (Louvain, 1643).

Ó Coileáin, Seán (?1754–1817), poet and scribe. Born in West Carbery, Co. Cork, he was educated for the priesthood on the Continent before returning to Myross, near Glandore, where he lived by teaching and is reputed to have led a rakish life. His extant poems are few: his best-known 'Machtnamh an Duine Dhoilíosaigh', written in 1813, is a reflection on the ruins of Timoleague Abbey in his native place. A sombre poem, it unites romanticism with Gaelic tradition, and for this reason was a favourite of 19th-cent. translators such as *Ferguson and *Mangan.

Ó Coistealbha, Seán (1930–), poet and dramatist; born in Indreabhán, Connemara. Many of his poems, selected in *Buille Faoi Thuairim Gabha* (1987), have passed into oral tradition in the *Gaeltacht. His plays, among them *An Tincéara Buí* (1962), and *Pionta Amháin Uisce* (1978), are based on stock situations.

Ó Conaill, Peadar (1755–1826), lexicographer. Born near Kilrush, Co. Clare, he spent some time with Charles *O'Conor the Elder in Co. Roscommon. His main interest was in the older forms of Irish.

Ó Conaill, Seán (1835–1931), a traditional story-teller, and a farmer and fisherman of the village of Cill Rialaig,

Co. Kerry. His repertoire was published as *Leabhar Sheáin I Chonaill* (1949).

Ó Conaire, Pádhraic Óg (1893–1971), novelist and short-story writer. Born in Ros Muc, Connemara, and educated locally, he was one of Patrick *Pearse's first pupils at St. Enda's. He joined the IRB [see *IRA] in 1913, spent twenty years as a travelling teacher for the *Gaelic League, and worked for the Government Translation Service, 1931–58. His well-crafted stories include *Seóid ó'n Iarthar Órdha* (1924), *Ceol na nGiolcach* (1939), and *Déirc an Díomhaointis* (1972).

Ó Conaire, [Sean-]Phádraic (1882–1928), novelist and short-story writer. Born in Galway, abandoned by his father in 1888, and orphaned in 1893, he went to live with an English-speaking uncle in Ros Muc. He was sent to the local national school, and later attended Rockwell and Blackrock Colleges. He went to London in 1899, joined the *Gaelic League, and started to write. He began to drink heavily, left London in 1914, and spent the rest of his life roaming around Ireland, living off meagre earnings from hastily scribbled articles and stories. He died destitute in the Richmond Hospital, Dublin. Ó Conaire's best writing, the short-story collections *Nóra Mharcuis Bhig agus Sgéalta Eile* (1909) and *An Chéad Chloch* (1914) and his bleak novel, *Deoraíocht* (1910), dates from his period in London. He was amongst the first modernist writers of fiction in Irish. Ó Conaire's is a world without hope or salvation. Twelve of his rural sketches, translated by Cormac Breathnach with illustrations by Micheál *MacLiammóir, were collected as *Field and Fair* (1929).

Ó Conghaile, Micheál (1962–), writer of fiction; born in Inis Treabhair, Co. Galway, and educated at UCG, he founded Cló Iar-Chonnachta at Indrea-bhán in 1985, which proved to be a major force in the Irish-language movement in the 1990s. *Mac an tSagairt* (1986) and *An Fear a Phléasc* (1997) were short story collections; *Sna Fir* (2000) a novel. Ó Conghaile's style is energetic and fluent, reflecting contemporary Gaeltacht speech-patterns; his material is frequently the exciting and danger-ous underworld of homosexual encounters.

O'Connell, Daniel (1775–1847), the dominant political figure of post-*Union Ireland. Born at Cahirciveen, Co. Kerry, and brought up at Derrynane House, he was called to the Irish Bar in 1798. He was involved in the agitation for *Catholic Emancipation from 1804, achieving it in 1829. He then cam-paigned for *Repeal. Following his climb-down in agreeing to cancel a mass meeting at Clontarf in 1843, he was convicted of seditious conspiracy in a state trial of 1844. Released on appeal after four months, he sought new alli-ances but never regained his former dynamism. O'Connell's political ideas were those of an advanced secular rad-ical, supporting parliamentary govern-ment, manhood suffrage, equality of opportunity, and the separation of Church and State. Yet his success depended on his ability, working in close alliance with the Catholic clergy, to channel the complex blend of con-crete grievances, sectarian animosities, and vague aspirations towards social transformation that animated the Catholic masses. He combined an apocalyptic and often inflammatory rhetoric with the pursuit of limited objectives by constitutional means. See Oliver MacDonagh, *Daniel O'Connell* (2 vols.: *The Hereditary Bondsman*, 1988; *The Emancipist*, 1991).

O'Connor, Dermod (Darby) (*fl.* 1720), author of a translation of Geoffrey *Keating's *Foras Feasa ar Éirinn* which appeared in 1723. He was a member of the Dublin circle of Gaelic scholars gathered round Tadhg *Ó Neachtain, and was employed to transcribe Gaelic *manuscripts by Anthony *Raymond, a Church of Ireland clergyman and antiquarian.

O'Connor, Frank (pseudonym of Michael O'Donovan) (1903–1966), short-story writer, translator, and nov-elist. Born in Cork, he was raised in poverty by his mother largely in the absence of his father, a British soldier and Irish nationalist. O'Connor's for-mal education ended at 12, but there-after he read voraciously, encouraged by Daniel *Corkery, who directed him to Russian fiction, Gaelic poetry, and nationalism. During the *Civil War O'Connor took the Republican side and was interned in Gormanstown in 1923. The romantic idealism of the struggle for independence coupled with the barbarism of guerilla warfare and a general sense of betrayal shaped two of his most powerful books: his first volume of short stories, *Guests of the Nation* (1931), and the highly parti-san study of Michael *Collins, *The Big Fellow* (1937). After his release O'Con-nor became a librarian and quickly established himself as a disruptive presence in Dublin literary circles. He came under the influence of W. B. *Yeats, with whom he established the Irish Academy of Letters in order to oppose *censorship. *Guests of the Nation* was followed by a novel, *The Saint and Mary Kate* (1932), and *The Wild Bird's Nest* (1932), a volume of translations from the Irish published by the *Cuala Press from which Yeats happily adapted material as the need arose. The genial but detached narrator of O'Connor's short stories emerged in a second collection, *Bones of Contention* (1936), while the poems in *Three Old Brothers* (1936) were more stilted and mannered. *In the Train* (1937) and *Moses' Rock* (1938) were written for the *Abbey Theatre, which he served as a director 1935–9. In 1939 O'Connor married the Welsh actress Evelyn Bowen, and settled in Woodenbridge, Co. Wicklow. *Crab Apple Jelly* (1944) focuses on the frustrations and repressions of respectable middle-class Ireland in tales such as 'The Lucys' and 'The Mad Lomasneys'. Much of his best work in the 1940s was banned under the Censorship Act as indecent, notably the novel *Dutch Interior* (1940) and a vigorous translation of Brian *Merriman's *Cúirt an Mheán-Oíche*, as *The Midnight Court* (1945). Also proscribed were two volumes of short stories: *The Common Chord* (1947), a collection focused on the theme of love, and *Traveller's Samples* (1951). In 1951 he was invited to lecture in the USA, and there he married Harriet Rich. Out of his university teaching in America grew three critical works: *The Mirror in the Roadway* (1956), a study of the novel; *The Lonely Voice*, an analysis of the short story (1962); and *The Backward Look* (1967), a history of Irish literature from the earliest times. His attachment to Gaelic poetic tradition culminated in the collection of translations, *Kings, Lords and Commons* (1959). See James Matthews, *Voices: A Life of Frank O'Connor* (1983).

O'Connor, Joseph (1963–), novelist and playwright; born in Dublin and educated at UCD, Oxford, and Leeds. *Cowboys and Indians* (1991) was a novel, followed by *True Believers* (1991), short stories. *Desperadoes* (1994) and *The Salesman* (1998) were further novels; *Red Roses and Petrol* (1995), *The Weeping of Angels* (1998), and *True Believers* (1999) plays; and *Sweet Liberty* (1996) a book of travels in Irish America. He scripted *Ailsa* (1994), a film based on one of his stories; and *The Chosen Few* (2000) from his first novel.

O'Connor, Kevin (1941–), playwright; born in Limerick, he was educated there before becoming an actor, then journalist and radio producer. Plays include *Friends* (1970) staged at the *Abbey Theatre, *Bourke and Blake* (1992), and *The Ante-Room* (1996) adapted from Kate *O'Brien. *Sweetie* (1999) was a biography of Charles J. Haughey.

O'Connor, Ulick (1928–), man of letters. Born in Dublin and educated at UCD, he was called to the Irish Bar in 1951. He was sports correspondent for *The Observer*, 1955–61, having gained a reputation as a boxer. His biography *Oliver *St. John Gogarty* (1964) was followed by the more controversial *Brendan *Behan* (1970). A collection of poems, *Lifestyles* (1973), included some versions from the Irish. *The Celtic Dawn* (1984) is a study of the *literary revival. *Executions* (1993) is a play dealing with the execution of Republican prisoners by the new *Irish State in 1922.

O'Conor, Charles, the Elder (1710–1791), Irish scholar and founder of the Catholic Committee. Born in Co. Sligo, and educated by an Irish-speaking Franciscan, he made his first journey to Dublin in 1727, meeting Gaelic scholars and Anglo-Irish antiquarians there. During the 1750s O'Conor issued a number of lengthy pamphlets, often pseudonymously or by proxy, arguing for the relaxation of the *Penal Laws. O'Conor's chief work is *Dissertations: An Account of the Ancient Government, Letters, Sciences, Religion, Manners and Customs of Ireland* (1753), the second edition of which includes a refutation of *Macpherson's assertions about Gaelic literature (1766). In 1756 he was co-opted with Sylvester *O'Halloran onto the *RDS committee charged with founding the Royal Irish Academy (*RIA). Throughout his career O'Conor worked in close association with John *Curry, founding the Catholic

Committee with him and others of the Catholic gentry party. As a pamphleter and letter-writer he campaigned tirelessly against the misrepresentations of the *Rebellion of 1641 in the Anglo-Irish *chronicles. The O'Conor family at Belanagare were hosts to Carolan (Toirdhealbhach *Ó Cearbhalláin), whose harp remains in the library at Clonalis. At some time O'Conor came into possession of the *Book of the O'Conor Don. See Joseph Th. Leerssen, *Mere Irish and Fíor-Ghael* (1986).

O'Conor, Charles, the Younger
(1764–1824). Catholic priest and antiquarian. A grandson of Charles *O'Conor the Elder, he was born in Belanagare, Co. Roscommon, and educated in Rome, where he was ordained in 1791. His *Rerum Hibernicarium Scriptores Veteres* (1814–28) was a pioneering work in Irish historiography.

Ó Corcráin, Brian
(d. ?1624), poet and prose writer. A member of a prominent ecclesiastical family also noted for its musicians and scholars, he lived near Enniskillen, Co. Fermanagh, and was a friend and neighbour of Eochaidh *Ó hEódhasa. He based the prose romance *Eachtra Mhacaoimh an Iolair (Adventure of the Boy of the Eagle)* on a summary of a French tale.

Ó Criomhthain, Tomás,
(1856–1937), author of *An t*Oileánach* and other autobiographical writings; born on the Great Blasket Island off the Dingle Peninsula, the youngest of a large family, he was educated in English on an island school, and grew up amid conditions of poverty and hardship in a tiny community living in a village on the east side of the island facing Dunquin. Considered delicate as a child, young Ó Criomhthain continued to be breastfed to the age of 4, but ultimately outlived all of his contemporaries. Married in 1878 to Máire Ní Chatháin, they went on to produce ten children. An uncle, Diarmuid, acted as a kind of mentor to the young Ó Criomhthain, though he was also a rakish partner in drinking bouts. Ó Criomhthain was the first islander to achieve literacy in Irish, having taught himself to read and write the language. In 1917 Brian Ó Ceallaigh went to the island, met Ó Criomhthain, and urged him to write from his experience. Ó Ceallaigh persuaded Ó Criomhthain to send him a journal of island impressions, and these were edited by Pádraig *Ó Siochfhradha, using his pseudonym 'An Seabhac', as *Allagar na hInise* (1928). 'An Seabhac' edited Ó Criomhthain's classic Irish autobiography *An tOileánach* the year after. A third work, *Seanchas ón Oileán Tiar (Lore from the Western Island)* (1956), was compiled from his story-telling by Robin *Flower. Ó Criomhthain's writings reveal an individual and a community poised between medieval ways of living and the steadily increasing influence of the modern world. See Seosamh Céitinn, *Tomás Oileánach* (1992).

O'Crohan, Thomas,
see Tomás *Ó Criomhthain.

Octoroon, The;
or *Life in Louisiana* (1859), a melodrama by Dion *Boucicault, based on Mayne *Reid's novel *The Quadroon* (1856). George Peyton, who tries to run the Terreborne Plantation, loves Zoe, a slave. She commits suicide after the connivings of the villain M'Closkey ruin her life.

Ó Cuirnín, Ádhamh
(fl. 1410), member of a learned family of north Connacht. He made a copy of *Lebor Gabála in 1418.

O'Curry, Eugene
(Eoghan Ó Comhraí), (1796–1862), scholar. Born in Dunaha near Carrigholt, Co. Clare, he was the son of a story-teller, and

collector of *manuscripts. After a period spent labouring and teaching in his native locality he moved to Limerick, where he was employed in the lunatic asylum in about 1828. In 1835 he was appointed to the Topographical Section of the Ordnance Survey [see George *Petrie], working out of the office in Petrie's home at North Gt. Charles St., Dublin, together with his brother-in-law John *O'Donovan and others such as the poet J. C. *Mangan. In 1851 J.H. *Todd and Charles Graves commissioned him to make a copy of the *Book of Achill*, a legal text, and advised the Government to establish a commission to undertake a large-scale edition of ancient Irish *law. In 1853, O'Curry and John O'Donovan were appointed co-editors of the *Senchas Már* [see *law in Gaelic Ireland]. It finally appeared after O'Curry's death in 1865. In 1854 O'Curry was appointed Professor of Irish History and Archaeology at the Catholic University [see *universities], and there he delivered in 1855–6 his *Lectures on the Manuscript Materials of Ancient Irish History* (1861). *Arnold based many judgements on them in his own lecture series, *On the Study of Celtic Literature* (1866). O'Curry's *Lectures* supplied the earliest systematic account of such crucial issues as the manuscript sources of Irish literature and history; and the *Fionn, *mythological, *historical, and *Ulster cycles of sagas. In a second lecture series, *On The Manners and Customs of the Ancient Irish* (3 vols., 1873), O'Curry proceeded to treat comprehensively of the *political divisions, and kinship [see *fine] system of Gaelic Ireland. O'Curry's two Irish lecture series amount to an authoritative interpretation of Gaelic society and culture. See Pádraig Ó Fiannachta (ed.), *Eoghan Ó Comhraí: Saol agus Saothar* (1995).

Ó Dálaigh, a learned *bardic family which came to prominence in the early 12th cent., after the bardic families began to consolidate their position as the influence of the monasteries started to decline [see *monasticism]. Cú Chonnacht Ó Dálaigh was great-grandfather to Donnchadh Mor *Ó Dálaigh (d. 1244) and Muireadhach Albanach *Ó Dálaigh (fl. 1220). They had a school in Cork at Dunamark, near Bantry, as early as the late 12th cent. Gofraidh Fionn *Ó Dálaigh (d. 1387) traced the family origin to Dálach, a pupil of *Colmán mac Lénéni, the 6th-cent. patron saint of Cloyne, Co. Cork.

Ó Dálaigh, Aonghus Fionn (fl. 1590), poet and head of the branch of the *Ó Dálaigh learned family that supplied poets to the MacCarthys of Desmond. All but four of the fifty-five poems attributed to him are on religious themes, a third of them being devoted to the Virgin Mary.

Ó Dálaigh, Aonghus Ruadh (na nAor, 'of the Satires') (d. 1617), poet. He was hired by Lord Mountjoy [see under Hugh *O'Neill] and Sir George Carew to arouse enmity amongst the Irish by writing satires on the leading families. John *O'Donovan published his satires in *The Tribes of Ireland* (1852), appending James Clarence *Mangan's verse translations.

Ó Dálaigh, Cearbhall, (fl. 1620), poet to whom many *dánta grádha are ascribed, as is the often-translated 'Eibhlín a Rúin'.

Ó Dálaigh, Donnchadh Mór (fl. 1220), poet. Donnchadh Mór was trained in *bardic learning, but also in the subjects taught by the monastic schools [see *monasticism], not yet extinguished. He is chiefly noted as a religious poet, and, while more than 160 religious poems have been attributed to him (if somewhat dubiously), he has only one extant secular poem to his credit, a piece on the Uí Mhorna of east Ulster.

Ó Dálaigh, Gofraidh Fionn (d. 1387), poet; born probably in Duhallow, Co. Cork, and probably educated in a *bardic school of the Mac Craith learned family. The *Annals of the Four Masters* describe him as the chief ollam of his time [see *áes dána]. As a professional poet he served the MacCarthys, the Earls of Desmond, and the O'Briens of Thomond. Gofraidh's praise-poetry is indicative of the political ambivalence of the bardic poets. In 'Mór ar bhfearg riot, a rí Saxan', he compares Maurice Fitzmaurice, Earl of Desmond, to the Tuatha Dé Danann deity Lug [see Irish *mythology]; however, Maurice is also said to be the fosterling of the King of England. Gofraidh was respected as a moral and religious poet, one of his best-known compositions being 'Mairg mheallas muirn an tsaoghail', a poem on the vanity of human wishes which contains a vivid fable about a child born in prison whose knowledge of the outside world is restricted to a shaft of light through an auger-hole. See Lambert McKenna (ed.), *Dioghluim Dána* (1938) and *Aithdíoghluim Dána* (1939).

Ó Dálaigh, Muireadhach Albanach (*fl.* 1220), poet and member of the *Ó Dálaigh learned family. Most likely born in Co. Meath, a brother of Donnchadh Mór *Ó Dálaigh, he studied *bardic poetry and may also have attended monastic schools. According to the *Annals of the Four Masters*, in 1213, when he was living at Lisadell, Co. Sligo, a steward of Domhnall Mór Ó Domhnaill tried to exact tribute in an insulting fashion, and Ó Dálaigh instantly cut him down with an axe. He fled to Riocard de Búrc (Richard Fitz William Fitz Adelm de Burgo) in Clanrickard, whose protection he sought in the poem 'Créd agaibh aoidhigh i gcéin', praising de Burgo for his 'foreign beauty' and for adapting so completely to Gaelic culture. But Ó Dálaigh was forced to go on to Thomond, Limerick, then Dublin, before leaving for Scotland, where he remained in exile for some time. In Scotland—whence his sobriquet 'Albanach'—his offspring took the name Mac Muireadhaigh, thus establishing the Scottish poetic family called Mac Mhuirich. 'M'anam do sgar riomsa a-raoir' mourns the death of his wife and recalls the physical beauty of her body. While in exile he went to the Holy Land and re-visited Ireland afterwards, dedicating a poem to Murchadh Ó Briain, a descendant of *Brian Bóroime, in which he expresses a renewed confidence and spirit. According to tradition he ended his days in a monastery. See Lambert McKenna, *Aithdioghluim Dána* (1939). Alan *Titley's *An Fear Dána* (1993) is a novel based on the surviving evidence about Ó Dálaigh and on the poetry.

Ó Dálaigh, Tadhg Camchosach (*fl.* 1375), poet and member of the *Ó Dálaigh learned family who appears to have gone to the Continent to become a Franciscan. The poem 'Dá grádh do fhágbhas Éirinn' expresses his sorrow at parting from his people and describes his spiritual reasons for doing so.

O'Daly, John (1800–1878), editor and publisher. Born in Farnane, Co. Waterford, he was educated in *hedge schools before moving to Dublin, where he opened a bookshop in Anglesea St. He issued Edward *Walsh's *Reliques of Irish *Jacobite Poetry* (1844) in parts. His teaching-text, *Self-Instruction in Irish* (1846), appeared under his own imprint at about the time when he involved J. C. *Mangan in the making of the anthology, *Poets and Poetry of Munster* (1st series, 1849). Mangan's biographer, Fr. C. P. Meehan, tells how the poet would lean on the counter in O'Daly's shop and versify literal translations for ready cash. He followed this with a second series of *Poets and Poetry of Munster* (1860) with translations by George *Sigerson. The *Ossianic Society was founded in his Anglesea St. house in 1853. Douglas *Hyde purchased O'Daly's books at the auction after his death.

O'Davoren (Ó Duibhdábhoireann), learned family whose members were lawyers in the territory of Corcomroe, Co. Clare, at least as early as the 14th cent. The most important document associated with them is the manuscript now known as Egerton 88 (British Library). It was compiled between 1564 and 1569, and contains copies of some important law texts, as well as some versions of Old Irish tales.

Ó Direáin, Máirtín (1910–1988), poet; born in the Irish-speaking community of Inishmore, Aran Islands, and educated locally. He left the island in 1928 to work in the Post Office in Galway city, and there became involved in Irish-language theatre through the *Gaelic League. He transferred to the Civil Service in Dublin in 1938 and began to write poems, publishing two collections, *Coinnle Geala* (1942) and *Dánta Aniar* (1943), at his own expense. *Rogha Dánta* (1949) is a landmark in modern poetry in Irish, while *Ó Morna agus Dánta Eile* (1957) established him as a poet with a powerful and distinctive voice. Ó Direáin's work advances from nostalgic recollections of life in Aran to a later exploration of an urban environment, using bleak imagery based on the uncompromising landscape of the island. The poem 'Stoite' in *Rogha Dánta* engages with the theme of uprooted man adrift from the moral sanctions of traditional rural life, a subject that receives its most exhaustive treatment in *Ar Ré Dhearóil* (1963), where he explores a moral crisis inherent in 'an chathair fhallsa' (the false city).

Attractively simple in theme and language, his work shows a capacity for acute observation. A striking feature is the repeated use of a simple vocabulary in which words such as cloch, cré, carraig, and trá (stone, clay, rock, and strand), serve to evoke the values which the poet sees as being eroded by modern urban society. Ó Direáin received awards from the Irish-American Cultural Institute Award, and the Freiherr Von Stein Foundation, Hamburg, as well as an honorary degree from NUI. He remained in the Civil Service until his retirement in 1975, and died in Dublin. See Frank *Sewell, *Extending the Alhambra* (2000).

Ó Doibhlin, Breandán (1931–), novelist, critic, and translator. Born in Rooskey, Co. Tyrone, he was educated at St Colum's College in Derry and Maynooth before becoming Professor of French and Modern Languages there. He edited *Irisleabhar Mhá Nuad* and pioneered the application of critical methods to the works of modern writers in Irish. The novel *Néal Maidine agus Tine Oíche* (1960) deals with cultural values and their transmission in modern society, while *An Branar Gan Cur* (1979) depicts the attitudes of an alienated northern Catholic. He translated *Iseáia* (1975), which became part of *An Bíobla Naofa* (1981) [see *Bible in Irish].

Ó Doirnín, Peadar (?1700–1769) poet. Born near Dundalk, he spent most of his life in that area; he is buried in Urney on the Louth-Armagh border. Most of the details about him derive either from *folklore or from accounts written by antiquarians in the 19th cent., and are not very trustworthy. He became a schoolmaster at Forkhill, Co. Armagh, having married Rose Toner. According to tradition he was active as a Jacobite Whiteboy and lived a wild life. Personal and somewhat enigmatic, his love-poems combine derived themes with originality in language, metre, and imagery; they include 'Mná na hÉireann', and the well-known 'Úr-Chnoc Chéin Mhic Cáinte'.

Ó Domhnaill, Maghnus (?–1563), poet and hagiographer. Inaugurated as lord of Donegal in 1537 at Kilmacrenan, he was married to Eleanor Fitzgerald. In 1555 he was deposed by his son Calbhach, who held him prisoner. Though not a professional scholar, Maghnus was deeply interested in literary affairs and composed a life of *Colum Cille, Betha Colaim Chille*, which was written under his direction at his castle in Lifford in 1532. Maghnus composed a number of poems of the *dánta grádha type, including a lament for his wife ('Cridhe lán do smuaintighthibh'). *Betha Cholaim Cille* was translated into Latin by John *Colgan (in *Acta Sanctorum*, 1645) and translated into English by Brian Lacey (1998). Seán *Ó Tuama's play *Gunna Cam agus Slabhra Óir* (1967) is based on his life.

Ó Domhnaill, Uilliam, see William *Daniel.

Ó Dónaill, Niall, (1908–1995), lexicographer and writer; born in the Donegal *Gaeltacht, educated at St Eunan's College, Letterkenny, and UCD. He spent some years translating novels for An *Gúm before becoming editor of *Foclóir Gaeilge-Béarla* (1977) in 1959. Apart from thirteen translations, he wrote a life of John *Mitchel (*Beatha Sheáin Mistéil*, 1937) and a historical account of life in the Rosses (*Na Glúnta Rosannacha*, 1952).

Ó Donnchadha, Tadhg (pseudonym 'Tórna') (1874–1949), scholar and poet. Born in Carrignavar, Co. Cork, at that time still, to an extent, Gaelic-speaking, he was educated at the North Monastery, Cork, then at St Patrick's College, Drumcondra. He edited *Irisleabhar na Gaedhilge*, 1902–9. His *Leoithne Andeas* (1905) was the first collection of poems

in Irish of the *literary revival. He edited the work of many poets, among them Aodhagán *Ó Rathaille and Pádraigín *Haicéad.

Ó Donnchadha an Ghleanna, Séafraidh (?1620–1678), poet and chief of the O'Donoghues of Glenfesk near Killarney, Co. Kerry. He took part in the Irish attack on Tralee Castle in 1641, but managed to retain his estate through the *Cromwellian period. Among the surviving poems ascribed to him is an unusual piece lamenting the death of a dog which had choked on a mouse.

O'Donnel, a National Tale (1814), a novel by Lady *Morgan. Written in support of *Catholic Emancipation, the novel represents its hero, a cultured Irish gentleman, as innately superior to Lady Llanberis and her English society friends who parade him as a fashionable curiosity.

O'Donnell, Frank Hugh (1848–1916), politician and author. Born in Co. Donegal and educated at Queen's College, Galway [see *universities], he entered Parliament as nationalist MP for Dungarvan, Co. Waterford, 1877–85. In *Souls for Gold* (1899) he argued that *Yeat's The *Countess Cathleen* was blasphemous. He followed up this assault on the *Abbey Theatre with The *Stage-Irishman of the Pseudo-Celtic Revival* (1904), attacking *Synge in particular.

O'Donnell, John Francis (pseudonym 'Caviare') (1837–1874), journalist and poet. Born and educated in Limerick, he joined the Catholic *Universal News* in London in 1860. He returned to Dublin briefly as a staff writer on The *Nation, 1861–2. In 1863–4 he edited the Fenian journal *The Irish People*, and then moved on to *The Tablet*, 1865–8. A novel about the swindler John *Sadlier and another on land agents and evictions appeared in *The Nation* and *The

Lamp respectively in the early 1870s. His *Memoirs of the Irish Franciscans* (1871) commemorates the Counter-Reformation in Ireland. Richard Dowling edited his *Poems* (1891) for the Irish Literary Society. O'Donnell's work shows surprising modernity of feeling, especially in the self-questioning monologues that express a sense of alienation common to many Irishmen living in England.

O'Donnell, Peadar (1893–1986), Republican socialist and novelist. Born at Meenmore in Donegal, he was educated at St Patrick's College, became a teacher, and acted as a Union organizer. He fought in the *Anglo-Irish War and then in the *Civil War on the anti-Treaty side. He edited the *IRA paper *An Phoblacht* from its foundation in 1925 to 1931. His first novels, *The *Storm* (1925) and *Islanders* (1928), reflect his concern with poverty on the west coast of Ireland. *Adrigoole* (1929) is based on an actual case involving a mother and child who starved to death while her Republican husband was in prison. *The *Knife* (1930) deals with sectarian violence in the Lagan Valley, 1915–25. In 1934 O'Donnell split from the IRA to form the Republican Congress, and began to organize Irishmen to fight against Franco in 1936. He was Sean *O'Faolain's deputy editor and business manager on *The *Bell* from 1940, becoming editor in 1946. *The Big Windows* (1955), a novel, was followed by a volume of autobiography, *There Will Be Another Day* (1963). *Proud Island* (1975) was a late novel.

O'Donnell, Red Hugh (Aodh Ruadh Ó Domhnaill) (?1571–1602), Ulster chieftain of the Tyrconnell dynasty of Donegal, and son-in-law of Hugh *O'Neill. He was captured by the Lord Lieutenant, Sir John Perrot, by pretended hospitality on shipboard at Lough Swilly, and held in Dublin Castle as surety for O'Neill. At Christmas 1591

he escaped through the sewers of the Castle and found refuge with the O'Byrnes in Glenmalure. He became The O'Donnell in 1592 [see *inauguration]. According to tradition, it was he who drew O'Neill into the rebellion. O'Donnell took Sligo and joined forces with Hugh Maguire and O'Neill to effect a crushing victory over Sir Henry Bagenal at the Battle of the Yellow Ford on 14 August 1598. In 1600 he persuaded the Irish leaders to meet the Spanish expedition that had arrived at *Kinsale. There he encouraged O'Neill to make a precipitate attempt to relieve the besieged town, leading to their defeat by Lord Mountjoy (Charles Blount). O'Donnell sailed to Spain seeking further aid and died in Simancas on 10 September 1602. Irish tradition has ascribed his death to poison, as in the version in *Ulrick the Ready* (1892) by Standish James *O'Grady, who also dealt with his escape from Dublin in *The Flight of the Eagle* (1897). *Beatha Aodha Ruaidh Uí Dhomhnaill*, a life of O'Donnell by Lughaidh *Ó Cléirigh, depicts him as a courtly and heroic man of action.

Ó Donnghaile, Eoghan (*fl.* 1680), poet; member of a Tyrone family who fostered Seán an Díomais (Shane the Proud) Ó Néill (1530–67), and in whose memory Ó Donnghaile seems to have composed the poem beginning 'Ceist ar eólchaibh iath Banbha'. He may have written the prose tale *Comhairle Mhic Clámha*.

O'Donoghue, Bernard (1954–), poet; born Knockduff, Co. Cork, educated at Lincoln College, Oxford, becoming a Fellow of Wadham in 1995. Collections include *The Absent Signifier* (1990), *Gunpowder* (1995), and *Here Nor There* (1999). He also wrote *Seamus Heaney and the Language of Poetry* (1994).

O'Donoghue, D[avid] J[ames] (1866–1917), literary historian. Born in

Chelsea, London, he educated himself at the British Museum Library. In 1886 he joined the Southwark Irish Literary Society [see *literary revival] and later served as secretary to its successors in London and in Dublin. He settled in Dublin in 1896, becoming librarian at UCD in 1909. W. B. *Yeats's sketch of him in *Autobiographies fails to recognize him as the chief literary biographer and bibliographer of his period. His *Poets of Ireland* (1892-3), containing entries on 2,000 authors, was much enlarged in 1912 and still serves as a valuable reference work. His *Life of William* *Carleton (1896) includes autobiographical remnants and some letters recovered from that writer's sisters, whom O'Donoghue rescued from poverty, while his *Life and Writings of James Clarence* *Mangan (1897) likewise integrates autobiographical writings and uncollected letters with its narrative.

O'Donovan, Gerald (baptized Jeremiah) (1871-1942), novelist. Born in Co. Down, the son of a travelling pier-builder from Cork, he was educated in Maynooth and ordained in 1895. He left the priesthood in 1904 following disagreements with Thomas O'Dea, the conservative Bishop of Clonfert. Moving to Dublin and then London, he worked for the British propaganda department in the First World War and wrote a patriotic novel about the Home Front (*How They Did It*, 1920). His other novels are set in Ireland. The semi-autobiographical *Father Ralph* (1913) recounts the gradual disillusionment of an energetic and intelligent young priest who leaves the priesthood when the Pope condemns modernism. *Waiting* (1914) concerns the social ostracism of a Catholic who marries a Protestant. *Conquest* (1920) takes the form of dinner-table discussions on the *Anglo-Irish War, coming down on the side of Irish freedom. Other novels dealing with the

obstacles to freedom of conscience are *Vocations* (1921) and *The Holy Tree* (1922). O'Donovan's experience of the Church inspired the priest characters in Moore's 'Fugitives' and *The *Lake*.

O'Donovan, John (1806-1861), scholar. Born at Attateemore, Co. Kilkenny, he was educated locally at a *hedge school and in Waterford. In 1822 he opened a hedge school himself but the following year moved to Dublin. He worked as a scribe for James *Hardiman from around 1827. In 1828 he started teaching Irish to Lieutenant Thomas Larcom, Director of the Ordnance Survey [see George *Petrie], and when Edward *O'Reilly died in 1830, he became Gaelic adviser to the Survey. During 1834-41 he travelled the length and breadth of Ireland, sending back detailed accounts of the language, *folklore, and *place-names of the localities he visited. During 1836-40 he also worked for J. H. *Todd on the catalogue of Irish manuscripts at TCD. Thereafter he was employed by the *Irish Archaeological Society, for whom he edited a text each year between 1841 and 1844. In 1844 he had begun work on an edition and translation of the *Annals of the Four Masters* for the publisher George Smith (6 vols., 1848-51). In 1849 he was appointed to the Chair of Celtic, in Queen's College, Belfast. Though he had no students there, O'Donovan delivered annual lectures from 1850 and successfully resisted attempts to make him live in Belfast. In 1852 John *O'Daly published his edition and translation of *The Tribes of Ireland* by Aonghus Ruadh *Ó Dálaigh. After some difficulties O'Donovan and Eugene *O'Curry were appointed co-editors of the ancient Irish *laws. The language of the texts proving extremely difficult to interpret, the commission appointed others to the editorial team, but meanwhile O'Donovan and O'Curry—by now brothers-in-law—were bickering with each other and uneasy with their employers. The law texts were finally published, under the general editorship of Robert Atkinson, as *Ancient Laws of Ireland* (6 vols., 1865–1901). See Éamonn de hÓir, *Seán Ó Donnabháin agus Eoghan Ó Comhrai* (1962).

O'Donovan, John [Purcell] (1921–1985), playwright. Born in Dublin and educated at Synge St. Christian Brothers, he was an enthusiastic admirer of *Shaw, whom he once visited at Ayot St Lawrence. His plays produced at the *Abbey Theatre included *The Half Millionaire* (1954), *The Shaws of Synge Street* (1960), and *Copperfaced Jack* (1962).

O'Donovan Rossa, Jeremiah (1831–1915), *Fenian. Born at Rosscarbery, Co. Cork, he had a grocery shop in Skibbereen. Rossa became a Fenian and manager of *The *Irish People*, was imprisoned 1865–71, and then went to America. There he edited *The United Irishman* and set up a 'skirmishing fund' subsequently used to finance a dynamiting campaign in England. His funeral at Glasnevin was the occasion for a celebrated oration by Patrick *Pearse.

O'Driscoll, Ciaran (1943–), poet. Born in Callan, Co. Kilkenny, he was educated at National Schools and at St Francis College, Rochestown, Co. Cork. After working as a civil servant in Dublin, 1961–4, he attended UCC before lecturing at UCC and Limerick. His collections include: *Gog and Magog* (1987), *The Poet and his Shadow* (1990), *The Myth of the South* (1992), *Listening to Different Drummers* (1993), and *The Old Women of Magione* (1997). His verse is full of detailed observation and concerns itself with issues of social justice.

O'Driscoll, Dennis (1954–), poet. Born in Thurles, Co. Tipperary, he was

educated there and at UCD. He joined the Civil Service in 1970, rising to the rank of Assistant Principal Officer. His first volume, *Kist* (1982), was followed by *Hidden Extras* (1987), *Long Story Short* (1993) *The Bottom Line* (1994), *Quality Time* (1997), and *Weather Permitting* (1999).

Ó Dubhagáin, Seaán Mór (O'Dugan) (?–1375), poet. A member of a learned family associated with the compilation of the *Book of Uí Mhaine* and residing at Ballydoogan, Co. Galway, he is best-known for 'Triallom timcheall na Fódla', a topographical poem that provides a genealogical survey of Ulster, Connacht, and Co. Meath.

O'Duffy, Eimar [Ultan] (1893–1935), satirical novelist. Born in Dublin, the son of a dentist, O'Duffy went to Stonyhurst, in England, and returned to UCD. He graduated in dentistry but did not practise. He wrote plays for Edward *Martyn's Irish Theatre, 1914–16 (*Walls of Athens; Bricriu's Feast*), and joined the Irish Republican Brotherhood [see *IRA]. In March 1916 O' Duffy was sent to Belfast to call off the insurrection there. His first novel, *The Wasted Island* (1919, rev. 1929), is a personal account of the period, built around the character of Bernard Lascelles. *The Lion and the Fox* (1922), set in 1600–3, is a study of Hugh *O'Neill's vain efforts to enlist the support of Munster in his war against the English. *Printer's Errors* (1922) and *Miss Rudd and Some Lovers* (1923) are light-hearted novels. In 1925, he moved to London with his family and lived by writing. *King Goshawk and the Birds* (1926), the first of the fantasy novels that make up his *Cuanduine trilogy of economic satires, was followed by *The Spacious Adventures of the Man in the Street* (1928); *Asses in Clover* (1933), completed the series. This mock-heroic use of Irish *mythology has occasioned comparison with Flann *O'Brien.

Ó Duibhdábhoireann, learned family, see *O'Davoren.

Ó Duibhgeannáin, a learned family of historiographers to the Ó Fearghails at their ancestral home in Anghaile (Annaly, Co. Longford).

Ó Duilearga, Séamus (James Hamilton Delargy) (1899–1980), folklorist. Born in Cushendall, Co. Antrim, he was raised in Dublin and educated at Castleknock College and UCD, becoming a lecturer in Irish, then Director of the *Irish Folklore Commission in 1935, and finally Professor of Irish Folklore at UCD in 1937. He edited the folklore journal *Béaloideas* from 1928 to 1970, and issued *The Gaelic Story-Teller* (1945). His best-known work is a classic edition of the repertoire of a celebrated Kerry storyteller, *Leabhar Sheáin Í Chonaill* (1948).

Ó Dúill, Greágóir (1946–), poet and critic. Born in Dublin, he was raised in Co. Antrim and educated at QUB. He worked as a civil servant before becoming literary editor of *Comhar. His collections of poetry include *Innílt Bhóthair* (1981), *Dubhthrian* (1985), *Blaoscoileán* (1988), and *Saothrú an Ghoirt* (1994). An anthology of contemporary Ulster poetry in Irish, *Filíocht Uladh* (1986), was followed by a literary biography, *Samuel *Ferguson: Beatha agus Saothar* (1993), and *Garbh Achadh* (1996), another collection.

Ó Duinnín, an tAthair Pádraig [S.] (Fr. Patrick Dinneen) (1860–1934), lexicographer and editor; born in Rathmore, Co. Kerry, attending school there and at Meentogues. He entered the Jesuit order at Milltown Park, Dublin, in 1880 and taught at Clongowes Wood. He joined the *Gaelic League and came to know Patrick *Pearse. He left the order in 1900 to devote himself to Irish scholarship, and set about producing

editions of the poems of Aodhagán *Ó Rathaille (1900), Piaras *Feiritéar (1903), and others. His *Foclóir Gaedhilge agus Béarla: An Irish–English Dictionary* (1904, enlarged edns. 1927, 1934) is an indispensable resource for learners and scholars alike.

óenach, a popular assembly held periodically at fixed locations associated with dynastic burial sites. The óenach involved games, races, contests, and artistic narrative performances that renewed the social and human order whilst honouring the otherworld [see *sidh].

Oengus, see *mythological cycle, *mythology, and *Aislinge Oenguso.

O'Faolain, Eileen (née Gould) (1900–1988), author and children's novelist; born in Cork, wife of Sean and mother of Julia *O'Faolain. Among her children's novels, which deal sympathetically and imaginatively with animals, children, and fairies, were *The Little Black Hen* (1940), *The King of the Cats* (1941), *Miss Pennyfeather and the Pooka* (1949), and *High Sang the Sword* (1959).

O'Faolain, Julia (1932–), novelist and short-story writer; daughter of Sean and Eileen *O'Faolain, born in London and educated at UCD. The satirical stories in *We Might See Sights!* (1968), were followed by *Man in the Cellar* (1974). Her first novel, *Godded and Codded* (1970) deals with an Irish *ingénue* in Paris. Subsequent novels include *No Country for Young Men* (1980), *The Irish Signorina* (1984), and *The Judas Cloth* (1992).

O'Faolain, Sean (1900–1991), man of letters. Born John Whelan in Cork city, into a family recently moved from the country. His father was a member of the Royal Irish Constabulary, while his mother ran a boarding house in Half Moon Street catering for artists working at the nearby Opera House. He was educated by the Presentation Brothers and was influenced by Daniel *Corkery, who cultivated his literary interests but whose cultural politics he later repudiated. In 1918 he entered UCC and became involved in the Republican movement. As a member of the *Gaelic League, he visited the West Cork *Gaeltacht, taking cycling holidays with the slightly younger Frank *O'Connor. During these expeditions he met his future wife, Eileen Gould (*O'Faoláin). O'Faolain's childhood and formative years are described in his autobiography *Vive Moi* (1964). It recounts how he took the Republican side in the *Civil War, becoming a director of propaganda for the *IRA. He returned to studies and took an MA at Harvard on a Commonwealth scholarship, 1926–9, marrying in Boston in 1928. A period was spent teaching at Strawberry Hill College in England before his return to Ireland as a writer in 1933. O'Faolain's early fiction arises from these experiences. *Midsummer Night Madness and Other Stories* (1932) draws on the initial romance of and later disillusionment with nationalist revolutionary activity. In the next phase, with a series of historical novels, *A Nest of Simple Folk* (1934), *Bird Alone* (1936), and *Come Back to Erin* (1940), he constructed a family saga extending from the *Fenian Rising to the War of Independence and the years following. His fictional studies of idealism were paralleled by biographies of political figures in *Eamon *de Valera* (1933, 1939); *The King of the Beggars* (1938), a life of Daniel *O'Connell; and *The Great O'Neill* (1942), a life of Hugh *O'Neill. In *Newman's Way* (1952) he found an opportunity to develop his own conception of a liberal tradition of Catholicism. *The Irish* (1948), a study of national character, brought together many of his ideas on tradition, culture,

and the modern intellectual. His second volume of stories, *A Purse of Coppers* (1937), reflects the bleak conditions of life in Ireland in the 1930s. In *Teresa and Other Stories* (1947) and *The Man Who Invented Sin* (1949), a detached yet human perspective on Ireland emerges. In these and subsequent volumes (*I Remember, I Remember*, 1948; *The Heat of the Sun*, 1966; *The Talking Trees*, 1971; and *Foreign Affairs*, 1976) technique becomes more assured as moral awareness deepens. From 1940 to 1946 O'Faolain edited *The *Bell, the literary journal he founded, commissioning articles of a documentary and social nature while analysing aspects of contemporary life and thought in his editorials, which frequently lashed out against the cultural and religious climate of a period still dominated by the *Censorship Act of 1928. His polemical hostility to traditionalism is evident in his impatience with the Catholic and Gaelic ideal of Ireland, and in his attacks on his mentor Daniel Corkery's attempt to formulate a criterion for literary value based on cultural identity. *The Collected Stories* appeared as three volumes (1980–2). See Maurice Harmon, *Sean O'Faolain: A Life* (1994).

Ó Farach*in, Roibe*rd (Robert Farren) (1909–1984), poet. Born into a Dublin working-class family, he was educated at St Patrick's Training College and UCC, before joining Radio Éireann [see *RTÉ] in 1939, becoming Controller of Programmes, 1953–74, and a Director of the *Abbey Theatre, 1940–73. His verse plays include *Convention at Druim Ceat* and *Lost Light*, both performed at the Abbey in 1943. *Fíon gan Mhoirt* (1938) is an Irish short-story collection. Poetry published under his English name includes *Thronging Feet* (1936); *Rime Gentlemen, Please* (1945); and *The First Exile* (1944), an epic of the Life of St *Colum Cille. His verse reflects the influence of

*Sigerson and Austin *Clarke in its adoption of Gaelic prosodic patterns.

Ó Fiaich, Tomás (1923–1990), scholar and Cardinal; born in Creggan, Co. Armagh, and educated at Maynooth. Ordained in 1948 he became Lecturer in History at Maynooth, 1953, then Professor in 1958, and President in 1974. He was made Archbishop of Armagh in 1977 and a Cardinal in 1979. *Gaelscrínte i gCéin* (1960) is an account of Irish missionaries to Europe in the 7th–9th cents. See Diarmaid Ó Doibhlin (ed.), *Ón Chreagán go Ceann Dubhrann* (1992).

Ó Fiannachta, Pádraig (1927–), poet and translator; born in Ballymore, Dingle, Co. Kerry, and educated at Maynooth, and UCC, he was ordained in 1953. He was appointed Professor of Early and Middle Irish at Maynooth in 1959. With George Thomson he translated Augustine's *Confessions* as *Mise Agaistín* (1967). *Ponc* (1970) was a collection of poems, followed by *Rúin* (1971) and *Deora Dé* (1988). *Ag Siúl na Teorann* (1985) was a novel, and *Gailílí agus Iarúsailéim sa Bhaile Againn* (1999) a long poem. His crowning achievement was *An Bíobla Naofa* (1981), the Maynooth Irish Bible, of which he was chief translator.

O'Flaherty, Liam (1896–1984), novelist; born in Gort na gCapall on Inishmore in the Aran Islands, the ninth of ten children. He was educated at Oatquarter National School, Inishmore, and then at Rockwell College, Co. Tipperary. In 1915 he joined the Irish Guards Regiment as Bill Ganly, using his mother's maiden name. He was wounded in a bombardment at Langemarck, September 1917, and discharged after a year's medical treatment for acute melancholia. He engaged in radical politics and ran up the red flag over the Rotunda in Dublin. He began writing with *Thy Neighbour's Wife* (1923),

published on the recommendation of Edward Garnett, who helped him to write his next novel, *The *Black Soul* (1924) and introduced him to the Russian masters Dostoevsky and Gogol. In consequence his ensuing novels, *The *Informer* (1925), *Mr *Gilhooley* (1926), and *The *Assassin* (1928), were permeated by a St Petersburg gloom, while two collections of short stories, *Spring Sowing* (1924) and *The Tent* (1926), established him as a writer with profound insights into peasant life. *The *Return of the Brute* (1930), *The *Martyr* (1935), and *Hollywood Cemetery* (1935) reveal the author's obsessions. *The *House of Gold* (1929) and *Skerrett* (1932) present a vision of society through a range of characters independent of his own psychic dilemmas. *Two Years* (1930) and *Shame the Devil* (1934) are volumes of autobiography. His last novels, *Famine* (1937), *Land* (1946), and *Insurrection* (1950), form a historical trilogy tracing the rise of modern Irish nationalism. The publication of his short stories in Irish under the title *Dúil (Desire)* (1953), gained O'Flaherty a new audience. In his later years he became a recluse. See Patrick Sheeran, *The Novels of Liam O'Flaherty* (1976).

O'Flaherty, Roderick (1629–1718), historian. Born in Moycullen Castle, Co. Galway, he was educated in classics by John *Lynch in Galway, and studied traditional *bardic learning under Dubhaltach *Mac Fhir Bhisigh. *Ogygia* (1685) was an alternative to the Anglo-Irish *chronicles and the first work of *Gaelic historiography to be printed in London. A poor translation of *Ogygia* was made in 1793 by Revd James Hely of TCD, assisted by Theophilus O'Flanagan [see *Gaelic Society]. He was buried in the grounds of his own house at Park, Co. Galway.

O'Flanagan, James Roderick (1814–1900), novelist. Born in Fermoy,

Co. Cork, he graduated from TCD and practised law in Munster. He moved to London in 1870 but returned to the family home in Fermoy to found the *Fermoy Journal* in 1885, when his sight was already failing. Following a first novel on an *ascendancy legitimacy case (*Gentle Blood*, 1861), O'Flanagan wrote several others, notably *The Life and Adventures of Bryan O'Regan* (1866) and *Captain O'Shaugnessy's Sporting Career* (1873) in the tradition of W.H. *Maxwell.

O'Flanagan, Theophilus, see *Gaelic Society of Dublin.

Ó Flannghaile, Tomás (T.J. Flannery) (1846–1916), poet. He was born near Ballinrobe, Co. Mayo, but when he was 7 his family moved to Manchester. Having learnt to write Irish in his youth, he was one of the early poets of the language revival movement, producing the popular hymn 'Dóchas Linn, Naomh Pádraig'. From 1883 he taught Irish classes in the Southwark Literary Society [see *literary revival]. He circulated the proposal to establish the Irish Texts Society. Works edited by him include Donncha Rua *Mac Conmara's *Eachtra Ghiolla an Amaráin* (1897).

Ó Flatharta, Antoine (1953–), dramatist; born in Leitir Mealláin, Co. Galway, he was educated in the Connemara *Gaeltacht. His first play *Gaeilgeoirí* (1981), at the *Abbey Theatre, revealed a harsh dramatic realism brought to bear on the contemporary Gaeltacht community. This was followed by *Imeachta na Saoirse* (1983) the TV play *Grásta I Meiricea* (1989), *Ag Ealaín in Éirinn* (1985), and *An Solas Dearg* (1995), the latter a play dealing with crossed lives in a Gaelic-speaking radio station. *Bloody Guilty* (1989) was in English.

Ó Floinn, Críostóir (1927–), writer

in Irish and English; born in Limerick, educated at UCD and TCD. Novels include *Lá Dá bhFaca Thú* (1955) and *Learairí Lios an Phúca* (1968). His poems have been published in *Aisling Dhá Abhann* (1977) and other collections; and *Sanctuary Island* (1971) is a collection of stories in English. The controversial 1966 *Oireachtas prize-winning play, *Cóta Bán Chríost*, brought Ó Floinn widespread recognition. Other plays are: *Is É A Dúirt Polonius* (1973), *Mise Raifteirí an File* (1974), and an absurdist piece, *Homo Sapiens* (1985). *Centenary* (1985) is a long poem on the GAA; *There is an Isle* (1998) and *Consplawkus* (1999) are autobiographies.

ogam (or ogham), an alphabet for the Irish language based on twenty-five characters represented by a system of strokes or notches, developed probably in the 4th cent. AD. Examples of this form of writing preserved in stone are found all over Ireland as well as in Wales, the Isle of Man, Cornwall, and Scotland. Since 70 per cent of surviving ogam stones have been found in Cork and Kerry, the cult of erecting such monuments seems to have originated in the south-west of Ireland. The characters of the ogam alphabet had names taken from trees, where e.g. b, signified by a single stroke, was known as beithe (birch), or s, signified by four strokes, was known as sail (willow). Discussions of ogam are to be found in a number of medieval texts, amongst which *Auraicept na nÉces* and *In Lebor Ogaim* (*The Book of Ogam*) are the most significant. A knowledge of ogam apparently survived into the 19th cent.

Ogilby, John (1600–1676), born in Edinburgh, founder of the Theatre Royal at *Werburgh Street, Dublin, the first permanent playhouse in Ireland. Ogilby arrived in 1633 as a member of the household of the Viceroy, Thomas Wentworth, and was created Master of

Revels. In 1635 he recruited the dramatist James *Shirley to write plays and
prologues for the new theatre.

Ogle, Sir George, the Younger,
(?1740–1814), poet and politician, born
in Co. Wexford. A member of the
*Monks of the Screw, he wrote a num-
ber of frequently anthologized Anglo-
Irish lyrics including notably 'Banna's
Banks', 'Molly Astore', and 'Banish
Sorrow', the last a drinking song. He
represented Wexford in the *Irish Parliament after 1796, supported legislative independence but doggedly
opposed *Catholic Emancipation.

Ó Gnímh, a *bardic family with lands
near Larne, Co. Antrim, recorded as
practitioners of bardic poetry in the
16th and 17th cents. They received
the patronage of the Ó Néills and the
Antrim Mac Domhnaills. One Eoin
Agniw, a latter-day member of the family, sold manuscripts to Edward *Lhuyd
in Larne in 1699.

Ó Gnímh, Fear Flatha (?1540–
?1630), a poet who succeeded his father
Brian as head of the *Ó Gnímh bardic
family, ollams [see áes dána] to the Ó
Néill dynasty in Co. Antrim. He may
have travelled with Shane O'Neill on his
visit to Elizabeth I in London, 1562. His
poetry laments the anglicization of Ireland, the disregard for learned orders,
and the demise of the Irish aristocracy
that patronized them. His best-known
poem, 'Mo thruaighe mar táid Gaoi-
dhil', written around 1612, compares
the Irish people to a returning funeral
party. One of Ó Gnímh's most appealing
compositions is 'A Nioclás nocht an
gcláirsigh', a eulogy of the Kerry harper
Nioclás Dall Pierce.

Ó Gormáin, Muiris (?1720–1794),
poet and scribe. Born in Ulster, he
taught Irish to Charles *Vallancey,
among others, and he fell foul of Peadar

*Ó Doirnín because of a supposed lack
of competence in English. Though he
spent most of his later life in Dublin,
where he was a member of the *Ó
Neachtain circle of scholars, he resided
for a while in Belanagare transcribing
material for Charles *O'Conor the
Elder; and he helped Charlotte *Brooke
in compiling and translating *Reliques of
Irish Poetry* (1789).

O'Grady, Desmond (1935–), poet.
Born in Limerick, he was educated by
the Cistercians, then at UCD and Har-
vard. In the 1950s he lived in Paris for a
time. A first collection, *Chords and
Orchestrations* (1956), was followed by
many others, including *Reilly* (1961), *The
Dark Edge of Europe* (1967), *The Dying Gaul*
(1968), *A Limerick Rake* (versions from the
Irish, 1978), *Headgear of the Tribe* (1979),
Seven Arab Odes (1991), and *The Road
Taken* (1996), a volume of collected
poems. He has translated *The Gododdin*
(1977) and Cavafy (1998). He moved to
Italy in 1961 and became a friend of
Ezra Pound.

O'Grady, Standish Hayes (1832–
1915), Gaelic scholar. Born at Erinagh
House, Castleconnell, Co. Limerick, into
an Anglo-Irish naval family, he was a
cousin of the novelist Standish James
*O'Grady. He learnt Irish in the Gaelic-
speaking district of his childhood but
was educated at Rugby School in England before going to TCD. O'Grady
sought out John *O'Donovan, and
Eugene *O'Curry, the leading scholars
of the period, together with the book-
seller and publisher John *O'Daly.
He was a founding member of the
*Ossianic Society in 1853, becoming
President in 1855–7. His verse translation of *The Adventures of Donncha Ruadh
Mac Conmara was published by O'Daly
in 1853 over the name 'S. Hayes', while
the third volume of the *Transactions*
(1857) of the society, edited by O'Grady
himself, contains his translation-edition

of *Tóraigheacht Dhiarmada agus Ghráinne. Silva Gadelica* (2 vols., 1892) was a miscellany of medieval prose tales with elegant translations in the second volume. He worked on a catalogue of Irish *manuscript material in the British Museum but left it unfinished, Robin *Flower later using his work in his 3-volume *Catalogue.*

O'Grady, Standish James (1846–1928), novelist and cultural activist. Born at Castletown Berehaven, Co. Cork, where his father was Church of Ireland rector, he was educated at Tipperary Grammar School and TCD, and called to the Bar in 1872. Standish Hayes *O'Grady was a cousin. A chance encounter with Sylvester *O'Halloran's *Introduction to the Study of the History and Antiquities of Ireland* (1772) led him to undertake a thorough investigation of the extant sources of Irish myth and legend, and an ambitious series of legendary histories and fictions. Within four years he published the *History of Ireland: The Heroic Period* (1878), *Early Bardic Literature, Ireland* (1879), *History of Ireland: Cuculain and his Contemporaries* (1880), *History of Ireland: Critical and Philosophical* (1881), and *Cuculain: An Epic* (1882). He adopted a style at once high-flown and graphic to convey the grandeur of the *Ulster and other cycles. These books had a profound effect on younger writers, Yeats included. O'Grady thought that the Anglo-Irish *ascendancy should have taken over the leadership of the Gaelic people which he believed *Cú Chulainn provided for 'bardic' Ireland. *Toryism and Tory Democracy* (1886) implored the Anglo-Irish to embrace their nation and to take advantage of the native instincts for service, loyalty, and bravery. In the novel *Red Hugh's Captivity* (1889, rev. 1897 as *The Flight of the Eagle*), O'Grady deals with the Elizabethan reconquest of Ireland, arguing in a preface that a closer union with England had been

necessary. He continued to produce fiction, turning to the *Fionn cycle for *Finn and His Companions* (1892). *The Coming of Cuculain* (1894) was the first part of a trilogy, completed by *In the Gates of the North* (1901) and *The Triumph and Passing of Cuculain* (1920). These books, intended for children, retell the stories of Cú Chulainn in the style of the adventure story. He edited *The Kilkenny Moderator* and the *All-Ireland Review. The Queen of the World* (1906) was a science fiction novel, published under the pseudonym 'Luke Netterville'. In 1918 for health reasons he moved to the Isle of Wight.

Ó Grianna, Séamus (1889–1969) ('Máire'), novelist. Born in Ranafast, in the Donegal *Gaeltacht, he was educated locally and qualified as a teacher at St Patrick's College. The elder brother of Seosamh *Mac Grianna, he absorbed the *folklore and traditions of the region from their father, Féilimí Dhónaill Phroinsias Green. He was interned 1922–4, having taken the Republican side in the *Civil War. In 1932 he became a civil servant. His novels *Caisleán Óir* (1924) and *Mo Dhá Róisín* (1921), and the short stories *Cith is Dealán* (1927) are his best-known works. The social history and customs of Ranafast are recounted in *Rann na Feirsde* (1942), *Nuair a Bhí Mé Óg* (1942), and *Saoghal Corrach* (1945). See Nollaig Mac Congail, *Máire: Clár Saothair* (1990).

O'Growney, Fr. Eugene (an tAthair Eoghan Ó Gramhnaigh) (1863–1899), Irish-language activist; born in Ballyfallon, Co. Meath, and educated at Maynooth [see *universities]. While at Maynooth he spent summers in many *Gaeltacht areas. After ordination in 1889 he became curate of Ballynalargy, Co. Westmeath, and contributed articles to *Irisleabhar na Gaedhilge,* becoming its editor in 1891, when he was appointed Professor of Celtic Literature and Language at

Maynooth. His friendship with Douglas *Hyde led to his becoming Vice-President of the *Gaelic League on its foundation in 1893. In *Irisleabhar na Gaedhilge* and *The Weekly Freeman* he published the series that was issued by the League as *Simple Lessons in Irish* (1894), a book that sold in thousands.

Ogygia, seu Rerum Hibernicarum Chronologia (1685), a chronology of Irish history written in Latin and published by Roderick *O'Flaherty in London. The title derives from Plutarch's name for an island west of Britain supposedly visited by the Greeks, including Hercules, where the god Chronos was said to lie imprisoned in a cave.

O'Halloran, Sylvester (1728–1807), surgeon and historian; born in Limerick, where he studied with Seán Clárach *Mac Domhnaill. For further education he went to Paris and Leiden, but returned to practise ophthalmic medicine in Limerick, founding the Infirmary there in 1760. With *An Introduction to the Study of the History and Antiquities of Ireland* (1772) he became an out-spoken critic of the Anglo-Irish *chronicles. When Thomas *Leland produced his conservative *History of Ireland* (1773), O'Halloran replied with *Ierne Defended* (1774), asserting the value of Irish *manuscripts. His *General History of Ireland* (1774), defended the civilization of pre-Norman Ireland. Maria *Edgeworth merged him with Henry *Brooke to create a studious Catholic gentleman in *The *Absentee* (1812).

O'Hanlon, Canon John (pseudonym 'Lageniensis') (1821–1905), hagiographer. Born in Stradbally, Co. Laois, and ordained in 1847 in St Louis, Missouri, he returned to Ireland in 1853 and pursued a writing career of great activity, publishing his *Lives of the Irish Saints* (9 vols., 1875), a *History of Queen's Country* (Laois) (1907), and a number of pieces drawing on his experience in America.

Ó hAnnracháin, Peadar (1873–1965), poet; born near Skibbereen, Co. Cork. In 1901 he was a *Gaelic League organizer, and in 1913 joined the *Irish Volunteers, spending periods in gaol between 1916 and 1921. *Fé Bhrat an Chonnartha* (1944) is one of several accounts of his work for the League. His verse was collected in *An Chaise Gharbh* (1918) and *An Chaise Riabhach* (1937). A play, *Stiana* (1944), was produced at the *Abbey Theatre.

Ó hAodha, Séamus (1886–1967), poet and playwright. Born in Cork and educated there by the Christian Brothers and in UCC, he taught until 1923, when he became a primary-school inspector. His collections include *Uaigneas* (1928), *Caoineadh na Mná agus Dánta Eile* (1939), and *Ceann an Bhóthair* (1966). *Donnchadh Ruadh* (1939), a play about the poet Donncha Rua *Mac Conmara was produced in the *Abbey Theatre.

O'Hara, Kane (1714–1782), author of *Midas*, the first musical burlesque in English. Born in Sligo and educated at TCD. *Midas* was produced by amateurs at Capel St. Theatre, but soon went on to London. *The Golden Pippin* (1773) was revived by John *O'Keeffe as *Olympus in an Uproar* in 1796.

O'Hegarty, P[atrick] S[arsfield], (1879–1955), historian and bibliographer. Born in Carrignavar, Co. Cork, and educated by the Christian Brothers, he worked in the Post Office, resigning in 1918 when compelled to take the oath of allegiance. Author of studies of John *Mitchel (1917) and Terence *MacSwiney (1922) as well as bibliographies of *Mangan, *Allingham, and Joseph *Campbell, he edited magazines including *An tÉireannach* for the *Gaelic League

(London), and *The Irish World*. His historical works *Indestructible Nation* (1918), *The Victory of Sinn Féin* (1924), and *A History of Ireland under the Union, 1801–1922* (1952) reveal strong nationalist convictions.

Ó hÉigeartaigh, Pádraig see P.S. *O'Hegarty.

Ó hÉigeartaigh, Seán Sairséal (1917–1967), publisher; born in Welshpool, Montgomeryshire, where his father P. S. *O'Hegarty worked in the Post Office. Educated at St Andrew's College, Dublin, and TCD, he entered the Irish Civil Service. An enthusiastic language revivalist, he founded Craobh na hAiséirí and An Comhchaidreamh in conjunction with the student societies of the day, becoming first director of *Comhar* in 1942, and then establishing An Club Leabhar in 1948. In 1945 he founded with his wife, Bríd Ní Mhaoileoin, the Irish-language publishing company Sairséal agus Dill, which issued original works by many writers.

Ó hEithir, Breandán (1930–1990), novelist and journalist in Irish. A nephew of Liam *O'Flaherty, he was born on Inis Mór, the Aran Islands, and educated there, at Coláiste Éinde in Galway, and at UCG. From 1957 to 1963 he was Irish Editor of *The Irish Press*. He also edited *Comhar*. His first novel, *Lig Sinn i gCathú* (1976), is a bawdy narrative of Galway undergraduate life. His second, *Sionnach Ar Mo Dhuán* (1988), aroused controversy for its frank depictions of sex. Works in English include *Over The Bar* (1984) on the *GAA.

Ó hEódhasa, a learned family, originally from Ceinéal Tighearnaigh, an unidentified part of Ulster. Several members of the family resided between 1586 and 1603 on what may earlier have been church lands at Ballyhose (Baile Uí Eódhusa), Lower Lough Erne, Co. Fermanagh, as shown in Elizabethan state records.

Ó hEódhasa, Eochaidh (?1560–1612), poet; head of the Ó hEódhasa poetic family and ollam [see *áes dána] to three successive Maguire chieftains of Fermanagh: Cú Chonnacht (d. 1589), Hugh (d. 1600), and Hugh's half-brother, Cú Chonnacht. The family home was at Ballyhose on Castlehume Lough, Lower Lough Erne, where his principal teacher was probably his father, Maoileachlainn Óg. Maguire gave Ó hEódhasa lands at Currin, near Ballinamallard, but the poem 'T'aire riot a rí ó nUidhir' complains that the holding is not commensurate with his status as ollam; and that he is too far from Hugh himself whose affection he both craves and demands. Another poem, 'Mór an t-ainm ollamh flatha', rehearses the rights due to a chief-poet in similar terms. In 1600 Maguire joined Hugh *O'Neill in Munster, where he was fighting the English and awaiting Spanish reinforcements. Ó hEódhasa stayed in Fermanagh, and a personal poem, 'Fuar leam an adhaighse d'Aodh', expresses his fear for his patron's safety, and his concern that Hugh is exposed to the bitter cold of a winter's night while on campaign. This poem is the basis of a passionate adaptation by James Clarence *Mangan. Ó hEódhasa's poems to Maguire allow an insight into the very close relationship between poet and patron. Hierarchical and conventional, they embrace a personal dimension as well, animating the traditional expressions of devotion and loyalty. Hugh's half-brother Cú Chonnacht succeeded him in the chieftainship. Ó hEódhasa wrote the inaugural ode 'Fada léighthear Eamhain a n-aontomha', and when Cú Chonnacht went south in 1601 to join the Spaniards who had landed at Kinsale his ollam accompanied him. However, Ó hEódhasa was wounded in a skirmish and returned to Fermanagh, where he wrote 'Fada óm intinn a hamharc' for Cú Chonnacht. Of more than fifty surviving poems, about half are to the Maguires. He also dedicated poems to Red Hugh *O'Donnell, Toirdhealbhach Luineach Ó Néill, and the O'Byrnes of Wicklow, to the widow of one of whom he is said to have proposed marriage. 'Mór theasda dh'obair Óivid' celebrates the accession of James I in 1603. A poem addressed to Hugh O'Neill, 'Fríoth an uainse ar inis Fáil', written before the *Flight of the Earls, urges him to resume the war against the English. See Pádraig A. Breatnach, 'The Chief's Poet', *Proceedings of the RIA*, 83/C (1983).

Ó hEódhasa, Giolla Brighde (also Bonaventura, OFM) (?–1614), poet and divine; Guardian of St Anthony's College, *Louvain, born probably in Ballyhose, Co. Fermanagh, to the *Ó hEódhasa learned family. After a period spent training in the native learning, he went abroad in the 1590s to study at Douai. In 1607 he joined the newly established Irish Franciscan College of St Anthony of Padua at Louvain. He was ordained in 1609 and lectured in theology there. His *An Teagasg Críosdaidhe* (Antwerp, 1611; Louvain, 1614) was the first in a series of works in Irish by the Louvain Franciscans for pastoral use. Secular poems by him include a farewell to Ireland ('Truagh an t-amharcsa a Éire'), and an address to Red Hugh *O'Donnell composed about 1592. His manuscript treatise on the Irish language, *Rudimenta Grammaticae Hibernicae*, contains the first classification of Irish nouns by declension.

Ó hIfearnáin, Liam Dall (?1720–1803), poet; born in Lattin, Co. Tipperary, and trained at a latter-day *bardic school in Co. Limerick. He was probably weak-sighted rather than blind (dall), and an albino according to folk memory

in his native place. His poetry, written in the conventional amhrán metre of the time [see Irish *metrics], deals mostly with love and politics, his sympathies being strongly *Jacobite. His best-known composition is an *aisling entitled 'Pé in Éirinn Í'. Elsewhere he bestows on Ireland the name of Caitlín ní Uallacháin (*Cathleen Ni Houlihan), which subsequently became a familiar personification. The extant poems have been edited by Risteárd Ó Foghludha in *Ar Bhruach na Coílle Muaire* (1939).

Ó hIfearnáin, Mathghamhain (*fl.* 1585), poet, living in the Shronell district of Co. Tipperary in the late 16th cent., who wrote poems on the decline of the profession of poetry. 'Ceist, cia do cheinneóchadh dán?' describes his passage from one Munster market cross to another in search of a buyer for a well-wrought poem.

O'Higgins, Brian (pseudonym 'Brian na Banban') (1882–1949), nationalist author. Born in Kilscyre, Co. Meath, he was TD for Clare (1922), and later President of the Irish College at Carrigholt. He wrote much poetry and song. His fiction includes *By a Hearth in Eirinn* (1908) and *Hearts of Gold* (1918), reflecting on the hardships of rural life in Ireland.

Ó hOdhráin, Mícheál (1932–), writer of fiction and playwright. Born in Co. Mayo and educated at St Jarlath's College, Tuam, and UCG. Two collections of short stories, *Slán leis an gComhluadar* (1961) and *Sléibhte Mhaigh Eo* (1964), treat gently of traditional life. *Ar Son na Treibhe* (1964), *Cine Cróga* (1964), and *An Tine Bheo* (1966) are historical novels for children.

Ó hÓgain, Dáithí (1949–), poet, scholar, writer of fiction; born in Bruff, Co. Limerick, he was educated at UCD, where he became Professor in 1998. *Breacadh* (1973) was a volume of short stories, followed by the poetry collections *Cois Camhaoireach* (1981), *Cóngar na gCrosán* (1985), *Idir an Dá Dhealbh* (1988), and *Gadaí an Cheoil* (1994). *An File* (1982) was a study of the Gaelic poet. Further literary and folklore research included: *The Hero in Irish Folk History* (1985), *Fionn Mac Cumhaill* (1988), *Celtic Warriors* (1999), and *The Sacred Isle* (1999).

Ó hUid, Tarlach (1917–1990), man of letters. Born in London of Unionist parents, he learned Irish at an early age, joined the *IRA, and was interned in *Northern Ireland during the Second World War. *Ar Thóir mo Shealbha* (1960) recounts his early life. *Faoi Ghlas* (1985), a second volume of autobiography, deals with his years in prison. *An Bealach chun a'Bhearnais* (1949), his first novel, has a black descendant of 17th-cent. Irish slaves as its main character. Both *An Dá Thrá* (1952) and *Adios* (1975) deal with political tensions in Northern Ireland. Ó hUid worked on *Inniu* for many years before finally becoming editor.

Ó hUiginn, a famous learned family, which kept a *bardic school at Ceall Cluaine (Kilcloney), near Ballinasloe, Co. Galway.

Ó hUiginn, Tadhg Dall ('Blind') (1550–1591), poet and best-known member of the *Ó hUiginn *bardic family. Born at Dougharane, Leyney, Co. Sligo, he was fostered in Donegal. One of his first patrons was Cathal Ó Conchobhair, chief of the Ó Conchobhair family of Sligo who had retained the Ó hUiginns for generations. Tadhg Dall lived for a time at Coolrecuill in Kilmactigue, a parish of Leyney, where he was a man of some substance. According to tradition, he was murdered by six members of the Ó hEaghra family. The forty or so compositions attributed to Tadhg Dall which survive are copied in numerous *manuscripts such as the *Book of the O'Conor Don*. Most are entirely conventional in style and theme, and dedicated to members of the Gaelic aristocracy, displaying a remarkable technical command deepened with intelligence and emotion. In one of his most powerful poems, 'D'fhior chogaidh comhailtear síothcháin', Tadhg Dall urges Brian Ó Ruairc to make total war against the English. The poem ends with a vision of extreme violence. Aside from formal and professional verse, he is probably the author of a humorous poem on a lump of rancid butter. See Eleanor Knott (ed. and trans.), *The Bardic Poems of Tadhg Dall Ó hUiginn* (2 vols., 1922, 1926).

O'Hussey, see *Ó hEodhasa, learned family.

Oidheadh Chloinne Lir and Oidheadh Chloinne Tuireann, see *Three Sorrows of Storytelling.

Oidheadh Chonlaoich (*Violent Death of Conlaoch*), an Early Modern Irish [see *Irish language] retelling of *Aided Oenfhir Aífe narrating how *Cú Chulainn kills his son Conlaoch (called Connle in the older version).

tOileánach, An (1929), the autobiography of the Blasket Islander Tomás *Ó Criomhthain, written at the suggestion of Brian Ó Ceallaigh, a language revivalist who visited the island in 1917. The narrative deals with events of early childhood and boyhood, then courting, matchmaking and marriage, and afterwards the tragedy of dead children, as well as the stress of emigration and the unremitting harshness of a life close to and dependent upon nature. The book ends on an elegiac note of assured eloquence when he declares that he has written accurately of island life so that some account of its culture will survive, since 'ní bheidh ár leithéidí arís ann (our likes will never be seen again)'. *An tOileánach* was edited by Pádraig *Ó

Siochfhradha ('An Seabhac') in 1929 and revised by Pádraig Ó Maoileoin in 1973.

tOireachtas, An (lit. 'the assembly for business or pastime'), the premier Irish-language literary and cultural festival, held annually for ten days in October. The festival accommodates all aspects of Gaelic tradition—storytelling, music, art, drama, and in particular *sean-nós singing.

Oisín, son of *Fionn mac Cumhail, poethero of the *Fionn cycle, and original of James *Macpherson's Ossian (whence 'Ossianic'). He is lured to Tír na nÓg [see *sídh] by Niamh, where he spends hundreds of years. By his return Ireland has been Christianized, and much Fionn lore is devoted to the exchange, mostly acrimonious, between St *Patrick and the pagan survivor.

O'Kearney, Nicholas (*c.* 1802–*c.* 1865), scribe, editor, and occasional poet. Born in Thomastown near Dundalk, Co. Louth, he spent most of his life in Dublin, leaving behind a considerable collection of manuscripts. He edited tales from the *Fionn cycle: *Cath Gabhra* (1853) for John *O'Daly and *Feis Tighe Chonáin* (1885) for the *Ossianic Society.

O'Keeffe, John (1747–1833), playwright. Born in Dublin, he was educated in classics and French by a Jesuit. He worked under Henry *Mossop at *Smock Alley as an actor and an author, before moving to London. His writings, which include more than thirty-five comedies, farces, adaptations, comic operas, and other light-hearted stage entertainments, were collected in 1798. His *Recollections* (2 vols., 1826) are valuable for Irish and English theatrical history. He launched himself at the Hay-market Theatre with a follow-up to *Goldsmith's *She Stoops to Conquer* (1773) which he called *Tony Lumpkin in Town*

(1778). *Wild Oats* (1791) played for many years in London and Dublin. *The She-Gallant* (1767) was first performed at Smock Alley and revived in London in 1782; it features an Irish servant, Thady MacBrogue; of the rest, Irish material occurs in the following: *Harlequin Teague* (1782), a pantomime featuring the Giant's Causeway; *The Banditti*, a comic opera, includes music by Carolan [see Toirdhealbhach *Ó Cearbhalláin]; *The Toy, or Lie of the Day* (1789), has a character called Young O'Donovan, a needy Irishman in England; *The Poor Soldier* (1783) and its sequel, *Patrick in Prussia* (1786) have Irish characters and settings as has *The Prisoner at Large* (1788); *The Wicklow Gold Mine* (1796) is an opera with Irish town and country types; and *Tantara-rara Rogues All!* (1788) is in Paris but including the characters Sir Ulick Liffydale and O'Toole, alias Lord Limavaddy. In other plays he expressed disapproval of Irish absenteeism, as in *The Prisoner at Large* (1788). Ireland provided O'Keeffe with material for *stage-Irishmen and women, and opportunities for effusions on the natural beauty of 'Shamrockshire'.

O'Kelly, Charles (1621–1695), soldier and author of *Macariae Excidium, or the Destruction of Cyprus* (1692), a 'secret' history of the *Williamite War masquerading as a translation of a work of one Philotas Philocypres. Born in Screen, Co. Galway, of mixed Irish and English parentage, O'Kelly served in the Royalist army in Ireland, 1642–51, escaped to Spain, and joined Charles II in France.

O'Kelly, Seumus (?1875–1918), playwright and writer of fiction. Born near Loughrea, Co. Galway, he joined *The Southern Star* in 1903, which he rose to edit, as also *The Leinster Leader, The Dublin Saturday Post*, and *Sinn Féin's *Nationality*. *The Shuiler's Child* (1909) was produced at the *Abbey, and other plays include *Meadowsweet* (1912), *The Bribe* (1914), and *The Parnellite* (1919). His two novels are: *The Lady of Deer Park* (1917), a *big house romance set in Co. Galway, and *Wet Clay* (1922), the story of a returned emigrant who takes to farming with tragic results. In the novella 'The Weaver's Grave' a young widow awakens to new love while looking for the right grave for her husband. Collections of his short stories and fairy-tales include *By the Stream of Kilmeen* (1906), *Hillsiders* (1909), and *Waysiders* (1917). He died of a heart attack in the Sinn Féin offices when they were raided three days after the Armistice.

Ó Laighteís, Ré (1953–), poet and writer of fiction; born in Sallynoggin, Co. Dublin, he was educated at UCG and Boston. His first short stories appeared in *An Punk agus Scéalta Eile* (1988), then *Ciorcal Meiteamorfach* (1991), and *Ecstasy agus Scéalta Eile* (1994, translated into English, 1995; and Italian, 1997). His works include *An Taistealaí* (1990), *Sceoin sa Bhoireann* (1995), and *Gofa* (1996).

Ó Laoghaire, An tAthair Peadar (Fr. Peter O'Leary) (1839–1920), writer of fiction. Born on a small farm in the parish of Clondrohid, Co. Cork, he attended local schools before entering Maynooth [see *universities] in 1861, where, he tells us, he was reproached by Archbishop John *MacHale for failing to mention Irish writers in a prize-winning essay on literature. He was later to refer to Irish and English as twin armouries of the mind, in *Mo Sgéal Féin* (1915). After ordination in 1867 he finally settled as parish priest at Castlelyons in 1891. With the foundation of the *Gaelic League in 1893, Ó Laoghaire began writing in Irish. He was acknowledged as the chief advocate of the use of the living speech ('caint na ndaoine') as a suitable idiom for a new literature. His output included original works such as *Séadna* (1904) and *Niamh* (1907); and

modernizations of tales from the older literature such as *An Craos-Deamhan* (1905), *Eisirt* (1909), *An Cleasaidhe* (1913), *Lughaidh Mac Con* (1914), *Bricriu* (1915), and *Guaire* (1915).

Old Boys, The (1964), a novel by William *Trevor, it concerns the committee of an Old Boys' Association which meets to elect a new President.

Old English, term for Anglo-Norman families in Ireland [see *Norman invasion] and, more generally, those settled before the English Reformation.

Old Heads and Young Hearts (1844), a comedy of manners by Dion *Boucicault, written for the Haymarket Theatre, London. With its complicated plot involving two interlocking love triangles, mistaken identities, disguises, and sudden reversals, it follows the pattern of Restoration comedy.

Old Irish, term used for aristocratic families of Gaelic stock in Ireland as distinct from the *Old English and the New English, the latter being planted stock of the 16th cent. and after.

Old Jest, The (1979), a novel by Jennifer *Johnston, set in the period of the *Anglo-Irish War. Nancy Gulliver, an orphan, lives with her spinster aunt and senile grandfather in a Wicklow *big house on the point of being sold up by her reduced Anglo-Irish family.

Old Lady Says 'No', The (1929), Denis *Johnston's first play. Staged at the Peacock Theatre by the Gate Company after Lady *Gregory had refused it for the *Abbey, it uses expressionist techniques to measure the materialism and hypocrisy of the Irish Free State [see *Irish State] against the political idealism embodied by Robert *Emmet. Appearing as a flower-seller, *Cathleen Ni Houlihan takes the forms of a seductive young woman and a bloodthirsty old hag.

Old Woman Remembers, The (1923), by Lady *Gregory, first performed at the *Abbey Theatre by Sara *Allgood, is a dramatic poem about Irish rebellions against English rule across the centuries, the old woman lighting a candle for the leader of each.

O'Leary, John (1830–1907), revolutionary and man of letters. Born in Co. Tipperary, he had enough private means to study desultorily at TCD, Cork, and Galway. O'Leary belonged to the left wing of the *Young Ireland movement with James Fintan *Lalor, and was released from prison after 1848 on condition that he leave the country. During 1863–5 he edited The Irish People. Charged with treason-felony, he endured brutal treatment in English prisons. In 1885 he returned to Ireland, and became the centre of a literary circle that included W. B. *Yeats, Maud *Gonne, and Arthur *Griffith. O'Leary called his memoirs Recollections of Fenians and Fenianism (1896).

O'Leary, Fr. Peter, see An tAthair Peadar *Ó Laoghaire.

ollam, see *áes dána.

Ó Lochlainn, Gearóid (1884–1970), playwright, and author. Born in Liverpool, he was brought as a child to Ireland, and returned again after training in Copenhagen's Alexandrateater. He was a founding member of An Comhar Drámaíochta (1923), established to promote Gaelic Theatre. His Irish plays include Na Fearachoin (1946). Ealaín na hAmharclainne (1966) is a concise account of the development of drama with particular reference to Ireland, as well as a personal memoir of the *Abbey, the *Gate, and An *Taibhdhearc.

Ó Loinsigh, Pádraig, see *Gaelic Society of Dublin.

Ó Longáin, a learned family associated with Carrignavar, Co. Cork, from 1764, when Mícheál mac Peadair (1693–1770) arrived there from Ballydonoghue, Co. Limerick, where he had been a hereditary land steward to the Fitzgeralds, Knights of Glin. His only child, Mícheál Óg *Ó Longáin (1766–1837), was assisted by his sons, Peter (1801–?) and Paul (1808–66), who transcribed *manuscripts for Bishop John Murphy of Cork while still in their teens.

Ó Longáin, Mícheál Óg (1766–1837), poet and scribe; born to the *Ó Longáin learned family in Carrignavar, Co. Cork. His father, Mícheál mac Peadair, died when he was 4 and his mother when he was 8, and he supported himself as a cowherd before returning to school at 18. In 1797–8 he was a courier for the *United Irishmen and was in tune with the politics of Republicanism, unlike most *Jacobite poets in Munster. 'Buachaillí Loch Garman' praises the Boys of Wexford for kindling the fire, and bitterly laments Munster's failure to rise in 1798. In 1800 he married, and eked out a living as a scribe, a labourer, and a teacher. In one poem he expressed his helplessness on seeing his wife and children clinging together for warmth ('Fuacht na scailpe seo'). In 1814 the Catholic Bishop of Cork, John Murphy, employed him as a teacher and scribe. One of the most prolific of the later scribes, he produced some 150 extant manuscripts containing contemporary literature, but also material from earlier periods not collected elsewhere.

O'Loughlin, Michael (1958–), poet; born in Dublin, and educated at TCD, he co-founded the Raven Arts Press with Dermot *Bolger and Colm *Tóibín in the late 1970s, before leaving to teach abroad in Barcelona, Denmark, and Amsterdam. His collections include: *Stalingrad: The Street Dictionary* (1980), *Atlantic Blues* (1982), *The Diary of a Silence* (1985), and *Another Nation* (1996). His poetry has a marked visual quality.

O'Mahony [or O'Mahoney], John (1819–1877), revolutionary and translator. Born in Kilbeheny, Co. Limerick, and educated at TCD, he took part in the *Young Ireland rising of 1848, fled to France, and went to join John *Mitchel in New York in 1853. He issued a translation of *Keating's *Foras Feasa ar Éirinn* as *The History of Ireland* (1857), but the wholesale inclusion of notes from John *O'Donovan's edition of the *Annals of the Four Masters* (1848–51) prevented its sale in Ireland. The work includes a commentary of his own comparing the modern struggle against English rule in Ireland with the ethos of the *Fionn cycle, giving currency to the term most widely used for the *Fenians. In 1859 he founded the Fenian Brotherhood, the American wing of the Irish Republican Brotherhood (IRB).

O'Malley, Ernie [Ernest] (Earnán Ó Máille) (1898–1957), revolutionary. Born in Castlebar, Co. Mayo, and raised in Dublin, he was a medical student at TCD when the *Easter Rising broke out, and he joined with the insurgents. *On Another Man's Wound* (1936) gives an account of his career in the *IRA during the *Anglo-Irish War. *The Singing Flame* (1978), edited by Frances-Mary Blake from a manuscript, relates his involvement in the occupation of the Four Courts at the outbreak of the *Civil War.

O'Malley, Grace (called Gráinne Mhaol, Granuaile) (?1530–1600), pirate and figure of legend. She was born in Co. Mayo and assumed command of her family's maritime domain on the west coast of Ireland, gaining notoriety among the English colonists of the period. At her encounter with Queen Elizabeth I in London she is said to have assumed regal prerogatives and used Irish.

O'Malley, Mary (1954–), poet; born in Connemara, she was educated there and at UCG. She lived in Portugal 1978–86, teaching at the University of Lisbon 1983–6, when she returned to Galway. Her poetry, which combines lyrical force and a mythic resonance, was issued in *A Consideration of Silk* (1990), *Where the Rocks Float* (1993), and *The Knife in the Wave* (1997).

Ó Maoilchonaire, learned family, originally from Teffia (Tethbha), east of Lough Ree. Their principal seats were in north Roscommon at Cluain Polcáin and Cluain na hOidhche, the birthplace of Flaithrí *Ó Maoilchonaire.

Ó Maoilchonaire, Flaithrí (Florence Conry) (?1560–1620), theologian and Archbishop of Tuam; born at Cluain na hOidhce, Co. Roscommon, a seat of the *Ó Maoilchonaire learned family. He was trained in native learning before entering the Franciscan order in Salamanca. In 1601 he accompanied Don Juan del Aquila to Kinsale, later joining Red Hugh *O'Donnell, to whom he was spiritual director in Spain after the *Flight of the Earls. In 1606 he persuaded Philip III to establish St Anthony's College at *Louvain in the Spanish Netherlands. An authority on the writings of St Augustine, his *Emanuel or *Sgáthán an Chrábhaidh* (*Mirror of Faith*) (1616), generally called *Desiderius*, was largely based upon the Catalan work *El Desseoso* (1615).

Ó Maoileoin, Pádraig (1913–), novelist. Grandson of Tomás *Ó Críomhthain, he was born in Dunquin, Co. Kerry. He spent thirty years in the Garda

Síochána before being employed on Niall *Ó Dónaill's *Irish–English Dictionary* (1977). The autobiographical *Na hÁird Ó Thuaidh* (1960) is a study of change in the author's native Corca Dhuibhne. His first novel, *Bríde Bhán* (1967), had a modern heroine, while *De Réir Uimhreacha* (1968) was based on his police experience.

Ó Maolmhuaidh, Proinsias (Francis Molloy) (?1614–1684), Franciscan theologian, and grammarian. Born probably in Co. Offaly, he was educated at St Anthony's in Rome from 1632, and was appointed Professor of Theology at St Isidore's in Rome in 1650. Author of *Disputatio Theologica de Incarnatione Verbi* (1645) and *Cursus Philosophiae* (1666), he also composed poetry in Latin. His devotional text *Lóchrann na gCreidmheach* (*Lucerna Fidelium*) (1676) was produced for the Irish and Scottish missions, and for the spiritual welfare of Irish soldiers in Continental armies [see *Irish Brigade].

O'Meara, Kathleen (pseudonym 'Grace Ramsay') (1839–1888), novelist. Born in Dublin, she lived nearly all of her life in Paris. Her novels such as *Robin Redbreast's Victory* are pro-Catholic and seek to illustrate how improved understanding between denominations may help to solve landlord and tenant problems in Ireland. *The Battle of Connemara* (1878) advances similar views.

Ó Muireadhaigh, [An tAth] Réamonn (1938–), poet. Born in Co. Armagh, he was educated at Maynooth. After ordination in 1962 he worked for some time as a priest in Belfast before returning to Armagh. His collections include *Athphreabadh na hÓige* (1964), and *Arán ar an Tábla* (1970).

Ó Muirgheasa, Énrí (1874–1945), scholar and folklorist. Born in Donaghmoyne, Co. Monaghan, he trained as a teacher in St Patrick's College, Drumcondra. He collected *folklore and *folksong from some of the last speakers of Irish in Tyrone and elsewhere. Ó Muirgheasa's collections include *Céad de Cheoltaibh Uladh* (1915), *Dhá Chéad de Cheoltaibh Uladh* (1934), *Dánta Diadha Uladh* (1936), and *Amhráin na Midhe* (1933). Ó Muirgheasa's collection of manuscripts is held by UCD and his library by UUC.

Ó Muirthile, Liam (1950–), poet. Born in Cork, the son of a carpenter from Ballinacarraige, near Dunmanway, he was educated at Coláiste Chríost Rí, and UCC, where he came under the influence of Seán *Ó Tuama and Seán *Ó Ríordáin, and was involved with the group of poets associated with *Innti magazine. The title poem of his first collection, *Tine Chnámh* (1984), is a long poem dealing with his memories of St John's Eve bonfires [see *festivals] in Cork city. *An Peann Coitianta* (1991) is a selection of journalistic prose; other collections include: *Dialann Bóthair* (1993) and *Walking Time* (2000). *Ar Bhruach na Laoi* (1995) was a novel; *Fear an Tae* (1999) and *Liodán na hAbhann* (1999) poetic dramas.

Ó Murchadha, Seán (na Ráithíneach) (1700–62), poet and scribe. A member of a learned family he was born and educated in Carrignavar, Co. Cork, where he presided over a court of poetry (*cúirt éigse). Almost thirty *manuscripts have survived spanning 1719–62, the greatest number for any Irish-language poet of the period. He was bailiff for the petty sessions in Glanmire, but his loyalties were with the Catholic cause. 'Tá an bhliadhain seo ag teacht' (1744) looks forward to a coming rebellion. Ó Murchadha's notebooks for 1720–45 are extant, providing a unique insight into Gaelic life of the period.

On Baile's Strand, see *Cuchulain cycle.

Ó'n Cháinte, Fear Feasa (*fl.* 1600), poet; born and lived in Co. Cork. The uncompromising force of his work is seen to good effect in a poem urging Conchubhar Ó hEidirsceóil to make war against the English.

Ó Neachtain, Seán (?1650–1729), poet and scribe. Born and brought up in Co. Roscommon, he moved to Dublin as a young man. He wrote *Jacobite verse, love-poems, and elegies; and also literary burlesques, such as 'Cath Bearna Chroise Brighde', based on *Pairlement Chloinne Tomáis. His prose works include Stair Éamuinn Uí Chléire (*History of Eamonn O'Cleary*), an allegorical tale based on his own life. His best-known poem is 'Rachainn fón gcoill leat', in which the poet asks his beloved to go with him into the world of nature.

Ó Neachtain, Tadhg (1670–1749), poet and scribe. Son of Seán *Ó Neachtain, he was born in the Liberties, Dublin, where he spent most of his life. His houses were meeting-places for Irish scholars from about 1700. In 1726 a poem of his, 'Sloinfead scothadh na Gaoidhilge grinn', names twenty-six Gaelic scholars working in Dublin and its environs, among them Pól Mac Aogáin, a Franciscan priest, and other Catholic clergy. One of his patrons was Anthony *Raymond (Uaithne Réamonn), Fellow of TCD, for whom he wrote a panegyric.

O'Neill Daunt, William Joseph, see *Daunt, William Joseph O'Neill.

Ó Néill, Eoghan Ruadh (Owen Roe O'Neill) (?1584–1649), commander of native Irish forces in the *Confederation of Kilkenny. A nephew of Hugh *O'Neill, he was born in Co. Armagh, and served in the Spanish army in Flanders for nearly forty years before returning to Ireland in 1642, when he took command of the Ulster army. On 6 June 1646 he resoundingly defeated Robert Munro's Scottish army at Benburb, a victory celebrated by Pope Innocent X in Rome.

O'Neill, Hugh [3rd Baron of Dungannon; 2nd Earl of Tyrone] (?1550–1616), leader of the Irish forces in the War of 1595–1603. After the assassination of his father by Shane O'Neill (?1530–1567) in 1558, he was brought up by Sir Henry Sidney at Penshurst. He commanded a troop of horse against the Irish in the Desmond War in the 1570s. He secured his position against dynastic enemies in Ulster by building up a range of strategic connections with major Gaelic families, including his own marital alliance with the O'Donnells of Tír Conaill (Co. Donegal). In 1585 he was made Earl of Tyrone, but soon began to resist attempts to extend Tudor control over Ulster, making political overtures to Philip II of Spain. In 1592 he organized the escape of Red Hugh *O'Donnell from imprisonment in Dublin Castle. O'Neill continued an outward show of loyalty to the Crown, but in February 1595 he captured the Blackwater Fort, and was proclaimed a traitor. On 14 August 1598 O'Neill defeated and killed Sir Nicholas Bagenal at the Battle of the Yellow Ford. O'Neill now extended his authority through the midlands and into Munster, whilst O'Donnell consolidated Connacht. In September 1601, when the long-promised Spanish expeditionary force landed at Kinsale under Don Juan del Aquila, O'Neill was persuaded by O'Donnell to attempt to release the Spaniards from the siege laid by Charles Blount, Lord Mountjoy and his Irish allies. A premature attack on Mountjoy's forces resulted in a rout by his cavalry and a long retreat back to Ulster through a hostile countryside.

O'Neill's submission resulted in a lenient treaty. The expansion of English power in Ulster proceeded rapidly in the following years and O'Neill came under increasing suspicion as Rory O'Donnell and the Maguires continued their entanglement with Spain. In 1607 O'Neill joined the other principal Ulster lords in the *Flight of the Earls. Hugh O'Neill was an adept politician and gifted soldier who made the most of limited resources in a period of rapid change. See Hiram Morgan, *Tyrone's Rebellion* (1993).

O'Neill, John (1778–1858), poet; born in Waterford, he was a cobbler in Carrick-on-Suir before leaving for London where he sought the success which evaded him until *The Drunkard* (1840) his temperance poem reflecting his own reformation of character. Other works include *The Triumph of Temperance* (1852) and *Handerahan the Irish Fairyman; and Legends of Carrick* (1854).

O'Neill, Joseph (Séosamh Ó Néill) (1878–1953), novelist; born in Tuam, Co. Galway, and educated at UCG. In 1903 he gave up a lecturership at Galway in order to study Irish under Kuno *Meyer. He went on to study comparative philology with Rudolf *Thurneysen in Freiburg. In 1908 he joined the Civil Service. In the novel *Wind from the North* (1934) a clerk is transported to 11th-cent. Dublin on the eve of the Battle of *Clontarf and transformed into a Viking. *Land Under England* (1935) envisages a society of cruel automata descended from the Roman legionaries in Britain, while *Day of Wrath* (1936) nervously predicts the overthrow of European civilization by Africa and Japan. *Philip* (1940) follows the tragic efforts of a Hellenized Jew to discover his identity in Jerusalem at the time of Christ's death. *Chosen by the Queen* (1947) explores the personality of the Earl of Essex as seen through his secretary's eyes. O'Neill worked as Permanent Secretary for Education, 1923–44. In 1949 he moved to France with his wife, Mary (*O'Neill) but soon returned.

O'Neill, Maire, see Molly *Allgood.

O'Neill, Mary (née Devenport) (1879–1967), poet. Born in Galway, she attended a convent school and then the Metropolitan Art School. After a long friendship she married Joseph *O'Neill in 1908. Her sole volume was *Prometheus* (1929). Her plays *Bluebeard* (1933) and *Cain* (1945) were both performed by the Abbey Theatre Ballet Company, the former being choreographed by Ninette *de Valois.

O'Neill, Moira (pseudonym of (Agnes) Nesta Skrine, neé Higginson) (1865–1955), poet; born in Cushendun, Co. Antrim. Following *Elf-Errant* (1893), she wrote a series of extremely popular poems in *Hiberno-English, collected as *Songs of the Glens of Antrim* (1901).

O'Neill, Owen Roe, see Eoghan Ruadh *Ó Néill.

Ó Néill, Séamus (1910–1981), writer of fiction. Born in Co. Down, he studied at QUB, UCD, and Innsbruck, and taught at Carysfort College, Dublin. He published two collections of short stories, *An Sean-Saighdiúr agus Scéalta Eile* (1945) and *Ag Baint Fraochán* (1955); two novels, *Tonn Tuile* (1947) and *Máire Nic Artáin* (1959); a number of plays, including *Iníon Rí Dhún Sobhairce* (1960) and *Faill ar an bhFeart* (1967); two volumes of poetry, *Dánta* (1944) and *Dánta do Pháisti* (1949); and two collections of essays, *Súil Timpeall* (1951) and the posthumous *Lámh Dhearg Abú* (1982).

Only Jealousy of Emer, The, see *Cuchulain cycle.

O'Nolan, Brian, see Flann *O'Brien.

'On the Necessity for de-Anglicising Ireland', see Douglas *Hyde.

On the Study of Celtic Literature, see Matthew *Arnold.

Ó Nualláin, Brian, see Flann *O'Brien.

Ó Nualláin, Ciarán (1910–1983), writer and language activist; born in Strabane, Co. Tyrone. One of twelve children, he was especially close to his brother Brian (pseudonym 'Flann *O'Brien'). Like him he was educated at home, then at UCD. *Oíche i nGleann na nGealt* (1939) and *Eachtraí Pharthaláin Mhic Mhórna* (1944) were novels which have as their central character an amateur solver of mysteries. *Óige an Dearthár* (1973) was a memoir of Flann O'Brien.

O'Rahilly, T[homas] F[rancis] (1883–1953), scholar. Born in Listowel, Co. Kerry, he was educated at Blackrock College and UCD. He founded *Gadelica* (1912–13), an influential journal even though it did not run beyond the first volume. He edited *Dánta Grádha* (1926), a collection of Irish love-poetry in syllabic verse. An anthology of *bardic poetry, *Measgra Dánta*, i and ii (1927), followed. *Irish Dialects, Past and Present* (1932) established a methodology for the discipline. The somewhat contentious findings of his later years are summarized in *Early Irish History and Mythology* (1946).

Orange Order, the, a Protestant society founded in Loughgall, Co. Armagh, in 1795, its name commemorating King William III, Prince of Orange, whose victory at the *Boyne in 1690 secured the Protestant interest in Ireland.

Ó Rathaille, Aodhagán (?1670–1729), poet; born at Scrahanaveele in Co. Kerry. After training in poetry, possibly at a latter-day *bardic school, he appears to have spent some time in Iveleary between Macroom and Bantry. 'Créachta Críoch Fódla', written after the *Battle of the Boyne, mourns the wounds inflicted upon Ireland. Ó Rathaille removed to Corcaguiney in Co. Kerry, where in *c.* 1708 he wrote 'Is fada liom oíche', a heartbroken lament, expressing his grief at the shamefulness of the life he now has to lead. Ó Rathaille continued to lead an unsettled life, spending periods of time in Kerry and Limerick. 'Tionól na bhFear Muimhneach' is an *aisling describing Jacobite preparations in Munster for a forthcoming invasion. Other aisling poems, in particular 'Mac An Cheannaí', 'Maidean sul smaoin Titan', and 'Gile na Gile', bring the form to a striking level of originality. In 'Mac an Cheannaí' Ireland, described as a beautiful maiden, looks south every day, hoping for the ships to come. In 'Gile na Gile' the maiden the poet encounters in the wilderness is Éire [see *Ériú], but is not named as such. Ó Rathaille describes how the spéirbhean leads him to a mansion where she is held in thrall by an idiot. 'Cabhair ní Ghoirfead', probably written in 1729, describes his moral and physical devastation. The rhythmic energy of Ó Rathaille's verse owes a great deal to his ability to infuse the amhrán metre [see Irish *metrics] with the vitality of impassioned speech. Ó Rathaille has been an inspiration and challenge to translators since *Mangan's version of 'Gile na Gile' in *Poets and Poetry of Munster* (1849). See Seán *Ó Tuama, *Filí faoi Sceimhle* (1978).

Order of the Golden Dawn, a hermetic order founded in London in 1888 by the coroner Dr William Wynn Westcott, Dr W. E. Woodman, and Samuel Liddell [MacGregor] Mathers (1854–1918), who later adopted the title of Comte de Glenstrae. The Order was devoted to the study of ancient wisdom.

Mathers invited W.B. *Yeats to join the
Order in 1893; Miss Annie *Horniman,
the tea heiress and *Abbey patron, was
a member from 1890, as was Maud
*Gonne.

Ordnance Survey Commission,
see Sir George *Petrie.

Ó Reachtabhra, Antoine, see
Antoine *Raiftearaí.

O'Reilly, Edward (?1770–1829),
Irish scholar. Born probably in Co.
Cavan, he moved to Dublin in about
1790 and probably learnt Irish there,
going on to compile *Sanas Gaoidhilge/
Sags-Bhéarla* (1817), an Irish–English dictionary. He published *A Chronological
Account of Nearly Four Hundred Irish
Writers with a Descriptive Catalogue of their
Works* (1820).

O'Reilly, John Boyle (1844–1890),
poet. Born at Dowth Castle, Co. Louth,
he worked as a journalist there before
enlisting in a British regiment in 1863,
with a view to recruiting soldiers for the
*Fenian movement. By 1876 he was editor of the *Boston Pilot*, which he made
the leading Irish-American newspaper
and host to Irish writers including W. B.
Yeats and Douglas *Hyde. His poems
were issued in collections such as *Songs
from Southern Seas* (1873) and *Songs,
Legends, and Ballads* (1878). He also wrote
on boxing but was best known for his
orations.

Orgain Denna Rig (*The Destruction of
Dinn Ríg*), an Old Irish saga preserved in
the *Book of Leinster* and in the *Yellow
Book of Lecan*. It relates how Labraid
Loingsech kills his great-uncle Cobthach Cóel and takes the kingship of
Leinster.

Ó Riada, Seán (1931–1971), composer. Born in Adare, Co. Limerick, he
was educated there and at UCC. In 1963

he went to live in Cúil Aodha in the
West Cork *Gaeltacht on appointment
to a lecturership in Irish music at UCC.
Ó Riada is best known for his work with
Ceoltoirí Chualann, the influential
music group he founded to give the performance of Irish traditional music a
new direction, releasing the original
airs from the metronomic conventions
of the céilí band.

'Orinda', see Katherine *Philips.

Ó Ríordáin, Seán (1916–1977), poet;
born in Ballyvourney in the West Cork
*Gaeltacht and educated locally until
1932, when the family moved to Iniscarra, near Cork, where he attended the
North Monastery. In 1937 he joined the
Cork Corporation, where he worked as
a clerk. He suffered from pulmonary
tuberculosis. In Cork he became friends
with Daniel *Corkery, Seán *Ó Tuama,
and An tAthair Tadhg Ó Murchú (a language activist), all of whom influenced
him. His first collection *Eireaball Spideoige* (1952) draws upon Gaelic tradition
but also reflects his receptiveness to
European modernism. Dún Chaoin
(Dunquin, Co. Kerry), which he began to
visit from the early 1950s, came to symbolize Gaelic culture, but when he
writes of it and of Peig *Sayers their fragility is registered as much as their
authenticity. The collection *Brosna*
(1964) confronts, in poems such as 'Fiabhras' or 'Na Leamhain', the possibility
that the self may be an illusion. In 1965
Ó Ríordáin resigned from the City Hall,
suffering from fibrosis of the lungs.
With Séamus Ó Conghaile he compiled
Rí na hUile (1967), modern versions of
medieval Irish religious poetry. From
1967 he began to contribute a column
to *The Irish Times* which he continued
until shortly before his death. In 1969
he was appointed to a part-time lecturership in UCC, where he influenced
*Innti poets such as Michael *Davitt and
Nuala *Ní Dhomhnaill. *Línte Liombó*

(1971) contains further meditations on personal and cultural uncertainty. *Tar Éis mo Bháis* (1979) was issued posthumously. See Seán Ó Coileáin, *Seán Ó Ríordáin: Beatha agus Saothar* (1982).

O'Riordan, Conal Holmes O'Connell (pseudonym 'F. Norreys Connell') (1874–1948), playwright and novelist. Born in Dublin, the son of a QC, and educated at Belvedere and Clongowes Wood College, he was prevented from following an army career by a horse-riding injury. His early fiction reveals an indifference to social convention. *In the Green Park* (1894), a short-story collection, comprises tales of Greek deities transported to a London club in the hallucinated imaginings of a concussed man. *Strange Women* (1895) is a tangled novel of upper-class bohemian life with an energetic Foreign Legion plot. Other books were *The Fool and His Heart* (1896), *How Soldiers Fight* (1899), *The Nigger Knights* (1900), *The Follies of Captain Daly* (1901), and *The Pity of War* (1906). Among three short plays for the *Abbey Theatre was *The Piper* (1908), a humane critique of Irish nationalism set in 1798. After *Synge's death O'Riordan was appointed theatre-manager at the *Abbey. During the First World War he went to the front with the YMCA rest units. On his return he commenced working on twelve novels tracing the history of an upper-middle-class Irish family. He started with the 'Adam' series (*Adam of Dublin*, 1920; *Adam and Caroline*, 1921; and *Adam and Marriage*, 1922) before turning to the chronologically earlier 'Soldier' series (comprising chiefly *Soldier of Waterloo*, 1928; *Soldier's Wife*, 1935; and *Soldier's End*, 1938). Others in the series deal chiefly with loveless marriages, as in *The Age of Miracles* (1925), *Judith Quinn* (1939), and *Judith's Love* (1940).

Ormond (1817), a novel by Maria *Edgeworth, written during her father's final illness. Harry Ormond, an aristocratic orphan, grows up in the Anglo-Irish society of his guardian Sir Ulick O'Shane's demesne, Castle Hermitage. Harry buys the Black Island from 'King Corny' and becomes an improving landlord.

Ormond[e], James Butler, 1st Duke of (1610–1688), soldier, statesman, and patron of the arts. Born in London, he distinguished himself by loyalty in politics and toleration in religion. Ormond commanded the Royalist army under the Earl of Stafford and fought against the *Confederation of Kilkenny at the outbreak of the *Rebellion of 1641. In 1644 Charles I made him Lord Lieutenant. Ormond maintained a diplomatic relationship with *Cromwell and with Parliament until the execution of Charles I. He returned as Lord Lieutenant at the Restoration, and remained so, with intermissions, until the strongly pro-Catholic policy of James II forced him to resign. The date of Ormond's arrival on 27 July 1662 coincides with the advent of neo-classicism to Dublin and the beginning of the period of ambitious planning during which the centre of the city was laid out along the spacious lines that determined its modern character.

Ormsby, Frank (1947–), poet; born in Enniskillen, Co. Fermanagh, educated at QUB. In his first collection, *A Store of Candles* (1977), he registers loss. In *A Northern Spring* (1986) and *The Ghost Train* (1995), he questions the familiarity of home ground. Editor of *The Honest Ulsterman*, 1969–89, he also edited the anthologies: *Poets from the North of Ireland* (1979); and *Northern Windows: An Anthology of Ulster Autobiography* (1987); and the *Collected Poems of John *Hewitt* (1991).

Oroonoko, or *The Royal Slave* (1696), a verse tragedy by Thomas *Southerne about an African prince whose beloved, Imoinda, is sold into slavery by the jealous king, Oroonoko's grandfather.

O'Rourke, Edmund, see Edmund *Falconer.

Orr, James ('the Bard of Ballycarry') (1770–1816), *weaver poet. Born at Broad Island, Co. Antrim, he became a member of the *United Irishmen and contributed poetry to *The Northern Star*. Orr frequently wrote in the vernacular, and is acknowledged to be the best Ulster-Scots poet by John *Hewitt and others.

Ó Séaghdha, Pádraig (pseudonym 'Conán Maol') (1855–1928), fiction-writer. Born near Kenmare, Co. Kerry, he was educated at the local national school and entered the Customs service. A pioneer of the short story in Irish, his early work was published in the collection *An Buaiceas* (1903), highly regarded as an attempt to modernize Gaelic narrative. Other writings include the novel *Eoghan Paor* (1911) and a play, *Aodh Ó Néill* (1902).

Ó Searcaigh, Cathal (1956–), poet. Born near Gort a' Choirce (Gortahork) in the Donegal *Gaeltacht, he was educated at Maynooth [see *universities], where he read Celtic Studies. He lived for a time in London and Dublin, before returning to the Gaeltacht, where he farmed. His collections include *Miontraigéide Cathrach* (1975) and *Túirlingt* (1978) with Gabriel *Rosenstock; *Súile Shuibhne* (1983); *Suibhne* (1987); *An Bealach 'na Bhaile* (1991); and a selected poems in 1993, with translations by Seamus *Heaney and others. *Na Buachaillí Bána* (1996) is a volume notable for its sexual openness, as was the bilingual *Out in the Open* (1997).

O'Shea, John Augustus (1839–1905), journalist and novelist. Born in Nenagh, the son of a journalist, and educated at the Catholic University, Dublin [see *universities], he wrote the novels *Military Mosaics* (1888) and *Mated in the Morgue* (1889) about life in France.

O'Siadhail, Micheal (1947–), poet; born in Dublin, he was educated at Clongowes Wood, then TCD and the University of Oslo before becoming a Lecturer in Irish at TCD, 1969–73. He joined the *DIAS, and became Assistant Professor (1980–7). *An Bhliain Bhisigh* (1978) was followed by *Runga* (1980) and *Cumann* (1982). *Springnight* (1983), *The Image Wheel* (1985), and *The Chosen Garden* (1990) were collections in English, and *Hail! Madam Jazz* (1992) includes translations from the volumes in Irish. *A Fragile City* (1995) was followed by *Our Double Time* (1998).

Ó Siochfhradha, Pádraig (pseudonym 'An Seabhac') (1883–1964), fiction-writer. Born near Dingle, Co. Kerry, he was educated by the Christian Brothers before joining the *Gaelic League and working as a teacher and organizer. *An Baile Seo 'Gainne* (1913) was a volume of humorous sketches. *Seáinín nó Eachtra Mic Mírialta* (1922) is a picaresque novel. His classic comic tale, *Jimín Mháire Thaidhg* (1922), is narrated by the young boy Jimín. *Caibidlí as Leabhar Mhóirín* (1934) was an attempt to repeat *Jimín's* success, with a girl narrator.

Ó Snodaigh, Pádraig [Oiliféar] (1935–), poet, publisher, and man of letters. Born in Carlow, he was educated by the Christian Brothers there before becoming a clerk for the Electricity Supply Board, 1951–63, and assistant keeper of the National Museum, 1963–88. He attended UCD and developed his interest in Irish, becoming Chairman of Clódhanna Teo, a *Gaelic League imprint, before taking it over and running it himself as Coiscéim, a major publishing outlet for writing in Irish in the 1980s and 1990s. *Comhghuallaithe na Réabhlóide* (1966), a study of Irish revolutionaries, was followed by *Hidden Ulster* (1973), and *Óh Droichead go dtí an Duibheagán* (1997). Amongst his collections of poetry are *Cumha agus Cumann* (1985), *Cúl le Cúl* (1988), and *Ó Pharnell go Queenie* (1991). *Rex* (1981) was a novel and *Linda* (1987) a work of short fiction.

Ossianic cycle, see *Fionn cycle.

Ossianic Society, The (1853), founded on St Patrick's Day, 1853, with the aim of preserving and publishing *manuscripts of the *Fionn cycle. Standish Hayes *O'Grady was the President, John *O'Daly, the Secretary.

Ó Súilleabháin, Amhlaoibh (1780–1838), author of the first known diary in Irish; born in Killarney. His family moved to Co. Kilkenny, then largely Irish-speaking, when his father, a *hedge school-master, settled there. From 1827 to 1835 he kept a diary, It reflects the tastes and interests of a cultured and lively mind, full of intellectual curiosity.

Ó Súilleabháin, Diarmaid (1932–1985), novelist. Born in Eyeries, west Cork, he was educated locally before becoming a primary teacher in Co. Wexford. His novel *Dianmhuilte Dé* (1964) is set in the Beara peninsula in west Cork. *Caoin Tú Féin* (1967) examines the sterile life of the teacher Ian Ó Murchú. *An Uain Bheo* (1988) concerns Louis Stein, a *déraciné* Irish Jew moving in a society of empty satisfactions. *Maeldún* (1972) [see *Immram Curaig Maíle Dúin] is a vicious attack on economic expansionism and materialistic values. *Ciontach* (1983) is based on a three-month prison sentence in Mountjoy Gaol on suspicion of *IRA activities. Besides the posthumous *Bealach Bó Finne* (1988), several other novels remain unpublished.

Ó Súilleabháin, Eoghan Rua (1748–1784), poet. Known as 'Eoghan an Bhéil Bhinn' (of the Sweet Mouth) on account of the musicality of his verse, he was admired for the wit and skill of his satires and lyrics, and also became a folk-hero for his philandering and wildness. He was born in Meentogues near Killarney, Co. Kerry, and attended a local *hedge school at Faha. He made a living as a schoolmaster and a spailpín (itinerant labourer). He joined—or was press-ganged into—the navy, and served under Admiral Rodney. On a visit to Killarney in 1784, he was knocked on the head with a fire-iron by servants of a local landowner and yeomanry colonel whom he had satirized. He fell into a fever and died. Ó Súilleabháin's versions of the *aisling are recognized as masterpieces of atmospheric euphony, among them 'Ceo draíochta i gcoim óiche do sheol mé' and 'Ag taisteal na Blárnan'. A poem requesting a blacksmith to provide him with a spade for potato-digging is gracious but also seditious.

Ó Súilleabháin, Muiris (1904–1950); author of *Fiche Blian ag Fás (1933), an autobiographical account of life on the Great Blasket Island off Co. Kerry. Born on the island, he was raised in an orphanage in Dingle after his mother's death in 1905, returning to the Great Blasket in 1911. In 1923 the scholar George Thomson urged him to join the police force of the *Irish State (the Garda Síochána). Ó Súilleabháin was posted to Indreabhán in the Connemara *Gaeltacht, and there he wrote his book, following the example of Tomás *Ó Criomhthain in *An t*Oileánach* (1929). Ó Súilleabháin quit the Garda Síochána in 1934 and settled in Connemara as a writer, producing a sequel, *Fiche Blian Fé Bhláth (Twenty Years in Bloom)*, which was rejected by publishers.

Ó Súilleabháin, Seán (Seán O'Sullivan) (1903–1996), *folklorist. Born in Tuosist, Co. Kerry, he joined the *Irish Folklore Commission in 1935. *Diarmuid na Bolgaighe agus a Chómhursain* (1937) is a study of a poet from his native parish, while *Scéalta Cráibhtheacha* (1952) is a collection of religious legends. *Caitheamh Aimsire ar Thórraimh* (1964) was translated as *Irish Wake Amusements* (1967). Other studies include *A Handbook of Irish Folklore* (1942), and *The Folklore of Ireland* (1974).

Ó Súilleabháin, Tadhg Gaelach (?1715–1795), poet, acclaimed especially for his verses on religious subjects. He was born in the Tournafulla district of Co. Limerick, travelled to East Cork, and remained there for about thirty years. He was in contact with poets such as Liam Inglis and Eadbhard de Nógla of Cork city, and Donncha Rua *Mac Conmara. During the latter part of his life, spent in Waterford, he wrote numerous religious compositions. His secular poems include variations on the *aisling theme. First published in Clonmel as *Timothy O'Sullivan's Pious Miscellany* (1802), his religious poems went through numerous editions, indicating their popularity among the Irish-speakers of Munster.

O'Sullivan, Seumas (pseudonym of James Sullivan Starkey) (1879–1958), poet, and editor. Born in Dublin, he attended Wesley College before becoming an apprentice in his father's pharmacy. He married the artist Estella Solomons in 1926. His first book of poems, *Twilight People* (1905), reflected the mood of the *literary revival. *The Earth-Lover and Other Verses* (1909) focuses on Dublin life. This is evident in *Requiem and Other Poems* (1917), some of which respond to the *Easter Rising of 1916. His contribution to Irish cultural life came in his editorship of *The *Dublin Magazine* (1923–58).

O'Sullivan Beare, Philip (?1590–?1634), historian; born on the Beare Peninsula, Co. Cork, and educated at Compostella in Spain. He served in the Spanish navy before turning to propagandist literature in defence of Ireland and the Catholic cause, his *Historiae Catholicae Iberniae Compendium* (Lisbon, 1621), giving a Gaelic version of the Tudor conquest. *Zoilomastix*, written in 1626, though not printed until 1960, is a vigorous defence of the dignity of Irish culture.

otherworld, see *sídh.

Ó Tiománaidhe, Mícheál (1853–1940), folklorist. Born at Cartron, near Crossmolina, Co. Mayo, he emigrated to Australia and returned home in 1894, when he began to collect *folklore. In 1906 he published two volumes, *Abhráin Ghaedhilge an Iarthair*, an anthology of songs, and *Targaireacht Bhriain Ruaidh Uí Chearbáin*, an account of a local prophet of the 18th cent. with some other items of folk history.

O'Toole, Fintan (1953–), journalist and critic; born in Dublin and educated there. He worked for *In Dublin* Magazine and on the *Irish Times*. He wrote *The Politics of Magic* (1987 and 1995) on the plays of Tom *Murphy; and *The Traitor's Kiss* (1998) on Richard Brinsley *Sheridan.

Ó Tuairisc, Eoghan (Eugene Rutherford Watters) (1919–1982), poet and novelist. Born in Ballinasloe, Co. Galway, the son of a shoemaker, and educated at Garbally College, Ballinasloe, and St Patrick's College, Drumcondra, he worked as a teacher in Dublin, 1940–69. He edited *Feasta, 1963–6. His first novel, *Murder in Three Moves* (1960), is a thriller set in Galway. *L'Attaque* (1962), a novel about the *United Irishmen's Rebellion of 1798, was followed in 1964 by the publication of his long poem *The *Week-End of Dermot and Grace* and the collection *Lux Aeterna*, which contains 'Aifreann na Marbh', his poetic Mass for the Hiroshima victims. In 1965 his first wife, the artist Una McDonnell, died suddenly while he was working on *Dé Luain* (1966), a novel about the 1916 *Easter Rising. Ó Tuairisc left Dublin and over the next five years produced little more than a series of intensely personal lyrics, later published as *New Passages* (1973). In 1969 he moved to the Wicklow/Carlow border where he began to write again. In 1972 he married the writer Rita *Kelly. The major works of this later period were An *Lomnochtán* (1977), an autobiographical novel; *Dialann sa Díseart* (1981), a joint poetry collection with Rita Kelly; and the play *Fornocht do Chonac* (1981). See Máirín Nic Eoin, *Eoghan Ó Tuairisc: Beatha agus Saothar* (1988).

Ó Tuama, Seán (an Ghrinn, 'of the Merriment') (?1708–1775), poet. Born probably near Kilmallock, Co. Limerick, he studied at the same school as his friend Aindrias *Mac Craith, with whom he was one of the best-known filí na Máighe (poets of the Maigue). Ó Tuama settled in Croom, worked as a water-bailiff, and for many years kept an inn which became a meeting-place [see *cúirt éigse] for poets. Among these were Seán Clárach *Mac Dómhnaill. 'Aonach Chromadh an tSubhachais' celebrates the hospitality and friendship to be found in Croom on fair-day. In the *aisling, 'A chuisle na héigse', Ireland calls upon her poets to anticipate joyously the return of the Stuart [see *Jacobite poetry]. When Mac Dómhnaill died in 1754, Ó Tuama wrote a majestic elegy.

Ó Tuama, Seán (1926–   ), poet, playwright, and critic. Born in Cork, he was educated at UCC, where he studied Irish and English and was taught by Daniel *Corkery. *Nuabhéarsaíocht* (1950), his anthology of modern poetry in Irish,

drew attention to the modernism of contemporary Irish poetry. A founder of Compántas Chorcaí, a Cork drama group, he spent 1955–6 in France studying modern theatre. In 1961 he published a collection of poems, *Faoileán na Beatha*, which contains personal lyrics and dramatic meditations. Inspired by the innovations of European theatre, he wrote plays that combined song, direct narration, and swift transitions in mood. These early plays were issued as *Moloney agus Drámaí Eile* (1966) and *Gunna Cam agus Slabhra Óir* (1969), the latter about Maghnus *Ó Domhnaill. A sense of betrayed idealism underlies many poems in *Saol Fó Thoinn* (1978). With Thomas *Kinsella he edited and translated *An Duanaire 1600–1900: Poems of the Dispossessed* (1981). *An Bás i dTír na nÓg* (1988) contains delicate elegies for his parents. *Death in the Land of Youth* (1997) has selected poems with translations by Peter *Denman.

Otway, Revd Caesar (1780–1842), author and controversialist. Born in Co. Tipperary, he was educated at TCD. In 1825 he founded, with Joseph Henderson Singer, *The *Christian Examiner and Church of Ireland Magazine*. He encouraged William *Carleton to write for the *Examiner*. His own *Sketches in Ireland* (1827), *A Tour in Connaught* (1839), and *Sketches in Erris and Tyrawly* (1841) show that the influence worked both ways.

Owenson, Robert (1744–1812), actor-manager, and father of Lady *Morgan. Born in Tirawley, Co. Galway and an Irish-speaker, he became an associate of *Goldsmith and Garrick, appearing at Covent Garden Theatre from 1774. In 1784 he leased the Fishamble Street Theatre in Dublin to mount a 'National Theatre' with the support of the patriot aristocracy.

Owenson, Sydney, see Lady *Morgan.

Pacata Hibernia: *Ireland Appeased and Reduced* (1633), an English account of the campaign against Hugh *O'Neill, 1601-3, compiled by Thomas Stafford from papers of Sir George Carew, President of Munster.

Pairlement Chloinne Tomáis (*Parliament of Clan Thomas*), an anonymous burlesque on upstarts. The first of two parts was probably written in Co. Kerry at the beginning of the 17th cent. and the second in Leinster shortly after the Restoration of 1660.

Párliament na mBan (*Parliament of Women*), a 17th cent. didactic prose work in Irish by the Cork priest, Dr Domhnall Ó Colmáin, addressed to James Cotter (1689–1720), to whom Ó Colmáin was tutor consisting of a series of sermons presented as the proceedings of a parliament of women.

Pakenham, Christine, see Lady *Longford.

Pakenham, Edward Arthur Henry, see Lord *Longford.

Pale, the, see *Irish State.

Parker, Stewart (1941–1988), playwright. Born in East Belfast, he was educated at Ashfield Boys' Secondary School and at QUB. His first play was *Spokesong (1974). Catchpenny Twist* (1977) concerns two Belfast songwriters. A trilogy of 'history plays' dramatizes the struggle between individual creativity and the forces of the age. The first, *Northern Star (1984), deals with the *United Irishmen's Rebellion of 1798. Heavenly Bodies* (1986) is a collage of the career of the Irish

dramatist Dion *Boucicault. *Pentecost* (1987), written for *Field Day, tells the story of four ordinary Belfast people caught up in the Ulster Workers' Strike of 1974. For television he wrote *I'm a Dreamer, Montreal* (1979), *Ruby in the Rain* (1981), *Blue Money* (1985), and *Lost Belongings* (1987).

Parnell and His Island (1887), a revised edition of a series of satirical articles that George *Moore wrote for *Le Figaro* and afterwards published as *Terre d'Irlande*.

Parnell, Anna and Fanny, see *Land League.

Parnell, Charles Stewart (1846–1891), nationalist leader. Born in Avondale, Co. Wicklow, and educated at Cambridge, he was elected MP for Co. Meath in 1875 and Cork City in 1880. He established his reputation as an advanced nationalist through obstruction tactics in Parliament. Following the alliance with the *Fenians in the New Departure and his presidency of the *Land League, with the support of Michael *Davitt, he was elected leader of the *Irish Parliamentary Party. Land League agitations, typified by the practice of boycotting (after Captain *Boycott), led to his imprisonment in October 1881. Thereafter he directed Irish energies away from the agrarian struggle towards a strictly constitutional campaign for self-government. Parnell's political career was destroyed by the party split that followed his citation as co-respondent in the O'Shea divorce petition of December 1889, and his failure to defend the action. The Irish Party split in a bitter division in Committee Room 15 of the House of

Commons. His tragedy entered the fabric of Irish literary memory in works such as James *Joyce's A *Portrait of the Artist as a Young Man (1914).

Parnell, Thomas (1679–1718), poet; born in Dublin and educated at TCD. In 1713 he published a verse Essay on the Different Styles of Poetry. Homer's Battle of the Frogs and Mice with the Remarks of Zoilus (1717) is a mock-heroic attack on contemporary critics.

Parra Sastha, or The History of Paddy Go-Easy and His Wife Nancy (1845), a didactic novel by William *Carleton, written in nine days for James *Duffy. Paddy Go-Easy becomes conscious of his own shortcomings and is transformed into a steady, industrious, and persevering farmer.

Parsons, Julie (1951–), novelist; born in New Zealand, she lived in Ireland since she was a child. Educated in Dublin, she worked in *RTÉ before publishing the suspense thrillers Mary, Mary (1998), followed by The Courtship Gift (1999).

Partholón, see *Lebor Gabála Érenn.

partition, see *Irish State and *Northern Ireland.

Pastorini, pseudonym of Charles Walmsley (1722–1797), Catholic bishop. Born in Lancashire and educated in seminaries in France, he wrote his General History of the Christian Church (1771), which foretells the triumph of *Catholicism in 1825 from the Apocalypse of St John, a forecast circulated as Prophecies of Pastorini in chapbook editions during the period of the *United Irishmen's Rebellion. Thereafter Pastorini became a household word in rural Ireland.

Patrick, St (d. ?493), Christian missionary and patron saint of Ireland. He was born near the west coast of Roman Britain, and had the given name Succat. His father, Calpurnius, was a deacon and a municipal official. After being captured by Irish raiders at 15, he was made a servant in Ireland for six years, herding pigs for Milchu on Mount Slemish, Co. Antrim. There, in the first of seven dream-visions, as tradition relates, he was instructed how to escape on a ship exporting wolfhounds. After his return to Britain, he dreamt he heard the voices of the Irish calling to him. He confronted the *druidic order at the court of the High King Laegaire at *Tara [see also *kingship]. In the tradition, he destroys the idol Crom Cruaich and banishes snakes from the country. The conversion of Ireland to Christianity appears to have occurred within his lifetime, and Patrick records that he baptized thousands in his journeys through Ireland, ordaining clergy and founding churches. The Confessio provides an autobiographical account of his work in Ireland. The *Lorica or Breastplate of St Patrick is believed to be of later provenance, and has no historical connection with the saint.

Patrick Pearse Motel, The (1971), a farce by Hugh *Leonard concerning married couples living in a fashionable Dublin suburb who are determined to enjoy the uninhibited life-style of the seventies.

Patrick's Purgatory, St, see *Lough Derg.

Patriot King, The, or the Irish Chieftain (1773), a verse tragedy by Francis *Dobbs. Set in the time of the *Viking invasion, it was performed at *Smock Alley Theatre.

Patterson, Glenn (1961–), novelist; born in Belfast and educated at QUB. Burning Your Own (1988), his first novel,

presented a view of the Northern
*Troubles from a Protestant perspec-
tive. In *Fat Lad* (1992) the narrative
moves back and forth in time to create a
complex picture of a family with its
internal hurts and divisions. He was
writer in residence, first at UCC, then at
QUB in 1994. *Black Night at Big Thunder
Mountain* (1995) is set during the construction of Disney World in Paris; *The
International* (1999) in a Belfast hotel in
the 1970s.

Paulin, Tom (Thomas Neilson)
(1949–), poet; Born in Leeds, he grew
up in Belfast and took degrees at Hull
and Oxford. The poetry collections *A
State of Justice* (1977), *The Strange Museum*
(1980), *The Book of Juniper* (1982), *Liberty
Tree* (1983), *Fivemiletown* (1987), *Walking a
Line* (1994), and *The Wind Dog* (1999)
respond to the political culture of modern Ireland, Britain, and Europe with an
imagery of surveillance and siege. In *A
New Look at the Language Question* (1983)
he advocated the use of *Hiberno-
English, later editing *The Faber Book of
Vernacular Verse* (1990). Paulin has also
written drama: *The Riot Act* (1985), a play
based on Sophocles; *The Hillsborough
Script* (1987), a dramatic satire; and *Seize
the Fire* (1990), a version of Aeschylus'
Prometheus Bound. As a critic, he followed
a study of Thomas Hardy (1975) with
essays collected as *Ireland and the English
Crisis* (1984) and *Minotaur: Poetry and the
Nation State* (1992). His biography of
Hazlitt, *The Day Star of Liberty*, appeared
in 1998.

P-Celtic, see *Celtic languages.

Peacock Theatre, see *Abbey
Theatre.

Pearse, Patrick H[enry] (Pádraig
Mac Piarais) (1879–1916), educationalist, author, and revolutionary. Born in
Dublin to an English stone-mason
father and an Irish mother, he was
educated by the Christian Brothers, and
at the Royal University, Dublin [see
*universities]. He joined the *Gaelic
League in 1896, and became editor of its
journal, *An *Claidheamh Soluis*, from
1903 to 1909. In 1907 he founded Sgoil
Éanna (St Enda's School). In late 1913 he
was one of the founders of the *Irish
Volunteers, and was recruited into the
secret Irish Republican Brotherhood
[see *IRA], becoming commandant-
general of the Republican forces on
*Easter Monday, 1916. After the sur-
render he was sentenced to death by a
British court matrial, and executed by
firing-squad in Kilmainham Jail on 3
May 1916. *From a Hermitage* (1915)
brought together a series of essays first
published in the IRB publication *Irish
Freedom*. *Ghosts*, *The Separatist Ideal*, *The
Spiritual Nation*, and *The Sovereign People*,
all published in 1916, were intended to
demonstrate the legitimacy of his political creed. *The Murder Machine* (1916)
contains a statement of his ideals as an
educationalist. His writings in Irish
included two collections of short stories, *Íosagán agus Sgéalta Eile* (1907) and
An Mháthair agus Sgéalta Eile (1916). His
Irish poetry, published in *Suantraidhe
agus Goltraidhe* (1914), adapts traditional
conventions to contemporary and often
personal situations.

Penal Laws, to contemporaries the
Popery Laws, the name given to anti-
Catholic legislation enacted after the
*Williamite War. The legislation of the
1690s formalized political exclusion by
requiring MPs, office-holders, and lawyers to take an oath renouncing central
Catholic doctrines. Other statutes forbade Catholics to keep weapons or
horses fit for military purposes (the
notorious ban on horses valued at more
than £5), to send children abroad for
education, or to maintain schools. The
main victims of the Penal Laws were
the small Catholic landed class. From
the 1760s propertied Catholics began to

campaign for a relaxation of legal restrictions, aided by liberal Protestants such as Henry *Brooke and Edmund *Burke.

Penny in the Clouds, A (1968), a volume of autobiography by Austin *Clarke, giving an account of his years as a student at UCD, and subsequently as a young writer in Dublin and in London.

Personal Sketches of His Own Times, see Jonah *Barrington.

Peter Waring (1937), a novel by Forrest *Reid. Peter, estranged from his father, forms a deep friendship with Mrs Carroll, of the nearby *big house, and falls in love with her niece Katharine, who comes to stay during the holidays.

Petrie, (Sir) George (1790–1866), artist and archaeologist. Born in Dublin, he was educated at Samuel *Whyte's school and became a prolific recorder of Irish antiquities in watercolour. His interest in Irish culture extended to *manuscripts and artefacts, as well as prompting the purchase of such treasures as the Ardagh Chalice, and the Tara Brooch. In 1824 an English parliamentary committee recommended the establishment of an Irish Ordnance Commission. Lt. Thomas Larcom engaged Petrie to take charge of a Topographical Section. Petrie assembled a team of scholars to undertake the work, such as John *O'Donovan, Eugene *O'Curry, W. F. Wakeman, and Samuel *Ferguson. In 1832–3 Petrie edited with Caesar *Otway the fifty-six issues of the Dublin Penny Journal, in which he wrote many of the antiquarian articles himself. In 1840–1 Petrie launched the Irish Penny Journal, aiming to develop a broader appreciation of Irish culture. The Ancient Music of Ireland (2 vols., 1855–82),

reflected his lifelong interest in the music of Ireland.

Petty, (Sir) William (1623–1687), cartographer and economist. Born in Hampshire, Petty studied medicine at Leiden, Paris, and Oxford, where he was appointed Professor of Anatomy in 1651. In Ireland he began in 1654 the 'Down Survey' (a term referring to the laying down of measuring chains), published in 1684, one of the first attempts to conduct an accurate mensuration on a national scale. After the Restoration he wrote his Political Anatomy of Ireland (1691).

Philadelphia, Here I Come! (1964), a play by Brian *Friel, set in the village of 'Ballybeg', Co. Donegal. The action takes place the night before a young man, Gar O'Donnell, emigrates to America. His part is split into Public Gar and Private Gar and played by two actors, the second revealing the emptiness of the first's bravado and sparking much plangent comedy.

Philanderer, The (1905), a play [see *Plays Pleasant . . .] by George Bernard *Shaw, written in 1893, and which he described as being about 'the fashionable cult of Ibsenism and "New Womanism"'. The action concerns the triangular relation between Leonard Charteris, Grace Tranfield, and Julia Craven.

Philips, Katherine (née Fowler), called 'Orinda' (1631–1664), author of *Pompey (1663), a heroic play based on Corneille, and the first drama to be written for the *Smock Alley Theatre. She came to Ireland as the wife of a wealthy English man of affairs in 1662, and founded a Society of Friendship with exclusively female members.

Philips, William (1675–1734), dramatist. Born in Derry, the son of the

Governor, he was educated at TCD and bought a captain's commission after the appearance of his first play, *The Revengeful Queen* (1698), in London. Two years later *St Stephen's Green or The Generous Lovers* (1700), a conventional social comedy, appeared at *Smock Alley. *Hibernia Freed* (1722), staged at Lincoln's Inn Fields, is a historical tragedy set during the *Viking invasion. He also wrote *Belasarius* (1724).

Phillips, Charles (1789–1859), lawyer and author. Born in Sligo and educated at TCD. Besides *Recollections of Curran and His Contemporaries* (1818), his other writings include *Specimens of Irish Eloquence* (1819) and a *Historical Sketch of Wellington* (1852).

Picture of Dorian Grey, The (1891), Oscar *Wilde's only novel, it gives a melodramatic account of a beautiful youth who keeps his good looks while his portrait changes to reflect its subject's every vice and profligacy.

Pictures in the Hallway, see *Autobiographies* [Sean O'Casey].

Pie-Dish, The (1908), a play by George *Fitzmaurice, first staged at the *Abbey Theatre, and an allegory of the artistic life, rich in character and language.

Pigeon Irish (1931), a novel by Francis *Stuart. While the powerful army of a materialistic and scientific civilization is set to take over the country, Ireland, with its unique blend of 'the physical and the spiritual', represents the last stronghold of Western culture.

Pigott, Richard (1828–1889), journalist and forger. Born at Ratoath, Co. Meath, he began his journalistic career as an errand boy in *The *Nation* office, progressing to ownership of *The Irishman* in 1865, a paper strongly supporting the *Fenian movement. He found

willing recipients for letters appearing to show *Parnell's complicity in the Phoenix Park Murders [see *Invincibles] and the violent tactics of the Land War. As the traitor of the *Irish Parliamentary Party he features in James *Joyce's *Finnegans Wake*.

Pilkington, Laetitia (née Van Lewen) (1712–1750), autobiographer and memoirist of Jonathan *Swift; born in Dublin, the daughter of an obstetrician. In 1732 she married Revd Matthew Pilkington but was left by him when she committed adultery. Though undependable, her *Memoirs* (1748–54; repr. 1929) gave domestic details of Swift's later years which contributed to the traditions that surround him.

Pillar of Cloud, The (1948), a novel by Francis *Stuart based on his wartime experiences. In the bleak ruins of Marheim, Germany, just after the war, the Irish poet Dominic Malone finds companionship with the sisters Halka and Lisette. Forced by necessity into prostitution, Halka has survived imprisonment in a concentration camp and later an asylum.

place-names in Ireland reflect human life on the island for at least 2,000 years. The Gaelic name of the country, Éire (earlier *Ériú > Ireland), may have been taken over by the Érainn from the Picts, whose own name (Latin Pretani > Pretanic, or British, Isles) is reflected in local names such as Ráth Cruithne ('mound of the Picts'), now Crown Mound, Co. Down. The names of many of the early Celtic tribes survive in regional names such as Ulster (Cúige Uladh, 'the fifth of the Ulaid') and Corcaguiny (Corca Dhuibhne, 'the seed of Duibhne'). The vast majority of the names originate in the Irish language. The *Vikings left a small number of Norse names mainly on the coast (e.g. Carlingford, Waterford). The

French-speaking *Normans, while greatly influencing the Irish language, left just a few French names (e.g. Carton). The English likewise introduced very few new place-names, mostly coinages imposed by the later landlords enshrining their own family name (e.g. Manorhamilton).

plantation, the seizure of Irish land and the allocation of it to new owners on the condition that they settle it with an English tenantry, or with Irish or Scots sympathetic to English rule. Plantation occured broadly within the period 1550–1700 and was frequently a response to Irish rebellion against the English Crown. Queen Mary (r. 1553–8) gave approval for the plantation of Leix and Offaly. There were plantations in Munster following the rebellion of Gerald Fitzgerald, Earl of Desmond, 1579–80; in Ulster, after the wars between Elizabeth I and Hugh *O'Neill, 1594–1603; and in Wexford.

Play (1963), a short play by Samuel *Beckett, in which three grey urns, from each of which a head protrudes, stand side by side on a darkened stage.

Playboy of the Western World, The (1907), a play by J. M. *Synge. It tells how Christy Mahon arrives in a Co. Mayo village and wins the hearts of the local women by boasting that he has killed his father. His prowess at the local sports confirms him in the role of hero and as fitting mate for Pegeen Mike. When old Mahon appears, they turn upon their hero despite his offer to 'slay his da' a second time. Escaping from their clutches, he tames his father, and the two leave the stage disdainful of the gullible Mayo peasants. The play was condemned by nationalists as a travesty of western Irish life, and treated as a *stage-Irish libel evoking a peasantry of alcoholics and fantasists rather than a people ready to assume self-government.

Plays for Puritans, see *Three Plays for Puritans.

Pléimeann, Séan, see John *Fleming.

Plough and the Stars, The (1926), a play by Sean *O'Casey, first produced at the *Abbey Theatre, where, as an anti-heroic depiction of tenement life before and during the *Easter Rising, it caused a riot. The recently married Jack and Nora Clitheroe share a tenement with the alcoholic Fluther Good, the irascible Peter Flynn, and others. Clitheroe's patriotism reawakens when he is promoted to officer rank in the Irish Citizen Army, but he is killed in the fighting. Vociferous arguments raging between the characters provide a satirical view of contemporary Irish passions.

Plunkett, Edward, see Lord *Dunsany.

Plunkett, Sir Horace (1845–1932), English-born social reformer; son of the 10th Baron Dunsany. Educated at Oxford, he became interested in agricultural co-operative movements on his return to Ireland. In 1894 he set up the Irish Agricultural Organization Society (IAOS), which helped a great many Irish farmers adapt to the modernizing period. Plunkett appointed George *Russell as organizer and editor of the Society's journal, The *Irish Homestead.

Plunkett, James (pseudonym of James Plunkett Kelly) (1920–), writer of fiction. Born in Sandymount, Dublin, but reared in the inner-city area, he was educated by the Christian Brothers. Leaving school at 17 for a clerkship, he became an active trade unionist and worked under James *Larkin. He began publishing in The *Bell from 1942 the short stories collected as The Trusting and Maimed (1955). Big Jim, his Larkin play, was broadcast in 1954 and later adapted as The Risen People (1958) for the *Abbey Theatre. In 1955 he joined Radio Éireann, becoming a television producer in 1960. *Strumpet City (1969) is a novel giving a comprehensive picture of Dublin from 1907 to 1914. Plunkett's next novel, Farewell Companions (1977) is concerned with Irish society in the aftermath of the First World and *Anglo-Irish Wars. The Circus Animals (1990) continues Plunkett's anatomy of modern Irish society into the 1940s and the 1950s.

Plunkett, Joseph Mary (1887–1916), revolutionary and poet. Born in Dublin he was educated at Belvedere College and UCD. Persistent ill health caused him to live much of the time abroad. He sought out Thomas *MacDonagh to learn Irish from him and they became friends. The Circle and The Sword (1911) was Plunkett's first collection. In 1913–14 he was editor of The *Irish Review. With MacDonagh and Edward *Martyn he founded the Irish Theatre in Hardwicke Street to perform Irish plays and foreign masterpieces. Although recovering from an operation on his throat, he joined the *Easter Rising and was a signatory to the Proclamation of the Irish Republic. On the eve of his execution he married Grace Gifford in his cell.

Plunkett, St Oliver (1629–1681), Catholic archbishop and martyr. Of Hiberno-Norman descent, he was born in Co. Meath and ordained in Rome, where he became Professor of Theology. Sent to Ireland as Archbishop of Armagh in 1670, he was arrested in 1679 during the panic following Titus Oates's allegations of a Catholic plot, and subsequently executed in London.

poem-book, see *duanaire.

Poetry Ireland (first series 1948–54; second series 1963–8; third series 1981–), a poetry journal founded by David *Marcus.

Poets and Dreamers (1903), a volume of essays on *folklore and translations from Irish by Lady *Gregory, based on material she and W. B. *Yeats had collected in the Galway region after 1896.

political poetry in Irish of the 17th and 18th cents. reflects the outlook of the native intelligentsia and documents their reaction to contemporary affairs. This writing is marked by a providential mode of thought, it reflects the role prophecy had in political affairs, and it recognizes the centrality of *Catholicism to the cultural identity of Ireland after the Battle of *Kinsale. In a series of political poems written c. 1640–60 the fortunes of the Catholic Church are linked inextricably with the fortunes of the body politic. The enemy, who is destined to be driven from Ireland, is identified as being both Protestant and English-speaking. In these poems, represented in Cecile O'Rahilly's edition (see below), a communal voice emerges, the narrator speaking in the first person plural on behalf of a dispossessed people. One of their constant sources of hope was the house of Stuart. To the poets of the 1680s, witnessing the unprecedented reforms implemented by *James II, it seemed that a prophecy was being fulfilled. To Dáibhí *Ó Bruadair it was evident that the Irish now 'had a real king'. In exile in France James assumed an idealized role as the perfect Irish king destined to return and save his people. His son and grandson also inherited that role, and for most of the 18th cent. the main focus of Irish political poetry was the house of Stuart and the Jacobite cause. See Cecile O'Rahilly (ed.), *Five Seventeenth-Century Political Poems* (1952).

Pompey (1663), a version of Pierre Corneille's *Mort de Pompée* in heroic verse by 'Orinda' (Katherine *Philips), and the first original play to be presented at *Smock Alley.

Poor Mouth, The, see An *Béal Bocht.

popular theatre, 1820–1899, was the chief form of drama in Ireland from the closure of *Crow St. to the foundation of the *Abbey Theatre. In 1820 the Covent Garden manager, Henry Harris, bought the theatrical patent and built the Theatre Royal (later Royal Theatre), Hawkins St., Dublin. It opened in 1821 with a performance of *The Comedy of Errors*. From 1871 the Royal Theatre was rivalled by the Gaiety Theatre on King St. under the management of the brothers John and Michael Gunn (opening with *She Stoops to Conquer*); and following a disastrous fire at the 'Old' Royal in 1880 the Hawkins St. building remained derelict until reopened by a consortium in 1897. The Gaiety stuck to its well-tried popular repertory of melodramas, comedies, and musicals, though both theatres scheduled touring opera companies throughout the year. At the Queen's Royal Theatre—first opened on Great Brunswick St. (now Pearse St.) as the Adelphi in 1829 and rebuilt in 1844—there emerged a national theatre in the sense that the political melodramas mounted by the English actor-manager J. W. *Whitbread between 1880 and 1907 attracted Dublin audiences with a mixture of patriotism and theatricality. One-third of the typical season at the Queen's involved Irish touring companies performing plays on Irish themes, while Boucicault's Irish trio, *The *Colleen Bawn* (1860), *Arrah-na-Pogue* (1864), and *The *Shaughraun* (1874), were often revived

there. Also regularly staged were Hubert *O'Grady's political melodramas, while others who followed in the tradition established by Whitbread and O'Grady were P. J. *Bourke and Ira Allen (1884–1927). After the foundation of the Abbey and *Gate Theatres, the popular theatre persisted at the Gaiety and the Olympia on Dame St., throwing up such comic stars and favourites as Jimmy O'Dea and Maureen Potter.

Porter, (Revd) James (1753–1798), Presbyterian minister and author who contributed a series of letters to *The Northern Star* in 1796, satirizing local landlords. These were published as *Billy Bluff and Squire Firebrand* in the same year (repr. 1810, 1829). At the outbreak of the Rebellion of 1798 [see *United Irishmen] he was captured and hanged outside his meeting-house at Grey Abbey, Co. Down. He is the subject of Séamus *Ó Neill's *Faill ar an bhFeart* (1967).

Portrait of the Artist as a Young Man, A (1916), an autobiographical novel by James *Joyce. In five chapters, it deals with Stephen Dedalus's spiritual liberation from the bonds of family, nationality, and religion which he comes to see as the defining characteristics of Irish society. The main episodes roughly correspond to events from infancy to 1902, when Joyce made his first journey to Paris.

Pot of Broth, The (1902) a play by W. B. *Yeats and Lady *Gregory performed at the *Abbey Theatre, with William *Fay in the role of the tramp.

Power, Marguerite (Countess of Blessington) (1789–1849), poet and novelist. Born in Knockbrit, Co. Tipperary. After marrying Charles Gardiner, Earl of Blessington, in 1817 she lived on the Continent, returning to establish a literary circle at Mayfair. Her popular

Conversations of Lord Byron (1834) arose from a close friendship with the poet in Genoa. *The Idler in Italy* (1839) and *The Confessions of an Elderly Lady* (1838) are works of fiction based on her experiences in Regency society. Her novels set in Ireland, *The Repealers, or Grace Cassidy* (1833) and *Country Quarters* (1850), are romances of high society.

Power, M[aurice] S. (1935–), novelist. Born in Dublin, he settled in the south of England. *The Killing of Yesterday's Children* (1985), *Lonely the Man Without Heroes* (1986), and *A Darkness in the Eye* (1989) formed a trilogy about *Northern Ireland. His other novels are *Crucible of Fools* (1990) and *Come the Executioner* (1991).

Power, Richard (1928–1970), novelist. Born in Dublin, he was educated by the Christian Brothers and entered the Civil Service. *Úll í mBarr an Ghéagáin* (1959) recounted his experiences on the Aran Islands and with Gaelic-speaking labourers in London. *The Hungry Grass* (1969) concerns the last year in the life of an Irish country priest.

Power, [William Grattan], Tyrone (1797–1841), actor, and novelist, born near Kilmacthomas, Co. Waterford. He joined a company of travelling players, arriving in London in 1821. His career began with a series of Irish roles at Covent Garden in 1826, after which he appeared frequently in London and Dublin, and America from 1833, his first journey resulting in the publication of *Impressions of America* (2 vols., 1836). Besides several romantic novels such as *The King's Secret* (1831), he wrote and also presented a number of farcical comedies.

Praeger, Robert Lloyd (1865–1953), naturalist. Born in Holywood, Co. Down, and educated at QUB. He became a civil engineer and later joined the National Library of Ireland, 1893–1924. His numerous works include *The Botanist in Ireland* (1934), *Some Irish Naturalists* (1949), *Natural History of Ireland* (1950), and *Irish Landscape* (1953). He is best remembered for his topographical classic *The Way that I Went* (1947), an Irish travel journal.

Priests and People: *A No Rent Romance* (1891), an anonymous novel, attacking the criminality of the *Land War and the corrupting influence of the Catholic Church.

Principles of Human Knowledge, The (1710), the chief philosophical work of George *Berkeley, in which he presents the case for the immaterialist theory, asserting that the existence of physical things consists solely in their being perceived, for which proposition he coined the Latin tag *esse est percipi*.

Prior, Thomas (1682–1751), economist and founder of the *RDS. Born in Rathdowney, Co. Laois, and educated at Kilkenny Grammar School and TCD. His *List of Irish Absentees*, first issued in 1729, gives estimates of the income spent abroad by Irish landlords to the detriment of their country.

Prisoner of Grace (1952), a novel by Joyce *Cary, first in his second trilogy, the others being **Except the Lord* (1953) and **Not Honour More* (1955). Adopted by an aunt, Nina Woodville becomes pregnant by her cousin, Jim Latter, an army officer, after which Chester Nimmo, a radical politician on the make, marries her for her fortune. The novel is a study of the exploitation of kindness by force and cruelty.

Proposal for the Universal Use of Irish Manufacture, A (1720), a polemic on Irish affairs published anonymously by Jonathan *Swift, his first such pamphlet after becoming

Dean of St Patrick's. In it he attacks the English mercantilist policy which is draining Ireland of her wealth.

Protestantism. In 16th-cent. England the State successfully sponsored the realignment, over two generations, of popular religious allegiances. In Gaelic Ireland, the Reformation made virtually no headway. The *Old English of the Pale [see *Irish State], a conservative provincial élite, were willing to accept royal supremacy, but showed little enthusiasm for reformed doctrine and liturgy. Even within the Church of Ireland, many of the first generation of clergy were no more than nominal adherents to the new faith. In the decades that followed the *plantations of Munster and Ulster, the Church of Ireland made little attempt to break out of its minority status. The growing numbers of Scots settling in Ulster brought Presbyterianism with them. The restoration of monarchy in 1660 meant a renewal of an episcopal Church of Ireland. Dissent in the three southern provinces, still seen as a major problem in the 1660s, thereafter dwindled into insignificance. Quakers now shed their radical origins to become a prosperous, largely self-contained sect. After 1691 the Government sponsored around twenty small colonies of Huguenots, refugees from France. A second immigrant sect were the Palatines, Protestant refugees from the Rhineland, who arrived in 1709. The shrinkage of dissent in the south was not matched in Ulster, where Presbyterians, already by the mid-17th cent. the largest single denomination, continued to grow in numbers and strength. Yet relations with the established Church remained tense. Much of the party conflict of Whig and Tory in these years centred on the question of whether it was Catholics or dissenters that presented the greater threat to

the established Church. The sacramental test, introduced in 1704 and not repealed until 1780, excluded Presbyterians as well as Catholics from offices of trust or profit under the Crown. But the radicalism of the Ulster *United Irishmen in the 1790s, and the vitality of Ulster Liberalism up to the Home Rule crisis of 1885–6 [see *Irish Parliamentary Party], were based in part on continued Presbyterian antipathy towards what they perceived as an Anglican-dominated establishment. The Church of Ireland of the 18th cent. enjoyed both wealth and legal privilege, while serving only one-eighth or so of the population. Lower-class members were thinly scattered in the rural south, but were more numerous in Ulster, and also in many of the towns of Munster and Leinster; Dublin was, up to the middle of the century, a predominantly Protestant city. Following a tradition established by Archbishop James *Ussher in the 1620s, historians emphasized the continuity between the Church of Ireland and the early Christian Church, appropriating to themselves the idealized image of an island of saints and scholars. All denominations of Irish Protestantism were affected, from the end of the 18th cent., by movements of religious revival. John Wesley visited Ireland twenty-one times between 1747 and 1789 and Irish Methodism continued to expand rapidly in the early 19th cent. From Samuel *Ferguson and his colleagues in the 'Orange Young Ireland' of the 1840s to *Yeats and other participants in the *literary revival, there were repeated attempts to construct a historical and cultural tradition that would reconcile Protestantism and Irishness. At another level there was a ruthless and pragmatic struggle to maintain privilege. After 1922 this formerly dominant minority found themselves in an *Irish State whose official ideology advanced the interests of the Catholic majority. Between 1926 and 1971 the Protestant population of independent Ireland fell by more than 40 per cent, partly as a result of the tough line taken by the Catholic Church on the upbringing of children of religiously mixed marriages (*Ne Temere*). In Northern Ireland, meanwhile, Unionism continued to appeal to an explicitly Protestant identity, reinforced by the threat, real and imagined, of Catholic nationalism. See S. J. Connolly, *Religion, Law, and Power: The Making of Protestant Ireland 1600–1760* (1995).

Proust (1931), a critical study by Samuel *Beckett of Marcel Proust's *À la recherche du temps perdu* (1913–27). Written in Paris in 1930, it describes the French novelist's art in hermetic prose as a quest for the real through involuntary memory and latent consciousness.

Prout, Fr., see Francis Sylvester *Mahony.

Prút, Liam [F.] (1940–), poet and writer of fiction. Born in Nenagh, Co. Tipperary, he joined the Christian Brothers in 1953. His poetry collections include *Fíon As Seithí Óir* (1972), *Asail* (1982), *An Dá Scór* (1984), and *An Giotár Meisce* (1988); he published short stories, *Sean-Dair* (1985), a novella, *Geineasas* (1991), and *Désirée* (1989), a novel.

publishing in English. The first printing press was established in Ireland by Humfrey Powell in 1550, who published *The Book of Common Prayer* (1551) in Dublin. During the 17th cent. Dublin remained the centre for Irish publishing, and various King's printers were appointed there. As the 1709 British Copyright Act did not apply in Ireland, printing during the early 18th cent. was devoted almost exclusively to the cheap and profitable production of works which had been published in Britain. By the mid-century, several publishers had produced about 5,000 editions of Latin authors, and works by Irish writers such as George *Berkeley and Jonathan *Swift (*Collected Works*, 1735). The best-known publisher of the period was George *Faulkner, whom Swift called the 'Prince of Dublin printers'. James *McGlashan took over from William Curry (d. 1846) in publishing the burgeoning Irish fiction industry in the 19th cent.; James *Duffy established the nucleus of Irish literary nationalism in his press at Anglesea St., printing *The *Spirit of the Nation* in 1843. The two series of William *Carleton's *Traits and Stories of the Irish Peasantry* were also published in Dublin—the first by Curry and the second by W. F. Wakeman. 19th-cent. Irish fiction and verse was published by Ward & Downey [see Edmund *Downey] and D. & J. Sadlier [see Mary *Sadlier], as well as other houses established by Irishmen in England and America. Some early publications of the Irish *literary revival were issued by T. Fisher Unwin of Paternoster Row in London. *Maunsel and Co., with offices in Dublin and in London, served as publisher to the *Abbey Theatre and also issued much of the *Anglo-Irish poetry of the early decades of the 20th cent. The Talbot Press, Browne & Nolan, and M. H. Gill provided the major outlets for authors in Ireland up to the Irish publishing renaissance spearheaded by Liam Miller's *Dolmen Press, consciously perpetuating the aesthetic tradition of the *Cuala Press. In Ulster, the early period of the *literary revival was served by publishing houses such as Marcus Ward and Erskine Mayne. Fiction and poetry were produced in the mid-century by the Mourne Press [see Richard *Rowley]. Contemporary Irish writing appears under the imprints of an increasingly large number of smaller houses including the Appletree, Arlen, Attic, Blackstaff, Brandon, Dedalus, Gallery, Town House, Lagan, Lilliput, Mercier, O'Brien, Poolbeg, Raven Arts, Salmon, and Wolfhound presses.

publishing in Irish began with *Foirm na nUrrnuidheadh* (1567), a devotional work for Irish and Scottish Presbyterians issued in Edinburgh by Seon *Carsuel. This was followed by Seán *Ó Cearnaigh's *Aíbidil Gaoidheilge & Caiticiosma* (1571), a catechism and prayerbook for the use of the Church of Ireland, printed in Dublin on founts paid for by *Elizabeth I. Uilliam Ó Domhnaill [see William *Daniel] saw to the publication of an Irish New Testament in 1603 [see *Bible in Irish], printed in Dublin by Seon Franche. A counter-offensive was launched at St Anthony's College in *Louvain, where the Franciscans devised an Irish fount and issued Aodh *Mac Aingil's *Sgáthán Shacramuinte na hAithridhe* (1618), and other books. William *Bedell organized the translation of the Old Testament, completed by 1640 but not published until 1685. *Keating's *Foras Feasa* was not published until 1811 (vol. i only), although an English translation was published by Dermod *O'Connor (1723). The work of Mícheál *Ó Cléirigh on the *Annals of the Four Masters* remained in manuscript until edited by John *O'Donovan (1848–51), but his glossary *Foclóir nó Sunasán Nua* was published in Louvain (1643). By the 18th cent., with the *Penal Laws in force and English gaining ground as a spoken and written language, there was less demand for devotional works in Irish. Nevertheless, in 1722 Francis *Hutchinson published *The Church Catechism in Irish* for use on Rathlin Island. James *Gallagher published Catholic sermons in Irish in 1767. Charlotte *Brooke's *Reliques of Irish Poetry* (1789) was the first volume which contained specifically literary material in Irish. In the 19th cent. a new interest in history and antiquities led to the founding of learned societies, among them the *Ossianic Society, and the *Irish Archaeological Society. Cultivation of Modern Irish was encouraged by the *Society for the Preservation of the Irish Language (1876), which published elementary texts from 1877 to 1887. The *Gaelic League published many volumes of folklore and creative writing. The Irish Texts Society, founded in 1900, began to publish editions of classic Irish texts with full scholarly apparatus. A government agency, An *Gúm, established in 1925, had by 1950 published over 1,000 books. Sáirséal agus Dill, founded in 1947 by Seán *Ó hÉigeartaigh, published works by modern writers such as Máirtín *Ó Cadhain. Notwithstanding a small readership, a greater number of books in Irish have been published in the fifty years to the end of the century than were published during the previous 400 years, and the number published annually has been steadily increasing, not least because of the industry of Pádraig Ó Snodaigh's Coiscéim imprint.

Purcell, Deirdre (1945–), novelist; born in Dublin and educated there, she was a member of the *Abbey company, and worked as a journalist for *RTÉ. Her works include *A Place of Stones* (1991), *That Childhood Country* (1992), *Full Circle* (1995), *Sky* (1995), and *Love Like Hate Adore* (1997).

Purdon, Katherine F[rances] (1852–1918), novelist. Born in Hotwell, Enfield, Co. Meath, she was educated at Alexandra College. Her first novel, *The Folk of Furry Farm* (1914), tells of local eccentricity at 'Ardenoo' (Hotwell), narrated in *Hiberno-English. *Dinny of the Doorstep* (1918), is a study of children's lives in Dublin slums.

Purgatory (1938), a late play by W. B. *Yeats, first produced at the *Abbey

Theatre. An old pedlar and his 16-year-old son return to the ruined *big house where the father was conceived. The old man kills his son in a vain attempt to stop the nightmare of the past repeating itself.

Puritan, The (1932), a novel by Liam *O'Flaherty. Francis Ferriter, a Dublin journalist, murders a prostitute for supposedly religious motives, but he comes to understand that he has acted out of sexual jealousy.

Purple Dust, The (1940), a 'wayward comedy' by Sean *O'Casey, in which two English would-be gentlemen vainly attempt to restore the ruins of a Tudor castle in Ireland.

Pygmalion: A Romance in Five Acts (1914), a play by George Bernard *Shaw, it presents a comic version of the classical myth of Pygmalion. Henry Higgins, a professor of phonetics, undertakes to turn a cockney flower-girl, Eliza Doolittle, into a plausible replica of a duchess by teaching her how to speak English in an upper-class manner.

Q-Celtic, see *Celtic languages.

Q-Celts, see *Celts.

Quare Fellow, The (1954), a play by Brendan *Behan, set in a Dublin prison. It concerns the execution of a murderer, the 'quare fellow'.

Queen's Colleges, see *universities.

Queen's Theatre, see *popular theatre.

Querist, The, George *Berkeley's study of economics and social matters, particularly as they relate to Ireland.

Quiet Man, The, see Maurice *Walsh.

R

Radio Telefís Éireann, see *RTÉ.

Raiftearaí, Antoine (Anthony Raftery) (1779–1835), poet; born in Cill Liadáin (Killedan) near Kiltimagh, Co. Mayo. Blinded by smallpox in childhood, Raiftearaí became a wandering minstrel, spending most of his time in south Co. Galway. According to an enemy, Peatsaí Ó Callanáin, he 'went with' a woman, Siobhán, and they had two children. He is buried in Killeenin near Craughwell in Co. Galway. His poetry and song deal with contemporary events, many of them reflecting his radical political views. His virulent attitude towards the Protestant religion was influenced by the writings of the Catholic propagandist *Pastorini. 'Cill Liadáin' is an evocation of his native place. 'Eanach Dhúin' is a lament for about twenty people who were drowned in Lough Corrib in 1828. Pre-*Famine Ireland, densely populated, unruly, dangerous, but energetic, is vividly portrayed in his verse.

Rann (1948–53), a quarterly of Ulster poetry edited by Roy *McFadden with Barbara Edwards. It ran to twenty issues.

rapparee, an 18th-cent. Irish Jacobite irregular, from ropairí (half-pikes), the customary weapon of the Catholics who attacked Protestants in the period of the *Williamite War. At the collapse of the Jacobite cause in Ireland the term became largely synonymous with the more commonplace *tory, a highwayman or bandit.

Rapparee, The (1870), a historical melodrama by Dion *Boucicault, set in the west of Ireland after the Battle of the *Boyne, and dealing with the defeated Irish gentry on the Jacobite side in the *Williamite War.

Rat-Pit, The (1915), a novel by Patrick *MacGill. A companion to *Children of the Dead End*, it deals with the lives of female migrant workers from Co. Donegal.

Ray, R. J. (pseudonym of Robert J. Brophy) (?1865–?), dramatist. Born in Cork, he worked as a journalist on newspapers in Cork and Dublin, and became known as one of the Cork realists for plays dealing with prejudice and brutality in Irish life, the best-known being The Casting-Out of Martin Whelan (1910) and The Gombeen Man (1913), both produced at the *Abbey Theatre.

Raymond, Anthony (1675–1726), antiquary and translator. Born in Ballyloughran, Co. Derry, he was educated at TCD becoming a Fellow in 1699. He employed scribes from the circle gathered around Tadhg *Ó Neachtain in Dublin to copy manuscripts for him.

RDS (Royal Dublin Society), a chartered society for 'Improving Husbandry, Manufactures, and other useful Arts and Sciences'. Derived from the Dublin Philosophical Society of 1683, it was founded by Thomas *Prior, Samuel ('Premium') *Madden, and others in 1731.

Read, Charles [Anderson] (1841–1878), novelist and anthologist; born near Sligo, to a landowning family. He wrote two popular Irish novels, *Savourneen Dheelish* (1869) and *Aileen Aroon* (1870), the former dealing with the same episode as *Carleton's

'*Wildgoose Lodge', He is best remembered for *The Cabinet of Irish Literature*, compiled 1876-8.

Reading in the Dark (1996), an atmospheric autobiographical novel by Seamus *Deane, set in Derry, and employing an episodic structure to unfold a family secret. Its action extends from the mid-1940s to the 1970s and it depicts individual stress against the backdrop of the *Troubles.

Real Charlotte, The (1894), a novel by *Somerville and Ross. Charlotte is a plain-looking Protestant of 40 making her way up the social scale in the West Cork village of Lismoyle. The principal victim of her ambition is her pretty young cousin Francie Fitzpatrick, whom Charlotte cheats out of her inheritance.

Reavey, George (1907-1976), poet and publisher. Born at Vitebsk in Russia, where his father managed a flax-mill, he went to Cambridge and co-founded the literary magazine *Experiment*. His Europa Press published early collections of verse by *Beckett and Denis *Devlin. *The Colours of Memory* (1955) was a collection of his own verse.

Rebellion of 1641. The Rebellion broke out in Ulster on the night of 22/3 October, led by Rory O'More and Sir Phelim O'Neill, members of a Gaelic aristocracy increasingly apprehensive about their property rights. On one side was an unstable alliance of the *Old English and the *Old Irish known as the *Confederation of Kilkenny; on the other was a combination of Irish Royalists and Parliamentarians. In 1642 Eoghan Ruadh *Ó Néill returned from service in the Spanish army to lead the Confederation forces. A year-long truce struck with James Butler, Earl of *Ormond, foundered after the Battle of Benburb, when Ó Néill routed an English army in Co. Tyrone in 1646. In spring of 1649 *Cromwell arrived with his New Model Army. Within six months the Confederation had collapsed, and after the notorious massacres at Drogheda and Wexford many Irish towns capitulated. In the English Parliament, an Act of Settlement (1652) and an Act of Satisfaction (1653) were passed legitimizing the confiscation of all property in Catholic hands east of the Shannon. A virulent propaganda literature describing alleged atrocities committed by the Catholic insurgents against Protestant planters flourished in the years after the outbreak of the Rebellion.

Rebellion of 1798, see *United Irishmen.

Recruiting Officer, The (1706), a play by George *Farquhar first produced at Drury Lane Theatre, London. The free-living Captain Plume, who is enlisting soldiers in and around Shrewsbury, seeks Silvia's affections while his shy friend Worthy dithers over the coquettish Melinda.

Red and the Green, The (1965), a novel by Iris *Murdoch. Set in Dublin during the 1916 *Easter Rising, it contrasts the British officer Andrew Chase-White and his Anglo-Irish family with the Republicans Pat and Cathal Dumay.

Red Branch, see *Conchobor mac Nessa.

Red Hand of Ulster, The (1912), a novel by George A. *Birmingham, dealing with a revolution instigated by Conroy, an Irish-American millionaire and *Fenian, which leads to an independent Ulster.

Red Hanrahan, a romantic poet and *hedge schoolmaster who appears as a character in W. B. *Yeats's *Stories of Red Hanrahan* (1897) and elsewhere in his works.

Red Roses for Me (1942), a play by Sean *O'Casey, based on his experiences of the 1913 Lock-out Strike [see James *Larkin]. Ayamonn Breydon, leader of the transport workers, sacrifices his love for Sheila Moorneen to the cause and is killed in a demonstration.

Redemption (1949), a novel by Francis *Stuart. Ezra Arrigho returns from wartime Germany to a small Irish town. Kavanagh, a local fishmonger, murders the shopgirl, Annie. Arrigho's dying aunt Nuala joins a commune living over Kavanagh's fish-shop while awaiting his arrest.

Red-Leaguers, The (1904), a novel by Shan *Bullock about a fictional Republican rising in Co. Fermanagh.

Redmond, John [Edward] (1856–1918), nationalist leader. Born in Ballytrent, Co. Wexford, he was educated at TCD. Elected MP for New Ross in 1881, Redmond was imprisoned in 1888, supported the leader in the *Parnell Split, and became head of the Parnellite faction after his death, reuniting the *Irish Parliamentary Party in 1900.

Reeves, William (1815–1892), churchman and antiquarian. Born in Charleville, Co. Cork, he studied medicine at TCD. His *Life of Columba* (1857) collated *Adamnán's life with other sources, including Maghnus *Ó Domhnaill's biography. He acquired the *Book of Armagh* for the TCD Library.

Reflections on the Revolution in France [and the proceedings of certain societies in London relative to that event] (1790), a counter-revolutionary treatise by Edmund *Burke. Burke claimed that an orderly State requires some means of correction, whereby it can adjust to change when necessity ordains, but only to retain its continuity with ancient laws and privileges. Democracy, Burke argues, becomes tyranny, a

condition which he illustrates by describing the French Assembly taking orders from a mob. The British distrust innovation and cling to their 'prejudices' and the latent wisdom inhering in them, thereby protecting themselves from the lunacy of 'calculators' and 'sophists'.

Reid, Christina (1942–), playwright; born in Belfast and educated there, she was writer-in-residence at the *Lyric Theatre in Belfast 1983–4, and at the Young Vic in London 1988–9. Plays include *Tea in a China Shop* (1983), *Joyriders* (1986), *The Belle of Belfast City* (1986), and *My Name, Shall I Tell You my Name* (1989).

Reid, Forrest (1875–1947), novelist; born in Belfast, educated at the Royal Belfast Academical Institute and then apprenticed to the tea trade before going to Cambridge, where he was encouraged to write by E. M. Forster. The fifteen books that he produced after his return to Belfast were chiefly fictional and autobiographical studies of boyhood and adolescence. The earlier of two autobiographies, *Apostate* (1926), reveals a rebellious disdain for middle-class Protestant ethics. The earliest novel, *The Kingdom of Twilight* (1904), elicited detailed comments from Henry James, who repudiated the dedication of his next (*The Garden God*, 1905) because of its homosexual overtones. During the next four decades, Reid lived privately in Belfast and established himself as a noted stylist. *Peter Waring* (1937) is a radical revision of the earlier *Following Darkness* of 1912, which tells of a boy's troubled upbringing. *The Bracknels: A Family Chronicle* (1911), rewritten as *Denis Bracknel* in 1947, portrays a harsh father. *Brian Westby* (1934) tells of the reunion of a father and his teenage son from whom he has been separated by divorce. In the *Tom Barber novels a boy's life is examined at successively earlier stages (*Uncle Stephen*, 1931; *The Retreat*, 1936; and *Young Tom*, 1944). *At the Door of the Gate* (1915) is his one novel about working-class Belfast. A second autobiography, *Private Road* (1940) describes Reid's meeting and discussions with George *Russell.

Reid, Graham (1945–), playwright. Born in Belfast, he left school at 15, subsisting on unemployment benefit after service in the British army. In his late 20s he studied at QUB and became a teacher, but gave it up to write full-time in 1980. Reid's first plays, *The Death of Humpty Dumpty* (1979) and *The Closed Door* (1980), deal with the *Troubles. In *The Hidden Curriculum* (1982) and *Remembrance* (1984), this is only one factor among many with which working people have to contend. The Billy trilogy (*Too Late to Talk to Billy*, 1982; *A Matter of Choice for Billy*, 1983; *A Coming to Terms for Billy*, 1984), written for television, centres on intra-familial pressures amid violent social conflict. *Ties of Blood* (1985), also for television, deals with the army and its impact on civilians. *You, Me and Marley* (1992) concerns a Belfast teenager who is rejected by the *IRA.

Reid, Mayne (pseudonym of Thomas Mayne) (1818–1883), boys' novelist. Born in Ballyroney, Co. Down, he left home and reached Louisiana in 1838, working as a slave-overseer, teacher, and Indian-fighter. He enlisted in the Mexican-American War, suffering serious wounds at Chatultepec, 1847. *The Scalp-Hunters* (1850) was a phenomenal success with the boy-audience for which he wrote some thirty further titles. His best-known titles included *Rifle-Rangers* (1850), *Boy Hunters* (1853), *Castaways* (1870), and *The White Squaw* (1871). As a champion of the sport, he wrote a croquet treatise in 1863.

Repeal of the Union. Calls for a repeal of the Act of *Union were made from time to time in the years after 1800. Following the success of the *Catholic Emancipation campaign, Daniel *O'Connell announced that repeal was now his main objective, founding the Repeal Association in July 1840. The Repeal movement revived the tactics of the Catholic Emancipation campaign, with local societies collecting a 'Repeal rent', and active co-operation from the Catholic clergy.

Republic of Ireland, see *Irish State.

Responsibilities (1914), a collection of poems by W.B. *Yeats in which he assesses those people and inheritances that still command his loyalty after disappointment in love, betrayal by one-time friends, and despair at modern Ireland.

Resurrection, The (1931), a prose play by W. B. *Yeats. Three characters, a Greek, a Hebrew, and a Syrian, witness events surrounding the resurrection of Christ.

Retreat, The, see *Tom Barber trilogy.

Return of the Brute, The (1929), a novel by Liam *O'Flaherty based on the author's experience as an Irish Guardsman during the First World War.

rhyming weavers, see *weaver poets.

Rhys, Grace (née Little) (1865–1929), novelist. Born in Boyle, Co. Roscommon, she married the Welsh poet Ernest Rhys. Her novels include *Mary Dominic* (1898), concerning a girl rejected by her parents after being seduced by a wealthy man. *The Wooing of Sheila* (1901) and *The Prince of Lisnover* are romantic love-stories.

RIA (Royal Irish Academy), a learned body dedicated by its charter to 'the cultivation of Science, Polite Literature, and Antiquities'; it came into being in 1785 with James Caulfield, Lord *Charlemont, as its first President. The RIA was the immediate successor to the Hibernian Antiquarian Society, 1779–83, itself arising from the work of a Select Committee of the *RDS, set up in 1772. In the 19th cent. it became the focus for philological, archaeological, and architectural studies. The RIA library became a major centre for the preservation of the literary and historical remains of Gaelic society. It now contains the *Book of the Dun Cow, *Leabhar Breac, the *Book of Lecan, and an original autograph copy of part of the *Annals of the Four Masters, along with 1,400 *manuscripts of various kinds.

Rice, Adrian (1958–), poet; born in Belfast, educated in Ballyclare and at UUJ he worked as a freelance writer and founded the Abbey Press with Mel McMahon in 1997. Collections include *Impediments* (1997) and *The Mason's Tongue* (1999); *Signals* (1997) was an anthology of poetry and prose.

Richardson, John (1664–1747), translator and clergyman. Born in Armagh and educated at TCD, where he took holy orders. His commitment to proselytizing Catholics led to *Seanmora ar na Priom Phoncibh na Chreideamh* (1711), a collection of sermons by himself and others. In preparing *Leabhar na nOrnaighteadh cComhchoitchionn* (1712), a translation of *The Book of Common Prayer*, he had the assistance of Cathal Ó Luinín, a member of the *Ó Neachtain circle of Gaelic scholars in Dublin.

Riddell, Charlotte, Mrs J. H. (née Cowan) (1832–1906), novelist; born in Carrickfergus. She wrote more than forty-five books and edited *St James's Magazine*. Many of her novels, such as *George Geith of Fen Court* (1864), the story

of a hardworking accountant, show a detailed knowledge of commercial life in London. Only a few draw on Irish material: *Maxwell Drewitt* (1865), set in Connemara; *Berna Boyle* (1884), set in Co. Down; and *The Nun's Curse* (1888), set in Dunfanaghy, Co. Donegal.

Riders to the Sea (1904), a one-act play by J. M. *Synge. Performed at the *Abbey, with George *Russell's *Deirdre*, it tells of an old woman, Maurya, who has lost her husband and five of her sons to the sea, and who begs the last not to undertake a treacherous crossing which also proves to be fatal.

Rising of the Moon, The (1907), a one-act play by Lady *Gregory, set in a coastal town. As a police sergeant is putting up a poster of a wanted rebel, the man himself arrives disguised as a pedlar, but the sergeant does not betray him.

Rivals, The (1774), a comedy of manners by Richard Brinsley *Sheridan. Lydia Languish, a wealthy young lady in Bath, welcomes the advances of Ensign Beverley, really Jack Absolute in disguise. A farcical plot involving misunderstandings and the threat of violence ends happily for the young lovers.

Rivals, The (1829), a short novel by Gerald *Griffin, published in tandem with *Tracy's Ambition*. The melodramatic plot concerns Esther Wilderming, a Methodist beauty loved by two suitors, one a romantic rebel named Francis Riordan, the other a Justice of the Peace, Richard Lacy.

Robert Emmet (1884), an Irish political melodrama by Dion *Boucicault dealing with the 1803 *United Irish Rising and its leader. For the most part the play follows the historical events faithfully, enlisting the familiar characters of the legend, yet preserving a balance between private and public action, and concluding with *Emmet's famous speech from the dock.

Roberts, George, see *Maunsel & Company.

Robinson, [Esmé Stuart] Lennox (1886–1958), playwright and theatre manager, born in Douglas, Co. Cork. His father became a clergyman in middle age and moved to a rectory in Ballymoney, Co. Cork. A visit by the *Abbey Theatre Company at the Cork Opera House in 1907 introduced him to Irish nationalism, as documented in *A Young Man from the South* (1917), an autobiographical novel. His first play, *The *Clancy Name*, enjoyed a long run at the Abbey in 1908, and was followed by *The Cross Roads* (1909) and *Harvest* (1910), all studies of provincial life in Co. Cork. Following the death of *Synge in 1909, Robinson was taken on as manager and director at the Abbey. In 1910 he incurred the wrath of Annie *Horniman by failing to close the theatre in mourning for Edward VII. *Patriots* (1912) and *The Dreamers* (1915) describe the clash of political idealism with reality. On leaving the Abbey in 1914 Robinson became a librarian for the Carnegie Trust under Sir Horace *Plunkett. His first and most enduring comedy was *The *Whiteheaded Boy* (1916), followed by *The Lost Leader* (1918), a play based on *Parnell. In 1918 he returned to the Abbey as manager and producer. In 1923 he was appointed a member of the Board of Directors, and was for many years director of the Abbey School of Acting. During the ensuing years he wrote numerous plays, of which the best-known are *The Big House* (1926), *The Far-Off Hills* (1928), and *Drama at Inish* (1933). *In Three Homes* (1938) and *Curtain Up* (1941) are volumes of autobiography. *Ireland's Abbey Theatre, 1899–1951* (1951) was an official history.

Robinson, Tim (1935–), artist and topographer; born in London and educated at Cambridge, he went to live on the Aran Islands in 1972, learning Irish and studying the history of the landscape. *Stones of Aran* appeared as two volumes: *Pilgrimage* (1986) followed by *Labyrinth* (1995). These are volumes of cultural analysis as well as evocations of landscape and history.

Roche, Billy [William Michael] (1949–), novelist and dramatist; born in Wexford, and educated there before working in various jobs. *Tumbling Down* (1986) was a novel, followed by *A Handful of Stars* (1988), the first play in a 'Wexford Trilogy', the others being *Poor Beast in the Rain* (1989) and *Belfry* (1991). These plays depict the frustrations of contemporary small-town Irish life. The plays are written in *Hiberno-English dialogue of such bite and accuracy that it becomes a kind of poetry. *Amphibians* (1992), *The Cavalcaders* (1993), and *Tumbling Down* (1994) were further plays, *Trojan Eddie* (1997) a screenplay.

Roche, Regina Maria (née Dalton) (1764–1845), novelist. Born in Waterford, she wrote a number of sentimental novels featuring hot-tempered lords and ladies in Gothic settings, of which *Children of the Abbey* (1796) was her greatest success. Other works were: *The Munster Cottage Boy* (1820), *The Bridal of Dunamore* (1823), and *The Castle Chapel* (1825).

Rodgers, W[illiam] R[obert] (1909–1969), poet. Born in Belfast, he was educated at QUB, and installed as Presbyterian Minister at Loughgall, Co. Armagh. The poems in his first volume, *Awake! And Other Poems* (1940), exhibit verbal exuberance. In 1945 he accepted a job with the BBC in London. The poems in *Europa and the Bull* (1952), are remarkable for their vigorous sensuality.

Rolleston, T[homas] W[illiam] (1857–1920), translator and poet. Born in Shinrone, Co. Offaly, he was educated at TCD. He edited *Poems and Ballads of Young Ireland* (1888) with W. B. *Yeats and others. He became Secretary to the Irish Literary Society in London in 1892, returning to Dublin in 1894. *Sea Spray: Verses and Translations* (1909) contained his version of 'The Dead at Clonmacnois', as well as a curious piece on the pleasures of cycling. Other works include *Myths and Legends of the Celtic Race* (1911).

romantic tales in Irish are of comparatively late origin, first appearing in *manuscripts in the 15th cent. They are rambling tales of magic and conflict frequently centred on the quest motif, and often featuring a kingly hero seeking territorial or amorous conquest in foreign lands. Among these tales are *Eachtra Mhelóra agus Orlando (Adventure of Melora and Orlando)*, and *Bás Cearbhaill agus Farbhlaidhe (Death of Cearbhall and Farbhlaidh)*, telling of a tragic love affair involving the poet Cearbhall *Ó Dálaigh.

Roper, Mark (1951–), poet; born in Derbyshire, educated at Reading and Oxford Universities, and worked as a teacher in Ireland from the 1980s. Collections include *The Hen Ark* (1990), *Catching the Light* (1996), and *The Home Fire* (1998).

Rory O'More (1837), a novel by Samuel *Lover derived from his popular ballad. Choosing the background of the 1798 Rebellion, Lover succeeded in producing a light-hearted, sentimental work which would not challenge his readers.

Ros, Amanda McKittrick (1860–1939), novelist. Born in Drumaness, Co. Down, she trained as a teacher and found a post at Larne. She published two romances, *Irene Iddlesleigh* (1897) and *Delina Delany* (1898), both in an

idiosyncratic manner that provides unconscious comedy of a high order. Her two volumes of verse, *Poems of Puncture* (1913) and *Fumes of Formation* (1933), evince a virulent hostility to lawyers and literary critics. A last novel, *Helen Huddleston* (1969), was completed by Jack Loudan.

'Rosa Alchemica' (1897), a short prose romance in W. B. *Yeats's mystical triptych with 'The *Adoration of the Magi' and 'The *Tables of the Law'. Michael Robartes visits the narrator in Dublin, and transports him to a mystical temple in the west of Ireland.

roscad, with rosc, from which it derives, comes from the verbal root sech- ('speak, utter'), and is used of legal maxims and aphorisms quoted in early Irish legal texts. It is also used to refer to an early form of Irish *metrics. The roscad utterances are composed in a form of structured diction, or rhymeless verse. Roscad preceded the rhyming, syllabic verse which came into use in the 7th cent. and thereafter dominated Irish poetry until the 17th. Because of its esoteric aura it is sometimes used of extempore and mantic chants.

Roscommon, Earl of, see Wentworth *Dillon.

Rose and Crown, see *Autobiographies [Sean O'Casey].

Rosenstock, Gabriel (1949–), poet and translator. Born in Kilfinane, Co. Limerick, he was educated at UCC, where he was one of the *Innti group of poets. He moved to Dublin, where he became editor at An *Gúm. His first collection, *Susanne sa Seomra Folctha* (1973), was followed by *Túirlingt* (1978), *Méaram!* (1981), *Om* (1983), *Nihil Obstat* (1984), *Migmars* (1985), *Rún na gCaisleán* (1989), *Ní Mian Léi an Fhilíocht Níos Mó* (1993), among others. Rosenstock is a prolific translator, tackling Seamus *Heaney in *Conlán* (1989), Georg Trakl in *Craorag* (1991), as well as numerous versions from Arab tradition. *Bróg Kruschev* (1998) is a short story collection.

Ross, Martin (pseudonym of Violet Florence Martin) (1862–1915), novelist, and second cousin of Edith Œnone *Somerville, with whom she formed the writing partnership *Somerville and Ross. In 1872 Violet Martin and her mother went to live in Dublin, where Violet attended Alexandra College. The two cousins met for the first time in 1886 and soon embarked on their literary collaboration. Violet spent much time at Drishane House in Castletownshend, Co. Cork, the Somerville home, and it was there that most of their writing was done.

Rotherick O'Connor King of Connaught, or *The Distressed Princess* (1719), a history play by Charles *Shadwell. Performed at *Smock Alley Theatre, it narrates the events of the *Norman invasion of Ireland, presenting Rory O'Connor, last High King of Ireland (d. 1198), and 'Catholicus', Archbishop of Tuam, as malignant tyrants. Ireland is delivered by Strongbow.

Rowley, Richard (pseudonym of Richard Valentine Williams) (1877–1947), poet, playwright, and publisher; born in Belfast, he ran the family cotton firm until its collapse in 1931. During the Second World War he founded the Mourne Press. *The City of Refuge* (1917), celebrates industrial Belfast, while later collections such as *Ballads of Mourne* (1940) make use of rural settings and Ulster Scots. His play *Apollo in Mourne* (1926) is a study of peasant life.

Royal Dublin Society, see *RDS.

Royal Irish Academy, see *RIA.

Royal Theatre, see *popular theatre.

Royal University of Ireland, see *universities.

RTÉ (Radio Telefís Éireann), the Irish national broadcasting service. Irish public-service broadcasting began on 1 January 1926, when the radio station 2RN was inaugurated. The national radio service was called Radio Éireann from 1937 to 1966, when it merged with Telefís Éireann, established in 1962, the new body being known as Radio Telefís Éireann. RTÉ has been successful in maintaining a distinctively Irish broadcasting service in regard to news, current affairs, sport, and light entertainment.

Russell, George [William] (pseudonym 'AE' from Greek 'Æon') (1867–1935), poet, mystic, social reformer; born in Lurgan, Co. Armagh. The family moved to Dublin in 1878, and he was educated at Rathmines School and the Metropolitan School of Art, where he met W. B. *Yeats. From 1884, when he began to experience waking visions, he became increasingly involved in spiritual research. His first collection of poetry, *Homeward: Songs by the Way* (1894), contained ethereal poems, intent on evoking spiritual and contemplative states. His other collections continued more or less in this vein, and include *The Earth Breath and Other Poems* (1897), *The Divine Vision and Other Poems* (1904), and *Collected Poems* (1913). In 1897 Russell joined Sir Horace *Plunkett's Irish Agricultural Organization Society (IAOS), supervising the setting-up of co-operative banks in the west of Ireland. His version of *Deirdre* (1902), performed by the *Abbey Theatre's precursor, had Constance *Markievicz in the title-role. He edited The *Irish Homestead, the journal of the IAOS, 1905–23, using its columns to encourage many young writers, including Padraic *Colum, Seumas *O'Sullivan, and Eva *Gore-Booth. In 'On Behalf of Some Irishmen Not Followers of Tradition', he attacked the deployment of myth to enlist nationalist feelings, a poem fiercely criticized by Joseph Mary *Plunkett in 1913. In that year he supported the Dublin Strikers during the Lock-out [see James *Larkin]. The outbreak of the First World War seemed to confirm man's severance from the sources of wisdom, and *Gods of War, With Other Poems* (1915) challenges the prevailing war fever. *The National Being* (1916) presents a synthesis of his ideas on non-militant nationalism, spiritual concerns, and idealistic principles. Other prose works include *The Candle of Vision* (1918), a collection of essays describing his inner life. Two novels, *The *Interpreters* (1922) and *The Avatars* (1933), outline his spiritual message. In 1922 he became editor of *The *Irish Statesman*, which incorporated *The Irish Homestead*, and continued in that role until 1930. He went on writing poems and prose, publishing collections such as *Enchantment and Other Poems* (1930) and *The House of the Titans and Other Poems* (1934). The prose work, *Song and Its Fountains* (1932), continues the enquiry begun in *The Candle of Vision*. Escaping from a 'nation run by louts' he went to live in England after 1933, first in London and then in Bournemouth. See Henry Summerfield, *That Myriad-Minded Man: A Biography of G. W. Russell, 'AE'* (1975).

Russell, T[homas] O'Neill (1828–1908), novelist (pseudonym, 'Reginald Massey') and founding member of the *Gaelic League with Douglas *Hyde and others. Born in Co. Westmeath of Quaker stock, he first stated the case for language revival in *The Irishman* (1854). The hero of *Dick Massey* (1860) is a member of a landowning family who works passionately for the victims of the *Famine. In *True Heart's Trials* (1872) the scene shifts between the Irish midlands and American backwoods.

Ryan, Desmond (1893–1964), man of letters; born in London, son of W. P. *Ryan, he came to Ireland and was educated at Patrick *Pearse's school, St. Enda's, becoming a teacher there and secretary to Pearse. He saw active service in the *Easter Rising and was interned at Frongoch. He wrote *The Man Called Pearse* (1919), and *The Sword of Light* (1939), a study of the survival of Gaelic tradition in the 18th and 19th centuries. Novels include *The Invisible Army* (1922) and *St. Eustace and the Albatross* (1935).

Ryan, Fred[erick] (1876–1913), socialist and playwright. Born in Dublin, he was Secretary of the Irish National Theatre Society [see *Abbey Theatre], contributing a play, *The Laying of the Foundations* (1902), satirizing county council corruption. With John *Eglinton he edited the short-lived *Dana*.

Ryan, Richard (1946–), poet; born in Dublin and educated there, he entered the Diplomatic Service. His collections include *Ledges* (1970) and *A Northern Spring* (1986).

Ryan, W[illiam] P[atrick] (also 'Liam P. Ó Riain') (1867–1942), novelist. Born in Templemore, Co. Tipperary, he was active in the Irish Literary Society in London, and wrote an account of *The Irish *Literary Revival* (1894). Ryan wrote several novels, most notably *The Plough and the Cross* (1910), based on his experiences as a liberal editor.

Ryves, Elizabeth (1750–1797), poet and translator. An Anglo-Irish woman who lost her property through process of law, she went to London to make a living as a writer, but died in destitution. Robert Dodsley, published her *Poems on Several Occasions* (1771). Her novel, *The Hermit of Snowden* (1790), published in Dublin, tells the story of an authoress, Lavinia, as unsuccessful as herself.

Saddlemyer, Ann (1933–), scholar; born in Saskatoon, Canada, she became Professor of English and Drama at the University of Toronto, and served as Chairman of the International Association for the Study of Irish Literatures. She made a special contribution to the study of Irish drama, beginning with an edition of Synge's plays (1968), followed by *In Defence of Lady Gregory, Playwright* (1977), an edition of Lady Gregory's plays in four volumes in the Coole edition (1971–9), and of the correspondence between Yeats, Lady Gregory, and Synge in their management of the *Abbey (1982).

Sadleir (sometimes Sadlier), John (1814–1856), politician and embezzler. Born in Co. Tipperary and educated at Clongowes, he became an agent for the railways and MP for Carlow and for Sligo in 1847 and 1853. With George Henry Moore (George *Moore's father), William Keogh, and others he founded the Catholic Defence Association, also known as 'the Pope's Brass Band'. Sadleir embezzled large sums from Irish and English concerns before committing suicide by poison on Hampstead Heath.

Sadleir, Mary [Anne] (née Madden) (1820–1903), author of novels addressing mainly an Irish-American female audience. Born in Cootehill, Co. Cavan, she emigrated to Canada in 1844 and married the publisher James Sadleir in 1846. *Father Sheehy* (1845), her earliest book, narrates the story of a priest wrongfully executed at Clonmel in 1766. Many of her works are patriotic historical romances (*The Confederate Chiefs*, 1859; *The Red Hand of Ulster*, 1850: *The Daughters of Tyrconnell*, 1863; *MacCarthy More*, 1868). Others deal with the trials of newly arrived emigrants (*Willy Burke*, 1850; *The Blakes and the Flanagans*, 1855; *Bessy Conway*, 1861; *Simon Kerrigan*, 1864; and *Confessions of an Agnostic*, 1864). Several of her novels are frame-stories for the recitation of tradition, legend, and song. Such are *The Old House by the Boyne* (1865) and *The Heiress of Kilorgan* (1867).

Saint Joan: *A Chronicle Play in Six Scenes, and an Epilogue* (1923), by George Bernard *Shaw. Written shortly after the canonization of the 15th-cent. French girl, it counters the 19th-cent. sentimentalization of her story. Shaw's Joan is forthright, energetic, and strong of will.

St. Patrick for Ireland (1640), a play by the English dramatist James *Shirley, then in Dublin, and the first to take Irish history for its subject-matter. On his arrival in Ireland, St *Patrick converts a nobleman called Dichu, whose sons are then condemned to death by King Loegarius. Archimagus, the druid saves them.

St. Patrick's Day, *or the Scheming Lieutenant* (1775), a play by Richard Brinsley *Sheridan. O'Connor, the Irish Lieutenant, aided by Doctor Rosy, disguises himself as a country bumpkin, Humphry Hum, to become a servant to Justice Credulous, who is violently opposed to the Lieutenant's marrying his daughter Lauretta.

saints' lives. Lives of Irish saints were most often composed to assert property or territorial claims, and date mainly from periods when such claims were being put forward for the first time or being contested. The earliest lives, in Latin, belong to the second half of the 7th cent. Two lives of St *Patrick of Armagh were compiled by *Muirchú and *Tírechán. A life was also composed for St *Brigit of Kildare by Cogitosus. At Iona *Adamnán wrote a life of *Colum Cille shortly before 700. From c.850 to 950 a group of vernacular lives were written. The earliest of these was that of Brigit of Kildare; the latest a life of Adamnán, composed shortly after 950 at Kells.

Sáirséal agus Dill, an Irish-language publishing house founded in 1945 by Seán *ÓhÉigeartaigh and his wife Bríd Ní Mhaoileoin. The company's relationship with its authors was free from the bureaucratic and political constraints characteristic of An *Gúm. Sáirséal agus Dill quickly built up an impressive list based on an upsurge in creativity during the later 1930s. In 1981 the imprint was purchased by Caoimhín Ó Marcaigh and thence continued as Sáirséal Ó Marcaigh.

Salkeld, Blanaid (1880–1959), poet; born in Chittagong, India (now Pakistan) where her father was in the colonial service, she was educated in Dublin. Her work includes *Hello, Eternity* (1933), *A Dubliner* (1942), *The Fox's Covert* (1935), and *Experiment in Error* (1955).

Sally Cavanagh, or the Untenanted Graves (1869), a novel by Charles *Kickham, written during his imprisonment for *Fenian activities. Loosely episodic in structure, the story outlines the plight of Sally Cavanagh and her children after her husband and eldest boy emigrate to America following the land-grasping activities of a corrupt agent.

Salomé (published in French, 1893; in English, 1894), a one-act tragedy by Oscar *Wilde; written in French and translated by Alfred Douglas. A superior English translation by Wilde's son Vyvyan Holland appeared in 1957. It was first performed in Paris during Wilde's imprisonment in 1896.

Saltair na Rann (*Psalter of Verses*) is a narrative poem of 162 cantos recounting the story of the creation of the heavens and the earth, the creation and fall of Man, Old Testament history, the life of Christ, and the Last Judgement.

Samhain [see also *festivals], the quarter-day marking the beginning of winter and the New Year, celebrated on 1 November, from which season-day the month is named in Irish. The vigil is known as Oíche Shamhna. Samhain had an important place in Celtic *mythology as a time when the normal order is suspended to allow free passage between the natural and supernatural worlds.

Samhain (1901–6, six issues; 1908, one issue), the organ of the Irish Literary Theatre [see *Abbey Theatre], following *Beltaine, and edited by W. B. *Yeats.

Sanas Chormaic, see *Cormac mac Cuilennáin.

Sarr, Kenneth (pseudonym of Kenneth Reddin) (1895–1967), novelist and playwright. Born in Dublin and educated at UCD, he was imprisoned for a time for Republican activities. After the *Anglo-Irish War he became a District Justice. Sarr wrote a number of plays for the *Abbey Theatre in the manner of T. C. *Murray, then turned to fiction with *Somewhere to the Sea* (1936), which depicts Dublin during the *Troubles. *Another Shore* (1945) and *Young Men with a Dream* (1946) are further studies of the revolutionary period.

Sarsfield, Patrick (?1655–1693), Jacobite commander, created Earl of

Lucan by *James II in 1691. Born into an *Old English family with estates in Dublin and Kildare, he was commissioned and rapidly promoted in the army of James II. During the *Williamite War he emerged as the most popular Irish Jacobite commander, especially after his daring expedition to Ballyneety (11 August 1690) to destroy Williamite siege equipment heading for Limerick.

Savage, Marmion W[ilmo] (1805–1872), journalist and author of *The Falcon Family* (1845), a satire on *Young Ireland in which that name was supposed to have first occurred. He also wrote novels such as *The Bachelor of Albany* (1848) and *Reuben Medlicott, or The Coming Man* (1852).

Sayers, Peig (1873–1958), Irish storyteller. Born into a story-telling family in Vicarstown, Dunquin, Co. Kerry, she went into domestic service in Dingle at the age of 14. She was rescued from a second, less kindly employer by an arranged marriage to Pádraig Ó Gaoithín from the Great Blasket Island. Her contemporary fame as a story-teller increasingly attracted visitors until, encouraged by Máire Ní Chinnéide, she dictated her autobiography *Peig* (1936) to her son, Mícheál, being unable to write Irish herself. *Machtnamh Seana-Mhná* (1939) contains further recollections. Seosamh Ó Dálaigh recorded 360 of her tales, which remain unpublished, for the *Irish Folklore Commission. In her last years Peig Sayers settled on the mainland prior to the official evacuation of the Blasket Islands in 1953.

Scéla Alaxandair (History of Alexander), a Middle Irish saga which tells 'how Alexander son of Philip took the kingship and empire of the world', being an adaption of Orosius' 5th-cent. text, *Historiae Contra Paganos*.

Scéla Cano meic Gartnáin (Story of

Cano, Son of Gartnán), a 9th-cent. king tale [see *historical cycle], surviving in the *Yellow Book of Lecan. Cano, an exiled Scottish prince, visits Marcán, king of Uí Maine in Connacht. Marcán's wife Créd, who is in love with Cano, drugs the guests at a banquet and elicits from Cano the promise that he will return, but their plans are thwarted.

Scéla Mucce meic Dathó (Story of Mac Datho's Pig), a short tale of the *Ulster cycle, preserved in the *Book of Leinster and dating from the early 9th cent. Ailill and *Medb of Connacht and *Conchobor of Ulster each ask Mac Dathó, King of Leinster, for his great hound Ailbe. To decide the issue he invites both sides to a feast, at which a contest takes place regarding the first carving of the pig prepared for them.

School for Scandal, The (1777), a comedy of manners by Richard Brinsley *Sheridan, first produced at Drury Lane. The hypocritical Joseph Surface wants to marry Maria, the young ward of Sir Peter Teazle, for her money, while his younger brother, Charles, is in love with her. Joseph is finally unmasked when he attempts to seduce Lady Teazle.

Scottus Eriugena, see John Scottus *Eriugena.

Scully, Maurice (1952–   ), poet; born in Dublin and educated at TCD, he worked in Italy and Africa before returning to lecture at DCU. Collections include *Love Poetry and Others* (1981), *The Basic Colours* (1994), and *Steps* (1998). He edited *Súitéar na nAingeal* (1999), a journal devoted to Irish experimental poetry, with John *Goodby.

Scythe and the Sunset, The (1958), Denis *Johnston's play about the *Easter Rising. Set in a small café opposite the General Post Office, with roles

roughly corresponding to main participants in that event, it offers an alternative perspective to The *Plough and the
Stars*.

Sea, The Sea, The (1978), a novel by
Iris *Murdoch purporting to be the
memoirs or diary of Charles Arrowby, a
theatrical director who has retired to a
coastal village where he discovers his
childhood sweetheart, Hartley. She is
happily married, but Charles obses-
sively refuses to believe she is content.
A fantastic tone arises with the mysticism and magic of Charles's cousin
James and the symbolic presentation of
the sea as a place of purification.

Seabhac, An, see Pádraig *Ó
Siochfhradha.

Séadna (1904), the best-known work of
an tAthair Peadar *Ó Laoghaire. It was
intended to provide reading material
for learners of Irish. Séadna, a shoemaker, succumbs to the forces of evil in
the person of an Fear Dubh by accepting
money, with the promise that he will go
with him at the end of thirteen years. At
the end Séadna outwits the devil with
the help of the Blessed Virgin.

Seán An Chóta, see Seán *Ó
Caomhánaigh.

seanchaí bearer of 'old lore' (seanchas). Since the 18th cent. the word has
come to refer to an oral story-teller who
possesses a wide repertoire of lore
involving shorter forms of narrative.

'Seanchas na Sceiche' ('History of
the Bush'), a poem by Antoine
*Raiftearaí which treats of persons and
events from Noah and the Flood to
Patrick *Sarsfield and the Treaty of
Limerick [see *Williamite War], using a
question-and-answer form.

'Seandún', see Tadhg *Ó Murchadha.

sean-nós (lit. 'old style'), a term used
to denote the native song tradition in
Irish, although it is sometimes also used
of traditional instrumental music. The
song tradition is an oral one, handed on
from one singer to another, and there-
fore the songs are, to an extent, in a
continual state of evolution, with
singers varying them from one performance to another. Most traditional
songs are anonymous, and form part of
the body of Irish *folklore.

Search Party, The (1909), a comic
novel by George A. *Birmingham. Set in
a small west of Ireland town, Clonmore
(based on Westport, Co. Mayo), it tells of
the disappearance of the dispensary
doctor, the blacksmith, and two visiting
MPs. Lucius O'Grady, the doctor,
appears in several other novels by
Birmingham.

secret societies became a common
feature of Irish rural life in the second
half of the 18th cent. Commencing with
the Whiteboy movement in Tipperary
and adjoining counties in 1761–5, there
were major outbreaks of rural protest in
every decade up to the 1840s. Such protest was generally the work of small
local groups, linked by no more than
the adoption of a common name—
Whiteboys, Oakboys, Steelboys,
Threshers, Carders, Cravats, Rockites,
Terry Alts—or at most by the transmission from place to place of an oath of
association. Rival Protestant and Catholic secret societies, the Peep o'Day Boys
and the Defenders, emerged in south
Ulster in the 1780s. After 1795 the Peep
o'Day Boys were replaced, and to some
extent absorbed, by the *Orange Order.
Ribbonism, emerging around 1812, was
a direct successor to Defenderism.
Appealing mainly to wage-earners and
petty traders, it kept alive something
of the nationalist and Republican sentiments of the 1790s. The great age of
the secret societies ended with the

*Famine. Traditional techniques of protest did not disappear: *Parnell, in 1881, could still warn that if he were arrested 'Captain Moonlight' would take his place.

Sedulius Scottus (*fl. c.*850), Latin poet and moralist. Born probably in Leinster, he enjoyed the patronage of Charles the Bald, great-grandson of the Emperor Charlemagne. He addressed poems to Bishop Hartgar of Liège. He also wrote hymns and devotional poems. His religious verse was translated by George *Sigerson in *The Easter Song of Sedulius* (1922).

Senchán torpéist, see *Dallán Forgaill.

Senchas Már, see *law in Gaelic Ireland.

Sentimental Journey through France and Italy, A (1768), a travel book by Laurence *Sterne, loosely based on his own trips to the Continent after 1762. Parson Yorick recounts his travels, which take him no further than Lyons. Fine feelings interest him more than landscapes, and he engages with people of all classes, especially attractive women.

Serglige Con Chulainn and Óenét Emire (*Wasting Sickness of Cú Chulainn* and *The Only Jealousy of Emer*), a linked pair of stories of the *Ulster cycle with elements of the echtra *tale-type, preserved in the *Book of the Dun Cow. When Cú Chulainn tries to kill two magical birds, he is horsewhipped in a dream by two women of the *sídh. In a further vision, he is told that if he fights Labraid's enemies in the otherworld he will win the love of Fand, and he accepts the challenge. He sleeps with Fand but after a month he leaves, making a tryst with her at Newry. Emer plans to kill Fand at the meeting-place, but instead

each woman offers to surrender her love.

Sewell, Frank (1968–), poet; born in Belfast and educated at QUB and UUC; he has published *Outside the Walls* (1997, with Francis O'Hare) and *Out in the Open* (1997), a volume of translations of Cathal *Ó Searcaigh. He was Irish editor of *The Honest Ulsterman* (1994–9). Criticism includes *Extending the Alhambra* (2000), a study of modern poetry in Irish.

Sgeilg, see Séan *Ó Ceallaigh.

Shadow of a Gunman, The (1923), a play by Sean *O'Casey, set in a Dublin tenement in May 1920 during the *Anglo-Irish War. Donal Davoren considers himself a poet, but also enjoys being taken for an *IRA gunman on the run, with tragic consequences, including the death of Minnie Powell.

Shadwell, Charles (?1675–1726), English dramatist. A son of Thomas *Shadwell, he wrote plays, mostly versions of French farces treated in the English manner and transposed to Irish settings, for the *Smock Alley Theatre. They include: *The Hasty Wedding* (1716), *Irish Hospitality* (1717), *The Sham Prince* (1718), *The Plotting Lovers* (1719), and a tragedy, *Rotherick O'Connor* (1719).

Shadwell, Thomas (?1642–1692), English dramatist. John Dryden dubbed him 'MacFlecknoe' in a retaliatory satire of 1682, using the Irish patronymic to imply a kinship with the 'prince of Dulness' Richard *Flecknoe, who—unlike Shadwell—was an Irishman. Shadwell capitalized on anti-Catholic feeling with a play, *Teague O'Divelly, the Irish Priest* (1681) that represents an extreme of *stage-Irish sectarian stereotyping.

Shake Hands with the Devil, see Reardon *Conner.

Shame the Devil (1934), one of three autobiographical books by Liam *O'Flaherty, the others being *Two Years* (1930) and *I Went to Russia* (1931). It depicts a manic-depressive character who reappears in different guises in many of O'Flaherty's novels.

Shan Van Vocht, The (Jan. 1896–Apr. 1899), a short-lived nationalist literary magazine—formerly *The Northern Patriot*—edited in Belfast by Ethna *Carbery and Alice *Milligan.

Share, Bernard [Vivian] (1930–), novelist. Born in Dublin and educated at TCD. He wrote two comic novels in the tradition of Flann *O'Brien, *Inish* (1966) and *Merciful Hour* (1970). *The Finner Faction* (1989) is a thriller.

Sharp, William (pseudonym 'Fiona MacLeod') (1855–1905), man of letters. Born in Paisley, Scotland, he wrote tales of magic, mystery, and peasant life in the *Celtic Twilight mode using a female alias. Amongst the writings published under that name are tales, *Pharais* (1893) and *The Mountain Loves* (1895); and plays, *The Immortal Hour* (1900) and *The House of Usna* (1903).

Shaughraun, The (1875), a political melodrama set on the west coast of Ireland, in which Dion *Boucicault's sympathetic version of the *stage-Irishman stereotype has advanced to the title-role. Conn the Shaughraun, a good-hearted wanderer, helps Robert Ffolliott to escape from Australia where he had been transported as a *Fenian rebel.

Shaw, George Bernard (1856–1950), playwright; born in Dublin, he was the third child of a down-at-heel family with pretensions to respectability. Shaw detested the several schools he attended. In 1876, he moved to London where his mother had been living for some years, in flight from an alcoholic marriage. He wrote five novels in four years, 1879–83: *Immaturity, The Irrational Knot, Love Among the Artists, Cashel Byron's Profession*, and *An Unsocial Socialist*. During his early years in London he was converted to socialism and became a vegetarian in 1881 after reading a tract by Shelley. In 1884 he joined the Fabian Society. He had an affair with Jenny Patterson, who subsequently became jealous of rivals such as the actress Florence Farr. *The *Philanderer*, written in 1893, draws on Shaw's experiences in this triangular relationship. In 1898, aged 42, he married Charlotte Payne-Townshend, a cousin of Edith *Somerville. Shaw's literary reputation was first established as a music, art, and theatre critic for various London periodicals. He frequently invoked the plays of Ibsen as a foil to the banality of contemporary English drama. A lecture of 1890 was published in expanded form as *The Quintessence of Ibsenism* (1891). Another early hero of Shaw's was Wagner, about whom he wrote *The Perfect Wagnerite* (1898), a treatise on *The Ring*. Shaw's career as a playwright began in 1892 with *Widowers' Houses*. By 1896 he had completed the seven plays which were gathered under the title *Plays Pleasant and Unpleasant* (1898). The three further works completed by the end of the century were published as *Three Plays for Puritans* (1901). *Arms and the Man* (1894), the first of the 'plays pleasant', had its première at Florence Farr's Avenue Theatre with W. B. *Yeats's *The Land of Heart's Desire* as a curtain-raiser. In *Three Plays for Puritans* he attacked a narrow and unimaginative conception of religion, making the wrathfully vindictive Mrs Dudgeon in *The *Devil's Disciple* (1897) an epitome of joyless and rigid Puritanism. During 1901–2 Shaw began the composition of *Man and Superman* (1905), which explored his new 'religion' of Creative Evolution. He adopted the notion of the Life Force as a response to the 19th-cent. debates concerning will, power, evolutionism, and the role of the individual in thinkers such as Nietzsche, Darwin, and later Bergson. Shaw's reputation increased markedly in the first decade of the 20th cent. *John Bull's Other Island* (1904), *Major Barbara* (1905), and The *Doctor's Dilemma* (1906) were all produced at the Court Theatre by the actor-manager Harley Granville-Barker. *John Bull's Other Island*, originally commissioned by Yeats for the *Abbey, was not produced there for political reasons, but when The *Shewing-Up of Blanco Posnet* (1909) was banned in England, it was staged at the Dublin theatre. *Pygmalion* (written 1912) crowned his success in the pre-war period. His love affair with the 'perilously bewitching' Mrs Patrick Campbell began in 1912. Her captivating but often exasperating personality is reflected in the characters of Hesione in *Heartbreak House* (1921), the Serpent in *Back to Methusaleh* (1923), and Orinthia in The *Apple Cart* (1929). Immediately after the outbreak of the First World War, Shaw wrote the polemical essay, *Common Sense About the War* (1914), in which he attacked the official British rationale for entry into the struggle. Shaw's outspoken criticism of the execution of the leaders of the *Easter Rising did little to commend him to British public opinion. His major creative achievement in the war years was *Heartbreak House*, written in the atmosphere of doom evoked by Zeppelin air raids on civilian targets in London and other English cities. The horror of the war left a deep imprint on *Back to Methusaleh: A Metabiological Pentateuch* (1922). In the 1920s *Saint Joan* (1923) was acclaimed on both sides of the Atlantic, and in 1925 Shaw was awarded the Nobel Prize for Literature. The political character of The Apple Cart (1928) is partly explained by the fact that he had been engaged in writing The *Intelligent Woman's Guide to Socialism and Capitalism* (1928) since 1925. Many of Shaw's later plays are remarkable for their experimental character. Plays such as *Geneva* (1936), portraying the age of Fascist ideologies, reveal a sense of near despair about national and international political organizations. He died following an illness precipitated by a fall from an apple-tree he was pruning in his garden at Ayot St Lawrence. Most of the plays of Shaw's early and middle period, up to and including *Heartbreak House*, were developed from the mould of late 19th-cent. naturalism. With the science fiction scenario of *Back to Methuselah*, Shaw entered the final phase of his play-writing career. In later plays such as *Too True to Be Good* (1931) fantastic incidents become increasingly common. Whereas the characters in Shaw's early and middle plays are drawn with psychological insight, in later work the characterization tends towards allegory and cartoon. As an iconoclast with an Irish sense of distance from the English life he enjoyed and mocked, he employed his gifts in the exposure of humbug and hypocrisy in his time, and in the subversion of sanctimonious value systems. A Shaw play leaves not so much the sense of a proven thesis as an awareness of open-ended possibilities and irreducible complexity, and of the depth, subtlety, and humour of his treatment of human relationships. See Michael Holroyd, *Bernard Shaw* (4 vols., 1988–92).

She Stoops to Conquer (1773), a comedy by Oliver *Goldsmith, produced at Covent Garden. Young Marlow and his friend Hastings travel down the country so that Marlow can see Miss Kate Hardcastle, whom his father intends him to marry. Losing their way, they meet Kate's wastrel stepbrother Tony Lumpkin, who directs them to the family home while telling them it is an inn-house. Marlow, shy with social equals and overbearing towards inferiors, treats Mr Hardcastle as the landlord and, mistaking his daughter for a servant, courts her. With the arrival of Marlow's father, Sir Charles, the tale of mistaken identities finally unravels.

Sheares, John (1776–1798), *United Irishman and poet. Born in Cork, and educated at TCD, he was a leader of the Dublin society of United Irishmen, and was arrested, tried, and hung for treason with his elder brother Henry (b. 1753) in May–July 1798.

Shee, (Sir) Martin Archer (1769–1850), painter and poet. Born in Dublin and trained at the *RDS Art School, he went to London in 1788. He wrote poetry (*Rhymes on Art*, 1805), drama (*Alasco*, 1824), novels (*Old Court*, 1819; and *Harry Calverley*, 1835), and a memoir of Sir Joshua Reynolds.

Sheehan, Patrick Augustine (Canon Sheehan) (1852–1913), priest and novelist. Born in Mallow, Co. Cork, and educated at Maynooth [see *universities], he became parish priest of Doneraile, Co. Cork, in 1894. Between 1895 and 1913 he produced ten novels in addition to essays, poems, and sermons. Writing for a Catholic audience, he represented their religion as the essence of Irish nationhood in an effort to counteract the influence of reformers and socialists. His first two novels, *Geoffrey Austin: Student* (1895) and *The Triumph of a Failure* (1899), were 'sermons in print' on the importance of Catholic teaching. Sheehan's themes

thereafter were the land, labour, social unrest (in *Lisheen, *Miriam Lucas, and *The Queen's Fillet*); the national question (in *Glenanaar and The *Graves of Kilmorna); and the religious life (*My New Curate, *Luke Delmege, and The *Blindness of Dr. Gray*). Primarily a novelist of clerical life in rural Ireland, Sheehan outlined in fiction the kind of firm leadership he felt was needed if the Church was to preserve its influence in modern times.

Sheehan, Ronan (1953–), fiction writer; born in Dublin and educated at Gonzaga College, and UCD, he was a member of the Irish Writers' Co-op with Dermot *Bolger and others. His first novel, *Tennis Players* (1977), deals with contrasting sexual moralities in the changing Ireland of its decade. *Boy with an Injured Eye* (1983) is a collection of stories. *The Heart of the City* (1988) is a study of Dublin in the millenium year.

Sheehy-Skeffington, Francis (1878–1916), feminist and pacificist. Born in Bailieborough, Co. Cavan, he attended the Royal University [see *universities]. He founded *The National Democrat* with Fred *Ryan in support of Michael *Davitt in 1907. A campaigner against wartime conscription in Ireland, he went out unarmed to prevent looting during the *Easter Rising. His arrest and murder in Portobello Barracks caused widespread horror. His works include a historical novel, *In Dark and Evil Days* (1916).

Sheil, Richard Lalor (1791–1851), playwright and politician. Born in Drumdowney, Co. Kilkenny, he was educated at TCD. His first tragedy, *Adelaide, or the Emigrants* (1814), appeared at *Smock Alley and went on to London. *The Apostate* (1817) was played at Covent Garden. Other successful works were *Bellamira, or the Fall of*

Tunis (1818) and *Evadne, or the Statue* (1819). In 1820 he helped John *Banim with his tragedy *Damon and Pythias* (1821).

Sheridan, Frances (née Chamberlaine) (1724–1766), novelist and playwright. Born in Dublin, she wrote a novel at 15. Richard Brinsley *Sheridan was one of the five children of her marriage to Thomas *Sheridan. Her novel, *Memoirs of Miss Sidney Bidulph* (2 vols., 1761–7), was dedicated to Samuel Richardson. David Garrick appeared in her social comedy *The Discovery* (1762); in the same year *The Dupe* was criticized for licentiousness and failed. *The History of Nourjahad* (1767), a romance, appeared after her death.

Sheridan, Richard Brinsley (1751–1816), dramatist and politician; born in Dublin, son of the actor-manager Thomas *Sheridan and Frances (*Sheridan), and grandson of *Swift's friend Thomas *Sheridan. He was educated at Samuel *Whyte's school in Dublin. The family moved in 1770 to Bath, where his observations of social life provided him with the mainstay of his comedies. In the following year he eloped to France with Elizabeth Ann Linley, and married her while both were minors. Sheridan began writing for the stage to make money. His first play, *The *Rivals* (1775), was successful, and this was followed in the same year by *St. Patrick's Day*, a farce, and then by *The *Duenna*, a comic opera. Sheridan's initial misgivings about involvement with theatre soon gave way to grandiose ambition. In 1776 he bought out David Garrick's half-share in Drury Lane with borrowed money and became its manager. In 1776 he staged *A Trip to Scarborough*, to be followed in 1777 by *The *School for Scandal*. *The Critic* (1779) was his last original play. *Pizarro*, produced in the same year, was an adaptation of a tragedy in

German by Kotzebue. In 1780 he entered politics as MP for Stafford, making his mark as an orator with his maiden speech on the Begum of Oude in support of Edmund *Burke's impeachment of Warren Hastings. Sheridan was ruined when Drury Lane burnt down in 1809. Failing to get reelected in 1812, he diverted into his personal finances funds lent him by the Prince Regent to buy a seat, and spoiled the friendship. His last, wretched, years were marred by drunkenness and the depredations of the bailiffs, who carried off his household furniture. The first biography was written by Thomas *Moore. See James Morwood, *The Life and Works of Richard Brinsley Sheridan* (1985).

Sheridan, Thomas (the Elder) (1687–1738), poet, translator, and friend of Jonathan *Swift. Born in Co. Cavan, he was educated at TCD and established a school in Capel St., Dublin. His prose translations of Persius and Juvenal appeared in 1739. Sheridan's verse was mainly comic in works such as *Ars Punica, or the Flowers of Languages* (1719). Quilca House, his Cavan home, was well known to Swift. Many poems were exchanged between them, and the two collaborated closely on the twenty issues of *The Intelligencer* (1728–9).

Sheridan, Thomas (the Younger) (1719–1788), actor and educationalist; born in Dublin or possibly at Quilca, Co. Cavan, the son of Thomas *Sheridan, whose friend Jonathan *Swift was his godfather. After some years at his father's school in Dublin he went to TCD. In 1743 *Smock Alley produced his farce, *The *Brave Irishman, or Captain O'Blunder*. In 1744 he travelled to London and acted in rivalry to David Garrick, whom he enticed back to Dublin for the season of 1745–6, having become manager of a united Aungier

St. and Smock Alley company. His *British Education: Source of Disorders* (1756) was followed up with a lecture proposing the foundation of an academy of English in Dublin. An ambitious *Plan of Education for the Young Nobility and Gentry of Great Britain* (1769) was followed by *A Life of the Rev. Dr. Swift*, and Swift's *Works* (17 vols., 1784).

Shewing-up of Blanco Posnet, The

(1909), a one-act play by George Bernard *Shaw. Banned in London for alleged blasphemy, the work was first performed at the *Abbey Theatre in defiance of Dublin Castle. The setting is a seedy American town in the post-Gold Rush era, the themes hypocrisy and justice.

Shiels, George

(1886–1949), playwright. Born in Ballymoney, Co. Antrim, and educated locally, he emigrated to Canada, where he was crippled in a railway accident in 1913. On his return to Ireland he began writing drama. His earliest plays, written as 'George Morshiel', were performed by the *Ulster Literary Theatre. His association with the *Abbey Theatre, begun in 1921 with the one-act *Bedmates*, continued with some thirty plays. Early work such as *Paul Twyning* (1922), *Professor Tim* (1925), *Cartney and Kevney* (1927), and *Grogan and the Ferret* (1933) are comedies, though often with a sardonic edge which Abbey productions generally down-played. From about the mid-1930s the satirical aspect of his work became more pronounced, notably in *The Passing Day* (1936). A major theme of Shiel's drama is the conflict between traditional habits of feeling and modern values, a tension that dominates *The New Gossoon* (1930). *The Rugged Path* (1940) and its sequel, *The Summit* (1941), are more serious plays, showing how the Dolis clan arouses atavistic fears in order to bully the progressive farmers in the valley.

Shiels's plays were conventionally realistic in form, though the use of stark situations often makes a disconcerting impact.

Shirley, James

(1596–1666), English dramatist. He was invited to *Werburgh St. Theatre Royal by John *Ogilby, whom he knew at Oxford, and remained in Ireland, 1635–41. Among the plays he wrote was *St. Patrick for Ireland* (1640). Others were *The Royal Master* (1637), *The Doubtful Heir* (1638), *The Constant Maid* (1640), and *The Politique Father* (1641). Dublin editions of his works appeared in 1720 and 1750.

Short View of the State of Ireland, A

(1728), a pamphlet by Jonathan *Swift attacking those who seek political favour by pretending that Ireland is a prosperous nation.

Shorter, Dora Sigerson

(1866–1918), poet. Born in Dublin, eldest child of George *Sigerson and Hester Varian (herself a writer), she formed a friendship with Katharine *Tynan and Alice Furlong in the early years of the Irish *literary revival. Much of her prolific output of verse in volumes such as *Ballads and Poems* (1899) and *New Poems* (1912), was influenced by her father's interest in Irish *metrics. She also wrote narrative poems such as the *The Fairy Changeling* (1897) and *Madge Linsey* (1913). *The Tricolour: Poems of the Revolution* (1922) contains elegies for each of the executed 1916 leaders.

Shortland, Gaye

(1948–), novelist; born in Cork, and educated in the Presentation Convent, Bandon, and UCC. After graduating she taught in Leeds and then in Ahmadu Bello University, Nigeria, then at Niamey University, Niger, where she married a Tuareg, returning in 1989 to write full-time. Her novels include *Mind That, 'Tis My Brother* (1995), *Turtles All the Way Down* (1997),

Polygamy (1998), and *Harmattan* (1999). She became editor at Poolbeg Press in 1998.

Siabhradh Mhic na Miochomhairle (*Delusion of the Son of Foolish Council*), an anonymous late 17th-cent. prose burlesque, interspersed with ribald verse and composed in south-east Ulster. Mac na Miochomhairle happens upon a castle inhabited by an enchanter and his beautiful daughter. When he awakes in the morning the castle has gone.

sídh (modern spelling: sí), a fairy rath (or fort) where the fairies are said to live. They are also known as aos sí ('fairy folk'), slua sí ('fairy host'), and daoine maithe ('good people'). According to a life of St *Patrick in the 9th-cent. *Book of Armagh* the sídh were the pagan gods of the earth over whom Christianity has triumphed, but according to Gaelic tradition they were the Tuatha Dé Danann, the ancient gods of Ireland residing in the fairy mounds all over the country [see *mythology]. They feature most prominently in the *mythological cycle in tales such as *Cath Maige Tuired* or *Tochmarc Étaíne*; in the *Ulster cycle in *Táin Bó Cuailnge*, *Togail Bruidne Da Derga*, and many other tales; and throughout the *Fionn cycle, where Fionn's own *genealogy involves otherworld beings. A number of Anglo-Irish writers in the second half of the 19th cent. began collecting the folklore traditions of Ireland, notably T. C. *Croker and Lady *Wilde. These were joined by others more in tune with the native culture such as J. J. *Callanan, Patrick *Kennedy, and Canon John *O'Hanlon. The *literary revival gave rise to a renewed interest in the fairy-lore of Ireland, which came to be seen as a unique body of almost sacred literature of Celtic origin, encapsulating realities occluded by the advance of a materialistic civilization. The slua sí carry off mortals, most often children, if they are beautiful or otherwise exceptional, leaving a changeling (síofra or síobhra) behind. They also appear on coastlines, as mermaids (murúch, *Hiberno-English merrow). Solitary fairies are known variously as the leipreachán, represented as a cobbler; the clúracán, or drunken fairy; the fear dearg ('red man', the otherworld colour), or trickster; the fear gorta ('hunger-man'), a phantom appearing at times of famine; the dallacán, a headless sprite who rides on the death-coach (cóiste bodhar, 'silent coach'); the leannán sí, a fairy lover, who drives his or her mortal lover to distraction; and the bean sí (*banshee), who appears combing her red hair at the deaths of members of certain families. The púca (anglicé 'pooka') is the Irish form of the sprite familiar in English folklore as the night-mare.

Sigerson, Dora, see Dora Sigerson *Shorter.

Sigerson, George (1836–1925), translator and physician. Born at Holy Hill near Strabane, Co. Tyrone, he was educated at Letterkenny, then at Queen's College, Cork [see *universities], where he graduated in medicine in 1859. He became Professor of Botany, then Zoology at UCD. In 1860 appeared his *Poets and Poetry of Munster*, a second series of texts and verse translations issued by John *O'Daly. His *History of the Land Tenures and Land Classes of Ireland* (1871) influenced Gladstone's thinking on Irish land reform. In August 1892 he inaugurated the National Literary Society with a lecture on Irish Literature. Sigerson's major work was *Bards of the Gael and Gall* (1897), an anthology of Irish poetry in translation, arranged historically and prefaced by an introduction that presents the variety of Irish poetry across its different phases of development. His bold contention in the preface that Irish poetry was a major European tradition in its own right influenced subsequent Irish literature in English and in Irish. Douglas Hyde, Thomas *MacDonagh, Austin *Clarke, Robert Farren (*Ó Faracháin), F. R. *Higgins, and John *Montague were all indebted to him. *The Easter Song of *Sedulius* (1922) is another translation.

Silent People, The (1962), a panoramic novel by Walter *Macken, dealing with the events affecting the 'small people' of Ireland from the agitation for *Catholic Emancipation to the Great *Famine.

Silva Gadelica, see Standish Hayes *O'Grady.

Silver Tassie, The (1928), an anti-war play in four acts by Sean *O'Casey, first produced at the London Fortune Theatre. While on leave, Harry Heegan, a young Dublin labourer serving in the British army during the First World War, leads his football team to win the prize cup of the title. Returning to France, he is seriously wounded, and sent home paralysed and impotent. Its rejection by the *Abbey Theatre led to O'Casey's self-imposed exile.

Simmons, James [Stewart Alexander] (1933–), poet and songwriter. Born in Derry and educated at Campbell College, Belfast, and the University of Leeds, he taught in NUU (now UUC), and was writer in residence at QUB, 1985–8. In 1969 he founded *The *Honest Ulsterman*, and in 1990 established the Poets' House at Islandmagee with his third wife, later removing to Falcarragh in the Donegal Gaeltacht. His poetry speaks of a society not so much Irish or British as ordinary and modern, free from formulaic convictions. *Aíkin Mata* (1966), a version of Aristophanes'

Lysistrata with Tony Harrison, was followed by a first collection *Late But in Earnest* (1967). Other collections include *In the Wilderness* (1969), *Energy to Burn* (1971), *No Land Is Waste, Dr Eliot* (1973), *West Strand Visions* (1974), *Judy Garland and the Cold War* (1976), *Constantly Singing* (1980), *From the Irish* (1985), *Poems 1956–1986*, ed. Edna *Longley (1986), and three LPs of his own songs.

Singing-Men at Cashel, The (1936), a novel by Austin *Clarke set in early Christian Ireland, dealing with the three marriages of Queen Gormlai, according to tradition a 9th-cent. poet [see *Gormfhlaith].

Sinn Féin, meaning 'ourselves' in Irish, a term coined by Máire Butler in 1904. The first party of that name, led by Arthur *Griffith, was formed in 1907. Although Sinn Féin played no part in the *Easter Rising (as distinct from some of its members), it was widely labelled the Sinn Féin rebellion, and it was under the name Sinn Féin that a new nationalist movement committed to achieving an Irish republic, with *de Valera as Party President, took shape from 1917. At the end of the *Anglo-Irish War the name Sinn Féin was retained by Republicans who rejected the Treaty of 1921. De Valera resigned as President in 1926, establishing Fianna Fáil, and electorally crushed Sinn Féin in 1927. Following developments within the *IRA in 1970, however, Sinn Féin split into Provisional and Official wings, the latter becoming Sinn Féin, the Workers' Party, and then The Workers' Party.

Siris: *A Chain of Philosophical Reflexions and Inquiries* (1744), George *Berkeley's last and most puzzling book. The 'chain' referred to connects tar-water (a concoction formed by boiling up in water the tar exuded from pine or fir bark) with theology by tenuous links.

Sirr, Peter (1960–), poet; born in Waterford and educated at TCD, he taught abroad and acted as director of the Irish Writers' Centre in Dublin from 1991. Collections include: *Marginal Zones* (1984), *Talk, Talk* (1987), *Ways of Falling* (1991), and *The Ledger of Fruitful Exchange* (1995).

Sister Teresa, see **Evelyn Innes.*

Sisters, The, the initial story in James **Joyce's **Dubliners* (1914). It establishes the theme of spiritual paralysis with a clerical example.

Sive (1959), a play by John B. **Keane. It tells the melodramatic story of an orphan girl whose love affair is fatally thwarted by her aunt and uncle, with the stark simplicity of folk poetry.

Skerrett (1932), a novel by Liam **O'Flaherty set on 'Nara' (Inishmore, Aran Islands), and dealing with a struggle between the national schoolteacher Skerrett and the parish priest Fr. Moclair.

Small Window, The (1967), a novel by Janet **McNeill. Middle-aged Julia appears to fit the roles of wife and mother, but when her husband Harold dies suddenly, she is launched on a journey of self-discovery.

Smith, Michael (1942–), poet and publisher. Born in Dublin and educated at UCD, he established the New Writers' Press in the late 1960s, publishing contemporary poetry by Augustus **Young and Trevor **Joyce as well as reissuing the works of Brian **Coffey and Thomas **MacGreevy. His own work includes *Times and Locations* (1972), *Del Camino* (1974), a translation of the poet Antonio Machado, *Stopping to Take Notes* (1979), and *Lost Genealogies and other Poems* (1993).

Smith, Paul (1935–), novelist. Born in Dublin, he travelled widely. His first novel, *Esther's Altar* (1959, reissued as *Come Trailing Blood*, 1977), is a hectic evocation of Dublin tenement life. *Stravanga* (1963) is a satire set in the west of Ireland.

Smith, Sydney Bernard (1936–), poet and novelist; born in Glasgow, and raised in Portstewart, Co. Derry, he was educated at Clongowes and TCD after which he taught, retiring in 1970 to Inishbofin. Poetry includes *Girl with Violin* (1968) and *Scurrilities* (1981); *The Book of Shannow* (1991) is an autobiographical fiction.

Smithson, Annie (1873–1948), novelist. Born in Dublin. She briefly practised in Ulster in 1901 before settling in Dublin as a district nurse. The elaborately romantic plots of her highly popular novels—nineteen in all—were built on elements of her own experience, including a protracted and painful involvement with a married doctor. Her women heroes are strong and noble-minded in novels such as *Carmen Cavanagh* (1921), *The Walk of a Queen* (1922), *The Laughter of Sorrow* (1925), *The Light of Other Days* (1933), and *The Weldons of Tibradden* (1940). Political loyalty to Ireland provides the main interest in books such as *Margaret of Fair Hill* (1939) and *By Shadowed Ways* (1943). *Myself and Others* (1944) is an autobiography.

Smock Alley Theatre (1662–1786), the first Dublin playhouse to be built after the Restoration. It succeeded **Werburgh St. Theatre as the home of the Theatre Royal up to 1759, continuing intermittently thereafter as the Smock Alley Company. Standing in Essex St. West (variously called Blind Quay, Orange St., and Smock Alley), it was opened by John **Ogilby and Thomas Stanley, who were joint holders of the Master of Revels patent for Ireland. In 1735 the theatre was rebuilt completely. Smock Alley was demolished to make way for the Catholic Church of St Michael and St John in 1813. The theatre was controlled by actor-managers of whom the most important were Joseph *Ashbury after 1666, Thomas Elrington after 1720, Thomas *Sheridan the Younger after 1745, and Henry *Mossop from 1760. The first recorded performance was *Wit Without Money* by John Fletcher in 1662. Later in the season, Katherine *Philips's *Pompey* was played. John *Dancer's tragicomedy *Agrippa, King of Alba* (1675) appeared in 1669. Charles *Shadwell was resident playwright from 1715 to 1720, his earliest production in this capacity being *The Hasty Wedding* (1716) and his latest *Rotherick O'Connor* (1719). In 1732, when the old building was declared unsound, the company removed to Aungier St.

Smuggler, The (1831), the last novel by John *Banim. Michael Mutford is a Yorkshireman dispossessed of family property and estates through legal chicanery who is finally driven to crime and exile in order to support his ruined family.

Smythe, Colin (1942–), publisher and bibliographer; born in Maidenhead, Berkshire, he was educated at Bradfield and TCD, after which he founded Colin Smythe Ltd, and began the Coole edition of the works of Lady *Gregory with T. R. *Henn in 1970, acting as editor of some of the volumes himself. He began an Irish Literary Studies series in 1977 which reclaimed to critical view many Irish writers and their literary contexts. With Henry Summerfield in 1978 he began publishing the collected works of George *Russell. When the *Dolmen Press folded after Liam Miller's death he took over management of the titles. His activities greatly facilitated the development of Irish literary scholarship 1970–2000.

Snake's Pass, The (1890), Bram *Stoker's first novel, serialized in 1889. The narrator, Arthur Severn, a young Englishman on a visit to Connemara, becomes involved in thwarting the land-grabbing designs of Murtagh Murdock, a melodramatically sinister 'gombeen man'.

Society for the Preservation of the Irish Language, The, founded on 29 December 1876 to encourage the use of the language by establishing classes for its instruction and to promote a modern literature in Irish. Professor Brian O'Looney of TCD chaired the first meeting.

Some Experiences of an Irish R.M. (1899), the first volume of a series of stories by *Somerville and Ross, written for the monthly *Badminton Magazine* and speedily published as a book. The Resident Magistrate of the title is Major Sinclair Yeates, sent to Skebawn, Co. Cork, where he becomes involved in hilarious escapades, many of them contrived by the redoubtable Flurry Knox. *Further Experiences of an Irish R.M.* (1908) and *In Mr. Knox's Country* (1915) were sequels, all three being issued as *The Irish R.M.* in 1956.

Somerville, Edith Œnone (1858–1949), novelist. Born in the island of Corfu where her father's regiment was stationed, she grew up at Drishane House, Castletownshend, Co. Cork. She was educated by governesses, then at Alexandra College in Dublin. She developed an early interest in drawing and studied painting for a term at the South Kensington School of Art in her late teens. In January 1886 she first met her cousin Violet Martin (pseudonym 'Martin *Ross') with whom she was to form the literary partnership of

*Somerville and Ross. Together, before Martin's death in 1915, they published five novels as well as the three volumes of 'R.M.' stories. After Violet's death, Edith continued writing in the belief that her cousin's spirit was supporting her from beyond the grave. In 1932 she received a D.Litt. from TCD.

Somerville and Ross was the joint pseudonym of the celebrated literary partnership of cousins Edith *Somerville (1858–1949) and Violet Martin (1862–1915; see Martin *Ross). They met for the first time at Castletownshend in 1886, an encounter that Edith was later to describe as 'the hinge of my life'. Their first literary joint venture was An *Irish Cousin (1889). By the time of Violet's death in 1915, they had collaborated on five novels (An Irish Cousin, 1889; *Naboth's Vineyard, 1891; The *Real Charlotte, 1894; The Silver Fox, 1898; and *Dan Russel the Fox, 1911), and had achieved fame as the authors of the 'Irish R.M.' stories, issued in three separate volumes (*Some Experiences of an Irish R.M., 1899; Further Experiences of an Irish R.M., 1908; and In Mr. Knox's Country, 1915). They also travelled together in Ireland, Wales, France, and Denmark, writing up some of these trips in books such as Through Connemara in a Governess Cart (1892), In the Vine Country (1893), and Beggars on Horseback (1895). Although they began in a spirit of playfulness their collaboration quickly produced a masterpiece, The *Real Charlotte, where the theme of social decline is worked out against a background encompassing a broad spectrum of Irish life. The excitement and discipline of working together developed a capacity for caustic wit and unsentimental appraisal of human nature. Their comic vision, and the accompanying air of dispassionate calm troubled by a touch of cruelty, influenced other writers, among them Dorothea *Conyers, Elizabeth *Bowen, and John *Banville. After Violet's death in 1915 Edith published five more novels, the most impressive of which was The *Big House at Inver (1925).

Song of Dermot and the Earl, The (?1210), a narrative poem in Norman French by Morice Regan, secretary to Dermot MacMurrough, dealing with the latter's journey to Aquitaine to enlist the support of Henry II in regaining the *kingship of Leinster.

Southern[e], Thomas (1660–1746), dramatist; born in Oxmanstown, near Dublin. While at TCD in 1676–80 he attended plays at *Smock Alley Theatre. He presented his first play, The Loyal Brother, or the Persian Prince (1682), at Drury Lane. The Disappointment, or the Mother in Fashion (1684) was played at Smock Alley. Southerne received an army commission but his military career ended when James II lost the throne in 1688. He returned to the stage with Anthony Love, or The Rambling Lady (1690), the most ribald of his plays. His best-known works, The Fatal Marriage, or, Innocent Adultery (1694) and *Oroonoko, (1695), were both tragedies based on novels by Aphra Behn. Later plays include The Spartan Dame (1719) and Many the Mistress (1726).

Spacious Adventures of the Man in the Street, The see *Cuanduine trilogy.

Spanish Gold (1908), a novel by George A. *Birmingham. Set like many of his books in a thinly disguised Co. Mayo, it is an adventure celebrating the beauty of the terrain and the energy of the people, with much paradoxical but telling commentary on the Irish questions of the day.

Speckled Book, see *Leabhar Breac.

Spenser, Edmund (?1552–1599), poet. Born in London, he studied at Pembroke Hall, Cambridge, and was briefly in the service of *Elizabeth I's favourite, Robert Dudley, Earl of Leicester. *The Shepheardes Calendar* (1579), marked the arrival of a poet of even greater promise than Philip Sidney, to whom the poem is dedicated. In 1580 he became secretary to Arthur Grey, Lord Wilton, Viceroy of Ireland, and accompanied him to Dublin. Grey was recalled after two years, charged with cruel and dishonourable conduct against the Irish. Spenser never wavered in his support for the methods used to suppress the Desmond Rebellion. After Grey's disgrace he stayed on to become clerk to the council of the Munster *plantation and later Sheriff of Cork. Spenser's rank secured him Kilcolman Castle with a large estate near Doneraile in Co. Cork, granted in 1586 and confirmed in 1590. There he lived with his family from 1588 to October 1598, when his home was burnt down by the Earl of Desmond during Hugh *O'Neill's rebellion. He died shortly after his return to London and was buried in Westminster Abbey. While living in Ireland Spenser wrote *The Faerie Queene* (I–III, 1590; IV–VI, 1596), the first great English poem since Chaucer, as well as most of his other works. *Colin Clouts Come Home Againe* (1595) expresses his pleasure at coming home to Kilcolman after seeing the first volumes of *The Faerie Queene* through the press in London. *Amoretti and Epithalamion* (1595), a sonnet sequence and marriage-poem, celebrates his wedding to Elizabeth Boyle in 1594, and evokes the topography of Cork city and county in one of the masterpieces of English Renaissance poetry. *The Faerie Queene* comprises a series of allegorical quests by knights who symbolize the Protestant virtues (temperance, etc.) and who encounter magicians, sorceresses, and wicked Saracens intent on diverting them from their duty. Ireland and its conflicts are present in different ways in the poem: in Arthegall, Knight of Justice in Book v, who embodies Lord Grey's attributes; in the pastoral landscapes of vi, derived from the rivers and mountains around Kilcolman; and in the cannibals, also in vi, who are part Irish kerns (soldiers for hire), part Virginian savages. The 'Mutabilitie Cantos', which are all that survive of the seventh book, are set on Galteemore (called Arlo by Spenser, after Aherlow), in the Galtee mountain range. In *A *View of the Present State of Ireland* (1596) Spenser associates the most culpable form of degeneracy not with the native Irish but with the Old English, who have adopted their language, laws, and customs. Ireland provided Spenser with wealth and leisure enough to enable him to write the greatest English Renaissance epic.

'Speranza', see Jane *Wilde.

Spirit of the Nation, The (1843); a collection of poems and ballads originally published in *The *Nation*, printed by James *Duffy for the editors, and sold at sixpence a copy. A second part was issued in 1844.

Spokesong (1974), Stewart *Parker's first stage play. It is set in the Belfast bicycle-shop of Frank Stokes, who is under threat from urban planners and *IRA bombs. A gentle idealist, Frank sees the bicycle as representing freedom and democracy.

Spreading the News (1904), a one-act comedy about rumour by Lady *Gregory staged on the opening night of the *Abbey Theatre.

Stacpoole, Henry de Vere (1863–1951), novelist. Born in Kingstown (Dun Laoghaire), Co. Dublin, he was educated in England and travelled as a ship's doctor before becoming an author of light fiction. *The Blue Lagoon* (1908) is a love-story of adolescent castaways who end their idyll by taking never-wake-up berries as they drift through shark-infested waters. Stacpoole followed with other exotic stories such as *Pools of Silence* (1910), and *Poppyland* (1914). Several novels are set in Ireland: *Patsy* (1908), *Garryowen* (1910) and *Father O'Flynn* (1914).

Stafford, Thomas, see **Pacata Hibernia*.

stage-Irishman, a term for stereotypical Irish characters on the English-language stage from the 17th cent., also applied to characters in fiction in whom Irish national characteristics are emphasized or distorted. As a product of colonialism, the first stage-Irishman reflected a desire to stigmatize the native Irish as savages or anathematize them as traitors, while later versions sought more commonly to provide amusement to English audiences by exaggerating the traits which differentiated the Irish from the English. His chief identifying marks were disorderly manners and insalubrious habits, together with the *Hiberno-English dialect or brogue and a concomitant propensity for illogical utterance increasingly identified as his exclusive property and called 'the Irish bull'. The *Irish Hudibras* (1689) by James Farewell and its companion piece, *Hesperi-Neso-Graphia* (1716), are key texts in the evolution of the stereotype. To these ludicrous features was added an intense and seemingly inapposite pride in his native country. A small number of Irishmen are to be found in plays by Shakespeare and his contemporaries, the best known of these being Captain Macmorris in *Henry V*. The stage-Irish stereotype first emerged after the Restoration of the English monarchy with Teg in Sir Robert Howard's *Committee*

(1662). In late 17th- and 18th-cent, plays by authors such as Thomas D'Urfey, George Powell, John Durant Brevel, and Moses Mendez, the names of stage-Irishmen such as MacBuffle, Mactawdry, Mackafartey, and Machone, as well as Phaelim O'Blunder and a beggarwoman called Bet Botheram O'Balderdash, all indicate the chronic deprecation of Irish identity in metropolitan Britain during the period following the *Williamite War. Numerous stage-Irishmen were created by playwrights from Ireland such as Isaac *Bickerstaffe, Hugh *Kelly, John *O'Keeffe, and Richard Brinsley *Sheridan, often inventing obsequious and ridiculous characters in order to ingratiate themselves with London audiences. In *Love á la Mode* (1759) Charles *Macklin added Sir Callaghan O'Brallaghan to the repertoire of loyalist Hibernians. He followed this with *The *True-Born Irishman, or The Irish Fine Lady* (1762), a play which demonstrated the possibility of taking pride in Irish origins. Cultural patriotism was again attempted in *Variety* (1782) by Richard *Griffith. As political and economic conditions in Ireland deteriorated throughout the 19th cent. a stereotype evolved in which the apparent vagaries of the Irish peasant were served up in a racist concoction known as 'Irish drama'. In the Victorian period several authors successfully exploited their Irish background to produce such regional characters as Samuel *Lover's *Rory O'More* (1837) and *Handy Andy* (1842). From Charles *Lever to *Somerville and Ross, sketches of rural buffoonery made up a recurrent element in Irish writing. Not all successful images of the Irish peasant were so demeaning. Boucicault created *Arrah-na-Pogue* (1864) around an Irish peasant whom audiences would laugh with rather than at. In *John Bull's Other Island* (1904) George Bernard *Shaw pronounced authoritatively on the extravagances of the stereotype. With the growth of the independence movement at the turn of the century, the stage-Irishman came under vehement attack. *Synge's *The *Playboy of the Western World* (1907) was sufficiently offensive to nationalism to cause riots in Dublin. The course of Irish drama in the 20th cent. was significantly influenced by the determination of playwrights and actors to avoid the appearance of trivializing Irish character. See G.C. Duggan, *The Stage Irishman* (1937).

Stair an Bhíobla (?1726), a history based on the Bible narrative by Uaitéar Ó Ceallaigh.

Stand and Give Challenge (1934), the first of Francis *MacManus's trilogy of novels dealing with the career of Donncha Rua *Mac Conmara and set in *Penal days, the others being *Candle for the Proud* (1936), and *Men Withering* (1939). In *Stand and Give Challenge* Mac Conmara returns from the Continent, and runs off with the sister of the local rebel leader. In *Candle for the Proud* the poet converts to *Protestantism to save his daughter from beggary. He returns to his faith, and in *Men Withering* he spends his final days, with his son and daughter.

Stanford, W[illiam] B[edell] (1910–1984); classical scholar. Born in Belfast and educated at TCD, where he became Professor of Classics. Besides his early scholarly studies including *Greek Metaphor* (1936), he produced an edition of Homer's *Odyssey* (2 vols., 1947–8). *Ireland and the Classical Tradition* (1976) embraces the Gaelic, Hiberno-Latin, and *Anglo-Irish responses.

Stanyhurst (or Stanihurst), Richard (1547–1618), historian and classicist; born in Dublin, educated at Kilkenny Grammar School and at University College, Oxford, where his tutor was the English Catholic martyr Edmund Campion (d. 1581). Stanyhurst compiled a 'Description of Ireland' and part of the 'History of Ireland' for the first edition of Holinshed's *Chronicles* (1577). Stanyhurst converted to *Catholicism, settling in the Netherlands, from where he engaged in a controversy on religion with James *Ussher. He is perhaps best known for his hexameter version of Virgil, *The First Four Bookes of Virgil his Aeneis translated into English Heroical Verse* (Leiden, 1582).

Star Turns Red, The (1940), a play by Sean *O'Casey, dealing with the confrontation between trade unions and a Fascist organization, the latter supported by State and Church. Red Jim, the central figure, is based on the Irish labour leader Jim *Larkin.

Starkey, James Sullivan, see Seumas *O'Sullivan.

Starkie, Enid [Mary], (1897–1970), literary biographer. Born in Killiney, Co. Dublin, she was educated at Alexandra College, and the Sorbonne, before becoming a Fellow of Somerville College, Oxford. Her chief works are biographies of Rimbaud (1947), Baudelaire (1957), and Flaubert (1967).

Starkie, Walter [Fitzwilliam] (1894–1976), Romance scholar and gypsy author. Born in Dublin at Killiney, the brother of Enid *Starkie, he was educated at TCD, becoming Professor of Spanish and Italian between 1926 and 1947. His travels as a fiddler with Romany gypsies in the Balkans produced the well-liked *Raggle-Taggle* (1933), which he followed with *Spanish Raggle-Taggle* (1934) and *Gypsy Folklore and Music* (1935). He was an *Abbey Theatre Board Member, 1927–42 and spent the war years at the British Institute in Madrid.

Statutes of Kilkenny, the, passed in the Irish Parliament of 1366, were brought forward by Lionel Duke of Clarence. They sought to arrest the hibernicization of the Anglo-Normans by forbidding intermarriage or alliances with the native Irish, and by proscribing the adoption of Irish language and culture.

Steele, Sir Richard (1672–1729), playwright, essayist, and moralist. Born in Dublin, son of an attorney, he was educated at Christ Church, Oxford, which he left to join the Life Guards (1694). In 1700 he fought a duel with another Irishman, Kelly, leaving the latter seriously wounded. His remorse inspired the high moralizing tone of his first play, *The Christian Hero* (1701). This was followed by *The Funeral* (1701), *The Lying Lover* (1703), and *The Tender Husband* (1705). In 1709 he turned his journalistic talents to a partnership with Joseph Addison in *The Tatler*. The venture failed in 1711, and from then on he and Addison ran *The Spectator* (1711–12), *The Guardian* (1713), and *The Englishman* (1713–14). His final play, *The Conscious Lovers* (1722), is a fine example of 18th-cent. sentimental comedy.

'Stella', a sobriquet used by Jonathan *Swift for his friend and companion Esther Johnson (1681–1728). He first met her in 1689, when he became her tutor. During the years 1710–13, while he was in London propagandizing for the Tories, he wrote the *Journal to Stella* (published 1766–8), a personal diary of sixty-five letters. Her replies were not preserved by Swift.

Stephen Hero (1944), an early draft of *A *Portrait of the Artist as a Young Man* by James *Joyce, written 1904–7 and published posthumously. The draft contains several characters and episodes absent from its successor and is written in strictly chronological form. The work remains interesting as an account of the period of the *literary revival from Joyce's personal standpoint.

Stephens, James (1825–1901), founder of the *Fenian movement. Born in Kilkenny, he was a civil engineer before participating in the *Young Ireland rising of 1848. Escaping to Paris he immersed himself in revolutionary organizations before returning in 1856, while his close associate John *O'Mahony went to New York. In 1857 he gave a candlelit oration at the funeral-rally for Terence Bellew McManus in Glasnevin Cemetery. He organized secret Fenian cells in Ireland with himself as 'Head Centre' and planned a rising for 20 Sept. 1865. On 15 Sept. he was arrested but escaped from Richmond Prison. On his return to America Stephens warned against a premature rising planned for 1867 and was deposed by the American leadership of the movement.

Stephens, James (?1880–1950), poet and writer of fiction. Born in Dublin and sent to an orphanage, his social origins and date of birth remain obscure. In 1896 he began to work as a clerk-typist in a solicitor's office. From 1907 he contributed to Arthur *Griffith's nationalist newspaper *Sinn Féin. George *Russell, whom he met in 1907, introduced him to *Yeats, Lady *Gregory, and George *Moore. *Insurrections* (1909), his first volume of poetry, is a series of angry vignettes of Dublin slum life. Two novels, *The *Charwoman's Daughter* (1912) and *The *Crock of Gold* (1912), together with another volume of poetry, *The Hill of Vision* (1912), showed his ability to combine realism and fantasy. *Here Are Ladies* (1913) is a realistic short-story sequence. *The *Demi-Gods* (1914) completed his trilogy of novels, which centre on the experience of young girls coming to womanhood. Following the success of

The Crock of Gold Stephens became a full-time writer and moved to Paris. He returned to Dublin in 1915 to become Registrar of the National Gallery of Ireland. New volumes of poetry, *Songs from the Clay* (1915) and *The Adventures of Seamas Beg* [with] *The Rocky Road to Dublin* (1915), are in the pastoral mode. *The *Insurrection in Dublin* (1916) is an eyewitness account of the *Easter Rising. *Reincarnations* (1918), a volume of adaptations from the Irish, recreates poems of Aodhagán *Ó Rathaille, *Keating, and others. *Hunger* (1918), a harrowing short story concerning inner-city deprivation, describes the reality of poverty. *Irish Fairy Tales* (1920) draws upon the *Fionn cycle; while the *Ulster cycle provided the subject-matter for *Deirdre* (1923) and *In the Land of Youth* (1924). In 1925, Stephens moved to England and settled in a London suburb. *Collected Poems* (1926, rev. 1954) is a selective gathering, omitting many early poems. From around 1927 Joyce and he developed a close friendship, Joyce suggesting that Stephens complete *Finnegans Wake* if he could not do so. *Etched in Moonlight* (1928) is a collection of short stories of nightmarish vividness. Three further collections of verse, *Theme and Variations* (1930), *Strict Joy* (1931), and *Kings and the Moon* (1938), were influenced by his study of Eastern philosophy. See Augustine Martin, *James Stephens: A Critical Study* (1977).

Sterling, James (1701–1763), poet and playwright. Born probably in Dublin and educated at TCD. In the dedication to *The Rival Generals* (1722) he claims to be the first Irish tragedian. He issued his *Poetical Works* (1735) in Dublin.

Sterne, Laurence (1713–1768), novelist and clergyman; born in Clonmel, Co. Tipperary, where his father was stationed. Sterne's mother (née Herbert) was Irish. He was sent to school in Yorkshire at 10, and entered Jesus College, Cambridge, in 1733. In 1738 he obtained a living at Sutton-on-the-Forest. The first two volumes of *The *Life and Opinions of Tristram Shandy* appeared in 1759, and succeeding volumes came out at intervals up to 1767. The immediate popularity of *Tristram Shandy* made Sterne a celebrity. Sterne acquired a living at Coxwold in Yorkshire in 1760, and settled there at the house he called Shandy Hall. Sterne made trips to France, 1762–4, and France and Italy, 1765–6. *A *Sentimental Journey* (1768) was based on his Continental travels. After the funeral his body was recognized in a Cambridge lecture-hall, having been sold by grave-robbers.

Stewart, Robert, see Viscount *Castlereagh.

Stoker, Bram [Abraham] (1847–1912), novelist. Born in Dublin, he studied at TCD after a sickly childhood, and followed his father into the Civil Service. From 1871 he contributed drama reviews and other pieces to the *Dublin Evening Mail*. In 1878 he moved to London to become the actor Henry Irving's manager, an arrangement which lasted until Irving's death in 1905. A first novel, *The *Snake's Pass* (1891), is set in Co. Mayo. *Dracula* (1897), his novel of vampirism, was influenced by Sheridan *Le Fanu. It was followed by a steady stream of other publications: *Miss Betty* (1898), *The Mystery of the Sea* (1902), and *The Jewel of the Seven Stars* (1903). *The Man* (1905) and *Lady Athlyne* (1908) are, like *Miss Betty*, romantic novels. In *The Lair of the White Worm* (1911) a legendary monster returns to prey on 19th-cent. Staffordshire.

Stokes, Whitley (1830–1909), Celtic philologist. Born in Dublin, he was educated at TCD. He joined the English Bar in 1855 and after several years' practice went to India, where he was prominent in legal administration. His study of Sanskrit led to an edition of *Hindu Law Books* in 1865. Numerous editorial works on the *glosses culminated in the *Thesaurus Palaeohibernicus* (1901–3; repr. DIAS, 1975), edited with John Strachan, a compilation based on material in Continental as well as Irish libraries. His other editions include *The Calendar of Oengus the Culdee*, and an Irish version of Lucan's *Pharsalia*. His two-volume edition of *The Tripartite Life of St. *Patrick* (1887) presents text, translation, and commentary on *Bethu Phátraic*.

Storm, The (1925), Peadar *O'Donnell's first novel, the storm of the title being an actual event and a symbol for the *Anglo-Irish War of 1919–21.

Story of the Injured Lady, The (1746), Jonathan *Swift's first pamphlet on Irish affairs. Written while he was Vicar of Laracor, Co. Meath, it is a protest at England's Act of Union with Scotland, settled in May 1707.

Story-Teller's Holiday, A (1918), a collection of stories by George *Moore, based on medieval Gaelic tales and on incidents from his own life. The book describes a journey from London to Mayo and back, with tales told by Moore and by the *seanchaí Alec Trusselby of poets, monks, and nuns.

Stott, Thomas (pseudonym 'Hafiz') (1755–1829), artisan and poet. Born at Hillsborough, Co. Down, he was a member of Bishop Thomas Percy's antiquarian circle at Dromore with Samuel *Burdy. He contributed poetry to the *Northern Star*. His *Song of Deardra* (1825) is a translation of *Longes mac nUislenn*.

Strange Occurrence on Ireland's Eye (1956), a play by Denis *Johnston,

based on a famous murder trial, and reflecting his concern about justice in society.

Strike at Arlingford, The (1893), a play by George *Moore. John Reid, a trade union official, is organizing a strike at Arlingford Collieries, owned by Lady Anne Travers, a young widow whom he loved when he was her father's secretary.

Strings Are False, The (1965), an autobiography by Louis *MacNeice, written in 1940–1 and posthumously collated from several manuscripts by E. R. Dodds. Beginning with his Ulster childhood, the writer sets out the experiences and impressions which conditioned his imagination.

Strong, Eithne (née O'Connell) (1923–1999), poet and writer of fiction. Born in Glensharrold, Co. Limerick, she was educated at TCD. She worked in the Civil Service, 1942–3. Her first collection, *Songs of Living* (1961), was followed by *Sarah in Passing* (1974), *Flesh—the Greatest Sin* (1980), *Cirt Oibre* (1980), *Fuil agus Fallaí* (1983), *My Darling Neighbour* (1985), *Aoife Faoi Ghlas* (1990), *An Sagart Pinc* (1990), *Spatial Nosing* (1993) and *Nobel* (1999). *The Love Riddle* (1993) was a novel.

Strong, L[eonard] A[lfred] G[eorge] (1896–1958), man of letters. Born in Plymouth of Anglo-Irish parents, he was educated at Wadham College, Oxford. His poetry collections included *Dublin Days* (1921), *The Lowery Road* (1924), and *Call to the Swan* (1936). Among more than twenty novels and fiction collections, those dealing with Irish material include *The Bay* (1931), *Sea Wall* (1933), and *The Director* (1944). In *The Light Above the Lake* (1958), set in Co. Wicklow, an elderly doctor comes to communicate with his dead wife.

Strumpet City (1969), a novel by James *Plunkett. Set in Dublin 1907–14, it concerns the strike leading to a lock-out of trade union members by an employers' cartel in 1913.

Stuart, [Henry] Francis [Montgomery] (1902–2000), novelist. Born Townsville, Australia, of Ulster parents, he was educated at Rugby School in England. In 1920 he married Iseult Gonne, daughter of Maud *Gonne, and took part in the *Civil War on the Republican side. He was interned at the Curragh until November 1923. *We Have Kept the Faith* (1924, enlarged 1992), a small collection of poems, was selected by W.B. *Yeats for an award. Stuart's first novel, *Women and God* (1931), explores the way that Irish society is being eroded by increasing material-ism. The next two novels, *Pigeon Irish* (1932) and *The *Coloured Dome* (1932) explore the role of the outcast and the redemptive value of suffering. In 1933 *Men Crowd Me Round* was performed at the *Abbey Theatre. *Things to Live For* (1934) is an account of events which helped to shape his philosophy and beliefs. Of the novels published in the years leading up to the war, *The *White Hare* (1936), *The Bridge* (1937), *Julie* (1938), and *The Great Squire* (1939), the first two show real artistic merit. By 1939 Stuart's career had reached a low ebb and he accepted a lecturing post at Berlin University, despite the onset of war. Stuart agreed, in 1942, to broad-cast from wartime Germany to Ireland. His weekly talks, dealing with literary subjects and Irish politics, continued until 1944. Shortly after the war, Stuart and his companion Gertrud ('Madeleine') Meissner, whom he later married, were arrested by French forces and imprisoned until July 1946. Stuart wrote a trilogy of novels, *The *Pillar of Cloud* (1948), *Redemption*, (1949), and *The *Flowering Cross* (1950), which drew on these experiences and display a brooding intensity. Following a move to London in 1952, Stuart published five novels, *Good Friday's Daughter* (1952), *The Chariot* (1953), *The Pilgrimage* (1955), *Victors and Vanquished* (1958), and *The Angels of Providence* (1959). Returning to Ireland he began to work on a 'memoir in fictional form'. The publication of *Black List, Section H* (1971) heralded a new phase in Stuart's career. Merging fact and fantasy, Stuart updates old themes and turns from a mystical to a neuro-logical quest. The success of *Black List, Section H* encouraged Stuart to write a more experimental form of fiction, and to explore the obsessive, alogical nature of minds like his own. *Memorial* (1973), *A *Hole in the Head* (1977), *The *High Consistory* (1981), *Faillandia* (1985), and *A *Compendium of Lovers* (1990) use struc-tural and narrative techniques to undermine the reliability of the text. See Anne McCartney, *In One Mind* (2000).

Stuart, James (1764–1840), anti-quarian. Born in Armagh and educated at TCD, he was editor of the *Newry Telegraph* in 1812 and the *Belfast News Letter* in 1821. His *Historical Memoirs on the City of Armagh* (1819) emphasized the importance of St *Patrick. *Poems* (1811) includes a verse essay on the history of Armagh.

Sublime and Beautiful, A *Philosophical Enquiry into the Origin of our Ideas of the* (1757, rev. 1759), a treatise on aesthetics by Edmund *Burke, ana-lysing the ways in which the senses are affected by different stimuli, how the mind is in turn influenced by these sensory perceptions, then dif-ferentiating between two separate categories of mental and emotional reaction, classified as the sublime and the beautiful.

Sullivan, A[lexander] M[artin] (1830–1884), journalist and politician.

Born in Bantry, Co. Cork, he succeeded Charles Gavan *Duffy as editor and proprietor of The *Nation. His Story of Ireland (1870) epitomized the constitutional nationalist view of Irish history. A son and namesake (A. M. Sullivan, 1871–1959) maintained his father's antagonism to revolutionary politics, but acted for Roger *Casement at his trial in 1916. Old Ireland (1927) and The Last Sarjeant (1952) are his memoirs.

Sullivan, T[imothy] D[aniel] (1827–1914), politician and poet; born in Bantry, Co. Cork, the elder brother of A. M. *Sullivan, whom he succeeded as editor-publisher of The *Nation from 1876. His Lays of the Land League (1887) reflect his involvement in land agitation, while Prison Songs (1888) were composed in Tullamore Gaol during a six-month sentence. Besides numerous anthologies, his volumes of poetry include Dunboy (1861), and Blanaid (from the Irish) (1891).

Sun Dances at Easter, The (1952), a prose romance by Austin *Clarke set in medieval Ireland. Orla, a childless young wife, is sent by a saint to St Naal's Well to be made fertile.

Sunset and Evening Star, see *Autobiographies (Sean O'Casey).

Suzuki, Hiroshi (1928–), scholar; born in Toyama, Japan, and educated at Waseda University, Tokyo. His life's work was the interpretation of W. B. *Yeats to a Japanese readership. He published Yeats-shi Jiten (1996), a commentary on the poetry; and he translated the Collected Poems (1982), A Vision (1978), and Ideas of Good and Evil (1974). He was a Professor at Waseda until his retirement in 1999.

Sweeney, see *Buile Shuibne.

Sweeney, Matthew (1952–), poet. Born in Lifford, Co. Donegal, he was educated at UCD and the Polytechnic of North London. His first collection, A Dream of Maps (1981), was followed by A Round House (1983), The Lame Waltzer (1985), Blue Shoes (1989), Cacti (1992) and The Bridal Suite (1997). His poems sketch brief worlds, lucid evocations combining menace with sadness. The Flying Spring Onion (1992) and Fatso in the Red Suit (1995) are books of children's verse.

Swift, Carolyn (1923–), playwright, screen-writer, children's author; born in London, and educated in schools in Sussex, she wrote The Millstone (1951) after marrying, in 1947, the Irish director Alan Simpson, who produced this play about adoption in Dun Laoghaire. With Simpson she founded the Pike Theatre, which staged Brendan *Behan's The Quare Fellow and Samuel *Beckett's Waiting for Godot in 1953. Other plays were Resistance (1977) and Lady G (1987). She was a series editor and writer for a number of series on *RTÉ radio and television, including children's programmes.

Swift, Jonathan (1667–1745), man of letters. Born in Dublin, he was educated at Kilkenny School and TCD. In 1689 he left Ireland and became personal secretary to Sir William Temple, a retired diplomat. He lived with him at Moor Park, Surrey, where he met Esther Johnson (*'Stella'). In 1694 he took holy orders and was appointed to Kilroot, Co. Antrim, where he began A *Tale of a Tub (1704), an attack on religious extremism. In 1699 Swift returned to Dublin, where he served as chaplain to the Earl of Berkeley, and obtained the vicarage of Laracor, Co Meath, the following year. In 1701 he published Contests and Dissensions between the Nobles and the Commons in Athens and Rome, supporting a system of checks and balances in government. In 1707 he wrote *The *Story of the Injured Lady* (1746), protesting that the Union between England and Scotland of that year was a betrayal of Ireland in favour of Scotland. In 1710 he was courted by the new Tory ministry, and began the *Journal to Stella* (1766–8). Over the next three years Swift worked for the Tories, taking on the editorship of *The Examiner* (1710–11), a weekly paper, and writing essays defending government foreign policy, such as *The Conduct of the Allies* (1711). While in London he met Esther Vanhomrigh, whom he later named 'Vanessa' [see *Cadenus and Vanessa*]. He was also introduced to Alexander Pope and enjoyed the literary company of the Scriblerus Club. Swift reluctantly accepted the Deanery of St. Patrick's having hoped for an English post. After six years of relative silence Swift produced *A *Proposal for the Universal Use of Irish Manufacture* (1720), the first of many anonymous pamphlets by the new Dean on Irish affairs. He also began work on *Gulliver's Travels*, but in 1724 this was interrupted by the controversy over Wood's half-pence, to which Swift contributed the famous *Drapier's Letters*, earning him the contemporary title of *'Hibernian Patriot'. In 1726 he visited London with a copy of *Gulliver's Travels*, which was published in October of that year. *A Short View of the State of Ireland* (1728) expresses deep pessimism in relation to Ireland's unstable economy. He continued to write polemical pamphlets, the most bitter of which, *A *Modest Proposal*, appeared in 1729. He spent increasing amounts of time with friends outside Dublin, especially with Thomas *Sheridan (the Elder) at Quilca, Co. Cavan. Together they produced *The Intelligencer* (1729), a weekly paper on literary, economic, and social topics. With the author's assistance, George *Faulkner published the first edition of Swift's *Works* in 1735. In 1742 he was declared 'of unsound mind and memory', and for the next three years he was looked after by close friends. Although he repeatedly referred to himself as 'an Englishman born in Ireland', he came to feel increasingly alienated from, and vengeful towards, England. See Irvin Ehrenpreis, *Swift: The Man, His Works and the Age* (3 vols., 1962–83).

Swift, Theophilus (1746–1815), barrister and author. He was educated at Oxford and the Middle Temple. His poetical works include *The Gamblers* (1777), *The Temple of Folly* (1787), and *The Female Parliament* (1789).

Sword of Welleran, The, and Other *Stories* (1908), a collection of twelve supernatural stories by Lord *Dunsany. In the title-story the Welleran gives his sword to a young man who saves his people's city of Merimna.

Synge, [Edmund] J[ohn] M[illington] (1871–1909), playwright. Born in Rathfarnham, Co. Dublin, to a family of ecclesiastics and landowners. In childhood Synge began to study Charles Darwin, and found it increasingly difficult to accept his mother's religious outlook. Educated at TCD, where he learnt Irish, his interest in the language was rewarded with the Irish Prize (1892). He travelled to Germany, where he studied music; but, turning to literature, he settled in Paris in 1895. He attended lectures on Celtic civilization given by Henri d'Arbois de Jubainville at the Sorbonne, and wrote criticism for various journals. In 1896 in Paris Synge met W. B. *Yeats, recently returned from Aran. Yeats urged Synge to abandon the attempt to make himself an interpreter of French literature in England, but to go to Aran and—as Yeats put it—'express a life that has never found expression'. In 1897 Synge suffered the first attack of the Hodgkin's disease which would kill him. In May

1898 he visited Inishmore, largest of the Aran Islands, before moving on to Inishmaan. He returned to Aran in the summers of 1899, 1900, 1901, and 1902, amassing his notes for The *Aran Islands. Later visits to the congested districts of Connemara and Mayo, as well as to West Kerry, further enriched his knowledge of the west; but he did not give up his residence in Paris until 1903. In translations from *Keating and other Irish originals Synge attended to the distinctive codes and rhythms of Irish; and drawing also upon the persistence in Hiberno-English of Gaelic speech patterns, he forged his uniquely bilingual dramatic language. *Hyde had employed a similar technique in Love Songs of Connacht (1893), but no one prosecuted this method with the wide-awake linguistic intelligence of Synge. Calling for a theatre which would once again reconcile reality and joy, Synge achieved this fusion in a language based on the actual speech of Irish people. Synge, recognizing that there was no tradition of Irish-language drama, and that none of the *Abbey actors was a native speaker, decided that his dramatic language would be a form of English based on the syntax and locutions of Irish. Synge's early work, such as Vita vecchia (1895–7) and Étude morbide (1899), fails through mawkishness and over-subjectivity. He completed The Aran Islands late in 1901, and in it he describes the shock of his encounter with the reality of people living their lives in close contact with nature and the elements. In 1902 he wrote *In the Shadow of the Glen (produced 1903); and *Riders to the Sea (produced 1904), based on an incident

he had heard recounted on Aran; and drafted the comedy The *Tinker's Wedding (produced 1909). By the time the Abbey Theatre opened in 1904 Synge was accepted by Yeats and Lady Gregory as the leading playwright of the literary revival, becoming a Director in 1905, and Managing Director in 1908. In 1905 the Abbey staged The *Well of the Saints, a play brutally contrasting the world of illusion with that of harsh fact. The *Playboy of the Western World, in many respects the master-work of the Abbey Theatre, was staged in January 1907, provoking riotous demonstrations. The hero, a verbal master drawing upon the vocabulary of Connacht love-song, is also cowardly and vicious. The play subjects imagination to unflinching moral scrutiny. The riots occurred because the play offended a nationalist audience who wanted simpler images of the Western world. The role of Pegeen Mike was created for Molly *Allgood, to whom Synge became engaged; but then Hodgkin's disease recurred, leading to the postponement of their marriage plans. The realization that his disease was fatal hangs over the mood of his last play, unfinished at his death, *Deirdre of the Sorrows. Synge's poetry, published in Poems and Translations (1911), reflects his view that verse would have to become brutal if it was to recover its full humanity. Synge based his work on his own experience of Irish country people, and his writing reflects a 'collaboration', a term he used in the Playboy preface, between hardship and imagination. See Declan Kiberd, Synge and the Irish Language (1979); and Mary C. King, The Drama of J. M. Synge (1985).

'Tables of the Law, The' (1897), a short prose romance in W. B. *Yeats's triptych on a mystical theme which also includes *'Rosa Alchemica' and 'The *Adoration of the Magi'.

Taibhdhearc, An, the Irish-language theatre in Galway, founded in 1927 by Séamus Ó Beirn of Oranmore. Liam Ó Briain of UCG secured a state grant from Ernest *Blythe, Minister for Finance in the Cosgrave Government, and got Mícheál *Mac Liammóir to stage his *Diarmaid Agus Gráinne* for the opening production.

Tailor and Ansty, The, see Eric *Cross.

Táin Bó Cuailnge (*Cattle Raid of Cooley*), the central saga of the *Ulster cycle and one of the oldest stories in European vernacular literature. Already very old when it was written down, it survives in three main manuscript recensions: in the *Book of the Dun Cow, the *Book of Leinster, and the *Yellow Book of Lecan. The *Book of Leinster* version, though it produces a consistent narrative, is florid in style, whereas the other two preserve earlier and starker forms of the tale, written perhaps in the 8th cent. The *Táin* tells how *Medb, Queen of Connacht, makes a raid on the Ulaid (Ulstermen) to carry off the Donn (Brown) Cuailnge, a great bull from Cooley in Co. Louth, so that she can rival her husband, Ailill, who possesses a comparable bull called Finnbennach (White-Horned). When the Connacht army reaches Ard Cuillenn they find the first sign of *Cú Chulainn, the hero of the narrative. A boy of 17, he defends Ulster alone since the Ulstermen are suffering a debility laid on them by Macha [see *mythology] for compelling her to race while pregnant. Cú Chulainn attacks the Connacht army in a series of devastating night raids, but the army still advances. Fergus makes an agreement with Cú Chulainn, committing him to a bout of single combat each day. A troop of boys, training in arms at *Emain Macha and exempted from Macha's sickness because of their youth, now come against Medb and are killed. When Cú Chulainn awakes and finds that the boy-troop has been destroyed, he goes into a 'warp-spasm' (riastrad): in this enraged condition, he makes a great slaughter. According to a late and highly formulaic accretion to the story, Ferdia, Cú Chulainn's foster-brother, is persuaded to enter combat against him. The heroes fight for three days at Áth Fhirdia (Ardee, Co. Louth). Finally Cú Chulainn sends a lethal weapon called the gae bolga downstream, killing Ferdia when its barbs open out inside his body. After a fierce struggle between the bulls the Donn carries Finnbennach's carcass on his horns across Ireland. See Thomas *Kinsella's *The Tain* (1969), a translation which has a valuable introduction and maps.

Táin Bó Fraích (*Fraech's Cattle Raid*), a tale of the *Ulster cycle and a pre-tale to *Táin Bó Cuailnge. Fraech woos Findabair, daughter of Ailill and *Medb of Connacht. The marriage is agreed, provided that Fraech bring his cattle on the raid (táin) against Ulster, but they have been stolen in his absence. Fraech regains them with the help of *Conall Cernach.

Taking Chances (1929), a novel by Molly *Keane. Maeve Sorrier invites

Mary Fuller to be her bridesmaid. On the eve of the wedding, Mary sleeps with the groom and becomes pregnant.

Talbot's Box (1979), a two-act play by Thomas *Kilroy, first produced in 1977. Catholic ascetic Matt Talbot (d. 1925), is less a hero than an individualist and a visionary victimized by the social and economic forces that exploit his reputation for sanctity.

Tale of a Tub, A (1704), a prose satire by Jonathan *Swift on religious fanaticism. It tells the story of three brothers, Peter (Catholicism), Martin (Anglicanism), and Jack (Dissent), representing the main branches of the Christian Church.

tale-types. The extensive narrative literature preserved in Irish *manuscripts is now usually classified into four groups or cycles, the *mythological cycle (or cycles of the gods and goddesses), the *Ulster cycle, the *Fionn (or Ossianic) cycle, and the king or *historical cycle. The earlier classification, however, was according to the first word of the title of the story. *Togail Bruidne Da Derga was classed among the Togla (Destructions), *Táin Bó Cuailnge among the Tána (Cattle Raids), and so on.

Tales and Sketches *Illustrating the Character, Usages, Traditions, Sports and Pastimes of the Irish Peasantry* (1845), a collection of twenty-one short prose pieces by William *Carleton, often confused with his better-known *Traits and Stories (1843–4). *Tales and Sketches* is built up around grotesquely eccentric members of peasant society, as in 'Buckram Back, the Country Dancing Master', and 'Barney M'Haigney, the Irish Prophecy Man'.

Tales by the O'Hara Family, a collection of Irish novels by John and Michael *Banim containing *Crohoore of the Billhook, The *Fetches, and *John Doe in the first series (1825), with The *Nowlans and Peter of the Castle following in the second (1826).

Tales of Fashionable Irish Life, see Maria *Edgeworth.

Tales of My Neighbourhood (1835), the last collection of stories by Gerald *Griffin to appear during the author's lifetime, ranging in character from lively rustic humour to moralizing about agrarian violence.

Tales of the Munster Festivals (1827), a volume of three long tales by Gerald *Griffin: 'Card Drawing', 'Suil Dhuv the Coiner', and 'The *Half-Sir'.

Tales of War (1918), a collection of stories and sketches about the First World War by Lord *Dunsany.

Talis Qualis or *Tales of the Jury Room* (1842), a collection of stories by Gerald *Griffin. An English visitor to Ireland strays into the jury-room of a courthouse in a town in the south of Ireland. Concealing himself in a cupboard to escape detection, the visitor listens while the twelve jurors each tell a story.

Tara (Old Irish Temair, Modern Irish Teamhair, meaning 'place of assembly'), the seat of the High King (ard-rí) of Ireland for centuries, and the site of his *inauguration. Known as Temair na Rig (Tara of the Kings), it comprises a complex of earthworks and lies south-east of Navan, Co. Meath. It was a place of ritual burial from c.2000 BC, long before the arrival of the *Celts in Ireland. A large oval enclosure called Ráth na Ríg (Fort of the Kings) contains two earthworks known as Forad (Royal Seat) and Tech Cormaic (Cormac's House). A pillar-stone at the latter is referred to as *Lia Fáil, the inauguration stone of the High King, but it is unlikely that this is the original monument. A rectangular earthwork is known as Tech Midchuarta and is said to have been a banqueting-hall. The five main roads of Ireland radiated from Tara. Tara symbolized the unity of Ireland, which had its human embodiment in the King inaugurated at the site. The ritual known as Feis Temrach (Mating of Tara), where the King was mated with the tutelary goddess of Ireland, confirmed the monarch's sovereignty [see Irish *mythology].

Tarry Flynn (1948), a novel by Patrick *Kavanagh set in the mid-1930s. It deals with the conflict in Tarry's mind between his poetic aspirations and his desire to marry and settle down on the family smallholding.

Tate, Nahum (1652–1715), dramatist and poet. Born in Dublin, the son of a clergyman, he was educated at TCD before moving to London, where he became known for his adaptations of Shakespeare. In 1696 he produced *A New Version of the Psalms* with Nicholas Brady. He wrote almost all of the second part of *Absalom and Achitophel* (1682), following in John Dryden's footsteps. Tate became Poet Laureate in 1692.

Taylor, Alice (1938–), memoirist; born in Newmarket, Co. Cork, she was educated at Drishane Convent. *To School Through the Fields* (1988) is an account of an idyllic childhood, and was followed by *Quench the Lamp* (1991), and *The Night Before Christmas* (1994).

Taylor, Geoffrey (1900–1956), poet and editor. Born Geoffrey Basil Phibbs in Norfolk and brought up in Sligo, he worked in various jobs including the Irish Guards and schoolteaching in Cairo before settling in Ireland. Besides his own collections *Withering of the Figleaf* (1927) and *A Dash of Garlic* (1933), he compiled *Irish Poets of the Nineteenth Century* (1958), and *Irish Poems Today* (1944), a gathering of contributions to

*The *Bell*, which he served as poetry editor.

Tecosca Cormaic (*Teachings of Cormac*), a 9th-cent. *gnomic text in Old Irish attributed to the legendary King *Cormac mac Airt. A dialogue between the King and his son, Cairbre, it is largely concerned with the proper behaviour of kings. One section advocates an acquaintance with *law and other branches of learning, as well as patronage of craftsmen. The text castigates women for silliness and vanity, and even for reacting tearfully to music.

Teevan, Colin (1968–), playwright; born in Dublin, educated at Belvedere and the University of Edinburgh. He was artistic director of the Gallowglass Theatre Company in Clonmel 1990–4, and from 1997 was writer-in-residence then lecturer in drama at QUB. *The Big Sea* (1990) was first produced in Clonmel, then in Paris (1992) and other locations. *Tear Up the Black Sail* (1994) followed in Dublin, while *Vinegar and Brown Paper* opened at the *Abbey Theatre. *Iph* (1999) was produced at the *Lyric, Belfast, and *The Walls* (1999) at the National Theatre. London.

Temple, Sir John (1600–1677), government official and author. Born in Dublin, son of a TCD Provost, he was imprisoned for siding with the Parliamentarians in the Civil War. His *History of the Irish Rebellion* (1644), subtitled *together with the barbarous cruelties and bloody massacres which ensued thereupon*, identifies English rule with God's will, and depicts the Irish Catholics as ingrates.

Thackeray, William Makepeace (1811–1863), English novelist, essayist, and travel writer, who visited Ireland in 1840 and then in 1842, under contract to produce *The Irish Sketch Book* (1843). Charles *Lever, in whose home it was completed, claimed that the author avoids passing judgement on the dominant political questions of the day; however, Thackeray persistently points out examples of sectarian prejudice on both sides, while a preface supporting Home Rule [see *Irish Parliamentary Party] was suppressed by the publisher. Thackeray's journey took him to all the major towns and scenic places. He warmed to the Irish people, making much of their good humour and intelligence. *The Adventures of Mr James Freney* (1764), a chap-book life of a *rapparee found in a Galway hotel, gave him a model for The *Luck of Barry Lyndon* (1844). His friendship with Lever broke down when he produced a parody of the latter's prose and verse in 'Phil Fogarty, by Harry Rollicker', one of the *Novels from Eminent Hands* (1847), and he was caricatured as Elias Howle in *Roland Cashel* (1850) in return.

That Lady (1946), a novel by Kate *O'Brien. Set in 16th-cent. Spain, it explores the difficulties experienced by women in a patriarchal society.

Theatre of Ireland, see Edward *Martyn.

Theatre Royal, a title designating the theatrical company whose manager held the royal patent of Master of the Revels, or was appointed by one so licensed. The patent was obtained from the Lord Lieutenant or Viceroy, rather than from the King. In Irish theatrical history it was first held at *Werburgh Street, 1635, then at *Smock Alley, 1662, later at *Crow Street, 1786, and finally by the Theatre Royal in Hawkins St., 1820, which came to be called the Royal Theatre.

Third Policeman, The (1967), a novel by Flann *O'Brien, written in 1940. With Divney, who has managed his property since his parents' deaths

during his childhood, the unnamed narrator carries out the murder of a wealthy farmer called Mathers. A mysterious journey brings him to a police station, where he is confronted with the puzzling activities of the eccentric constabulary. Fox, the third policeman, operates the machine which generates eternity. This anti-conventional and nihilistic novel satirizes the sloth and self-absorption that O'Brien discerned in Irish society.

Thomas Muskerry (1910), a play by Padraic *Colum. The title-character, a workhouse master, himself becomes an inmate, having been tricked by his avaricious and uncaring relatives who profit by his weakness.

Thompson, Sam (1916–1965), playwright. Born in Belfast and educated locally, he began working as an apprentice painter in the Harland and Wolff shipyard at 14. With encouragement from Sam Hanna *Bell, he started writing radio features on the dockyards and plays such as *Brush in Hand* (1956). His first and best-known play, *Over the Bridge* (written 1956), shows ordinary trade unionism being overwhelmed by vicious sectarianism in the shipyard. *The Evangelist* (1961), his second play, concerns a canting hypocrite.

Thompson, William (1785–1833), socialist reformer and author. Born in Rosscarbery, Co. Cork, he established an ill-fated agrarian co-operative on his estate there. In *An Enquiry into the Principles of the Distribution of Wealth most Conducive to Human Happiness* (1824), he noted that manufacture tended to impoverish still further the working classes. Thompson also issued *An Appeal of one Half of the Human Race, Women, against ... Civil and Domestic Slavery* (1825), written in collaboration with Anne Wheeler.

Thompson in Tir na nÓg, see Gerald *MacNamara.

Thomson, Samuel, see *weaver poets.

Thoughts on the Cause of the Present Discontents (1770), a political tract by Edmund *Burke written against the background of the riots that followed the election of the radical John Wilkes at Middlesex, and his subsequent expulsion from Parliament.

Three Dialogues Between Hylas and Philonous (1713), by George *Berkeley, expounding his doctrine that physical objects are dependent on mind.

Three Plays for Puritans (1901), a collection of plays by George Bernard *Shaw, containing *Caesar and Cleopatra, *Captain Brassbound's Conversion, and The *Devil's Disciple. The plays are linked by their critique of established religious and ethical codes.

Three Shafts of Death, The, see Geoffrey *Keating.

Three Sorrows of Storytelling (Trí Truaighe na Sgéalaigheachta), a collective title for the stories of the Exile of the Sons of Uisliu [or Uisneach; see *Longes mac nUislenn], the Death of the Children of Tuireann (Oidheadh Chlainne Tuireann), and the Death of the Children of Lir (Oidheadh Chlainne Lir). In *manuscripts from the 16th cent. these three tales are often found together, and they were given their collective title in the 15th or 16th cent. The story of the Sons of Uisliu and Deirdre belongs to the *Ulster cycle; the other two tales are related to the *mythological cycle.

Three Weeks After Marriage (1776), a comedy by Arthur *Murphy. It was first presented at Drury Lane as What We Must All Come To in 1764, and failed. Comic dialogues illustrate the breakdown of relations between ill-matched couples, pointing up the folly of crossing social barriers.

Threshold (1957–), a literary magazine founded in connection with the *Lyric Players Theatre and edited at first by Mary O'Malley with John *Hewitt as poetry editor.

Threshold of Quiet, The (1917), a novel by Daniel *Corkery, dealing with the problems of a lower-middle-class Catholic community in Cork city as they experience the disrupting influence of modernization. It begins with the suicide of Frank Bresnan, which the narrative sets about explaining as a consequence of loss of identity and faith.

Thurneysen, Rudolf (1857–1940), scholar. Born in Basle, Switzerland, he taught at the Universities of Jena, 1885–7, Freiburg, 1887–1913, and Bonn, where he trained many leading Celtic scholars who were to be associated with the *DIAS, among them Osborn *Bergin, D. A. *Binchy, Myles *Dillon, and James *Carney. He was a pioneer in the application of historical and comparative linguistics to Old Irish. His Handbuch des Altirischen (2 vols., 1909) described the grammatical structure of Old Irish and was translated by Bergin and Binchy as A Grammar of Old Irish (1946). Other major works include Die irische Helden- und Königsage (The Irish Sagas of Heroes and Kings) (1912), a study of the *Ulster and *historical cycles of tales.

Thurston, Katherine Cecil (née Madden) (1875–1911), novelist; born in Cork, and educated privately. In 1901 she married the English novelist Ernest Temple Thurston (d. 1938). She first published The Circle (1903) and then had considerable success with John Chilcote M.P. (1904), a political thriller. The

Gambler (1906) and *The Mystics* (1907) were followed by *The Fly on the Wheel* (1908, repr. 1987), which is set in Waterford. Her last novel, *Max* (1910), appeared in the year that she divorced her husband.

Thy Tears Might Cease (1963), a semi-autobiographical novel by Michael *Farrell, unpublished during his lifetime and edited by Monk *Gibbon after his death. Martin Matthew Reilly is the cherished child of a prosperous household in the Ireland of John *Redmond. His Catholic education makes him bleakly anti-clerical while the *Easter Rising overwhelms his constitutional nationalism, so that he enters enthusiastically into the armed struggle.

Tighe, Mary (1772–1810), poet; born in Dublin, she lived in Woodstock Co. Kilkenny. A poet of some celebrity in her day, her long poem *Psyche: Or the Legend of Love* (1805), in Spenserian stanzas, is said to have influenced Keats.

Tinker's Wedding, The (1909), a comedy by J. M. *Synge, set in Wicklow. It received its first production in London in 1909, W. B. *Yeats having decided not to present it at the *Abbey, as it was likely to antagonize Catholic and nationalist sensibilities already outraged by The *Playboy of the Western World (1907). Sarah Casey, a tinker, wants the priest to marry her and her partner, Michael Byrne, However, he refuses to go through with the ceremony, eventually calling down the curse of God on them as they run off.

Tír na nÓg, see *sídh.

Tírechán (*fl.* 650), author of a Latin Life of St *Patrick preserved in the *Book of Armagh in a unique copy. He was from Tirawley, Co. Mayo.

Tithe Proctor, The: *Being a Tale of the Tithe Rebellion in Ireland* (1849), a novel by

William *Carleton, arguing that the levy of Church of Ireland tithes on Catholics generates support for the Ribbonmen [see *secret societies].

Tithe War, a campaign during 1830–3 against the levy on agricultural produce payable to the Church of Ireland [see *Protestantism] which began as a movement of passive resistance, but Government attempts to enforce payment by the seizure of goods and livestock quickly led to bloodshed.

Titley, Alan (1947–), novelist. Born in Cork and educated at Coláiste Chríost Rí and St Patrick's College, Drumcondra, he taught in Nigeria during the Biafran war, before settling in Dublin and lecturing in his old college. *Méirscrí na Treibhe* (1978), set in 'Zanidia' in West Africa, deals with the turmoil of post-independence States. His technical and artistic skills were further developed in the novel *Stiall Fhial Feola* (1980) and in *Eiriceachtaí agus Scéalta Eile* (1987), a volume of stories. A wayward and sardonic humour, drawing upon the angry comedy of Gaelic burlesque, is increasingly evident, especially in *Tagann Godot* (*Abbey, 1991), a play which is both homage and response to Samuel *Beckett. *An Fear Dána* (1993) is a novel based on the life and travels of Muireadhach Albanach *Ó Dálaigh, the medieval poet. *Fabhalscéalta* (1995) and *Leabhar Nóra Ní Anluain* (1998) are volumes of Borges-like fables and stories. Titley is also the author of *An tÚrscéal Gaeilge* (1991), an overview of the novel in Irish; *Chun Doirne* (1997) contains essays.

To Be a Pilgrim (1942), a novel by Joyce *Cary, the second of the Gulley Jimson trilogy, which also includes *Herself Surprised (1941) and The *Horse's Mouth (1944). It is the testimony of old Tom Wilcher, a lawyer, evangelical, and political liberal, who wants to marry

Sara Monday. Caught molesting girls, he is judged insane and put into the charge of Ann, a doctor niece, in Devon.

Tochmarc Emire (*Wooing of Emer*), one of the longer sagas of the *Ulster cycle. *Cú Chulainn sets out to woo Emer, daughter of Forgall Monach. Forgall contrives to have Cú Chulainn sent abroad to learn the martial arts, from the woman-warrior Scáthach. Cú Chulainn is summoned back to Ireland, attacks the fortress of Forgall, who falls to his death. Cú Chulainn brings Emer home with him.

Tochmarc Étaíne (*Wooing of Étaín*), a trilogy of early Irish sagas which tells of the love between Midir, a deity figure, and Étaín. An incomplete text is found in the *Book of the Dun Cow, while the whole is preserved in a 14th-cent. manuscript which originally formed part of the *Yellow Book of Lecan.

Todd, James Henthorn (1805–1869), scholar. Born in Dublin and educated at TCD. In 1840 he founded the *Irish Archaeological Society with Eugene *O'Curry and others. Todd became Regius Professor of Greek in 1849, TCD Librarian in 1852, and then was President of the *RIA, 1856–62. His *St. Patrick Apostle of Ireland* (1864) draws upon classical sources, early Irish *saints' lives, and *Gaelic historiography to describe his mission.

Todhunter, John (1839–1916), poet and playwright. Born in Dublin, he lectured in English at Alexandra College, Dublin, before setting up as a literary man in London. His early poetry (*Laurella and Other Poems*, 1876) shows the pervasive influence of Shelley. A growing interest in Irish topics, inspired by Standish James *O'Grady, led to *Banshee and Other Poems* (1888); *Three Irish Bardic Tales* (1894); *A Life of Patrick *Sarsfield* (1901); and *From the Land of Dreams*

(1918). He was persuaded to write *A Sicilian Idyll* (1890) by W. B. *Yeats.

Togail Bruidne Da Derga (*Destruction of Da Derga's Hostel*), an early Irish saga [see *tale-types], dealing with the tragic life and early death of Conaire Mór, a prehistoric King of *Tara. The main recension of the saga was apparently compiled in the 11th cent. from two 9th-cent. versions. Considered part of the *Ulster cycle, it is also linked to the *mythological cycle by the figure of Étaín [see *Tochmarc Étaíne]. Conaire is brought up as the son of Eterscéle, king of Tara, but a supernatural being advises him to go to Tara where he will be made king. Conaire falls foul of ill-luck, breaking a series of gessa [taboos, see *geis]. Eventually he meets his death at Da Derga's hostel. This narrative of foreign invasion facilitated by inner division attracted Samuel *Ferguson, who based 'Conary' on it.

Togail Troí (*Destruction of Troy*), a free and much-expanded translation into Middle Irish of the late Latin prose narrative of the Trojan War, *De Excidio Troiae Historia*, attributed to Dares Phrygius, who was said to have fought on the Trojan side.

Tóibín, Colm (1955–   ), journalist and novelist; born in Enniscorthy, Co. Wexford and educated at UCD. *The South* (1990) was a novel set in Spain, where Katherine Proctor flees her Anglo-Irish background. *The Heather Blazing* (1992) concerns an Irish high court judge dealing with issues of constitutional and criminal law against the background of a changing Ireland. *Walking Along the Border* (1987) and *Homage to Barcelona* (1989) record journeys, while *The Trial of the Generals* (1990) selects his journalism. *Travels in Catholic Europe* (1994) assesses the state of the continental Church. *The Story of the Night* (1996) is a novel, and it was followed by *The Blackwater Lightship*

(1999), which deals with the death of an AIDS-victim.

Toland, John (1670–1722), deist philosopher and controversialist; born in Inishowen, Co. Donegal. Baptized by his own account Janus Junius (though more probably Seán Ó Tuathaláin), he was a native speaker of Irish. He appears to have converted to Presbyterianism at 15, studying thereafter in Glasgow and Leiden. As a thinker he advanced from theological liberalism to deism, then pantheism and possibly to atheism. His first work, *Christianity not Mysterious* (1696), opposes sacerdotal authority and fideism. Toland was vehemently attacked by Church of Ireland contemporaries such as William *King, and Robert *Clayton. His approach gave rise to a fertile period of philosophical thought, engaging Francis *Hutchinson and Edmund *Burke besides the clerical writers, while *Berkeley opposed his freethinking in *Alciphron* (1732). At Oxford in 1694 he appears to have told the antiquarian Edward *Lhuyd that he would establish the kinship of Irish and Welsh in the Celtic family of languages. *Nazarenus* (1718) describes an Irish manuscript of the gospels, with an account of ancient Irish religion sounding remarkably like deism. His *History of the *Druids* (1726) attributes pantheistic ideas to the ancient Irish. He is also believed to have had a hand in Dermod *O'Connor's translation of Keating's *Foras Feasa ar Éirinn*.

Tom Barber trilogy, the (1931–1944), novels by Forrest Reid, comprising *Uncle Stephen* (1931), *The Retreat* (1936), and *Young Tom* (1944), each treating of a progressively earlier period in the title-character's boyhood.

Tom Burke of 'Ours' (1844), a novel by Charles *Lever, in which an orphan, cheated of his patrimony, is given succour by the *United Irishman Darby the Blast.

Tomelty, Joseph (1911–95), playwright and novelist. Born in Portaferry, Co. Down, he left school aged 12 and became a house-painter. In 1939 he co-founded the *Ulster Group Theatre, serving as General Manager until 1951. Among his plays produced there were *Barnum Was Right* (1940) and its sequel *Right Again, Barnum* (1946), as well as *Idolatry at Inishargie* (1942), *Poor Errand* (1943), and *The End House* (1944), the latter concerning the disintegration of a working-class Catholic family in Belfast. The Group also staged *All Souls' Night* (1948), a tragedy combining realistic and supernatural elements, and *Is the Priest at Home?* (1954), a sympathetic depiction of a priest's daily life. A number of his plays were produced successfully at the *Abbey. His novels, *Red is the Port Light* (1948) and *The Apprentice* (1953), are realistic but with melodramatic elements.

Tomorrow (Aug.–Sept. 1924; two issues), a controversial literary magazine launched by H. [Francis] *Stuart and Cecil Salkeld.

Tone, Theobald Wolfe (1763–1798), Republican and revolutionary; born in Dublin, he entered TCD in 1784, and was called to the Bar in 1789. In the following year he published a Gothic novel, *Belmont Castle, or The Suffering Sensibility* (1790). His radical thinking is evident in his *Argument on Behalf of the Catholics of Ireland* (1791), written some weeks before he founded with Thomas *Russell a Dublin branch of the Society of *United Irishmen. Tone's political thinking was informed by French revolutionary theories adapted to Irish conditions as a doctrine of non-sectarian Republican separatism. He became involved with William *Jackson, who had been sent by the French government to investigate prospects for an invasion of England and, following Jackson's arrest in April 1795, Tone was obliged to accept the government's offered alternative of emigration to America. In 1796 he travelled to France and convinced the Directory of the probable success of a French invasion of Ireland. Tone accompanied the fleet, which was prevented by bad weather from landing in Bantry in December 1796. A second projected invasion in 1797 with Dutch help likewise came to nothing. His third attempt in September 1797 ended in disaster at Lough Swilly, when he was captured. He was sentenced to hang. He cut his throat a few hours before the sentence was to be carried out. Tone's remains lie at Bodenstown, Co. Kildare, an annual site of Republican pilgrimage.

Tonna, Charlotte Elizabeth (née Browne) (1790–1846), poet and novelist. The daughter of a Norwich clergyman, she wrote religious tracts for a Dublin evangelical society as 'Charlotte Elizabeth' and more than thirty novels, mainly addressing social problems, as in *Helen Fleetwood, a Tale of the Factories* (1841). *The Rockite* (1838) and *Derry, a Tale of Revolution* (1839) attack *Catholicism. Her best-known poems are anonymously printed *ballads such as 'The Maiden City'.

Tony Butler (1864), a novel by Charles *Lever set partly on the north Antrim coast and partly in Naples at the time of Garibaldi's bid for Italian liberty. Tony Butler, the son of an impoverished widow, lives in a cottage on the Causeway coast under the shadow of Lyle Abbey, a *big house. The novel chronicles Butler's struggle to free himself from his circumstances.

Too True to be Good: *A Political Extravaganza* (1931), a play by George Bernard *Shaw, written in 1931 and reflecting the combination of political allegory and fantasy found in Shaw's later plays.

Topographia Hibernica, see *Giraldus Cambrensis.

Tóraigheacht Dhiarmada agus Ghráinne (*Pursuit of Diarmaid and Gráinne*), a tale of the *Fionn cycle. The earliest surviving version is preserved in a manuscript in the *RIA which was written by Dáibhí *Ó Duibhgeannáin in 1651. *Fionn mac Cumhaill, the ageing leader of the Fianna, is promised the young Gráinne as his wife. At a feast in *Tara she puts Diarmaid Ó Duibhne under *geis (taboo) to take her with him. Eventually peace is made between Fionn and the lovers, who go to live at Keiscorran, Co. Sligo. Years later, while hunting on Ben Bulben, Fionn is joined by Diarmaid, even though the latter is under geis not to hunt the boar. In the ensuing chase, Diarmaid is wounded and dies.

Tórna, see Tadhg *Ó Donnchadha.

tory, probably from Irish tóraí, meaning pursuer or robber, was first used in English by the Duke of *Ormond to describe 'idle-boys' robbing on the public roads. Tory later became synonymous with royalists who refused to lay down their arms after the *Rebellion of 1641, as well as the outlaws who disrupted the Cromwellian settlement [see *plantation]. Éamonn an Chnoic (Ned of the Hill) and his contemporary Seán Ó Duibhir an Ghleanna are examples of such outlaws celebrated in Irish *folksong. After the Restoration of Charles II in 1660 the term was used to describe common robbers. In the latter part of the 1670s the word gradually filtered into English politics. See also *rapparee.

Tower, The (1928), a volume by W. B. *Yeats containing some of his greatest lyric poems. 'Sailing to Byzantium', turns away from time to the consolation of artifice. The title-poem addresses the problem of age and mortality. 'Meditations in Time of Civil War' surveys the troubles of modern Ireland, while poems such as 'Among Schoolchildren' and 'All Souls' Night' pose questions about the mutability of life.

Town of the Cascades, The (1864), Michael *Banim's last novel, set among the poor peasantry in Ennistymon, Co. Clare.

Tracy, Honor [Lilbush Wingfield] (1913–1987). English-born novelist who settled in Ireland after the Second World War and wrote satirical fiction and essays. A collection, *Mind You, I've Said Nothing* (1956) includes broad caricatures of literary Dublin. In *The Straight and Narrow Path* (1958), *The Prospects Are Pleasing* (1958), and *The Quiet End of Evening* (1972), among many other novels, she gives a comical account of Irish rural life.

Tracy's Ambition, a short novel by Gerald *Griffin, published in tandem with *The *Rivals* in 1829. Abel Tracy, a Protestant middleman or land agent, is ruined by obsessive ambition.

Traits and Stories of the Irish Peasantry (1830; 2nd series, 1833; definitive edn. 1843–4); a collection of prose pieces by William *Carleton. The 'definitive' 1843–4 edition, which revises most of the tales, includes two novella-length works (*'Denis O'Shaughnessy' and 'The Poor Scholar'), short tales reflecting an oral tradition ('The Three Tasks'), and accounts of peasant traditions ('Shane Fadh's Wedding'). The authorial voice shifts abruptly from vivid *Hiberno-English dialogue to formal commentary.

translation from the Irish into English and Latin began when scholars, chroniclers [see Anglo-Irish *chronicles], and ideologues sought to describe

the culture of a civilization whose written records were exclusively preserved in *manuscript form. One of the first records of translation having been made from the Irish occurs in Edmund Spenser's *A *View of the Present State of Ireland* (?1596, published 1633), where he expresses concern that the invention he found in *bardic poetry is being abused for seditious purposes. In 1627 Conall *Mac Geoghegan translated the *Annals of Clonmacnoise* into English, thereby saving this material from oblivion, as the original text was subsequently lost or destroyed. While Geoffrey *Keating was finishing *Foras Feasa ar Éirinn* Michael Kearney from Ballyloskye, Co. Tipperary, was translating it into English. Meanwhile a co-ordinated programme of research, based in St Anthony's College in *Louvain, was amassing hagiographical material in Irish and Latin throughout Ireland, resulting in John *Colgan's *Acta Sanctorum Hiberniae* (1645). In Ireland James *Ware employed Dubhaltach *Mac Fhir Bhisigh to translate for him as he studied early Irish history. In 1660 John *Lynch translated Keating into Latin. In the early years of the 18th cent. there was a renewal of interest in Gaelic material, especially in Dublin. Dermod *O'Connor produced a translation of Keating's history. By the middle years of the 18th cent. the first wave of Celticism had begun to make itself felt in the literary culture of London and Edinburgh. James *Macpherson's *Ossian* stimulated a widespread debate about the quality and authenticity of Scottish and Irish materials. Joseph Cooper *Walker's *Historical Memoirs of the Irish Bards* (1786) was the first major literary outcome of the influence of Celticism in Ireland. Charlotte *Brooke, one of Walker's contributors, went on to compile an anthology of translated Irish verse, *Reliques of Irish Poetry* (1789). Thomas *Moore drew upon the story of Deirdre [see *Longes mac nUislenn] in

'Avenging and Bright' in the *Irish Melodies* (1808–34). Theophilus O'Flanagan's *Transactions of the Gaelic Society* (1808) included translations from the Deirdre story, but also a translation of Tadhg mac Dáire *Mac Bruaideadha's hortatory ode to Donnchadh Ó Briain. From the early 19th cent. there is a steady flow of translated Irish material, particularly poetry, but also, with the foundation of bodies such as the *Irish Archaeological and *Ossianic Societies, scholarly translations of prose texts. Amongst the 19th-cent. poets who adapted and translated Gaelic material are: J. J. *Callanan; Samuel *Ferguson; Edward *Walsh; James Clarence *Mangan; Standish Hayes *O'Grady; George *Sigerson; and Douglas *Hyde. Scholars who edited and translated Irish prose texts include Eugene *O'Curry and John *O'Donovan. A second wave of Celticism broke out in the 1890s, leading to the founding of the *Gaelic League, which had a policy of editing and translating Gaelic texts. This new Celticist impluse had as one of its manifestations the popularist cult of the so-called *Celtic Twilight; but it also led to the foundation of the School of Irish Studies in Dublin, and the beginnings of a distinguished tradition of modern Irish scholarship. See Michael Cronin, *Translating Ireland* (1996).

translation into Irish of literary material is thought to have begun in the 9th cent. with classical stories from Latin [see *classical literature in Irish]. These versions include translations of the destruction of Troy (*Togail Troí) and the wanderings of Aeneas (*Imtheachta Aeniasa*) and have the distinction of being the earliest vernacular translations of classical texts in existence. Non-literary genres were not neglected: standard medical works such as the *Rosa Anglica* of John of Gaddesden, and the *Aphorisms* of Hippocrates were translated, wholly or

in part. The impact of the Reformation led to Uilliam Ó Dómhnaill [see William *Daniel] and William *Bedell's translations of the Bible. The 18th and 19th cents. saw little in the way of translation into Irish, although Archbishop John *MacHale translated Homer's *Iliad* (1844–71) and Moore's *Melodies* (1871). In the 20th cent. translation into Irish of a wide range of writing was steady. An tAthair Peadar *Ó Laoghaire translated *Don Quixote*, while George *Moore had the stories that eventually became *The *Untilled Field* done into Irish as *An tÚrghort* (1902) by Tadhg *Ó Donnchadha ('Torna'). The poet Liam S. *Gógan translated poets as diverse as Horace, Goethe, Verlaine, and Keats. Denis *Devlin made versions of poems by Rimbaud. The most ambitious of all translators was Pádraig *de Brún, who made versions of Sophocles (*Antioghoine*, 1926), and a rhythmically compelling version of Homer's *Odyssey* (*An Odaisé*, 1990). *An Bíobla Naofa* (1981), translated by a team of scholars under the direction of Pádraig *Ó Fiannachta at Maynooth [see *universities], formed the basis of a new Catholic liturgy in Irish [see also *Bible in Irish]. Translating activity increased in the 1970s, 1980s, and 1990s, examples being Michael *Hartnett's adaptations of the Hungarian poet Ferenc Juhász in *An Damh-Mhac* (1987); Pearse *Hutchinson's versions from Catalan poets in *Le Cead na Gréine* (1989); and Gabriel *Rosenstock's renderings of Seamus *Heaney in *Conlán* (1989).

Translations (1980), a historical play by Brian *Friel, set in 1833, when a detachment of British soldiers arrives to map Ballybeg, Co. Donegal, for the Ordnance Survey [see George *Petrie]. The enforced translation of Gaelic placenames into English provides a dramatic metaphor for the Anglo-Irish historical relationship.

Treaty, Anglo-Irish (1921), see *Anglo-Irish War.

Trecheng Breth Féne (*Triad of Judgements*), see *triads.

Trench, [Frederick] Herbert (1865–1923), poet. Born in Avonmore, Co. Cork, he was educated at Oxford. *Deirdre Wedded* (1901) is a narrative poem based on *Longes mac nUislenn*, and tells the Deirdre story in an impressionistic manner. *Apollo and the Seaman* (1907) is another narrative poem. *Poems with Fables in Prose* (2 vols., 1918) collected his published verse and prose pieces.

Trench, Richard Chenevix (1807–1886), philologist poet, and Protestant Archbishop; born in Dublin and educated at Cambridge. Trench was best known for his popular philological works, *Study of Words* (1851) and *English Past and Present* (1856). He is credited with a motion at the Philological Society on 7 January 1858 which led to the creation of the *Oxford English Dictionary*. Besides verse included in *Justin Martyr* (1835), *Honor Neale* (1838), and *Poems from Eastern Sources* (1842), he translated Christian hymns (*Sacred Latin Poetry*, 1849).

Trench, William Steuart (1808–1872), land agent and author of *The Realities of Irish Life* (1868), a detailed account of the *Famine and later *Land League period in Ireland from the standpoint of a 'progressive' agriculturist. Born near Portarlington, Co. Laois, to a clerical family and educated at TCD, Trench issued a novel, *Ierne* (1871), based on material gathered for a history of the Land War.

Trevor, William (pseudonym of William Trevor Cox) (1928–), short-story writer and novelist. Born the son of a bank official in Mitchelstown, Co. Cork, he attended St Columba's College in Dublin, then TCD. After teaching for a time, he turned to sculpture and started writing when he tired of modern abstraction, producing his first novel, *A Standard of Behaviour*, in 1958. Trevor's talent for the depiction of eccentrics is evident in *The *Old Boys* (1964), and since then he has been a prolific writer of black comedies. Besides Basil Jaraby, a child-molester in *The *Old Boys*, the gallery of nasty characters figured in Trevor's fiction includes Septimus Tuam in *The Love Department* (1966), Timothy Gedge in *The Children of Dynmouth* (1976), and Francis Tyte, the villain of *Other People's Worlds* (1980). In the 1980s Trevor devoted a number of novels to Irish political violence. Among these, *Fools of Fortune* (1983) and *The Silence in the Garden* (1988) encapsulate the turbulence of historical experience. Similar issues are explored in a number of short stories such as 'Beyond the Pale' and 'Attracta'. Some other short stories have been televised successfully: of these, *The *Ballroom of Romance*, title-story of a 1972 collection, was hugely popular. *Two Lives* (1990) was a pair of novellas. *Felicia's Journey* (1994) recounts the fate of a girl from the Irish midlands who falls into the hands of a sexual psychopath. *The Collected Stories* appeared in 1992. *Excursions in the Real World* (1993) is a book of memoirs; other works include *Mrs Eckdorf in O'Neill's Hotel* (1969), *Elizabeth Alone* (1973), and *Death in Summer* (1998).

Trí Truaighe na Sgéalaigheachta, see *Three Sorrows of Storytelling.

triads, a prominent genre in early Irish literature. *Trecheng Breth Féne (Triad of Judgements of the Irish)*, the most extensive collection, probably dates from the 9th cent. Some triads are based on observations of natural phenomena ('three cold things which bubble: a well, the sea, new ale').

Trial of Father Dillingham, The (1981), a novel by John *Broderick, dealing with the illness and suicide of Maurice O'Connell and its impact on a circle of friends living as tenants in a Georgian house in Fitzwilliam Square, Dublin.

Trinity College, Dublin, see *universities.

Tristram Shandy, see The *Life and Opinions of Tristram Shandy.

Triumph of Failure, The (1901), see under *Geoffrey Austin: Student.

Triumph of Prudence over Passion, The (?1781), an epistolary novel advocating the legislative independence of *Grattan's Parliament, written probably by a woman.

Trollope, Anthony (1812–1882), English novelist. Living in Ireland as a Post Office surveyor and later inspector between 1841 and 1859, he worked out of Banagher, Co. Offaly, and Clonmel, Co. Tipperary. After an unhappy childhood and some years drudging in London, Ireland liberated Trollope from asthma and gave him the impetus to start writing. In his first novel, The *Macdermots of Ballycloran (1847), he deals with the tragedy that overwhelms a reduced Catholic gentry family. In The *Kellys and the O'Kellys (1848) he sets an upper-class love-story in Dunmore, Co. Galway, among the landed families of *ascendancy Ireland. Castle Richmond (1860) concerns a rivalry between a widow and her daughter over Owen Fitzgerald, an Irish aristocrat. Phineas Finn (1869) and Phineas Redux (1874), though the title-character is Irish and supposedly modelled on John *Sadleir, focus on political life at Westminster. An Eye for an Eye (1879), set at the Cliffs of Moher, is a tale of seduction. The Landleaguers (1883) was the last of nearly fifty novels;

it deals with the persecution of an English family who buy an estate in Co. Galway.

'Troubles, the', a term commonly used to refer to two separate but related periods of crisis in modern Irish history, the first being the years of the *Anglo-Irish War and the *Civil War from the *Easter Rising of 1916 to the ceasefire of 1923; the second being of much longer duration, from the outbreak of violence in *Northern Ireland in 1968 following civil-rights demonstrations to the Good Friday Agreement of 1998. At the heart of both conflicts lies the question, still unresolved, as to the form or forms the State or States of Ireland should take which would be representative of the differing cultural identities and religious convictions of the people of Ireland, North and South.

Troy, Una (1918–), novelist and playwright; born Fermoy, Co. Cork, and educated at Loreto Convent, Dublin. Her first two novels, Mount Prospect (1936) and Dead Man's Light (1938), were written under the pseudonym 'Elizabeth Connor'. She subsequently published fourteen novels under her own name. We are Seven (1955) and Out of the Everywhere (1976) deal with highly irregular domestic situations in a humorous and sympathetic manner. A small-town world is depicted in novels such as Caught in the Furze (1977) and So True a Fool (1981).

True-Born Irishman, The, or the Irish Fine Lady (1762), an Irish comedy by Charles *Macklin. First played at *Smock Alley, it concerns the affectations of the wife of Murrough O'Dogherty, an MP in the *Irish Parliament. However, she is cured of 'the London vertigo'. It was adapted by Brian *Friel as The London Vertigo (1991).

tuath, see *political divisions.

Tuatha Dé Danann, see *mythology, *mythological cycle, and *Lebor Gabála Érenn.

Twenty Years a-Growing, see *Fiche Blian ag Fás.

Twice Round the Black Church (1962), a volume of autobiography by Austin *Clarke consisting mainly of recollections of childhood and adolescence, and the more forbidding aspects of Clarke's Catholic upbringing.

Twin Rivals, The (1702), a play by George *Farquhar first produced at Drury Lane Theatre, London. Hermes Wouldbe, the elder brother, is going to be swindled out of the family estate and the hand of his fiancée, Constance, by the younger, Benjamin, with the help of an attorney, Subtleman, who offers to bring a cargo-load of perjuring witnesses from Ireland. The *stage-Irish servant Teague exposes the villains.

Twisting of the Rope, The, see *Casadh an tSúgáin.

Two Days in Aragon (1941), a novel by Molly Keane, set during the period of the *Troubles in the 1920s, and exploring the precarious situation of the Anglo-Irish *ascendancy at the time.

'Two Gallants', a story in James *Joyce's *Dubliners* (1914), written in 1906.

Two young men living by their wits connive in cadging money from a servant-girl, working in Merrion Square.

Tynan, Katharine (1861–1931), poet and novelist. Born in Dublin, daughter of a cattle-dealer, she was educated at the Dominican Convent in Drogheda. Her first poetry collection, *Louise de la Valliere* (1885) established her as a prominent figure of the *literary revival, and inaugurated her life-long friendship with W. B. *Yeats. In 1893 she married the barrister and writer Henry Albert Hinkson and moved with him to England, returning in 1914 when he became a Resident Magistrate in Co. Mayo, living at Brook Hill outside Claremorris. She completed over 100 novels, twelve collections of short stories, and three plays. Her four volumes of memoirs (*Twenty-Five Years*, 1913; *The Middle Years*, 1916; *The Years of Shadow*, 1919; and *The Wandering Years*, 1922) contain valuable literary portraits. Her eighteen volumes of poetry, of which *The Wind Among the Trees* (1898) is the best, chiefly contain nature lyrics.

Tyrrell, Robert Yelverton (1844–1914), classical scholar; born at Ballygarry, Co. Tipperary, he was educated at TCD, where he became Professor of Latin, Greek, and Ancient History. He edited Euripides, Sophocles, Terence, and Cicero, and co-founded the TCD journal *Hermathena* in 1874.

ua [. . .], names commencing with [e.g. Ua Maoileoin], see under Ó [. . .].

Uisneach, sons of, see *Longes mac nUislenn.*

Uladh (Nov. 1904–Sept. 1905; four issues), a literary and cultural magazine founded on the model of *Samhain* and *Beltaine* by a group associated with the *Ulster Literary Theatre that included Joseph *Campbell and Bulmer *Hobson.

Ulick and Soracha (1926), a historical romance by George *Moore. Continuing the partnership between the author and Alec Trusselby of A *Story-Teller's Holiday, it traces Sir Ulick de Burgo's pursuit of the Princess Soracha in 14th-cent. Ireland.

Ulster cycle, a group of heroic tales relating to the Ulaid, a powerful prehistoric people of the north of Ireland, from whom the name of Ulster derives. Their territory extended from Donegal to the mouth of the Boyne and their traditional seat was at *Emain Macha, now Navan fort near Armagh. Their opponents were the Connachta, associated with the province of that name, who had their seat at Cruachain in Co. Roscommon. The conflict between the Ulaid and Connachta forms the basis of the tales grouped in this cycle, the most famous of which is *Táin Bó Cuailnge, where the Ulster hero is *Cú Chulainn. At the time in which the cycle of tales is set, *Conchobor mac Nessa is King of the Ulaid and *Medb, wife of Ailill, is Queen of the Connachta. The tales reflect a dynastic struggle between these two peoples, while Medb retains associations with the goddess of sovereignty [see Irish *mythology]. The world depicted in the tales reflects the culture of pre-Christian Celtic Gaul and Britain as described in classical writers such as Diodorus Siculus: it is warlike; combat is often from chariots, manned by warrior and charioteer; the heads of opponents are cut off and used as trophies; the hero gets the finest cut of meat; druids, magic and prophecy are central to society; and the otherworld is always close [see *Celts]. Cú Chulainn is Lug's son [see *mythological cycle]; *Conall Cernach is related to Gaulish Cernunnos, the horned god depicted on the Gundestup Cauldron from the 1st cent. BC. Tales in this cycle include: *Aided Chon Culainn, *Fled Bricrenn, *Longes mac nUislenn, *Scéla Mucce Maic Dathó, *Serglige Con Chulainn, *Tochmarc Emire, and *Togail Bruidne Da Derga.

Ulster Group Theatre, the (1940–1960), formed when the Ulster Theatre, the Jewish Institute Dramatic Society, and the Northern Irish Players amalgamated after a successful season of separate productions at the Ulster Hall that included Joseph *Tomelty's first play, Barnum Was Right (1940). The cooperative venture began with St John *Ervine's Boyd's Shop (1941), and this was followed by Tomelty's Idolatory at Inishargie (1942) and Poor Errand (1943), and George *Shiel's The Old Broom (1944) and Borderwine (1946). A season was planned to include Sam *Thompson's Over the Bridge in 1958, but its suppression led to the rapid dissolution of the Group. Actors launched included Colin Blakeley, J. G. Devlin, and Denys Hawthorne.

Ulster Literary Theatre, the (1902–1934), founded in Belfast by Bulmer

*Hobson and David Parkhill (pseudonym 'Lewis Purcell') with the aim of fusing the principles of Theobald Wolfe *Tone and the *United Irishmen to the ideals of the Irish Literary Theatre [see *Abbey Theatre]. Though not initially encouraged by W. B. *Yeats, they opened with his *Cathleen Ni Houlihan and James *Cousins's The Racing Lug in November 1902, describing themselves as the Ulster Branch of the Irish Literary Theatre. In 1904, they again produced Cathleen alongside George *Russell's Deirdre, and were served, from Dublin, with notice that they lacked authority to use the name. Changing to the Ulster Literary Theatre, they founded the short-lived literary journal *Uladh and announced the intention of writing their own plays. Lewis Purcell's The Reformers (1904), a satire on municipal jobbery, and Hobson's Brian of Banba (1904), incorporating elements from Irish *mythology in Yeats's manner, were produced. In ensuing seasons, plays based on local issues, such as The Enthusiast (1905) by Purcell and Turn of the Road (1906) and The Drone (1908) by Rutherford Mayne [see Samuel *Waddell], were staged with others on heroic themes such as Joseph *Campbell's Little Cowherd of Slainge (1905). These two strands were drawn together in Suzanne and the Sovereigns (1907), a satire on sectarianism in Ulster by Gerald *MacNamara, with help from Purcell. Thompson in Tír na nÓg (1912), MacNamara's best-known play, combines the matter of *Tóraigheacht Dhiarmada agus Ghráinne with the idioms of Ulster *Orangeism to comic effect. Other writers included Shan *Bullock, Lynn *Doyle, St John *Ervine, George *Shiels, and Helen *Waddell; but there was a decline in the 1930s.

Ulster Volunteer Force (1913), an organization established by the Ulster Unionist Council in January 1913 in response to the imminence of Home Rule [see *Irish Parliamentary Party]. The membership quickly reached 23,000 and began to drill openly. Southern nationalists responded by forming the *Irish Volunteers, the nucleus of the later *IRA, and both forces began to arm themselves. The outbreak of the First World War led to the shelving of Home Rule, and the energies of the Ulster Volunteers were redirected to the war effort. The Ulster Volunteers, renamed the 36th (Ulster) Division, suffered huge casualties at the Somme in 1916. In 1966 a new Ulster Volunteer Force was set up in response to the perceived renewal of the nationalist threat.

tUltach, An (1924–), the journal of Comhaltas Uladh, a northern alliance of branches of the *Gaelic League, founded to promote writing in Irish.

Ulysses (1922), a novel by James *Joyce, dealing with the events of one day in Dublin, 16 June 1904, and modelled on episodes in Homer's Odyssey. The central characters, Stephen Dedalus, Leopold Bloom, and his wife Marion ('Molly'), correspond to Telemachus, Ulysses, and Penelope, while several others also have Homeric counterparts. The chapters are known by the titles Joyce used during composition, though these do not appear in the published text: 'Telemachus', 'Nestor', 'Proteus', jointly called the Telemachiad; 'Calypso', 'Lotuseaters', 'Hades', 'Aeolus', 'Lestrygonians', 'Scylla and Charybdis', 'Wandering Rocks', 'Sirens', 'Cyclops', 'Nausicaa', 'Oxen of the Sun', 'Circe', jointly called the Odyssey; and 'Eumaeus', 'Ithaca', and 'Penelope', jointly called the Nostos. Highly experimental in form from the outset, and increasingly so in successive chapters, it makes extensive use of the techniques of stream of consciousness (or 'interior monologue') and stylistic parody. The separate itineraries of Stephen and Bloom are treated in alternate sections before they meet in the Holles St. National Maternity Hospital ('Oxen of the Sun'), after which Bloom follows Stephen to the brothel quarter ('Circe') and takes him home via the cabman's shelter to 7 Eccles St. ('Eumaeus'). Stephen accepts refreshment but refuses an offering of lodgings and departs alone ('Ithaca'). Later Molly, in bed upstairs, mulls over her life as girl and woman in a soliloquy composed of four long, unpunctuated sentences, ending with a sexually compliant and life-affirming 'Yes' ('Penelope'). Stephen Dedalus's day begins at the Martello Tower which he shares with Malachi ('Buck') Mulligan ('Telemachus'). Stephen departs to teach for the last time at Mr Deasy's preparatory school ('Nestor'). Reviewing his position as he walks on Sandymount Strand, he reflects on problems of perception, identity, and their relationship with nascent art ('Proteus'). Drawing on the life and works of Shakespeare, he argues that art is a sublimation of personal experience in the National Library ('Scylla and Charybdis'). In the offices of The *Freeman's Journal* he rejects the rhetoric of nationalist Irish culture ('Aeolus'). When Bloom arrives at the Holles St. Hospital to pay his respects to a woman in labour, Stephen is drinking with medical students ('Oxen of the Sun'). In Bella Cohen's brothel Stephen is visited by a ghoulish hallucination of his mother ('Circe'). He smashes the lamp in the brothel and is knocked down by a soldier. Bloom, who has already taken charge of his money, effects a rescue. Leopold Bloom is an advertising canvasser married to an amateur singer. Sexual relations have ceased after the death in infancy of their son Rudolph some years before. Their one living child, Milly, is working as a photographer's assistant in Mullingar. Molly is having an affair with 'Blazes' Boylan, the manager of her

musical tour. Bloom begins the day by making breakfast for Molly ('Calypso'). Later, he collects a letter from a female correspondent, enters a Catholic church, and visits the Turkish baths ('Lotuseaters'). At Paddy Dignam's funeral he extends his reflections on religion and its influence on Irish conduct, travelling to the Glasnevin cemetery with Stephen's father, Simon Dedalus, and several other Dubliners ('Hades'). He visits the *Freeman's Journal* offices to place an advertisement and crosses paths with Stephen, whom he has already spotted on the journey to Glasnevin ('Aeolus'). He takes a sandwich and a glass of wine in Davy Byrne's pub, reflecting on food and sensual appetite ('Lestrygonians'). He goes to the Ormond Bar to answer his letter of the morning, hears Simon Dedalus and Ben Dollard singing, and glimpses Boylan setting out on a jaunting-car for his assignation with Molly ('Sirens'). In Barney Kiernan's pub he is attacked by an intransigent nationalist, asserts his Irish nationality, defends the Jews, and declares against violence in politics ('Cyclops'). Sexually aroused by Gerty MacDowell's display of underwear on Sandymount Strand near the Dignam household where he has gone to make insurance arrangements, he masturbates ('Nausicaa'). In 'Circe' his anxiety spills into masochistic fantasy. In the penultimate chapter, we learn that Bloom's temperate reaction to his wife's infidelity includes the 'antagonistic sentiments' of 'envy, jealousy, abnegation, equanimity' ('Ithaca'). *Ulysses* was first conceived as an additional story for *Dubliners*, to be based on the occasion when a Dublin Jew called Alfred Hunter rescued Joyce after he had been knocked down in the street by the escort of a young woman in January 1904. The streets and houses of contemporary Dublin are portrayed with an exhaustive precision which owes its thoroughness to Joyce's use of Thom's *Dublin Directory* (1904), which enabled him to claim that the city could be rebuilt from the information in his novel. See Stuart Gilbert, *James Joyce's Ulysses* (1930); and Don Gifford, *Ulysses Annotated* (1989).

Uncle Silas (1864), a sensational novel by Joseph Sheridan *Le Fanu. The narrator, Maud, is the child of Austin Ruthyn, who lives as a mystic and recluse on his estate. When he dies, the will requires that Maud live under her uncle Silas's guardianship. Silas attempts to bring about a marriage between Maud and his boorish son Dudley and, when that fails, to arrange her undetected murder.

Uncle Stephen, see *Tom Barber trilogy.

Under the Net (1954), Iris *Murdoch's first novel, a playful study in language, communication, and self-knowledge. Jake Donaghue is searching for affection and tries to renew emotional contact with the actress Anna Quentin, and with the taciturn Hugo Belfounder. He fails to win Anna but does rediscover Hugo.

underworld, see *sídh.

Unfortunate Fursey, The, see Mervyn *Wall.

Unicorn, The (1963), a novel by Iris *Murdoch. Marian Taylor, appointed governess at a *big house in the west of Ireland, finds herself companion to Hannah Crean-Smith, kept prisoner after attempting to kill her husband seven years previously.

Union, Act of (1800), the parliamentary measure that abolished the *Irish Parliament by providing for Irish representation at Westminster only,

effective from 1 January 1801. The idea of a political Union had been debated for more than a century, but was ultimately passed in the aftermath of the *Rebellion of 1798. The passage of the Act through Parliament in Dublin was secured by an unprecedented use of government patronage. Once established, opposition to the Union was focused by Daniel *O'Connell's abortive *Repeal Association, and later by the Home Rule movement of the *Irish Parliamentary Party. The political initiative later passed to *Sinn Féin and militant Republicanism when faced with intransigent Unionism in Ulster [see *Northern Ireland].

United Irishman, The (1899–1906), a nationalist weekly paper edited in Dublin by Arthur *Griffith for its proprietor, William Rooney. Griffith propounded his separatist philosophy in its columns, leading to the establishment of the *Sinn Féin party.

United Irishmen is the name generally given to the insurgents of 1798 (or 'Ninety-Eight), whether in Ulster, Leinster, Munster, or Connacht, in spite of the different character of the various uprisings in regard to leadership, motivation, and progress. Strictly speaking the term refers to a political society founded in Belfast in October 1791 by Samuel McTier and Robert Simms. Originally intended as a response to the continuing failure of the *Irish Parliament to reform itself, the Society aimed at securing a measure of parliamentary reform, and for several years pursued its goal by constitutional means. It was hoped to unite all Irishmen in the pursuit of universal male suffrage; but despite the rapid establishment of a Dublin branch by Wolfe *Tone and Thomas Russell, the Society's early membership was drawn mostly from the Ulster Protestant community. In May 1794 the Dublin Society was included in the wave of proscription which was then afflicting most anti-government organizations. Following the disastrous revelation of the Government's 'gradualist' approach to *Catholic Emancipation, the United Irishmen re-emerged as a secret, oath-bound, elaborately organized and centrally-directed body. It was now Republican in outlook and aimed to separate the two kingdoms. Connections were established with the Defenders [see *secret societies], originally a clandestine Catholic defence organization. The chief episodes of the 1798 Rebellion as reflected in popular tradition began with the brutal attacks on Presbyterian Republicans by militia and the yeomanry unleashed by General Lake throughout east Ulster. An early victim of judicial murder was William Orr, whose hanging for sedition in Antrim on 14 October 1797 became the subject of a famous ballad by William *Drennan. In Leinster the organization was counting on a rising of an estimated 300,000 insurgents on 23 May, but the arrest of members of the Dublin Directory, including Lord Edward *Fitzgerald, broke the chain of command. Martial law was declared on 30 March. In Co. Wexford, even though many Protestants joined the insurgents, the rising developed into a sectarian war with atrocities on both sides. The chief town fell to Fr. John Murphy of Boolavogue on 30 May. On 5 June, however, the insurgents under Bagenal Harvey were defeated at New Ross by British contingents led by Major-General Henry Johnson. The ruthless destruction of the insurgent remnant at Vinegar Hill, where Fr. Murphy and some 10,000 rebels were encamped outside Enniscorthy on 21 June, epitomized for folk memory the fate of the Croppies—so-called because of the short hair-cut of French revolutionary activists—who faced muskets and ordnance with pikes and farming implements. During the ensuing reprisals Fr. Murphy was brutally flogged, beheaded, and burnt in pitch. In Ulster the insurgents were mainly Presbyterians in religion and Republicans in politics. Martial events began with an attack on Antrim town on 7 June, resulting in the capture of Henry Joy *McCracken on Slemish Mountain and his execution by hanging in Belfast. In Co. Down Henry Monro led the insurgents at Saintsfield, and again in a pitched battle at Ballynahinch on 13 June. As in Wexford so in Co. Down: after the defeat of the insurgents, the militia and yeomanry indulged in several days of indiscriminate killing, with the connivance of General Lake. The final chapter of the 1798 Rebellion occurred in Mayo following the landing of French forces under General Humbert at Killala on 22 August. After an initial victory at the Races of Castlebar, when a large contingent of mixed British forces was ignominiously routed on 27 August, came the defeat of the 1,000-strong French party with their Irish allies when General Cornwallis surrounded them at Ballinamuck. Some time later the *Hoche* was taken in Lough Swilly by the British navy, and Wolfe Tone arrested on board. His death by suicide in order to avoid hanging ended the 'conspiracy' of the United Irishman. Robert Emmet's Rising of 1803, conducted in the same political spirit, is traditionally regarded as a separate event, chiefly because the Anglo-Irish *ascendancy was stampeded into passing the Act of *Union in the interim. The large literature of the 1798 Rebellion begins with the patriotic ballads by *weaver poets and others, to which may be added Thomas *Moore's *Irish Melodies* and the commemorative poems that later appeared in *The *Nation*, notably 'Who Fears to Speak of '98' by J. K. *Ingram, and 'The Croppy' by William McBurney (d. ?1902). R. R. *Madden's *Lives and*

Times of the United Irishmen (7 vols., 1842–6) and W.J. Fitzpatrick, in *Lord Edward Fitzgerald and His Betrayers* (1869) and *Secret Service under Pitt* (1892), were nationalist apologies for the rebels. The lives, loves, and betrayals of the insurgents became one of the most enduring themes of 19th and 20th cent. Irish literature. See Stephen Brown, *Ireland in Fiction* (Appendix C) (1919) and James Cahalan, *Great Hatred, Little Room: The Irish Historical Novel* (1983).

universities. University education in Ireland commenced in 1591 with a royal charter for the foundation of Trinity College, Dublin. Among the first students to enter when it opened in 1592 were William *Daniel and James *Ussher, the latter making a journey to London in 1603 with Dr Luke Challoner in order to buy books to form the nucleus of a university library. By the 18th cent. it had come to include many Irish *manuscripts, including the *Book of Kells, the *Book of Leinster, and the *Book of Durrow. Under the Act of *Union, TCD Library acquired entitlement to copies of all books published in the Kingdom. From the outset the University was essentially an Anglican foundation with the primary purpose of promoting the Reformation. TCD became a large landowner under the *plantations. It remained the only chartered institution of higher learning in the country until 1795, when St Patrick's College, Maynooth, was founded as a Roman Catholic centre of higher education. It was not until 1970 that the Catholic clergy removed the 'ban' on Catholics entering TCD, although Presbyterians had been increasingly numerous there since the turn of the century. In 1800 Maynooth was opened to lay students, but within a short time it became an exclusively clerical seminary, granting awards of the Pontifical University in Rome.

Because of the Anglican ethos of TCD, pressure mounted from the Roman Catholic and Presbyterian Churches in the early decades of the 19th cent. for what each could regard as appropriate third-level institutions. In 1845 legislation was passed establishing the Queen's University of Ireland, with constituent colleges in Belfast, Cork, and Galway. These were opposed as 'godless colleges' by many Presbyterians and by the Catholic hierarchy; and, because of their allegedly secular ethos and the absence of guarantees protecting Catholic educational interests, neither Queen's College, Cork, nor Queen's College, Galway, achieved the full support of Catholics. The Belfast College, catering for the predominantly Presbyterian population of the northeast, enjoyed greater success, however. In 1854, in an attempt to provide university education for Catholics from its own resources, the Church hierarchy founded the Catholic University of Ireland under the rectorship of Cardinal John Henry *Newman. However, it lasted only four years. Increased pressure on government from an ever more confident Catholic clergy and middle class led to the abolition of the Queen's University and the establishment of the Royal University of Ireland in 1879. The Royal University was an examining body, publishing syllabuses and setting papers for which candidates were prepared mainly in various recognized colleges throughout the country, notably the Queen's Colleges and University College, Dublin (UCD). The latter was established on St Stephen's Green, in buildings that formerly housed the Catholic University, with members of the Society of Jesus for the most part as its lecturers, and it was here that James *Joyce received his university education. Also associated with the Royal University was Magee College in Derry, founded in 1865 as a Presbyterian theological institution. The Royal University was notable in that it was the first university in Ireland to admit women to degrees. In 1908 the National University of Ireland (NUI) and the Queen's University of Belfast (QUB) were established as two new and separate teaching universities. The National University was a federal university consisting of the University Colleges in Cork (UCC), Dublin (UCD), and Galway (UCG). St Patrick's College, Maynooth, became a recognized university institution within NUI. At the same time Magee College became an associate college of the University of Dublin (TCD), retaining this link until it was affiliated to the New University of Ulster (NUU) established at Coleraine in 1968. In 1984 NUU was amalgamated with the Northern Ireland Polytechnic to form the University of Ulster (UU), with campuses at Jordanstown (UUJ), Belfast (UUB), Coleraine (UUC), and Derry (UUM, though still known as Magee). Further additions to the university system in Ireland resulted from the transformation of the two National Institutes of Higher Education (NIHE) in Limerick and Dublin into the University of Limerick (UL) and Dublin City University (DCU) in 1989, St Patrick's College, Drumcondra, later becoming affiliated to the latter.

Unnamable, The (in French as *L'Innommable*, 1953; in English, 1958), a novel by Samuel *Beckett, last in a trilogy that includes *Molloy* and *Malone Dies*. Compelled to speak in spite of a longing for extinction and silence, the disembodied narrator's voice bemoans time wasted in telling of *Murphy, Molloy, and Malone, when he could have been speaking of himself. Several possible identities are rehearsed; voices express an intense loathing of language as well as the obsessive need to go on talking.

Untilled Field, The (1903), a volume of short stories by George *Moore, set in Mayo and in the Dublin area in the 1880s. First published as *An tÚrGhort* (1902) in Irish translations by Tadhg *Ó Donnchadha and Pádraig Ó Súilleabháin of TCD, the collection arose from Moore's plan to provide the *Gaelic League with something distinctly modern to read in Irish. The stories tell of lonely and frustrated people for whom the only escape is rebellion or exile, as well as depicting a world of heretofore unexamined lives.

Untouchable, The (1997), a novel by John *Banville, based on the Cambridge spy and art historian Anthony Blunt, and his experiences in the upper reaches of English society. Banville makes his Blunt-figure, Victor Maskell, Irish, and gives him a background very like that of Louis *MacNeice, whom Blunt knew. A sombre novel, it emits a sad and despairing gloom to evoke the worlds of espionage and covert homosexuality.

Uraicecht Becc, see *áes dána.

Ussher, James (1581–1656), ecclesiastical historian. Born in Dublin, he was one of the first entrants to TCD, becoming Professor of Divinity in 1607, and later Bishop of Meath, 1621, and Archbishop of Armagh, 1625. As an Irish churchman, he secured the adoption of the Anglican articles of faith by the Irish Church, and is known for estimating the creation of the world at 23 October 4004 BC in his *Chronology (Annales Veteris et Novi Testamenti,* 2 vols., 1650–4). His collection of Irish *manuscripts was part of an attempt to furnish the Protestant Church in Ireland with an ancient pedigree independent of Rome. *A Discourse of the Religion Anciently Professed by the Irish and the British* (1631) was the polemical fruit of this, but other works in Latin, such as *Veterum Epistolarum Hibernicarum Sylloge* (Dublin, 1632), are more impartially interested in the historical record.

Ussher, [Percival] Arland (1899–1980), essayist and translator. Born in Battersea, London, and descended from a collateral branch of the family of James *Ussher, he studied at Cambridge for some time, and returned to manage the family farm in Co. Waterford before moving to Dublin in 1953. In 1926 he published a translation of *The Midnight Court* (*Cúirt an Mheán-Oíche). He published *The Face and Mind of Ireland* (1949), challenging the legacy of institutional puritanism, and *Three Great Irishmen* (1952), studies of *Shaw, Yeats, and *Joyce.

Vain Fortune (1891), a novel by George *Moore. Herbert Price, author of a moderately successful play, is saved by a legacy from an uncle. He goes to live with the disinherited niece, Emily, who kills herself when her love for him is not returned.

Valentine M'Clutchy, the Irish Agent or *The Chronicles of Castle Cumber* (1845); a melodramatic novel by William *Carleton. M'Clutchy is the dishonest agent of an absentee landlord. His son Phil wants to marry Mary M'Loughlin; her refusal provokes a campaign of persecution against the family in which M'Clutchy is helped by Solomon M'Slime. At the end M'Clutchy is assassinated.

Vallancey, Charles (1721–1812), military engineer and Irish antiquarian. Born in Windsor, he came to Ireland with the British army in 1762 and rose to the rank of General. The journal that he founded, *Collectanea de Rebus Hibernicis* (1770–1804), was devoted to native Irish culture, embracing language, religion, architecture, literature, and *law. He never learnt Irish and his philological arguments tended to invoke specious homophones and improbable etymologies. He postulated a Phoenician source for Irish, associating it with the language of the Carthaginians, the Persians, and even the Chinese. In his *Grammar of the Hiberno-Celtic or Irish Language* (1773), Vallancey took pains to characterize Gaelic as 'masculine' and 'nervous'. Vallancey was a founder-member of the *RIA in 1782. He initiated the modern study of *ogam with an essay on the Mount Callan Stone in 1785.

Valley of the Squinting Windows, The (1918), a novel by Brinsley *MacNamara. Nan Brennan, a fallen woman, has pinned all her hopes on her legitimate offspring, John, and his future as a priest. However, John is led astray by his dissipated half-brother Ulick Shannon, whom he eventually kills. The book was greeted by stormy protests; in the author's village, Delvin, Co. Westmeath, the book was burnt and his father boycotted.

Vera, or *the Nihilists* (1880), Oscar *Wilde's first play, produced in New York by Marie Prescott. The title-character is a Siberian peasant who leads a conspiracy to assassinate the Tsar.

'Verses on the Death of Dr Swift' (1733), an ironic review of his life by Jonathan *Swift, dealing with his Irish career.

Vicar of Wakefield, The (1766), a novel by Oliver *Goldsmith. Dr Charles Primrose, an Anglican priest, goes bankrupt, loses his living at Wakefield, and moves to a small farm. Mr Burchell befriends the family and rescues Primrose's daughter Sophia from drowning. When Primrose cannot pay his rent the villainous landlord, Thornhill, puts him in gaol. Mr Burchell turns out to be a wealthy benefactor, and marries Sophia.

View of the Present State of Ireland, A (1596, printed 1633), a colonial tract by Edmund *Spenser, written in dialogue form from the standpoint of the Anglo-Irish *chronicles. Irenius and Eudoxus, two Englishmen, discuss how to make the Irish submit to the Tudor State. Irenius, who has lived in Ireland for some years, considers its subjugation by war and famine necessary and justified if the country is to be 'reformed' and made over into tillage under the control of English settlers, with garrisons, judiciaries, and schoolmasters maintained by taxes. He castigates especially the *Old English who have adopted the *Irish language and *laws, and ridicules the common people who regard themselves as kinsmen of the chiefs whose names they share [see *fine].

Viking invasion. The first Irish incursions of the Norsemen, comprising ship-borne martial groups from Norway and Denmark, occurred in 795, when Rechru (now Lambay Island) in Dublin Bay was raided. The shallow-draught boats of the Vikings rendered many of the waterways of Ireland navigable to them, and by 820 they had consolidated their estuarial encampments and established control over the Shannon, the Nore, the Bann, and other rivers. Having first been raided in 795, the monastery founded by *Colum Cille on Iona was extensively pillaged in 802, while in 806 sixty-eight members of the community were slaughtered. The political activities of the Vikings in Ireland were consolidated in 831 with the arrival of Turgesius (Thorgest). In 852 Olaf the White landed in Dublin and established the chief Scandinavian centre in Ireland. The Norsemen suffered their first major defeat at the hands of Mael Sechlainn II (Malachi), the last undisputed Uí Néill High King of Ireland, in a battle at *Tara in 980 [see *kingship]. In 994 Mael Sechlainn captured Dublin and installed as king Sitric Silkenbeard. A clash in 998 between Mael Sechlainn and *Brian Bóroime, the dominant king in Munster, resulted in an agreement to share the country north and south. The following year Brian captured Dublin, defeating a Viking and Leinster alliance, and

reinstalled Sitric as king. Further hostilities broke out, according to tradition, when Brian's son Murchad insulted Maelmorda, King of Leinster, who turned for help to Sigurd, Earl of Orkney, and Brodir, King of Man. The forces assembled at Dublin by this alliance were defeated by Brian at the Battle of *Clontarf on 23 April 1014, bringing Viking dominance to an end. The chief impact of the Viking invasion of Ireland, as elsewhere, was the disruption of the Christian institutions that formed the nucleus of literary culture in the early Middle Ages. The Viking trading colonies of littoral Ireland are usually regarded as the earliest prototypes of urban development in the country. Contemporary Irish accounts of the Vikings in Ireland are to be found in the *annals, as well as in *Cogadh Gaedhel re Gallaibh.

Vindication of Natural Society, A
(1756), a political tract by Edmund *Burke. Subtitled *A View of the Miseries and Evils Arising to Mankind from Every Species of Artificial Society*, it was published anonymously, in response to Henry St John, Viscount Bolingbroke's attack on orthodox belief as superstition, and his advocacy of natural religion.

Virtue Rewarded, *or the Irish Princess* (1693), an anonymous romance set in Ireland during the *Williamite War. It concerns a German prince who courts an Irish lady in Clonmel, Co. Tipperary.

Vision, A (1925; rev. edn. 1937), a prose work of mystical philosophy by W. B. *Yeats, based on the automatic writings of his wife Georgie. This material encouraged him to systematize the theory of masks already outlined in *Per Amica Silentiae Lunae* (1918). Much of the work is given over to locating types of human personality and historical ages between the poles of extreme subjectivity and extreme objectivity, according to their place in a cyclical scheme of interesting *gyres.

Vision of Adamnán, see *Fís Adamnáin.

Vision of mac Conglinne, see *Aislinge meic Conglinne.

visions, see under individual titles [*Vision of..., Fís...] and *tale-types.

Visions and Beliefs in the West of Ireland (1920), a collection of *folklore made by Lady *Gregory over the previous twenty-five years, some of which had already been published in versions by W. B. *Yeats.

Vita Sancti Columbae, see *Adamnán and *Colum Cille.

volunteers, see *Irish Volunteers (1782), *Irish Volunteers (1913), and *Ulster Volunteer Force (1913).

Volunteers, (1975), a play by Brian *Friel. A group of political prisoners have volunteered for an archaeological dig in Dublin city centre before the site, which contains relics of Irish history from the *Viking to the Georgian periods, is developed as a basement swimming-pool in a tourist hotel.

Voyage of Bran, see *Immram Brain maic Febail.

Voyage of Brendan, see *Navigatio Sancti Brendani Abbatis.

Voyage of Mael Dúin, see *Immram Curaig Maele Dúin.

Voynich, Ethel Lilian (née Boole) (1864–1960), novelist; born in Cork, her father George Boole being Professor of Mathematics at the Queen's College [see *universities]. She was educated partly in Berlin, and in Russia met the exiled Polish Count Wilfrid Voynich (d. 1930). Her first book, *Stories from Garshin* (1893), was followed by *The Gadfly* (1897), a romantic story of Young Italy, the revolutionary brotherhood of 1848. *An Interrupted Friendship* (1910) was a sequel, followed by a third part, *Put Off Thy Shoes* (1945).

Waddell, Helen [Jane] (1889–1965), scholar and author. Born in Tokyo, where her father was a Presbyterian missionary and an orientalist, she was educated at QUB, and at Oxford. She worked from 1923 for Constable, her publisher. Her best-known work, *The Wandering Scholars* (1927), is a historical study and translation-anthology of the Goliards. Her only novel, *Peter Abelard* (1933), combines an evocation of the medieval world with a sympathetic treatment of erotic love. Besides *Medieval Latin Lyrics* (1929), her works include translations and studies of early Church Fathers.

Waddell, Samuel J[ohn] (pseudonym 'Rutherford Mayne') (1878–1967), actor and playwright. Born in Japan, the son of a Presbyterian missionary and brother of Helen *Waddell, he was educated at the Royal Belfast Academical Institute, qualified as an engineer at the Royal University [see *universities], and worked for the Irish Land Commission. He acted and wrote for the *Ulster Literary Theatre, providing them with their first noted success, *The Drone* (1908). In *The Troth* (1909), a Catholic and a Protestant farmer unite in a plan to murder an oppressive landlord. *The Red Turf* (1911) is a Galway story of land hunger and agrarian murder. Waddell wrote little for many years, returning to the stage with *Peter* (1930) and *The Bridgehead* (1934), both for the Abbey. He was married to Josephine Campbell, the sister of the poet Joseph *Campbell.

Wadding, Luke (1588–1657), theologian and scholar. Born in Waterford, he was orphaned at 14 and sent to the Jesuit seminary at Lisbon, but soon afterwards entered the Franciscan novitiate in Oporto. He studied theology and Hebrew in Salamanca and became President of the college in 1617, moving to Rome in 1618. His appointment as head of a commission charged with writing the history of the Franciscans resulted in the publication of *Annales Ordinis Minorum* (8 vols., 1625–54). He published in 1639 a monumental edition in twelve volumes of the works of Duns Scotus. He succeeded in having the feast-day of St *Patrick inserted in the liturgical calendar (17 March).

Waiting for Godot (published in French as *En attendant Godot*, 1952; in English, 1954; first performed in Paris, 1953, and in London and Dublin, 1955), a play by Samuel *Beckett in which—according to Vivian *Mercier's well-known summary—nothing happens, twice. While waiting on a country road for the mysterious Godot, Vladimir and Estragon divert themselves with conversational sallies that parody ideas of philosophy, poetry, and theatre. The tyrannical Pozzo arrives with Lucky, an abject slave tethered by a neck-rope. A boy arrives to tell the pair that Godot will not be coming till the next day. In the second act they fend off despair and suicide in the same manner. The play caused a sensation at its first performance at the Théâtre Babylone, Paris.

Walker, George (Revd) (?–1690), author of *A True Account of the Siege of Londonderry* (1689). Born in Co. Tyrone, possibly in 1618, and educated at Glasgow, he held two Church of Ireland parishes before becoming Rector of Donoghmore near Dungannon in 1674. Walker raised a regiment at Dungannon in 1688 and acted as joint Governor of

Derry with Henry Baker and then John *Michelburne. In July 1689 he carried a loyal address to William III in England, where he wrote the *Account*.

Walker, Joseph Cooper (1761–1810), antiquarian. Born in Dublin and educated at Thomas Ball's school, he spent some time in Italy for reasons of health before settling in Bray, Co. Dublin, where he entertained many Irish antiquarians of the time, among them Charles *O'Conor (the Elder), Charles *Vallancey, Sylvester *O'Halloran, and Charlotte *Brooke. A founder-member of the *RIA, he was infected with the contemporary enthusiasm for Celticism. His *Historical Memoirs of the Irish Bards* (1786) outline the progress of Irish poetry and music from the earliest times, making use of primary sources such as Fear Flatha *Ó Gnímh and Carolan (*Ó Cearbhalláin), with the assistance of scholars such as Theophilus O'Flanagan [see *Gaelic Society of Dublin] and Charlotte Brooke.

Wall, Eamonn (1955–), poet; born in Enniscorthy, Co. Wexford, he was educated at UCD, Wisconsin-Milwaukee, then at Creighton University, Omaha. His collections include *Fire Escape* (1988), *The Tamed Goose* (1990), *Dyckman – 200th Street* (1994) and *Iron Mountain Road* (1997).

Wall, Mervyn [Eugene Welply] (1908–1997). Born in Dublin and educated at Belvedere College and at UCD, he worked throughout his career as a civil servant. Following early *Abbey plays, *Alarm among the Clerks* (1940) and *The Lady in the Twilight* (1941), he wrote a burlesque of monastic Ireland in *The Unfortunate Fursey* (1946), the story of a simple-minded brother whose cell in *Clonmacnoise becomes a refuge of the devil. *The Return of Fursey* appeared in 1948. *Leaves for the Burning* (1953) and *No Trophies Raise* (1956) expound a disaffected view of Irish life in the post-Independence period. *Hermitage* (1982) is the first-person narrative of Tony Langton, a convicted murderer.

Waller, John Francis (pseudonym 'Jonathan Freke Slingsby') (1809–1894), poet and editor. Born in Limerick and educated at TCD. One of the founder-members of the *Dublin University Magazine*, he edited it in its declining years when he bought it from J. S. *Le Fanu. His comic and sentimental contributions to it in verse and prose were collected as *The Slingsby Papers* (1852).

Walsh, Catherine (1964–), poet; she was born in Dublin and educated there, after which she worked in Barcelona and Eastbourne before settling in Limerick. She founded hardPressed Poetry with Billy *Mills. Publications include *Macula* (1986), *Making Tents* (1987), *Pitch* (1994), and *Etruscan Books Reader No 1* (1997).

Walsh, Edward (1805–1850), poet and translator; born in Derry, he was educated in a *hedge school in Millstreet, Co. Cork, becoming a schoolmaster himself. In the 1830s he contributed nationalist verses to George *Petrie's *Dublin Penny Journal*. He became a national schoolteacher but was dismissed from Glounthane in 1842 for publishing 'What Is Repeal, Papa?' in *The *Nation. In Dublin he met John *O'Daly, the publisher who issued his *Reliques of Irish Jacobite Poetry* (1844) in penny weekly parts. A collection of Jacobite lyrics, it contained many *aislingí by 18th-cent. practitioners of the genre such as Eoghan Rua *Ó Súilleabháin. Walsh's metrical translations mirrored the assonance of the originals. *Irish Popular Songs* (1847), also published by O'Daly, was an anthology mainly of love-songs, again with faithful metrical versions by Walsh. He taught young convicts on Spike Island, where he met John

*Mitchel as he was being deported to Van Diemen's Land.

Walsh, Francis (Proinsias Bhailís), OFM (1654–1724), Franciscan priest and lexicographer. Born probably in Co. Dublin, and ordained in Prague in 1677, he lectured in philosophy and theology at *Louvain and in Italy before returning to Ireland. In 1706 he compiled in manuscript an Irish–Irish dictionary derived from Mícheál *Ó Cléirigh's *Foclóir no Sanasán Nua* (1643).

Walsh, Maurice (1879–1964), writer of fiction. Born at Ballydonoghue near Listowel, Co. Kerry, he was educated at local schools and St Michael's College in Listowel before joining the Customs and Excise service in 1901, serving mostly in the Scottish Highlands which provide the settings for many of his stories. His novels and stories are mostly romantic adventures. His first novel, *The Key Above the Door* (1926), was followed by *While Rivers Run* (1928). In *Blackcock's Feather* (1932), set during the Elizabethan period, David Gordon joins the rebel O'Cahans of Tyrone after the execution of Mary Queen of Scots. *Green Rushes* (1935) contains the story 'The Quiet Man' on which John Ford based his famous film (1952). Other novels include *Danger Under the Moon* (1954) and *A Strange Woman's Daughter* (1956).

Walsh, Peter (?1614–1688), Franciscan writer on politics and religion. Born in Kildare, he became the main promoter of the Remonstrance, a Catholic declaration of loyalty to the restored English monarchy, in works such as *The History and Vindication of the Loyal Formulary of Irish Remonstrance* (1674).

Wanderings of Oisin, The (1889), a long poem by W. B. *Yeats, recounting the adventures of *Oisín, the poet of the *Fionn cycle. The warrior son of Fionn, he spends 300 years in the otherworld with Niamh. Troubled by memories of the Fianna, Oisin returns to Ireland, where his years descend on him when he falls to the ground from his horse.

War of Independence, see *Anglo-Irish War.

Ward, bardic family, see *Mac an Bhaird.

Ware, Sir James (1594–1666), antiquarian. Born in Dublin, son of the auditor-general and later auditor-general himself, as well as Irish MP, and Privy Councillor in 1639, he was educated at TCD, where he was encouraged by James *Ussher. He served the Duke of *Ormond on diplomatic missions to Charles I. Ware's extensive library, which now forms the largest part of the Clarendon Collection in the Bodleian, includes Irish *manuscripts which he commissioned from Dubhaltach *Mac Fhir Bhisigh. His own works on Irish literary and ecclesiastical antiquities, written in Latin, began to appear in 1626 and were later published in translation by his son Robert as *The Antiquities and History of Ireland* (1705). In 1633 Ware issued historical works by Edmund *Spenser and Edmund Campion. Ware's complete works were edited with additions in two folio volumes (1739 and 1746) by Walter *Harris, who also brought up to date his *History of the Writers of Ireland* (1764), first published in Latin in 1639.

Wasting Sickness of Cuchulain, see *Serglige Con Culainn.

Waters, John (1955–), journalist and cultural critic; born in Castlerea, Co. Roscommon, he was educated there before working in various jobs and then as a journalist on the *Irish Times* and elsewhere. *Jiving at the Crossroads* (1991) is a study of forces and themes in Irish culture, while *Race of Angels: Ireland and* the *Genesis of U2* (1994) anatomizes the origins and formations of Irish creative energy.

Watt (1953), a novel by Samuel *Beckett, in which the title-character arrives from town to take up a domestic position in the country at the *big house of a Mr Knott. Watt's arrival causes the departure of his predecessor, Arsene, and in each of the four sections he progresses through the domestic hierarchy floor by floor until he reaches the master's bedroom, after which he himself is ejected.

Watters, Eugene Rutherford, see Eoghan *Ó Tuairisc.

weaver poets, or rhyming weavers, terms used to describe a group of rural, working-class Ulster poets of the later 18th and early 19th cents. During this period much poetry was written by Ulster men and women, but a distinctive group of peasant and rural craftsmen poets can be discerned who made use of the Ulster-Scots variety of *Hiberno-English in their work. Many of these poets came from the south Antrim-north Down area, where Scottish influence was particularly strong. The Antrim poets James Campbell (1758–1818) and James *Orr were members of the *United Irishmen and were imprisoned for a time. Both were weavers, unlike Samuel Thomson (1766–1816), also from Antrim, who was a schoolmaster and whose *Poems on Different Subjects Partly in the Scottish Dialects* (1793) carried the names of prominent United Irishmen on its subscription list. James Campbell's volumes were *Posthumous Works* (1820) and *Poems and Songs* (1987). David Harbison (1800–1870), 'The Bard of Dunclug', was the most prolific of the Antrim poets. He published *Midnight Musings* (1848) and *The Snow Wreath* (1869). From Co. Down there was Francis Boyle (?1730–?), who

issued *Miscellaneous Poems* (1811); and Robert Huddleston (1814–1889), whose *First Collection* and *Second Collection* appeared in 1844 and 1846.

Webb, Alfred John (1834–1908), Irish biographer. Born in Dublin to a Quaker family, he was educated there before joining his father's printing firm. In 1878 he issued a *Compendium of Irish Biography*, giving an alphabetical account of some 350 distinguished Irishmen and women.

Wedlocked, (1994), a novel by Emma *Cooke, set in Co. Clare, and dealing with the promiscuously intertwined lives of two couples who have nine children between them.

Week-End of Dermot and Grace, The (1964), a narrative poem by 'Eugene Rutherford Watters' (Eoghan *Ó Tuairisc). Based on *Tóraigheacht Dhiarmada agus Ghráinne* from the *Fionn cycle, it explores global concerns such as nuclear warfare, and moral and theological issues such as sex and salvation.

Welch, Robert (1947–), novelist, poet, critic; born in Cork, he was educated by the Presentation Brothers, at UCC, and Leeds University. He taught at Leeds, in Nigeria, and Cork, before becoming Professor of English at UUC in 1984. His critical work includes *Irish Poetry from Moore to Yeats* (1980), *A History of Verse Translation from the Irish* (1988), *Changing States: Transformations in Modern Irish Writing* (1993), and *The Abbey Theatre 1899–1999: Form and Pressure* (1999). He edited the *Oxford Companion to Irish Literature* (1996) and this *Concise* version (2000). His poetry includes *Secret Societies* (1997) and *The Blue Formica Table* (1999). Fiction titles are *The Kilcolman Notebook* (1994), *Tearmann* (1997, in Irish), *Groundwork* (1997), and *The Kings Are Out* (2001).

Weldon, John, see Brinsley *MacNamara.

Well of the Saints, The (1905), a play by J. M. *Synge. Set in Co. Wicklow, it tells of a blind couple whose sight is restored by a travelling 'saint'.

Wellington, (Arthur Wellesley) 1st Duke of (1769–1852), soldier and statesman; born in Ireland, educated at Eton and a military academy in Angers, France. He was commander of British armies in India, 1797, and in Spain, 1809–14, Secretary of State for Ireland, 1807–9, victor at Waterloo, 1815, and British Prime Minister, 1828–30, 1834, and 1841–6. As an Irish MP he supported the extension of the franchise to Catholics (barring their entry into Parliament), but resisted electoral reform and *Catholic Emancipation.

Werburgh Street, Theatre Royal (1637–1641), the first permanent playhouse in Ireland, built by John *Ogilby in the fashionable parish of St Werburgh, adjacent to Dublin Castle. The English dramatist James *Shirley wrote prologues and plays for the Werburgh Street company, including *The Royal Master* (1637). Some local works such as Shirley's *St. Patrick for Ireland* and Henry *Burnell's *Landgartha* were also performed.

West, Anthony C[athcot] (1910–1988), novelist. Born in Co. Down, he was brought up in Cavan before going to America in 1930–8. He served in the Second World War as an RAF navigator and later moved to Wales, where he farmed. His first novel, *The Native Moment* (1961), describes the wild excursions of young Simon Green. Simon's early career is recounted in *The Ferret Fancier* (1963), a turbulent account of growing up. *As Towns with Fire* (1968) deals with the emotional development of a young poet.

Whaley, Thomas ('Buck Whaley') (1766–1800), famed for a wager of £20,000 that he would reach the walls of Jerusalem and return within two years, a journey accomplished in 1788–9. Whaley's *Memoirs* (1797) was edited in 1906.

Wharton, Anthony P., see *McAllister, Alexander.

Wheatley, David (1970–), poet; born in Dublin, and educated in Bray and at TCD, after which he worked as a reviewer and piano teacher. He edited with Justin Quinn the abrasive journal *Metre* from 1996. *Thirst* (1997) was a first collection.

Where There Is Nothing (published 1902, performed 1904), a prose play written jointly by W. B. *Yeats, Lady *Gregory, and Douglas *Hyde. The play concerns Paul Ruttledge, a landlord who joins a band of tinkers and remains a vagabond until illness forces him to enter a Franciscan monastery, where he disturbs the community with his visions and his laughter. It was written to keep George *Moore from stealing the plot. A revised version, *The Unicorn from the Stars*, was performed in 1908.

Whitbread, J[ames] W[illiam] (1847–1916), an English actor-manager who leased the Queen's Royal Theatre in Dublin from 1880 to 1907. He altered the staple diet of Irish *popular drama, largely supplied by English touring companies, by writing and producing political melodramas that appealed greatly to Dublin audiences. These included *Shoulder to Shoulder* (1886), *The Nationalist* (1891), *Spectres of the Past* (1893), *Wolfe Tone* (1898), and *The Irish Dragoon* (1905).

White, [Herbert] Terence de Vere (1912–1994), novelist. Born in

Dublin, he practised law before becoming literary editor of *The Irish Times*, 1961–77. His dozen novels, including *An Affair with the Moon* (1959), *The March Hare* (1970), *The Radish Memoirs* (1974), *My Name Is Norval* (1978), and *Johnnie Cross* (1983), are mostly in the vein of social comedy. *The Distance and the Dark* (1973) deals with the Northern *Troubles. *The Fretful Midge* (1959) is an autobiography. Besides a study of *The Parents of Oscar *Wilde* (1967), he wrote biographies of Isaac *Butt (1946), and Thomas *Moore (1977). *The Anglo-Irish* (1972) is a treatise on the *ascendancy.

White, Victoria (1962–), writer of fiction; born in Dublin, and educated at TCD, she was arts editor of the *Irish Times* from 1997, and published the collection *Raving Autumn* (1990).

White, William John ('Jack') (1920–1980), journalist and novelist. Born in Cork and educated at Midleton College, Cork, and TCD, he became London editor of *The Irish Times* and later Controller of *RTÉ. He wrote three novels, *One For the Road* (1956), *The Hard Man* (1958), and *The Devil You Know* (1962), all dealing with modern Irish metropolitan life. *The Last Eleven* (1968) is a play about a declining Church of Ireland community.

White Cockade, The (1905), a 'folkhistory' play by Lady *Gregory produced by the *Abbey Theatre and set at the time of the *Williamite War. After his defeat, *James II tries to escape by hiding in a barrel but is discovered. Patrick *Sarsfield tries to restore his courage but fails, and pretends to be king in his place, while James escapes.

White Hare, The (1936), a novel by Francis *Stuart. Hylla Canavan comes to stay with the brothers Patrick and Dominic de Lacy and they both fall in love with her. Patrick marries Hylla, and all three move to Dublin. Patrick goes to sea and is drowned in mid-Atlantic.

Whiteboy, The: a *Story of Ireland* (1845), a novel by Anna Maria *Hall set in 1822 against a background of political tension and armed rebellion. Edward Spencer, a young absentee landlord, arrives in the country determined to bring prosperity to his tenants through improvements.

Whiteboys, see *secret societies.

Whiteheaded Boy, The (1916), a three-act comedy by Lennox *Robinson which provided a model of realistic comedy. Denis Geoghegan returns home from Dublin, where he has been at medical college. He is the whiteheaded boy who exploits his special place in a loving if indulgent family.

Whoroscope (1930), a prize-winning poem on the theme of time by Samuel *Beckett.

Whyte, Laurence (?1700–?1755), poet. Born in Liverpool, probably a cousin of Samuel *Whyte, he taught in Dublin. Two separate collections of his poetry appeared as *Poems on Various Subjects* (1740) and *Original Poems* (1742).

Whyte, Samuel (1733–1811), schoolmaster and poet; best known as the teacher of R. B. *Sheridan, Thomas *Moore, and the Duke of *Wellington at his school on Grafton Street which he opened in 1758. He was brought up in Dublin by the Sheridans. In 1772 he edited *The Shamrock; or, Hibernian Cresses*, an anthology of poems mostly by himself.

Widowers' Houses (1892), a play [see *Plays Pleasant ...] by George Bernard *Shaw dealing with problems of economic exploitation and middle-class hypocrisy.

Wild Geese, the, Irish soldiers serving in Europe following the evacuation of the Irish army to France under the terms of the Treaty of Limerick, 1691, as well as the succeeding waves of recruits to Irish brigades in Continental armies of the 18th cent. and—by extension—in American and Latin American wars of later periods. Typically the 'Wild Geese' went either to France, where Irish troops formed a distinct *Irish Brigade, to Spain, which also had specifically Irish regiments in its army, or, in smaller numbers, to Austria and Hungary. The most prominent Wild Geese were Patrick *Sarsfield; Thomas Arthur Lally; Ricardo Wall; and Ambrose O'Higgins, Viceroy of Peru, whose illegitimate son Bernardo was to be the hero of Chilean independence.

Wild Irish Boy, The (1808), a novel by Charles Robert *Maturin, and a failed attempt to emulate the financial success of The *Wild Irish Girl by Sidney Owenson (Lady *Morgan). The illegitimate Ormsby Bethel becomes heir to his rich Irish uncle, De Lacy, and, though he loves and woos the unhappily married Lady Montrevor, ends up marrying her daughter Athanasia.

Wild Irish Girl, The (1806), a novel and idealized self-portrait by Sidney Owenson, later Lady *Morgan. Set in Tireragh, Co. Sligo, where it was actually written, it deals with the romantic courtship of Glorvina, an heiress, and Mortimer, who has been banished to the family estate in Connacht by his impecunious absentee father the Prince of Inishmore.

Wild Oats, or the Strolling Gentlemen (1791), a play by John *O'Keeffe first performed at Covent Garden. Set in Hampshire, the plot concerns the attempt of Jack Rover, a young actor, to woo Amelia by impersonating her cousin and his friend, Harry Thunder.

Wilde, Lady (née Jane Francesca Elgee) (1821–1896), poet and mother of Oscar *Wilde, born in Wexford. She contributed to The *Nation under the pen-name 'Speranza'; when she replaced Charles Gavan *Duffy as leader-writer during his imprisonment in 1848, she issued a call to arms on behalf of the *Young Irelanders. In 1851 she married William *Wilde, an eye and ear surgeon with interests in *folklore and topography. In 1854 she was taken to court by Mary Travers, a patient with whom her husband had an affair. The court found in favour of Mary Travers but indicated its view by awarding her a farthing damages. Lady Wilde moved to London after her husband's death. She published her husband's unfinished *Ancient Legends, Mystic Charms and Superstitions of Ireland* (1887) and *Ancient Cures, Charms and Usages of Ireland* (1890), *folklore collections which impressed W. B. *Yeats for their circumstantiality.

Wilde, Oscar [Fingal O'Flahertie Wills] (1854–1900), dramatist. Born in Dublin, the son of Sir William *Wilde and Jane Francesca *Wilde ('Speranza'), he was educated at Portora at Enniskillen, Co. Fermanagh, and TCD, where he was taught by the classicist John Pentland *Mahaffy. At Oxford, he won the Newdigate Prize for Poetry, and his chief mentor was Walter Pater. His first book, *Poems* (1881), hints at his themes of homosexuality, individualism, and Republican indifference to authority. In 1879 Wilde set up in London as a self-styled 'Professor of Aesthetics', intent on a crusade to civilize the English through lectures and essays on the reform of English dress and on house decoration, but also by his own example. So considerable was the impact of his self-promotion that he was engaged to undertake a lengthy lecture tour of North America during 1882. Although Wilde developed his public image considerably in this period ('I have nothing to declare but my genius'), it was also a time when he consolidated the ideas which were to underpin his best satirical writings. Returning from America, he settled down to the career of a man of letters. For eighteen months he edited *The Woman's World* (in 1887–9), soliciting contributions from society ladies including his wife, Constance Lloyd. Together they made their Chelsea home at 16 Tite St. into the 'House Beautiful'. Wilde's unsatisfactory Russian melodrama *Vera, or the Nihilists* was produced in New York in 1883. His literary fortunes began to rise in 1890 with The *Picture of Dorian Gray* in *Lippincott's Magazine*, and this was followed by the publication of his collected essays and dialogues under the title of *Intentions* in 1891. From 1886 Wilde had been having sexual relationships with men, beginning with Robert Ross, who was to become his literary executor. In 1891 he met Lord Alfred Douglas, a young man sixteen years his junior. In his company Wilde ventured with increasing recklessness into the London world of boy-prostitution. At the same time, his writing began to deal more explicitly with homosexual themes. Wilde's liberationist outlook was further developed in The *Soul of Man Under Socialism* (1891), an aesthete's version of Marxism. *Lord Arthur Savile's Crime and Other Stories* (1891) and *A House of Pomegranates* (1892), were volumes of tales for a more adult audience than The *Happy Prince* (1888), which had originated in his children's nursery. In 1891 he also wrote *Lady Windermere's Fan*, inaugurating the drama of epigrammatic dandyism and moral paradox on which his fame is based. The performance of this play in the following year greatly increased his notoriety.

Thereafter Wilde concentrated on three matters: the perpetuation of his stage success with *A Woman of No Importance* (1893), *An *Ideal Husband*, and The *Importance of Being Earnest* (both produced in 1895); a life of self-indulgence principally in company with Douglas; and a series of works of a religious nature which include *Salomé* (in French, 1893; in English, 1894), as well as *A Florentine Tragedy* and *La Sainte Courtisane*. In 1895 he was lured into instigating an action for criminal libel against Douglas's father, the Marquess of Queensberry, who had left a card in the Albemarle Club inscribed 'To Oscar Wilde, posing as a somdomite' [*sic*]. Forced to abandon the prosecution under cross-examination by Edward *Carson, Wilde was charged with gross indecency, convicted by jury on 25 May 1895, and sentenced to two years' hard labour. Towards the end of his imprisonment at Reading, Wilde wrote an account of his relationship with Alfred Douglas, first published by Ross in abridged form as *De Profundis* (1905). After his release in 1897, Wilde immediately left England and drifted aimlessly around France and Italy, sometimes with Douglas, sometimes with Ross, using the pseudonym 'Sebastian Melmoth'. Writing nothing other than The *Ballad of Reading Gaol*, he indulged heavily in drink and sex. Wilde died in 1900, most likely of meningitis. See Richard *Ellmann, *Oscar Wilde* (1987).

Wilde, Sir William R[obert Wills]

(1815–1876), antiquarian and surgeon. Born in Castlerea, Co. Roscommon, he was educated at Elphin Diocesan School and the Royal College of Surgeons. The success of his *Narrative of a Voyage to Madeira, Teneriffe, &c* (1839), based on a voyage made as a personal physician, enabled him to continue his medical education in Berlin and Vienna before settling in Dublin. He became ophthalmologist to the viceregal household in 1853. With Lady *Wilde, whom he married in 1851, he had three children, among them Oscar *Wilde. His topographical and ethnographical writings include *The Beauties of the Boyne and the Blackwater* (1849) and *Lough Corrib and Lough Mask* (1867), as well as materials published posthumously in Lady Wilde's *Ancient Legends, Mystic Charms, and Superstitions of Ireland* (1887).

'Wildgoose Lodge' (1830), a story by William *Carleton, first published as 'Confessions of a Reformed Ribbonman' in the *Dublin Literary Gazette*, and later revised for *Traits and Stories of the Irish Peasantry* (2nd series, 1833). The narrator is summoned to a meeting of Ribbonmen [see *secret societies] at a Catholic chapel in the dead of night. Paddy Devann, schoolteacher and parish clerk, leads the party out to wreak revenge on a Protestant neighbour branded an 'informer'.

Williamite War, 1689–1691, fought between supporters of *James II and William III, who had invaded England on 5 November 1688 and become joint sovereign with his wife Mary (James's daughter) on 13 February 1689. In Ireland the Lord Lieutenant Richard Talbot, Earl of Tyrconnell, committed himself to James. Protestant resistance in Bandon, Co. Cork, and other parts of the south was quickly suppressed, and a Protestant force was also defeated in Co. Down. But the city of Derry, where citizens had closed the gates against a Jacobite army on 7 December 1688, withstood a lengthy siege (18 April–13 June), while Enniskillen Protestants defeated Jacobite forces at Belleek (7 May) and Newtownbutler (31 July). A Williamite army under Marshal Schomberg landed at Belfast in August 1689, but failed to move beyond Ulster until William arrived and took personal charge on 14 June 1690. Victory at the *Battle of the Boyne allowed the Williamites to take Dublin. In 1691 the Williamites captured Athlone and won a major victory at Aughrim (12 July). The Jacobites under *Sarsfield held out in Limerick, surrendering on terms (the Treaty of Limerick) on 3 October. The Williamite victory, followed by the enactment of the *Penal Laws, confirmed Protestant *ascendancy in Ireland.

Williams, Richard D'Alton (pseudonym 'Shamrock') (1822–1862), poet. Born in Dublin, he studied medicine in Dublin, and joined the *Young Ireland movement. He wrote verses for *The *Nation* from 1842 under his pseudonym.

Wills, James (1790–1868), poet and biographer; born in Willsgrove, Co. Roscommon, and educated at TCD. He took holy orders in 1822. His *Lives of Illustrious and Distinguished Irishmen* (6 vols., 1840–7) was a historical compendium of Irish biography. Collections of his poetry appeared as *The Disembodied* (1831), *Dramatic Sketches* (1845), and *The Idolatress* (1868). Other works are *Philosophy of Unbelief* (1835) and *Moral and Religious Epistles* (1848).

Wills, W[illiam] G[orman] (1828–1891), playwright, painter, and novelist; born in Kilkenny city a son of James *Wills, and educated at TCD. He began writing for the stage in 1865 and went on to compose thirty-three historical plays, performed mostly at the London Lyceum, where he revived popular verse drama with *Charles I* (1872). Other plays include *Hinko, The Headman's Daughter* (1871); *Medea in Corinth* (1872); *Eugene Aram* (1873); and *Faust* (1885), based on *Anster's translation of Goethe. His novels include *Notice to Quit* (1863) and *The Love That Kills* (1867), dealing melodramatically with landlord-peasant relations after the *Famine.

Wilson, Charles Henry (1757–1808), translator and dramatist. Born in Bailieborough, Co. Cavan, he studied law at TCD and became a parliamentary reporter. He edited *Beauties of Edmund *Burke* (1798) and wrote two comedies, *Poverty and Wealth* (1799) and *The Irish Valet* (1811). He was associated with the Brooke family, and edited the papers of Henry *Brooke (*Brookiana*, 2 vols., 1804); he anticipated Charlotte *Brooke's *Reliques of Irish Poetry* (1789) by several years with his *Poems Translated from the Irish Language into the English* (1782).

Wilson, R[obert] A[rthur], 'Barney Maglone' (?1820–1875), journalist and poet. Born in Dunfanaghy, Co. Donegal, he taught in Ballycastle, Co. Antrim, emigrated to America, then returned and wrote for newspapers in Enniskillen and Belfast. He made his name as 'Barney Maglone' with a series of sketches of town-hall figures, chiefly for the Belfast *Morning News* (1865). His *Almeynack for All Ireland an' Whoever Else Wants It* (1871) was in the same vein of dialect humour.

Wilson, Robert MacLiam (1964–), novelist; born in Belfast, he was educated there and at Cambridge, which he left before taking a degree to write his first novel, *Ripley Bogle* (1989). *Manfred's Pain* (1992) concerns a dying man who recalls how he destroyed love through marital violence. Wilson was writer in residence at UUC 1991–4. *Eureka Street* (1996) was a bitter novel of the endgame of the northern *Troubles.

Wind Among the Reeds, The (1899), a collection of poems by W. B. *Yeats, heavy with symbolism and driven by sensuality and frustration, reflecting his love affair with Olivia Shakespear, and his unrequited passion for Maud *Gonne.

Windele, John (1801–1865), scholar and antiquarian. Born in Cork, he was one of a group of literary men who cultivated an interest in *folklore and antiquities. With J. J. *Callanan and Thomas Crofton *Croker he formed a group called the Anchorites. His collection of *ogam stones are now kept at UCC. During 1826–30 he edited *Bolster's Quarterly Magazine*. His topographical interests are reflected in *Historical and Descriptive Notes of the City of Cork* (1839).

Winding Stair, The (1913), a collection of poems by W. B. *Yeats which appeared in its first version in 1929, containing some of his greatest poetry. Its central symbol is the stair that ascends from actuality into the darkness of death and eternity, but the collection is animated by an interaction between life and death, self and soul, vision and reality in 'Coole Park and Ballylee', 'Byzantium', and the Crazy Jane poems.

Wingfield, Sheila (neé Beddingfield) (1906–1992), poet. Born in Hampshire, she married Viscount Powerscourt in 1932 and lived at Enniskerry, Co. Wicklow. She published *Poems* (1938); *Beat Drum, Beat Heart* (1946); *A Cloud Across the Sun* (1949); *A Kite's Dinner* (1954); *The Leaves Darken* (1964); *Admissions* (1977); and *Collected Poems* (1983). *Real People* (1952), an autobiography, was followed by *Sun Too Fast* (1974), exploring her background.

Within the Gates (1934), a modern morality play by Sean *O'Casey, set in a London park. Jannice, a young prostitute dying of heart disease, encounters opposing attitudes towards human life in three men she has been involved with.

Without My Cloak, (1931), a novel by Kate *O'Brien, set in her native

Limerick. It tells the story of the Considine family whose fortunes were founded by 'honest John' and perpetuated by his son Anthony.

Woffington, Peg [Margaret] (?1718–1760), actress; born in Dublin, she was introduced to the *Smock Alley management by Charles *Coffey. In 1739 she was Sir Harry Wildair in *Farquhar's The *Constant Couple. She travelled with Coffey to London in 1740. There she persuaded Christopher Rich to cast her as Silvia in The *Recruiting Officer. During 1742–5 she visited Dublin with Garrick. Her affair with Garrick and acrimonious rivalry with Kitty *Clive are part of English theatrical legend. Her beauty and acting were said to be mesmeric.

Wolfe, Charles (1791–1823), clergyman and poet. Born in Dublin or possibly Co. Kildare, and educated at TCD, he became curate of Donoughmore, Co. Down, in 1814. He is known as the author of 'The Burial of Sir John Moore', an elegiac response to a much-commemorated event at Corunna during the Peninsular War, that he did not witness, which quickly became a staple of declamation after its discovery by Byron.

Woman, or Ida of Athens (1800), romantic novel by Sydney Owenson, later Lady *Morgan. Ida, whose lover has fled Greece after an unsuccessful revolt against the Turks, travels to London with a self-indulgent English aristocrat, before being reunited with her Greek lover.

Women, or Pour et Contre (1818), a novel by Charles Robert *Maturin, set in and around contemporary Dublin. Charles de Courcy, an orphan and heir to property in the south of Ireland, comes to Dublin as a 17 year-old student, where he falls in love with Eva, is

captivated by Zaira, Eva's mother, then dies.

Wonderful Tennessee (1993), a play by Brian *Friel, in which three couples arrive at a pier in Ballybeg intending to visit Oileán Draíochta (Magic Island), an island on which the ruined bookie and concert-promoter Terry has taken an option. The sadness and disappointment of their intertwined lives are revealed.

Wood of the Whispering, The (1953), a play by M. J. *Molloy, Sanbatch Daly, a derelict, camps outside a ruined castle in the west of Ireland, living in a coffin-shaped box. The nearby wood, formerly called 'whispering' because of courting couples, is now silent.

Woods, MacDara (1942–), poet. Born in Dublin and educated at Gonzaga College and UCD, he travelled in Europe and North Africa before settling in Dublin, where he founded the literary magazine Cyphers in 1975, and married Eiléan *Ní Chuilleanáin in 1978. He has published Decimal D. Sec Drinks in a Bar in Marrakesch (1970); Early Morning Matins (1972); Stopping the Lights in Ranelagh (1987); Miz Moon (1989); The Hanged Man Was Not Surrendering (1990); and The Country of Blood-Red Flowers (1993). His poems show a love of colour and the exotic including the hallucinatory and bizarre, with a strong satiric vein. He edited The Kilkenny Anthology in 1991.

Woods, Vincent (1960–), playwright. Born in Tarmon, Co. Leitrim, he was educated at the College of Journalism, Rathmines. He worked as a current affairs presenter at *RTÉ until 1989. His plays take the legacy of Irish history as their primary theme. John Hughdy and Tom John were produced as a double bill by the *Druid Company in 1991. *At the Black Pig's Dyke* (1992) is an energetic study of cultural and political divisions in the border territory [see *Northern Ireland]. *Song of the Yellow Bittern* (1994) is based on a case of 1829 when Daniel *O'Connell defended a Catholic priest. *The Colour of Language* (1994) is a book of poems.

Words Upon the Window Pane, The (produced 1930, published 1934), a play about Jonathan *Swift by W. B. *Yeats. A group of people assemble for a seance in an old Dublin house which belonged to friends of *'Stella' where lines from a poem of hers are cut upon the window-pane.

Workhouse Ward, The (1908), a one-act comedy by Lady *Gregory. Two old men, neighbours since youth, quarrel incessantly in the paupers' infirmary.

World of Love, A (1955), a *big house novel by Elizabeth *Bowen. It concerns the disruption in the Montfort home when the young Jane Danby finds a packet of old love-letters written by the deceased former owner, Guy.

Wylder's Hand (1864), a novel by Joseph Sheridan *Le Fanu. Mark Wylder, engaged to Dorcas Brandon, disappears mysteriously. Letters arrive from the Continent renouncing his claim on her, whereupon she marries Stanley Lake. Lake, it emerges, has killed his rival and arranged for the letters to be forged.

Wyndham Land Act of 1903, promoted by George Wyndham (1863–1913), great-grandson of Lord Edward *Fitzgerald and Secretary for Ireland 1900–5. The Act provided treasury stock to facilitate the sale of estates by tenant farmers, on terms of sixty-eight-year repayment. The articles of the Act were formulated by *Land League leaders and the *Irish Parliamentary Party at the Land Conference of 1902. It spelt the end of the Anglo-Irish *ascendancy class. By 1923, when the transfer of six million acres of land had been effected, the term 'peasant', which permeates Irish literature from *Carleton to *Yeats, had ceased to apply in fact.

Yeats, Jack Butler (1871–1957), painter and author. Born in London, the youngest child of John Butler *Yeats and brother of W. B. *Yeats, he grew up mainly in Sligo, and attended art schools in London. He became a friend of J. M. *Synge, with whom he shared walking tours in the west of Ireland, leading to a joint commission to produce a series of articles for the *Manchester Guardian* (1905), which furnished the illustrations later used for Synge's *The *Aran Islands* (1907). He returned to live in Ireland in 1910, first at Greystones, Co. Wicklow, then in Dublin. Yeats began working consistently in oil from 1905. The mystical atmosphere of his later canvases reflects his conviction that there is a higher reality. Yeats wrote a number of plays. *Harlequin Positions* (1939), *La La Noo* (1942), and *In Sand* (1949) were produced at the *Abbey's Peacock Theatre. Three further plays, *Apparitions*, *The Old Sea Road*, and *Rattle*, appeared in a single volume in 1933. In their indifference to normal dramatic convention, and the openings they create for metaphysical surmise, they anticipate the stagecraft of Samuel *Beckett, a personal friend. Yeats also published a number of idiosyncratic works of pseudo-autobiography and fantastic narrative. *Sligo* (1930), *Sailing, Sailing Swiftly* (1933), *The Charmed Life* (1938), *Ah, Well* (1942), *And To You Also* (1944), and *The Careless Flower* (1947) display a liking for free association. In *The Amaranthers* (1936) James Gilfoyle, a Dubliner, makes a journey to a magical isle off the west of Ireland.

Yeats, John Butler (1839–1922), portrait-painter, the father of W. B. *Yeats and Jack Butler *Yeats. Born at Tullylish, Co. Down, where his father was Rector, he was educated at TCD. In 1863 he married Susan Pollexfen, sister of his school-friend George. In 1867 Yeats moved to London. In the 1870s and 1880s the family moved frequently between Dublin, London, and Howth, the children often staying in Sligo with the Pollexfens. After his wife died in 1900 he settled in Dublin with his daughters Susan ('Lily') and Elizabeth ('Lollie'). Sir Hugh *Lane commissioned him to paint a series of portraits of leading figures of the Irish *literary revival, amongst them *Synge, *Moore, Lady *Gregory, and Susan *Mitchell. In 1908 he accompanied Lily to New York, where he made many new friends, including the lawyer John Quinn and Isadora Duncan. In New York he wrote essays and reviews (*Essays Irish and American*, 1918).

Yeats, W[illiam] B[utler] (1865–1939), poet, playwright, founder of the *Abbey Theatre, and driving force of the Irish *literary revival; born in Dublin, the son of John Butler *Yeats, a portrait-painter whose own father was a Church of Ireland clergyman. Yeats's mother, Susan Pollexfen, came from a Sligo family that owned mills and a small shipping company. From 1867 to 1872 the Yeatses lived mainly in London, from 1872 to 1874 in Sligo, then in London again from 1874 to 1881. Yeats went to the Erasmus Smith High School in Dublin, 1881–3. In 1884 he entered the Metropolitan School of Art, and met George *Russell. In 1885 he met John *O'Leary, who introduced him to translations of Irish literature into English. Stimulated by reading Standish James *O'Grady's histories and fictions, he determined to give the legends and *mythology of Ireland new literary expression by writing poetry about Irish places. At the same time his interest in Indian thought and theosophy led him to the Dublin Hermetic Society. His first volume, *Mosada: A Dramatic Poem*, appeared in 1886. *The *Wanderings of Oisin* (1889), a long poem based on the *Fionn cycle, was published in the year when 'the troubling of his life' began in the meeting with Maud *Gonne. In 1892 Yeats wrote his play *The *Countess Cathleen* for her, and addressed to her over the years many wistful love-poems. The marriage proposal that he made in 1891 was refused. In 1890 he joined the Hermetic *Order of the Golden Dawn; interested in magic, astrology, and the Cabbala, he made a study of Blake (whose poems he edited with Edwin J. Ellis in three volumes, 1893), as well as reading Swedenborg. His *Representative Irish Tales* and *John Sherman* and *Dhoya* were published in 1891, the year of *Parnell's death. He began planning a new Irish Literary Society in London, hoping that a cultural revival could be launched. In the following June in Dublin he inaugurated the National Literary Society at a meeting in the Rotunda. *Irish Fairy Tales* and *The Countess Kathleen and Various Legends and Lyrics* were published in 1892. In this period his poetry became more obscure, while a collection entitled *The *Celtic Twilight* (1893) gave its name to the kind of poetry then being produced by imitators. This 'Celtic' poetry reached its ultimate development in the symbolic lyrics of his *The *Wind Among the Reeds* (1899). Having first met Lady *Gregory in London during 1894 he visited her at *Coole Park, her country house in Co. Galway in 1896 and spent long periods there during the summer for many years. Coole provided Yeats with a peaceful routine, and he did much work there, Lady Gregory rekindling his interest in folk tales and peasant speech. While staying at Coole in the summer of 1897, Yeats planned the Irish Literary Theatre with Lady Gregory, and another Co. Galway land owner, Edward *Martyn at Duras House, in Kinvara [see *Abbey Theatre]. Yeats became a member of the *Irish Republican Brotherhood to please Maud Gonne, but soon grew disillusioned with revolutionaries, especially after the Dublin riots of 1897. In 1902, Maud Gonne acted in the title-role of *Cathleen Ni Houlihan*, a play which made a great impression on Irish nationalists, causing Yeats to wonder later in reference to the leaders of the 1916 *Easter Rising if it had 'sent out certain men the English shot'. He was shattered by her sudden marriage to John MacBride in 1903, but continued to write love poetry to and about her. As President of the Irish National Dramatic Society, and Director of the Abbey Theatre, Yeats was deeply immersed in theatre policy and management during this period. Poems in *The *Green Helmet* (1910) and *Responsibilities* (1914) express disillusion. *On Baile's Strand* (1904) was the first of his plays about the Irish hero *Cú Chulainn. An inveterate letter-writer, he also composed many essays: *Ideas of Good and Evil* (1903) and *Discoveries* (1907) were followed in 1916 by *Reveries over Childhood and Youth*, being the first part of *Autobiographies*. His continuing interest in aristocratic art was reflected in imitations of the Japanese Noh, and 1916 saw a production of *At the Hawk's Well*, the first of his *Four Plays for Dancers* (1921). When the 1916 Rising took place in Dublin, Yeats realized that the Irish leaders executed for their part in it had been transformed into national martyrs through the 'terrible beauty' of their sacrifice. Among them was John MacBride. Yeats went to Normandy, where Maud Gonne was living with Seán (born 1904), her son by MacBride, and Iseult (1894–1954), her second child by Lucien Millevoye, a French right-wing politician. There he proposed marriage, was refused, and next proposed to Iseult, who gave no definite answer. In 1917, on receiving a final refusal, he turned to Georgie Hyde Lees, whom he married in 1917. Marriage transformed Yeats's life. His wife's automatic writing underpinned the views on history and human personality sketched in the prose *Per Amica Silentia Lunae* (1918) and which he systematized in *A *Vision* (1925). Ownership of Thoor Ballylee, a medieval tower in Co. Galway, and of a town house at 82 Merrion Square gave him the sense of being rooted in Ireland. He became a senator of the Irish Free State [see *Irish State] in 1922, chairing the committee on the new Irish coinage, and later causing a controversy with his defence of divorce in June 1925. He was awarded the Nobel Prize for Literature in 1923. Of the collections in this period, *Michael Robartes and the Dancer* (1921) included a bleak vision of the future in 'The Second Coming', and praise of ceremony in 'A Prayer for my Daughter'. The magnificent poems of *The *Tower* (1928) focused on legends surrounding Thoor Ballylee, the problem of age, inherited characteristics, civil war, and love. *The *Winding Stair and Other Poems* (1933) continued this rhetorical poetry. Various medical conditions took their toll, though Yeats's output continued impressively with *Collected Poems* (1933), *Collected Plays* (1934), *Wheels and Butterflies* (1934), *A Full Moon in March* (1935), and *Dramatis Personae* (1935). After editing *The Oxford Book of Modern Verse* (1936), Yeats revised *A Vision* (1937), published *New Poems* (1938), planned *On the Boiler* (1939) and composed *Purgatory* and *The Death of Cuchulain*. Riversdale became his last Irish residence in 1932. He died at Roquebrune, Cap Martin in the South of France. The leading literary figure in Ireland in his time, who virtually invented modern Irish literature in

English, and one of the greatest modern poets in any language, Yeats has cast a long shadow. See: A. N. Jeffares, *W. B. Yeats: Man and Poet* (1948); and R. F. Foster *W. B. Yeats: A Life* (1997 and 2001).

Yellow Book of Lecan, an Irish compilation of sixteen *manuscripts, bound together by Edward *Lhuyd, compiled, in part, by Giolla Íosa *Mac Fhir Bhisigh in about 1392 at Leacán (Lackan, Co. Sligo). The manuscript is preserved in TCD.

Yellow Ford, Battle of, See Hugh *O'Neill.

You Never Can Tell (1899), a play by George Bernard *Shaw, written in 1895–6, celebrating, as the title indicates, life's surprises, contradictions, and ever-changingness.

Young, Arthur (1741–1820), English agronomist, travel writer, and author of *A Tour of Ireland* (1780). Arriving in June 1776, he covered some 1,500 miles, but did not travel much beyond the Shannon. His attention was mostly drawn to economic matters and social practices relating to them. He was shocked by the improvidence of the landed class and the idleness of the tenantry. Before returning to England in 1779, Young spent a period as agent to Lord Kingsborough's estate at Mitchelstown, Co. Cork. Young's copious records were stolen on the way to London, so that he had to rely on a more informal journal kept in 1776–7.

Young, Augustus (pseudonym of James Hogan), (1943–), poet. Born in Cork and educated at Christian Brothers College, before studying dentistry at UCC; he then became an epidemiologist and medical consultant. His first volumes, *Survival* (1969) and *On Loaning Hill* (1972), were followed by the evocative

Rosemaries (1976), a sequence about growing up in Cork. *The Credit* (bk. i, 1980; bks. ii and iii, 1986) owes something of its philosophical wit to the example of Brian *Coffey. *Dánta Grádha* (1975, repr. 1980) contains versions of the genre [see *dánta grádha]. *Lampion and his Bandits* (1994) contains essays and poetry. *Lightning in Low Places* (1999) also returned to Cork.

Young Ireland, a romantic nationalist group established in October 1842 and associated with *The *Nation* newspaper. Its leading members were Thomas *Davis, Charles Gavan *Duffy, and John Blake Dillon (1816–66), later joined by William Smith *O'Brien and John *Mitchel. Initially part of the *Repeal movement, Young Ireland revolted against Daniel *O'Connell's pragmatism. When O'Connell provoked a confrontation over theoretical attitudes to physical force in July 1846, Young Ireland stood behind Thomas Francis *Meagher ('of the Sword'), and seceded from the Repeal movement. Young Ireland can be taken as representing the advent of Romantic nationalism in Ireland. Its members are mainly remembered as the first to make language and culture central to the concept of national identity. Attempts to organize an Irish rising in 1848 led only to a confrontation with police at Ballingarry, Co. Tipperary, subsequently derided as 'the battle of the Widow McCormick's cabbage patch'.

Young, Robert (1800–1870), poet, the 'Fermanagh True Blue'; born near Irvinestown he was a nailor but later became a printer on the *Londonderry Sentinel*. He was placed on the Civil List in the 1860s in recognition of his stalwart loyalism. Works include *Poems and Songs* (1854) and his *Works* (1863). He died in the Derry Lunatic Asylum.

Young Tom, see *Tom Barber trilogy.

Zeuss, Johann Kasper (1806–1856), philologist and grammarian; born in Vogtendorf in southern Germany. After a delicate and bookish childhood he studied at Munich University. Having first completed an impressive work on the German peoples, he turned to the Celtic languages, and especially Irish. He studied the interlinear *glosses in the devotional Latin tracts of central European monasteries frequented by early Irish monks. From these he developed an ordered grammatical system, published as *Grammatica Celtica* (Leipzig, 1853).

Zimmer, Heinrich (1851–1910), Celticist. Born in the Mosel district of Germany, he became Professor of Sanskrit in Greifswald in 1881 and was founding Professor of Celtic at Berlin in 1901. The first volume of his *Keltische Studien* (1881) and the text of the *Würzburg Glosses* (1881) were the beginnings of an impressive series of Celtic studies. His *Ueber die Bedeutung des irischen Elements für die mittelalterliche Kultur* (1887; translated as *The Irish Element in Mediaeval Culture*, 1891) praised Irish influence in Europe.

Zoilomastix, see Philip *O'Sullivan Beare.

Zozimus, pseudonym of Michael Moran (?1794–1846), ballad- and comic song-writer, so named after the bishop who converts the lady in his best-known performance, 'St Mary of Egypt'. Born in Faddle Alley, off Black Pitts in the Liberties, he was blind from infancy and lived by busking, earning great renown as a Dublin 'character'.